*For Mike McCarthy whose clear mind
is both a challenge and a comfort.
And for the other great conversational partners of my life:
Jenny, Ben, Jocelyn Sr., and my father, Michael,
violinist and language master.*

BRIEF CONTENTS

PART ONE
WRITING: ITS MOTIVES, METHODS, AND PROCESSES   1
    CHAPTER ONE
    Motives   3
    CHAPTER TWO
    Methods   14
    CHAPTER THREE
    Processes   22

PART TWO
CRITICAL READING, RESEARCH, AND WRITING   57
    CHAPTER FOUR
    Critical Reading and Responding   59
    CHAPTER FIVE
    Primary Research   97
    CHAPTER SIX
    Secondary Research   114

PART THREE
RESPONDING TO SITUATIONS   137
    CHAPTER SEVEN
    Responding to Personal Experience   139
    CHAPTER EIGHT
    Responding to Processes   189
    CHAPTER NINE
    Responding to Controversial Issues   240

PART FOUR
RESPONDING TO TEXTS   299
    CHAPTER TEN
    Responding to Essays   301
    CHAPTER ELEVEN
    Responding to Fiction and Film   365

PART FIVE
STRATEGIES FOR WRITING IN THE ACADEMIC COMMUNITY   455
    CHAPTER TWELVE
    Writing the Research Paper   457
    CHAPTER THIRTEEN
    Strategies for Responding to Essay Questions   494

PART SIX
STRATEGIES FOR ASSESSMENT AND PROCESS-BASED REVISION   505

CONTENTS

**PART ONE: WRITING: ITS MOTIVES,
METHODS, AND PROCESSES**   **1**

CHAPTER ONE: MOTIVES   3
Writing Is Conversation   3
   Critical Thinking and Critical Writing   4
Writing Is Persuasion   4
  Writer-Based General Purposes   5
  Audience-Based General Purposes   6
Writing Is Expression   6
  The Role of Critical Thinking in Expressive Writing 7
  Interview: A Student Writer Talks about Critical
     Writing and Thinking   9

CHAPTER TWO: METHODS   14
■ **Sample Journal Entry:** Getting Started   14
Writer's Tools   15
  ■ **Computer Tip:** Enter and Save   16
Responsive Journal Writing: Exploring Your Attitudes   17
  The Writing Place   17
Responsive Journal Writing: Evaluating Your Own Writing
     Place   17
  The Right Time to Write   18
  Thinking Time   18
Research and Writing   18
The Role of Collaboration in Writing   20
  Informal Collaborative Relationships   20
  Formal Collaborative Relationships   21
  Collaboration and Learning   21

CHAPTER THREE: PROCESSES   22
The Writing Situation   22
Writing Is a Process   23
Responsive Journal Writing: Assessing Past Experience   24
Entering the Conversation   25
  Write to Encounter a Subject   25

■ **Journal Entries of a College Freshman, Sylvia Plath**   25
    Critical Reading Assignment: Highlighting and
        Annotating   30
    Sample Highlighting and Annotating   31
  Responsive Writing Assignment: Responding to Text and
        Situation   32
    Write to Analyze the Choices and Constraints of the
        Writing Situation   32
  Responsive Journal Writing: Exploring Audience and
        Purpose   33
  Write to Expand and Clarify Your Responses   33
  Responsive Prewriting Exercise: Conversing Actively with
        Text and Experience   34
    Sample Exploratory Response: Agreement Statement   34
    Collaborative Writing Assignment: Questioning Your
        First Response   35
    Sample Questions   36
  Responsive Prewriting Assignment: Responding to Your
        Questions   36
    Sample Responses to Questions   36
  Write to Revise Your Thinking by Drafting   38
  Continue to Revise by Rewriting   39
■ **Final Draft:** Fire on the Plains   39
■ **Sample Draft** with Collaborative Partner's Annotations   40
Choices Writers Make   48
  Choices in Voice   48
  Choices in Development   49
  Choices in Arrangement   49
  Choices in Mechanics   50
  Interview: A Student Writer Talks about Writing   50
Assessing Your Performance by Writing Critically   53
  Final Note   53

PART TWO: CRITICAL READING, RESEARCH, AND WRITING   57

CHAPTER FOUR: CRITICAL READING AND
RESPONDING   59
Listen—Read Texts for Meaning   59
  Reading for Meaning: A Model for the Process   61
    A Guide to the Critical Reading Model   61
  Preread   61

■ **Being Black and Feeling Blue, Shelby Steele** 62
Implicitly and Explicitly Expressive Writing 68
  Explicit 68
  Implicit 69
Collaborative Writing Assignment: Exploring Steele's
  Text 69
Responsive Journal Writing: Exploring Your Experience 72
Responsive Journal Writing: Changing Perspectives 73
■ **Sample Journal Entry** 73
Learn—Read with an Eye to the Writer's Craft 75
  Focus on Language Communities 75
  Focus on Purpose, Audience, and Message 76
  Focus on Persuasion in Audience-Based Writing 77
Collaborative Writing Assignment: Focus on the
  Writer's Choices 79
Respond—Develop a Perspective Through Writing 81
  Reading and Responding 81
■ **Student Writing:** Without Success There Can Be No
  Motivation 81
■ **Student Writing:** Smelling Foreigner 83
**Responsive Writing Assignment: Writing a Response
  Statement** 85
A Guide to the Writing Process 86
  Assess Your Past Performance 86
  Explore the Writing Situation 86
  Prewrite 88
Responsive Prewriting Exercises 88
  Focus on Audience and Purpose 90
  Focus on a Working Message 91
  Focus on Your Choices 92
  Draft 91
    ■ **Computer Tip:** Drafting on Computer 92
    ■ **Computer Tip:** Cutting and Adding 93
    ■ **Computer Tip:** Moving Material 94
  Rewrite 95
Assess Your Performance by Writing Critically 96

CHAPTER FIVE: PRIMARY RESEARCH 97
Collaborative Research 98
Critical Reading 99
Interviewing 99
Observing 103
  ■ **Computer Tip:** Writing Up Your Results 106

Questionnaires   106
   Collaborative Writing Assignment: Research and
      Credibility   110
■ **Howling, Dierdre McNamer**   110

CHAPTER SIX: SECONDARY RESEARCH   **114**
Secondary Research in the Academic Community   115
Secondary Research Sources   116
   Reference Sources   116
   Specialized Sources   117
      Explore Reference Sources   117
      Experts   117
      ■ **Computer Tip:** The Internet   118
      Reference Librarians   118
      The Central Catalogue   119
      ■ **Computer Tip:** Print and Electronic Sources   119
      Bibliographies   120
      Indexes   120
      Reference Books   121
         Dictionaries   121
         Biographical Dictionaries   121
         Almanacs and Yearbooks   121
         Atlases   121
   Other Library Sources   122
      Microforms   122
      Interlibrary Loan   122
   Evaluate Specialized Sources   122
      Gather Varied Sources   122
      Read Titles Critically   122
      Note the Name of the Author   123
      Note the Publisher   123
      Think Critically about the Date of Publication   123
      Consider the Length of the Work   123
      Make Use of Annotated Bibliographies, Indexes and
         Reviews   123
      Preview Likely Sources   124
   Read Specialized Sources Critically   124
   Collaborative Writing Assignment: Reading Critically   124
■ **The Roots of Language Protectionism, Harvey A.**
      Daniels   125
Acknowledge Sources   135

Questionnaires 106

  Collaborative Writing Assignment: Research and
Credibility 110

■ **Howling, Dierdre McNamer** 110

CHAPTER SIX: SECONDARY RESEARCH 114

Secondary Research in the Academic Community 115

Secondary Research Sources 116

  Reference Sources 116

  Specialized Sources 117

    Explore Reference Sources 117

    Experts 117

    ■ **Computer Tip:** The Internet 118

    Reference Librarians 118

    The Central Catalogue 119

    ■ **Computer Tip:** Print and Electronic Sources 119

    Bibliographies 120

    Indexes 120

    Reference Books 121

      Dictionaries 121

      Biographical Dictionaries 121

      Almanacs and Yearbooks 121

      Atlases 121

    Other Library Sources 122

      Microforms 122

      Interlibrary Loan 122

  Evaluate Specialized Sources 122

    Gather Varied Sources 122

    Read Titles Critically 122

    Note the Name of the Author 123

    Note the Publisher 123

    Think Critically about the Date of Publication 123

    Consider the Length of the Work 123

    Make Use of Annotated Bibliographies, Indexes and
Reviews 123

    Preview Likely Sources 124

  Read Specialized Sources Critically 124

  Collaborative Writing Assignment: Reading Critically 124

■ **The Roots of Language Protectionism, Harvey A.
Daniels** 125

  Acknowledge Sources 135

■ **Being Black and Feeling Blue, Shelby Steele**   62
   Implicitly and Explicitly Expressive Writing   68
      Explicit   68
      Implicit   69
   Collaborative Writing Assignment: Exploring Steele's
      Text   69
Responsive Journal Writing: Exploring Your Experience   72
Responsive Journal Writing: Changing Perspectives   73
■ **Sample Journal Entry**   73
Learn—Read with an Eye to the Writer's Craft   75
   Focus on Language Communities   75
   Focus on Purpose, Audience, and Message   76
   Focus on Persuasion in Audience-Based Writing   77
   Collaborative Writing Assignment: Focus on the
      Writer's Choices   79
Respond—Develop a Perspective Through Writing   81
   Reading and Responding   81
■ **Student Writing:** Without Success There Can Be No
      Motivation   81
■ **Student Writing:** Smelling Foreigner   83
**Responsive Writing Assignment: Writing a Response
      Statement**   85
A Guide to the Writing Process   86
   Assess Your Past Performance   86
   Explore the Writing Situation   86
   Prewrite   88
Responsive Prewriting Exercises   88
   Focus on Audience and Purpose   90
   Focus on a Working Message   91
   Focus on Your Choices   92
   Draft   91
      ■ **Computer Tip:** Drafting on Computer   92
      ■ **Computer Tip:** Cutting and Adding   93
      ■ **Computer Tip:** Moving Material   94
   Rewrite   95
Assess Your Performance by Writing Critically   96

CHAPTER FIVE: PRIMARY RESEARCH   97
Collaborative Research   98
Critical Reading   99
Interviewing   99
Observing   103
      ■ **Computer Tip:** Writing Up Your Results   106

PART THREE: RESPONDING TO SITUATIONS

137

CHAPTER SEVEN: RESPONDING TO PERSONAL
EXPERIENCES   139
The Writer's Scenario   139
Responding to Personal Experiences: Professional Writing   140
Techniques for Responding to Personal Experience   140
■ **Ordinary Spirit, Joy Harjo**   141
■ **Getting to Know Mister Lincoln, Beverly Lowry**   147
■ **If I Could Write This in Fire, I Would Write This in
    Fire, Michelle Cliff**   152
Encounter the Subject   168
   Research Opportunity: Expanding Your Response   168
Responsive Journal Writing: Changing Perspectives   168
Listen—Read Carefully for Meaning   169
   Collaborative Writing Assignment: Reading for
     Meaning   169
Responsive Journal Writing: Explaining Changes   170
   Collaborative Research Opportunity: Questioning   171
Responsive Journal Writing: Recording Your Findings   171
Learn—Read with an Eye to the Writer's Craft   171
   Focus on Dramatic Activity in Personal Experience
     Writing   171
   Focus on Persuasion in Personal Experience Writing   171
   Collaborative Writing Assignment: Focus on the
     Writer's Choices   173
Respond—Develop a Perspective through Writing   174
■ **Student Writing:** July 7th, 1991   174
■ **Student Writing:** I Can Wash My Rugs on Sunday   176
**Responsive Writing Assignment: Responding to Personal
   Experience**   178
A Guide to the Writing Process   179
   Assess Your Past Performance   179
   Explore the Writing Situation   179
   Prewrite   182
Research Opportunity: Expanding Your Response   182
Responsive Prewriting Assignments   182
   Focus on Audience and Purpose   184
   Draft   185
   Rewrite   187
Assess Your Performance by Writing Critically   188

CHAPTER EIGHT: RESPONDING TO PROCESSES   189

The Writer's Scenario   189

Techniques for Responding to Processes   190

Responding to Processes: Professional Writing   190

■ **Learning to Read, Malcolm X**   191

■ **The Beekeeper, Sue Hubbell**   202

■ **The Ruination of the Tomato, Mark Kramer**   205

Encounter the Subject   212

   Research Opportunity: Expanding Your Response   212

Responsive Journal Writing: Changing Perspectives   213

Listen—Read Carefully for Meaning   213

   Collaborative Writing Assignment: Reading for
      Meaning   213

Responsive Journal Writing: Explaining Changes   215

   Research Opportunity: Questioning   215

Responsive Journal Writing: Recording Your Findings   216

Learn—Read Closely for Craft   216

   Focus on Causality in Process Writing   216

   Collaborative Writing Assignment: Focus on
      Arrangements and Development in Process
      Writing   216

   Focus on Persuasion in Process Writing   218

   Collaborative Writing Assignment: Focus on the
      Writer's Choices   218

Respond—Develop a Perspective through Writing   220

■ **Student Writing:** Bringing Home the Red Lantern   220

   Collaborative Student Writing: Getting into Bob Weir
      Hot Springs   225

   Interview: Two Student Writers Talk about Collaborative
      Writing   228

Responsive Writing Assignment: Responding to a Process   230

A Guide to the Writing Process   230

   Assess Your Past Performance   230

   Explore the Writing Situation   230

   Prewrite   232

   Research Opportunity: Expanding Your Response   232

   Draft   235

   Rewrite   238

Assess Your Performance by Writing Critically   239

CHAPTER NINE: RESPONDING TO CONTROVERSIAL
ISSUES   240
The Writer's Scenario   240
Techniques for Responding to Controversial Issues   242
■ **Forestry: Only God Can Make a Tree, But . . . , Michael
    Frome**   243
■ **Gays in Arms, Jacob Weisberg**   252
■ **HIV Testing: Voluntary, Mandatory, or Routine,
    Theresa L. Crenshaw**   260
Encounter the Subject   270
    Research Opportunity: Expanding Your Encounter   271
Responsive Journal Writing: Changing Perspectives   271
Listen—Read Carefully for Meaning   272
    Collaborative Writing Assignment: Reading for
        Meaning   272
Responsive Journal Writing: Changing Perspectives   273
    Research Opportunity: Questioning   274
Responsive Journal Writing: Recording Your Findings   274
Learn—Read with an Eye to the Writer's Craft   274
    Focus on Research in Responses to Controversy   274
    Focus on Persuasion in Responses to Controversy   274
    Collaborative Writing Assignment: Focus on the
        Writer's Choices   278
Respond—Develop a Perspective through Writing   279
■ **Student Writing:** The Politics of Prohibition and the
    Death of the American Dream   280
■ **Student Writing:** In Defense of American Education   283
**Responsive Writing Assignment: Responding to a
    Controversial Issue**   287
A Guide to the Process   287
    Assess Your Past Performance   287
    Explore the Writing Situation   288
    Prewrite   289
    Research Opportunity: Expanding Your Response   289
Responsive Prewriting Exercises   290
    Draft   292
    Rewrite   295
Assess Your Performance by Writing Critically   296

PART FOUR: RESPONDING TO TEXTS   299

CHAPTER TEN: RESPONDING TO ESSAYS   301
The Essay Writer's Scenario   301
Techniques for Responding to Essays   302
Responding to Essays: Professional Writing   302
  ■ **Death and Justice: How Capital Punishment Affirms**
        Life, Edward I. Koch   303
  ■ **The Death Penalty, David Bruck**   308
Encounter the Subject   313
  Research Opportunity: Expanding Your Encounter   314
Responsive Journal Writing: Changing Perspectives   314
Listen—Read Carefully for Meaning   315
  Collaborative Writing Assignment: Reading for
        Meaning   315
Responsive Journal Writing: Changing Perspectives   316
A Brief Anthology of Essays   316
  ■ **Dangerous Parties, Paul Keegan**   316
  ■ **Marriage and Love, Emma Goldman**   333
  ■ **Three Faces of Greed, Jane O'Reilly**   341
Respond: Explore Your Perspective by Writing   345
  ■ **Student Writing:** Marriage and Love   345
  ■ **Student Writing:** Marriage and Love   348
Responsive Writing Assignment: Responding to an Essay   352
A Guide to the Writing Process   352
  Assess Your Past Performance   352
  Explore the Writing Situation   352
  Research Opportunity: Expand Your Response   354
  Read the Essay for Meaning   354
  Read with an Eye for the Writer's Craft   355
  Focus on Persuasion in Essay Writing   355
  Prewrite   357
Responsive Prewriting Exercises   357
  Draft   359
  Rewrite   362
Assess Your Performance by Writing Critically   363

CHAPTER ELEVEN: RESPONDING TO FICTION
AND FILM   365
The Writer's Scenario   365
Techniques for Responding to Fiction and Film   367
Responding to Fiction and Film: Primary Texts   367

Preread Fiction 367

■ **Hills Like White Elephants, Ernest Hemingway** 368

Preview Film 372

Listen—Analyze Fiction and Film for Meaning 373

  Collaborative Writing Assignment: Reading for
     Meaning 373

  A Guide to Reading Fiction and Film for Meaning 373

    Know the Text 373

    Search for Meaning in the Text 374

    Consider Theme 378

  Responding to Fiction and Film: Secondary Responses 379

  Focus on the Conversational Nature of Interpretive
     Writing 379

  Secondary Responses to "Hills Like White Elephants" 379

■ **J. F. Kobler** 380

■ **Gary D. Elliot** 381

■ **Mary Dell Fletcher** 383

  Research Opportunity: Expanding Your Response 385

Responsive Journal Writing: Changing Perspective 386

  A Secondary Response to *Unforgiven* 386

■ **Clint Eastwood and the Machinery of Violence, John C.
   Tibbetts** 386

  Research Opportunity: Expanding Your Response 400

Response Journal Writing: Changing Perspectives 400

  Listen—Read Responses to Fiction and Film Carefully for
     Meaning 400

  Consider Community When Reading Interpretive
     Responses 400

  Collaborative Writing Exercise: Reading Secondary
     Response for Meaning 401

  Research Opportunity: Questioning 404

Responsive Journal Writing: Recording Your Findings 404

Learn—Read Responses to Fiction and Film with an Eye to
     Improving Your Own Technique 405

  Focus on Persuasion in Interpreting Fiction and Film 405

  Collaborative Writing Assignment: Focus on the
     Writer's Choices 405

Responding to Fiction: Student Responses 408

■ **Student Writing:** Hills Like White Elephants 408

■ **Student Writing:** Hills Like White Elephants 410

■ **Student Writing:** Unforgiven 412

Respond—Develop Perspective Through Writing 413

**Responsive Writing Assignment: Responding to Fiction or
          Film**   413
A Guide to the Writing Process   414
  Encounter a Primary Text   414
A Brief Anthology of Short Fiction   414
  ■ **Girl, Jamaica Kincaid**   414
  ■ **Cathedral, Raymond Carver**   416
  ■ **Roman Fever, Edith Wharton**   431
A Brief List of Suggested Films   444
  Assess Your Past Performance   444
  Explore the Writing Situation   445
  Read the Primary Text for Meaning   446
  Collaborative Writing Assignment   446
  Prewrite   447
  Research Opportunity: Expanding Your Response   447
  Draft   449
  Rewrite   451
Think Critically about Your Performance   452

PART FIVE: STRATEGIES FOR WRITING IN THE ACADEMIC COMMUNITY   455

CHAPTER TWELVE: WRITING THE RESEARCH PAPER   457
The Writer's Scenario   457
Some Considerations   457
  Consider Time Restraints   457
  Prewriting Will Be Extended and Interrupted   457
  Keep a Research Journal   458
    ■ **Computer Tip:** Notetaking   458
Prewrite to Explore What You Know and Believe   458
  Consider Context   458
  Formulate a Working Hypothesis   458
Research to Increase Your Knowledge and Understanding   460
  Confirm or Deny by Interviewing a Mentor   460
Journal Writing: Reevaluating Your Working Hypothesis   460
  Locate Pertinent Sources   461
    Secondary Sources   461
      ■ **Computer Tip:** Using Computerized Catalogs   461
      ■ **Computer Tip:** Searching for Information   462
    Evaluating Secondary Sources   464
  Primary Sources   465

Gather and Analyze the Results of Your Research   465
  Primary Sources   465
Responsive Journal Writing: Writing Up the Results of
       Your Research   465
  Secondary Sources   466
    Read Secondary Sources Critically   466
Responsive Journal Writing: Writing Up the Results of
       Your Research   466
Drafting   466
  Avoiding Plagiarism   467
    Using and Documenting Sources   468
      Punctuating Quoted Material   468
      Paraphrasing Material   469
    Styles of Documentation   470
    Conventions for Citations in Your Text   470
    Conventions for Lists of Sources   472
      Books   473
      Articles   474
      Electronic Sources   475
      Other Sources   476
■ **Sample Draft** with Collaborative Partner's Annotations   477
■ **Final Draft:** Beautiful Fire   485
Interview: A Student Writer Talks about Researching   489

**CHAPTER THIRTEEN: STRATEGIES FOR
RESPONDING TO ESSAY QUESTIONS**   494
Long-Term Study Strategies   494
  Practice Critical Thinking   495
    Engage in Challenging Conversation   495
    Listen Actively   495
    Take Thorough, Well-Organized Notes   495
    Read Your Notes Critically   496
    Research Any Unknowns   496
    Apply Concepts   496
    Supply Evidence   496
  Practice Critical Reading   496
    Preread   496
    Read Carefully for Meaning   496
  Practice Critical Writing   497
    Keep Course Journals   497
    Keep a Personal Journal   497

497

Strategies for Studying for Exams   497
  Explore the Writing Situation in Advance   497
    Consider Your Past Performance   497
    Analyze Your Audience   497
    Formulate Possible Questions   498
    Write Out the Answers to the Questions   498
    Pose Study Questions   498
    Focus Your Study to Fill in Gaps   498
    Reformulate Questions and Rewrite   499
    Memorize Key Elements and Spellings   499
Strategies for Taking Exams   499
  Read Over the Entire Exam   499
  Proportion Your Time   499
  Write Legibly and Correctly   500
  Start with the Easiest Question   500
  Supply Specific Examples, Reasons, and Evidence   500
  Read Over the Exam and Make Corrections   500
Practice What You Have Learned   500
■ **Being a Man, Paul Theroux** (excerpt)   501
  Collaborative Writing Assignment: Formulating Possible
       Exam Questions   502
**Responsive Writing Assignment: Answering Practice
       Questions**   502
Assess Your Performance by Writing Critically   503

**PART SIX: STRATEGIES FOR ASSESSMENT
AND PROCESS-BASED REVISION**   **505**

Introduction   507
A Guide to Process-Based Revision   508
  Collaborate to Assess Your Problem Areas   508
Problems with Voice   509
  Common Artistic Problems with Voice   509
    Pretentious Voice   509
    Inconsistent Voice   510
    Casual Voice   511
  Think Critically about Your Performance   513
  Common Technical Problems with Voice   513
    Map Your Errors   513
    Common Technical Problems with Voice   514
    Fragmented Sentences   515
      Exercise for Practice   516

Lack of Parallel Structure   516
   Exercise for Practice   516
Misplaced and Dangling Modifiers   517
   Exercise for Practice   517
Faulty Subject-Verb Agreement   517
   Exercise for Practice   518
Faulty Pronoun-Antecedent Agreement   518
   Exercise for Practice   519
   Exercise for Practice   519
Faulty Pronoun Reference   520
   Exercise for Practice   520
   Exercise for Practice   521
Shift in Person   521
   Exercise for Practice   521
Shift in Tense   521
   Exercise for Practice   522
Faulty Denotation and Inappropriate Connotation   523
Think Critically about Your Performance   524
Problems with Development   525
Common Problems with Development   525
Strategies for Process-Based Revision   526
   Exercise for Practice   529
Freewriting   529
Looping   529
Double-Entry Notes   530
Sketching   531
Clustering   532
Summarizing   533
Outlining   533
Bridge Strategies   533
Problems with Arrangement   535
Problems with Logical Order   535
Bridge Strategies   537
Illustrating Judgment   537
Comparing and Contrasting   537
Defining   539
Considering Causes and Effects   539
Dividing and Classifying   540
Narrating   540
Analogy   541
Describing   541
Transitional Devices   541

Inclusion of Unrelated Material   545
Problems with Mechanics   546
Common Problems with Mechanics   547
Run-On Sentences   547
Blatant Run-Ons   547
Comma Splice Run-Ons   548
Exercise for Practice   548
Lack of Comma in Compound Sentence   549
Exercise for Practice   549
Lack of Comma to Separate Items in a Series   549
Exercise for Practice   550
Lack of Comma(s) around Non-Restrictive Elements   550
Exercise for Practice   551
Lack of Comma after Introductory Element   551
Exercise for Practice   551
Incorrect Semicolon Use   551
Exercise for Practice   552
Omission of Apostrophe to Signal Possession   552
Exercise for Practice   552
Incorrect Colon Use   553
Exercise for Practice   554
Incorrect Dash Use   554
Exercise for Practice   554
Problematic Words   554
Exercise for Practice: its/it's   555
Exercise for Practice: supposed to, used to   555
Exercise for Practice: there/their/they're   556
Exercise for Practice: whose/who's   556
Exercise for Practice: past/passed   557
Exercise for Practice: have/of   557
Exercise for Practice: to/too   557
Index   559
Credits   566

PREFACE

TO THE STUDENT

There's no doubt that the ability to write with clarity of thought and elegance of language is extraordinarily empowering. On a purely practical level, students who are good writers get better grades than students who aren't; and professionals and even nonprofessionals who write well are more likely to succeed in the work force than their counterparts who don't write well. But even more significant than the worldly success associated with writing skill is the fundamental role language (and its visible form, writing) plays in human existence; language is all we have at our disposal to make meaning out of experience and to communicate that meaning to other people. The epistemology that drives this book is based on the following assumptions, all of which have as their ground the meaning-making function of language in human life.

WRITING IS RESPONSIVE

Like conversation, writing is responsive. Sometimes it's actually conversational response organized and written out; one writer will read what another writer has written and write back in response. Other times the response is to situations that exist in the world. For this reason, rather than basing major writing assignments on a particular writing strategy, like narration or causal analysis, or even on a purpose, like explaining or informing, I've based the formal writing assignments in *The Responsive Writer* on the subjects of writing and placed the critical thinking, critical reading and research that make up the writer's encounter with subject at the top of the writing process. A finished piece of writing is, after all, an organized critical response to a subject, and that subject first must be understood and interacted with by the writer in order to be written about. Therefore, I've introduced research early on and integrated it into every reading and writing assignment, and I've replaced the text specific "questions for discussion" that usually follow readings with a critical reading model that connects the reading and writing processes and allows students to see that there are general principles that can be applied in the reading of all texts. In addition, this book emphasizes that the writer's response to subject always takes place in a particular rhetorical context with its own unique system of choices and constraints; both the

"Collaborative Writing Assignments" that accompany the readings and the formal "Responsive Writing Assignments" give students practice in analyzing the rhetorical choices and constraints inherent in any writing situation.

WRITING IS PERSUASION

Like every communicative act, writing creates meaning to accomplish some purpose—to effect some change in knowledge, thought or action in its intended audience. And it's precisely because writing communicates meaning to accomplish a purpose, that all writing is to some degree persuasive. The critical reading model included in *The Responsive Writer* helps students discern the purposes of the texts they encounter, and emphasizes the specific ways (logos, pathos, ethos) writers use language to effect change in their audiences. In addition, all the writing assignments (both the private "Responsive Journal Writing" assignments and the transactional "Responsive Writing Assignments") emphasize purpose.

WRITING IS EXPRESSION

Just as virtually all writing is persuasive to some extent, all writing is expressive to one degree or another. Expressiveness in writing can take many forms—from the expression of simple interest in a subject to the expression of powerful judgments on it. However, since the best writing is both expressive *and* critical, *The Responsive Writer* aims to help students develop the self-critical internal audiences that will enable them to become critical readers of their own thinking and writing. "Responsive Journal Writing" assignments throughout the book invite students to examine and analyze how and why their perspectives on texts or situations have been changed by engaging in research or discussion; and the critical reading model encourages students to think critically about their responses to written texts by requiring them to supply evidence for every assertion they make.

COLLABORATION IS ESSENTIAL
TO LEARNING

More often than not, we extend and clarify our knowledge of the world by interacting with others. We listen to other people's speculations and conclusions, and we learn from them; then we respond by constructing our own ideas about the meaning of experience. Furthermore, the association between collaboration and growth as a reader and writer is overwhelmingly apparent. With this in mind, I've designed assignments that stress learning through informal and formal collaboration throughout the reading and writing processes.

ASSESSMENT IS ESSENTIAL TO WRITING INSTRUCTION

Clarity of thought and precision of language should be stressed in writing instruction. Writing is a communicative act, and the mistakes students make while writing affect the meaning they're trying to communicate. Furthermore, rather than being mysterious and insurmountable, weaknesses in writing are habitual and writer-specific, indicating real gaps in knowledge or chronic misuses of the writing process. Unlike any other handbook, Part Six of *The Responsive Writer* presents an individual diagnostic method for assessment and process-based revision that provides students with strategies for recognizing and overcoming their particular areas of writing weakness. In addition, assessment and process-based revision are integrated into every formal writing assignment.

SUMMARY OF SPECIAL FEATURES

- The unique "Critical Reading Model" connects the reading and writing processes and allows students to see that there are general principles that can be applied in the reading of all texts.

- The "Reading with an Eye to the Writer's Craft" sections in major assignment chapters provide students with a model for craft study that focuses on the rhetorical choices writers make during the writing process.

- "Focusing on Persuasion" subsections within the craft study model help students discern the persuasive purposes of the texts they encounter by emphasizing the specific ways (logos, pathos, ethos) writers use language to effect change in their audiences.

- Realistic writing assignments give students practice in analyzing the rhetorical choices and constraints inherent in any writing situation.

- Research techniques are introduced early on, and "Research Opportunities" throughout the book integrate research into every reading and writing assignment.

- "Computer Tips" throughout the book demystify computer literacy and show students how to use computers for writing and research.

- The unique handbook (Part Six) presents an individual diagnostic method for assessment and process-based revision that gives students specific strategies for recognizing and overcoming their particular areas of writing weakness.

- "Assess Your Performance" self-assessment exercises integrated into every formal writing assignment help students evaluate their progress as writers.

TO THE INSTRUCTOR
OVERVIEW OF THE TEXT
PART ONE
"Writing; Its Motives, Methods, and Processes"

The three brief chapters that make up Part One of *The Responsive Writer* introduce students to the why's and how's of writing.

Chapter One, "Motives," invites students to join the ongoing intellectual conversation and clearly defines writing as a responsive, meaning-making activity that involves critical reading and thinking. In addition, the chapter stresses the persuasive nature of all writing and introduces students to the general writer and audience-based purposes. Chapter One ends with an interview with a student writer that illustrates the importance of critical writing and thinking in the academic community and beyond.

Chapter Two, "Methods," uses the student interview from Chapter One as a illustrative starting place to introduce (and get students using) methods regularly employed by most working writers. The chapter includes discussions about the subjects of writing; the writer's use of tools, place, and time (including journal writing and writing on the computer). The chapter also includes discussions about the important roles that research and collaboration play in writing and learning.

Chapter Three, "Processes," gives students a hands-on introduction to the writing process (and to concepts presented in Chapters One and Two) as they work side by side with a real student writer through the book's first formal writing assignment. New concepts introduced and illustrated in this process chapter include the "writing situation," the recursive nature of the writing process, and the importance of assessment and process-based revision to the development of writing proficiency.

PART TWO
"Critical Reading, Research, and Writing"

The three chapters that make up Part Two of *The Responsive Writer* introduce students to the critical reading and research strategies necessary for college level writing.

Chapter Four, "Critical Reading and Responding," connects the reading and writing processes and introduces students to general principles that can be applied to the reading of all texts. This chapter adds critical reading and craft-study models to the writing process model previously introduced in Chapter Three. New subjects introduced and illustrated in this chapter include communities of discourse, the Aristotelian persuasive techniques (logos, pathos, and ethos), and implicitly and explicitly expressive writing.

Chapters Five and Six, "Primary Research" and "Secondary Research," provide an introduction to research sources and methods and invite students to make research part of all reading and writing assignments.

PARTS THREE AND FOUR
"Responding to Situations" and "Responding to Texts"

The five chapters that make up Parts Three and Four of *The Responsive Writer* use the critical reading, craft-study and process models introduced in Chapter Four to give students practice reading different kinds of texts, and practice writing in response to a variety of texts and situations.

PART THREE

Chapter Seven, "Responding to Personal Experiences," introduces students to reading and constructing personal experience texts. The ability to critically read and write personal experience texts is useful in the academic community and in the world at large. The reading assignments in this chapter challenge students to think more deeply about their own lives by introducing them to ways of living and thinking beyond their own experience. In addition, since who a person is (and where that person has been) profoundly influences the critical judgments he or she makes about the world, writing critically about personal experiences can help students discover how who they are influences how and what they think.

Chapter Eight, "Responding to Processes," is designed to give students practice reading and writing process texts. The ability to critically read and write texts that describe and analyze complex processes is crucial in the academic community and the world at large. The world we live in is a world of complex and interrelated processes, and the more students practice thinking critically about the processes they encounter by reading and writing critically about them, the more thoroughly they'll understand those processes.

Chapter Nine, "Responding to Controversial Issues," underscores the argumentative nature of most higher-level academic writing and gives students practice reading and writing texts that respond to controversy.

PART FOUR

Chapter Ten, "Responding to Essays," is designed to give students practice reading and responding to brief analytical, interpretative texts. Since a great deal of college level writing is done in response to brief, analytical, interpretative texts—formal essays or chapters in book-length books—the ability to read essays critically and then to respond interpretatively is a crucial element in students' academic success.

Chapter Eleven, "Responding to Fiction and Film," is designed to give students practice thinking critically and writing interpretatively about fictional works. The ability to critically read and effectively interpret works of fiction is important in the academic community and the world at large. Since fictional works are a large part of the record of human existence, interpreting them can help students think critically about their own cultures and about the ways human thought has evolved. In addition, interpreting fictional works encourages students to reflect on their own lives and values, and challenges them to personal growth and change.

PART FIVE

"Strategies for Writing in the Academic Community"

Chapter Twelve, "Writing the Researched Paper," is a step-by-step process-oriented guide to writing researched essays. Chapter Twelve is designed to be used in concert with any one or all of the major assignment chapters.

Chapter Thirteen, "Strategies for Responding to Essay Questions," provides students with hands-on experience preparing for, and responding to, essay questions.

PART SIX

"Strategies for Assessment and Process-Based Revision"—This unique handbook presents an individual diagnostic method for assessment and process-based revision that gives students specific strategies for recognizing and overcoming their habitual areas of writing weakness.

TIPS FOR TEACHING WITH
THE RESPONSIVE WRITER

Although there are many ways to teach composition, the one thing that all effective writing teachers have in common is that they have developed a personal pedagogical philosophy by thinking critically about the ways writing is taught and by reflecting on their own experiences with the process of writing. Since there are many ways to teach writing effectively, the best way to use this book and the other pedagogical resources available to you is to use them actively and critically. As you read the teaching suggestions and student activities included in this book, consider how you agree and disagree with them; then, use the ones you agree with and amend the ones you disagree with to bring them in line with your own pedagogical philosophy. The general suggestions for using *The Responsive Writer* that follow are based on my own experiences as a writer and teacher of writing; however, this book is designed to be flexible enough to accommodate a variety of teaching philosophies and styles.

The Classroom as Writing Community—Perhaps the two most valuable things you can communicate to your students are that writing is not a solitary activity nor an effortless one. Even the best writers struggle with language and get help from editors and peers. Because the journey toward becoming a better writer has a powerful collaborative element, writing classes are most effective when they function as student-centered writing communities, rather than as teacher-centered lecture classes. In the best writing classroom, the teacher is a coach and facilitator who listens and reads student work carefully and offers problem-solving advice. In addition, effective writing teachers are writers themselves; they understand the writing process from the inside out because they continue to struggle with it and reflect on it themselves. The best writing teachers also make themselves members of the classroom writing community by sharing their own struggles with and reflections on the writing process with their students.

Assessment—Although "Part Six" of *The Responsive Writer*, "Strategies for Assessment and Process-Based Revision" is written to a student audience, it's also designed to help writing teachers diagnose students' individual areas of writing weakness. Based on research that indicates that writing problems are habitual and writer-specific, the individual diagnostic method for assessment I present in this book focuses on the causes of writing weakness and matches assessment criteria with problem-solving strategies designed to help students become better writers by filling in gaps in knowledge and by revising the ways they use the writing process as individuals.

The journal entries and assessed draft of Jesse Richter's "Fire on the Plains" in Chapter Three provide an illustration of the idiosyncratic nature of writing weakness; Jesse's writing samples reveal discrete problems that are repeated again and again. Furthermore, the problems that were revealed in Jesse's writing samples weren't mysterious and insurmountable; they merely indicated gaps in his knowledge or chronic ways he misused the writing process. In addition, from his prior struggles with the writing process, Jesse had a pretty good idea of what some of his writing weaknesses were by the time he came into my class; he knew he had problems with development and with what he calls in his interview in Chapter Three "glossy writing." Looking at my annotations on Jesse's draft of "Fire on the Plains" and reading through "Part Six" will give you an introduction to the individual diagnostic method for assessment. However, for a full explanation of the method (including discussions of self-assessment and peer assessment) see the assessment ancillary that accompanies the annotated instructor's edition of *The Responsive Writer*.

Critical Reading and Craft Study Models—I've designed the critical reading and craft study models in *The Responsive Writer* as concept-based replacements for the "questions for discussion" found in most readers and rhetorics. The major problem I've always had with "questions for discussion" is that they're leading and specific rather than being interactive and conceptual. Because such questions usually call for a specific "correct" answer about the essay in question, instead of inviting interaction with the text, they tend to close interaction and discussion down. In addition, the specific nature of the questions doesn't allow student readers to see that there are general principles that can be applied to the reading and writing of all texts.

My purpose in creating both models was to provide clear conceptual connections between the reading and writing processes. The critical reading model (under the rubric, "Listen; Read Texts for Meaning") is an inductive paradigm designed to help students discover meaning in texts through the application of Aristotelian concepts. Rather than leading students toward a particular "correct" judgment of a given text's meaning, the model invites students to read interactively by making evidence-supported cases for their judgments of meaning; any judgment that can be supported with evidence from the text is considered a credible judgment.

The craft study model, appearing as "Learn; Read with an Eye to the Writer's Craft" in each major assignment chapter, connects the reading and writing process by focusing on the rhetorical choices writers make during the writing process. In addition, "Focusing on Persuasion" subsections within the craft study model help students discern the persuasive purposes of the texts they encounter by emphasizing the specific ways (logos, pathos, ethos) writer's use language to effect change in their audiences. The concepts and vocabulary from critical reading and craft study models are then carried over into the writing process section of each chapter (under, "Respond; Develop a Perspective through Writing").

The most effective way to use both the critical reading and craft study models is in a student-centered rather than teacher-centered classroom. Rather than taking an active role in the classroom conversation, I play the part of facilitator and arbiter. I listen carefully and jump in only on occasion—to ask for more evidence; to slow down the conversation while a student with a minority opinion clarified his or her ideas; or to note a subtle connection between one student's judgments and another's. I also make a point of celebrating those moments when students give up positions that aren't credible.

Research—I've designed this book to allow for a full integration of research into every reading and writing activity. My purpose in doing so is to allow students to see that research isn't something added on to the writing process, but, rather, an integral part of critical reading, writing and thinking.

However, to integrate research into assignments, you'll have to be knowledgeable about the research resources on your campus. Since most college libraries are changing rapidly because of the introduction of new and more effective electronic sources, it's a good idea to keep up to date on the workings of your library by regularly consulting the person on your campus who is responsible for information literacy. **Information literacy specialists** are particularly useful because they're trained to see research sources from the perspective of the least experienced researcher.

In addition to providing research information that is specifically aimed at undergraduate needs, an information literacy specialist can also help you integrate the learning of research strategies into particular reading and writing assignments. For example, working collaboratively with a library staff member, you might design an assignment that combines a self-guided tour of the library with the "Research Unknowns" step of the critical reading model or with any one of the "Research Opportunities" included in this book; in addition, you might combine one of the "Responsive Prewriting Exercises" with CD-ROM lab instruction. Your students will learn the workings of the campus library much more thoroughly if that learning is an integral part of real reading and writing assignments.

Collaborative Writing Assignments—I've presented the **critical reading** and **craft study** models included in the major assignment chapters of *The Responsive Writer* in the form of "Collaborative Writing Assignments" to give students the opportunity to test and expand their ideas in small groups (in or outside of the classroom) before they make their judgments totally public in classroom discussion. However, I've designed these assignments to be flexible enough so that you can make full collaborative use of them in every chapter or vary their use by focusing on different assignments or on only parts of each assignment as you work through the book. For example, in one chapter, you might focus on critical reading, and in the next, on craft study; or you might have your students do part of an assignment as a collaborative activity and part as an individual activity.

In addition, since a great deal of writing in the academic community and in the world at large is collaborative, I've designed the text to be flexible enough for instructors to incorporate collaboration into research activities and formal writing assignments. Chapter Eight, "Responding to Processes," contains an essay written collaboratively by student writers Brian Ricker and Anthony Pollner; the chapter also contains an interview in which Brian and Anthony discuss the negative and positive aspects of collaborative writing.

ACKNOWLEDGMENTS

From working out the ideas, to getting the language right, this book has been a collaborative enterprise. My greatest debts are to Aristotle and Kenneth Burke, and to the thousands of students who have challenged and inspired me since the first day I walked into a classroom and picked up that teacher's piece of chalk. However, I would also like to acknowledge others whose work has clearly contributed to the ideas and pedagogical principles included in this book: Linda Flower and John Hayes, Toby Fulwiler, Andrea Lunsford, Donald Murray, Mike Rose, John Warnock, and Tillie Warnock. In addition, I would like to thank two exceptional mentors and friends: Bill Kittredge, who taught me the importance of voice (and a great many other things about writing as well); and Larry Riley J.D., whose lawyerly way of thinking had a profound effect on me and on the shape of this book.

I also owe debts to friends and colleagues in the academic and writing communities in Missoula, Montana. I would like to thank the members of the Rattlesnake Salon (Sharon Barrett, Kate Gadbow, Patricia Goedicke, Deirdre McNamer, Megan McNamer, Caroline Patterson, Connie Poten, and Marnie Prange), who for the past ten years have been careful, critical readers of my work; I would particularly like to thank Kate who has been a close colleague, a wise critic, and an extraordinary friend for more than a decade. In addition, I wish to thank colleagues at The University of Montana whose ideas found their way into this book: literature and writing teachers Bill Bevis, Debra Earling, Mark Medvetz, and Lois Welch; and Sue Samson, Humanities Librarian and information literacy specialist at The University of Montana's Mansfield Library. I'm grateful also for the support of my friend and chair, Bruce Bigley, and for the very remarkable support of friends Virginia Carmichael and Janet Whaley.

I've been especially fortunate to develop and publish this book with Harcourt Brace. The people at Harcourt taught me the true meaning of the word "collaboration." Michael Rosenberg, editor and friend, was enthusiastic and savvy from the very beginning. Christi Grider tirelessly did the detective work to gather the permissions. Graduate student intern Kim Allison made astute comments about the book's arrangement that led me to cut a ponderous chapter and integrate material throughout the text. Copy editor, Donald Pharr, clarified the book's voice and made invaluable final suggestions. Debra Jenkin and John Haakenson guided the final manuscript gracefully through the production process, and designer, Vicki Whistler, made the book a work of art. However, my greatest thanks go to developmental editor, Camille Adkins, whose knowledge and skill and good humor were with me at every stage of the writing process, and who kept on saying, "Just one more draft." It was also Camille who chose the extraordinary reviewers from across the country who carefully read the manuscript through several drafts and challenged me to clarify my thinking and writing:

Chris Burnham, New Mexico State University
Patricia E. Connors, University of Memphis
Allene Cooper, Boise State University
Jonathan S. Cullick, University of Kentucky
Elizabeth Curtin, Salisbury State University
Kitty Dean, Nassau Community College
Margaret Baker Graham, Iowa State University
Maureen Hourigan, University of Nevada
C. Jeriel Howard, Northeast Illinois University
Ted E. Johnson, El Paso Community College Valle Verde
Sarah Liggett, Louisiana State University
Lisa J. McClure, South Illinois University Carbondale
James C. McDonald, University of Southwestern Louisiana
Patricia Murray, California State University Northridge
Irvin Peckham, University of Nebraska at Omaha

Jane Peterson, Richland College
Ken Smith, Rutgers University
Victoria Stein, University of Arizona
Camille Taylor, College of Lake County
Irwin Weiser, Purdue University
Stephen Caldwell Wright, Seminole Community College

Finally, I'd like to thank my family: my parents and brother who set the stage for this book by loving language and argument; Ben, whose joy energized me; Jenny who talked me through the rough spots; and Mike who was there every step of the way, and who never for a moment doubted I could do it.

THE RESPONSIVE WRITER

PART
ONE

WRITING:
ITS
MOTIVES,
METHODS,
AND
PROCESSES

CHAPTER
ONE
MOTIVES

WRITING IS CONVERSATION

Imagine that you enter a parlor. You come late. When you arrive, others have long preceded you, and they are engaged in a heated discussion, a discussion too heated for them to pause and tell you exactly what it is about. In fact, the discussion had already begun long before any of them got there, so that no one present is qualified to retrace for you all the steps that had gone before. You listen for a while, until you decide that you have caught the tenor of the argument; then you put in your oar. Someone answers; you answer him; another comes to your defense; another aligns himself against you, to either the embarrassment or gratification of your opponent, depending upon the quality of your ally's assistance. However, the discussion is interminable. The hour grows late, you must depart. And you do depart, with the discussion still vigorously in progress.
—KENNETH BURKE, from *Philosophy of Literary Form*

Underlying all language is the simple and wonderful fact that we are not alone. We live in community with other people. We converse. We encounter the world, and we speak to one another about what we've encountered. How does writing fit into all of this? A finished piece of writing is language made visible on the page. Like conversation, writing is responsive. Sometimes it's actually conversational response organized and written out; one writer will **read** what another writer has **written** and write back in response. Other times the response is to **situations** that exist in the world; writers will respond to injustice or oppression, to the beauty they see around them, or to significant relationships they have with other people.

In the writing you'll be doing at your college or university, the response will be to the subject matter of courses. You might be asked to respond to a lecture, to a written text, to an observed event, or to any combination of the three. Whatever the **text** or **situation** might be, it will speak to you, and when you write, you will speak back. The whole history, the whole evolution, of human thought is really just one long conversation, one long dialogue. People wrote, other people read what was written, and the readers wrote in response. And it has just gone on and on.

What does all of this mean, and how is it important to the writing you are and will be doing at your college or university? You are entering (in fact, you have already entered) the great conversation, the great exchange and evolution of ideas that began when our first ancestor equipped with vocal chords and a reflexive jaw spoke the first sound that had meaning to a partner who was similarly equipped. That first cave man or woman said something like ''Oogh,'' and his or her conversational partner answered with a thoughtful ''OOgh, bah'' (*bah* meaning ''but''). And that was how it all got started.

CRITICAL THINKING AND CRITICAL WRITING

What entering the conversation means is that you'll get to test and expand your conclusions about experience by engaging in discussion with others. You'll be presented with other people's ideas and knowledge, and you'll compare and combine those ideas and that knowledge with your own experience and then respond. But in order to respond effectively (in order to be listened to), you'll have to learn to read and listen carefully and critically, both to the messages coming from outside and to your responses to those messages. You'll have to examine and analyze what other people are saying, but you'll also have to examine and analyze what you think in response. What all this examination and analysis add up to is **critical thinking.**

I'm using the word *critical* in a positive sense here; being critical doesn't necessarily mean being negative. The word comes from the Greek *kritikos,* meaning being able to discern or judge. To communicate effectively in writing you'll have to be discerning and judgmental in three different ways. You'll have to **read critically** to discern the **meaning** that others have discovered in experience. You'll have to **think critically** to decide what *you* think. You'll have to **write critically** to refine your ideas and communicate them to others.

WRITING IS PERSUASION

Wherever there is ''meaning'' there is ''persuasion.''
—KENNETH BURKE

To **communicate** is to create **meaning.** Certainly, when you add your critical judgments to the ongoing conversation about a text or situation by writing, you create meaning. However, even the most "mindless" forms of communication—the self-communication of daydreaming, the idle chatter of small talk—create meaning. When you daydream, you create a meaningful scenario in you head; when you engage in small talk, the conversation may not be profound, but it has meaning. The simple "No!" of a parent to a toddler has meaning. The lawyer's complex legal brief probably contains many meanings.

Furthermore, every act of communication creates meaning to accomplish some **purpose.** You daydream to entertain yourself or to give yourself hope for the future. You engage in small talk to relieve boredom or to ward off that uncomfortable feeling of having nothing to say. The parent says no to keep the child from injuring herself or breaking something. The lawyer writes the legal brief to win a case.

And it's precisely because communication creates meaning to accomplish a purpose that all successful communication is to some degree **persuasive.** If your daydreams aren't compelling, they won't entertain you, and you'll stop daydreaming. If the small talk you engage in isn't interesting enough to relieve your boredom or discomfort, you'll make some excuse and be on your way. If the parental "No!" isn't convincing, the child will keep right on heading for the stairs. If the lawyer's brief isn't credible enough to sway the jury, the case will be lost.

The point is, since writing is a communicative activity, virtually every written text you encounter attempts to persuade you to some degree. Think of all the texts you've encountered in the last twenty-four hours: billboards and news stories, textbooks and flyers, bills and letters, notes and reminders. Now think of the **purpose** of each text—the **change the text sought in your knowledge or thought or action.** The change the text sought in you may have been subtle and only in the mind: know that there was an earthquake in California; know that your roommate won't be home until ten o'clock; consider the dangers of smoking; think about your insensitive behavior. Or the change the text sought may have been dramatic and physical: put money in an envelope and send it to the earthquake victims in California; stay home until your roommate gets there; crush out that cigarette; clean up after yourself.

WRITER-BASED GENERAL PURPOSES

Sometimes the general purpose for writing is **writer-based.** Journals and class notes are examples of writer-based writing. If your purpose is writer-based, you'll write to **change** your own knowledge or way of thinking or acting, with no external audience in the writing equation. You might write in a journal to **learn** and **understand** by exploring what you think. And as you learn and understand, you might **express** your ideas and feelings about the subject of your writing. At other times, or at the same time, you might write to **remember.** The process of writing will help you fix facts or concepts or your own emotional responses in your memory. You might also write to **observe** sensory experiences; writing down what you receive through your senses will help you understand your sensory experiences more clearly.

However, the writing you do for yourself alone will be meaningful only if it is sufficiently **persuasive.** If the class notes that you take are disorganized and incomplete, they'll probably wind up confusing you instead of helping you learn and remember. If your personal journal is dishonest and slight, you'll probably wind up being bored with yourself instead of learning what it is you think and feel.

AUDIENCE-BASED GENERAL PURPOSES

Often, though, you'll be writing primarily to **change** an audience other than yourself. Your general purpose for writing might be to **inform** your audience or to **explain** concepts, to change your audience's knowledge or understanding. You might write to formally **persuade** others to accept a particular point of view or take some course of action. At other times, your purpose will be to **explore** ideas with your audience by sharing your reflections and posing questions. In addition, or in combination with other purposes, you might write to **entertain** your audience by engaging their wit and imagination.

When you write to an audience other than yourself, the persuasive stakes are raised higher than when you're writing only for yourself. Writing to change your own knowledge or understanding is one thing; writing to change an audience who doesn't know and feel what you know and feel is another. When you write, you have to get beyond yourself and imagine your audience's possible responses, and deal with those responses as you present your view of things.

Whatever your audience-based purposes for writing, your intent will also be to **express** yourself. Since critical writing conveys your own ideas and judgments about experience, that unique human being, you, will always be to some degree present in your writing.

WRITING IS EXPRESSION

The more a writer is **personally invested** in a piece of writing, the more **expressive** that piece of writing is. And just as virtually all writing is persuasive to some extent, all writing is expressive to one degree or another. When writers write expressively, they're **responding** to the subjects of their writing with interest or belief. And the way they achieve that interest or belief is by framing agreements and disagreements and by making judgments. Personal journals and creative writing are the kinds of writing we most readily think of when we think of expressive writing, but all kinds of writing—from journalism to scientific writing—can be *highly* expressive. Expressiveness in writing can take many forms—from the expression of simple interest in a subject to the expression of powerful judgments on it.

THE ROLE OF CRITICAL THINKING IN EXPRESSIVE WRITING

Just writing expressively won't make you a great writer, or even a good one. If you merely express without thoughtfully testing your responses, your writing, just like your untested thinking, is apt to be gushing and superficial.

Following are two passages excerpted from longer pieces of writing. In the first, from the "Beauty Helpline" column of *Cosmopolitan* magazine, the writer has made specific word choices to express and communicate interest in the subject being written about. Read it carefully, and see if you can locate the words that express the writer's interest.

> To "volumize" a wimpy mane, try the following technique (from Rodney Groves, of New York City's Vartali Salon): Apply setting lotion to freshly shampooed hair from roots to ends, then toss hair over one side of the head and blow dry from underneath, section by section—builds body. (Once each layer is dry, pull back to where it normally falls.) Next, wind hair on large velcro rollers. (To speed setting process, attach new-age hair cap to blow dryer—acts like old-fashioned hood dryer. Stay under cap for five minutes.) Remove rollers, and for added fullness, tease roots with fine-tooth comb. Finally, brush hair into place and spritz with hair spray. Voila . . . fat, sexy tresses.

In the second passage, excerpted from *Sunrise with Seamonsters*, writer and teacher Paul Theroux expresses powerful judgments on the subject he's writing about. Read it carefully, and locate as many of Theroux's judgments as you can.

> The youth who is subverted, as most men are, into believing in the masculine ideal is effectively separated from women and he

spends the rest of his life finding women a riddle and a nuisance. Of course, there is a female version of this male affliction. It begins with mothers encouraging little girls to say (to other adults) "Do you like my new dress?" In a sense, little girls are traditionally urged to please adults with a kind of coquettishness, while boys are enjoined to behave like monkeys toward each other. The nine-year-old coquette proceeds to become womanish in a subtle power game in which she learns to be sexually indispensable, socially decorative and always alert to a man's sense of inadequacy.

Although the excerpt from *Cosmopolitan* contains expressive words that suggest the writer's interest (adjectives like *wimpy* and *sexy,* nouns like *mane* and *tresses,* verbs like *toss* and *spritz*), of the two excerpts, only the Theroux passage contains the thoughtful **judgments** about experience characteristic of critical writing. Both excerpts are roughly the same length, and both create **meaning** to **change** an audience's knowledge or way of thinking or acting. However, the second contains sophisticated ideas, and the first doesn't. Those ideas are conclusions that Theroux has drawn about the customary ways that boys and girls are raised, and how those ways of being raised go on to influence the behavior of adult males and females. Consider your own responses to the two passages. The *Cosmopolitan* excerpt wouldn't be likely to spark a discussion. There aren't any conclusions in it with which you'd be likely to agree or disagree. At best, your response might be to try the technique on your own hair. However, the Theroux excerpt makes you respond in a different way. You may totally agree with Theroux, you may totally disagree, or you may agree with some of his judgments and disagree with others.

The point is that critical writing involves a whole lot more than simply being personally invested in a subject. With interest and belief, there also comes the responsibility to be knowledgeable about your subject and critical about your responses to that subject. In order to write expressively *and* critically, you'll have to develop a **self-critical internal audience** that will allow you to become a critical reader of your own thinking and writing. You'll have to learn how to agree and/or disagree with your own responses to the texts and situations you encounter by searching for evidence that will either support or oppose those responses.

None of this will be easy, but, like physical exercise, the more you do it, the less difficult it will get. The critical thinking that leads to effective writing is hard work. But, because writing critically allows us to clarify and express our own ideas and judgments, it's one of the most rewarding and important kinds of work any of us will ever do.

However, don't just take my word for all of this. Read the transcript of a conversation I had with a student, and listen to what she says about her continuing growth as a critical writer and thinker.

Stephanie Wing is a senior majoring in English and art. When I met Stephanie four years ago in a basic writing class (the lowest level writing course our university offers), she thought that improving her writing skills was something she'd better do to make it through college. The year after she was in my class she took a literature class and decided to major in English as well as art. These days, when her grandparents ask her what she's going to do with her double degree, she says only half teasingly, "Be a famous writer."

Over the years, Stephanie and I have kept in touch. In her interview she mentions three teachers who have been important influences on her writing: William Bevis and Lois Welch, both professors of literature, and Debra Earling, a professor of creative writing. As you read, focus on how Stephanie's perspective on the usefulness of writing has changed since she took her first writing class.

A STUDENT WRITER TALKS ABOUT CRITICAL WRITING AND THINKING

J. S.: When you were in my class, one of the first things you said to me was that you weren't a good writer. Can you remember back to when you thought you weren't a good writer?

S. W.: (laughs) Of course, there are still times when I don't think I'm a good writer.

J. S.: Why did you think you weren't a good writer?

S. W.: It wasn't just my writing. From the time I was young in school, I felt really insufficient as a reader. In fifth grade when they went around the room, I would dread when my paragraph came up, but when I was a sophomore in college I found out I had a learning disability. I was pretty depressed about the whole thing, but I was relieved, too. It wasn't that I had done all that badly in school. I could get by. I could always find another way to learn things. When I found out about the learning disability, I said to myself, you'll just have to work on this. You can't just give up.

continued on page 10

continued from page 9

J. S.:   How did you work on it?

S. W.:   The suggestions that were given to me by the student support services—things like reading out loud and reading as much as I could—which I still don't do enough of.

J. S.:   The first time I told you you were a good writer, you protested; I remember you said, ''But you don't know how long it takes me. It's such an incredible amount of work.''

S. W.:   I do work hard on my writing. I have to. I have to work hard because I have something to say. Sometimes when I write and I go back over things that I've written in my journal, I almost amaze myself. Sometimes I don't even remember having written it—I look at something and I think, I can't believe I wrote that. The things that I write that I really like, I go back to—even if it's just a group of words or a part of something that I believe has power. And I read them over and over and think about what they mean and the way they connect in your ear.

J. S.:   You once told me you hadn't read or written much when you graduated from high school.

S. W.:   I read about five books in high school and only wrote one research paper in a history class. Writing the research paper was an important experience.

J. S.:   Why was writing a research paper important?

S. W.:   Now, after being in college and having to do analytical writing, I think that it's important to know how to do both analytical and more ''creative'' types of writing. If you have the base of the analytical writing and also know how to be creative, then you've got it made.

J. S.:   Why are both elements important?

S. W.:   If you have a hold of how language works and you also know the power behind the language, then you'll be able to communicate what you think and feel clearly. When I write, I want—and it doesn't work all the time—I want people to understand what's really on my mind. I feel that I've been lucky in having professors who push me to take my analytical writing further.

J. S.:   Who, for example?

continued to next page

S. W.: Bill Bevis. Last semester I wrote a paper on Gertrude
Stein, and he gave it back and said, "You know, this is
an 'A' paper, but I want Chapter Two." The thing that
was so neat about that paper was that I kind of went
out on a limb—when I first read Gertrude Stein, I said,
"What in the hell is this???!!!" I mean, it didn't make
any sense. And then I kept reading, and she does this
repeating, saying something once and then repeating it
in a little different way, and I thought, oh geez. And
then I thought she must have some sort of purpose for
the structure that she used, and that's when I started
reading more of her things, because you can't just read
one thing of any writer. Then a friend lent me a book of
Gertrude Stein's collected works, and there was one
paragraph she wrote and it talked about language,
about the beauty of language, and from that I kind of
felt that there is beauty in the way language is spoken
and written and the story it tells. What was amazing
was that it was almost like I had *known* that, but I
didn't *think* it until I began writing about it and could
get hold of it. Bill [Bevis] really encouraged my own
thinking about the subject. He didn't just want to hear
what he had to say back at him, which was important.
It gave me kind of confidence in myself and confidence
in my own thinking. Still, sometimes when I think
about it, I feel so young in my thinking. I've learned a
lot in the past three years, but I still feel like I have so
much more to learn about language and writing.

J. S.: Is that a good feeling or a bad feeling?

S. W.: It's scary, because it's going to take a lot of work to get
to where I want to be. I know that I want to write, but I
also want to understand what I'm writing and why I'm
writing. A lot of the time I feel out of control. I don't
understand what gives me this urge—I mean, at this
point I can't *not* write. I keep trying to put names to the
urge, to understand it. Maybe it's because when I was a
little kid I was told I couldn't do it, I wasn't worth
anything, and you know how you get that little "Well,
I'll show you." But mainly it's because writing helps me
look at myself and see how I fit into the world. It helps

continued on page 12

continued from page 11

me get my thinking clear. I have a relative who ignores life. She's one of those people who doesn't think deeply. That sounds kind of harsh. I think of how her life has been led—the pain and the suffering that she's gone through. And I think it's because she doesn't listen to herself or isn't able to listen to herself. I'm thankful that I think deeply because I feel like I'll avoid a lot of the suffering that she's experienced. She has no control over the decisions she has in her life. People say you make your choices, but if you aren't thoughtful you're unable to see the other choices out there.

When I took your class, I thought, this is something I have to do to get through college and do well. Writing was a college survival skill. Even though you gave me a good grade, it's almost like I didn't know what I really had until I was in Lois Welch's class and she told me. And then later Debra Earling told me, too.

J. S.:   You mean you thought I was being nice to you when I gave you a good grade? You thought it was a pity thing?

S. W.:   (laughing) Well, you know. No. It's almost like *you* have to decide—*I* had to decide. I had to believe in myself; I had to believe that what I had to say should be heard.

Of course, not all of you reading this book will decide in the next few years that you want to be famous writers. However, I think Stephanie has made a pretty good case that critical reading, writing, and thinking can be more than just academically useful. Certainly, being a good writer can help you get good grades in college and a better job when you graduate. (Look in the classified section of any newspaper under "Professional Positions," and you'll notice how often the phrase "skill in written communication" comes up.)

However, for Stephanie, getting an "A" on a paper from literature professor Bill Bevis wasn't enough; she had to go on and really "get hold" of what she thought by reading and writing more. In the final analysis, Stephanie doesn't "work hard" at her writing to get good grades or a good job (although her grades are good and her job prospects are excellent); Stephanie writes to develop herself more fully as a thinker and a human. She writes to "get [her] thinking clear." And that clear thinking gives her power over the decisions she makes in her own life; it enables her to "see the other choices out there."

In addition to making a case that critical thinking and writing can help you develop as a human being, Stephanie's conversation also reveals that becoming a good writer isn't something that happens overnight. Like any other complex skill—skiing, for example, or playing the piano—learning to write takes instruction and continual practice. And, as with skiing or playing the piano, the first step toward becoming a good writer or a better one is the conscious decision to do it.

CHAPTER
TWO
METHODS

Stephanie Wing

GETTING STARTED (JOURNAL ENTRY)

I write in a couple—actually three—stages. First, I think. It's not like I consciously think about what I'm going to write. I'm walking down the street, and I think about what I see, or I listen to people's conversations. This includes people that I don't know and people I know. Sometimes I even think when I'm by myself in my room or in my living room. I think pretty constantly. I'm kind of a daydreamer. Then what I do is write in my journal about the situations that I find have a lot of power, or I write about things I've read. I write in my journal in my room in my bed, usually at night. Sometimes, I write out my frustrations—I kind of explode. And then once I get an idea I go to my dad's house and use his computer. When I'm actually composing a piece of writing, I don't write it in my journal; I can't see it. I compose on the computer. I feel like when I'm on the computer I'm plugged in. When I handwrite it takes too long. On the computer I can think faster and my thoughts are displayed on the screen in front of my face so I can see what they look like. If I don't like the way they look or the way they sound after I read them out loud, it's easy to fix them.

THE SUBJECTS OF WRITING   Any subject worth thinking about is worth writing about. This is especially true of the subject matter of your college courses. Even if you don't *have* to write in a particular class, writing about the texts and situations you encounter in that class can help you understand them more fully. Writing about the content of your classes will make you generally more thoughtful about what you're learning, and the more thoughtful you are, the more likely what you learn will come to have relevance to your life.

Make writing a part of your daily routine, as Stephanie does, by keeping some kind of **journal.** You might keep a **course journal,** either in a notebook or in a computer file, for each class you take. Keeping course journals will help you make connections between ideas and knowledge encountered in one class and ideas and knowledge encountered in another. In addition, the journals can be used as resources for writing formal papers and as a study guides for exams. Chapter Four, "Critical Reading and Responding," contains a course journal entry written by student writer Lance Hummel.

You may also want to keep a **personal journal.** Use it to respond to movies that you see and books that you read outside your college classes. Use it also to explore your ideas about situations in your personal and family life and in the world in general. Then compare your personal journal with your course journals. Finding corresponding ideas and circumstances in the two types of journals will help connect what you're learning in your classes with what's going on in your personal life and in the world at large. Later in the next chapter you'll encounter personal journal entries written by the poet Sylvia Plath when she was a freshman in college.

Keep in mind as you write in your journals that journal entries are not "assignments" to be turned in and evaluated. Your purpose for journal writing is to come to an understanding of your own intellectual and emotional responses. Think of your journal as your own personal writing space, and aim for honesty and exploration.

WRITER'S TOOLS   Before the widespread use of computers for word processing, the tools writers chose were as individual as the times when they chose to write. Some writers were typers; some wrote in longhand with sharp number-two pencils. But these days most professional writers work primarily on the computer.

If you have the opportunity to write on a computer, start doing it as soon as possible. The fact that writing is a process of discovery and clarification makes writing on a computer a natural. As you discover new ideas, it's simple to go back and revise your emerging text in light of your discoveries. Learning the basics of word processing is incredibly easy. In twenty minutes you can learn all you need to know to get started, and with the help of a manual and a computer lab assistant you'll continue to learn. Don't worry if you're not a good typist. Writing on a computer isn't just typing. Because you're composing rather than copying, you don't have to have a high keyboarding speed. In addition, formatting texts is simple, rewriting is much easier on the computer, and for bad spellers like me, there's that wonderful feature called spellcheck.

It's also useful to purchase a small notebook (a three-by-five spiral is perfect) to keep with you at all times. As ideas come to you, you can write them down in the form of notes to yourself.

COMPUTER TIP

The two basic things you need to know to start writing on a computer or word processor are how to "enter text" and how to "save" the text you've entered. Entering text is simply typing into the machine so you can see what you've written on the screen. If you're writing on a word processor (the nineties version of the typewriter—an electronic machine with word processing but not computational capability), just start the word processor. When the screen flashes on, begin striking the letter keys. The cursor (a blinking line in some cases; a colored or lighted rectangle in others) will mark the spot on the screen where the next character you enter will appear.

If you're writing on a computer, you'll probably have to get into the word processing program by typing the appropriate letters or choosing the appropriate icon with your mouse. Once you get a screen with a cursor, you can begin writing.

After you've created text, you can "save" it, either on the hard disk of the machine or on floppy disks. "Save" commands differ from one word processing program to another, so you'll have to find out the appropriate command for the program you use.

Most colleges and universities have computer centers where students can find handouts explaining the basics of word processing.

THE WRITING PLACE   Although the best way to begin writing is to start doing it, you can't write just anywhere. Every writer has a particular place where writing is easiest. Stephanie Wing has more than one writing place; she writes in her journal in her room and then composes on her dad's computer. However, Jesse Richter (the student whose writing appears at the end of this chapter) doesn't write at his dad's computer; he does his best writing in a particular campus computer lab. But Jesse's writing partner, Lennace Nelson, never writes in the computer lab; she

RESPONSIVE JOURNAL WRITING

Explore your attitude toward writing in the form of a journal entry (if possible, write this journal entry on a word processor or computer). If writer-based writing (writing only for yourself) has ever been pleasurable or satisfying, explain why and under what circumstances. If you've never written only for your own pleasure or satisfaction, speculate about why you haven't. If you have trouble getting started, focus on your experience as a writer and free-write (write nonstop without worrying about what you get down) for ten minutes.

does her best writing in the converted pantry behind her kitchen. For another student writer, the writing place is a windowless attic room. For yet another, it's the front desk of the dorm, where he works the graveyard shift. Ernest Hemingway's writing place, his study in Key West (it's still there, by the way), was reachable only by a rope bridge. What all these places have in common is that they're distraction-free.

If your dorm room or home is a zoo, look around for a more suitable place to work. Try the library or a study lounge or, better yet, a computer lab. Once you're comfortable working on a computer, the combination of screen and keyboard can become a kind of writing place in itself.

The more you write, the more important the writing place will become to you. Once you've found a place where writing seems easier, stay with it. The ritual of returning to the same place time after time will help you to establish writing as a habit and a discipline.

RESPONSIVE JOURNAL WRITING

Assess the suitabiity of your own "writing place" by writing critically. Describe in detail the place where you do (or have done) your most successful writing. Why do you (or did you) write there? What elements make it a good environment for writing? What elements make it less than ideal?

THE RIGHT TIME TO WRITE   Some writers are five A.M. people; others don't start the writing day until after midnight. However, your writing time should depend on your energy level at different times of the day, rather than on your chosen lifestyle. Don't decide that you're a late-night writer only because you always put off writing papers until after midnight. To discover your best personal writing time, chart your energy level over a couple of average weekdays. If you're wide awake at seven in the morning, don't schedule early-morning classes; set a couple of morning hours aside as writing time, and get yourself as quickly as possible to your writing place.

Although *when* you choose to write is important, *how* you choose to use that time is even more important. Since writing is a process, the use of time is probably the single most important factor in the writing equation. And using the time you have well means saying no. Professional writers probably say no more than people in any other profession. They say no to going out to lunch or out for coffee. They say no to answering the door or the telephone. And they say no to themselves: "No, I won't turn on the TV." "No, I won't go out tonight." "No, I won't do the dishes; they can wait until later."

Writers also ask for help; if their friends or families are demanding too much of them, they quietly take their friends or family members aside and say, "I care for you, but I need this time. Please help me find it." Writers set aside time for their writing, and they keep that time for writing.

THINKING TIME   Writing is thinking made visible, and because it is, you won't only need time to write and a place to write; you'll also need time to think. For some writers, the best, and least intimidating, place to begin writing is not in front of a computer screen or blank sheet of paper but in the mind. Use time that you have free that is not your writing time to think about the subjects of your writing. If you have an assignment due in a history class, think about it while you're exercising or driving to school or making dinner. Just as you set aside and keep time for writing, set aside and keep time for thinking about the subjects of your writing.

RESEARCH AND WRITING

When you write critically, you don't passively record experience. Instead, you make **evidence-supported judgments** about the texts and situations you encounter in the world. However, to formulate the kind of ideas that will stand up under the pressure of criticism, you have to have knowledge of your subject. Simply put, you can't write effectively unless you *know* what you're talking about. And the most efficient way of knowing more is to actively engage in **research.** If you've explored this book, you'll have noticed that the research chapters (Chapter Five, "Primary Research," and Chapter Six, "Secondary Research") are at the front rather than at the back. Research is at the beginning rather than at the end of the writing process.

Engaging in research can be as simple as reading a text that someone else has written or even asking for a classmate's opinion. Whenever you reach beyond yourself for further knowledge of a subject or for someone else's perspective on it, you engage in research. The point is, without actively being aware of it, you're already a researcher. However, the more you formalize the research process by doing it actively and critically, the more use the knowledge you accumulate will have for you.

As well as being part of the library research process, **critical reading** is a research activity in itself. Critical reading is the interactive process of **listening** to, **learning** from, and **responding** to written texts. When you read critically, you are actively **conversing** with the texts you encounter; you listen to what other writers have written and learn from them, and then decide for yourself what *you* think. Reading texts critically not only gives you the opportunity to share in other people's perspectives and ideas but also gives you the knowledge to thoughtfully agree and disagree with other people's points of view. And careful, critical reading can help you unlock texts that at first seem beyond your understanding. Stephanie Wing's journey from a first response of "What the hell is this???!!!" to an "A" paper was the result of critical reading.

The critical reading exercises included in this book are designed to help you clarify your own responses to written texts in the context of classroom conversation. The more different perspectives you have on a given text, the more meaningful that text will become. Listening to your classmates' responses and forming agreements and disagreements with those responses will challenge you to think more deeply and creatively.

However, although critical reading is a research activity, it's only a part of the research process. As soon as possible, explore and begin using the formal research resources your campus has to offer. Take a library tour, and set aside a couple of hours to get acquainted with the library on your own. Do a library search, and focus on a subject from the class you're enrolled in this term that you enjoy the most. Then do some background reading.

Use other students and instructors as resources as well. Invite a classmate to coffee, and discuss what's going on in class. Stop by an instructor's office for further conversation. Reach beyond yourself. Even when research isn't required, make a habit of incorporating at least one research activity into each of your reading and writing assignments. Practicing your research skills when research isn't *required* will make required research that much easier.

THE ROLE OF COLLABORATION IN WRITING

In spite of what you may have heard, writing isn't solitary. Look at the acknowledgments in the front of this book, and you may begin to get an idea of how many people helped me write it. And I mean *really* helped. From working out the ideas to getting the language right, the book you're reading was a collaborative enterprise. Family and friends, students, university colleagues, instructors from other universities, and professional editors read and criticized several drafts of this book and gave me good advice about how to make it better.

INFORMAL COLLABORATIVE RELATIONSHIPS

Working writers are constantly helping each other write better. They **collaborate informally** by attending **workshops** and forming **editorial relationships** with other writers and with editors. In informal collaborative relationships, the members or editors **assess** a text and offer advice to the writer about improving the text by **revising** it. The word *revise* means "to see again." Having others read drafts of your work and conversing with them about their responses can help you see old ideas in a new light and push you to discover new ones. Stephanie Wing collaborated informally with her literature professor and then went on to write Chapter Two of her paper on Gertrude Stein.

In workshops, the collaboration is reciprocal; the members are usually peers who take turns reading one another's work. All the members will read each text produced in the group and then give specific advice about how the writer whose text is being focused on can revise by **cutting** or **adding** material, or by **rearranging** or **rewording.** Editorial relationships are less reciprocal. Although editors give the same kind of advice as workshop partners, they're usually more like mentors than peers. They may know more than the writer about the writing process in general, or they may have more experience with an aspect of the particular writing assignment than does the writer. For example, the editor of a popular magazine would probably know more about the concerns of the magazine's readers than a writer would. In the writing community of your class, your classmates are more likely to function as workshop partners, while your instructor is more likely to serve in an editorial function.

FORMAL COLLABORATIVE RELATIONSHIPS

Writers also **collaborate formally** to **research, draft,** and **revise** entire texts. When writers collaborate formally, each person in the group has a part in every step of the writing process. Most governmental writing and a great deal of academic, business, and screen writing is produced by collaborative committees or by two or three writers working together. However, on occasion, even fiction writers and poets collaborate formally. Chapter Eight contains an essay written collaboratively by students Anthony Pollner and Brian Ricker. Accompanying that essay is the transcript of an interview in which Anthony and Brian talk about the delights and difficulties of collaborative writing.

COLLABORATION AND LEARNING

In addition to helping you produce or revise a particular text, collaboration also gives you access to other people's thinking processes. More often than not, we extend and clarify our knowledge of the world by interacting with others. We **listen** to other people's conclusions and speculations, and we **learn** from them; then we **respond** by constructing our own ideas about the ''meaning'' of experience.

The best way to make use of your college experience is to think of yourself as belonging to a community of other writers and thinkers—writers and thinkers who will help and challenge you. Write to them, and read what they write. Speak with them, and listen carefully to their responses. Use them as collaborative partners to test and expand your ideas.

The informal and formal collaborative assignments you'll find in this book are designed to introduce you to group-based strategies regularly employed by most working writers.

CHAPTER
THREE
PROCESSES

THE WRITING SITUATION

Subject
Writer
Audience
Purpose

Being a college or university student means being a working writer. In the next few years you'll probably write more and under greater pressure than you ever have before. Just as professional writers—journalists and technical writers and magazine writers—are given "assignments" by their employers, you'll be given writing assignments by your instructors. And each writing assignment will be a **writing situation,** with its own unique system of choices and constraints. A writing situation is defined by the **writer** who is writing, the **audience** to whom the piece of writing is addressed, the **subject** that is being written about, and the **purpose** that the writer is trying to accomplish. When you write to fulfill an assignment, all four of the elements that define the writing situation interact and influence the final form of the written text you create.

Certainly, the **subject** you're writing about—the text or situation you're responding to—determines the choices you make as you write. However, what you write is ultimately created by you, the **writer,** an individual human being with unique personal and educational histories. Given the same writing **assignment,** no two people will produce exactly the same text. Every text you've ever created in response to a subject has been different from those created by others given the same assignment. The responsive journal entries you've written so far while working through this chapter are different from those your classmates wrote.

And just as the person you are influences what you choose to put down on the page, the **audience** to whom you're writing also influences your choices. No matter what your age, a letter to your mother describing your weekend activities will be very different from a letter to your best friend describing the same weekend. You'll make different choices as you write to each of your audiences, emphasize different things, leave out different things, include different things.

What you write will also be affected by the **purpose** you have for writing. Your purpose in any writing situation is the specific **change** in knowledge or thought or action you desire from your audience. The change you want can be as mild as getting your audience to know factual information or as demanding as getting the audience to change its position on a controversial issue. When you write to an audience hoping to accomplish one purpose, you'll make one set of choices. But when you write to that same audience with a different purpose in mind, you'll make another set of choices altogether. If you were writing about a campus issue only to inform your audience about it, you would include one kind of information. However, if you were writing to that same audience with the purpose of persuading them to agree with your position on the issue, you would develop your text in a different way; you would include your judgments and the evidence to back those judgments up.

Some writing situations—some writing assignments—will allow you to make a great many choices as a writer; you may be free to choose your audience, subject, or purpose—or, perhaps, all three. And those essential choices will allow you new, more detailed, choices. With other assignments, your choices will be limited; your choice of audience or subject or even purpose may be constrained. For example, the assigned journal entries in this chapter all limit your choices in some way.

Although operating under constraints might seem to add up to negative pressure, you can use the pressure created by constraints to your intellectual advantage in creative and dynamic ways. Constraints reflect the conversational nature of writing, and rather than throttling you down, they can give you a starting place, a challenging structure to push off against. The challenge of writing for a specific and demanding audience can force you to put critical pressure on your own ideas. And the more you think critically about your own conclusions, the more refined and solid those conclusions become. Some ideas fall under the pressure, but others grow stronger and send out branches that lead to new discoveries.

WRITING IS A PROCESS

All college writing assignments **(writing situations)** are constrained by deadlines, and because they are, it's crucial to recognize that **writing is a process.** In its simplest form, the writing process looks like this:

Encounter a Subject
Respond by Thinking
Respond in Writing
Rewrite the Response

You have to encounter a subject before you can think about it, and you have to be thoughtful about the subject before you can write effectively about it, and you have to write before you can rewrite. Sounds neat, but what complicates the neatness is that you don't finish one step of the process and go on to the next. Instead, you're constantly rethinking and rewriting *as* you're writing, and rethinking and writing *as* you're rewriting. Writing is **recursive.** Writing is recursive because thinking is recursive. We don't think one thought and then forget it. One thought leads to another, and the second thought often makes us change our minds, however slightly, about the first. We've all had those moments when the mental lights go on. We think a new thought, and suddenly we understand something we didn't understand before. When that happens, we're thinking recursively; we're conversing with ourselves, and we're discovering through that conversation new ways of looking at old bits of experience and information. We can see evidence of this phenomenon even in the simplest pieces of writing. For example, the shopping lists or notes we write to ourselves often contain additions or corrections.

And not only is the process of producing a single text recursive; your own process of becoming a better writer is also recursive. The more you write, and the more you study the way *you* write, the more effective your writing will become. Just as we all have strengths and weaknesses in our personalities, we also all have strengths and weaknesses in our writing. One writer may be able to produce the most elegant sentences but have trouble developing ideas. And just as understanding the strengths and weaknesses in our personalities can help us grow as people, understand-

RESPONSIVE JOURNAL WRITING

Begin assessing your writing weaknesses by writing critically. Reflect on your past experiences with writing, and focus on the best experience you've had as a writer (either in a school setting or on your own). Next, write at least a page in which you explore and explain your strengths as a writer. In addition, focus on the worst experience you've had as a writer. Then write a page in which you explore and explain your writing weaknesses.

ing our writing strengths and weaknesses by assessing our writing in collaboration with others can help us grow into more effective writers. See Part Six for detailed process-based strategies for assessment and revision.

ENTERING THE CONVERSATION

Since the best way to learn any skill is through practice, it's probably time for me to step back and let you and your classmates actively enter the conversation. To practice the concepts I've already presented and encounter a few more, join a particular student writer and work through the formal writing assignment that ends this chapter.

Jesse Richter is a student at The University of Montana. Although Jesse is a guitarist and composer, he isn't sure of his major yet; he's giving himself some time for exploration before he decides what direction he'll take. Let's work with Jesse through the recursive process of writing one paper, and then listen as he talks about writing the paper and about his own recursive growth process as a writer. Keep in mind that Jesse's use of the process is only an example. One of the things I want you to begin to see is that how a person writes is a very individual thing. No two people do it in exactly the same way. And no one writer does it in exactly the same way each time he or she writes. As you are about to do, Jesse started the process by **encountering a subject.**

WRITE TO ENCOUNTER A SUBJECT

Encounter the following "journal entries" by reading and then writing about them. In addition to being highly **expressive,** these journal entries also contain the **evidence-supported judgments** characteristic of critical writing. They were written by the poet Sylvia Plath when she was a freshman at Smith College. As you read them, compare **your experiences and perspectives** with the experiences and perspectives of the speaker in the **text.**

JOURNAL ENTRIES OF A COLLEGE FRESHMAN
Sylvia Plath

The reason that I haven't been writing in this book for so long is partly that I haven't had one decent coherent thought to put

continued on page 26

continued from page 25

down. My mind is, to use a disgustingly obvious simile, like a wastebasket full of wastepaper, bits of hair, and rotting apple cores. I am feeling depressed from being exposed to so many lives, so many of them exciting, new to my realm of experience. I pass by people, grazing them on the edges, and it bothers me. I've got to admire someone to really like them deeply—to value them as friends. It was that way with Ann.[1] I admired her wit, her riding, her vivacious imagination—all the things that made her the way she was. I could lean on her as she leaned on me. Together the two of us could face anything—only not quite anything, or she would be back. And so she is gone, and I am bereft for a while. But what do I know of sorrow? No one I love has ever died[2] or been tortured. I have never wanted for food to eat, or a place to sleep. I have been gifted with five senses and an attractive exterior. So I can philosophize from my snug little cushioned seat. So I am going to one of the most outstanding colleges in America; I am living with two thousand of the most outstanding girls in the United States; what have I to complain about? Nothing much. The main way I can add to my self-respect is by saying that I'm on scholarship, and if I hadn't exercised my free will and studied through high school I never would be here. But when you come right down to it, how much of that *was* free will? How much was the capacity to think that I got from my parents, the home urge to study and do well academically, the necessity to find an alternative for the social world of boys and girls to which I was forbidden acceptance? And does not my desire to write come from a tendency toward introversion begun when I was small, brought up as I was in the fairy-tale world of Mary Poppins and Winnie-the-Pooh? Did not that set me apart from most of my schoolmates? [And] the fact that I got all A's and was "different" from the rough-and-tumble—*how* I am not quite sure, but "different" as the animal with the touch of human hands about him when he returns to the herd.

I am jealous of those who think more deeply, who write better, who draw better, who ski better, who look better, who love better, who live better than I. I am sitting at my desk looking out at a bright antiseptic January day, with an icy wind whipping the sky

continued to next page

into a white-and-blue froth. I can see Hopkins House, and the hairy black trees; I can see a girl bicycling along the gray road. I can see the sunlight slanting diagonally across the desk, catching on the iridescent filaments of nylon in the stockings I hung over the curtain rod to dry. I think I am worthwhile just because I have optical nerves and can try to put down what they perceive. What a fool!

After being conditioned as a child to the lovely never-never land of magic, of fairy queens and virginal maidens, of little princes and their rosebushes, of poignant bears and Eeyore-ish donkeys, of life personalized, as the pagans loved it, of the magic wand, and the faultless illustrations—the beautiful dark-haired child (who was you) winging through the midnight sky on a star-path in her mother's box of reels—of Griselda in her feather cloak, walking barefoot with the Cuckoo in the lantern-lit world of nodding mandarins, of Delight in her flower garden with the slim-limbed flower sprites, of the Hobbit and the dwarves, gold-belted with blue and purple hoods, drinking ale and singing of dragons in the caverns of the valley—all this I knew, and felt, and believed. All this was my life when I was young. To go from this to the world of "grown-up" reality. To feel the tender skin of sensitive child-fingers thickening to feel the sex. . . . To feel the sex organs develop and call loud to the flesh; to become aware of school, exams (the very words as unlovely as the sound of chalk shrilling on the blackboard), bread and butter, marriage, sex, compatibility, war, economics, death, and self. What a pathetic blighting of the beauty and reality of childhood. Not to be sentimental, as I sound, but why the hell are we conditioned into the smooth, strawberry-and-cream Mother-Goose-world, Alice-in-Wonderland fable, only to be broken on the wheel as we grow older and become aware of ourselves as individuals with a dull responsibility in life? • To learn snide and smutty meanings of words you once loved, like "fairy." To go to college fraternity parties where a boy buries his face in your neck or tries to rape you if he isn't satisified with burying his fingers in the flesh of your breast. • To learn that there are a million girls who are beautiful and that each day more leave behind the awkward teenage stage, as you once did, and embark on the adventure of being loved and petted. • To be aware that you must compete somehow, and yet that wealth

continued to page 28

continued from page 27

and beauty are not in your realm. • To learn that a boy will make a careless remark about "your side of town" as he drives you to a roadhouse in his father's latest chromium-plated convertible. • To learn that you might have been more of an artist than you are if you had been born into a family of wealthy intellectuals. • To learn that you can never learn anything valid for truth, only momentary, transitory sayings that apply to you in your moment, your locality, and your present state of mind. • To learn that love can never come true, because the people you admire, like Perry,[3] are unattainable since they want someone like P. K. • To learn that you only want them because you can't have them. • To yearn for an organism of the opposite sex to comprehend and heighten your thoughts and instincts, and to realize that most American males worship woman as a sex machine with rounded breasts and a convenient opening in the vagina, as a painted doll who shouldn't have a thought in her pretty head other than cooking a steak dinner and comforting him in bed after a hard 9–5 day at a routine business job.

There comes a time when you walk downstairs to pick up a letter you forgot, and the low confidential voices of the little group of girls in the living room suddenly ravels into an incoherent mumble and their eyes slide slimily through you, around you, away from you in a snaky effort not to meet the tentative half-fear quivering in your own eyes. And you remember a lot of nasty little tag ends of conversation directed at you and around you, meant for you, to strangle you on the invisible noose of insinuation. You know it was meant for you; so do they who stab you. But the game is for both of you to pretend you don't know, you don't really mean, you don't understand. Sometimes you can get a shot back in the same way, and you and your antagonist rival each other with brave smiles while the poison darts quiver, maliciously, in your mutual wounds. More often you are too sickened to fight back, because you know the fear and the inadequacy will crawl out in your words as they crackle falsely on the air. So you hear her say to you, "We'd rather flunk school and be sociable than stick in our rooms all the time," and very sweetly, "I never see you. You're always *studying* in your room!" And you keep your mouth shut. And oh, how you smile!

contiued to next page

Linda is the sort of girl you don't remember when you meet her for the second time. She is rather homely, and nondescript as an art gum eraser. Her eyes are nervous and bright like neurotic goldfish. Her skin is muddy; maybe she has acne. Hair: straight, brown, oily. But she left some of her stories with you. And she can write. Better than you ever dreamed of writing. She tossed off conversation that breathed love and sex and fear and infatuation and yet was only a series of sharp, brief pistol-shot sentences. You took out your story—the one that won third prize in *Seventeen*. You felt sick as you reread the paragraphs of lyrical sentimentality that seemed so real and genuine a few months ago. You couldn't even say it was antiseptic and understated: it was hideously obvious. So you got rid of your astonishment that someone could write so much more dynamically than you. You stopped cherishing your aloneness and poetic differentness to your delicately flat little bosom. You said: She's too good to forget. How about making her a friend and competitor—you could learn a lot from her. So you'll try. So maybe she'll laugh in your face. So maybe she'll beat you hollow in the end. So anyhow, you'll try, and maybe, possibly, she can stand you.

Frustrated? Yes. Why? Because it is impossible for me to be God— or the universal woman-and-man—or anything much. I am what I feel and think and do. I want to express my being as fully as I can because I somewhere picked up the idea that I could justify my being alive that way. But if I am to express what I am, I must have a standard of life, a jumping-off place, a technique—to make arbitrary and temporary organization of my own personal and pathetic little chaos. I am just beginning to realize how false and provincial that standard, or jumping-off place, must be. That is what is so hard for me to face.

Perry said today that his mother said, "Girls look for infinite security; boys look for a mate. Both look for different things." I am at odds. I dislike being a girl, because as such I must come to realize that I cannot be a man. In other words, I must pour my energies through the direction and force of my mate. And yet, it is as I feared: I am becoming adjusted and accustomed to that idea. . . .

continued to page 30

continued from page 29

I am part man, and I notice women's breasts and thighs with the calculation of a man choosing a mistress . . . but that is the artist and the analytical attitude toward the female body . . . for I am more a woman; even as I long for full breasts and a beautiful body, so do I abhor the sensuousness which they bring. . . . I desire the things which will destroy me in the end. . . . I wonder if art divorced from normal and conventional living is as vital as art combined with living; in a word, would marriage sap my creative energy and annihilate my desire for written and pictorial expression, which increases with this depth of unsatisfied emotion . . . or would I [if I married] achieve a fuller expression in art as well as in the creation of children? . . . Am I strong enough to do both well? . . . That is the crux of the matter, and I hope to steel myself for the test . . . as frightened as I am. . . .

---

[1] A close friend during freshman year who left Smith but kept up her friendship with Sylvia.

[2] Her father, Otto Plath, died when she was eight.

[3] The brother of Dick Norton, an important boyfriend. Sylvia was also very attracted to Perry.

COLLABORATIVE WRITING ASSIGNMENT

Now start **actively thinking** about the subject you've encountered by conversing and writing in collaboration with your classmates. Break into groups of three or four, and respond collaboratively to the prompts you'll find below. Keep your books open as you talk, and focus on the **responsive** nature of Plath's writing. After ten minutes or so, open the discussion up to full-class conversation.

1. To focus on the responsive nature of writing, search through Plath's journal entries and identify (mark them with a highlighter or pen) the written **texts** (books, stories, etc.) and **situations** (relationships between people, human conditions, etc.) the speaker is responding to. Make sure you mark specific pas-

continued on page 32

she is gone, and I am bereft for a while. But what do I ← *situation*
know of sorrow? No one I love has ever died2 or been
tortured. I have never wanted for food to eat, or a
place to sleep. I have been gifted with five senses and
an attractive exterior. So I can philosophize from my ← *sit.*
snug little cushioned seat. So I am going to one of the
most outstanding colleges in America; I am living
with two thousand of the most outstanding girls in
the United States; what have I to complain about?
Nothing much. The main way I can add to my self- } *privilege?*
respect is by saying that I'm on scholarship, and if I   *How much free will?*
hadn't exercised my free will and studied through
high school I never would be here. But when you
come right down to it, how much of that *was* free will? ← *situation*
How much was the capacity to think that I got from
my parents, the home urge to study and do well academically, the necessity to find an alternative for the
social world of boys and girls to which I was forbid- ← *compensation*
den acceptance? And does not my desire to write
come from a tendency toward introversion begun
when I was small, brought up as I was in the fairy-tale
world of Mary Poppins and Winnie-the-Pooh? Did
not that set me apart from most of my schoolmates? ← *texts*
[And} the fact that I got all A's and was "different"
from the rough-and-tumble – *how* I am not quite sure,
but "different" as the animal with the touch of human
hands about him when he returns to the herd.

I wonder, does everyone think, I'm different?

continued from page 30

sages from the **text** as **evidence** for each text or situation you identify.

2. Focus on Plath's ability to **think critically** by studying the text and identifying (using a highlighter or pen) passages where the speaker questions or criticizes her own former ways of viewing the world. When you've identified as many critical passages as you can, **annotate** each passage by summarizing Plath's judgment about it in two or three words. Be prepared to support your own conclusions with **specific evidence from the text.** Here's how Jesse marked and annotated part of the text (page 31). Don't worry if your annotations are slightly different from Jesse's. We are all individuals and bring to the reading of any text our own unique knowledge and experience.

Like you, Jesse encountered a subject; he read Plath's journal entries and engaged in collaborative critical thinking activities. Then he was given the following writing assignment.

RESPONSIVE WRITING ASSIGNMENT

In paragraph three of Plath's journal entry, the speaker contrasts her childhood's "lovely never-never land of magic" with "the world of 'grown-up' reality." After reflecting on your own childhood and considering your agreements and disagreements with Plath's text and with your collaborative group members, write a two- or three-page responsive paper directed at your classmates in which you explore the differences between your childhood view of the world and the view you presently hold.

WRITE TO ANALYZE THE CHOICES AND CONSTRAINTS OF THE WRITING SITUATION

In addition to being complicated by the way we think, the process of constructing any given text is affected by the writing situation itself— before you can begin work on any assignment, you have to understand precisely what the assignment is asking you to do. So let's add an analysis of the writing situation to the steps of the process.

The first thing Jesse did was read over the assignment and analyze it by writing in his course journal. And what his analysis amounted to was an **exploration** of the choices and constraints of the writing situation. Jesse's **subject** was given; he had to write about the differences and similarities between his childhood view of the world and the view he presently holds. Jesse's **audience** and purpose were also given; he was to write an exploratory paper to the other members of his class. And as Jesse analyzed the writing situation, he realized that reading Plath's "Journal Entries" and discussing them had triggered his thinking about the subject even before he'd been given this particular assignment. Before Jesse had actually begun writing his paper, he was well into the writing process.

RESPONSIVE JOURNAL WRITING

Explore the writing situation as Jesse did by writing in your journal. Study the prompt and think about how you as a **writer** respond to this particular **subject.** Has reading and discussing Plath's journal entries made you think about the differences between your childhood view of the world and the view you presently hold? If so, how?

Now consider your **audience.** What are your classmates like? What values and perspectives have they revealed in their conversations? How have these values and perspectives influenced your own thinking on the subject?

Finally, focus on your **purpose** for exploring. Although a lot of exploratory writing is writer-based, when writers explore *with* an external audience, they share their reflections about experience with others. Exploration is the least constrained of the writer-based purposes. The whole point of doing it is to push your thinking to places it hasn't gone before. So take risks. And feel free to pose questions you may not be able to fully answer.

WRITE TO THINK—EXPAND AND CLARIFY YOUR RESPONSES BY PREWRITING

Since **writing is thinking made visible** on the page, the next thing Jesse did was begin to "get hold" of his responses by engaging in the following **prewriting** exercise.

RESPONSIVE PREWRITING EXERCISE

Now, like Jesse, it's time for you to **actively converse** with Sylvia Plath. Explore your responses to Plath's journal entries by comparing your own **judgments about experience** with hers. Choose one of Plath's judgments you located in Collaborative Exercise 2 that you agree with and one that you disagree with. Write a page-long response explaining why you agree and another page-long response explaining why you disagree. Keep the **persuasive** nature of writing in mind, and make sure you back up your judgments with **evidence** from your own experience.

Like you, what Jesse was doing when he wrote his exploratory response was conversing with himself and with Plath. He was considering what Plath said, and he was responding to her and to his own experience at the same time. He was saying, yes, I understand what you say, and I agree or disagree, and this is why I do. However, at this stage Jesse wasn't consciously writing to communicate to other people; he was writing to and for himself—to **understand** what he felt and to **express** his feelings by exploring them. Here's the result of Jesse's exploration.

Jesse Richter

SYLVIA PLATH—AGREEMENT STATEMENT

Plath has excellent insight into the loss of innocence—that transition period between the playground and the "awkward teenage stage." This period is usually the time when we start on the road to defining ourselves as individuals in terms of our goals, interests, relationships with parents, and our social worlds. As Plath puts it, "we become aware of ourselves as individuals with a dull responsibility in life."

The transition between the fantasy world Plath so nostalgically describes and the adult world happened early in my life. My parents divorced very early in my childhood and I was pulled between the bacheloresque lifestyle of my father and the safe en-

continued to next page

vironment my mother tried to provide. I remember riding the train and the bus at age eight and roaming around the town of Chester, Montana while other kids played in the fenced yards of their babysitters.

I understand Plath's feeling of not being accepted by groups, but always somehow being on the outside. The same kind of parties Plath talks about happened for me in seventh grade, where a couple would disappear into a room for several hours and come out a little ruffled—the girls slightly sheepish and the guys beaming with pride. I used to go up to our summer cabin with my father at age seven or so, and remember groups of guys and girls skinnydipping in the river. All these things led me out of that fairytale world and into a more ''real'' world of sexuality and interactions with more ''real'' people.

Sometimes I feel a little bit sad, as it seems Plath does, about this loss of innocence so early on. I also wonder if I had lived in a different environment if things would be different now.

After Jesse had written his exploratory response, he tested his thinking by **collaborating** with some classmates. After reading his responses, Jesse's collaborative partners had wanted to know more. They thought Jesse made judgments but didn't give enough evidence to make them believable. What about ''not being accepted by groups''? What about the ''father's bacheloresque lifestyle''? And what about that last sentence, ''I also wonder if I had lived in a different environment if things would be different now''? Jesse responded by being self-critical; he used his partners' questions to help him **assess** the effectiveness of the writing he'd done so far, and he decided he hadn't included enough evidence to **persuade** his readers. Collaborate informally, as Jesse did, by engaging in the following activities.

COLLABORATIVE WRITING ASSIGNMENT

To test and expand your conclusions about Plath's text, break into collaborative groups of three or four, and exchange and read the agreement and disagreement statements you wrote in response

continued on page 36

continued from page 35

to the above prewriting exercise. As you read your group members' responses, focus on any judgments or experiential evidence you have questions about. For example, if one of your partners makes a judgment but doesn't support it with evidence, write down a word or two as a reminder to yourself.

After you've read all the responses in your group, use your notes as a starting place to formulate and write out at least three questions for each of your group members.

However, before you begin formulating questions for your group members, read the questions that Jesse's collaborative partners came up up with.

What exactly was your "father's bacheloresque lifestyle?"
What specifically was your "environment" like, and how do you think things would be different now if you'd been brought up differently?
How weren't you accepted by groups?

RESPONSIVE PREWRITING ASSIGNMENT

Think critically about your responses to Plath's text by continuing your prewriting. Choose two of the questions posed by your group members in the above exercise, and write at least a page in response to each of them. Here's how Jesse responded to two of the questions his partners formulated.

Journal Entry

"BACHLORESQUE DAD"

I spent many years at my father's place during a period he was divorced. That is excluding the three month marriage to Dorothy, the bar maid from some dusty trailer community in eastern

continued to next page

Montana. Most summers it was just my brother and I. Dad was a completely happy bachelor though. Most nights we would call the pharmacy up and see if we could make the special call to tasty freeze. A half-hour later he'd pull up and Jeremy and I would devour the greasy bags of food while dad had us listen to his favorite records. It only took and hour though and down he'd go, out for at least a couple hours.

Other nights I'd fall asleep to the sound of my dad's band as they rehearsed in the garage. The sound seemed to put me right to sleep. Sometimes I'd wake up to find dad and his friends smoking, drinking and talking late into the night. When I stumbled into the room they would hoot and holler and razz me until I went back to bed. I'd always try to stay awake and catch snippets of their conversations.

Jeremy and I would always go to the pharmacy where dad worked. It was an amazing place filled with treasures of every kind. Dad would let us drink soda and eat candy till we were blue in the face. In fact he went through a six pack of coke a day himself. Sometimes would talk rather loud to us in the back about a customer at the counter, it would always make me nervous that the customer might hear.

Dad seemed always to have a girl friend, most younger than himself. He was always charming to women and only occasionally made a remark that would turn me red in the face. It has always seemed he felt most comfortable during this divorced period. Even though he was lonely, he had a firm grasp of who he was. As his third and final marriage wore on he seemed to become more restless and less amiable.

Journal Entry

"DIFFERENT ENVIRONMENT, DIFFERENT ME"

I've often imagined how my life might have been different had the circumstances of my upbringing been different. At times

continued on page 38

continued from page 37

I feel as if I'm preprogrammed, I react to a situation and wonder where on earth that response came from. With out doubt we are the products of our environment. We can struggle against its influence, but we can never shake it.

I grew up in a split household, summers with dad and school with mom. Mom's house was a haven of security and comfort. Joe my stepfather is a very straight forward, honest man. His presence always was the controlling factor of the household. He saw to it that my forays into individuality were kept in check. The security of the household gave me a lot of confidence and opportunities, but it also kept me from pursuing many of my desires. For instance, I used to love to draw for hours on end, until it was decided I needed to spend more time with the family. I became very frustrated with the lack of space and respect that my parent had for my creative side. As a result I lost a lot of my ambition and felt depressed a lot. If I was given more encouragement to pursue my artistic side I would have had a much easier time accepting myself as an artist. Even now I question my ability and the choices I have made for my self.

Dad's place was the opposite, no security, very little comfort and always dealing with my father's moods. I felt embarrassed to bring friends over because the house was always a mess. The environment was very scattered, there was no organization in the house. I was left to do pretty much what I wanted. I've always felt that I never spent enough time with my dad at that young age. I was always at a sitter's house or at swimteam practice, but never with my dad. I've always felt a bit antisocial, but then again my dad never let me have friends over to play. So I was left to my own ends.

WRITE TO REVISE YOUR THINKING BY DRAFTING

As Jesse drafted, he realized that drafting wasn't all that different from **prewriting.** He was still exploring things and discovering things he hadn't understood before, and he was still expressing himself. However, **drafting** was significantly different from prewriting in one way. This assignment was an actual "paper," not just an exploratory exercise. The members of his class had been assigned as his audience, and some of them would read it. It had to be more "complete" than his response, because he had a specific **purpose** for writing. He wanted to **change** his classmates' (his audience's) thoughts and feelings by making them understand as fully as possible the way he felt about his own experience. He decided he needed to support the statements he'd made with evidence from his experience. But since he had only two or three pages to do it, he made a decision to focus on one issue from his response and write about it; that issue was his relationship with his father.

And because the text he was constructing had to be more complete, Jesse began **actively revising** as he drafted. He **added** some details and **cut** others; he **rearranged** the order of sentences and paragraphs; he **reworded** as he wrote to communicate what he meant as clearly as possible. And he did all of these things with his audience's responses in mind.

Draft as Jesse did. Use your agreement and disagreement statements and the results of your collaboration as starting places. Then continue to explore. Like Jesse, try to focus your thinking on one aspect of your experience. In addition, revise your thinking and writing as you draft by cutting unrelated material, by adding evidence or judgments, by rearranging or rewording to clarify your ideas for your readers.

CONTINUE TO REVISE BY REWRITING

When Jesse got his draft as close to "finished" as he could on his own, he took it to the same collaborative partners who had read the results of his prewriting. Since he hadn't developed things sufficiently before, he asked them to look particularly hard at how he had developed his paper. That draft, complete with his partners' criticisms begins on page 40.

Jesse read his partners' criticisms and decided that he hadn't finished **exploring** his subject. He focused on the places in his text that were problematic to his readers and thought about them for a day before **rewriting** the text into its final form. That rewriting took more revising. He cut the whole first paragraph. He added more detail and developed his ideas. And he reworded to clarify meaning and edit usage problems. Here's the final version of his text.

Jesse Richter

FIRE ON THE PLAINS

The summers spent at my father's house were long and easy. The town was small, the people slow, and the kids restless. My dad had settled in Chester, Montana out of what I see now must

continued on page 45

I awake with a start to the sound of a lawn mower. The clock says two a.m.. I pull myself heavily from my bed and glance out the window at the moon splashed yard. My dad nervously pushes the mower about in no particular pattern or direction. The mower occasionally scrapes on a chunk of wood or rock, and my Dad curses, muscles flexed, and heaves the mower away from its obstruction. There at the window, I realize my father is different. Different in what way I do not know--it is years later I learn of his drug addiction and the depression with which he continually struggles. I slip back under my cool sheets and wonder at my fathers behavior, smiling at his oddities.

Summers spent at my fathers house were long and easy. The town was small, the people slow, and the kids restless. My dad had settled in Chester out of what seems sheer convenience. His father owned several pharmacies, and my father found it easy to simply lease the one in Chester. The Richters were outsiders in Chester--we had built somewhat of a fortress one-half mile from town, complete with a mote (actually a gnatty creek bed). Our fortress was adorned with many of my fathers eccentricities: tractors, farm animals, full shop, vast supplies of every kind of anything a kid could want to grow up with.

Yes, my father was a slightly indulgent man. My brother paints an amusing picture of him in tight checkered pants with no underwear waltzing into his fortress around five. His fingers nervously produce a cascade of quarters, dimes and pills. All sorts of pills--green, white, big and small you name it; and out they tumbled anywhere and everywhere from his pockets on to the most convenient counter. From there he idles down the hallway singing, thus transforming himself from pharmacist into raving lunatic. One of these days my brother fatefully swallows a green pill from the tumult of lint, quarters and pills on the bathroom counter. Mother being mother went into a frenzy of mythical proportions. My brother and I rumor that this was the last straw leading to my parents divorce.

this one is correct

With my mother's absence my father became free to broaden his recklose enterprises. Sex, drugs and rock and roll took on new meaning as my father staggered through the tail-end of the seventies. None-the-less my father, brother and I developed an everlasting bond during this period. It's perhaps the height of the time I refer to as the wealthy bachelor/spoiled kids period. This time included weekend excursions to the "Dude Ranch" and two-week long trips to our cabin. My father found it easy to show his love through countless meals at Tastee Freeze and Circle K. There seemed to be no end to the toys, candy and freedom the summer days at my fathers house held for my brother and I. Long lazy days at the Chester swim pool, followed by movies or watching dads band at night. We were definitely Dads boys then, and we wor- *again, compound sentence* shipped him immensely.

The tides slowly turned with my fathers marriage. He seemed to slowly metamorphose into a different person; still very crazy, but no longer charmingly so. These changes came with the addition of three new children his new wife brought with her into the marriage. The house no longer pulsed with my fathers bacheloresque rhythm, but gurgled with nuclear family bullshit. There were after dinner bible lessons with the new wife at the helm. These kind of family affairs stifled the ol' Richter powerhouse of my brother, father and I. Life took on new dimensions with the addition of females to the house. Sexual discovery with the older become a dual source of shame and excitement. Things became complicated for my brother and I; we had to adjust to the outsiders.

explain this

My father and I grew apart during these years of adjustment. I could no longer connect with the mannerisms he had apparently developed with his new family. And then it happened--the BIG FIRE. The fire marked the end of any close relations between Dad and I. It happened on a hot day on a late summer afternoon. My younger brother Ahren by marriage of my father's new wife and I were fooling around in the "steel building." "The steel building" is an old combine storehouse turned Richter archive. The inside contents are slightly analogous to a roadcut in that you can trace the history of the Richters starting at the floor and working your way toward the ceiling. For instance, you might find the May 1971 issue of _Playboy_ towards the bottom, and set of encyclopedias towards the top. The Richter kids need not go much further than that megalithic building to find fun and excitement. On one of these days of discovery in the building Ahren and I stumbled upon a box of fireworks. Not your everyday hiss-pop variety, but the kind that rattle the foundations of surrounding buildings when they ignite. Dad made yearly trips to the Blackfoot Indian reservation in Browning, Montana to purchase and smuggle these illicit fireworks for our

this time you got it right

possession again

local festivities. These fireworks are illegal because their composition powder is twice that of domestic fireworks. Twice the bang, twice the danger, that's how dad likes it. And dangerous they proved to be. I pull a sparkler from the box and playfully run a flame close to its fuse. The fuse catches and I drop it not expecting it to ignite. I quickly extinguish the sparkler and I breathe a sigh of relief. Ahren and I smile at our luck and exit the building in search of other pleasures.

another tense shift— UNIFY

Moments later, what sounded like World War III broke out inside the building. I ran to the gaping doorway only to see shooting flames and red, blue, green and yellow fireworks crashing everywhere. I ran for the garden hose (a ridiculous reaction). As I rushed toward the building dragging the spouting hose, my father sped out of the house in the direction of the steel building. I foolishly yelled "Fire! Fire!" like some redundant dipshit. My father assessed the fire before entering and then dashed in with a heavy army blanket to douse the flames. Moments later the building thundered like the heavens of Zeus and bright flames shot from the door. Standing there, garden hose spouting, birds chirping, I realized I had just killed my father. He stumbled out seconds later, like the clumsy scarecrow in The Wizard of Oz. His hair mottled, fried and standing on end. Skin on his face and arms hung like shredded cobwebs and his arms crossed in front of him, still warding off some imaginary flames. I don't remember anything after this--I don't know how dad got to the hospital, etc. The following day came and I sheepishly climbed into the car to visit Dad. I was so ashamed I couldn't even look at him--

fragmented sentences LISTEN to the MEANING and make it PRECISE

again, compound sentence

inconsistent with the voice you've created

arms in bandages and suspended in various ropes. I
avoided the topic of how the fire started just as a criminal would. That was the last time I saw Dad that summer. Vacation was over and it was time to go back to
Mom's place.

again, not precise

The fire incident still lingers unresolved between
my father and I. When he rubs his scars, I look away
hastily and pretend not to notice. It took disaster for
me to realize that my father wasn't the superman I
thought him to be. I wonder and hope for the closeness of those long lazy days of summer before our
lives changed. I still love my father immeasurably but
I can no more tell him than I can take the scars from
his arms.

I/me confused, AGAIN

compound sentence AGAIN

What do you wonder? You need to think a bit more about the MEANING you're trying to get hold of in this last paragraph. Try some free writing.

Jesse,
    You've certainly had a DEVELOPMENT breakthrough. Absolutely stunning evidence in here that paints a clear picture of your father and your environment. If you look at my "AGAIN" notations and my connecting lines you'll see you need to work on the following:
    1.—Language precision—read out loud and listen to the meaning and reword for precision.
    2.—Lookup apostrophes to signal possession in the handbook and practice correct use.
    3.—Lookup using commas with coordinating conjunctions in compound sentences in the handbook and practice the proper convention.
    4.—You consistently use the subjective "I" when you should be using the objective "me."
    5.—Dad is capitalized when it's a proper noun—"Dad's Band." However, it's not capitalized when it's a common noun—"My dad had settled in Chester..."
    6.—Although the first paragraph is beautiful, the essay seems to open with the second pragraph. Save the first paragraph in your journal for later use. Note that all those marks on your paper only added up to six problem areas! The point is that as writers we just keep repeating the same few mistakes.

continued from page 39

have been sheer convenience. His father owned several pharmacies, and my father found it easy to simply lease the one in Chester. The Richters were outsiders in Chester—we had built a ridiculously large house one-half mile from town, complete with a mote (actually a gnatty creek bed). Our home was cluttered wall-to-wall with collections of my father's toys which he tirelessly brought home to add to his treasure horde. Lavish persian rugs covered the floors, but they frequently rolled up and put away when my brother and I walked too much. It was like growing up in a museum where you could look all you wanted, but never touch.

Yes, my father was a slightly self-indulgent man. My brother paints a amusing picture of him in tight checkered pants with no underwear, waltzing into castle around five. His fingers nervously produced a cascade of quarters, dimes and pills—all sorts of pills—red, white, green, big and small; you name it, out they tumbled anywhere and everywhere from his pockets on to the most convenient counter. There was an unwinding period after work where Dad would go competly nuts, singing and dancing madly about on the brink of hysteria. One of these days my brother fatefully swallowed a green pill from thr tumult of lint, quarters and pills scattered on the bathroom counter. Mother, being mother, went into a frenzy of mythical proportions. My brother and I still believe that this was the last straw leading to my parents' divorce.

With my mother's absence, my father became free to broaden his reckless enterprises. Sex, drugs, and rock and roll took on new meaning as my father staggered through the tail-end of the seventies. Nonetheless, my father, brother and I developed an everlasting bond during this period. It was the height of the time I refer to as the wealthy bachelor/spoiled kids period. This included weekend excursions to the "Dude Ranch" and two week long trips to our cabin. My father found it easy to show his love through countless meals at Tasty Freeze and Circle K. There seemed to be no end to the toys, candy and freedom the summer days at my father's house held for my brother and me. Long lazy days at the Chester swim pool, followed by movies or watching Dad's band at night. We were definitely Dad's boys then, and we worshipped him immensely.

continued on page 46

continued from page 45

The tides slowly turned with my father's remarriage. He seemed to slowly metamorphose into a different person; still very crazy, but no longer charmingly so. These changes came with the addition of three children his new wife brought with her into the marriage. The house no longer pulsed with my father's bachelor-esque rythym, but gurgled with nuclear family bullshit. I went from roaming freely, exploring the nooks and crannies of Chester, to watching "Days of Our Lives" and eating pb and j with a lazy babysitter in her den of bratty, crying children. I felt trapped into a whole new life blown in by some lady I was supposed to call mom. Things became complicated for my brother and me; we had to adjust to the outsiders.

My father and I grew apart during these years of his trying to assimilate his "new" family. I could no longer connect with the new mannerisms he had developed. And then it happened—the Big Fire. The fire marked the end of any close relationship between Dad and me.

It happened on a hot day on a late summer afternoon. My younger step-brother Ahren and I were fooling around in the "steel building." The steel building was an old combine storehouse turned Richter archive. The inside contents were slightly analogous to a roadcut in that you could trace the history of the Richters, starting at the floor and working your way towards the ceiling. For instance, you might find the May 1971 issue of "Playboy" towards the bottom, and a set of encyclopedias towards the top. The Richter kids need not go much further than that megalithic building to find fun and excitement.

On one of these days of discovery in the building, Ahren and I stumbled upon a box of fireworks. Not your everyday hiss-pop variety, but the kind that rattle the foundations of surrounding buildings when they ignite. Dad made yearly trips to the Blackfoot Indian reservation in Browning, Montana to purchase and smuggle these illicit fireworks for our local festitivities. These fireworks are illegal because their composition of explosive powder is twice that of domestic fireworks. Twice the bang, twice the danger, that's how Dad liked it, and dangerous it proved to be. I pulled a sparkler from the box and playfully ran a flame close to its fuse. The fuse caught and I dropped it, not expecting it to

continued to next page

ignite. I quickly extinguished the sparkler and breathed a sigh of relief. Ahren and I smiled at our luck and exited the building in search of other pleasures. Moments later, what sounded like World War III broke out inside the building. I ran to the gaping doorway to see shooting flames, and red, blue, green and yellow fireworks crashing everywhere. I ran for the garden hose (a ridiculous reaction). As I rushed toward the building dragging the spouting hose, my father sped out of the house in the direction of the steel building. I stupidly yelled, "Fire! Fire!" like some redundant idiot. My father assessed the fire before entering and then dashed in with a heavy army blanket to douse the flames. Moments later, the building thundered like the heavens of Zeus, and bright flames shot from the door. Standing there, garden hose spouting, birds chirping, I realized I had just killed my father. He stumbled out seconds later like the clumsy scarecrow from the *Wizard of Oz*. His hair was mottled, fried and standing on end. The skin on his face and arms hung like shredded cobwebs, and he had his arms crossed in front of him, still warding off some imaginary flames.

I don't remember anything after this—I don't even know how Dad got to the hospital. The following day came, and we climbed into the car to go visit my dad. I was so ashamed I couldn't even look at him—arms in bandages and suspended in various rope pulleys. He looked helpless and shell shocked, and I felt as if he were playing the role up. I avoided the topic of how the fire started just as a criminal would. That was the last time that I saw Dad that summer. Vacation was over and it was once again time to go back to Mom's place.

The fire incident still lingers unresolved between my father and me. It is one of those things that is avoided and rarely verbalized. I still harbor guilt about the event, although it was a product of my lunatic environment. When Dad rubs his scars, I look away hastily and pretend not to notice them. Often I fear that I have adopted my own crazy madness; different from that of my father, but equally manic.

The revisions Jesse made in his paper can be grouped into four categories: revisions in **voice, development, arrangement,** and **mechanics.** And those four categories are the types of **choices** writers make to **persuade** their audiences to change.

1. Choices in Voice Voice is the persona, the facet of personality, that the writer creates on the page through the choice of **words** and **sentence structure.** No writer has just one voice. No person has just one voice. We speak with different voices to different people. You speak in one voice to your closest friend and in another voice to your elderly neighbor. You choose different words and different sentences, with different lengths and complexities, depending on your audience. You even speak in different voices to the same person—one voice when you're discussing ideas with a particular friend, an entirely different one when he or she asks to borrow your credit card. Think of the person in the world you're closest to. Now think of all the different voices you use to speak to that person: one voice when you're communicating love, another when you're expressing anger; one when you're thinking out loud, another when you're giving directions; one when you're fascinated, another when you're bored. The words you choose and the sentence structures you use to frame those words not only reflect your own attitude but also change from person to person and from purpose to purpose.

Like competitive ice-skating, voice can be assessed on its artistic and on its technical merit. On the artistic side, a meritorious voice is **unified** and **appropriate** to the writer's **audience** and **purpose;** a well-chosen voice sounds like a single person addressing a particular and discernible audience. For example, a well-written artistic voice wouldn't switch back and forth between formal and casual language. On the technical side, a meritorious voice is **free of errors** in **sentence structure** and **diction** (word choice). For example, in a technically correct voice there are no sentence fragments or incorrectly used words.

Voice has always been Jesse's major strength as a writer. In fact, it was such a strength that it kept him from overcoming his major weakness as a writer (we'll get to that later). All through high school, Jesse got excellent grades on his papers because they "sounded" so wonderful, only to get to college and be surprised by mediocre grades. However, even though Jesse is a master of the artistic aspects of voice, he did make some technical voice errors in his draft. For example, his diction (word choice) was often not precise enough to communicate his meaning. Jesse habitually makes imprecise word choices because the sentences come out so easily and "sound" so good that he doesn't stop to consider his intended meaning. In addition, Jesse consistently uses the subjective case *I* when he should be using the objective case *me.* Although this error indicates a gap in Jesse's knowledge of proper pronoun use, what's really interesting about this particular mistake is the *reason* Jesse makes it. Jesse consistently chooses *I* when he should choose *me* because *I* sounds more like something an "educated" person would say.

2. Choices in Development Development is the material the writer chooses to **support the message** he or she is sending to the audience. Just stating the message isn't enough; since by nature we humans base our conclusions on evidence, human audiences need to be drawn in and convinced. Think about the people in your life you trust the most, and you'll realize you trust them for reasons. They've earned your trust by giving you **evidence** that you can trust them. For example, you may *hope* someone loves you when they declare it, but the only way you come to *trust* that love is if they treat you in a loving manner. Imagine how unsatisfying human communication would be without development; it would amount to nothing more than a long series of declarations and orders.

A well-developed paper contains **logically sound judgments** that are all supported with evidence and unified under a single, clear message. The message of a text is the text's main idea, thesis, or general claim. Usually, the more openly persuasive a text is, the more obvious the message will be. In exploratory writing, the message is more likely to be a dominant impression than an outright argumentative claim.

Like choices in voice, choices in development change from one audience to another. You may send the same message to many different audiences, but the evidence you supply to convince each audience that your message is credible will be different. For example, take the declaration "I love you." You'll demonstrate your love for your mother in one way and for your father in another; you'll demonstrate your love for your lover in a different way altogether.

Developing with **specific evidence** has always been Jesse's major area of writing weakness. For example, in his prewriting, he made a lot of statements he didn't go on to support with evidence. And the reason Jesse had problems with development was because he didn't **focus** on one aspect of a topic and really dig into it by thinking critically. His general statements "sounded" so good that he just kept stringing them together.

3. Choices in Arrangement Arrangement is the writer's chosen **pattern of organization.** We're constantly making choices in arrangement when we communicate with other people. We decide to place one thing before another because we believe our audience will understand our message more clearly if we do. Like voice and development choices, the choices we make in arrangement vary from audience to audience and from purpose to purpose. One audience will need developmental material arranged in one way; another audience will need it arranged in a different way. For example, if we've spoken about a subject extensively to someone before, we won't have to start our current communication with a great deal of background information. Likewise, if we're certain that someone will agree with us, we won't have to win this person over *before* we go on to present our case.

A well-arranged text moves logically from one cluster of judgments and evidence to another without including unrelated material. In addition, a well-arranged piece of writing contains transitional words and phrases that connect one cluster of judgments and evidence to another.

The only significant arrangement problem Jesse had was the inclusion of the unrelated first paragraph. And that problem was related to his personal writing process. Jesse, like a lot of writers, had to write his way into his paper. He had to get started drafting before he knew what direction his paper was going to take.

4. *Choices in Mechanics* I define correct mechanics in this book as **competency in the current conventions** of spelling and punctuation. Errors in mechanics not only undercut the **credibility** of your writing and make it less persuasive, but they can also interfere with the meaning you're trying to communicate. Punctuation and spelling errors aren't mysterious and insurmountable; they merely indicate gaps in your knowledge of the conventions. Use the **mapping** strategy in Part Six of this book to identify and rank habitual errors in mechanics. Then overcome your problems by learning and practicing the conventions. For example, Jesse didn't know how to punctuate compound sentences when he wrote his first draft, but he learned how as he wrote his second.

A STUDENT WRITER
TALKS ABOUT WRITING

Before you go on to the final step of the process, read this transcript of a conversation I had with Jesse, and listen as he talks about his continuing relationship with the writing process. As you read, focus on those places where Jesse is being actively critical about his own writing and thinking.

J. S.: What was the major trouble you had with writing in the past?

continued to next page

J. R.: I couldn't develop what I wanted to say. I didn't elaborate on anything. My ideas just came out in one sentence, and then I'd be on to the next idea. My writing was all unexplained conclusions. In high school, I wrote each idea I had on a different note card, and then I'd have to come up with some kind of scheme to relate them.

J. S.: What helped you deal with your problems with development?

J. R.: The responses I got from my readers. I listened, and finally I decided to just limit, just take one idea and kind of force myself to mull it over, and just stick with that idea. It's hard for me to think my ideas are all that fascinating, but now I think I can elaborate them. And when I do elaborate, people really respond to it. That surprised me, the response I got.

J. S.: How do you usually respond to your collaborative partners' criticisms?

J. R.: Usually I change the thing they comment on, but not necessarily the way my partners want me to. I usually don't take their ideas, but their comments let me see weaknesses in my writing—things I've left out or that are just weak. After we talk, I always go back and read their comments. What's funny is that their comments are usually about things I've questioned myself when I was drafting.

J. S.: What did you learn from being the reader in informal collaboration?

J. R.: As much as I discovered what I liked about other people's writing, I also discovered what I wanted to watch out for in my own writing. The things I didn't like in other people's writing were things I tended to do myself.

J. S.: Like what?

J. R.: One thing I don't like is glossy writing—the kind of writing where you can tell the person is trying to come off in a certain way to an audience. And I think what annoyed me was that I do that. Sometimes I change things to justify myself, to make myself seem better—to

continued on page 52

continued from page 51

make myself and the situation I'm writing about seem more cool. There was a guy in my group who did that, and I realized I didn't believe what he was writing. Overwriting is another part of the same thing. You use a big word that sounds good, but you're not quite sure of its meaning. You like the way the words are sounding, but you should be focusing on the meaning. It's like trying to sound intellectual when you don't have to be, when you could say it in a lot simpler way that's obvious.

J. S.:   Let's talk about you as the "the writer." How did who you are as a person affect your reading of Plath's "Journal Entries" and your writing in response to them?

J. R.:   I was getting into a relationship at the time we read the Plath text, and these things were in my head. I was thinking about my dad and how he affected my present state—not just my dad, my family—my past. I wanted to understand how the baggage of my past was affecting the present so I wouldn't mess up the relationship. And thinking about it by reading and then writing helped me understand things betters.

Rewrite as Jesse did, but before you begin, **assess your past performance as a writer.** Read over the journal entries you wrote as you worked through this chapter. What clues can your journal entries give you about your use of the writing process and about your strengths and weaknesses as a writer? Then, with your analysis of your strengths and weaknesses in mind, read over your draft and mark those passages you think might be problematic.

Finally, take your draft to the same collaborative partners you worked with before. Exchange your draft with other members in the group and read them in turn, until each member has read all the drafts. Use Part Six as a guide for focusing on problems in **voice, development, arrangement,** and **mechanics.** Look for correspondences between your own assessment of your strengths and weaknesses and your partners' assessments. Then, with both assessments in mind, continue to revise by cutting, adding, and rewording.

ASSESS YOUR PERFORMANCE BY WRITING CRITICALLY

Jesse's writing improved because he studied his own process. He identified his problem areas, and then he analyzed *why* he had those problems. He also listened to the responses of others, and he learned from them; then he took what he had learned into consideration when he wrote to fulfill later assignments. Begin **assessing your own personal writing process** by writing a page explaining what was most difficult about completing this assignment. Which choice category (voice, development, arrangement, or mechanics) gave you the most trouble? Why do you think that category gave you the most trouble? Then write a second page explaining what you learned (both about yourself and about the writing process) from writing this particular paper.

Consider this assignment a ''benchmark'' from which to begin assessing your growth as a writer during the course of the term. Keep your final draft and all the written work you did to produce it in a file folder or manila envelope, and compare and contrast it with each text you construct in the next few months. **Think critically** (the way Jesse did about his problems with focus and development). Throughout the term, **read the comments** you get from your collaborative partners and instructor carefully, and **look for patterns** in their questions, criticisms, and compliments. As you think and write now and in the future, **focus your attention** on how you do both and consider the recursive steps of the writing process.

A FINAL NOTE

Trust yourself; trust your mind. Certainly, you should test your ideas and conclusions about the world and be critical of them. But you should be equally critical and testing of other people's ideas and conclusions. The written texts, the books and articles you'll encounter in your courses, were written by human beings—intelligent, knowledgeable humans, but humans nonetheless, humans with a wide variety of viewpoints, whose points of view create many agreements and many disagreements. Likewise, your instructors are human. By saying this I am in no way trying to discredit their intelligence and knowledge or attack their good will. Instead, I'm saying that you can't be a passive receptor and still be a player in the great conversational game. The process of sorting through other people's ideas and judgments to arrive at your own is an active process. Knowledge isn't something you soak up; you're not an empty cup waiting to be filled. Knowledge is something you test and compare with your own experience and with the knowledge you've already accumulated, and the testing and comparing are invariably a struggle.

PART TWO

CRITICAL
READING,
RESEARCH,
AND
WRITING

CHAPTER
FOUR
CRITICAL READING
AND RESPONDING

Although we certainly learn to write by doing it, we also learn to write by reading. Reading carefully to discern the meaning others have discovered in experience moves us further along in our own knowledge and understanding of the world around us. Reading with an eye to the writer's craft by closely studying the elegance and beauty of excellent writing challenges us to be better writers and thinkers ourselves. Critically reading what other writers have written challenges us to sharpen and change old ideas we have about the world and invites us to formulate new ones.

To sum it up, if you want to become a good writer or a better one, read carefully for meaning; read closely for craft; read critically for your agreements and disagreements. And the summary of this summary reads like this: **listen, learn, and respond.**

LISTEN—READ TEXTS FOR MEANING

Reading written texts critically is like having the very best conversation; the whole point of doing it is to grow and change. Think about the people you most enjoy talking with, and you'll realize they're the ones who spark the greatest positive changes in you. When you're bored, they amuse you with their wit. When you're confused, they help you clarify your thoughts. When you're troubled, they comfort you. They're also good and active listeners. They don't bully you with their point of view, and they aren't passive and unresponsive. You trust them. And the reason you do is because their minds are open; you know they'll really listen and consider what you have to say. The same principle that holds true in conversation also holds true in reading; to grow and change, you have to keep your mind open to other people's perspectives. You have to consider what other people have to say.

However, keeping you mind open as you read isn't as easy as it sounds. Some of the very skills that make us rational creatures can, if you use them uncritically, close us down and blind us. As I suggested in the first chapter of this book, every one of us comes to a written text encumbered by ideas and conclusions already formed about the subject of that text.

We humans are by nature concluders. From the time we get the language to do it, we begin making sense of everything around us, sometimes with very peculiar results. When I was seven, I was certain that an island I could see off Brighton Beach in Brooklyn, New York, was France. This conviction made perfect sense to me. I was looking east, wasn't I? France was east, wasn't it? No matter how hard my mother tried to explain the curvature of the earth or the limits of human sight, I *knew* that I, at least, was seeing France. I also knew that dogs and cats were, respectively, male and female of the same species and that the antelope my father tried to point out on a hillside in Yellowstone Park were round melons like the ones we ate slices of topped with vanilla ice cream in the summertime. I didn't think these things might be true. I had drawn conclusions based on my own experience and knowledge that they were true, and I *knew*. The point is that sometimes the sense we make of things from our limited perspective doesn't actually make that much sense. And the lesson in respect to critical reading is this: don't let your prior conclusions and expectations block your ability to consider someone else's perspective; you may not actually *know* what you think you know.

Fortunately, however, in addition to being concluders, we humans are also by nature creatures who grow and change. When we're challenged by the knowledge, experience, and perspectives of others, we have the opportunity to escape from our limited, egocentric view of things. But the only way we can make that escape is by carefully listening, by considering what other people have to say. Although I didn't accept my mother as an authority when she tried to explain that France couldn't possibly be viewed from Brighton Beach, I remember very clearly the series of illustrations in our family encyclopedia that made me suddenly understand she was right. Those illustrations showed a three-masted sailing ship sinking down over the curve of the earth until all you could see was the pennant at the top of its tallest mast. I have to admit, I felt a little dumb; I was embarrassed that I had argued so strenuously. But the embarrassment was overwhelmed by a feeling of profound excitement, and when I saw my best friend, Lorraine, in the schoolyard the next morning, I amazed her with my newly discovered knowledge.

You might have noticed, however, that it was Lorraine I rushed to with my new-found knowledge, not my mother. The point here is that in addition to being concluders and changers, we humans also hate to admit we've been wrong. But to refine old ideas and discover new ones, we invariably have to do just that—admit we've been wrong. When we read what someone else has written, we always risk having our old ideas about the world challenged. And although we certainly have both the right and the responsibility to oppose some challenges, we must also have the courage to admit when someone else is right and we've been wrong. Giving up a position that isn't credible isn't giving up anything at all. Rather than being a loss, this kind of giving up is a gain. When I understood why I couldn't see France from a beach in Brooklyn, I hadn't been defeated. And the next morning when I ran into the schoolyard and spotted Lorraine, I felt elated. The two of us were always trading information, and she was going to be impressed by this amazing geographic news of mine.

READING FOR MEANING:
A MODEL FOR THE PROCESS

The reading process outlined here isn't a set of "rules" for reading. Instead, it's a model that I've experimented with and found to be useful. The same is true of the other analytic models you'll find in this chapter. I see the models here (like everything else presented in this book) as just a few of the many possible responses in the ongoing conversation about the teaching and learning of writing. They'll work best for you if you use them actively and critically. What I'm saying is, change them in any way that seems useful. Reorder and amend and expand on them. Then write me or give me a call. I'd like to know what you think.

A GUIDE TO THE CRITICAL READING MODEL

1. Read the text
2. Research unknowns
3. Analyze the speaker
   facts
      emotions
         attitudes
4. Determine the message
5. Determine the audience
6. Determine the purpose

PREREAD

Before you can read any text critically, you have to get an overview of what's going on in it by prereading. To familiarize yourself with the subject of the following selection, **read the first three paragraphs** slowly, focusing on those things you understand. When you get to the end of paragraph three, stop reading and take stock; **summarize** what you think has gone on in the text to that point. What do you know about the subject of the text so far? If you're confused, go back and focus on the sentences you don't understand and **reread** them, searching for meaning. Then **predict** what direction you think the text will take. As you continue to read, compare your predictions with what unfolds on the page. After each of the remaining paragraphs, pause again to summarize, reread if necessary, and predict. Preread, then reread the following text.

BEING BLACK AND FEELING BLUE
Shelby Steele

Shelby Steele teaches English at San Jose State University. This text is an excerpt from an essay that was originally published in The American Scholar *in 1989.*

In the early seventies when I was in graduate school, I went out for a beer late one afternoon with another black graduate student whom I'd only known casually before. This student was older than I—a stint in the army had interrupted his education—and he had the reputation of being bright and savvy, of having applied street smarts to the business of getting through graduate school. I suppose I was hoping for what would be called today a little mentoring. But it is probably not wise to drink with someone when you are enamored of his reputation, and it was not long before we stumbled into a moment that seemed to transform him before my very eyes. I asked him what he planned to do when he finished his Ph.D., fully expecting to hear of high aspirations matched with shrewd perceptions on how to reach them. But, before he could think, he said with a kind of exhausted sincerity, "Man, I just want to hold on, get a job that doesn't work me too hard, and do a lot of fishing." Was he joking, I asked. "Hell no," he said with exaggerated umbrage. "I'm not into it like the white boys. I don't need what they need."

I will call this man Henry and report that, until five or six years ago when I lost track of him, he was doing exactly as he said he would do. With much guile and little ambition he had

continued to next page

moved through a succession of low-level administrative and teaching jobs, mainly in black studies programs. Of course, it is no crime to just "hold on," and it is hardly a practice limited to blacks. Still, in Henry's case there was truly a troubling discrepancy between his ambition and a fine intelligence recognized by all who knew him. But in an odd way this intelligence was more lateral than vertical, and I would say that it was rechanneled by a certain unseen fear into the business of merely holding on. It would be easy to say that Henry had simply decided on life in a slower lane than he was capable of traveling in, or that he was that rare person who had achieved ambitionless contentment. But, if this was so, Henry would have had wisdom rather than savvy, and he would not have felt the need to carry himself with more self-importance than his station justified. I don't think Henry was uninterested in ambition; I think he was afraid of it.

It is certainly true that there is a little of Henry in most people. My own compulsion to understand him informs me that I must have seen many elements of myself in him. And though I'm sure he stands for a universal human blockage, I also believe that there is something in the condition of being black in America that makes the kind of hesitancy he represents one of black America's most serious and debilitating problems. As Henry reached the very brink of expanded opportunity, with Ph.D. in hand, he diminished his ambition almost as though his degree delivered him to a kind of semi-retirement. I don't think blacks in general have any illusions about semi-retirement, but I do think that, as a group, we have hesitated on the brink of new opportunities that we made enormous sacrifices to win for ourselves. The evidence of this lies in one of the most tragic social ironies of late twentieth-century American life—as black Americans have gained in equality and opportunity, we have also declined in relation to whites, so that by many socio-economic and other measures we are further behind whites today than before the great victories of the civil rights movement. By one report, even the black middle class, which had made great gains in the seventies, began to lose ground to its white counterpart in the eighties. Most distressing of all, the black underclass continues to expand rather than shrink.

Of course, I don't suggest that Henry's peculiar inertia singularly explains social phenomena so complex and tragic. I do

continued on page 64

continued from page 63

believe, however, that blacks in general are susceptible to the same web of attitudes and fears that kept Henry beneath his potential, and that our ineffectiveness in taking better advantage of our greater equality and opportunity has much to do with this. I think there is a specific form of racial anxiety that all blacks are vulnerable to that can, in situations where we must engage the mainstream society, increase our self-doubt and undermine our confidence so that we often back away from the challenges that, if taken, would advance us. I believe this hidden racial anxiety may well now be the strongest barrier to our full participation in the American mainstream—that it is as strong or stronger even than the discrimination we still face. To examine this racial anxiety, allow me first to look at how the Henry was born in me.

5   Until the sixth grade, I attended a segregated school in a small working-class black suburb of Chicago. The school was a dumping ground for teachers with too little competence or mental stability to teach in the white school in our district. In 1956 when I entered the sixth grade, I encountered a new addition to the menagerie of misfits that was our faculty—an ex-Marine whose cruelty was suggested during our first lunch hour when he bit the cap off his Coke bottle and spit it into the wastebasket. Looking back I can see that there was no interesting depth to the cruelty he began to show us almost immediately—no consumptive hatred, no intelligent malevolence. Although we were all black and he was white, I don't think he was even particularly racist. He had obviously needed us to like him though he had no faith that we would. He ran the class like a gang leader, picking favorites one day and banishing them the next. And then there was a permanent pool of outsiders, myself among them, who were made to carry the specific sins that he must have feared most in himself.

The sin I was made to carry was the sin of stupidity. I misread a sentence on the first day of school, and my fate was sealed. He made my stupidity a part of the classroom lore, and very quickly I in fact became stupid. I all but lost the ability to read and found the simplest math beyond me. His punishments for my errors rose in meanness until one day he ordered me to pick up all of the broken glass on the playground with my bare hands. Of course, this would have to be the age of the pop bottle, and there were

continued to next page

sections of this playground that glared like a mirror in sunlight. After half an hour's labor I sat down on strike, more out of despair than rebellion.

Again, cruelty was no more than a vibration in this man, and so without even a show of anger he commandeered a bicycle, handed it to an eighth grader—one of his lieutenants—and told the boy to run me around the school grounds "until he passes out." The boy was also given a baseball bat to "use on him when he slows down." I ran two laps, about a mile, and then pretended to pass out. The eighth grader knew I was playing possum but could not bring himself to hit me and finally rode off. I exited the school yard through an adjoining cornfield and never returned.

I mention this experience as an example of how one's innate capacity for insecurity is expanded and deepened, of how a disbelieving part of the self is brought to life and forever joined to the believing self. As children we are all wounded in some way and to some degree by the wild world we encounter. From these wounds a disbelieving *anti-self* is born, an internal antagonist and saboteur that embraces the world's negative view of us, that believes our wounds are justified by our own unworthiness, and that entrenches itself as a lifelong voice of doubt. This anti-self is a hidden but aggressive force that scours the world for fresh evidence of our unworthiness. When the believing self announces its aspirations, the anti-self always argues against them, but never on their merits (this is a healthy function of the believing self). It argues instead against our worthiness to pursue these aspirations and, by its lights, we are never worthy of even our smallest dreams. The mission of the anti-self is to deflate the believing self and, thus, draw it down into inertia, passivity, and faithlessness.

The anti-self is the unseen agent of low self-esteem; it is a catalytic energy that tries to induce low self-esteem in the believing self as though it were the complete truth of the personality. The anti-self can only be contained by the strength of the believing self, and this is where one's early environment becomes crucial. If the childhood environment is stable and positive, if the family is whole and provides love, the schools good, the community safe, then the believing self will be reinforced and made strong. If the family is shattered, the schools indifferent, the neighborhood a mine field of dangers, the anti-self will find evidence everywhere with which to deflate the believing self.

continued on page 66

continued from page 65

10   This does not mean that a bad childhood cannot be overcome. But it does mean—as I have experienced and observed it—that one's *capacity* for self-doubt and self-belief are roughly the same from childhood on, so that years later when the believing self may have strengthened enough to control the anti-self, one will still have the same capacity for doubt whether or not one has the actual doubt. I think it is this struggle between our capacities for doubt and belief that gives our personalities one of their peculiar tensions and, in this way, marks our character.

My own anti-self was given new scope and power by this teacher's persecution of me, and it was so successful in deflating my believing self that I secretly vowed never to tell my parents what was happening to me. The anti-self had all but sold my believing self on the idea that I was stupid, and I did not want to feel that shame before my parents. It was my brother who finally told them, and his disclosure led to a boycott that closed the school and eventually won the dismissal of my teacher and several others. But my anti-self transformed even this act of rescue into a cause of shame—if there wasn't something wrong with me, why did I have to be rescued? The anti-self follows only the logic of self-condemnation.

But there was another dimension to this experience that my anti-self was only too happy to seize upon. It was my race that landed me in this segregated school and, as many adults made clear to me, my persecution followed a timeless pattern of racial persecution. The implications of this were rich food for the anti-self—my race was so despised that it had to be segregated; as a black my education was so unimportant that even unbalanced teachers without college degrees were adequate; and ignorance and cruelty that would be intolerable in a classroom of whites was perfectly all right in a classroom of blacks. The anti-self saw no injustice in any of this, but instead took it all as confirmation of a racial inferiority that it could now add to the well of personal doubt I already had. When the adults thought they were consoling me—"Don't worry. They treat all blacks this way"—they were also deepening the wound and expanding my capacity for doubt.

And this is the point. The condition of being black in America means that one will likely endure more wounds to one's self-

continued to next page

esteem than others and that the capacity for self-doubt born of these wounds will be compounded and expanded by the black race's reputation of inferiority. The anti-self will most likely have more ammunition with which to deflate the believing self and its aspirations. And the universal human struggle to have belief win out over doubt will be more difficult.

And, more than difficult, it is also made inescapable by the fact of skin color, which, in America, works as a visual invocation of the problem. Black skin has more dehumanizing stereotypes associated with it than any other skin color in America, if not the world. When a black presents himself in an integrated situation, he knows that his skin alone may bring these stereotypes to life in the minds of those he meets and that he, as an individual, may be diminished by his race before he has a chance to reveal a single aspect of his personality. By the symbology of color that operates in our culture, black skin accuses him of inferiority. Under the weight of this accusation, a black will almost certainly doubt himself on some level and to some degree. The ever-vigilant anti-self will grab this racial doubt and mix it into the pool of personal doubt, so that when a black walks into an integrated situation— a largely white college campus, an employment office, a business lunch—he will be vulnerable to the entire realm of his self-doubt before a single word is spoken.

This constitutes an intense and lifelong racial vulnerability and anxiety for blacks. Even though a white American may have been wounded more than a given black, and therefore have a larger realm of inner doubt, his white skin with its connotations of privilege and superiority will actually help protect him from that doubt and from the undermining power of his anti-self, at least in relations with blacks. In fact, the larger the realm of doubt, the more he may be tempted to rely on his white skin for protection from it. Certainly in every self-avowed white racist, whether businessman or member of the Klan, there is a huge realm of self-contempt and doubt that hides behind the mythology of white skin. The mere need to pursue self-esteem through skin color suggests there is no faith that it can be pursued any other way. But if skin color offers whites a certain false esteem and impunity, it offers black vulnerability.

This vulnerability begins for blacks with the recognition that we belong quite simply to the most despised race in the human

15

continued on page 68

continued from page 67

community of races. To be a member of such a group in a society where all others gain an impunity by merely standing in relation to us is to live with a relentless openness to diminishment and shame. By the devious logic of the anti-self, one cannot be open to such diminishment without in fact being inferior and therefore deserving of diminishment. For the anti-self, the charge verifies the crime, so that racial vulnerability itself is evidence of inferiority. In this sense, the anti-self is an internalized racist, our own subconscious bigot, that conspires with society to diminish us.

So when blacks enter the mainstream, they are not only vulnerable to society's racism but also to the racist within. This internal racist is not restricted by law, morality, or social decorum. It cares nothing about civil rights and equal opportunity. It is the self-doubt born of the original wound of racial oppression, and its mission is to establish the justice of that wound and shackle us with doubt.

IMPLICITLY AND EXPLICITLY EXPRESSIVE WRITING

It's almost time for you to begin actively conversing with the text you've preread by reading it for meaning in collaboration with your classmates; however, before you do, let's pause for a moment and consider the finer points of expressive writing.

Behind every piece of writing is a writer, a unique human being using written language to express a point of view on the subject being written about. Sometimes the writer's expression is **explicit;** sometimes the writer's expression is **implicit.** In explicit writing, the writer's responses to the subject are fully and clearly expressed; however, in implicit writing, the writer's responses are suggested but not directly stated. The first of the following passages uses language explicitly to express the writer's responses to the scene; the second uses language implicitly.

EXPLICIT

I hated the place from the moment I saw it through the dirty fog. Even the ferry that brought us there was half broken down, its engine rattling and clanging as it shut off. As we sailed forward noiselessly toward the pier, I clutched Michael's hand tighter, filled with anxiety. With each passing second the shacks where the pathetic miners lived became more distinct. And above the squalid shanty village lining the harbor, the ugly, slag-covered hills became slowly visible. We were to spend the worst eight months of our lives in this place.

IMPLICIT

As we approached the island, the ferry's engines ground to a clanking, rattling stop, and we sailed noiselessly forward through the brown fog toward the looming pier. I clutched Michael's hand tighter. With each passing second the miners' shacks became more distinct, and beyond them the slag-covered hills became slowly visible. We were to spend eight long months in this place.

In the second passage, the language only implies the writer's responses to the subject. The responses are there but not explicitly stated: the fog is "brown" instead of "dirty"; the miners live in "shacks," not a "squalid shanty village"; the hills are "barren" instead of "ugly"; the months spent there are "long" as opposed to "the worst."

A lot that's only suggested in the second is actually stated in the first: that the speaker "hated the place," that the ferry was "half broken down," that the miners were "pathetic." Notice also how in the second passage the writer implies the "anxiety" that's openly stated in the first passage by juxtaposing "looming pier" with "I clutched Michael's hand."

Like all the other choices writers make, the choice of whether to be explicitly or implicitly expressive depends on the writer's purpose and audience. With one audience, implicit expression might be the best way to get desired audience response; with another audience, explicit expression might be better.

COLLABORATIVE WRITING ASSIGNMENT

Explore the meaning of Steele's text in collaboration with your classmates. Start the collaboration in groups of three or four. Think of yourselves as detectives. Your assignment here is to look closely at the language in the text, searching for the writer's

continued on page 70

continued from page 69

meaning, gathering evidence and finally drawing conclusions. Expect to have initial (or perhaps even lasting) disagreements about what the writer is actually saying, but keep debating and providing evidence until you get as close as you can to a consensus of meaning. After about twenty minutes, open the conversation to the whole class and share and discuss your conclusions. There is only one rule in this exercise—stay inside the text. You're free to make any judgment about the text as long as you can back up that judgment by citing specific evidence from the text. And remember, keep an open mind, and have the courage to give up positions that aren't credible.

RESEARCH UNKNOWNS.   The point of careful reading is to discern as closely as you can the meaning of a text. Therefore, it's important to **research** unknown words or references in the text you're reading. With this in mind, mark words or references in Steele's text that are unknown to you, and use the resources at your college or university to clarify their meaning. For example, if you don't know what the word *umbrage* means, look it up in a dictionary.

ANALYZE THE SPEAKER.   As I said earlier, behind every piece of writing is a writer, a unique human being using written language to express a point of view on the subject being written about. So let's start with this writer, but to be fair to Shelby Steele, we'll further refine the definition of *writer*. Shelby Steele is a human being with many more facets than are revealed in this particular text. This text reveals just one small, carefully constructed part, and we'll call that part **"the speaker."**

Using only the text of the selection as a source of evidence, respond to the following (make sure you cite specific passages from the text to support your assertions):

1. *Facts* List and support with evidence from the text as many **facts** as you can about the speaker (at least five). For example, the speaker is black. Evidence: paragraph 1, "with another black graduate student."

2. *Emotions* Where in the text does the speaker describe his own or another's emotional response(s)? What are those

continued to next page

responses? Example: after his experience with his teacher, the speaker feels such shame at his stupidity that he is afraid to tell his parents about the incident. Evidence: paragraph 11, ''My own anti-self . . . ,'' etc.

At this ''emotions'' stage of reading for meaning, it's useful to empathetically encounter the emotional reactions described in the text. Since we encounter the world emotionally as well as intellectually, empathizing can help us to grasp more of the text's meaning. Have you ever experienced one or more of the **emotions** described by the speaker? Think of a time in your own life, a specific instance, when you've experienced one of the emotional reactions described in the text (the situation doesn't have to be the same, just your emotional response), and share it with your classmates.

   3. Attitudes Unlike emotional responses, the speaker's **attitudes** are thoughtful conclusions, evidence-supported judgments that the speaker has drawn about the subjects being written about. Although an emotional response can, after thought, lead to an attitude, an attitude is an intellectual rather than an emotional response. Where in ''Being Black and Feeling Blue'' does the speaker express particular conclusions he's drawn about the subjects of his writing? What are these conclusions? What evidence does he use to support these conclusive attitudes? Find as many as you can; the more you find, the sharper the text's meaning will become for you. As an example, the speaker thinks that his feelings of inferiority were strengthened when black adults told him that all blacks were treated badly by whites. Evidence: paragraphs 12 and 13, ''When the adults thought they were consoling me . . . ,'' etc.

DETERMINE THE MESSAGE.   The **message** of a particular text is very specific; it's the **main idea** the speaker is trying to communicate. The writer wants the audience to agree with a particular message and then be moved to further thought or action. Look back over the conclusions you've come to in the first three steps of the reading process. With those conclusions in mind, what do you think the speaker's message is? In as few sentences as possible, write that message down and support it with specific evidence from the text.

continued on page 72

continued from page 71

DETERMINE THE AUDIENCE.   What **audience** or **audiences** (specific group or groups of people) do you think the speaker is addressing in the text? What evidence (language choices or choices of detail made by the writer) can you find in the text for your judgment of audience?

DETERMINE THE PURPOSE.   Purpose is always intimately connected to audience; the writer's **specific purpose** is the **change** he or she desires in the **audience's knowledge or way of thinking or way of acting.** Purpose is not as specific as message; a writer may send many different messages through the medium of many different texts while trying to accomplish the same purpose. In this text the writer wants the audience to *agree* with a particular message and be changed. With that in mind, and with your conclusions about message and audience also in mind, determine what purpose the speaker is trying to accomplish by sending his message.

RESPONSIVE JOURNAL WRITING

Since we apprehend meaning emotionally as well as rationally, explore your emotional responses to Steele's text by journal writing. Focus on a time in your life when you experienced an emotional response similar to one of the responses described in Steele's text. The situation doesn't have to be similar, but your emotional response should be. Then, in writing, describe the remembered situation and your response to it. For example, in paragraph eleven the speaker describes his own feelings of shame. If you've ever experienced shame, you might focus on a particular time in your life when you experienced that emotion and describe the situation and your emotional response.

RESPONSIVE JOURNAL WRITING

Assess the effect of the critical reading process by journal writing. Focus on what you learned from reading ''Being Black and Feeling Blue'' in collaboration with others. Was your perspective on the subject of the text changed in *any* way? If so, write a page in which you explain how your perspective was changed and what you learned about critical reading or yourself as a reader from reading this particular text. If your perspective wasn't changed, write a page explaining why it wasn't.

A STUDENT WRITES
ABOUT CRITICAL READING

The following course journal entry was written by student writer Lance Hummel in response to the journal writing assignment above. Hummel describes how his personal and educational history influenced his initial reading of Steele's text.

Several years ago, when I worked as a Peace Corps volunteer, I visited the tiny island of Goreé located off of the western coast of Senegal, Africa. On this island there were many dark, underground cells with hand and foot shackles, restraining chains, whipping posts, and devices of torture all for the purpose of subjugating and holding human beings to be sold into slavery. During the middle 1800's, Goreé had the reputation of being brutally efficient in supplying people to the slavers, due in large part to the manner in which the people were collected into slavery. It was mostly native blacks who knew the country, who knew where the villages were, who performed the abductions and brought the victims to Goreé to be held and sold to white slavers arriving by ship. When I asked the tour guide why the native blacks would bring their own people into slavery, he responded

continued on page 74

continued from page 73

that the victims were usually from inland tribes considered by coastal tribes to be inferior.

His answer came as a shock. The idea of blacks selling those of their own race into slavery was something that I was not prepared for. I was a recent college graduate, had supported the civil rights and anti-war movements, and had even taken a civil rights class in the Black Studies program. I was prepared to acknowledge white oppression, white business, and racism as the driving forces behind slavery, but instead was told of the crucial involvement of native blacks in slavery. Somehow it just didn't make sense, because if prejudices and discrimination against American blacks resulted from white oppression in a white-dominated society, then blacks in a black-dominated society should be free from these problems. This was certainly not the case. During my tour as a Peace Corps volunteer in Africa I had many experiences which confirmed the fact that prejudice and discrimination are commonplace among the blacks of Africa, and I eventually concluded that I found more racism in Africa than I had ever found in America.

In retrospect, I believe this revelation had something of a numbing effect on my attitude toward the black civil rights movement in America. Without realizing it, I became less sympathetic. Having seen ample evidence for prejudice and discrimination among blacks themselves, I subconsciously developed a bit more callous, almost skeptical attitude toward those who would blame these problems on white oppression in America. It seemed that some of the civil rights activists were using white oppression and the white dominated society as a convenient scapegoat to cover up their own inadequacies.

I persisted in my judgments for many years until only very recently, when I was challenged by a classmate during a discussion to rethink these judgments. I am now in the process of doing so and have come to understand some limitations of my judgments. I now see that I had not only developed a skeptical attitude towards civil rights in America, but that it was based on overly simplistic, flawed conclusions made years before during my Peace Corps experience. To compare the problems of African society to those of American society with the simple logic that I had used was totally unrealistic. Prejudice and discrimination are enor-

continued to next page

mously complex problems spanning all nations, all races, and probably all the time in which human beings have inhabited the earth.

However, the most significant limitation of my judgments is that I had unwittingly let them affect my perspectives. Whether it was reading about civil rights struggle in the newspapers, learning about it on TV, or even reading Steele's text, I had allowed my judgments to affect what I was learning. For example, I could *not* read Steele's text without forming my own arguments with him as I read and, as a result, I completely misinterpreted his message. I've not yet conquered this judgment problem, but at least I know it is there. And that is the first step.

LEARN—READ WITH AN EYE TO THE WRITER'S CRAFT

We humans come into the world with the remarkable, innate ability to learn language. Some researchers believe that even before we're born we begin the learning by listening to the voices of our mothers and those close by. As infants, we pick up our first words and expressions from the speakers around us. As young children, living exclusively within the community of our families, we talk the way our families talk; we use the vocabulary of our parents and siblings. Later, as we leave the exclusive language community of our homes and go out into the world, we learn to speak in other ways. We learn to speak in one way with our friends and in another way with our teachers. We learn the different vocabularies and speaking styles of the different communities we enter. And the more sophisticated the communities we enter are, the more our spoken language evolves.

Just as the spoken language we hear influences the way we speak, the written language we read influences the way we write. And just as our spoken language evolves and becomes more sophisticated as we grow and learn and enter more (and more sophisticated) language communities, so does our written language. By nature programmed to accept language, we humans unconsciously soak up the vocabulary and style of the texts we habitually read. More than in any other way, we enter a specific written language community by reading. In order to write an essay or a poem, you have to know what an essay or a poem is; the only way you can know what makes up an essay or a poem is by reading essays and poetry. Writers aren't born with the ability to write. When we enter a written language community, we immediately and unconsciously begin learning the conventions and expectations of that community through reading.

Establishing yourself as a member of a specific written language community is a gradual process that begins with your first experience with reading a text from that community. And the more texts you read, the more you'll learn the conventions and expectations of that community and the easier reading and writing in that community will become. Being a member of a specific written language community means being a student of the texts produced in that community. Just as apprentice carpenters learn the techniques of their craft by studying the performance of masters in the field, so do student writers. And like all crafts, writing involves making **choices.** A carpenter will choose different kinds and grades of wood and different finishes for different jobs, and in the actual building, a carpenter will choose one construction technique over another, depending on the assignment. The choices carpenters make, like the choices writers make, have everything to do with the **purpose** of the product they're creating. A kitchen cabinet that's used every day will have to have a durable finish; in the same way, a persuasive piece of writing will have to have evidence to make it convincing.

When we study a writer's performance in a particular text with an eye to improving our own technique, a good place to start is with the writer's purpose; all the choices the writer made in constructing the text were based on that purpose.

Let's look again at Shelby Steele's text and compare the judgments of purpose, audience, and message made by you and your classmates in the first collaborative writing assignment in this chapter with the judgments made by another group of students. Below are judgments of Steele's audience, purpose, and message made by a group of university students enrolled in a composition class. Don't be concerned if the analytic conclusions you arrived at were slightly different from theirs. Reading, like writing, is an interactive process. We don't have to come up with exactly the same judgments other people come up with; we just have to come up with something we can support with sufficient evidence from the text.

1. *Purpose* The student group concluded that Steele's purpose in writing the text was **to persuade his audience to further the advancement of blacks in American society.**

2. *Chosen Audiences* The group decided that Steele had two audiences, **well-educated black Americans and well-educated non-black Americans.** In addition, the group thought that Steele's underlying purpose was refined when he began to bring in the concept of audience (that intimate purpose-audience connection, again). Although Steele's purpose remained the same, his audiences were not the same, and because they weren't, he needed to change them in different ways. He wanted to persuade blacks to advance *themselves* in American society. And he wanted to persuade non-blacks to aid in that advancement.

3. *Message* Because Steele had two different audiences, the message of his text had to be directed toward changing both of them. He couldn't risk losing the attention of one audience by aiming his message solely at the other. The message of his text, then, had to be something both of his audiences would listen to. Here is the message the group of students decided Steele was sending: **because blacks have been "the most despised race" in American society, they have developed an "internal racist" that holds them back from full participation in that society.**

With audience, message, and purpose in mind, you can begin to study the choices that Steele made in crafting his text. And now you may be thinking, "But where do I start?" First, you have to remember that the choices writers make have to do with ways of transmitting meaning by using written language. Simply put, the writer says, "What are the best ways to use the language available to **persuade** my audience to change?" If you've read Chapter One of this book, you'll remember the writer's categories of choice:

Voice
Development
Arrangement

FOCUS ON PERSUASION
IN AUDIENCE-BASED WRITING

Before you and your classmates begin studying Steele's choices, let's slow down for a few minutes and take a closer look at just how it is that writers **persuade** their audiences. Aristotle identified three main persuasive techniques regularly employed in organized communication:

Logos—**persuading** the audience with reason
Pathos—**persuading** the audience with emotion
Ethos—**persuading** the audience by establishing credibility

LOGOS, PERSUADING WITH REASON   All effective writing makes some sort of appeal to the the reader's reason. We humans are by nature rational creatures. We gather evidence and draw conclusions; we find it appealing when things make sense to us. However, things that make sense to us aren't necessarily *true;* they're just plausible—they could, under the right circumstances, be true. For example, consider these sentences from paragraph two of Steele's text:

> It would be easy to say that Henry had simply decided on life in a slower lane than he was capable of traveling in, or that he was that rare person who had achieved ambitionless contentment. But, if this was so, Henry would have had wisdom rather than savvy, and he would not have felt the need to carry himself with more self-importance than his station justified. I don't think Henry was uninterested in ambition; I think he was afraid of it.

The speaker isn't presenting us with an absolute truth when he says that Henry is afraid of ambition; he's presenting us with evidence (Henry's "need to carry himself with more self-importance than his station justified") and inviting us to agree with his conclusive judgment.

PATHOS, PERSUADING WITH EMOTION   Just as we humans are rational creatures, we're also creatures of emotion. We're moved not only by logic but by how we feel about things. Appeals to our emotions are not necessarily weaker or more suspect than appeals to our reason. Certainly, appeals to emotion can be used dishonestly; however, appeals to reason can also be used dishonestly on naive audiences. The "reasonableness" of a given proposition very often depends on the perspective of the person proposing it; therefore, getting a reader to *feel* what it's like to be on the other side of a situation is a very effective way of moving that reader from one "reasonable" position to another. For example, when the speaker in Steele's text says "when a black walks into an integrated situation—a largely white college campus, an employment office, a business lunch—he will be vulnerable to the entire realm of his self-doubt before a single word is spoken," the speaker is presenting his audiences with an emotionally charged situation and inviting them to identify and empathize.

ETHOS, PERSUADING BY ESTABLISHING CREDIBILITY   Although the general credibility of writers depends to a large extent on the solidity of their reasonable and emotional appeals, there are other factors that can affect just how much we trust a given writer. One significant factor is the writer's status in the world. For example, the fact that the speaker in Steele's text is highly educated (he went to graduate school) might make him seem more credible to his audience.

Writers can also enhance their credibility by citing authorities or by including the results of other people's research in their texts. The speaker in Steele's text includes the results of someone else's research in paragraph three, when he says, ''By one report, even the black middle class, which had made great gains in the seventies, began to lose ground to its white counterpart in the eighties.''

One of the most powerful vehicles for credibility is the writer's created voice. The persona you create on the page reveals your attitude toward your audience as well as toward your subject. And if your audience begins to distrust your voice, your credibility is lost.

COLLABORATIVE WRITING ASSIGNMENT

Study the writer's choices in Steele's text in collaboration with your classmates. Start the collaboration in groups of three or four. Your assignment here is to look closely at how Steele constructed his text with an eye to improving your own technique. After about fifteen minutes, open the conversation to the whole class and share and discuss your conclusions.

VOICE   In crafting his text, Steele made choices in language and sentence structure that create a persona, a distinctive personality that's revealed on the page. These choices reflect the speaker's attitude toward his subject and his orientation to both of his audiences. Study the voice of the speaker in Steele's text in the following ways:

Audience
You've decided on the chosen audience. Now list specific language and sentence structure choices that are evidence for your decision.

Emotional Orientation
What would you judge to be the speaker's feelings about each of his audiences? What specific language in the text supports your judgments? How might the speaker's emotional orientation toward the audiences help establish the writer's credibility? Remember, give evidence from the text to support the judgments you make. For example, you may *think* that someone in the

continued on page 80

continued from page 79

speaker's position would be angry at non-black Americans, but you must have evidence in the form of language from the text if you make that assertion.

Rational Orientation

Where does the speaker place himself intellectually in terms of his audiences? Does he address his audiences as his equals? What evidence from the text supports your assertion? How might the speaker's rational orientation toward his audiences help establish his credibility?

DEVELOPMENT   Study the analysis of the speaker from the "reading for meaning" process. It's in that step of the process that the writer's choices in development are revealed. What different kinds of developmental material does Steele use to convince his audience? Identify what material is Steele's own and what comes from an outside source. When is he appealing to his audiences' emotions? When to their reason? When is he trying to persuade his audiences by establishing his credibility? Why do you think he chose the kinds of developmental material he did? Some of the developmental material Steele includes is his own; it comes from his experience or his process of thinking and drawing conclusions.

ARRANGEMENT   If you examine Steele's text, you will begin to see that there are blocks or segments of developmental material. Outlining these blocks by listing them can help you to see that Steele has made choices in order and grouping to create a movement of meaning.

Look back at the part of the reading for meaning process where you found examples in the text of the speaker's thoughtful conclusions—his "attitudes." Where in your outline do these expressions of attitude come? Why might Steele have chosen to place them where he did? Now repeat the process, focusing on the speaker's descriptions of "emotions" in the text. How are the expressions of "emotion" and "attitude" related in terms of their order? Why might Steele have chosen to order them the way he did? What kinds of material does he group together?

RESPOND—DEVELOP A PERSPECTIVE THROUGH WRITING

It's almost time for you to actively enter the conversation by responding to Steele's text in writing. However, before you do, read what two other student writers have to say about "Being Black and Feeling Blue."

READING AND RESPONDING: STUDENT WRITING

The two texts that follow were written in response to "Being Black and Feeling Blue." In the first, nursing student Anne Steenberg disagreed partially with Steele's perspective. In the second, Lutfi Han, a political science major from Turkey, voices strong disagreements with Steele's conclusions. As you preread and then read the texts critically, focus your attention on how these two writers use evidence from their own experience to support their conclusive judgments.

Anne Steenberg

WITHOUT SUCCESS THERE CAN BE NO MOTIVATION

I agree with Shelby Steele's message in this selection, but not completely. People struggling against self-limitation not only feel self-doubt, but become passive and are unable to help themselves.

This helplessness is learned. It comes from the evidence-supported belief that the odds are stacked against you, that power follows money, and in this country you get the best justice that you can afford. This may be linked with the sense of inferiority that Steele speaks of, but I think this learned helplessness is as damaging to progress as the "internal racist," if not more so. There are other self-internalized labels (welfare mother, juvenile delinquent, stupid) that are just as harmful to self-esteem as any racial slur.

After years of efforts to better yourself, the effort to keep on trying becomes harder and harder to justify, given the results. All attempts to succeed seem to be followed not only by failure, but

continued on page 82

continued from page 81

in some cases by personal attack. The reason for these attacks seems to be to keep you in your place.

In my own life, as an uneducated and mostly unskilled young woman, I drifted into the small town of Hall, Montana. I worked for a brutal man who met all complaints from the women on the crew with loud speculations about "that time of the month" to his cronies. My home life had degenerated into one typical of living with an abusive alcoholic. Perhaps the most depressing part of this life was the way that I accepted it. I expected things to go on pretty much as they always had.

It is not the major crises that create this apathy. People can overcome a major tragedy and go on with their lives. It is the small deadening, day-to-day cruelties and disappointments. You are shorted ten dollars on your paycheck and told to "prove it." Your spouse "forgets" that you need the car the day that you are to register for school. One day you look at your life and realize that unless something remarkable happens, this is as good as it is going to get.

I escaped because of a first, small success. Over the not-so-subtle objections of my husband I registered for a class at the vocational college. I was as surprised as he that I could keep up with the class, and that I could learn as quickly as any of the other students. The confidence I gained from that experience gave me the strength to make some hard decisions about my future and start working toward my goals. From that time on, I knew that it *was* possible for me to succeed, and that knowledge helped me change other, more important areas of my life. More significant than the initial success was the awareness that I could succeed if I so chose.

Shelby Steele's message seems to be that members of the black community need to break away from passivity and self-doubt and "pursue their dreams with discipline and effort, to be responsible for themselves." However, there is no motivation to be disciplined or responsible when no progress is made. If people never experience any success, then there is little chance that they will continue to pursue it. I agree with Steele that self-doubt is crippling the progress of many, but the helplessness learned from having to struggle against the odds is too often overlooked.

Lutfi Han

SMELLING FOREIGNER

The first job that I could find in America was washing dishes in one of the downtown restaurants in Missoula, Montana. Although washing dishes was not the position that I applied for, the manager told me that there was nothing else at the moment but as soon as possible I would be transferred to the dining room. I washed dishes for six months, and the restaurant kept hiring people for busing tables and waiting tables, but I was still washing dishes. Almost every day, the manager and the other workers would tell me that I was hard worker and a very fast dishwasher, and that they only wished they had someone like me for Saturdays and Sundays. As ignorant as I was, I had pride in doing a good job. I was hired only to do dishes, but the head cook would make me scrub the walls, clean the cooler and freezer, and wash the floors as well.

Although I had four years of experience waiting tables, bussing and tending bar, I realized that if I did not make any noise I would be washing dishes for as long as I worked there. I thought constantly of telling the manager that I did not want to wash dishes anymore. Every day I would work up my courage and get closer to telling the manager, but something in my throat would not let me. I was afraid of losing the dishwashing job.

One day one of the bussers quit, and I was so terribly tired of doing dishes that I went to the manager and told her that I did not want to wash dishes anymore. Since there was a opening in the dining room I would be really happy to do bussing. She looked at me and asked why I didn't like washing dishes. "What's wrong with doing dishes?" she asked. I did not want to tell her that I hated doing dishes, so instead I told her that I would be more helpful working in the dining room. I could tell she was not satisfied with my answer. I was ready to quit if I did not get that job. I guess she knew that I was going to quit. She told me she would see if there was anything that she could do about it. After couple of more weeks of doing dishes, I was finally allowed to bus tables. I was so proud of myself that I worked in the dining

continued on page 84

continued from page 83

room. After a few months bussing tables, I was allowed to wait tables, and I made four or five times more money than I had made bussing or washing dishes.

It has been almost two years that I have been working at this restaurant, and there hasn't been one day that the head cook hasn't had something for me to do. She would come out of the kitchen door, pass every single busser and waiter and come to tell *me* that there some silverware needed to be washed and polished, and if I didn't have anything else to do I should go and work in the kitchen.

All along I have done my best to do everything this cook told me to do. One day I went to work, and she was there. After I punched in my card and left to go to the dining room, she stopped me and started to smell me. I thought she was joking. After a few seconds, I realized that she was not joking. She said she had gotten some complaints the day before that I smelled. I asked her, "How come these complaints came to you instead of going to the restaurant manager?" She told me that that was not the point. The point was that I smelled. I asked her to smell me again to see if I still smelled, and she did and told me that I did not smell any more. I knew she was a liar, because the day that I was supposed to smell I had taken a shower, and that day that she was smelling I hadn't bathed yet. I was so upset that I did not know what to say to this woman. I went back to the break room and cried. I was twenty-five years old and for the first time in my life someone was telling me that I smelled. All my life passed in front of my eyes. I thought about the pride that I had in my country and the pride my family had in me. Here in America for the first time I was the object of racism. There was nothing I could do at the moment to lift up my pride and dignity. I was crushed to the floor like some useless piece of paper. I felt so small and so worthless that I asked Allah to take my life and not let me experience anything like this again. After I had been sitting in the break room for almost an hour, another waiter came and told me that the dining room was almost full, and that he needed me there to help him. Unwillingly, I went to work. All night long I felt that I had shamed myself and my parents by letting the head cook walk all over me. That night she was working with the assistant cook in

continued to next page

the kitchen. Purposely, they would not buzz me when my orders were ready in the kitchen so that my food would get cold. When I asked them to buzz me when my food was ready, the assistant cook told me that this was the way it was going to be. "If you don't like it," he told me, "you can get the f--- out of here."

Later that night, the restaurant manager and her helper came and spoke to me. They told me to go to the bookstore and find books about racism in America and learn more about it. Yes, a great deal of racism still exists in America. It is in the blood of a great many people, and it is going to take a long time, perhaps centuries, to get rid of it. It will be passed on in every day life from one generation to another. I and members of other minority groups might work hard and achieve, but that won't protect us from being humiliated by racists. Even though there are a lot of good people in America, there are bad people as well. And unfortunately the bad people are the ones who hold much of the power. It may be that America will never reach Martin Luther King's dream.

Reading a text without thinking about how you agree and disagree with it isn't authentically reading a text. Now that you've listened and learned by reading carefully and closely, it's your turn to respond. You've probably already begun to frame initial agreements or disagreements (or perhaps a combination of both) with Steele's view of things, but now it's time to explore and expand on your perspective through the process of writing.

RESPONSIVE WRITING ASSIGNMENT

After rereading "Being Black and Feeling Blue," write a response statement that explains your agreements or disagreements with the text's message. Use your experience and knowledge as supportive evidence for your position. Gradations of agreement and disagreement (yes or no, buts) are as valid as evidence-supported positions of total agreement or disagreement.

A GUIDE TO THE WRITING PROCESS

Assess Your Past Performance
Explore the Writing Situation
Prewrite
Draft
Rewrite

ASSESS YOUR PAST PERFORMANCE

Just as writing is a recursive process, the continuing journey toward becoming a better writer is also recursive. As you work through this assignment, **analyze how you think** and write: **learn from your previous experience,** and **respond by revising** your personal writing process. Read over the self-assessment you wrote when you finished your previous assignment(s), study the journal entry in which you assessed your strengths and weaknesses as a writer, and think about the comments you've gotten on papers you've constructed in the past. For example, you may have had a continuing problem focusing your writing around a clear message. If you've had problems focusing in the past, pay particular attention to the strategies included in this chapter that deal with message. Part Five provides detailed strategies for prewriting and process-based revision.

EXPLORE THE WRITING SITUATION

You've been given an assignment. Now it's time to **explore the choices and constraints** in the writing situation at hand. Open yourself to the passages that follow and see if they trigger any response from you.

SUBJECT   Although the subject for writing is given in this assignment (agree and/or disagree with the message of Steele's text), your essential agreements or disagreements will come entirely out of your own thoughtful conclusions about the subject.

AUDIENCE   In this particular assignment the choice of audience is open. You might choose to write to one or more of your classmates, to your instructor, or to the class community as a whole—anyone who has read the text might be a possible audience. You might directly respond to the speaker in the text. Or you might even write to someone who hasn't read the text. You might write to a friend with whom you'd like to share your responses, or you might choose as an audience a person with experiences and perspectives similar to Steele's or a person with experiences and perspectives that are radically different.

PURPOSE   Your general purpose in this assignment is given; you are to *explain* to an external audience why you agree or disagree with the message of Steele's text. However, as you *explain* you might also *inform* your audience or *entertain* them or *explore* with them. And in addition to having a general purpose for writing, you'll also have a specific purpose; you'll be writing to change your audience's knowledge or way of thinking or acting, and your specific purpose will be determined by the audience you choose to write to and your agreements and disagreements with the text's message.

THE WRITER   Focus on yourself, now. Explore your prior experiences with and prior knowledge of the subject of Steele's text. How might your personal and educational histories have affected your face-to-face encounter with the text? What specific parts of the text did you respond to most intensely? Consider why those particular parts might have drawn the responses they did.

TIME   Give yourself plenty of time, not only writing time, but thinking time as well. Start thinking about your response now. The active process of writing your response began with your face-to-face encounter with Steele's text; don't throttle that process down by purposely refusing to think about the subject because you've been given a formal, looming assignment.

If your exploration of the writing situation has triggered your choice of audience, answer the following questions as a way of exploring in writing your audience's knowledge of the subject and possible point of view. What is your audience's race, social class, age, gender, and cultural and educational history? Is your audience familiar with Steele's text? Even if your audience isn't familiar with the text, what developmental material in it would be most likely to change their perspective? How would they be changed by that material?

PREWRITE

Because writing (like thinking) is recursive, you can find yourself triggered into entering the process actively at any point. For example, some of you came to the exploration of the writing situation outlined above already prepared to begin drafting your response. You had your audience and message chosen, your purpose for writing was firmly set in your mind, and you had begun to gather the evidence you needed to get the audience movement you desired. However, for some of you it was the exploration that triggered choices, and for still others those choices remain to be made. You may need to prewrite, draft, or even rewrite before you discover who your chosen audience is, much less what your purpose and message are. Whether you have begun to make choices or not, leave yourself open to rethinking and discovery as you prewrite, draft, and rewrite. Even if you've already made choices, engage in one or more of the following responsive prewriting exercises.

RESPONSIVE PREWRITING EXERCISES

1. The situation Steele is responding to in his essay is something that he has encountered and judged to be a problem—**in spite of gains in equality, blacks have been held back from full participation in American society.** He has encountered the problem through evidence coming to him from the world around him. Some of that evidence has probably come to him from written texts. A great deal of that evidence has most likely come to him from his own observations and experience. Consider your own encounter with the problem, and explore your answers to the following questions in writing.

a. Situations contain **agents** or **active participants;** therefore, it's useful to isolate the active participants. Who in your judgment are the active participants in the situation? In other words, who is responsible for the problem? Steele would probably have listed blacks and non-blacks in response to these questions. Do you agree?

b. Since this particular situation is a *problem*, one way of analyzing it is by **mapping** its **causes** and **effects.** (Part Six provides

continued to next page

details about using causal analysis as a prewriting strategy.) The causes and effects of a given situation are related to the **actions of the active participants,** the **motives** behind those actions, and the **consequences** of both the motives and actions. With actions, motives, and consequences in mind, list as many possible **causes** of the problem as you can. The speaker in Steele's text probably would have listed the following causes. Do you agree with the speaker's analysis?

> racism in the culture
> hopelessness in the black community
> black shame and self-hatred brought about by personal
> experiences with racism

Now list possible **effects.** The speaker in Steele's text probably would have listed the following as effects. Do you agree with the speaker's analysis?

> expansion of the black underclass
> continued racism in the culture
> intensified black shame and self-hatred
> social and economic costs to the society

Now list possible **solutions.** The speaker probably would have listed the following as solutions. Do you agree?

> If non-blacks could understand the nature of racism—that
> it is an impulse driven by the racist's own feelings of
> inferiority—they might be moved to take a stronger stand
> against it.
> If non-blacks could achieve a fuller, more personalized
> understanding of the intensity of black shame and
> self-hatred, they might be persuaded to aid in black
> advancement.
> If blacks could be persuaded to understand that their
> feelings of shame and self-hatred have caused them to turn
> against themselves and create their own "internal racist,"
> they might be able to confront that "internal racist" and
> advance themselves in American society.

2. **Identify** the **specific passages** in Steele's text you disagree with; then use the **double-entry note** strategy in Part Six to identify and

continued on page 90

continued from page 89
explore evidence for your disagreements. After you've explored your disagreements, **repeat the process,** focusing on your agreements. After you've explored both, **read** what you've gotten down. Then immediately **freewrite** (write nonstop) about the subject for ten minutes. Part Six provides a detailed illustration of freewriting.

3. **Reread** those places in the text where the speaker described his or another's emotional reactions. Focus on one or more of these descriptions, and recall a time in your own life when you experienced a similar emotional response. Then **freewrite** about the situation and its effects on you as a person.

4. **Look back** on the in-class conversation you had about the text, and identify a person from the class whose comments either challenged you to consider a new way of looking at the text's subject or precipitated strong disagreement in you. Seek that person out and expand on the conversation. When the conversation is over, **freewrite** about it.

5. **Reread** the text yet again. Then immediately spend some time alone and **focus your thinking** on the subject of Steele's writing. Make sure you have a small notebook (or a piece of paper) and a pen available to record any ideas that come to you.

FOCUS ON AUDIENCE AND PURPOSE

After trying one or more of the above strategies, focus your thinking once again on the message of Steele's text. Do you essentially agree with the text's message, or do you disagree? If you have gradations of agreement or disagreement (yes or no, buts), write them out in one or two sentences. Then focus on the choices allowed to you in the writing situation and tentatively answer the following questions. If necessary, choose an experimental audience and purpose to explore in your draft.

AUDIENCE   Considering your agreements or disagreements, who is your chosen audience? Write out a brief analysis of your audience. What are their values, age, race, gender, and social or economic class? What knowledge do they have of Steele's text or of the subject of his writing?

PURPOSE   What change in knowledge, thought, or action do you desire from your chosen audience?

FOCUS ON A WORKING MESSAGE

Just as Steele's text has a specific message it's sending in order to accomplish its purpose, the text your produce in response to Steele's should also have a message. The message of a text is simply the text's main idea or thesis. In this particular assignment the message of your text will most likely center on the general *why* behind your agreement or disagreement. Focus your thinking on your agreement or disagreement (or on your gradation of either), and in as few sentences as possible write down why you agree or disagree. The result should be your **working message.**

DRAFT

DRAFT TO REVISE

The revision you engage in as you draft gives you the opportunity to expand on old ideas and formulate new ones. **Read** and **reread** your draft as you write, and look for new ways of viewing your subject. Pay particular attention to those areas that have given you trouble in previous writing assignments, and revise as you draft by cutting, adding, rearranging, and rewording.

   The more choices you have made up to this point, the easier the active drafting of your text will be. Your draft should flow right out of your prewriting. As you draft, keep the following in mind.

AUDIENCE   Imagine yourself in conversation with your audience as you write. What do they know and need to know? What is their possible point of view on Steele's text?

PURPOSE   Just how do you want to change your audience? Will what's emerging on your page or computer screen get the change you want?

MESSAGE   As you actively draft, keep your working message foremost (write it across the top of your draft or tape a written copy of it to the top of your computer screen) and test it frequently as you write your emerging text.

FOCUS ON YOUR CHOICES

VOICE   Certainly, the words and sentence structures that you use should **reflect your own attitude** toward the subject, but they should also be chosen carefully to **get the change you want** from your audience. Think about Steele's text. Although a person with Steele's background and experience might have reason to be angry with non-black Americans, there's no anger in the speaker's voice in the text. Both the non-black and the black Americans that Steele is speaking to are educated people who pride themselves on their rationality, and the tone of the voice in the selection is measured and rational; it's not whining, punishing, or entreating.

To maintain your own chosen voice as you draft, **think constantly about your audience** and the change you want in them. And above all else, **struggle for clarity of meaning.** Don't try to "talk up" to your audience by using words and sentence structures you don't yet control. If your **self-assessment** has helped you identify voice as a habitual problem area, see "Problems with Voice" in Part Six for specific strategies. Keep in mind as you write that **clear, evidence-supported writing is the key to communicating your ideas to an audience.** As you draft, read your emerging text aloud, and reword with your audience's responses in mind.

COMPUTER TIP

Drafting on a computer can help with voice problems because your emerging text is right in front of you where you can *see* it and reread and reword easily. In handwritten drafting the text becomes messier and harder to read as you reword, but in computer drafting your language tends to become clearer as you revise because you can delete as you reword. To reword on the computer, move the cursor to the word you want to change, then type in the new word, and delete the old word by backspacing or using the delete key.

DEVELOPMENT   Voice and development are very closely connected. When we write, language is all we have at our disposal to communicate what we mean to other people, and it's language that creates that meaning. If we start out writing in a contemptuous **voice,** the **details** that we choose to prove our position will follow our contemptuous language. Think about how the developmental details in the Steele text are wedded to the reasonable voice of the speaker. Think about his descriptions of emotional responses, for example. The speaker is not so much expressing his own strong emotions as he is attempting to elicit similar emotions from his audience.

The point is, don't let a badly chosen voice dominate your thinking. Consider the change you desire in your audience, and imagine their conversational responses. Then put critical pressure on each piece of **evidence** you include and each **conclusion** you draw. If **self-assessment** has helped you identify development as a habitual problem area, see Part Six ("Problems with Development?") for specific strategies. Look for ways of **cutting** developmental material that might lead your audience away from your focus. In addition, put pressure on your judgments and the evidence you supply to support them, and look for ways to expand and clarify your conclusions by **adding.**

COMPUTER TIP

Cutting and adding developmental material is much easier on the computer than off. To add judgments or evidence, move the cursor to the place where you want the additional material to go and start typing. To cut, just move the cursor and delete by backspacing or using the delete key.

In addition, if your computer or word processor has the capacity, you can use a split-screen or "window" to view relevant material as you draft. For example, you might want to view the prewriting you've done as you draft, or you might want to compare your emerging text with your introductory paragraph by viewing both as you draft.

ARRANGEMENT   Just as development is closely connected to voice, arrangement is wedded to development. Just as language creates meaning, so does the **order and grouping of our chosen details.** In his text, Steele sets up the concept of the anti-self first in order to draw his non-black audience in. The anti-self is a concept that all people can relate to, and Steele uses it as a way of setting up his own personal concept of "internal racist." Also worth noting is that Steele draws us in with anecdotes; he gets us to respond empathetically and rationally, and then hits us with some very bold conclusive statements later on in the text. For example, the idea that blacks belong to "the most despised race in the human community of races" is central to the message of his text, but he makes that statement only after he has set his audience up by **persuading** them with emotion and reason.

And the point here is, consider how to best order the details of your text to get the change you want from your audience. **Rearrange** the order of sentences or paragraphs or sections of your text with your audience's responses in mind. If **self-assessment** has helped you identify arrangement as a habitual problem, see Part Six ("Problems with Arrangement") for detailed strategies.

COMPUTER TIP

Use the block and move functions on the computer or word processor to rearrange sentences or paragraphs, or to cut unrelated material. To block text, put the cursor at the top or bottom of the area of text you want to move or cut, and select the block function. Then use the appropriate arrow keys to mark the text you want to move or delete. Prompts displayed at the bottom of the screen will direct you to your options.

DRAFTING IS ACTIVE AND RECURSIVE

As you write, new responses to Steele's text will come to you, and vague responses will be clarified into new ideas. Test your **working message** against your **new discoveries** and your discoveries against your working message. Go back and fill things in or, if you've established a momentum, leave yourself notes in your emerging text.

As you draft, you may come to resting places (perhaps you've finished relating an anecdote that illustrates your responsive position, or maybe you've drawn a significant conclusion). If you get stuck at one of these places, go back to the beginning of your draft and read out loud what you've gotten down so far. Reading can help you to find your next direction.

If you find the draft dying on you, analyze why. Go back through the process. Check your working message. If it seems workable, you may need to spend more time exploring your responses to Steele's text—a rereading of the text or a conversation with a member of the class or the instructor might help. Perhaps you need to think more deeply about the topic—solitary time with a notebook and pen might be the answer.

REWRITE

I know of no working writer who goes from draft to publication without editorial assistance. So, if possible, **workshop** your response in an informal collaborative group. Part Six provides strategies for workshops. The draft you bring to your collaborative partners should be your best effort—a finished piece of writing, not a "rough draft." Think of your workshop partners as your first line of defense against that judgmental audience down there at the end of the writing process. At the workshop you bring your piece of writing out into the world for its first official viewing, so your aim while rewriting should be to write for the most critical audience possible. As you work through the following strategies, be as actively self-critical as you can be; look constantly for opportunities to **revise** by **cutting, adding, rearranging,** and **rewording.**

- If possible, put your draft away for a day or two before you begin rewriting, but continue thinking critically about both the Steele text and your response to it. Getting a little distance from your writing while continuing your encounter with the subject can help you to see holes in your response that might need to be plugged.
- Re-examine your audience and purpose. Is the developmental material you supply to agree or disagree with Steele's message aimed at getting the change you desire in your audience? Can more be added? Think about *quality* as well as *quantity* of developmental material. Effective developmental material is evidence to support your position that has been critically tested with your audience's possible responses in mind.
- Read your draft out loud (preferably to another person), and listen to the sound of your language. Is your language clear? Does it convey the meaning you want it to convey? How would you characterize the tone of your written voice? Is that tone likely to persuade your audience?
- Consider the way your developmental material is arranged. Would rearranging things improve the impact the material has on your audience? Is there any meaningful material that might be added?
- If, as you rewrite, you find you have questions about how well parts of your text are working, write down your concerns in the form of brief notes, and take both your notes and your text to a

trusted classmate. Presenting a collaborative partner with specific questions can make rewriting more active and interactive.

EDIT TO FINAL FORM

Polish your text as you write the final draft. Focus on paragraphs, transitions, and any habitual problems with spelling, punctuation, and sentence structure. If **self-assessment** has helped you identify habitual problems with mechanics, see Part Six, ("Problems with Mechanics") for appropriate strategies.

PROOFREAD

If possible, put your response aside for at least a couple of hours before you proofread. Proofread for small careless errors by reading your text aloud, preferably to another person.

ASSESS YOUR PERFORMANCE BY WRITING CRITICALLY

After your paper has been evaluated, study your collaborators' and/or your instructor's comments and look for patterns in your writing weaknesses. Part Five provides strategies for analyzing evaluators' comments and mapping your own patterns of writing weakness. Focus on **voice, arrangement, development,** and **mechanics.** With which category did you mainly have trouble? After study and analysis, write a page explaining why you think you had trouble with that particular category. Then write a second page in which you explain what you might do to correct the problem.

CHAPTER
FIVE
PRIMARY RESEARCH

Primary research is the gathering of information from firsthand sources by **critically reading** texts, by **interviewing,** by **observing,** or by developing and administering **questionnaires.** Most of the finished texts we encounter involved some kind of primary research by their writers. Working writers are also working primary researchers, but even people who are never asked to write do primary research. **Whenever we seek the answer to a question, we engage in research.** When we make a major purchase, we'll most likely do research before we spend. We'll consult friends or local ''experts.'' We'll shop comparatively for the best price and listen to the salesperson at each store. Likewise, when we're attracted to another person, we'll research our subject before we make a permanent commitment. We'll observe how that person behaves with us and with other people. We'll ask mutual acquaintances about that person. When we do these things, we're gathering information, learning more, getting to know more so that our decisions will be informed decisions. And not only are informed decisions sounder than uninformed ones; they're also easier to make.

Just as research makes the decisions we make in everyday living easier, research also makes the choices we make during the writing process easier. Research isn't just a way of backing up our own judgments about a subject by citing authorities who agree with our conclusions; **research is a way of knowing,** and the more we know about a subject, the easier it is to write about that subject.

However, in addition to being a way of knowing, research is **a way of knowing differently.** The more new things we learn about a subject, the more our perspective about that subject changes. For example, consider your own experience with the college you attend. Before you came to your campus, you experienced the campus community only peripherally; an older relative or friend who attended your college may have described what it was like, or you may have read the catalogue or recruitment material or viewed a recruitment video; you may even have visited the campus. When you finally arrived on campus the first day as a student, you came with preconceived ideas and expectations about what life in the campus community would be like. However, now that you've had firsthand knowledge of campus life, it's likely that at least a few of your expectations have turned out to be false. Try comparing your expectations before you came to your campus with your perspective on campus life now that you've had firsthand experience with it. How has your perspective changed? Which of your preconceived ideas have held up? Which of your preconceived ideas have turned out to be false?

Since writing is responsive, it's virtually impossible to separate the firsthand gathering of information from the process of writing a meaningful text. Even texts as subjective as personal journals start with the gathering of information from real-world situations; journal writers encounter the world around them through observations and conversations. Then they record and respond to what they have observed and discussed. Think about the written texts you've produced in the last week—class notes and notes to friends, reminders to yourself, and letters—and you'll realize that in order to have written any one of them you had to have first gathered information from some outside source. The point is, you're constantly researching to write, even though you may be researching so informally that you're unaware of it. However, when you formalize the research process by doing it systematically and critically, your writing will become more credible because you'll know more about your subject and will have thought more deeply about it.

At college, you'll be required to do many different kinds of primary research. In a literature class you might be asked to **critically read** the primary text of a poem; in a sociology class you might be asked to **interview** a social work professional; in a biology class you might be asked to **observe** an experiment or a biological process; in a political science class you might have to develop and **administer a questionnaire** about an election. But even if primary research isn't required, almost any writing (or reading) assignment can be enhanced when some form of primary research is added to the writing process. This chapter introduces the three main primary research activities—interviewing, observing, and writing and administering questionnaires. In addition, subsequent chapters of this book contain "Research Opportunities" that give you suggestions for incorporating specific research activities into your own writing and critical reading processes.

COLLABORATIVE RESEARCH

Very few professional researchers work alone. The more sophisticated the research project, the more likely it is that a researcher will be a member of a "research team." Consider the concept of a think tank, a group or institution created for intensive research or problem solving. The image that comes to mind when you hear the phrase *think tank* is of a group of very smart people sitting around a table brainstorming better ways of doing things. And think-tank members have the right idea. One of the very things that makes them appear so smart is that they've learned to multiply their ideas by sharing the work load. Where research is concerned, two or three (or even more) heads really are better than one.

Although some instructors may require that you research on your own, you'll often be allowed to engage in research as a member of a collaborative team. Find out if collaboration is allowed; it it is, look for opportunities to research as a member of a team. Engaging in research as a member of a collaborative group can enhance the research process in significant ways. First, brainstorming with others can help you decide more easily which research activities will be most appropriate for a particular subject. Second, dividing up research tasks among a group will allow you to gather more in-depth information in a shorter time. Third, testing your conclusions in a group that's knowledgeable about your subject will help you to refine old ideas and develop new ones.

CRITICAL READING

As I suggested in Chapter Four, critical reading is crucial to every research activity. Whether you're reading the primary text of a short story for its meaning or gathering information from a secondary source after a library search, to research effectively you'll first have to read carefully to discern the meaning of the text you encounter; then you'll have to decide what *you* think. Chapter Four, "Critical Reading and Responding," provides detailed models and strategies for reading critically and responding in writing to what you've read.

INTERVIEWING

Interviewing is really nothing more than purposeful, focused conversation. From the time you were a small child you've learned about the world by asking the people around you questions. You've asked **closed questions** when you were seeking **specific information:** "What keeps airplanes up in the air?" "What does the word *ersatz* mean?" "Where is Senegal?" You've asked **open questions** when you wanted your conversational partner to **speculate,** or offer **opinions** or **interpretations:** "Why do people have to die?'' ''What did you think of that movie?'' ''Why did you decide to major in anthropology?'' And as you questioned, you also learned that some people were better at answering questions than others. They were more **credible sources;** the answers they gave were thorough and informed. For example, as a child you probably returned to the same parent or older brother or sister or family friend again and again with your questions. And as you grew older and developed interests beyond your family and extended family, you sought out people who knew more than you did about the things you were interested in. You may even have been lucky enough to have known a **research mentor**—the kind of person who, if he or she didn't know the answer to a question, would take you off on a quest to the local ''expert'' in the field (cyclist or musician or mechanic).

The point is, you've actually been interviewing all your life. However, the more you formalize your interviewing skills by practicing them thoughtfully and critically, the more effective interviewing will be for you as a way of gathering information. In order to improve the natural skills you already have, consider the following strategies.

USE INTERVIEWING AS A FIRST STEP IN THE RESEARCH PROCESS. It may be that your greatest problem as a researcher will be not knowing where to start. Consider the following scenario. You've been given an assignment that requires research. Being logical, you go off to the library (the most obvious place where research is done on your campus). You consult the card catalogue or access a computer database, and you find yourself faced with hundreds of sources and no way of knowing which sources will give you the information you need. Not knowing what else to do, you choose a few sources randomly and proceed with your paper, using whatever information comes your way as best you can. You struggle to write your paper and turn it in, only to have your instructor criticize the source you relied on most heavily, calling it ''biased.''

A good way to avoid a scenario similar to this one is to begin your research process by interviewing an expert. Colleges and universities are full of experts. Your instructors are experts in particular areas of their fields of study, and one of them might be used as a research mentor. Because they're familiar with the research sources in their fields of study, research mentors can help you sort through a list of possible sources and point you toward those sources that are likely to be most credible.

GIVE YOURSELF PLENTY OF TIME.   Because you have to arrange interviews around your own and your sources' schedules, and also because you may have to do follow-up interviews, from the very beginning, you'll need to consider time constraints.

SELECT CREDIBLE SOURCES.   The most important thing to keep in mind when you're creating your list of sources is credibility. Determining the credibility of a source will require critical thinking on your part. In noncontroversial subjects, a credible source has *thorough* and *up-to-date* knowledge of the subject. For example, if your subject is plant taxonomy, in order to be credible, your source must have knowledge of recent changes in plant classification.

However, determining the credibility of a source when your subject is controversial involves not only making judgments about thorough and up-to-date knowledge, but also making judgments about the reasonableness of your source's point of view. If your subject is controversial, you'll probably have to interview more than one person before you can make a judgment about how reasonable any one source may be. For example, imagine you're writing a paper about your campus's financial aid office, which has recently been under attack because of supposed insensitivity to student needs. Just whom should you interview? The leader of the student protest? The director of financial aid? A clerk in the financial aid office? A student waiting in line outside the office? To get a balanced picture of the issue, you may want to interview all four sources and then compare the results of your resarch.

PLAN AHEAD.   Planning ahead involves researching background information and developing effective interview questions. Do some preliminary critical reading and make decisions about what kind of information your source can give you that you won't be able to get from another research source. Then develop questions aimed at eliciting the kind of information you need. For example, if you've chosen to interview a clerk in your college's financial aid office, what information might that clerk be able to give you that you couldn't get from another source? Develop both open and closed questions. Then write your questions out and arrange them so that they follow a logical plan. If you were interviewing the clerk, you might develop the closed question "Would you describe the processing of a financial aid form?" and then follow it with the open question "In your opinion, what's the major cause of delays in the processing?" Keep in mind that a good interview is as complete as possible. The more questions you develop before the interview, the more information you'll have as a result. If you're interviewing more than one person, use answers from one interview as a source for developing questions for another.

Planning ahead also involves gathering the proper tools to interview efficiently. You'll need a notebook and more than one pen or pencil. A cardboard-backed spiral pad or a clipboard is good for interviews because its rigidity allows you to write easily without needing to depend on a desk or table. Although you may be tempted to take a tape recorder, think carefully about your source before you do. The presence of a tape recorder can make some people so uncomfortable that relaxed, revealing conversation becomes impossible. If you think that taping the interview might be a good way to go, make sure you ask your source's permission beforehand. Showing up with a tape recorder and then being denied permission will get your interview off to an awkward start.

INTERVIEW ACTIVELY.   Active interviewing means being on your toes, but it also means going slowly and deliberately through the process. In order to be relaxed and confident, allow yourself open conversation time at the beginning of the interview to make yourself and your source comfortable. Then, as you formally interview, give your source enough time to respond fully to each question. Make sure that you think critically about your source's responses. Is each answer complete? Does anything need to be clarified? Has the response triggered a new question that you hadn't anticipated while planning? If so, formulate a follow-up question, or leave yourself a reminder in your interview notes.

OBSERVE AS YOU INTERVIEW.   If the interview takes place on your source's home ground (workplace or home), what additional information can you gather through observing your surroundings? Is there some element in the surroundings that surprises or intrigues you? If so, it may lead to a follow-up question. Observe your source as well as your surroundings. What additional information can you gather from your source's style, body language, and tone of voice? Is your source irritated, frustrated, or pleased? You might develop a follow-up question.

TAKE EFFICIENT NOTES.   Think critically and sort out what's important as you listen. Don't try to get everything down. Focus on key words and concepts and on your source's judgments and conclusions. Abbreviate material that you may later want to quote verbatim. In addition, record the telling details of your observed impressions.

REREAD AND CONFIRM.   If you plan on quoting material, read it back to your source. Reading back to your source can give you confirmation that you have it right. It can also give your source the opportunity to expand on ideas and add additional information.

REVIEW.   Immediately after the interview, read over your notes and fill in the blanks between key words and concepts. Your notes are only reminders of all that went on in the interview, and you should add essential information while it's still fresh in your mind. Plan to spend about an hour thoughtfully reviewing and writing. Then write down your general impressions and conclusions, focusing on what you learned and what most surprised you about the interview. Make sure you give specific evidence for each impression. For example, if you concluded that your source was overworked, what observed and spoken information led you to your conclusion?

REWRITE.   Within the first twenty-four hours, formally write up your notes either in a notebook or in a computer file. Make connections with other researched materials as you go. If you've interviewed more than one source, look for points of comparison and contrast in your sources' responses.

Then **summarize the interview in writing.** What were your source's major points? Was there some idea or concern that was common to all of your source's points? For example, our hypothetical financial aid clerk might have focused again and again on student errors in filling out financial aid forms as a cause of delays in processing. After you've summarized, look over your results. If you have unanswered questions, you may need to do a follow-up interview.

Finally, explore your own judgments and conclusions in writing. What do *you* think about your source's responses? If the subject is controversial, to what extent do you agree with your source's conclusions? To what extent do you disagree? Then explain the reasons behind your agreements and disagreements.

THANK YOUR SOURCE.   Since your source has likely taken time out of a busy schedule to accommodate your interview, it's appropriate to send a note of acknowledgment and thanks within a week's time.

OBSERVING

Like interviewing, observing is a research skill you've practiced all your life. You've learned about the world by experiencing it through your senses. You've learned to interact with others by observing how the people around you interact. Think of all the times in your life when someone has said to you, "I'll show you how to do it," and you'll begin to understand just how much of what you've learned has come from observing.

And just as with interviewing, the more you formalize your observational skills by practicing them thoughtfully and critically, the more effective those skills will be and the more you'll learn from your observations. To improve the observational skills you already have, consider the following strategies.

CHOOSE A RELEVANT SITE.   Just as interviewing requires you to think critically in order to decide on credible sources, observing often requires that you consider where you need to go to get relevant information. Although sometimes your observational site will be the actual object of your research, other times you'll be able to choose the site to gather information about the subject of your writing. For example, if you're writing a paper about the financial aid office on your campus, what observational site (or sites) would give you the most useful information? Should you observe the goings-on behind the scene in the financial aid office? Should you observe a student engaged in filling out a financial aid form? Consider all the possibilities.

PLAN AHEAD.   Getting access to your chosen site is an important consideration. If your site has limited access (times or aspects that aren't officially open to the public), you'll want to make advance contact by calling or making a preliminary visit.

Planning ahead also involves considering your purpose and writing out research questions. Just what kind of information are you looking for? Gather background information by doing some preliminary critical reading or by interviewing relevant sources, and then write out key questions. For example, for the paper on your financial aid office you might interview the leader of the student protest and the director of financial aid, and use the interviews as a basis for developing questions ("Are there severe delays in processing?" "Who is responsible for delays?") for your observation.

OBSERVE ACTIVELY.   Give yourself plenty of time, and view the site from as many perspectives as possible. Get an overview; then zero in to observe the details of key elements. For example, if you were doing an observation of your campus financial aid office, you might start at the end of the line outside and do a walk-through, mentally (or in quick notes) recording centers of activity. After your walk-through, you could return to the centers of activity for thorough observation.

Actively observing requires focusing on significant details. Your purpose as a researching observer isn't just to record but also to analyze. Use your critical thinking skills to sort out the important details from the unimportant ones. Look for causal connections and for the hard evidence that details can provide. (Part Six provides instructions for using causal analysis as a critical thinking strategy.) If something is unclear, you might ask a person on-site for clarification. If questioning isn't possible, leave a reminder in your notes to do further research.

Observing often means using more than just your visual and auditory senses. For example, if you were observing the process of preparing and eating a pizza, smells, tastes, and textures would be as important as sounds and sights.

TAKE THOROUGH NOTES.   Although observing may give you a better opportunity to take extensive notes than interviewing, your attention should be on the site, not on your notes. In addition to writing, you may want to sketch what you're observing. Part Six gives you instructions for using sketching as a critical thinking activity.

Focus on your senses. What do you see? Consider both the big picture and the small details of the site. Describe the overall layout. Describe the people you see and their actions, the objects around you and their functions. What do you hear? Center in on conversations, significant noises, or even silences. What about your remaining senses? Are there significant smells, tastes, or textures?

Focus on your own responses. What do you think? What are your judgments and conclusions about the site or any of its details? What do you feel? What specific emotional responses do you have to the site or any of its details?

REREAD AND CONFIRM.   Before you leave the site, read over your notes and check for unanswered questions and any details you might have left out. Focus your attention on your recorded responses, and check the site for confirmation. Is there specific evidence for each of the conclusions you've drawn?

REVIEW.   Immediately after the observation, read over your notes and fill in any blanks you find in description or in your own responses. Plan to spend at least half an hour reviewing and rewriting. Then write down your general impressions and conclusions, focusing on what you learned and what was surprising about the observation. Make sure you provide specific evidence by noting details from your observation to support your conclusions. For example, if you were writing the hypothetical financial aid office paper and you concluded that student errors were the cause of delays in financial aid processing, you would have to have *seen* hard evidence (for example, a significant number of incorrect forms) to draw your conclusion. If you find that your conclusions don't match up with the evidence, you may have to do a follow-up observation as well as some other kind of research.

```
┌─────────────────────────────────────────────────────────────┐
│                                                             │
│                      COMPUTER TIP                           │
│                                                             │
├─────────────────────────────────────────────────────────────┤
│                                                             │
│  Writing up your results on the computer allows you to add, de- │
│  lete, and revise entries more easily than handwriting or typing. │
│                                                             │
└─────────────────────────────────────────────────────────────┘
```

REWRITE.   Within twenty-four hours, formally write up the results of your observation either in a notebook or in a computer file. Make connections with other research activities you may have engaged in as you go along. **Compare and contrast** the results of your observation with the results of other research activities, and **look for contradictions.** If you find any, you may have to do further research. Part Six provides a detailed discussion of comparing and contrasting.

Then **summarize your observation in writing.** (Part Five provides a detailed discussion of summarizing.) What were the key elements of the site? Was there any connection between the key elements? For example, were they part of a process, or were they alike in some way? If you judge the elements to be connected, speculate about the causes or results of their connection.

Finally, explore your own judgments and conclusions in writing. What do you think was significant about the site you observed? What did you learn? How was your perspective about the general subject of your writing changed by your observation? If your perspective was changed, what was it in your observation that brought about the changes?

QUESTIONNAIRES

Although you may never have administered a questionnaire, you're most certainly familiar with them. If you've ever filled out a customer satisfaction card in a restaurant, applied for a job, or filled out a college application, you've encountered a questionnaire. Like interviews, questionnaires are ways of gathering firsthand information from human sources.

You develop questionnaires in place of interviews when you want to gather specific kinds of information efficiently from large numbers of people. Questionnaires are more highly focused than interviews. Normally, you've already done preliminary interviews or other research and are trying to affirm or explore your earlier results by getting a wider sampling of information. For an example, let's return once more to our financial aid office paper. Suppose that you've interviewed the leader of the student protest, but you're still uncertain about how the rest of the student body feels about the subject. An efficient way of exploring the scope of student feeling would be to develop a questionnaire that polls student attitudes and gathers information about their experiences. To develop and administer effective informal questionnaires, consider the following strategies.

FOCUS ON YOUR PURPOSE. Questionnaires aren't starting places. The reason you decide to administer them in the first place is that *you* have questions. You develop a questionnaire when you *think* something might be true but aren't sure. Because questionnaires start with your own gaps in knowledge, the questions you develop should be designed to elicit the information that you're missing, without leading the respondents in a particular direction. Let's consider our hypothetical paper again. The information we're unsure of will direct us toward our purpose. Since we're not sure if there's widespread dissatisfaction with the way the financial aid office is run, the purpose behind our questions should be to find out if there is.

AVOID LEADING QUESTIONS. Since we're trying to get an unbiased view of the subject, we'll have to be careful not to ask **leading questions.** A leading question is one that pushes the respondent to answer in a particular way. Leading questions can be very tricky because there are no hard and fast rules that govern what is and what is not a leading question. For example, "How long have you been dissatisfied with the financial aid office" is certainly a leading question, but so is "Are you dissatisfied with the financial aid office?" The best way to avoid leading questions is to bend over backwards to allow your respondents as much room as possible in their responses. To avoid asking a leading question about the financial aid office, you might ask students to rate their level of satisfaction on a scale from one to five.

DEVELOP QUESTIONS WITH YOUR PURPOSE IN MIND. With purpose in mind, it's time to consider what kinds of questions we want to ask. We want to know as certainly as we can if there is student dissatisfaction with financial aid, and if so, what kind of dissatisfaction it is.

As in interviewing, there are two kinds of questions you can use when you develop questionnaires—**closed questions** and **open questions.** The following are some examples of **closed questions** that might be useful for our financial aid office questionnaire:

- What kind of financial aid do you currently receive?
    Pell Grant ____
    Work/Study ____
    Loan ____
    University Scholarship ____
    Other (specify) ____
    None ____
- How many years have you been on campus? ____
- In your experience, filling out financial aid forms has been
    very easy ____
    easy ____
    moderately easy ____
    moderately difficult ____
    difficult ____
    very difficult ____
    no basis for judgment ____
- Have you ever had a financial aid form returned because it was filled out incorrectly?
    yes ____
    no ____
- If your answer to the above question was yes, how many times has this occurred? ____
- Has your financial aid ever been delayed?
    yes ____
    no ____

Here are a few **open questions** that we might ask in order to elicit brief written responses:

- If your financial aid award has ever been delayed, briefly describe the reasons offered by the financial aid office for the delay.

    _____
    _____
    _____
    _____

- Considering your experiences with the financial aid office, what advice would you give fellow students about the application procedure or about dealing with the office?

    _____
    _____
    _____
    _____

- In your opinion, what might be done to improve the quality of the services offered by the financial aid office?

_____

_____

_____

_____

SUMMARIZE YOUR RESULTS.   Keep in mind that **summarizing is a critical thinking activity.** To make sense of the information you've gathered, you'll have to make judgments about the significance of your respondents' answers. You won't just be recording; you'll be analyzing and searching for meaning.

A good strategy for summarizing the information gathered from questionnaires is to start by getting an overview, and then going on to focus on **comparisons** and **contrasts** in individual questionnaires and among the survey group as a whole. Part Five contains a section that focuses on using comparison/contrast in critical thinking.

First, add up and record the responses to the closed questions on your questionnaire. Then look for patterns of similarity in your surveyed group's responses to the open questions, and group the similar responses into categories. For example, in response to "If your financial aid award has ever been delayed, briefly describe the reasons given by the financial aid office for the delay," eleven people might cite student errors as the reason for delay, twenty-five an understaffed financial aid office, six lost forms, and eight might say they were given no reason. These results point to understaffing as a problem.

After you've added up the closed responses and grouped the open ones, the next step in the process is to analyze the information by comparing and contrasting bits of it. Look for correspondences between individual responses to open questions and closed ones. For example, it may be that first-year students report more difficulties with the financial aid process than students who've been on campus for a year or more. Or it may be that students with work study grants overwhelmingly report delays and difficulties.

Then focus on patterns of responses in the group as a whole. Think critically and look for causal connections. (Part Six contains a section that focuses on using cause/effect as a critical thinking strategy.) As an example, let's consider the categories of response to the open question about the reasons for delays in processing: of fifty students responding, twenty-five cited lack of staff in the financial aid office, while another six cited lost forms. What might you infer from this information? Suppose that in addition to this information, a very high percentage of respondents had experienced delays and a very low percentage had had forms returned because of their own errors. What might these results suggest?

ANALYZE YOUR RESULTS.   Focus on the critical judgments you made while summarizing, and remember to be self-critical. Question your conclusions, and make sure you have evidence in the form of sufficient responses to support the judgments you've made. Keep in mind also that questionnaires aren't highly "scientific" instruments. Instead, they're an informal means of gathering information. When you administer a questionnaire, you're relying on the truth and accuracy of your human sources' responses. The information gathered from questionnaires *suggests* that things might be true; it doesn't *prove* that things are true.

COLLABORATIVE WRITING ASSIGNMENT

The following text, originally published in the "Talk of the Town" section of the *New Yorker*, isn't a formal research paper. However, novelist Deirdre McNamer engaged in field research to gather information about the subject of her writing. As you read, look for evidence that McNamer, a writer, is also an active researcher. After you've read the selection, form collaborative groups of three or four students and spend fifteen minutes or so isolating and responding to the passages from the text that required the writer to engage in field research. What kind of primary research activity did each passage you identified require? How did adding research to the writing process add to McNamer's credibility? After you've finished your small group work, open the conversation up and share the results of the collaboration with the class as a whole.

HOWLING
Deirdre McNamer

A young woman who lives in Montana writes:
   No one who meets Bob Ream would guess right off that he howls. He is in his early fifties, and is a large, calm person with

continued to next page

an unhurried stride, a Huck Finn grin, and a habit of saying nothing until he has something to say. He is also a state legislator, a forestry professor, and a wildlife researcher—that's where the howling comes in. For most of his adult life, Bob has studied the habits of wolves. It's a job that takes patience and imagination, because wolves are rare and ghostly, and people learn about them largely from the things they leave behind—scat, or a deer carcass, or a line of tracks across the snow. A long time ago, Bob taught himself a wolf howl and began to use it when he thought wolves were nearby. But it wasn't until March 1, 1985, at about ten o'clock in the morning, that the wolves finally talked back. He told me about it one afternoon as we drove up the snowy North Fork valley toward the Canadian border, where it had happened.

"It was one of those crystal-clear days," Bob said. "Twenty below zero. Two researchers and I travelled twelve miles by snowmobile to an elk that some wolves had killed. There wasn't room for all of us on the machine, so they pulled me on skis. We had to stop twice so I could warm my hands. Well, we got to the kill site and watched it for a while. A coyote and a bald eagle were there, and a bunch of ravens were hanging around. We thought the wolves were probably nearby, so I said, 'Let's try howling,' and we did. All three of us howled. And no sooner had we finished than a wolf answered. Then another, and another. It lasted from three to five minutes. They were only about two hundred yards away, and they were *loud*. And afterward it was so calm, so still. I'd been looking for wolves for years. It brought tears to my eyes."

The North Fork of the Flathead River, which the road follows, flows south from headwaters in British Columbia and forms the western border of Glacier National Park. Its drainage is a long valley of meadows and lodgepole pines flanked by rows of sharp, gleaming mountains. During the past decade, the valley has become a hot spot in the world of wolf research, because the animals have begun to reinhabit the area without coercion or encouragement from human beings. Wolves were wiped out in Montana and in most of the rest of the United States by about 1930, Bob told me, so their reappearance in numbers is big news anywhere it happens.

In 1979, Bob and his researchers trapped a female wolf who was roaming the North Fork alone, and put a radio collar on her.

continued on page 112

continued from page 111

They studied her travel patterns, and in the winter of 1982 they found that she had apparently teamed up with a very large male who was missing one toe on his left front foot. Those two were very likely the progenitors of what Bob and his team called the magic pack—magic because they were so elusive, even for wolves. The magic pack eventually divided into four packs, of twenty-two wolves in all.

When we reached the border, Bob and I were joined by Arnie and Helen Bolle, a couple in their early seventies, who had followed us in their car. (Arnold is a retired dean of forestry at the University of Montana.) Together, we headed out in Bob's truck for a spot where Bob hoped to pick up radio signals from one of the packs. Four of the wolves had collars, he told us. "Oh, boy!" Helen said. "One for each of us." It was a black, moonless winter night—the kind that makes you keep the headlights on high beam. Eventually, we stopped at the edge of the empty road, and Bob picked up some beeps on his radio receiver. He replaced the truck's whip antenna with a directional one, listened again, and pointed to a rectangle, several miles to the east, that was a shade or two lighter than anything else. "That meadow is probably where they are," he said. "And they're moving."

I realized then that my stereotype of a howling wolf—a voluble loner on a hilltop, silhouetted by a full moon—had nothing to do with the situation at hand. These wolves were loping together along an unlit valley floor. They were busy. Getting them to howl, I thought, would be like asking a howling team to stop and sing an opera.

"I think I'll try now," Bob said. Helen and Arnie and I waited what seemed like a long time. Bob didn't hurry. He took some deep, slow breaths. Then he cupped his mittened hands around his mouth, tipped his head back, and did it.

A wolf howl is to a domestic-dog howl what an air-raid siren is to my Toyota horn. The howl doesn't yip or whine; it soars. Bob's howl began in the bass register, as mournful as a foghorn, and swooped up to a muscular shriek that, frankly, raised my hackles. It descended slowly, with a couple of heartbreaking cracks, then levelled out and stopped and echoed off the mountains. The whole thing had a quality of utter extension and yearning in it, not unlike Marlon Brando calling for Stella.

continued to next page

This is a diagram I drew of Bob's wolf howl:

At first, I thought that it looked like some of the mountains that jut up from the edges of the North Fork valley. Then I decided that it looked like the profile of a seated, howling wolf.

Bob howled twice more, and stopped. We listened as hard as we could, hands cupped behind our ears. Then we heard them. Distance and an opposing breeze miniaturized the howls. But they were there—a thin, faint chorus.

The next day, hoping to find the wolves' tracks, we skied into a meadow that was on their route. Arnie and Helen and I tried some howls. Helen and I had problems with pitch—we sounded frail and yippy—but I thought I managed a convincing catch in my voice on the descent. Arnie was much more wolflike, although his timing was off and he didn't have the volume that Bob had built up over twenty years of howling.

Howling is a social activity, Bob said. Lone wolves rarely howl, because they have no one to howl at. But a pack might howl as a way of warning off any intruder wolves, or, when a pack spreads out to hunt, the members might howl simply as a way of counting noses. We howled again, for the heck of it, and Bob waved his arms like a conductor.

Helen and Arnie and I drove home together, leaving Bob to his work. "When I think about it, I think I've heard Bob howl before," Helen said. "But I can't put my finger on when it was. Did you ever hear him howl before, Arnie?"

"Yes," Arnie said, "At his fiftieth birthday party—remember? He howled, and somebody played it back to him on the saxophone."

CHAPTER SIX

SECONDARY RESEARCH

Writers engage in secondary research almost as often as they engage in primary research. Novelists, magazine writers, technical writers, and academic writers all regularly engage in some form of secondary research. The novelist Michael Crichton has made a stunningly successful career by writing novels that require months of research. Newspapers and magazines have their own research departments staffed with people who do nothing but research. Most of the instructors at your college or university engage in secondary research as part of their writing processes. But just as with primary research, even people who are never asked to write do secondary research.

Secondary research is the **gathering of information already compiled (and often analyzed) by someone else,** and hardly a day goes by when you don't unconsciously engage in some form of secondary research yourself. Secondary research sources are all around you. Whenever you watch the nightly news on television, read an informative article in your favorite magazine, look up a recipe in a cookbook, or consult a bus schedule, you engage in a form of secondary research. Without being actively aware of it, you're constantly gathering information that has been compiled by someone else.

A great many (perhaps even most) of the sources you'll encounter in the process of doing library research will be **secondary sources** rather than **primary sources. Primary sources** contain raw data or original, creative material that hasn't been analyzed or interpreted. For example, a transcript of a congressional hearing would be a primary source; likewise, if your assignment is to interpret a novel, the novel that you're responding to would be a primary source. On the other hand, **secondary sources** analyze or interpret written texts or situations that exist in the world. For example, an analysis of a congressional hearing would be a secondary source, as would an interpretation of a novel. However, when you read a secondary source that's packed with unfamiliar information and written in a voice that's dry and highly authoritative, it's easy to forget that the source has been **authored.** A person or a group of people has examined a subject and made critical judgments about it and is then imparting those judgments to an audience in the form of a written text.

And it's precisely because secondary sources have been authored that it's important to engage in secondary research carefully and critically. The information you gather changes you. What you learn shapes your values and your perspectives about the world. When you passively or haphazardly engage in research, you risk being, at best, confused and, at worst, misled.

SECONDARY RESEARCH IN THE ACADEMIC COMMUNITY

Because you're a member of an academic community, you're in the best possible position to engage in **active** and **critical** secondary research. Although secondary research sources are all around us, they're particularly abundant on college campuses. Campuses are centers of learning, not only for students but for instructors as well. In order to teach you effectively, your instructors must **remain active** and current in their fields of study by engaging in research as part of their daily work. Walk down the hall of any department on your campus and you'll see offices that contain instructors' personal book collections and mail rooms stacked with new books that have just come in. Go to the library or attend a college-sponsored film, and you'll probably notice one of your instructors actively engaged in learning more.

But even more significant than the amount of secondary research that goes on on campuses is the *kind* of secondary research that goes on. Because of the nature of the academic community, academic researchers have a special responsibility to **think critically** about the research sources they encounter. Colleges and universities are institutions devoted to open inquiry. Probably in no other human institution will you find such a level of commitment to free thought. You've probably already heard the phrase "academic freedom." Academic freedom is the freedom to pursue, teach, and discuss knowledge openly without constraint or interference, and it's a freedom that's assumed on college and university campuses.

However, part of the freedom to pursue knowledge openly is the freedom to criticize other people's ideas and conclusions. And when you do secondary research in the academic community, you'll find that this freedom to criticize amounts to a responsibility. To think and write effectively in the academic community, you'll have to be a critical researcher as well as an active one. You'll have to question and test the sources that you encounter.

Don't wait until you're assigned a formal research paper before you begin actively engaging in secondary research. Any reading or writing assignment can be enhanced when secondary research is added to the process. The more you know about a subject by gathering information about it and by exploring other people's perspectives on it, the more effective your written responses to that subject will be. Secondary research sources are all around. Practice your research skills by regularly incorporating research into your reading and writing assignments. Engaging in research isn't as daunting as you may think. For example, any textbook you've bought for a class this term can be used as a research source for that class or for another class.

This chapter is designed to help you begin engaging in secondary research actively, critically, and as soon as possible by introducing you to the secondary research sources available on your campus. Look for the "Research Opportunities" in subsequent chapters of this book; they provide specific strategies for incorporating some form of secondary research into your reading and writing activities.

SECONDARY RESEARCH SOURCES

Secondary research sources come in two kinds—**reference sources** and **specialized sources.**

Reference sources are the starting place in the secondary research process. If you don't know where to begin your research, reference sources can guide you and provide you with background information about your research area. Some reference sources help you locate specialized sources, and others provide you with general or statistical information.

REFERENCE SOURCES

Experts/Research Mentors
The Internet
Library Sources
    Reference Librarians
    Print and Electronic Sources
    The Central Catalogue
    Bibliographies
    Indexes
    Reference Books

The **specialized sources** that you'll locate by consulting reference works are the places you'll actively and critically gather the information that will augment your reading and writing activities. Just as there are different kinds of reference sources available on your campus, there are different kinds of specialized sources.

SPECIALIZED SOURCES

Books
Periodicals
Newspapers
Government Documents
Pamphlets
Nonprint Media
On-line and CD-ROM Sources

EXPLORE REFERENCE SOURCES

After you've read this chapter, set aside some time to explore the reference sources in your campus library. A free exploration of reference sources, without the pressure of an impending paper deadline, will help you understand the purposes and processes of scholarship by giving you an overview of the many research activities regularly engaged in by academic researchers.

Take a library tour and then spend a couple of hours exploring the library on your own. Find out how to use the resources that your campus library has to offer. The sooner you get to know the library and feel comfortable there, the sooner research will become an integral part of your reading and writing.

EXPERTS AS REFERENCE SOURCES College campuses are full of experts. Because your instructors regularly engage in critical research, they're current in their fields and can often point you toward the best, most credible sources. Use experts on your campus as **research mentors.** Begin the research process by **interviewing** one or more experts. (See Chapter Three, "Primary Research," for a full explanation of interviewing.) If necessary, go beyond the instructor who has assigned you research when you choose a mentor. Your instructor may not always be an expert in the field you're researching. For example, if you were engaging in research as part of the writing activity "Responding to Fiction and Film" in this book, you might consult your college catalogue to find a film expert on your campus.

After you've done an initial interview, check in from time to time with your mentor throughout the research process. In addition to pointing you

---

COMPUTER TIP

The Internet is a network of millions of computers worldwide that share information. Upwards of eighty percent of all colleges and universities are currently linked to the Internet, and most schools provide Internet access to students free of charge. Check with your college's office of computing services to see if Internet accounts are available. With an Internet account and access to an on-line computer, you can use databases all over the world, send and receive E-mail, and join in discussion groups about specific subjects. There are a number of excellent books available (probably right in your college bookstore) that will help you learn to negotiate "the Net." In addition to making research easier and conversation with people all over the world virtually instantaneous, information technology is the wave of the future, and the possession of networking skills can make you more employable.

Be warned, however, that a lot of the information on the Internet hasn't gone through the same processes of evaluation that normally published material has gone through. Anyone with enough time and the appropriate technology can put whatever they want on "the Net." Consult published Internet guides for lists of reputable sources, and evaluate on-line sources carefully.

---

toward the best, most credible sources, research mentors can introduce you to specific research techniques employed in particular disciplines.

REFERENCE SOURCES IN THE COLLEGE LIBRARY

REFERENCE LIBRARIANS   Just as your instructors are experts in their fields, college librarians are experts in library science. The people at the reference desk of your college library not only know what there is to know about libraries in general, they also know the ins and outs of your college library more thoroughly than any other people on campus. Although all libraries are organized in basically the same way, some libraries are larger and more technologically advanced than others. If you find your college library intimidating, don't be afraid to ask a reference librarian for help in locating or using sources. Teaching you how to make the best use of the resources your library has to offer is the main reason the people at the reference desk are there.

THE CENTRAL CATALOGUE   As the index in the back of a book helps you locate a particular bit of information, a central catalogue helps you find the location of particular sources in the library. Until just a few years ago, most libraries used card catalogues as reference systems. In card catalogues, books and other specialized research sources are cross-referenced under subject, author, and title on cards that are arranged alphabetically in file drawers.

However, more and more libraries are replacing card catalogue reference systems with computerized reference systems. Functioning much like card catalogues, these systems contain a cross-referenced listing of the library's holdings. Although these systems differ from library to library, most will provide you with a convenient printout of the sources you've called up.

In addition to systems that list the library's holdings, a great many libraries have networks that link them with other university libraries. The sophistication of these networks varies greatly. Some libraries belong to a limited library network, but others provide virtually unlimited access to libraries all over the world.

COMPUTER TIP

Until recently, libraries' reference works were all in printed form. However, publishers of reference sources are beginning to distribute their works in electronic form on-line or as CD-ROM databases. In computer language, "on-line" means connected to another computer, so on-line reference sources are sources that are stored in a library's powerful central computer or available via a telecommunications link through the central computer. You can do on-line reference searches either from a computer terminal in the library or from a personal computer equipped with a modem. CD-ROMs are compact disks that contain stored information. Most college libraries have CD-ROM sources as part of their reference holdings.

On-line and CD-ROM reference sources are easy to use and more efficient than print reference sources. Electronic sources allow you to do key word searches as well as the standard subject, title, and author searches. Most library terminals have instructional materials set up nearby. However, if you have questions about your library's system, sign up for an instructional session, or consult a reference librarian or library aide.

Nonprint media—records, videotapes, compact disks, photographs, slides, and other media—may be housed in a separate library on your campus or may be catalogued separately. If you're unsure of the location of nonprint media, consult a reference librarian.

BIBLIOGRAPHIES   Bibliographies are inventoried lists of sources on a particular subject. Bibliographies come in many forms; they're published in books, articles, and government documents, and available on-line and as CD-ROM databases. Some bibliographies are simple reference lists; others are full-blown scholarly works that include summaries and critical evaluations of the listed sources. Like card catalogues, print bibliographies list sources by author, title, and subject. However, electronic bibliographies allow you to search for sources by using key words. In addition, electronic bibliographies are updated more frequently than are print ones.

INDEXES   Generally, indexes are guides to specialized sources published in periodicals. Indexes are master lists to a particular group of sources, and they're updated frequently. Some indexes are general guides. For example, the *Bibliographic Index* is a general reference guide to bibliographies; the *Reader's Guide to Periodical Literature* indexes articles from general interest magazines. UNCOVER is an on-line index from which you can also order articles published in periodicals. Browsing the index is free, but ordering a fax copy costs $8.50 plus the copyright fee.

Some indexes are guides to specialized sources in particular fields; the *Art Index* and the on-line *Index—World Arts Resources* list recent journal and magazine publications in art by author and subject. Some specialized indexes are guides to kinds of documents; the *United States Governmental Publications Index* catalogues government documents. Still other indexes are guides to sources that represent particular ideological or cultural perspectives; the *Left Index,* for example, lists articles published in periodicals that present a Marxist or leftist point of view. Many indexes are available on-line or on CD-ROM. Ask your reference librarian about the availability of computer-accessed indexes on your campus.

REFERENCE BOOKS

Encyclopedias

Encyclopedias, whether general, like the *New Encyclopedia Britannica,* or specialized, like the *Encyclopedia of American History,* don't contain the detailed information or analysis that genuine specialized sources contain. Although almost every discipline has a specialized encyclopedia, even these are useful only as reference works. They can give you an overview of your subject and provide you with background and bibliographical information that can lead you to more specialized sources. All the major general encyclopedias and many of the specialized ones are available on CD-ROM.

Dictionaries

Although all dictionaries give definitions for words and details about their origins and proper usage, some dictionaries are more complete and extensive in their explanations than others. The more sophisticated unabridged dictionaries are more likely to give you obscure and archaic definitions for words as well as simple contemporary ones. The two most widely used unabridged dictionaries are *Webster's Third New International Dictionary* and the *Oxford English Dictionary.* In addition to giving comprehensive definitions, word histories, and grammatical information, both of them make fascinating and often amusing reading. They're loaded with quotations that illustrate quirky word origins and uses, and you literally won't be able to flip through two or three pages without encountering a word you've never seen before. Dictionaries, like encyclopedias, are available on CD-ROM.

Biographical Dictionaries

Biographical dictionaries provide brief biographies of noteworthy people in different professions and in the arts. Like unabridged dictionaries, biographical dictionaries can be fun to browse through even if you aren't actively engaged in a research project.

Almanacs and Yearbooks

Almanacs contain statistical and factual information. Like encyclopedias, some almanacs (the *World Almanac and Book of Facts,* for example) are general reference guides, while others are reference guides for particular fields.

Atlases

In addition to maps, atlases contain demographic and geologic information about different regions of the world. Like most other reference books, atlases are entertaining casual reading if you're fascinated by factual information.

OTHER LIBRARY SOURCES

Microforms

To save space and to protect valuable print sources, most libraries store some of their holdings in microform. The central catalogue will indicate if a source is in microform.

Interlibrary Loan

Many libraries belong to networks that allow you to borrow material from other libraries in your region. If you can't obtain a source at your library, you may be able to order it from another institution through Interlibrary Loan.

EVALUATE SPECIALIZED SOURCES

Being a critical researcher means being able to evaluate the specialized sources that you've located in terms of their **usefulness** and their **credibility.** Although you'll do a lot of this evaluating as you're actually *reading* specialized sources, being able to evaluate sources from the information given in indexes, bibliographies, and other reference sources can make the process of researching more efficient.

To begin the process of evaluating sources before you actually begin reading them critically, consider the following strategies.

GATHER VARIED SOURCES. The more sources (and the more different kinds of sources) you explore, the more likely you are to get an accurate picture of your research area. Remember, the information in specialized sources has been gathered and often interpreted by someone else. To formulate your own critical judgments about a subject, you have to get as close to an **unbiased view** of that subject as you can. And the best way to get an unbiased view is to **compare and contrast a variety of perspectives.** As you gather specialized sources for further exploration, consult different kinds of reference works, and strive for variety in source length and perspective.

READ TITLES CRITICALLY. A title will usually reveal the focus of a source. Read the entire title (subtitle included), and compare and contrast it with the subject you're researching. (In Part Six you'll find a discussion of comparison/contrast as a critical thinking strategy.) Does the title suggest that the source focuses on your area of research interest? If not, the source may not be useful for the research you're undertaking.

NOTE THE NAME OF THE AUTHOR.   The author's name can often tell you a lot about the credibility of a source. The author may be someone who has a reputation that is already known to you. In addition, the author may have been cited in other sources or be the writer of other books and articles on the subject. Look for the recurrence of an author's name in reference sources. A person who has published often in the field is likely to be an acknowledged authority.

NOTE THE PUBLISHER.   The publisher of a work also tells you a lot about a work's credibility. Reputable publishing houses, university presses, and scholarly journals have sophisticated review processes that ensure the credibility of the works they publish. Submissions are read critically by several experts before being accepted for publication. If you have questions about the credibility of a publishing house, consult your research mentor or reference librarian.

THINK CRITICALLY ABOUT THE DATE OF PUBLICATION.   In rapidly developing fields, an up-to-date source can be crucial. Even sources two or three years old can be out of date. Consider your area of research. Is it a field in which current sources would be more credible? On-line services update their lists monthly or bimonthly so that you can get the newest information.

CONSIDER THE LENGTH OF THE WORK.   Book-length works are often comprehensive and contain bibliographies that can lead to other sources. However, don't just assume that longer works are better than shorter ones. A long work will be useful only if it includes information that focuses on your particular research area. Think critically about your research area, and consider the title of the book. If you're still undecided, find the book in the library and check its table of contents and index to discover more.

MAKE USE OF ANNOTATED BIBLIOGRAPHIES, INDEXES, AND REVIEWS.   Bibliographies and indexes sometimes contain summaries and even evaluations of the sources they list. A summary can help you decide whether a source includes information that might be useful to you; an evaluation can help you decide if the source is credible or if it's biased in any way. Some indexes contain information about the ideological or political slant of the sources they list.

Reviews are more formal, comprehensive evaluations. A review both summarizes and evaluates a source. You can locate reviews by consulting book review indexes. However, keep in mind that you have to read reviews critically because they can be biased. A good strategy to test credibility is to read more than one review. Some on-line and CD-ROM indexes include abstracts that can be useful for evaluation.

PREVIEW LIKELY SOURCES. Once you've found a group of likely sources, you'll be ready to further evaluate them by previewing them. When you **preview,** you read a source to decide if it has any potential use. To preview articles, **read the first three paragraphs** slowly, focusing on those things that you know and understand. Then pause and **summarize** what's gone on in the text so far and **predict** what direction you think the text will take. If your prediction makes you think that the text has potential use, **read the remainder** of the article quickly to **confirm** your judgment.

To preview book-length works, explore the table of contents and the index, looking for entries that correspond to your research focus. Then preview the author's preface and/or any chapters that seem relevant.

READ SPECIALIZED SOURCES CRITICALLY

Although every chapter of this book provides you with strategies for the critical reading necessary to evaluate secondary sources, consider the following collaborative exercise to practice your evaluating skills.

COLLABORATIVE WRITING ASSIGNMENT

In the following text, professor of education Harvey A. Daniels uses his disagreements with English-only proponents as a starting place to present his view of things.

After reading the text carefully, form collaborative groups of three or four students and consider the following critical reading and research strategies.

- Make a paragraph outline of the text in order to focus on development. Summarize the information in each paragraph. Then focus on Daniels's critical judgments

continued to next page

about the informational and explanatory material he presents in the selection. Identify as many of Daniels's critical judgments as you can. With which of the studies or arguments he cites does Daniels agree? With which does he disagree? What are his reasons for agreement or disagreement?

- Focus on the language in the text, and explore Daniels's use of implicit language. Identify as many places in the text as you can where Daniels uses implicit language as a way of undercutting other people's arguments. Focus on the specific words and phrases that Daniels uses. What are their meanings? What do they imply about the arguments that Daniels rejects?

- Return to your paragraph outline and consider how Daniels chooses to arrange the informational and explanatory material he presents. Where in the selection does he place the arguments that he agrees with? Where does he place the arguments he disagrees with? Why might he have chosen to order them in this way?

- In collaborative research teams of three or four students, do a library search to find current sources that deal with the English-only movement. Locate at least one source that makes critical judgments similar to the judgments Daniels makes and at least two that make judgments that are different. Read the sources you've located critically, using the same strategies you used to explore Daniels's text. Then record the results of your research in writing.

THE ROOTS OF LANGUAGE PROTECTIONISM*
Harvey A. Daniels

The United States has always been a multilingual country. The history of the American people, the tory of the peoples native to this continent and of those who immigrated here from every corner of the world, is told in the rich accents of Cherokee, Spanish, German, Dutch, Yiddish, French, Menomonie, Japanese,

continued on page 126

*The writer of this essay has used the author-date documentation format described in The Chicago Manual of Style, 14 ed.

continued from page 125

Norwegian, Arabic, Aleut, Polish, Navajo, Thai, Portuguese, Caribbean creoles, and scores of other tongues. Of all the richnesses that define the compelx culture of this nation, none is more sparkling, more fascinating, or more evocative of our diverse origins than our plural heritage of languages.

Through much of our history, Americans have viewed this linguistic diversity as either a blessing or a simple fact of life. The founding fathers carefully omitted any constitutional provision establishing an official language—indeed, many of the founders were German-English bilinguals themselves. From the earliest days of nationhood, through both law and custom, the use of various languages other than English has been officially sanctioned in education, government, and commerce. The public and private use of a variety of languages has usually been treated as business-as-usual in a nation of immigrants.

But as Americans, we have also shared and treasured English, by custom and practice, and without challenge, as our common national language. While we trace our origins among peoples of many languages, we have always had our strong lingua franca. Indeed, America has developed one of the most efficient patterns of linguistic assimilation in the world. For more than two centuries, non-English speakers arriving in America typically have moved from their native language, through a bilingual stage, to monolingual English-speaking within three generations—and among some of today's immigrants, the process is occurring in only two generations (Veltman 1988).

The predominance and civic necessity of English is unquestioned in America; indeed, few countries in the world enjoy such a well-established, stable national language standard. For just one contemporary example of this acceptance: among a sample of contemporary Hispanic immigrants, 98 percent believe their children must learn to speak English "perfectly" in order to succeed—compared with 94 percent of Anglos holding the same opinion (Crawford 1989, 60). Of course, we Americans have also had our share of sociolinguistic conflicts, and . . . the most painful of these have occurred in the past seventy-five years. But still, the overwhelming fact of our national linguistic life has been the predominance of English and its remarkably quick mastery by new Americans.

continued to next page

Given this broad historic picture of linguistic stability and cultural consensus, then, it is somewhat surprising to find that language differences have become a searing political issue in the 1990s. Today, several powerful national lobbying groups are calling for the passage of both state and federal laws to officialize English, for cutbacks in bilingual education programs, and for a host of other legal measures designed to "legally protect" the common language. These groups argue that America is in a profound cultural crisis, that the very dominance of English is suddenly in peril, and that only concerted national legal action can save its central role in our culture. To these people, the image of Babel, a country confounded by a multiplicity of languages is not just a Biblical parable but an unfolding American reality.

According to U.S. English and other groups, the old pattern of language shift is no longer working; today's immigrants are different, and they are not assimilating like the Germans, Swedes, Poles, and Italians once did. Hispanics in particular are accused of actually *refusing* to learn English, instead demanding separate government-funded services delivered in their native language right to their ethnic neighborhoods. This new crop of immigrants, as one leader of the official English movement explains, prefers to hide in ethnic ghettos, "living off welfare and costing working Americans millions of tax dollars every year" (Horn n.d.).

The American public has been stirred by such accusations. How dare immigrants withhold this minimal act of allegiance—of plain simple respect—refusing to learn the common language of their adopted homeland? One need not be an ultrapatriot to be offended by such apparent intransigence and ingratitude. Nor has it been difficult for protectionist groups to spin frightening propaganda out of contemporary headlines. "I'm furious, and I'm scared," begins a solicitation letter from the director of El-Pac, the political lobbying arm of U.S. English. "I'm furious that the presidential nominee of a major American political party delivered a large portion of his acceptance spech *in a foreign language.* . . . Dukakis crossed a line that has never been crossed before. He signaled to all Americans that, in his search for Hispanic votes, he is willing to *embrace a new way of life* for us all—official bilingualism" (Zall n.d.).

Their fears stoked by such appeals, thousands of good-hearted, patriotic, loyal Americans—often consciously honoring

continued on page 128

5

continued from page 127

their own immigrant ancestry—have voted in large majorities to support official-English referenda recently appearing on the ballot in many states. By now, sixteen states have passed some version of an official-English law, and many more are considering such legislation. These states and the dates of their legislation are listed below:

Arizona	1988
Arkansas	1987
California	1986
Colorado	1988
Georgia	1986
Florida	1988
Illinois	1969
Indiana	1984
Kentucky	1984
Mississippi	1987
Nebraska	1923
North Carolina	1987
North Dakota	1987
South Carolina	1987
Tennessee	1984
Virginia	1981

*Hawaii and Louisiana have laws which give legal status to multiple languages.

What have been the outcomes of these state official-English statutes? The laws passed in the last few years have had a largely symbolic impact thus far. But from each of the new official-English states come reports of uncivil confrontations: in Colorado, a bus driver orders Hispanic children to stop speaking Spanish on the way to school ("English Only" 1989, 6); in Denver a restau-

continued to next page

rant worker is fired for translating the menu for a Hispanic customer (*EPIC* March/April 1988); in Texas, Spanish-language radio stations are the subject of FCC petitions (Bikales 1985); in Coral Gables, Florida, a supermarket checker is suspended without pay for speaking Spanish on the job (Gavin 1988); in Huntington Beach, California, court translators are forbidden to use Spanish in personal conversations (*EPIC* March/April 1988).

Still, large-scale official changes have not yet occurred in most areas. Few public officials—especially elected ones—have been eager to enforce English-only laws, especially when doing so would effectively terminate a previously available public service, and some, like the mayors of Denver and San Antonio have been outwardly defiant. And courts have struck down some English-only rulings, such as the Huntington Beach translators' case noted above. But, always keeping up the pressure, U.S. English and other groups continue to file specific challenges to particular practices, and these will gradually work their way through the legal system. It is not yet clear how the courts will rule, especially when language issues conflict with civil rights, a collision which is bound to occur frequently in these disputes.

10

What are some of the uses of non-English languages that U.S. English and others will try to terminate under the new statutes? Below are listed some practices and situations already targeted for abolition by U.S. English in one or more states:

- translators in public hospitals
- 911 emergency service
- voting materials, instructions, and ballots
- court reporters and other legal services
- bilingual education in public schools
- school materials, parent conferences, report cards
- driver's license regulations and examinations
- non-English radio and television broadcasting
- non-English holdings in public libraries
- street signs, park names, commemorative naming of public sites
- directory assistance
- telephone books and yellow pages
- tourist information
- public housing listings and information

continued on page 130

continued from page 129

- bus and train schedules and signs
- general advertising, business signs, billboards, menus
  (Zall n.d.; Crawford 1989; *EPIC*, 1988 both issues)

This list is a reminder, perhaps, of the degree to which public and private services already are routinely provided in non-English languages throughout America, in many cases to ensure public safety or simple justice.

As the list also suggests, U.S. English will probably not be satisfied when all immigrants learn English—they seem also to want all public reminders of the existence of other languages removed from America. They do not want to have to hear any Spanish in public, see any billboards, flip past any TV channels in languages other than English. Indeed, many U.S. English documents describe it as a violation of English speakers' civil rights to hear "foreign" languages in the street, to be made to feel a stranger in one's own country.

And as the above list further demonstrates, some English-only adherents feel that death is not too severe a penalty for an immigrant's failure to speak English. The denial of translator services in hospitals is one of the most telling planks in the official-English platform. The Florida director of U.S. English has specifically called not just for the termination of the 17 employees who translate between doctors and Spanish-speaking patients at Dade County's Jackson Memorial County Hospital, but also for elimination of prenatal, postnatal, and postsurgical materials and conferences in non-English languages (Robbins 1985). U.S. English is willing, in other words, to risk the lives of fellow Americans in the name of its language standards. As one U.S. English leader declared, just before going off to run for Congress from a Florida district, people who cannot explain a fire location or an ongoing crime in English have no right to police and fire protection through the 911 emergency number ("Florida English" 1986).

U.S. English holds an analogous view of education. Adherents essentially insist that being schooled immediately and exclusively in English is more important than achieving literacy or learning subject matter. Never mind that such an approach violates the best-proven educational practices and guarantees un-

continued to next page

necessary academic failure for many youngsters. As one widely distributed U.S. English promotional piece puts it, "If our society can't afford some scholastic failure, then we can't afford immigration" ("Frequently Used Arguments" n.d.). U.S. English proponents describe it as unrealistic and unattainable for immigrant children to succeed in school at the same rate as American-born children. Accordingly, U.S. English and the other language restrictionist groups oppose bilingual education, which has been amply shown to be the most educationally effective and socially benevolent approach to the education of non-English-speaking students.

For the time being, the national English-only lobby seems only modestly interested in enforcing its newly passed state laws. Instead, the movement's main energies are devoted to passing similar laws in additional states and attacking federal bilingual education policy. The overall strategy seems to be to get some official-English law on the books of a majority of states and to continually fan public resentment over schooling policies that "degrade English" and "cater" to immigrants. These activities seem aimed to develop momentum behind the English Language Amendment, the proposed federal constitutional amendment which has been stalled in committee for years, lacking the broad sponsorship that might coalesce if a snowballing public sentiment can be created.

LANGUAGE DEBATES IN THE TWENTIETH CENTURY

There has probably been more discord about language differences in America during the last seventy-five years than there was between Plymouth Rock and the turn of this century. A very distinct watershed occurred between 1915–20, when differences in language became a very contentious public issue. Emblematic of the period, Theodore Roosevelt asserted in 1919: "We have room for but one language here and that is the English language, for we intend to see that the crucible turns out people as Americans and not as dwellers in a polyglot boarding-house" (Crawford 1989, 23).

continued on page 132

15

continued from page 131

The increased concern with language differences was obviously related to the imminent World War, but it was also concurrent with a major shift in the quantity and type of immigration to the United States. After a steady flow of northern Europeans in the nineteenth century, there now appeared a growing number of southern and eastern European immigrants (members of the "Mediterranean" and "Alpine" races, according to the eugenicists of the day)—Italians, Poles, and Jews of various nationalities. This new type of immigrant was viewed darkly by many American politicians and educators, and thought to suffer from high levels of feeble-mindedness, disloyalty, Popery, and other shortcomings. In one of the more popular books of the day, Charles Benedict Davenport warned that

> the population of the United States will, on account of the great influx of blood from South-eastern Europe, rapidly become darker in pigmentation, smaller in stature, more mercurial, more attached to music and art, more given to crimes of larceny, kidnapping, assault, murder, rape, and sex-immorality . . . [and] the ratio of insanity in the population will rapidly increase. (Davenport 1911, 219)

During this period there were vociferous debates over how—and whether—persons so alien to the American "Nordic" race could assimilate. There was a vocal national concern that these immigrants were simply not of the quality and character of English or Scandinavian stock. While Germans were still viewed as genetically superior to Mediterranean types, the outbreak of war made the Germans the most despised people of all. The German accent was virtually eradicated from public use in America within a few years. In 1915, 24 percent of American high school students were studying German; by 1922 only 1 percent were doing so. Indeed, this period of linguistic intolerance caused a catastrophic drop in enrollments in *all* foreign languages from which our educational system has never recovered (Crawford 1989, 24).

Around this time, the fledgling National Council of Teachers of English, in its first decade of existence, hopped on the protectionist bandwagon by cosponsoring a national event called "Better Speech Week." In schools throughout America, students were

continued to next page

enlisted in "Ain't-less," "Final-G," and other assorted grammatical tag-days designed to heighten linguistic vigilance. The centerpiece of this annual festival, which ran for more than a decade, was the following pledge, recited by schoolchildren all around the country:

> I love the United States of America. I love my country's flag. I love my country's language. I promise:
> 1. That I will not dishonor my country's speech by leaving off the last syllable of words.
> 2. That I will say a good American "yes" and "no" in place of an Indian grunt "um-hum" and "nup-um" or a foreign "ya" or "yeh" and "nope."
> 3. That I will do my best to improve American speech by avoiding loud rough tones, by enunciating distinctly, and by speaking pleasantly, clearly, and sincerely.
> 4. That I will learn to articulate correctly as many words as possible during the year. (McDavid 1965, 9–10)

People familiar with the subsequent role of the NCTE in public language debates may be surprised to hear of the organization's entry on the side of prescriptivism, even overt nativism. But after this inauspicious launching, the NCTE promptly abjured popular, seat-of-the-pants notions about American speech and committed itself to the scholarly study of language. . . .

Today, in the controversy over the officialization of English, we are refighting the same old sociolingustic issues—the struggles of the 1970s, the 1920s, and other times and places. If anything is certain about the current episode, it is this: in fifty years, when we look back upon all this turmoil, we will recognize the English-only furor of the 1980s and 1990s as another incident in the long history of American intolerance of immigrants and minorities, another outburst of our fear and hatred of the stranger. Our era will seem and sound much like the early 1920s, and we will immediately notice the remarkable structural similarities between the immigration patterns—the sudden and large influx of ethnically diverse people from unfamiliar areas of the world.

In 1919, it seemed inconceivable that the American nation could possibly assimilate millions of dark-skinned, poor, largely

20

continued on page 134

continued from page 133

Catholic southern European immigrants without being "polluted" and destroyed. And yet, of course, we did gradually absorb all those peoples, and we have been immeasurably enriched in every aspect of our culture by doing so. Now those once-sinister Italians, Poles, and Jews have joined the old-timers in wondering: Can America absorb millions of Hispanics and Asians without being distorted, watered-down, and ruined?

Also when we look back fifty or seventy-five years from now, we will see that the English-only movement was built on misinformation, ignorance, and fear, but not on hatred. Whatever the politics of its leaders, the rank and file supporters, the ordinary citizens who marked official-English ballots and wrote small donation checks to U.S. English were not bigots. These were well-meaning, patriotic American citizens who supported language restrictionism out of genuine fear for the future of their country, or because they did not understand how language is actually learned and used, or because they had simply forgotten about the linguistic discrimination faced by their own immigrant ancestors. We will look back on the English-only movement, in other words, as a socially acceptable form of ethnic discrimination that passed from the scene just as soon as people understood its hidden meanings, its consequences, and the inhospitable messages it has sent to millions of our fellow citizens.

REFERENCES

Bikales, Gerda. [Executive Director of U.S. English.], "Petition for FCC Rule Making." Letter, 26 September 1985.

Crawford, James. *Bilingual Education: History, Politics, Theory, and Practice,* Trenton, N.J.: Crane Publishing Company, 1989.

Davenport, Charles Benedict. *Heredity in Relation to Eugenics,* New York: Henry Holt and Company, 1911.

"English Only Law Becomes a Matter of Interpretation." *Chicago Tribune, 6,* 15 January 1989.

EPIC Events (newsletter of the English Plus Information Clearinghouse). Washington, D.C.: January/February, March/April 1988.

"Florida English." *Education Week,* 19 March 1986.

continued to next page

"Frequently Used Arguments Against the Legal Protection of English," Flyer. Washington, D.C.: U.S. English, n.d.

Gavin, Jennifer. "Pena Outlaws Bias Based on Language," *Rocky Mountain News*, 29 December 1988.

Horn, Jim. "English First" solicitation letter. Falls Church, Va.: Committee to Protect the Family, n.d.

McDavid, Raven, ed., *An Examination of the Attitudes of the NCTE Toward Language.* Champaign, Ill.: National Council of Teachers of English, 1965.

Robbins, Terry. "An Open Letter to All the Governors in the United States." Florida English Campaign, Dade County, 30 March 1985.

Veltman, Clavin J. *The Future of the Spanish Language in the United States.* Washington, D.C.: Hispanic Policy Development Project, 1988.

Zall, Barnaby. "EL-PAC" solicitation letter, n.d.

ACKNOWLEDGE SOURCES

Because the academic community is devoted to **free and critical thought,** it's important to let your audience know if you've taken information or the analysis of information from a source beyond you. Your readers may want to read the source themselves to further explore the subject, or they may want to compare your perspective with the perspective voiced in the source. **Acknowledging sources** is a convention that's agreed upon in the academic community; when you don't acknowledge a source in academic writing, your readers will assume that the information or analysis is your own. If you don't acknowledge sources, you will be, perhaps without fully being aware of it, guilty of **plagiarism.** On college campuses plagiarism can have very serious consequences, among them failure of the course or even expulsion from the institution.

Chapter Twelve, "Writing the Research Paper," provides detailed information about using and acknowledging sources to avoid plagiarism. However, you'll learn how to use and acknowledge sources only if you're active about it. Ask your instructors for detailed information about the specific research activities and styles of **documentation** employed in their disciplines. In addition, as you read researched materials, pay attention to the ways writers use and document the sources that they cite.

PART THREE

RESPONDING TO SITUATIONS

CHAPTER
SEVEN
RESPONDING TO PERSONAL
EXPERIENCES

THE WRITER'S SCENARIO

A writer encounters a life **experience.** The experience might be traumatic, joyful, or puzzling. The experience might be fascinating, exciting, or terrifying. Whatever the experience is, something about it is so significant that the experience sticks in the writer's mind as a personal story that is revisited again and again. Eventually, after reflection, the writer responds to the experience by writing the story of it down in the form of a text.

Think about those experiences from your life that have remained with you to be revisited as personal stories—an event or series of events that affected your life in profound ways or taught you a simple but important lesson, a relationship with a person that challenged or shaped you, or even an experience so ordinary and seemingly unimportant that you can't understand why you've held on to it. What all of your revisited personal stories have in common is that they contain some **dramatic** element. Something has happened in them that has brought about a change. The change may have been subtle and only in the mind—a realization you've had or a delicate shift in your perspective. The change may have been a profound one that has radically altered the course of your life.

And just as the stories that stick with us mark changes in our lives, the texts we construct in response to those stories focus on the **drama of change.** Like short stories and novels, personal experience texts focus on **people** and on their **actions** in particular **places** and **times.** However, unlike fictional narratives, personal experience texts take as their subjects actual rather than imagined people and events.

The ability to critically read and write personal experience texts is useful in the academic community and in the world at large. Reading other people's stories will challenge you to think more deeply about your own life by introducing you to ways of living and thinking beyond your own experience. In addition, since who you are (and where you've been) profoundly influences the critical judgments you make about the texts and situations you encounter in the world, being able to understand and interpret your personal history is a crucial element in your continuing education as a thinker and a writer. Writing critically about your personal stories can help you discover how who you are influences how and what you think. To write critically about your own personal history, consider the following techniques.

TECHNIQUES FOR RESPONDING TO PERSONAL EXPERIENCES

1. Reconstruct in detail *where* and *when* the experience took place, and consider any necessary background information.
2. Focus on the dramatic activity in the experience by identifying and exploring in detail the *people* involved in the experience, the *significant actions* they engaged in, the *motives* behind those actions, and the actions' *consequences*.
3. Focus on the consequences of the entire experience by exploring the changes it brought about.
4. Determine your perspective on the experience by making or exploring an evidence-supported judgment about its meaning or importance.
5. Analyze your audience to determine what their possible point of view might be.
6. Present the experience and your perspective on it with your audience analysis in mind.

RESPONDING TO PERSONAL EXPERIENCES: PROFESSIONAL WRITING

FOCUS ON THE WRITER'S PURPOSE

Personal experience narratives can be written for any audience-based or writer-based purpose. As you actively preread and then read for meaning some or all of the following selections, focus your attention on the general purpose (or purposes) of each text.

PREREAD

To familiarize yourself with at least one of the following selections, preread. **Read the first three paragraphs** slowly, focusing on those things you understand. When you get to the end of the third paragraph, stop and consider what you've read. **Summarize** what's gone on in the text so far. If you're confused, go back and focus on the things that puzzle you and **reread** them, searching for meaning. Then **predict** the direction you think the text will take next. As you continue reading, compare your predictions with what unfolds on the page. After each of the remaining paragraphs, pause again to **summarize, reread** if necessary, and **predict.**

ORDINARY SPIRIT
Joy Harjo

Joy Harjo is a poet and teacher. The following essay was originally published in I Tell You Now *(1987), a collection of autobiographical essays by Native American writers.*

I was born in Tulsa, Oklahoma, on May 9, 1951, after a long hard labor that occurred sporadically for over a week. My mother didn't know it was labor because I wasn't due until mid-July. I also surprised her because I was a single birth; she had been told to possibly expect twins. The birth was hard on both of us. I was kept alive on a machine for the first few days of my life until I made a decision to live. When I looked around I saw my mother, only nineteen, of mixed Cherokee and French blood, who had already worked hard for her short life. And my father, a few years older, a tall, good-looking Creek man who was then working as a mechanic for American Airlines. I don't think I was ever what they expected, but I am grateful that they made my life possible and honor them for it.

I was the first of four children who were born evenly spaced over the next eight years or so. And much later had my own children, Phil and Rainy Dawn. We are descended from a long line of tribal speakers and leaders from my father's side. Menawa, who led the Red Stick War against Andrew Jackson, is our great-great (and possibly another great) grandfather. I don't know much about the family on my mother's side except there were many rebels and other characters. They are all part of who I am, the root from which I write, even though I may not always name them.

I began writing around the time I was twenty-two years old. I am now thirty-four and feel that after all this time I am just

continued on page 142

continued from page 141

beginning to learn to write. I am only now beginning to comprehend what poetry is, and what it can mean. Each time I write I am in a different and wild place, and travel toward something I do not know the name of. Each poem is a jumping-off edge and I am not safe, but I take more risks and understand better now how to take them. They do not always work, but when they do it is worth it. I could not live without writing and/or thinking about it. In fact, I don't have to think about it; it's there, some word, concept always being born or, just as easily, dying.

I walk in and out of many worlds. I used to see being born of this mixed-blood/mixed-vision a curse, and hated myself for it. It was too confusing and destructive when I saw the world through that focus. The only message I got was not belonging anywhere, not to any side. I have since decided that being familiar with more than one world, more than one vision, is a blessing, and know that I make my own choices. I also know that it is only an illusion that any of the worlds are separate.

5 It is around midnight. I often write at this time in my workroom near the front of an old Victorian-style house near downtown Denver. Tonight a thick snow has muffled the sounds of traffic. The world is quiet except for the sound of this typewriter humming, the sometimes dash of metallic keys, and the deep breathing of my dog who is asleep nearby. And then, in the middle of working, the world gives way and I see the old, old Creek one who comes in here and watches over me. He tries to make sense of this world in which his granddaughter has come to live. And often teases me about my occupation of putting words on paper.

I tell him that it is writing these words down, and entering the world through the structure they make, that has allowed me to see him more clearly, and to speak. And he answers that maybe his prayers, songs, and his belief in them has allowed him to create me.

We both laugh, and continue our work through many seasons.

This summer, during one of those sultry summer evenings when the air hums with a chorus of insects and there's the sound of children playing in the street, I sat, writing. Not actually writ-

continued to next page

ing but staring into that space above the typewriter where vision telescopes. I began remembering the way the world was before speech in childhood. A time when I was totally conscious of sound, and conscious of being in a world in which the webbed connections between us all were translucent yet apparent. I remember what it felt like to live within that space, where every live thing had a voice, and each voice/sound an aurora of color. It was sometime during that reminiscence that I began this poem:

SUMMER NIGHT

The moon is nearly full,
> *the humid air sweet like melon.*
Flowers that have cupped the sun all day
> *dream of iridescent wings*
under the long dark sleep.
> *Children's invisible voices call out*
in the glimmering moonlight.
> *Their parents play wornout records*
of the cumbia. *Behind the screendoor*
> *their soft laughter swells*
into the rhythm of a smooth guitar.
> *I watch the world shimmer*
inside this globe of a summer night,
> *listen to the wobble of her*
spin and dive. It happens all the time, waiting for you
> *to come home.*
There is an ache that begins
> *in the sound of an old blues song.*
It becomes a house where all the lights have gone out
> *but one.*
And it burns and burns
> *until there is only the blue smoke of dawn*
and everyone is sleeping in someone's arms
> *even the flowers*
even the sound of a thousand silences.

continued on page 144

continued from page 143

> *And the arms of night*
> *in the arms of day.*
> *Everyone except me.*
> *But then the smell of damp honeysuckle twisted on the*
> *vine.*
> *And the turn of the shoulder*
> *of the ordinary spirit who keeps watch*
> *over this ordinary street.*
> *And there you are, the secret*
> *of your own flower of light*
> *blooming in the miraculous dark.*
>
> *(from* Furious Light,
> *Watershed Foundation cassette, 1986)*

For years I have wanted to capture that ache of a summer night. This summer in Denver was especially humid, reminded me of Oklahoma. I wanted that feel, in the poem, of a thick, sweet air. And I wanted the voices I remembered, my parents' talking and scratchy, faint music of the radio. In the poem it is my neighbors I hear, and their old records of the *cumbia*. I also wanted to sustain a blues mood, pay homage to the blues because I love the blues. There was the sound of a sensuous tenor saxophone beneath the whole poem. I also added the part of everyone being in someone else's arms, "everyone except me," for the blues effect.

10

But I did not want to leave the poem there, in the center of the ache; I wanted to resolve it. I looked out the front door into the night and caught a glimpse of someone standing near the streetlight, a protecting spirit who was keeping watch over the street. I could have made that up, but I believe it is true. And I knew the spirit belonged in the poem and, because the spirit lives in the poem, too, helps turn the poem around to a place of tender realization. Hence, "And there you are, the secret/of your own flower of light/blooming in the miraculous dark."

When I first began writing, poetry was simply a way for me to speak. I was amazed that I could write anything down and have it come out a little more than coherently. Over the years the process has grown more complicated, more intricate, and the world within the poem more immense. In another recent poem the process is especially important:

continued to next page

TRANSFORMATIONS

This poem is a letter to tell you that I
have smelled the hatred you have tried
to find me with; you would like to destroy me.
Bone splintered in the eye of one you choose
to name your enemy won't make it better for you
to see. It could take a thousand years if you name it
that way, but then, to see after all that time, never
could anything be so clear. Memory has many forms.
When I think of early winter I think of a blackbird
laughing in the frozen air; guards a piece of light. I
saw the whole world caught in that sound. The sun
stopped for a moment because of tough belief. I don't
know what that has to do with what I am trying to tell
    you
except that I know you can turn a poem into something
else. This poem could be a bear treading the far
    northern
tundra, smelling the air for sweet alive meat. Or a
    piece
of seaweed stumbling in the sea. Or a blackbird,
    laughing.
What I mean is that hatred can be turned into
    something
else, if you have the right words, the right meanings
buried in that tender place in your heart where
the most precious animals live. Down the street
an ambulance has come to rescue an old man who is
    slowly
losing his life. Not many can see that he is already
becoming the backyard tree he has tendered for years,
before he moves on. He is not sad, but compassionate
for the fears moving around him.
That's what I mean to tell you. On the other side
of the place you live stands a dark woman.
She has been trying to talk to you for years.
You have called the same name in the middle of a
    nightmare,

continued on page 146

contined from page 145
from the center of miracles. She is beautiful.
This is your hatred back. She loves you.

When I began writing the poem, I knew I wanted an actual transformation to be enacted within it. I began with someone's hatred, which was a tangible thing, and wanted to turn it into love by the end of the poem. I was also interested in the process of becoming. I tried to include several states of becoming. The "process of the poem" becoming was one. I entered the poem very consciously with lines such as, "I don't know what that has to do with what I am trying to tell you," and "What I mean is. . . ." I also consciously switched tenses partly for that reason, and others. I often change tense within a poem and do so knowing what I am doing. It isn't by accident that it happens. Time doesn't realistically work in a linear fashion.

Within the poem is also the process of the "hater" becoming one who is loved, and who ultimately loves. The "I" is also involved in the process.

Earlier in the day an ambulance came into the neighborhood to pick up an elderly neighbor who had suffered a stroke and was near death. It was a major event. All who witnessed it walked carefully through the rest of the day. I was still thinking of him when I wrote the poem and knew that somehow he, too, belonged in the poem, for he was also part of the transformation.

I was not sure how the poem would end when I began writing it, but looking back I realize the ending must have originated in one of two places. One was a story I heard from a woman who during times of deep emotional troubles would be visited by a woman who looked just like her. She herself would never see her, but anyone passing by her room while she was asleep would see this imaginary woman, standing next to her bed. I always considered the "imaginary" woman as her other self, the denied self who wanted back in.

And I was reminded, too, of the woman who had followed me around at an all-night party in Santa Fe a few years before. We had all drifted around the house, talking, dancing, filled with music and whatever else we had tasted. She finally caught up with me around dawn and told me that she was sorry she was

15

continued to next page

white, and then told me that she believed white people had no souls. I was shocked and sad. And I saw her soul, starved but thinly beautiful, knocking hard on the wall of cocaine and self-hatred she was hiding behind.

So the poem becomes a way of speaking to her.

It is now very late and I will let someone else take over this story. Maybe the cricket who likes to come in here and sing and who probably knows a better way to write a poem than me.

It is not the last song, but to name anything that, only means that I would continue to be amazed at the creation of any new music.

GETTING TO KNOW MISTER LINCOLN
Beverly Lowry

Beverly Lowry is a journalist, fiction writer, and teacher. The following selection first appeared in the New York Times Magazine *(1995).*

In September, I moved to Washington to take up a teaching job at George Washington University. I was provided housing in a brownstone the college owns in a once-swampy area of town called Foggy Bottom. From my house, the White House was about five blocks east, the Kennedy Center about the same distance in the other direction. I found my way around Foggy Bottom quickly enough. Like that of many cities, the history of Washington is about water. There's always too much or too little. Less bossy than it used to be, the Potomac River now cradles Foggy Bottom. Parkland along the riverbank provides ample walking paths, north and south and across the river into Virginia. I walked and walked, to Cleveland Park, to Georgetown.

But the direction I headed most often was straight south down the street I lived on, past the small park where 10 to 20 — fear homeless men lived and on warm nights danced to a whammed-out beat on metal containers, past the huge, faceless State Department building, past one of the many kiosks selling three-for-$10 T-shirts and another one selling egg rolls, hot smokies and pretzels, across Constitution Avenue, to the Mall.

continued on page 148

continued from page 147

Everything is there: museums, a small lake, the Capitol, the Washington Monument, the Jefferson and Lincoln Memorials, not to mention people from all over the world. I went there all the time, to watch the people or go to a museum, often to see only one exhibit, or even one painting or statue. There was one funerary statue in the National Museum of African Art I grew particularly attached to. And afterward I would come back home feeling lively and nurtured and accompanied by the art I had seen, the observations from the walk, the people, the water, the wide long stretches of green. Because no building can be taller than the Capitol, there is a lot of sky in Washington, which I found comforting.

One night early in the fall semester I decided to go for a short run after class. But on my way home, I ran into a colleague and so by the time I had laced up my shoes and hit 21st Street, it was past 7:30 and dark.

I took the most lighted route, turning on Virginia Avenue toward the Washington Monument. The monument's up on a rise, and well lighted. When I got to 19th Street, I could see a number of people still wandering around its base.

I had my Walkman on, rock music pounding into my ears. When I got to Constitution, there was still a rosy glow in the sky but the light was failing fast. I would, I told myself, start straight back home as soon as I got to the monument, but once I did, and looked west down the reflecting pool toward the river, I stopped dead in my tracks.

After the assassination of Abraham Lincoln, it took nearly 50 years of hot dispute before a decision was made about what kind of memorial should be built in his honor, and where it should go. In the late 1800's, Tiber Creek met the Potomac on what would become Constitution Avenue. The water flowed all the way to the White House, often flooding Pennsylvania Avenue. The unfinished Washington Monument was an unsightly stump; the west end of the Mall, river bottom; the area around it, malarial marshes.

All kinds of suggestions were made: a triumphal arch, a grand memorial to the soldiers and statesmen of the Civil War. The emerging automobile industry favored a memorial highway

continued to next page

[Handwritten margin notes:]
She is from a small town
Showing her knowledge of A.L.

from Washington to Gettysburg, Pa. Railwaymen wanted a statue at Union Station. Finally, in 1912, the classic design of the architect Henry Bacon was chosen. By then, Tiber Creek had been covered over, the swamps dredged and filled, the land reclaimed. The west end of the Mall was still mosquito-ridden and jungly, but Bacon's supporters won the day and Congress voted to situate the memorial on a spot some 3,000 yards down the Mall from the Washington Monument, on an axis that went from the Capital across the river to Arlington Cemetery, and then to the house that until the Civil War had been the home of Robert E. Lee.

The sun sets behind the Lincoln Memorial, at an angle from its southernmost corner. That night it had already gone down, but that time of year sunset blessedly lasts for what seems like hours, and the sky was wildly ablaze, framing the memorial in a pulsating glow of deep reds, wild pinks and hot golds as lush and beautiful and vulgar as a cheap chiffon scarf.

I switched off my Walkman and stood there gawking, saying, "Look. Look at that," out loud and to nobody at all. The lights inside the memorial had gone on. There's a moment when, after that happens, the sky suddenly gets dark enough that the statue of Lincoln inside the memorial slowly makes a ghostly appearance from between the columns. From where I stood, I saw it happen. Like a picture coming into focus, gradually he was there, seated and in deep contemplation. With the sky on fire behind him, it was as if the whole thing had been staged, a drama of night and time, history and splendor. Beyond the memorial, the Memorial Bridge with its spotty sparkling lights pointed the way across the Potomac. In the reflecting pool, some geese honked a raucous chant, flapped their wings and took off. An airplane from National Airport flew in a diagonal line across the memorial, heading northeast.

I started for home. Beyond the statue of José de San Martín, there was a stretch of dark sidewalk to get through and—having read all the crime reports before arriving—I vowed if I made it home safely that night, never to go out that late again. But I wasn't sorry I had taken the risk. And afterward I began going to the Mall more often and for a more specific reason than for the people, the art or the sky. I went, as I said to myself in the way people alone speak aloud to themselves all the time, "to visit Abe."

continued on page 150

continued from page 149

Sometimes on a cool clear morning I would simply get up and go down there. The Wall, as the memorial to the veterans of the Vietnam War is called, is located just north of the Lincoln Memorial, and so I had to pass it on my way, and then the kiosks manned by Warriors Inc., and Friends of the Vietnam Veterans Memorial. No matter how early I got there, the kiosks were open, selling T-shirts and P.O.W. and M.I.A. bracelets. I would move on past them, and up the 58 steps to the memorial, where I paid Mr. Lincoln my respects, then came back home and made coffee, ready for the day.

I quickly began to develop a relationship with Abraham Lincoln. I read a couple of biographies, I went to Ford's Theater, where he was shot, and the house across the street, where he died. I stared at pictures of him for long minutes at a time. There was nothing about his life I did not find moving, and significant. And I began to depend on his presence. In my life as a visitor, Abraham Lincoln became a constant.

One day, standing on the top step leading to the reflecting pool, I heard this conversation from a group of boys in private-school jackets and ties:

"Which one is that?" He pointed.

"Lincoln I think. You taking a picture?"

"No, man. I only took Jefferson because Forrest Gump went there." And they moved on.

I have taken 10 or 12 photos of strangers who wanted a picture to take home, of themselves next to Lincoln. I would look in the lens and they would be standing there, those overhanging marble-booted toes high above them. They wouldn't do anything, not even smile, just stand there.

Not wanting to become jaded, I didn't always go up into the memorial itself. Sometimes I only walked past, looked to see who was around, nodded at the statue, and went on. About once a month, however, I allowed myself the pleasure. I devised a ceremony. I was strict. I did it the same way every time.

First I read the plaque at the foot of the steps, explaining that of the 38 columns in the memorial, 36 symbolize the 36 states that were a part of the Union during Lincoln's Presidency, all of which are named on the frieze above the columns. And then I would go

continued to next page

up the steps, reading the names of the states, noting that states from both the North and South are on the front facade: Massachusetts, Virginia, New York, Georgia.

Henry Bacon's design was an American version of a Greek Doric temple turned sideways, so that the long side became the front facade. The inner room, therefore, is comparatively shallow, and so when you walk inside the statue looks even bigger than it actually is, it's that close and in your face. Once I got past the columns, I stopped.

For the most part, visits to graves or memorial sites are a disappointment. You expect something to be there, to give you a sign, that all the marble and greenskeeping and landscaping mean something; that some version of the dead person is still around. And mostly nothing is there except trees, grass, the stone. In the Lincoln Memorial, however, I could swear some kind of magic has been accomplished. Henry Bacon's method of working was said to have been one of "ceaseless meditation." In the memorial, the presence of Lincoln seems to be all over the place.

I took my time looking up. He's up there, 11 feet of pedestal, 19 of statue. I concentrated first on his hands, the long fingers of the right one articulately, even delicately tensed as if about to make a gesture; the left one clenched in a loose, determined fist. After the hands I took in the huge booted feet and long legs, the broad shoulders and then finally—holding off, to extend the moment—I made my way to his magnificent face, those eyes. He is looking slightly down but mostly out, as if absorbed in his own thoughts yet knowing he must not sink too far or grow too introspective; there is a country to think of, and all those dead young men.

Beyond the top of his head, the inscription carved in the marble panel always fairly took my breath away: "In this temple/as in the hearts of the people/for whom he saved the Union/the memory of Abraham Lincoln/is enshrined forever." A newspaperman wrote those words, one Royal Cortissoz, then arts editor of the New York Herald Tribune. I would move from one side of the statue to another, taking it in from all angles. Aided by carefully orchestrated artificial lighting, sunlight falls softly through skylights in the ceiling, and bounces off the reflecting pool and on a clear day fills the memorial.

continued on page 152

continued from page 151

On either side of the statue are the limestone tablets on which are carved, on one side, the amazing Gettysburg Address and on the other, the even more moving and eloquent Second Inaugural Address. I made a point to read them, word by word, every time I went.

Hired to teach classes in the personal essay, I suggested to my students that when feeling confused about the form, they take a walk to the memorial and read those speeches. There they would find out the difference between certainty and smugness, between modesty and ambivalence.

I read those speeches many times. And every time I did, I felt moved and grounded again, as an American and as a writer. And afterward I would go down the steps feeling nourished and clean.

In writing the piece for the Times I somehow left out the name of the sculptor Daniel Patrick French, who designed and made the statue itself. Several people noted the ommission in letters I received. They were right; it should have been there.

Beverly Lowry

IF I COULD WRITE THIS IN FIRE, I WOULD WRITE THIS IN FIRE[1]
Michelle Cliff

Michelle Cliff is a writer and an academic. The following text is from her book The Land of Look Behind *(1985).*

I

We were standing under the waterfall at the top of Orange River. Our chests were just beginning to mound—slight hills on either side. In the center of each were our nipples, which were losing

continued to next page

their sideways look and rounding into perceptible buttons of dark flesh. Too fast it seemed. We touched each other, then, quickly and almost simultaneously, raised our arms to examine the hairs growing underneath. Another sign. Mine was wispy and light-brown. My friend Zoe had dark hair curled up tight. In each little patch the river-water caught the sun so we glistened.

The waterfall had come about when my uncles dammed up the river to bring power to the sugar mill. Usually, when I say "sugar mill" to anyone not familiar with the Jamaican countryside or for that matter my family, I can tell their minds cast an image of tall smokestacks, enormous copper cauldrons, a man in a broad-brimmed hat with a whip, and several dozens of slaves—that is, if they have any idea of how large sugar mills once operated. It's a grandiose expression—like plantation, verandah, outbuilding. (Try substituting farm, porch, outside toilet.) To some people it even sounds romantic.

Our sugar mill was little more than a round-roofed shed, which contained a wheel and woodfire. We paid an old man to run it, tend the fire, and then either bartered or gave the sugar away, after my grandmother had taken what she needed. Our canefield was about two acres of flat land next to the river. My grandmother had six acres in all, one donkey, a mule, two cows, some chickens, a few pigs, and stray dogs and cats who had taken up residence in the yard. Her house had four rooms, no electricity, no running water. The kitchen was a shed in the back with a small pot-bellied stove. Across from the stove was a mahogany counter, which had a white enamel basin set into it. The only light source was a window, a small space covered partly by a wooden shutter. We washed our faces and hands in enamel bowls with cold water carried in kerosene tins from the river and poured from enamel pitchers. Our chamber pots were enamel also, and in the morning we carefully placed them on the steps at the side of the house where my grandmother collected them and disposed of their contents. The outhouse was about thirty yards from the back door—a "closet" as we called it—infested with lizards capable of changing color. When the door was shut it was totally dark, and the lizards made their presence known by the noise of their scurrying

continued on page 154

continued from page 153

through the torn newspaper, or the soft shudder when they dropped from the walls. I remember most clearly the stench of the toilet, which seemed to hang in the air in that climate.

5   But because every little piece of reality exists in relation to another little piece, our situation was not that simple. It was to our yard that people came with news first. It was in my grandmother's parlor that the Disciples of Christ held their meetings.

Zoe lived with her mother and sister on borrowed ground in a place called Breezy Hill. She and I saw each other almost every day on our school vacations over a period of three years. Each morning early—as I sat on the cement porch with my coffee cut with condensed milk—she appeared: in her straw hat, school tunic faded from blue to gray, white blouse, sneakers hanging around her neck. We had coffee together, and a piece of harddough bread with butter and cheese, waited a bit and headed for the river. At first we were shy with each other. We did not start from the same place.

There was land. My grandparents' farm. And there was color. (My family was called "red." A term which signified a degree of whiteness. "We's just a flock of red people," a cousin of mine said once.) In the hierarchy of shades I was considered among the lightest. The countrywomen who visited my grandmother commented on my "tall" hair—meaning long. Wavy, not curly. I had spent the years from three to ten in New York and spoke—at first—like an American. I wore American clothes: shorts, slacks, bathing suit. Because of my American past I was looked upon as the creator of games. Cowboys and Indians. Cops and Robbers. Peter Pan.

(While the primary colonial identification for Jamaicans was English, American colonialism was a strong force in my childhood—and of course continues today. We were sent American movies and American music. American aluminum companies had already discovered bauxite on the island and were shipping the ore to their mainland. United Fruit bought our bananas. White Americans came to Montego Bay, Ocho Rios, and Kingston for their vacations and their cruise ships docked in Port Antonio and other places. In some ways America was seen as a better place

continued to next page

than England by many Jamaicans. The farm laborers sent to work in American agribusiness came home with dollars and gifts and new clothes; there were few who mentioned American racism. Many of the middle class who emigrated to Brooklyn or Staten Island or Manhattan were able to pass into the white American world—saving their blackness for other Jamaicans or for trips home; in some cases, forgetting it altogether. Those middle-class Jamaicans who could not pass for white managed differently—not unlike the Bajans in Paule Marshall's *Brown Girl, Brownstones*—saving, working, investing, buying property. Completely separate in most cases from Black Americans.)

I was someone who had experience with the place that sent us triple features of B-grade westerns and gangster movies. And I had tall hair and light skin. And I was the granddaughter of my grandmother. So I had power. I was the cowboy, Zoe was my sidekick, the boys we knew were Indians. I was the detective, Zoe was my "girl," the boys were the robbers. I was Peter Pan, Zoe was Wendy Darling, the boys were the lost boys. And the terrain around the river—jungled and dark green—was Tombstone, or Chicago, or Never-Never Land.

10

This place and my friendship with Zoe never touched my life in Kingston. We did not correspond with each other when I left my grandmother's home.

I never visited Zoe's home the entire time I knew her. It was a given: never suggested, never raised.

Zoe went to a state school held in a country church in Red Hills. It had been my mother's school. I went to a private all-girls school where I was taught by white Englishwomen and pale Jamaicans. In her school the students were caned as punishment. In mine the harshest punishment I remember was being sent to sit under the *lignum vitae* to "commune with nature." Some of the girls were out-and-out white (English and American), the rest of us were colored—only a few were dark. Our uniforms were blood-red gabardine, heavy and hot. Classes were held in buildings meant to recreate England: damp with stone floors, facing onto a cloister, or quad as they called it. We began each day with the headmistress leading us in English hymns. The entire school stood for an hour in the zinc-roofed gymnasium.

continued on page 156

contined from page 155

Occasionally a girl fainted, or threw up. Once, a girl had a grand mal seizure. To any such disturbance the response was always "keep singing." While she flailed on the stone floor, I wondered what the mistresses would do. We sang "Faith of Our Fathers," and watched our classmate as her eyes rolled back in her head. I thought of people swallowing their tongues. This student was dark—here on a scholarship—and the only woman who came forward to help her was the gamesmistress, the only dark teacher. She kneeled beside the girl and slid the white web belt from her tennis shorts, clamping it between the girl's teeth. When the seizure was over, she carried the girl to a tumbling mat in a corner of the gym and covered her so she wouldn't get chilled.

15

Were the other women unable to touch this girl because of her darkness? I think that now. Her darkness and her scholarship. She lived on Windward Road with her grandmother; her mother was a maid. But darkness is usually enough for women like those to hold back. Then, we usually excused that kind of behavior by saying they were "ladies." (We were constantly being told we should be ladies also. One teacher went so far as to tell us many people thought Jamaicans lived in trees and we had to show these people they were mistaken.) In short, we felt insufficient to judge the behavior of these women. The English ones (who had the corner on power in the school) had come all this way to teach us. Shouldn't we treat them as the missionaries they were certain they were? The creole Jamaicans had a different role: they were passing on to those of us who were light-skinned the creole heritage of collaboration, assimilation, loyalty to our betters. We were expected to be willing subjects in this outpost of civilization.

The girl left school that day and never returned.

After prayers we filed into our classrooms. After classes we had games: tennis, field hockey, rounders (what the English call baseball), netball (what the English call basketball). For games we were divided into "houses"—groups named for Joan of Arc, Edith Cavell, Florence Nightingale, Jane Austen. Four white heroines. Two martyrs. One saint. Two nurses. (None of us knew then that there were black women with Nightingale at Scutari.) One novelist. Three involved in white men's wars. Two dead in white men's wars. *Pride and Prejudice.*

continued to next page

Those of us in Cavell wore red badges and recited her last words before a firing squad in W.W. I: "Patriotism is not enough. I must have no hatred or bitterness toward anyone."

Sorry to say I grew up to have exactly that.

Looking back: To try and see when the background changed places with the foreground. To try and locate the vanishing point: where the lines of perspective converge and disappear. Lines of color and class. Lines of history and social context. Lines of denial and rejection. When did *we* (the light-skinned middle-class Jamaicans) take over for *them* as oppressors? I need to see when and how this happened. When what should have been reality was overtaken by what was surely unreality. When the house nigger became master.

"What's the matter with you? You think you're white or something?"

"Child, what you want to know 'bout Garvey for? The man was nothing but a damn fool."

"They not our kind of people."

Why did we wear wide-brimmed hats and try to get into Oxford? Why did we not return?

Great Expectations: a novel about origins and denial. about the futility and tragedy of that denial. about attempting assimilation. We learned this novel from a light-skinned Jamaican woman—she concentrated on what she called the "love affair" between Pip and Estella.

Looking back: Through the last page of *Sula.* "And the loss pressed down on her chest and came up into her throat. 'We was girls together,' she said as though explaining something." It was Zoe, and Zoe alone, I thought of. She snapped into my mind and I remembered no one else. Through the greens and blues of the riverbank. The flame of red hibiscus in front of my grandmother's house. The cracked grave of a former landowner. The fruit of the ackee which poisons those who don't know how to prepare it.

"What is to become of us?"

We borrowed a baby from a woman and used her as our dolly. Dressed and undressed her. Dipped her in the riverwater. Fed her with the milk her mother had left with us: and giggled because we knew where the milk had come from.

continued on page 158

continued from page 157

A letter: "I am desperate. I need to get away. I beg you one fifty-dollar."

I send the money because this is what she asks for. I visit her on a trip back home. Her front teeth are gone. Her husband beats her and she suffers blackouts. I sit on her chair. She is given birth-control pills which aggravate her "condition." We boil up sorrel and ginger. She is being taught by Peace Corps volunteers to embroider linen mats with little lambs on them and gives me one as a keepsake. We cool off the sorrel with a block of ice brought from the shop nearby. The shopkeeper immediately recognizes me as my grandmother's granddaughter and refuses to sell me cigarettes. (I am twenty-seven.) We sit in the doorway of her house, pushing back the colored plastic strands which form a curtain, and talk about Babylon and Dred. About Manley and what he's doing for Jamaica. About how hard it is. We walk along the railway tracks—no longer used—to Crooked River and the post office. Her little daughter walks beside us and we recite a poem for her: "Mornin' buddy/Me no buddy fe wunna/Who den', den' I saw?" and on and on.

I can come and go. And I leave. To complete my education in London.

II

Their goddam kings and their goddam queens. Grandmotherly Victoria spreading herself thin across the globe. Elizabeth II on our t.v. screens. We stop what we are doing. We quiet down. We pay our respects.

30   1981: In Massachusetts I get up at 5 a.m. to watch the royal wedding. I tell myself maybe the IRA will intervene. It's got to be better than starving themselves to death. Better to be a kamikaze in St. Paul's Cathedral than a hostage in Ulster. And last week Black and white people smashed storefronts all over the United Kingdom. But I really don't believe we'll see royal blood on t.v. I watch because they once ruled us. In the back of the cathedral a Maori woman sings an aria from Handel and I notice that she is surrounded by the colored subjects.

continued to next page

To those of us in the commonwealth the royal family was the perfect symbol of hegemony. To those of us who were dark in the dark nations the prime minister, the parliament barely existed. We believed in royalty—we were convinced in this belief. Maybe it played on some ancestral memories of West Africa—where other kings and queens had been. Altars and castles and magic.

The faces of our new rulers were everywhere in my childhood. Calendars, newsreels, magazines. Their presences were often among us. Attending test matches between the West Indians and South Africans. They were our landlords. Not always absentee. And no matter what Black leader we might elect—were we to choose independence—we would be losing something almost holy in our impudence.

WE ARE HERE BECAUSE YOU WERE THERE
BLACK PEOPLE AGAINST STATE BRUTALITY
BLACK WOMEN WILL NOT BE INTIMIDATED
WELCOME TO BRITAIN ... WELCOME TO SECOND-
   CLASS CITIZENSHIP

(slogans of the Black movement in Britain)

Indian women cleaning the toilets in Heathrow airport. This is the first thing I notice. Dark women in saris trudging buckets back and forth as other dark women in saris—some covered by loosefitting winter coats—form a line to have their passports stamped.

The triangle trade: molasses/rum/slaves. Robinson Crusoe was on a slavetrading journey. Robert Browning was a mulatto. Holding pens. Jamaica was a seasoning station. Split tongues. Sliced ears. Whipped bodies. The constant pretense of civility against rape. Still. Iron collars. Tinplate masks. The latter a precaution: to stop the slaves from eating the sugar cane.

A pregnant woman is to be whipped—they dig a hole to accommodate her belly and place her face down on the ground. Many of us became light-skinned very fast. Traced ourselves through bastard lines to reach the duke of Devonshire. The earl of Cornwall. The lord of this and the lord of that. Our mothers' rapes were the thing unspoken.

You say: But Britain freed her slaves in 1834. Yes.

Tea plantations in India and Ceylon. Mines in Africa. The Cape-to-Cairo Railroad. Rhodes scholars. Suez Crisis. The white

35

continued on page 160

continued from page 159

man's bloody burden. Boer War. Bantustans. Sitting in a theatre in London in the seventies. A play called *West of Suez*. A lousy play about British colonials. The finale comes when several well-known white actors are machine-gunned by several lesser-known Black actors. (As Nina Simone says: "This is a show tune but the show hasn't been written for it yet.")

The red empire of geography classes. "The sun never sets on the British empire and you can't trust it in the dark." Or with the dark peoples. "Because of the Industrial Revolution European countries went in search of markets and raw materials." Another geography (or was it a history) lesson.

40   Their bloody kings and their bloody queens. Their bloody peers. Their bloody generals. admirals. explorers. Livingstone. Hillary. Kitchener. All the bwanas. And all their beaters, porters, sherpas. Who found the source of the Nile. Victoria Falls. The tops of mountains. Their so-called discoveries reek of untruth. How many dark people died so they could misname the physical features in their blasted gazetteer. A statistic we shall never know. Dr. Livingstone, I presume you are here to rape our land and enslave our people.

There are statues of these dead white men all over London.

An interesting fact: The swearword "bloody" is a contraction of "by my lady"—a reference to the Virgin Mary. They do tend to use their ladies. Name ages for them. Places for them. Use them as screens, inspirations, symbols. And many of the ladies comply. While the national martyr Edith Cavell was being executed by the Germans in Belgium in 1915 (Belgium was called "poor little Belgium" by the allies in the war), the Belgians were engaged in the exploitation of the land and peoples of the Congo.

And will we ever know how many dark peoples were "imported" to fight in white men's wars. Probably not. Just as we will never know how many hearts were cut from African people so that the Christian doctor might be a success—i.e., extend a white man's life. Our Sister Killjoy observes this from her black-eyed squint.

Dr. Schweitzer—humanitarian, authority on Bach, winner of the Nobel Peace Prize—on the people of Africa: "The Negro is a child, and with children nothing can be done without the use of

continued to next page

authority. We must, therefore, so arrange the circumstances of our daily life that my authority can find expression. With regard to Negroes, then, I have coined the formula: 'I am your brother, it is true, but your elder brother.' " (*On the Edge of the Primeval Forest.* 1961)

They like to pretend we didn't fight back. We did: with obeah, poison, revolution. It simply was not enough.   45

"Colonies . . . these places where 'niggers' are cheap and the earth is rich."—W.E.B. DuBois, "The Souls of White Folk"

A cousin is visiting me from M.I.T. where he is getting a degree in engineering. I am learning about the Italian Renaissance. My cousin is recognizably Black and speaks with an accent. I am not and I do not—unless I am back home, where the "twang" comes upon me. We sit for some time in a bar in his hotel and are not served. A light-skinned Jamaican comes over to our table. He is an older man—a professor at the University of London. "Don't bother with it, you hear. They don't serve us in this bar." A run-of-the-mill incident for all recognizably Black people in this city. But for me it is not.

Henry's eyes fill up, but he refuses to believe our informant. "No, man, the girl is just busy." (The girl is a fifty-year-old white woman, who may just be following orders. But I do not mention this. I have chosen sides.) All I can manage to say is, "Jesus Christ, I hate the fucking English." Henry looks at me. (In the family I am known as the "lady cousin." It has to do with how I look. And the fact that I am twenty-seven and unmarried—and for all they know, unattached. They do not know that I am really the lesbian cousin.) Our informant says—gently, but with a distinct tone of disappointment—"My dear, is that what you're studying at the university?"

You see—the whole business is very complicated.

Henry and I leave without drinks and go to meet some of his   50
white colleagues at a restaurant I know near Covent Garden Opera House. The restaurant caters to theatre types and so I hope there won't be a repeat of the bar scene—at least they know how to pretend. Besides, I tell myself, the owners are Italian *and* gay; they *must* be halfway decent. Henry and his colleagues work for an American company which is paying their way through M.I.T. They mine bauxite from the hills in the middle of the island and

continued on page 162

continued from page 161

send it to the United States. A turnaround occurs at dinner: Henry joins the white men in a sustained mockery of the waiters: their accents and the way they walk. He whispers to me: "Why you want to bring us to a battyman's den, lady?" (*Battyman = faggot* in Jamaican.) I keep quiet.

We put the white men in a taxi and Henry walks me to the underground station. He asks me to sleep with him. (It wouldn't be incest. His mother was a maid in the house of an uncle and Henry has not seen her since his birth. He was taken into the family. She was let go.) I say that I can't. I plead exams. I can't say that I don't want to. Because I remember what happened in the bar. But I can't say that I'm a lesbian either—even though I want to believe his alliance with the white men at dinner was forced: not really him. He doesn't buy my excuse. "Come on, lady, let's do it. What's the matter, you 'fraid?" I pretend I am back home and start patois to show him somehow I am not afraid, not English, not white. I tell him he's a married man and he tells me he's a ram goat. I take the train to where I am staying and try to forget the whole thing. But I don't. I remember our different skins and our different experiences within them. And I have a hard time realizing that I am angry with Henry. That to him—no use in pretending—a queer is a queer.

1981: I hear on the radio that Bob Marley is dead and I drive over the Mohawk Trail listening to a program of his music and I cry and cry and cry. Someone says: "It wasn't the ganja that killed him, it was poverty and working in a steel foundry when he was young."

I flashback to my childhood and a young man who worked for an aunt I lived with once. He taught me to smoke ganja behind the house. And to peel an orange with the tip of a machete without cutting through the skin—"Love" it was called: a necklace of orange rind the result. I think about him because I heard he had become a Rastaman. And then I think about Rastas.

We are sitting on the porch of an uncle's house in Kingston— the family and I—and a Rastaman comes to the gate. We have guns but they are locked behind a false closet. We have dogs but they are tied up. We are Jamaicans and know that Rastas mean no harm. We let him in and he sits on the side of the porch and

continued to next page

shows us his brooms and brushes. We buy some to take back to New York. "Peace, missis."

There were many Rastas in my childhood. Walking the roadside with their goods. Sitting outside their shacks in the mountains. The outsides painted bright—sometimes with words. Gathering at Palisadoes Airport to greet the Conquering Lion of Judah. They were considered figures of fun by most middle-class Jamaicans. Harmless: like Marcus Garvey.

Later: white American hippies trying to create the effect of dred in their straight white hair. The ganja joint held between their straight white teeth. "Man, the grass is good." Hanging out by the Sheraton pool. Light-skinned Jamaicans also dredlocked, also assuming the ganja. Both groups moving to the music but not the words. Harmless. "Peace, brother."

III

My grandmother: "Let us thank God for a fruitful place." My grandfather: "Let us rescue the perishing world."

This evening on the road in western Massachusetts there are pockets of fog. Then clear spaces. Across from a pond a dog staggers in front of my headlights. I look closer and see that his mouth is foaming. He stumbles to the side of the road—I go to call the police.

I drive back to the house, radio playing "difficult" piano pieces. And I think about how I need to say all this. This is who I am. I am not what you allow me to be. Whatever you decide me to be. In a bookstore in London I show the woman at the counter my book and she stares at me for a minute, then says: "You're a Jamaican." "Yes." "You're not at all like our Jamaicans."

Encountering the void is nothing more nor less than understanding invisibility. Of being fogbound.

It is up to me to sort out these connections—to employ anger and take the consequences. To choose not to be harmless. To make it impossible for them to think me harmless.

Then: It was never a question of passing. It was a question of hiding. Behind Black and white perceptions of who we were—who they thought we were. Tropics. Plantations.

continued on page 164

continued from page 163

Calypso. Cricket. We were the people with the musical voices and the coronation mugs on our parlor tables. I would be whatever figure these foreign imaginations cared for me to be. It would be so simple to let others fill in for me. So easy to startle them with a flash of anger when their visions got out of hand—but never to sustain the anger for myself.

It could become a life lived within myself. A life cut off. I know who I am but you will never know who I am. I may in fact lose touch with who I am.

I hid from my real sources. But my real sources were hidden from me.

Now: It is not a question of relinquishing privilege. It is a question of grasping more of myself. I have found that in the real sources are concealed my survival. My speech. My voice. To be colonized is to be rendered insensitive. To have those parts necessary to sustain life numbed. And this is in some cases—in my case—perceived as privilege. The test of a colonized person is to walk through a shantytown in Kingston and not bat an eye. This I cannot do. Because part of me lives there—and as I grasp more of this part I realize what needs to be done with the rest of my life.

65   Sometimes I used to think we were like the Marranos—the Sephardic Jews forced to pretend they were Christians. The name was given to them by the Christians, and meant "pigs." But once out of Spain and Portugal, they became Jews openly again. Some settled in Jamaica. They knew who the enemy was and acted for their own survival. But they remained Jews always.

We also knew who the enemy was—I remember jokes about the English. Saying they stank. saying they were stingy. that they drank too much and couldn't hold their liquor. that they had bad teeth. were dirty and dishonest. were limey bastards. and horse-faced bitches. We said the men only wanted to sleep with Jamaican women. And that the women made pigs of themselves with Jamaican men.

continued to next page

But of course this was seen by us—the light-skinned middle class—with a double vision. We learned to cherish that part of us that was them—and to deny the part that was not. Believing in some cases that the latter part had ceased to exist.

None of this is as simple as it may sound. We were colorists and we aspired to oppressor status. (Of course, almost any aspiration instilled by western civilization is to oppressor status: success, for example.) Color was the symbol of our potential: color taking in hair "quality," skin tone, freckles, nose-width, eyes. We did not see that color symbolism was a method of keeping us apart: in the society, in the family, between friends. Those of us who were light-skinned, straight-haired, etc., were given to believe that we could actually attain whiteness—or at least those qualities of the colonizer which made him superior. We were convinced of white supremacy. If we failed we were not really responsible for our failures: we had all the advantages—but it was that one persistent drop of blood, that single rogue gene that made us unable to conceptualize abstract ideas, made us love darkness rather than despise it, which was to be blamed for our failure. Our dark part had taken over: an inherited imbalance in which the doom of the creole was sealed.

I am trying to write this as clearly as possible, but as I write I realize that what I say may sound fabulous, or even mythic. It is. It is insane.

Under this system of colorism—the system which prevailed in my childhood in Jamaica, and which has carried over to the present—rarely will dark and light people co-mingle. Rarely will they achieve between themselves an intimacy informed with identity. (I should say here that I am using the categories light and dark both literally and symbolically. There are dark Jamaicans who have achieved lightness and the "advantages" which go with it by their successful pursuit of oppressor status.)

Under this system light and dark people will meet in those ways in which the light-skinned person imitates the oppressor. But imitation goes only so far: the light-skinned person becomes an oppressor in fact. He/she will have a dark chauffeur, a dark nanny, a dark maid, and a dark gardener. These employees will be paid badly. Because of the slave past, because of their dark skin, the servants of the middle class have been used according

70

continued on page 166

continued from page 165

to the traditions of the slavocracy. They are not seen as workers for their own sake, but for the sake of the family who has employed them. It was not until Michael Manley became prime minister that a minimum wage for houseworkers was enacted—and the indignation of the middle class was profound.

During Manley's leadership the middle class began to abandon the island in droves. Toronto. Miami. New York. Leaving their houses and businesses behind and sewing cash into the tops of suitcases. Today—with a new regime—they are returning: "Come back to the way things used to be" the tourist advertisement on American t.v. says. "Make it Jamaica again." "Make it your own."

But let me return to the situation of houseservants as I remember it: They will be paid badly, but they will be "given" room and board. However, the key to the larder will be kept by the mistress in her dresser drawer. They will spend Christmas with the family of their employers and be given a length of English wool for trousers or a few yards of cotton for dresses. They will see their children on their days off: their extended family will care for the children the rest of the time. When the employers visit their relations in the country, the servants may be asked along— oftentimes the servants of the middle class come from the same part of the countryside their employers have come from. But they will be expected to work while they are there. Back in town, there are parts of the house they are allowed to move freely around; other parts they are not allowed to enter. When the family watches the t.v. the servant is allowed to watch also, but only while standing in a doorway. The servant may have a radio in his/her room, also a dresser and a cot. Perhaps a mirror. There will usually be one ceiling light. And one small square louvered window.

A true story: One middle-class Jamaican woman ordered a Persian rug from Harrod's in London. The day it arrived so did her new maid. She was going downtown to have her hair touched up, and told the maid to vacuum the rug. She told the maid she would find the vacuum cleaner in the same shed as the power mower. And when she returned she found that the fine nap of her new rug had been removed.

continued to next page

The reaction of the mistress was to tell her friends that the "girl" was backward. She did not fire her until she found that the maid had scrubbed the teflon from her new set of pots, saying she thought they were coated with "nastiness."

The houseworker/mistress relationship in which one Black woman is the oppressor of another Black woman is a cornerstone of the experience of many Jamaican women.

I remember another true story: In a middle-class family's home one Christmas, a relation was visiting from New York. This woman had brought gifts for everybody, including the housemaid. The maid had been released from a mental institution recently, where they had "treated" her for depression. This visiting light-skinned woman had brought the dark woman a bright red rayon blouse, and presented it to her in the garden one afternoon, while the family was having tea. The maid thanked her softly, and the other woman moved toward her as if to embrace her. Then she stopped, her face suddenly covered with tears, and ran into the house, saying, "My God, I can't, I can't."

We are women who come from a place almost incredible in its beauty. It is a beauty which can mask a great deal, and which has been used in that way. But that the beauty is there is a fact. I remember what I thought the freedom of my childhood, in which the fruitful place was something I took for granted. Just as I took for granted Zoe's appearance every morning on my school vacations—in the sense that I knew she would be there. That she would always be the one to visit me. The perishing world of my grandfather's graces at the table, if I ever seriously thought about it, was somewhere else.

Our souls were affected by the beauty of Jamaica, as much as they were affected by our fears of darkness.

There is no ending to this piece of writing. There is no way to end it. As I read back over it, I see that we/they/I may become confused in the mind of the reader: but these pronouns have always co-existed in my mind. The Rastas talk of the "I and I"—a pronoun in which they combine themselves with Jah. Jah is a contraction of Jahweh and Jehova, but to me always sounds like the beginning of Jamaica. I and Jamaica is who I am. No matter

continued on page 168

75

80

continued from page 167

how far I travel—how deep the ambivalence I feel about ever returning. And Jamaica is a place in which we/they/I connect and disconnect—change place.

---

[1] For this piece I owe a debt to Ama Ata Aidoo and her brilliant book *Our Sister Killjoy or Reflections from a Black-Eyed Squint* (Lagos and New York: Nok Publishers, 1979). [Author's note]

ENCOUNTER THE SUBJECT

All the texts included in this chapter take as their subjects experiences that have had lasting significance to their writers. Consider your encounters with the subjects of some or all of these texts—the process of writing, ambivalence about cultural identity, an important national monument. Are any of these subjects significant in your own life? What in your own personal and educational histories might have made them significant?

RESEARCH OPPORTUNITY

To expand on your encounter with at least one of these texts, research its subject. If you choose to focus on Harjo's text, you might explore Native American culture by doing a **library search** to find and critically read credible sources, or you might **interview** an expert in Native American studies on your campus. If you're focusing on Cliff's text, you might locate one of the many outside sources she cites and read it critically.

RESPONSIVE JOURNAL WRITING

Respond to the results of your research activities in the form of a journal entry. In what ways has researching your subject changed your perspective? In what ways has your initial perspective remained the same?

LISTEN—READ CAREFULLY FOR MEANING

COLLABORATIVE WRITING ASSIGNMENT

Explore the meaning of at least one of three essays in collaboration with your classmates. This collaboration can be done in the classroom or in small study and research groups beyond the classroom. Start the collaboration in groups of three or four. As you work, have one member of the group record your collaborative (or differing) conclusions. After concentrated group work, open the discussion up to full-class conversation.

RESEARCH UNKNOWNS.   When we read personal experience texts, we often encounter ways of living and thinking that are foreign to us. Some of these texts may contain cultural or experiential references that leave you with questions. If you have questions about anything in the text (or texts) you're exploring, use the resources on your campus to find answers.

ANALYZE THE SPEAKER.   Here you're going to start digging into the developmental material in the text. Your evidence-supported judgments about the speaker will help you focus on what's actually going on in the text.

Facts

From your reading, what factual information can you gather about each speaker? Make sure that you cite specific passages from the texts to support your judgments. In addition, can you gather factual information about the speaker from research?

Emotions

Where in each text does the speaker reveal her emotional reactions to the subject? What are those emotions, and how does the speaker communicate them to the reader?

Attitudes

Where in the texts does each speaker draw conclusive judgments about the subject, and what are those judgments?

DETERMINE THE MESSAGE.   Because personal experience texts can be written for any general audience-based purpose, they

continued on page 170

continued from page 169
can range in persuasiveness from the delicately exploratory to the openly argumentative. Texts at the argumentative end of the persuasive spectrum will have strong, clear-cut messages that are easily discerned. However, texts on the exploratory end of the spectrum are more likely to have subtle messages closer to dominant impressions than main ideas. To discern these subtle messages, you'll have to concentrate hard on the writer's revealed emotions and attitudes. With this in mind, after conversation with your collaborative partners, write down in as few words as possible your determination of each text's message.

DETERMINE THE AUDIENCE.   Making sure that you provide evidence from the text to support your judgments, describe in as much detail as possible the audience to whom each text is directed. As you make your determination, focus on age, gender, cultural background, educational level, and possible perspective.

DETERMINE THE PURPOSE.   As I said earlier, personal experience narratives can be written for any writer or audience-based purpose or for a mixture of purposes. With this in mind, make a determination of the general purpose (or purposes) of each text.

In addition, make a judgment about the specific purpose of each text. What specific change in knowledge, thought, or action does the writer seek from her audience?

RESPONSIVE JOURNAL WRITING

Assess the effect of the critical reading process by journal writing. If your perspective on the subject of the text was changed in any way by the critical reading process, write at least a page in which you explain the changes. If your perspective wasn't changed, write at least a page explaining why it wasn't.

COLLABORATIVE RESEARCH OPPORTUNITY

Now that you've read the text carefully, you may be left with questions about the writer or about the subject. Focus on your questions, and brainstorm research activities that might lead you to answers. Then pursue one or more of the activities that came out of your brainstorming. See Chapter Six, "Secondary Research," for more information about researching in a collaborative group.

RESPONSIVE JOURNAL WRITING

Respond to the results of your research by exploring your findings in a journal entry.

LEARN—READ WITH AN EYE TO THE WRITER'S CRAFT

FOCUS ON DRAMATIC ACTIVITY IN PERSONAL EXPERIENCE WRITING

Personal experience narratives center on the drama of change. As you proceed to collaboratively study the writers' choices in the texts you're exploring, focus your attention on the dramatic activity in each text. Who are the people involved in the experience? What significant actions do they engage in? What are the motives behind those actions, and what are the actions' consequences?

FOCUS ON PERSUASION IN PERSONAL EXPERIENCE WRITING

LOGOS.   **Persuading with Reason.** Effective personal experience writing appeals to our powers of reason just as all effective writing does. To draw us in and change us, the personal experience texts we encounter have to make sense to us. However, often (but not always) writers of personal experience texts don't openly state their conclusive judgments; instead, they tell us illustrative stories and make us do the work of drawing conclusions. Take, for example, paragraph 77 of Cliff's "If I Could Write This in Fire, I Would Write This in Fire," where Cliff presents a story and allows us to make a judgment about its significance:

> I remember another true story: In a middle-class family's home one Christmas, a relation was visiting from New York. This woman had brought gifts for everybody, including the housemaid. The maid had been released from a mental institution recently, where they had "treated" her for depression. This visiting light-skinned woman had brought the dark woman a bright red rayon blouse, and presented it to her in the garden one afternoon, while the family was having tea. The maid thanked her softly, and the other woman moved toward her as if to embrace her. Then she stopped, her face suddenly covered with tears, and ran into the house, saying, "My God, I can't, I can't."

In addition, often the developmental material in personal experience writing doesn't just make sense to us; it makes *surprising* sense. It reminds us of things from our own experience that we've forgotten, or it invites us to extend what is logical in our own experience into totally new situations. Lowry's description of herself as saying, " 'Look. Look at that,' out loud and to nobody at all" at the sight of the sky behind the Lincoln Memorial reminds us that talking out loud to no one at the sight of something beautiful is something most of us have experienced.

PATHOS.   **Persuading with Emotion.** Because personal experience narratives take as their subjects stories that have lasting significance to their writers, they invariably appeal to our emotions. However, because personal experience writing is dramatic and illustrative, the appeals employed often blend together so that a single action in a text can appeal both to our reason and to our emotions. For example, take Lowry's reaction to the sky behind the Lincoln Memorial: it makes sense to us, but it also invites us to respond emotionally.

ETHOS.   **Persuading by Establishing Credibility.** Although the general credibility of any writer in any writing situation depends to a large degree on the solidity of his or her reasonable and emotional appeals, more often than not, writers of personal experience texts establish their credibility by creating personas that are self-critical and fair, rather than self-serving and smug. Lowry makes this point very well in "Getting to Know Mister Lincoln":

Hired to teach classes in the personal essay, I suggested to my students that when feeling confused about the form, they take a walk to the memorial and read those speeches. There they would find out the difference between certainty and smugness, between modesty and ambivalence.

COLLABORATIVE WRITING ASSIGNMENT

In collaborative groups, study the writers' choices in the texts you're focusing on with an eye to improving your own skill at personal experience writing.

VOICE   In personal experience texts, voice is used as a developmental detail in itself; the writer creates a **persona** that reflects his or her attitude toward the subject being written about. Some of the essays included in this chapter have subtle voices that only suggest their writers' attitudes; the writers have made choices in wording and sentence structure that accumulate to create a dominant impression on the audience. In others, the writers' attitudes are direct and clearly defined. With what I've said in mind, describe in as much detail as possible (or draw a detailed picture of) the created persona in the text you're exploring. As usual, make sure you provide evidence from the text to support your determinations.

DEVELOPMENT   As I suggested earlier, the developmental material in personal experience narratives centers on the dramatic activity of people in particular places and times. Like short stories and novels, personal experience texts are narratives that contain **characters** who engage in **actions** (including the dramatic interaction of conversation) in **settings.** With this in mind, identify those passages in the text you're exploring where the writer describes people, actions, or places. In each passage you've identified, what conclusion does the writer invite you to make?

In addition, since personal experience texts take as their subjects experiences that have lasting significance to their writers, personal narratives are also apt to include writing that seeks **emotional responses** from their audiences. With this in mind,

continued on page 174

continued from page 173

identify those passages in the text where the writer is appealing to the audience's emotions.

ARRANGEMENT   All the selections included in this chapter proceed in chronologicl **order** to one degree or another. Personal narratives do, after all, center on dramatic situations that have proceeded through time. However, writers of personal narratives don't simply record experiences; they also interpret their significance. All these writers have made choices about where to begin and end their narratives and also about where to drop out of them and include commentary, and they've made those choices with the meaning they want to communicate in mind.

Working collaboratively, outline the texts you're focusing on. Then explore the possible reasons behind each writer's choices in arrangement.

RESPOND—DEVELOP A PERSPECTIVE THROUGH WRITING

It's almost time for you to respond to your own experience by writing. However, before you do, read what two other student writers have to say about their personal experiences.

Shiro Sakai

JULY 7th, 1991

Shiro Sakai is an exchange student from Japan majoring in business at The University of Montana.

I grew up with fairly little influence of family religion. The typical Japanese family is not inclined to force the daily practice of Buddhism on the younger generation. My parents seemed indifferent to religion. The only time I visited a temple, I was always

continued to next page

with my grandfather. Unlike my parents, he believed in the spirits of family ancestors that Buddhists usually pray for. He had a family Buddhist altar in his house, and every morning and night, he lit incense and a few candles, served little cups of food and water, and put his hands together to pray for another peaceful day.

He used to say that it was important to remember one's ancestors with respect and appreciate their protection over him. I was unsure if I could connect my feelings to the practices of Buddhism. It was far beyond me to believe in ancestors whom I had never seen nor spoken to. I simply went "through the motions" and considered Buddhist practice something that I was supposed to do.

My grandfather died on July 7th, 1991. I found out on July 14th, the day I came back from the United States. The plane landed at Narita International Airport two hours late. After a long, exhausting ten-hour flight from L.A., I was still overwhelmed with excitement and to see my family again. They were waiting for me on the other side of the gate. My year as a high school exchange student in the States had ended. I was home.

My parents looked tired and a little older. My little sister had grown up considerable in my absence. I was perplexed, not knowing where to start talking about my experiences in the States. I was so excited that I did not even notice a strange air around them. My father did not talk all the way to the hotel. I should have noticed something wrong. We checked into a hotel that night, so I could rest.

We were at the dinner table in the hotel when my father told me that my grandfather had died a week ago and they just finished his funeral a day before. I told him to stop joking, but then I saw the tears in my mother's eyes. All of my excitement disappeared right away, and I was thrown into sorrow. I wept and didn't care about people at the other tables. I wanted to ask someone why this could have happened to me, but I had no one to ask, nor was there anyone to blame.

That night was the most painful one in my life. I felt a great fatigue in my body, but I still couldn't sleep that night. I cried out through the night. I got up from the bed and walked around the hotel by myself. Small things from that early morning, somehow

continued on page 176

continued from page 175

very symbolic, remain vividly in my mind: the bitter taste of the tea I drank; the beautiful sunrise though the hotel window.

My grandfather was the one who had been the most excited about me coming back home; he'd wanted to hear a lot of stories about things I had experienced overseas. A year ago, I had said good-bye to my grandfather; I never expected it was for good. He was well until a few minutes before he died. As a matter of fact, he went to work in the garden, and all of a sudden, his heart stopped. He did not let anybody know that he was dying, not even my grandmother, his devoted wife. After his death, I regretted the fact that we could not spend as much time together as we should have. I still had a lot to learn from him.

I was back home when I saw the altar with my grandfather's name added to it. For the first time, I really spoke to the altar as if I would speak to him. I believed that this altar was a window and through it, my voice would reach him. My religious faith started in a very personal way, person to person, my grandfather and me.

It has been almost three years since the death of my grandfather. Though I am far away from home, I return every July to visit him. I try to remember him as much as I can, because memory is where he lives now. When I am home and stand in front of the altar, I feel a relief knowing my grandmother is not alone. She sits down in front of the altar and talks to him everyday, and does the same things he used to do. She lights incense and a few candles, serves little cups of food and water to him, then puts her hands together to pray for another peaceful day.

Susan Straw-Gusé

I Can Wash My Rugs on Sunday

Susan Straw-Gusé went back to school after twenty-two years. She is currently working on two college degrees, one in English and one in education.

continued to next page

Saturday morning, and Daddy is standing in front of the stove, making pancakes for his seven restless children who are crammed around the kitchen table. If a passerby looks in, they will assume that all is well in the Straw household. They will not notice that underneath there seems a feeling of forced calm. I sit and wonder when the normalcy of the morning will end.

I know from experience, that it could not, it would not last. Who or what will break the fragile aura of peacefulness that surrounds the kitchen? I look around the table and carefully consider each member of my family. I glare at my most likely choices, my older brothers, Randy and Kenny. I silently ask them, "Why do you have to ruin everything? Why can't you behave? Why did you have to be born?" They stare back at me in bewilderment.

I can only imagine what obscene incident they will create to throw the calm and my Daddy out of control. Maybe it will be one of my sisters. Diana, is too prim; Peggy, is too good; and Kathy is Daddy's pet. All that is left to consider is Jeffy, but he's just a baby. What if it is me?

My thoughts are interrupted as Daddy tells me to bring the pancake syrup from the counter to the table. I jump to do his bidding, before he can find fault with anything I might do. We are such a large family and our syrup comes in a glass gallon jug. It is clumsy and awkward, especially for a seven-year-old child. I carefully pull it from the counter into my waiting arms. But the jug doesn't stop. My arms can't seem to hold it. I can feel the panic as I struggle to gain control, but the bottle bangs off my knees and crashes to the floor. I watch as glass and sticky syrup fly everywhere. I can't seem to move; it's as if I am frozen in shock. Syrup is dripping off the hem of my nighty and running in steams down my legs and between my toes. The kitchen carpet, is hungrily soaking up the sticky mess like a sponge. I look up to see the look of horror on the faces around the table, but one face quickly turns to rage. It has happened so often. I know what is coming.

I know what to do. I must escape to the "other side." Daddy screams at the little girl in anger. Daddy hits the little girl, but he can't hurt Susie. I am too fast, I have to leave the little girl to suffer the blows. She must feel the hurt. I silently watch it all unfold

continued on page 178

continued from page 177

from the "other side." This is not a nice place, but it's a place I have been forced to create. It is a cold place of nothingness, blindingly bright. I find it hard for me to breath here. I must stay as an observer, until the worst is over. Nobody can touch me, but I still feel sad. I cry for the little girl.

When it is safe to return, I try to understand Daddy's anger. He must know that I didn't do it on purpose. Can't he see that it was an accident? Why doesn't my Mom help me? I will never treat my children like this. I am so sorry.

Years later I would marry a man, patterned after my Dad, but I refused to be like my Mom. I would never allow my boys to feel that fear. I could not always save myself, but I could protect them.

Boys will always track mud, and my sons were no different. I purchased multiple throw rugs, and it became my routine to turn or switch the rugs every day before their dad came home. It was really no extra effort to wash all the rugs on Sunday, and then start the new week fresh. We became expert co-conspirators in hiding minor mishaps from their dad. It was just easier for me to clean behind them. I did this as much for myself as I did for them. I still would suffer the blinding light of the "other side" when their Dad would punish them.

I have spoiled them terribly, and they are probably ruined for any other woman. They are grown now, and occasionally visit me on weekends. In spite of their Dad, they have become mature, sensitive men. I smile sadly as they still track mud on my rugs, but it is alright, for after they leave, I can wash my rugs on Sunday.

RESPONSIVE WRITING ASSIGNMENT

Write an essay in response to a significant personal experience. After thoroughly exploring the experience, construct a text in which you present both the experience and your perspective on it.

RESPONDING TO PERSONAL EXPERIENCES—A GUIDE TO THE PROCESS

Assess Your Past Performance
Explore the Writing Situation
Prewrite
Draft
Rewrite

ASSESS YOUR PAST PERFORMANCE

Just as writing is a recursive process, the continuing journey toward becoming a better writer is also recursive. As you work through this assignment, **analyze** how you think and write, **learn** from your previous experience, and **respond by revising** your personal writing process. If you've written an assessment of a past performance, read it over and consider your writing strengths and weaknesses. Identify the choice categories with which you had trouble. Did you have trouble with voice? Development? Arrangement? Usage? Then analyze why you had trouble, and focus on ways you might employ the writing process to avoid repeating your mistakes. For example, if the last text you constructed was disorganized, analyze why. Was it because you didn't consider what your audience might need to know? Was it because you "wrote your way into" the paper and then didn't go back and revise? To improve your performance, you'll have to focus more attention on audience analysis and revision in this assignment. Part Five provides detailed strategies for prewriting and process-based revision.

EXPLORE THE WRITING SITUATION

To find an initial direction for your essay, actively explore the choices and constraints of the writing situation.

THE WRITER   Because the subject of this assignment is your own life experience, I've varied the usual order of the writing situation and put you, "the writer," first. As you explore your possible choices of subject, audience, and purpose, **think critically** about your emotional and rational responses. To communicate your perspective on your own experience, you actually must have gained some perspective. And gaining perspective involves having the sufficient rational distance to make critical judgments about the meaning and importance of the experience you choose to write about. The point is, some subjects may be too charged with emotion for you to construct an essay about them at this time. You may have to revisit some experiences again and again (and experience other things) before their meaning becomes clear to you.

However, don't *necessarily* avoid emotionally charged subjects, but *do* think critically about your emotional and rational responses as you explore the writing situation. Personal experience writing focuses on the drama of change, and those events and relationships that change us are invariably emotionally charged. For example, the student essays included in this chapter take as their subjects experiences that were personally devastating to their writers.

SUBJECT   The subject of your essay is constrained only in one way—the experience you choose to write about must be one that is significant to you. Look back at the subjects of the texts included in this chapter for ideas. For example, Cliff's text is written in response to the continuing experience of being a Jamaican woman, while Sakai takes as his subject the death of his grandfather.

Don't get bogged down by thinking that your experiences aren't interesting enough to share with others. Instead, **explore** those **experiences** that have stuck with you over time, searching for the **element of drama** in them. Consider relationships in your life that have been or are deeply meaningful or charged with conflict. Make a list of people who have in some way shaped or challenged you, and focus on their influential actions. The people you list need not be relatives or long-term friends; a chance remark (a putdown or a word of unexpected praise) from someone you've known only briefly may have had a lasting effect on you.

Consider also actions you've undertaken that have challenged you. Make a list of activities you've engaged in that seem totally out of character—things you're proud to have accomplished or regret you were involved in.

In addition, focus on those things that passionately engage you. Make a short list of the activities, people, and places that you feel are crucial to your life (or about which you feel deeply ambivalent), and explore the reasons behind their significance.

AUDIENCE   Although the choice of audience is open in this assignment, because the subject of your writing is your own experience, to some extent you'll be writing to yourself and for yourself. All of the selections in this chapter have writer-based purposes as well as audience-based ones. Straw-Gusé, for example, writes to express her anger as well as to explore her subject with her audience.

However, since you're writing as a member of a community of writers, in addition to writing for yourself, you'll also be writing to an external audience. You might write to someone who shared in your experience or to the general community of your class. To **explore external audience choices,** identify the subjects from your lists of "possibles" that interest you the most. Then, with your emotional and rational responses in mind, consider a range of possible audiences for each subject. Keep in mind that you may be too emotionally encumbered to write comfortably to some audiences. Look over your determinations of audience for the selections you read in this chapter, and imagine how each selection might have been constructed if the writer had chosen to write to a different audience. For example, how might Straw-Gusé's text have been different if she'd chosen to write to her father or to one of her siblings? Why might Straw-Gusé have chosen to write to a distant audience rather than to one directly invovled in the experience?

PURPOSE   Because you'll be writing for yourself *and* for an external audience, you'll be writing for a mixture of general purposes. To **decide on an audience-based purpose** (or purposes), consider the impact each of your possible subjects had on you and the reasons you might want to share each experience with others. If the experience was funny and you think it might engage others, you might want to **entertain** your audience; if your experience was one through which you discovered something or learned a valuable lesson, you might want to **explore** your subject with your audience as Straw-Gusé, Harjo and Lowry do.

TIME   How much time you'll need for this assignment will depend on your subject. You may have been waiting for the opportunity to tell your story, and be ready to go. On the other hand, you may need time to explore the experience to discover its significance. In addition, keep yourself open to the possibility of researching. Although your essay will take as its subject a fragment of your own personal history, you may want (as Cliff and Lowry did) to enhance your perspective by engaging in research as part of the writing process.

If your exploration hasn't triggered a choice of subject, choose from your list of "possibles" and continue to explore it by prewriting.

PREWRITE

RESEARCH OPPORTUNITY

Just because your subject is your own personal history doesn't mean that **research** can't be useful in this assignment. If an experience has challenged or changed you, it's highly likely that a similar experience has challenged or changed other people. You might read a personal essay about an experience like your own to help you view your subject from a different perspective, or you might read a social scientist's analysis of similar situations to help you understand the impact of the experience on your life.

To add to your knowledge and understanding of your subject, **brainstorm** possible research activities. You might **interview** another person who participated in the experience, and widen your perspective by getting an alternative view of things. Or you might **observe** the places where specific actions in the experience occurred; revisiting a significant setting can revive memories and can also help you connect the present with past events. In addition, **consider library research** activities. Do a library search and locate and critically read personal essays or analytical works that deal with subjects similar to your own.

RESPONSIVE PREWRITING ASSIGNMENTS

1. If you've engaged in research, **explore** the findings of your research **in writing.** What additional information did you discover? How has your perspective on the experience been changed by your research? How has it remained the same? Why has it changed or remained the same?

continued to next page

2. Explore the **chronology** of the experience. Write out a **time line.** When did the experience start? How did it proceed? Has it come to an end? If so, when did it end?

3. Spend at least an hour recalling and exploring vivid **sensory details.** Start out by brainstorming or writing double entry notes. See "Problems with Development" in Part Six for more information about both of these prewriting techniques. Let yourself go with the exploration. Don't just record sense impressions that you think might be relevant. Push yourself toward new discoveries as you prewrite. The point is to reconstruct the experience in as much detail as possible to discover more that might be meaningful in it.

What did you **see?** Describe the place (or places), the people involved, and their actions.
What did you **hear?** Describe the sounds. Focus on people's voices and on their dialogue; focus on nonhuman noises— sounds made by machines or animals; focus on background noises or on the lack of background noise.
What did you **touch** or **feel** with your body? Describe the textures or sensations.
What did you **smell?** Describe the smells.
What did you **taste?** Describe the things you tasted as well as the way they tasted.

4. Explore the **dramatic activity** (include yourself in this exploration). **Brainstorm, freewrite,** or **employ double-entry notes.** Also consider drawing caricatures of the personalities of active participants. See "Problems with Development" in Part Six for further discussions of all these prewriting strategies.

Who participated in the experience?
What actions were engaged in?
What were the motives behind those actions?
What were the actions' consequences?

5. Explore your **emotional responses** and any **changes** in those responses. For ideas, consider emotional changes in the personal experience essays that you encountered in this chapter or through researching.

continued on page 184

continued from page 183

How *did* you feel about each person involved in the experience (including yourself)? Have your feelings changed in any way? If so, how?

How *did* you feel about the place? Have your feelings changed in any way? If so, how?

How *did* you feel about the experience in general? Have your feelings about it changes in any way? If so, how?

6. To determine your **perspective,** explore the consequences of the experience as a whole. How were you and/or others changed by the experience? Was the change subtle or profound?

FOCUS ON AUDIENCE AND PURPOSE

Look back over the results of your prewriting so far, and focus on your possible choices of audience and purpose.

AUDIENCE   Although you may want to write your essay partly for writer-based purposes, keep in mind that you're a member of a community of writers; even if you're writing primarily for yourself, someone else will read your essay. If you've made a choice of audience(s), proceed to analyze that audience. If you haven't yet chosen an audience, focus on people who might be interested in sharing in your experience, and make a tentative choice. Then write out a detailed description of your audience, focusing on their knowledge of the subject and possible perspective. Reread the results of your prewriting and identify those people, places, and actions that would be most interesting to your readers. Considering your audience's knowledge and perspective, are there any details that might be added to your prewriting?

PURPOSE   To get a clear idea of your general audience-based purpose or purposes for writing, reread the results of your prewriting and focus on how you want other people to be **changed** by sharing in your experience. Do you want to change their knowledge of the world by **informing** or **explaining?** Do you want to change the way they think by **exploring** or **explaining** or **entertaining?** Do you want to change the way they act by **persuading?**

Then focus on the specific change you desire in your audience. What specifically do you want them to know or think, or how do you want them to act as a result of reading your essay?

FOCUS ON A WORKING MESSAGE

The messages of your text will have a lot to do with your audience-based general purposes for writing. If your essay is argumentative, your message will most likely be openly stated. (See Chapter Nine for more information about formulating messages in argumentative writing.) If your text isn't argumentative, the message you send may be more like a dominant impression than a main idea. To focus on a subtle message, consider the impact the experience had on you, and explore that impact in writing. For ideas, look over your determinations of message for the selections in this chapter.

If you haven't yet chosen a working message, don't be overly concerned. You may actually have to begin drafting (or even complete an entire draft) before the meaning or importance of the experience becomes clear to you. However, *do* continue to be actively self-critical. Not being able to decide on a working message could be an indication that you're too close to the experience to write effectively about it for an external audience. Like Cliff, you may have to experience or learn more before you can understand the significance of the particular experience.

If you have decided on a working message, write it down in as few words as possible.

DRAFT

DRAFT TO REVISE

The **revision** you engage in as you draft gives you the opportunity to expand on old ideas and formulate new ones. **Read** and **reread** your draft as you write, and look for new ways of viewing your subject. Pay particular attention to those parts of the process that have given you trouble in the past, and **revise** as you draft by **cutting, adding, rearranging,** and **rewording.**

As you draft, keep foremost in your mind that personal experience essays focus on dramatic activity. The text you're constructing, like all personal experience texts, should show people acting and/or interacting to bring about change.

FOCUS ON YOUR CHOICES

VOICE   To create an appropriate voice, consider your attitude toward your subject. Harjo's wonder-filled voice, for example, communicates her attitude that writing is an open-ended, exploratory adventure. However, as you consider your attitude toward your subject, continue to be self-critical. If your attitude is not an honest one, your voice will reflect your dishonesty, and your choices in development will very likely follow that dishonesty. For ideas, study your characterizations of the voices in the essays you have read in this chatper. One of the main reasons we trust these writers is because they aren't self-serving; instead, they've created personas that are actively self-critical. Although Cliff and Straw-Gusé both communicate anger, the knowledgeable, clear-headed personas they create on the page keep their texts from being mere emotional rants. With your audience in mind, write a detailed description (or draw a detailed picture) of the voice you believe will most likely achieve your purpose. Then, as you draft, read your emerging text aloud, and **reword** with your audience's responses in mind.

DEVELOPMENT   As you make choices in development, focus on the dramatic activity in the experience you're writing about and on its connection to the message of your story. If you haven't yet chosen a message, search for meaning in the actions of yourself and others involved in the experience. Look for ways of **cutting** material that might lead your audience away from your focus. Flesh out the significant people (the characters) in your story by **adding** details that will make their significance apparent to your audience; identify and describe important actions they engaged in, including the dialogue of conversation; consider also the motives behind their actions and the consequences of those actions. For ideas, look back at the characters in the selections you've read in this chapter (and in any personal essays you may have read while researching).

Keep in mind, however, that personal experience texts need not be *purely* dramatic narratives. In addition to dramatic action, you may also wish to comment on your experience and/or cite outside sources. The developmental material in "If I Could Write This in Fire, I Would Write This in Fire" is a masterful mixture of experiential and scholarly writing. Cliff moves back and forth between telling stories and citing and commenting on outside sources to create a text that fully and purposefully integrates her personal and educational histories. Perhaps more than any other selection in this book, Cliff's piece illustrates the personal usefulness of an academic education.

Remember also that voice and development are very closely connected. The reason Cliff's voice is knowledgeable and authoritative instead of merely angry is because she provides convincing evidence that justifies her anger.

ARRANGEMENT   The essay you're constructing will be to some extent chronologically ordered. You are, after all, writing about an experience that proceeded through time to bring about a change. However, depending on your purpose and subject, you may choose to drop out of the straight chronology of your story to comment or add information. You may even choose to tell more than one story. Cliff, for example, tells Zoe's story, along with many other stories, as she tells the story of her continuing relationship with Jamaica.

As you draft, **rearrange the order** of sentences, paragraphs, or sections of your text with your audience's responses in mind. If you draft on a computer, use the block and move functions to rearrange. If you type or draft longhand, write on only one side of the page so that you can cut sections apart and rearrange them.

DRAFTING IS ACTIVE AND RECURSIVE

Continue to be self-critical throughout the process of drafting your essay. Question the conclusions you draw, and continue to search for new meaning in each action you describe.

REWRITE

To write an effective personal experience essay, you have to maintain a balance between audience and writer-based purposes. Remember, because the text you're constructing takes as its subject your own experience, part of your purpose for writing is undoubtedly writer-based. However, you're also writing to *move* an external audience in some way. Test the effectiveness of your draft by **workshopping** it in an informal collaborative group. (Part Six provides strategies for peer editing and workshops.) Ask your collaborative partners to read your essay carefully and to focus, first, on your voice. What attitude does your voice convey? Then ask them to focus on the dramatic activity in the text. What actions take place in your story? What are the changes brought about by those actions? Finally, ask them to determine what your audience and writer-based purposes are and what your message is.

ACTIVE REWRITING

Don't just make superficial style changes. Be active. Search for new discoveries as you revise. Consider your workshop partners' criticisms, your habitual writing weaknesses, and the techniques for responding to personal experiences. Read your draft critically, focusing on the following checklist, and continue to **cut, add, rearrange,** and **reword** with your audience's responses in mind.

- Does your text have clearly discernible writer and audience-based purposes?

- Does your text communicate a clear message or at least a dominant impression about the meaning or importance of your experience?
- Does your text focus on the dramatic activity in your story? Have you described significant people in sufficient detail? Have you focused on their actions and on the consequences of those actions?
- Have you focused on and described significant details in the setting (or settings) where the experience took place?
- Have you arranged the material in your essay with your audience in mind? Will the chronology be clear to an external audience?
- Is your text correct in terms of mechanics and the technical aspects of voice (spelling, punctuation, sentence structure, and diction)?

EDIT TO FINAL FORM

Polish your text as you write the final draft. Focus on paragraphing, transitions, and any habitual problems you may have with spelling, punctuation, and sentence structure. Part Six provides specific information and strategies.

PROOFREAD

If possible, put your response aside for at least a couple of hours before you proofread. Proofread for small, careless errors by reading your text aloud, preferably to another person.

ASSESS YOUR PERFORMANCE BY WRITING CRITICALLY

The process of writing any essay isn't completed until you've analyzed your performance. Study the comments on your evaluated paper, and focus on **voice, arrangement, development,** and **mechanics.** Part Six provides detailed strategies for analyzing your writing weaknesses and learning through self-criticism. With which category of choice did you mainly have trouble? Write a page explaining why you had trouble with that particular category. Then write a second page in which you explain what you might have done to correct the problem.

CHAPTER
EIGHT
RESPONDING TO PROCESSES

THE WRITER'S SCENARIO

A writer encounters a process. The process might be something the writer encounters in an academic discipline—cell division in biology or social mobility in sociology. The process might be something the writer encounters in personal life—beekeeping or childrearing or even (as you'll see later in this chapter) dog mushing. Then the writer continues to encounter the process by describing and/or analyzing it in writing.

Consider the processes you have encountered in your life. A process is a series of interrelated actions or operations that brings about a product or a result. Making a loaf of bread is a process. Writing a paper is a process. Reading a text critically is a process. Processes are chronologically ordered and causally connected, but the interrelated operations that make them up are not necessarily fixed. For example, when you make a cup of tea, you don't *have* to get a mug out of the cupboard *before* you put the kettle on. However, at some point you do have to make sure the dry tea and the water get together.

Every day, in the academic community and out of it, we encounter processes that vary in their complexity. Some of the processes we encounter are easy to understand (making a cup of tea, for instance), but the workings of some are complex and difficult to grasp. Think of the times in your own life when you tried to understand a complex process and wound up being frustrated and confused. You may have been assembling a bicycle, doing your taxes, or working out a mathematical proof, and some element in the process kept eluding you, blocking your ability to proceed.

The ability to critically read and write texts that describe and/or analyze complex processes is crucial both in the academic community and in the world at large. The world you live in is a world of complex and interrelated processes, and the more you practice thinking critically about the processes you encounter, the more you'll learn and understand. Understanding the process of property taxation in your community by critically reading texts that describe and analyze it will enable you to make an informed decision about which way to vote on a local mill levy. Writing critically about the complex processes you encounter in your college courses (child language acquisition in linguistics, the workings of the stock market in finance, the operations of a proof in mathematics) will enable you to understand those processes more thoroughly. Some of the process texts you'll produce in the context of your college classes will be written for outside audiences. However, process writing can also be highly useful as a study tool. To become an effective reader and writer of process writing, consider the following techniques.

TECHNIQUES FOR RESPONDING TO PROCESSES

1. Familiarize yourself with the process by researching or exploring it thoroughly.
2. Identify the actions or operations that make up the process, and analyze them to determine their significance and their relationship to each other and to the process as a whole.
3. Analyze your audience to determine what they know about the subject and what they need to know.
4. Present the process and your evidence-supported analysis with your audience's knowledge and perspective in mind.

RESPONDING TO PROCESSES: PROFESSIONAL WRITING

FOCUS ON THE WRITER'S PURPOSE

Although all process texts are to some extent **explanatory,** they are often written for additional audience-based or writer-based general purposes. Process texts range in their persuasiveness from the simply explanatory to the openly **argumentative.** In nonargumentative process writing, the analysis centers on the importance of particular operations in the process and on their relationship to one another and to the process as a whole. For example, if you were writing to an incoming freshman on your campus to explain the registration process, your analysis would most likely focus on the purpose and relative importance of each step in the process.

However, in an argumentative process text, the writer not only focuses on the importance of particular operations and on their significance, but also makes negative or positive judgments about those operations or about the process as a whole. For example, if you were writing to convince administrators on your campus to work to revamp the inefficient registration process, your analysis would include negative judgments about part or all of that process.

As you actively preread and study the selections included in this chapter, pay particular attention to the writer's purpose (or purposes) in each text.

PREREAD

To familiarize yourself with one or more of the following selections, actively preread. **Read the first three paragraphs** slowly, focusing on those things in the text you understand. When you get to the end of the third paragraph, stop and take stock. **Summarize** what's gone on in the text so far. If you're confused, go back and **reread,** searching for meaning. Then **predict** the direction you think the text will take next. As you continue reading, pause after each of the remaining paragraphs to **summarize, reread** if necessary, and **predict.**

LEARNING TO READ
Malcolm X

The following selection from the Autobiography of Malcolm X, *written by Malcolm X in collaboration with the late writer Alex Haley, was originally published in 1964, the year before Malcolm X's assassination.*

It was because of my letters that I happened to stumble upon starting to acquire some kind of a homemade education.

I became increasingly frustrated at not being able to express what I wanted to convey in letters that I wrote, especially those to Mr. Elijah Muhammad.[1] In the street, I had been the most articulate hustler out there—I had commanded attention when I said something. But now, trying to write simple English, I not only wasn't articulate, I wasn't even functional. How would I sound writing in slang, the way I would *say* it, something such as, "Look, daddy, let me pull your coat about a cat, Elijah Muhammad—"

Many who today hear me somewhere in person, or on television, or those who read something I've said, will think I went

continued on page 192

continued from page 191

to school far beyond the eighth grade. This impression is due entirely to my prison studies.

It had really begun back in the Charlestown Prison, when Bimbi[2] first made me feel envy of his stock of knowledge. Bimbi had always taken charge of any conversations he was in, and I had tried to emulate him. But every book I picked up had few sentences which didn't contain anywhere from one to nearly all of the words that might as well have been in Chinese. When I just skipped those words, of course, I really ended up with little idea of what the book said. So I had come to the Norfolk Prison Colony still going through only book-reading motions. Pretty soon, I would have quit even these motions, unless I had received the motivation that I did.

5   I saw that the best thing I could do was get hold of a dictionary—to study, to learn some words. I was lucky enough to reason also that I should try to improve my penmanship. It was sad. I couldn't even write in a straight line. It was both ideas together that moved me to request a dictionary along with some tablets and pencils from the Norfolk Prison Colony school.

I spent two days just riffling uncertainly through the dictionary's pages. I'd never realized so many words existed! I didn't know *which* words I needed to learn. Finally, just to start some kind of action, I began copying.

In my slow, painstaking, ragged handwriting, I copied into my tablet everything printed on that first page, down to the punctuation marks.

I believe it took me a day. Then, aloud, I read back, to myself, everything I'd written on the tablet. Over and over, aloud, to myself, I read my own handwriting.

I woke up the next morning, thinking about those words— immensely proud to realize that not only had I written so much at one time, but I'd written words that I never knew were in the world. Moreover, with a little effort, I also could remember what many of these words meant. I reviewed the words whose meanings I didn't remember. Funny thing, from the dictionary first page right now, that "aardvark" springs to mind. The dictionary had a picture of it, a long-tailed, long-eared, burrowing African

continued to next page

mammal, which lives off termites caught by sticking out its tongue as an anteater does for ants.

I was so fascinated that I went on—I copied the dictionary's next page. And the same experience came when I studied that. With every succeeding page, I also learned of people and places and events from history. Actually the dictionary is like a miniature encyclopedia. Finally the dictionary's A section had filled a whole tablet—and I went on into the B's. That was the way I started copying what eventually became the entire dictionary. It went a lot faster after so much practice helped me to pick up handwriting speed. Between what I wrote in my tablet, and writing letters, during the rest of my time in prison I would guess I wrote a million words.

I suppose it was inevitable that as my word-base broadened, I could for the first time pick up a book and read and now begin to understand what the book was saying. Anyone who has read a great deal can imagine the new world that opened. Let me tell you something: from then until I left that prison, in every free moment I had, if I was not reading in the library, I was reading on my bunk. You couldn't have gotten me out of books with a wedge. Between Mr. Muhammad's teachings, my correspondence, my visitors, . . . and my reading of books, months passed without my even thinking about being imprisoned. In fact, up to then, I never had been so truly free in my life.

The Norfolk Prison Colony's library was in the school building. A variety of classes was taught there by instructors who came from such places as Harvard and Boston universities. The weekly debates between inmate teams were also held in the school building. You would be astonished to know how worked up convict debaters and audiences would get over subjects like "Should Babies Be Fed Milk?"

Available on the prison library's shelves were books on just about every general subject. Much of the big private collection that Parkhurst[3] had willed to the prison was still in crates and boxes in the back of the library—thousands of old books. Some of them looked ancient: covers faded, old-time parchment-looking binding. Parkhurst . . . seemed to have been principally interested in history and religion. He had the money and the special

continued on page 194

10

continued from page 193

interest to have a lot of books that you wouldn't have in a general circulation. Any college library would have been lucky to get that collection.

As you can imagine, especially in a prison where there was heavy emphasis on rehabilitation, an inmate was smiled upon if he demonstrated an unusually intense interest in books. There was a sizable number of well-read inmates, especially the popular debaters. Some were said by many to be practically walking encyclopedias. They were almost celebrities. No university would ask any student to devour literature as I did when this new world opened to me, of being able to read and *understand*.

15

I read more in my room than in the library itself. An inmate who was known to read a lot could check out more than the permitted maximum number of books. I preferred reading in the total isolation of my own room.

When I had progressed to really serious reading, every night at about ten P.M. I would be outraged with the "lights out." It always seemed to catch me right in the middle of something engrossing.

Fortunately, right outside my door was a corridor light that cast a glow into my room. The glow was enough to read by, once my eyes adjusted to it. So when "lights out" came, I would sit on the floor where I could continue reading in that glow.

At one-hour intervals the night guards paced past every room. Each time I heard the approaching footsteps, I jumped into bed and feigned sleep. And as soon as the guard passed, I got back out of bed onto the floor area of that light-glow, where I would read for another fifty-eight minutes—until the guard approached again. That went on until three or four every morning. Three or four hours of sleep a night was enough for me. Often in the years in the streets I had slept less than that.

The teachings of Mr. Muhammad stressed how history had been "whitened"—when white men had written history books, the black man simply had been left out. Mr. Muhammad couldn't have said anything that would have struck me much harder. I had never forgotten how when my class, me and all of those

continued to next page

whites, had studied seventh-grade United States history back in Mason, the history of the Negro had been covered in one paragraph, and the teacher had gotten a big laugh with his joke, "Negroes' feet are so big that when they walk, they leave a hole in the ground."

This is one reason why Mr. Muhammad's teachings spread so swiftly all over the United States, among *all* Negroes, whether or not they became followers of Mr. Muhammad. The teachings ring true—to every Negro. You can hardly show me a black adult in America—or a white one, for that matter—who knows from the history books anything like the truth about the black man's role. In my own case, once I heard of the "glorious history of the black man," I took special pains to hunt in the library for books that would inform me on details about black history.

20

I can remember accurately the very first set of books that really impressed me. I have since bought that set of books and I have it at home for my children to read as they grow up. It's called *Wonders of the World*. It's full of pictures of archeological finds, statues that depict, usually, non-European people.

I found books like Will Durant's[4] *Story of Civilization.* I read H. G. Wells'[5] *Outline of History. Souls of Black Folk* by W. E. B. Du Bois[6] gave me a glimpse into the black people's history before they came to this country. Carter G. Woodson's[7] *Negro History* opened my eyes about black empires before the black slave was brought to the United States, and the early Negro struggles for freedom.

J A. Rogers'[8] three volumes of *Sex and Race* told about race-mixing before Christ's time; and Aesop being a black man who told fables; about Egypt's Pharaohs; about the great Coptic Christian Empires;[9] about Ethiopia, the earth's oldest continuous black civilization, as China is the oldest continuous civilization.

Mr. Muhammad's teaching about how the white man had been created led me to *Findings in Genetics* by Gregor Mendel.[10] (The dictionary's G section was where I had learned what "genetics" meant.) I really studied this book by the Austrian monk. Reading it over and over, especially certain sections, helped me to understand that if you started with a black man, a white man could be produced; but starting with a white man, you never

continued on page 196

continued from page 195

could produce a black man—because the white chromosome is recessive. And since no one disputes that there was but one Original Man, the conclusion is clear.

25   During the last year or so, in the *New York Times*, Arnold Toynbee[11] used the word "bleached" in describing the white man. His words were: "White (i.e., bleached) human beings of North European origin. . . ." Toynbee also referred to the European geographic area as only a peninsula of Asia. He said there is no such thing as Europe. And if you look at the globe, you will see for yourself that America is only an extension of Asia. (But at the same time Toynbee is among those who have helped to bleach history. He has written that Africa was the only continent that produced no history. He won't write that again. Every day now, the truth is coming to light.)

I never will forget how shocked I was when I began reading about slavery's total horror. It made such an impact upon me that it later became one of my favorite subjects when I became a minister of Mr. Muhammad's. The world's most monstrous crime, the sin and the blood on the white man's hands, are almost impossible to believe. Books like the one by Frederick Olmsted[12] opened my eyes to the horrors suffered when the slave was landed in the United States. The European woman, Fanny Kemble,[13] who had married a Southern white slaveowner, described how human beings were degraded. Of course I read *Uncle Tom's Cabin*.[14] In fact, I believe that's the only novel I have ever read since I started serious reading.

Parkhurst's collection also contained some bound pamphlets of the Abolitionist[15] Anti-Slavery Society of New England. I read descriptions of atrocities, saw those illustrations of black slave women tied up and flogged with whips; of black mothers watching their babies being dragged off, never to be seen by their mothers again; of dogs after slaves, and of the fugitive slave catchers, evil white men with whips and clubs and chains and guns. I read about the slave preacher Nat Turner, who put the fear of God into the white slavemaster. Nat Turner wasn't going around preaching pie-in-the-sky and "non-violent" freedom for the black man. There in Virginia one night in 1831, Nat and seven other slaves started out at his master's home and through the night they went

continued to next page

from one plantation "big house" to the next, killing, until by the next morning 57 white people were dead and Nat had about 70 slaves following him. White people, terrified for their lives, fled from their homes, locked themselves up in public buildings, hid in the woods, and some even left the state. A small army of soldiers took two months to catch and hang Nat Turner. Somewhere I have read where Nat Turner's example is said to have inspired John Brown[16] to invade Virginia and attack Harpers Ferry nearly thirty years later, with thirteen white men and five Negroes.

I read Herodotus,[17] "the father of History," or, rather, I read about him. And I read the histories of various nations, which opened my eyes gradually, then wider and wider, to how the whole world's white men had indeed acted like devils, pillaging and raping and bleeding and draining the whole world's non-white people. I remember, for instance, books such as Will Durant's *The Story of Oriental Civilization,* and Mahatma Gandhi's[18] accounts of the struggle to drive the British out of India.

Book after book showed me how the white man had brought upon the world's black, brown, red, and yellow peoples every variety of the sufferings of exploitation. I saw how since the sixteenth century, the so-called "Christian trader" white man began to ply the seas in his lust for Asian and African empires, and plunder, and power. I read, I saw, how the white man never has gone among the non-white peoples bearing the Cross in the true manner and spirit of Christ's teachings—meek, humble, and Christlike.

I perceived, as I read, how the collective white man had been actually nothing but a piratical opportunist who used Faustian machinations[19] to make his own Christianity his initial wedge in criminal conquests. First, always "religiously," he branded "heathen" and "pagan" labels upon ancient non-white cultures and civilizations. The stage thus set, he then turned upon his non-white victims his weapons of war.

I read how, entering India—half a *billion* deeply religious brown people—the British white man, by 1759, through promises, trickery, and manipulations, controlled much of India through Great Britain's East India Company. The parasitical British administration kept tentacling out to half of the sub-continent. In 1857, some of the desperate people of India finally mutinied—

30

continued on page 198

continued from page 197

and, excepting the African slave trade, nowhere has history recorded any more unnecessary bestial and ruthless human carnage than the British suppression of the non-white Indian people.

Over 115 million African blacks—close to the 1930's population of the United States—were murdered or enslaved during the slave trade. And I read how when the slave market was glutted, the cannibalistic white powers of Europe next carved up, as their colonies, the richest areas of the black continent. And Europe's chancelleries for the next century played a chess game of naked exploitation and power from Cape Horn to Cairo.

Ten guards and the warden couldn't have torn me out of those books. Not even Elijah Muhammad could have been more eloquent than those books were in providing indisputable proof that the collective white man had acted like a devil in virtually every contact he had with the world's collective non-white man. I listen today to the radio, and watch television, and read the headlines about the collective white man's fear and tension concerning China. When the white man professes ignorance about why the Chinese hate him so, my mind can't help flashing back to what I read, there in prison, about how the blood forebears of this same white man raped China at a time when China was trusting and helpless. Those original white "Christian traders" sent into China millions of pounds of opium. By 1839, so many of the Chinese were addicts that China's desperate government destroyed twenty thousand chests of opium. The first Opium War[20] was promptly declared by the white man. Imagine! Declaring *war* upon someone who objects to being narcotized! The Chinese were severely beaten, with Chinese-invented gunpowder.

The Treaty of Nanking made China pay the British white man for the destroyed opium; forced open China's major ports to British trade; forced China to abandon Hong Kong; fixed China's import tariffs so low that cheap British articles soon flooded in, maiming China's industrial development.

After a second Opium War, the Tientsin Treaties legalized the ravaging opium trade, legalized a British-French-American control of China's customs. China tried delaying that Treaty's ratification; Peking was looted and burned.

continued to next page

35

"Kill the foreign white devils!" was the 1901 Chinese war cry in the Boxer Rebellion.[21] Losing again, this time the Chinese were driven from Peking's choicest areas. The vicious, arrogant white man put up the famous signs, "Chinese and dogs not allowed."

Red China after World War II closed its doors to the Western white world. Massive Chinese agricultural, scientific, and industrial efforts are described in a book that *Life* magazine recently published. Some observers inside Red China have reported that the world never has known such a hate-white campaign as is now going on in this non-white country where, present birth-rates continuing, in fifty more years Chinese will be half the earth's population. And it seems that some Chinese chickens will soon come home to roost, with China's recent successful nuclear tests.

Let us face reality. We can see in the United Nations a new world order being shaped, along color lines—an alliance among the non-white nations. America's U.N. Ambassador Adlai Stevenson[22] complained not long ago that in the United Nations "a skin game"[23] was being played. He was right. He was facing reality. A "skin game" *is* being played. But Ambassador Stevenson sounded like Jesse James accusing the marshal of carrying a gun. Because who in the world's history ever has played a worse "skin game" than the white man?

Mr. Muhammad, to whom I was writing daily, had no idea of what a new world had opened up to me through my efforts to document his teachings in books.

When I discovered philosophy, I tried to touch all the landmarks of philosophical development. Gradually, I read most of the old philosophers, Occidental and Oriental. The Oriental philosophers were the ones I came to prefer; finally, my impression was that most Occidental philosophy had largely been borrowed from the Oriental thinkers. Socrates, for instance, traveled in Egypt. Some sources even say that Socrates was initiated into some of the Egyptian mysteries. Obviously Socrates got some of his wisdom among the East's wise men.

I have often reflected upon the new vistas that reading opened to me. I knew right there in prison that reading had changed forever the course of my life. As I see it today, the ability to read awoke inside me some long dormant craving to be

40

continued on page 200

continued from page 199

mentally alive. I certainly wasn't seeking any degree, the way a college confers a status symbol upon its students. My homemade education gave me, with every additional book that I read, a little bit more sensitivity to the deafness, dumbness, and blindness that was afflicting the black race in America. Not long ago, an English writer telephoned me from London, asking questions. One was, "What's your alma mater?" I told him, "Books." You will never catch me with a free fifteen minutes in which I'm not studying something I feel might be able to help the black man.

Yesterday I spoke in London, and both ways on the plane across the Atlantic I was studying a document about how the United Nations proposes to insure the human rights of the oppressed minorities of the world. The American black man is the world's most shameful case of minority oppression. What makes the black man think of himself as only an internal United States issue is just a catch-phrase, two words, "civil rights." How is the black man going to get "civil rights" before first he wins his *human* rights? If the American black man will start thinking about his *human* rights, and then start thinking of himself as part of one of the world's great peoples, he will see he has a case for the United Nations.

I can't think of a better case! Four hundred years of black blood and sweat invested here in America, and the white man still has the black man begging for what every immigrant fresh off the ship can take for granted the minute he walks down the gangplank.

But I'm digressing. I told the Englishman that my alma mater was books, a good library. Every time I catch a plane, I have with me a book that I want to read—and that's a lot of books these days. If I weren't out here every day battling the white man, I could spend the rest of my life reading, just satisfying my curiosity—because you can hardly mention anything I'm not curious about. I don't think anybody ever got more out of going to prison than I did. In fact, prison enabled me to study far more intensively than I would have if my life had gone differently and I had attended some college. I imagine that one of the biggest troubles with colleges is there are too many distractions, too much panty-

continued to next page

raiding, fraternities, and boola-boola and all of that. Where else but in a prison could I have attacked my ignorance by being able to study intensely sometimes as much as fifteen hours a day?

---

[1] *Elijah Muhammad:* U.S. clergyman (1897–1975); leader of the Black Muslims, 1935–1975.

[2] *Bimbi:* a fellow inmate whose encyclopedic learning and verbal facility greatly impressed Malcolm X.

[3] *Parkhurst:* Charles Henry Parkhurst (1842–1933); U.S. clergyman, reformer, and president of the Society for the Prevention of Crime.

[4] *Will Durant:* U.S. author and historian (1885–1981).

[5] *H. G. Wells:* English novelist and historian (1866–1946).

[6] *W. E. B. Du Bois:* William Edward Burghardt Du Bois, distinguished Black scholar, author, and activist (1868–1963). Du Bois was the first director of the NAACP and was an important figure in the Harlem Renaissance; his best-known book is *Souls of Black Folk.*

[7] *Carter G. Woodson:* distinguished African American historian (1875–1950); considered the father of Black history.

[8] *J. A. Rogers:* African American historian and journalist (1883–1965).

[9] *Coptic Christian Empire:* the domain of the Coptic Church, a native Egyptian Christian church that retains elements of its African origins.

[10] *Gregor Mendel:* Austrian monk, botanist, and pioneer in genetic research (1822–1884).

[11] *Arnold Toynbee:* English historian (1889–1975).

[12] *Frederick Olmsted:* Frederick Law Olmsted (1822–1903), U.S. landscape architect, city planner, and opponent of slavery.

[13] *Fanny Kemble:* Frances Anne Kemble, English actress and author (1809–1893); best known for her autobiographical *Journal of a Residence on a Georgia Plantation,* published in 1863 to win support in Britain for the abolitionist cause.

[14] *Uncle Tom's Cabin:* Harriet Beecher Stowe's 1852 antislavery novel.

[15] *abolitionist:* advocating the prohibition of slavery.

[16] *John Brown:* U.S. abolitionist (1800–1859); leader of an attack on Harpers Ferry, West Virginia, in 1859.

[17] *Herodotus:* early Greek historian (484?–425? B.C.).

[18] *Mahatma Gandhi:* Hindu religious leader, social reformer, and advocate of nonviolence (1869–1948).

[19] *Faustian machinations:* evil plots or schemes. Faust was a legendary character who sold his soul to the devil for knowledge and power.

[20] *Opium War:* 1839–1842 war between Britain and China that ended with China's cession of Hong Kong to British rule.

[21] *Boxer Rebellion:* the 1898–1900 uprising by members of a secret Chinese society who opposed foreign influence in Chinese affairs.

[22] *Adlai Stevenson:* U.S. politician (1900–1965); Democratic candidate for the presidency in 1952 and 1956.

[23] *skin game:* a dishonest or fraudulent scheme, business operation, or trick, with the added reference in this instance to skin color.

THE BEEKEEPER
Sue Hubbell

Sue Hubbell is a writer and farmer. The following essay originally appeared in the "Hers" column of the New York Times.

For the past week I've been spending my afternoons out in the honey house getting things ready for the harvest. I'm making sure the screens are all tight because once I get started clouds of bees will surround the place and try to get in, lured by the scent of honey. I've been checking the machinery, repairing what isn't running properly, and I've been scrubbing everything down so that the health inspector will be proud.

My honey house contains a shiny array of stainless-steel tanks, a power uncapper for slicing honeycomb open, an extractor for spinning the honey out of the comb and a pump to move it—machinery that whirs, whomps, hums and looks very special. My neighbors call it the honey factory, and I'm not above insinuating slyly that what I'm really running back here in the woods is a still.

The bees have been working since early spring, gathering nectar, first from wild plum, peach, and cherry blossoms, later from blackberries, sweet clover, water willow and other wildflowers as they bloomed. As they have gathered it, their enzymes have changed the complex plant sugars in the nectar to the simple ones of honey. In the hive young bees have formed into work crews to fan the droplets of nectar with their wings, evaporating its water until it is thick and heavy. Summertime heat has helped them, and now the honey is ripe and finished. The bees have capped over each cell of honeycomb with snowy white wax from their bodies, so the honey is ready for my harvest.

The honey that I take from the bees is the extra that they will not need for the winter; they store it above their hives in wooden boxes called supers. When I take it from them I stand behind the hives with a gasoline-powered machine called a bee blower and blow the bees out of the supers while the strong young men that I hire to help me carry the supers, weighing 60 pounds each, and stack them on pallets in the truck. There may be 30 to 50 supers

continued to next page

in every one of my bee yards, and we have about half an hour to get them off the hives and stacked before the bees realize what we are up to and begin getting cross about it.

The time to harvest honey is summer's end, when it is hot. The temper of the bees requires that we wear protective clothing: a full set of coveralls, a zippered bee veil and leather gloves. Even a very strong young man works up a sweat wrapped in a bee suit in the heat, hustling 60-pound supers while being harassed by angry bees. It is a hard job, harder even than haying, but jobs are scarce here and I've always been able to hire help.

This year David, the son of friends of mine, is working for me. He is big and strong and used to labor, but he was nervous about bees. After we had made the job arrangement I set about desensitizing him to bee stings. I put a piece of ice on his arm to numb it and then, holding a bee carefully by its head, I put it on the numbed spot and let it sting him. A bee stinger is barbed and stays in the flesh, pulling loose from the body of the bee as it struggles to free itself. The bulbous poison sac at the top of the stinger continues to pulsate after the bee has left, pumping the venom and forcing the stinger deeper into the flesh.

That first day I wanted David to have only a partial dose of venom, so after a minute I scraped the stinger out. A few people are seriously sensitive to bee venom; each sting they receive can cause a more severe reaction than the one before—reactions ranging from hives, breathing difficulties, accelerated heart beat and choking to anaphylactic shock and death. I didn't think David would be allergic in that way, but I wanted to make sure.

We sat down and had a cup of coffee and I watched him. The spot where the stinger went in grew red and began to swell. That was a normal reaction, and so was the itching that he felt later on.

The next day I coaxed a bee into stinging him again, repeating the procedure, but I left the stinger in place for 10 minutes, until the venom sac was empty. Again the spot was red, swollen and itchy but had disappeared in 24 hours. By that time David was ready to catch a bee himself and administer his own sting. He also decided that the ice cube was a bother and gave it up. I told him to keep to one sting a day until he had no redness or swelling and then to increase to two stings. He was ready for them the next

continued on page 204

5

continued from page 203

day. The greater amount of venom caused redness and swelling for a few days, but soon his body could tolerate it without reaction and he increased the number of stings once again.

10 Today he told me he was up to six stings. His arms look as though they have track marks on them, but the fresh stings are having little effect. I'll keep him at it until he can tolerate 10 a day with no reaction and then I'll not worry about taking him out to the bee yard.

I know what will happen to him there. For the first few days his movements will be nervous and quick and he will be stung without mercy. After that he will relax and the bees, in turn, will calm down.

The reason I am hiring David this year is that a young man I have used in the past has moved away. We worked well together and he liked bees though even he was stung royally at first. I admired his courage the first day we were out together, for he stood holding a super from which I was blowing bees while his arm was fast turning into a pin cushion from stings.

When we carried the stacked supers to the honey house's loading dock, he would scorn the hot bee veil as he wheeled the supers on the handtruck despite the cross bees flying around the dock. One time, as I opened the door for him to bring in the load, I noticed that his face was contorted in what I took to be the effort of getting the handtruck down the ramp. We quickly wheeled the load of supers up to the scale, where we weigh each load. He was going too fast, so that when he stopped at the scale he fell backward and 350 pounds of supers dropped on him. Pinned down, he loyally balanced himself on one fist so that he didn't harm the honey pump against which he had fallen. The reason for his knotted face and his speed was obvious for the first time: He was being stung on the forehead by three bees.

Good boss that I am, I did not choose that moment to go to the cabin and make myself a cup of coffee; I picked the supers off his chest, scraped off the stingers and helped him to his feet. It became one of our shared legends of working together. This year I miss him.

15 Now it is David, still shy about working for a friend of his parents, still a little nervous about bees. He is 19 and eager to

continued to next page

please. But he is going to be fine. In a month we will have finished and he will be easy and relaxed, and he and I will have our own set of shared legends.

THE RUINATION OF THE TOMATO
Mark Kramer

The following selection by writer and farmer Mark Kramer was first published in the Atlantic *in 1980.*

Sagebrush and lizards rattle and whisper behind me. I stand in the moonlight, the hot desert at my back. It's tomato harvest time, 3 A.M. The moon is almost full and near to setting. Before me stretches the first lush tomato field to be taken this morning. The field is farmed by a company called Tejon Agricultural Partners, and lies three hours northeast of Los Angeles in the middle of the bleak, silvery drylands of California's San Joaquin Valley. Seven hundred sixty-six acres, more than a mile square of tomatoes—a shaggy, vegetable-green rug dappled with murky red dots, 105,708,000 ripe tomatoes lurking in the night. The field is large and absolutely level. It would take an hour and a half to walk around it. Yet, when I raise my eyes past the field to the much vaster valley floor, and to the mountain that loom farther out, the enormous crop is lost in a big flat world.

This harvest happens nearly without people. A hundred million tomatoes grown, irrigated, fed, sprayed, now taken, soon to be cooled, squashed, boiled, barreled, and held at the ready, then canned, shipped, sold, bought, and after being sold and bought a few more times, uncanned and dumped on pizza. And such is the magnitude of the vista, and the dearth of human presence, that it is easy to look elsewhere and put this routine thing out of mind. But that quality—of blandness overlaying a wondrous integration of technology, finances, personnel, and business systems—seems to be what the "future" has in store.

Three large tractors steam up the road toward me, headlights glaring, towing three thin-latticed towers which support floodlights. The tractors drag the towers into place around an assembly

continued on page 206

continued from page 205

field, then hydraulic arms raise them to vertical. They illuminate a large, sandy work yard where equipment is gathering—fuel trucks, repair trucks, concession trucks, harvesters, tractor-trailers towing big open hoppers. Now small crews of Mexicans, their sunburns tinted light blue in the glare of the three searchlights, climb aboard the harvesters; shadowy drivers mount tractors and trucks. The night fills with the scent of diesel fumes and with the sound of large engines running evenly.

The six harvesting machines drift across the gray-green to-mato-leaf sea. After a time, the distant ones come to look like steamboats afloat across a wide bay. The engine sounds are dispersed. A company foreman dashes past, tally sheets in hand. He stops nearby only long enough to deliver a one-liner. "We're knocking them out like Johnny-be-good," he says, punching the air slowly with his right fist. Then he runs off, laughing.

5   The nearest harvester draws steadily closer, moving in at about the speed of a slow amble, roaring as it comes. Up close, it looks like the aftermath of a collision between a grandstand and a San Francisco tram car. It's two stories high, rolls on wheels that don't seem large enough, astraddle a wide row of jumbled and unstaked tomato vines. It is not streamlined. Gangways, catwalks, gates, conveyors, roofs, and ladders are fastened all over the lumbering rig. As it closes in, its front end snuffles up whole tomato plants as surely as a hungry pig loose in a farmer's garden. Its hind end excretes a steady stream of stems and rejects. Between the ingestion and the elimination, fourteen laborers face each other on long benches. They sit on either side of a conveyor that moves the new harvest rapidly past them. Their hands dart out and back as they sort through the red stream in front of them.

Watching them is like peering into the dining car of a passing train. The folks aboard, though, are not dining but working hard for low wages, culling what is not quite fit for pizza sauce—the "greens," "molds," "mechanicals," and the odd tomato-sized clod of dirt which has gotten past the shakers and screens that tug tomato from vine and dump the harvest onto the conveyor.

The absorbing nature of the work is according to plan. The workers aboard this tiny outpost of a tomato sauce factory are attempting to accomplish a chore at which they cannot possibly

continued to next page

succeed, one designed in the near past by some anonymous practitioner of the new craft of *management*. As per cannery contract, each truckload of tomatoes must contain no more than 4 percent green tomatoes, 3 percent tomatoes suffering mechanical damage from the harvester, 1 percent tomatoes that have begun to mold, and .5 percent clods of dirt.

"The whole idea of this thing," a farm executive had explained earlier in the day, "is to get as many tons as you can per hour. Now, the people culling on the machines strive to sort everything that's defective. But to us, that's as bad as them picking out too little. We're getting $40 to $47 a ton for tomatoes—a bad price this year—and each truckload is 50,000 pounds, 25 tons, 1100 bucks a load. If we're allowed 7 or 8 percent defective tomatoes in the load and we don't have 7 or 8 percent defective tomatoes in the load, we're giving away money. And what's worse, we're paying these guys to make the load too good. It's a double loss. Still, you can't say to your guys, 'Hey, leave 4 percent greens and 1 percent molds when you sort the tomatoes on that belt.' It's impossible. On most jobs you strive for perfection. They do. But you want to stop them just the right amount short of perfection—because the cannery will penalize you if your load goes over spec. So what you do is run the belt too fast, and sample the percentages in the output from each machine. If the load is too poor, we add another worker. If it's too good, we send someone home."

The workers converse as they ride the machine toward the edge of the desert. Their lips move in an exaggerated manner, but they don't shout. The few workers still needed at harvest time have learned not to fight the machine. They speak under, rather than over, the din of the harvest. They chat, and their hands stay constantly in fast motion. . . . Just a few years ago, when harvesting of cannery tomatoes was still done by hand, ten times the labor was required on the same acreage to handle a harvest that yielded only a third of what growers expect these days. The transformation of the tomato industry has happened in the course of about twenty years.

Much has been written recently about this phenomenon, and with good reason. The change has been dramatic, and is extreme. Tomatoes we remember from the past tasted rich, delicate, and

10

continued on page 208

continued from page 207

juicy. Tomatoes hauled home in today's grocery bag taste bland, tough, and dry. The new taste is the taste of modern agriculture.

The ruination of the tomato was a complex procedure. It required cooperation from financial, engineering, marketing, scientific, and agricultural parties that used to go their separate ways more and cross paths with less intention. Now larger institutions control the money that consumers spend on tomatoes. It is no more possible to isolate a "cause" for this shift than it is possible to claim that it's the spark plugs that cause a car to run. However, we can at least peer at the intricate machinery that has taken away our tasty tomatoes and given us pale, scientific fruit.

Let us start then, somewhat arbitrarily, with processors of tomatoes, especially with the four canners—Del Monte, Heinz, Campbell, and Libby, McNeill & Libby—that sell 72 percent of the nation's tomato sauce. What has happened to the quality of tomatoes in general follows from developments in the cannery tomato trade.

The increasingly integrated processors have consolidated, shifted, and "reconceptualized" their plants. In the fast world of marketing processed tomatoes, the last thing executives want is to be caught with too many cans of pizza sauce, fancy grade, when the marketplace is starved for commercial catsup. What processors do nowadays is capture the tomatoes and process them until they are clean and dead, but still near enough to the head of the assembly line so they have not yet gone past the squeezer that issues tomato juice or the sluice gate leading to the spaghetti sauce vat, the paste vat, the aspic tank, or the cauldrons of anything in particular. The mashed stuff of tomato products is stored until demand is clear. Then it's processed the rest of the way. The new manufacturing concept is known in the trade as aseptic barreling, and it leads to success by means of procrastination.

The growers supplying the raw materials for these tightly controlled processors have contracted in advance of planting season for the sale of their crops. It's the only way to get in. At the same time, perhaps stimulated by this new guaranteed marketplace—or perhaps stimulating it—these surviving growers of tomatoes have greatly expanded the size of their planting. The interaction of large growers and large processors has thus crowded many smaller growers out of the marketplace, not because

continued to next page

they can't grow tomatoes as cheaply as the big growers (they can) but because they can't provide large enough units of production to attract favorable contracts with any of the few canners in their area.

In turn, the increasing size of tomato-growing operations has encouraged and been encouraged by a number of developments in technology. Harvesters (which may have been the "cause" precipitating the other changes in the system) have in large part replaced persons in the fields. But the new machines became practical only after the development of other technological components—especially new varieties of tomato bred for machine harvesting, and new chemicals that make machine harvesting economical.   15

What is remarkable about the tomato from the grower's point of view is its rapid increase in popularity. In 1920, each American ate 18.1 pounds of tomato. These days we each eat 50.5 pounds of tomato. Half a million acres of cropland grow tomatoes, yielding nearly 9 million tons, worth over $900 million on the market. Today's California tomato acre yields 24 tons, while the same acre in 1960 yielded 17 tons and in 1940, 8 tons.

The increased consumption of tomatoes reflects changing eating habits in general. Most food we eat nowadays is prepared, at least in part, somewhere other than in the home kitchen, and most of the increased demand for tomatoes is for processed products—catsup, sauce, juice, canned tomatoes, and paste for "homemade" sauce. In the 1920s, tomatoes were grown and canned commercially from coast to coast. Small canneries persisted into the 1950s.

Tomatoes were then a labor-intensive crop, requiring planting, transplanting, staking, pruning. And, important in the tale of changing tomato technology, because tomatoes used to ripen a few at a time, each field required three or four forays by harvesting crews to recover successively ripening fruits. The forces that have changed the very nature of tomato-related genetics, farming practices, labor requirements, business configurations, and buying patterns started with the necessity, built so deeply into the structure of our economic system, for the constant perfection of capital utilization.

Some critics sometimes seem to imply that the new mechanization is a conspiracy fostered by fat cats up top to make their

continued on page 210

continued from page 209

own lives softer. But though there are, surely, greedy conspirators mixed in with the regular folks running tomato farms and tomato factories and tomato research facilities, the impulse for change at each stage of the tomato transformation—from the points of view of those effecting the change—is "the system." The system always pressures participants to *meet the competition*.

20

Even in the 1920s, more tomatoes were grown commercially for processing than for fresh consumption, by a ratio of about two to one. Today the ratio has increased to about seven to one. Fifty years ago, California accounted for about an eighth of all tomatoes grown in America. Today, California grows about 85 percent of tomatoes. Yet as recently as fifteen years ago, California grew only about half the tomato crop. And fifteen years ago, the mechanical harvester first began to show up in the fields of the larger farms.

Before the harvester came, the average California planting was about 45 acres. Today, plantings exceed 350 acres. Tomato production in California used to be centered in family farms around Merced. It has now shifted to the corporate farms of Kern County, where Tejon Agricultural Partners operates. Of the state's 4000 or so growers harvesting canning tomatoes in the late sixties, 85 percent have left the business since the mechanical harvester came around. Estimates of the number of part-time picking jobs lost go as high as 35,000.

The introduction of the harvester brought about other changes too. Processors thought that tomatoes ought to have more solid material, ought to be less acid, ought to be smaller. Engineers called for tomatoes that had tougher skins and were oblong so they wouldn't roll back down tilted conveyor belts. Larger growers, more able to substitute capital for labor, wanted more tonnage per acre, resistance to cracking from sudden growth spurts that follow irrigation, leaf shade for the fruit to prevent scalding by the hot sun, determinate plant varieties that grow only so high to keep those vines in rows, out of the flood irrigation ditches.

As geneticists selectively bred for these characteristics, they lost control of others. They bred for thickwalledness, less acidity, more uniform ripening, oblongness, leafiness, and high yield— and they could not also select for flavor. And while the geneticists

continued to next page

worked on tomato characteristics, chemists were perfecting an aid of their own. Called ethylene, it is in fact also manufactured by tomato plants themselves. All in good time, it promotes reddening. Sprayed on a field of tomatoes that has reached a certain stage of maturity (about 15 percent of the field's tomatoes must have started to "jell"), the substance causes the plants to start the enzyme activity that induces redness. About half of the time a tomato spends between blossom and ripeness is spent at full size, merely growing red. (Tomatoes in the various stages of this ripening are called, in the trade, immature greens, mature greens, breakers, turnings, pinks, light reds, and reds.) Ethylene cuts this reddening time by a week or more and clears the field for its next use. It recovers investment sooner. Still more important, it complements the genetic work, producing plants with a determined and common ripening time so machines can harvest in a single pass. It guarantees precision for the growers. The large-scale manufacturing system that buys the partnership's tomatoes requires predictable results. On schedule, eight or ten or fourteen days after planes spray, the crop will be red and ready. The gas complements the work of the engineers, too, loosening the heretofore stubborn attachment of fruit and stem. It makes it easier for the new machines to shake the tomatoes free of the vines.

The result of this integrated system of tomato seed and tomato chemicals and tomato hardware and tomato know-how has been, of course, the reformation of tomato business.

According to a publication of the California Agrarian Action Project, a reform-oriented research group located at Davis (some of whose findings are reflected in this article), the effects of an emerging "low-grade oligopoly" in tomato processing are discoverable. Because of labor savings and increased efficiency of machine harvesting, the retail price of canned tomatoes should have dropped in the five years after the machines came into the field. Instead, it climbed 111 percent, and it did so in a period that saw the overall price of processed fruits and vegetables climb only 76 percent.

There are "social costs" to the reorganization of the tomato processing industry as well. The concentration of plants concentrates work opportunities formerly not only more plentiful but more dispersed in rural areas. It concentrates problems of herbicide, pesticide, and salinity pollution.

25

continued on page 212

continued from page 211

As the new age of canner tomato production has overpowered earlier systems of production, a kind of flexibility in tomato growing, which once worked strongly to the consumer's advantage, has been lost. The new high-technology tomato system involves substantial investment ''up front'' for seed, herbicides and pesticides, machinery, water, labor, and for the ''management'' of growing, marketing, and financing the crop.

Today the cannery tomato farmer has all but ceased to exist as a discrete and identifiable being. The organizations and structures that do what farmers once did operate as part and parcel of an economy functioning at a nearly incomprehensible level of integration. So much for the tasty tomato.

ENCOUNTER THE SUBJECT

These three writers encountered the processes they describe and analyze in their texts long before they ever decided to write about them. Consider your own encounters with the processes of beekeeping, education, and high-tech farming. How might your encounters have been different from the encounters of these three writers? How might they have been similar? What in your personal and educational histories might have caused the similarities or differences?

RESEARCH OPPORTUNITY

To expand your encounter with one of these texts, **research** its subject or its writer. For example, you might **critically read** Malcolm X's entire autobiography, or you might do a **library search** focusing on Elijah Muhammad to find and explore sources that voice a variety of perspectives on the Black Muslim leader and on the Black Muslim religion in general. If Kramer's subject is your research focus, you might search for sources that strongly support technologically advanced agricultural practices in order to explore an opposing point of view.

RESPONSIVE JOURNAL WRITING

Respond to the results of your research activities in the form of an exploratory journal entry. In what ways has your perspective on the subject of your research changed? In what ways has it remained the same? Why do you think it has or hasn't changed?

LISTEN—READ CAREFULLY FOR MEANING

COLLABORATIVE WRITING ASSIGNMENT

Either in the classroom or in small study and research groups beyond the classroom, explore the meaning of at least one of the texts included above. Start the collaboration in groups of three or four. As you work, have one member of the group record your collaborative conclusions. If you have lasting disagreements with your collaborative partners, make sure you record your differences. After concentrated group work, open the discussion up to full-class conversation.

RESEARCH UNKNOWNS.   All of these texts, like most of the process texts you'll encounter in your college classes, were written by people who are "experts" in their subjects. Esoteric processes often have specialized vocabularies associated with them or involve the use of specialized tools that may cause you questions as a reader. If you have questions about words or references in the texts you're exploring, use the resources on your campus to find answers.

ANALYZE THE SPEAKER.   Now it's time to start actively exploring the developmental material in the texts you're focusing on. Your evidence-supported conclusions about the speakers will lead you toward the judgments that underlie their analytical positions. As you read, focus on the writer's purpose in each text—

continued on page 214

continued from page 213

although all of these speakers analyze the processes they write about, some of these selections are more openly argumentative than others.

Facts

From your reading, what factual information can you gather about the speaker? In addition, what information might you be able to gather by engaging in research?

Emotions

Where in the text you're exploring does the speaker reveal emotional reactions to the subject? Have you ever experienced similar reactions? If so, you might describe the circumstances and your responsive feelings to your collaborative partners.

Attitudes

Where in the text does the speaker make conclusive judgments about the subject, and what are those judgments?

DETERMINE THE MESSAGE.   Although each of the process texts included in this chapter has some kind of message, not all the process texts you'll encounter or write in your lifetime will. If, for example, you're writing out a mathematical proof to learn and understand its operations, the text you create will be "message-less." By the same token, the instructional text that comes in the box with your new (but unassembled) bicycle won't have a message.

The more openly argumentative a process text is, the easier for the reader to determine its message. For example, the Kramer text in this chapter is highly argumentative, and the message it sends comes through strong and clear. But some process texts have subtle or "fuzzy" messages that are more like dominant impressions than main ideas. These subtle messages will be harder to discern and pin down than straightforward ones; to discern what they are, you'll have to concentrate hard on the writer's revealed emotions and attitudes and on the developmental material the writer has included in the text. With this in mind, after concentration and exploration, write down in as few words as possible your judgment of the text's message.

continued to next page

DETERMINE THE AUDIENCE.   Making sure that you provide evidence from the text to support your judgments, describe the audience to whom the text is directed. Focus on the audience's prior knowledge of the process and possible perspective. Is the audience knowledgeable about the process? Is the audience likely to agree with the writer's perspective? What is the audience's probable educational level? What are the audience's values?

DETERMINE THE PURPOSE.   Although all process texts are explanatory, some are written for a combination of general purposes. With this in mind, determine the general purpose or purposes (beyond explaining) of the text you're focusing on. In addition, make a determination of the text's specific purpose. What change in knowledge, thought, or action does the text seek from its audience?

RESPONSIVE JOURNAL WRITING

Assess the effect of the critical reading process by journal writing. If your perspective on the subject of the text was changed in any way by the critical reading process, write at least a page in which you explain the changes. If your perspective wasn't changed, write at least a page explaining why it wasn't.

RESEARCH OPPORTUNITY

Now that you've read the texts carefully, you may be left with questions about the processes or about the writers' analyses. Focus on your questions, and brainstorm research activities that might lead you to answers. Then pursue one or more of the activities that came out of your brainstorming. The research chapters and Part Five provide more information about brainstorming.

RESPONSIVE JOURNAL WRITING

Respond to your research by exploring your findings in a journal entry.

LEARN—READ CLOSELY FOR CRAFT

FOCUS ON CAUSALITY IN PROCESS WRITING

Part of what writers of process texts engage in is **causal analysis.** Although the processes explained and analyzed in these texts vary in their complexity, all three writers focus on **cause/effect relationships.** A series of actions and operations bring about the final result in each text.

The emphasis on causality in process writing affects the choices writers make as they **develop** and **arrange** the material in their texts. Although most complex processes aren't linear and fixed, there comes a point in any process when one operation or action necessarily comes before another. For example, in order for Malcolm X to understand the texts he read, he first had to learn the meaning of words by systematically studying the dictionary. And what holds true when you're encountering a process also holds true when you're reading or writing about one. In order for their audiences to understand what's going on, writers of process texts have to describe and explain some actions or operations before they describe and explain others. For a hands-on illustration of the importance of **arrangement** and **development** in process writing, consider the following classroom exercise.

COLLABORATIVE WRITING ASSIGNMENT

For this exercise you'll need the following materials: blackboard, chalk, several sheets of newspaper, cellophane tape, and a small object (pen, eraser, or anything portable and of little value will do). By the way, the instructional text that follows is a process text.

continued to next page

Divide the class into two groups, and have one group leave the classroom with the mission of hiding the object mentioned above within easy walking distance. As the group proceeds on its mission, have a couple of members write a set of instructions that will direct the group left behind in the classroom to the hidden object. After the object has been hidden, get together and read over both sets of instructions and quickly revise the one you agree is most accurate. Then return to your classroom, but don't go inside until you've knocked and been given permission to enter.

While the "hiders" are on their mission, the group left behind should select a couple of "volunteers" from its ranks and have them collaboratively draw the figure of a person on the blackboard. As the volunteers draw, the rest of the group should collaboratively write a text that will allow the hiders to duplicate the person taking shape on the blackboard. When both the drawing and the collaborative text are finished, use the newspaper and the tape to completely cover the chalk drawing. Make sure you don't let any of the hiders into the classroom until the drawing is totally covered.

As soon as both groups are reunited in the classroom, exchange the texts the groups have produced. Now the group that produced the drawing should try to find the hidden object by following the other group's instructions. And the group that hid the object should try to duplicate the drawing with *only* the written text as a guide. As both groups proceed on their second missions, record any difficulties that they had in following the instructional texts.

When the entire class is once more reunited, unveil the covered drawing and compare it with its "duplicate." Then share the difficulties each group recorded, and respond collaboratively to the following questions:

1. Which of the two processes (duplicating the drawing or finding the object) was the more complex?
2. Which group had the most difficulty satisfactorily accomplishing its mission?
3. Which difficulties had to do with the way material was arranged in the instructional texts? Which had to do with the way material was developed (or left undeveloped)?

FOCUS ON PERSUASION IN PROCESS WRITING

LOGOS, PERSUADING WITH REASON   Because process texts take as their subjects complex interrelated operations, to be effective they must depend largely on appeals to our powers of reason. All three of the professional writers whose texts are included in this chapter clearly and logically lay out the processes they describe.

PATHOS, PERSUADING WITH EMOTION   Some process texts contain material that appeals to our emotions; others don't. A writer's decision to employ pathos in a process text will depend on the subject being written about and the writer's purpose for writing. Although all three of these selections contain appeals to our emotions, many of the informational process texts we regularly encounter are devoid of emotional appeals.

ETHOS, PERSUADING BY ESTABLISHING CREDIBILITY   The primary way writers establish their credibility in process writing is by demonstrating that they know what they're talking about. For example, you trust that the speaker in Kramer's text is an authority because he *knows* so much about corporate farming.

Although, as I suggested earlier, cause/effect relationships influenced the choices these writers made as they constructed their texts, their choices were also profoundly affected by the general and specific purposes they had for writing. For example, if Kramer's general purpose for writing had been simply explanatory rather than explanatory *and* persuasive, he would have made a different set of writer's choices; the text he created would have been substantially different from "The Ruination of the Tomato." Likewise, if Kramer's specific purpose had been to persuade his audience that high-tech farming was a positive development rather than a negative one, he would have made different choices to create a different text.

COLLABORATIVE WRITING ASSIGNMENT

In collaborative groups, comparatively study the writer's choices in at least one of these texts with an eye to improving your own technique. As you focus on each of the choice categories, keep in

continued to next page

mind the determination you made of the writer's specific and general purpose (or purposes); in addition, consider the impact of causality on the writer's choices in development and arrangement.

VOICE   In process texts that are openly argumentative, voice is employed as a vehicle for the writer's credibiltiy; how believable the writer is rests to a great extent on the trustworthiness of the persona he or she creates on the page. However, in process texts with subtle, nonargumentative messages, voice is more apt to be a kind of developmental detail in itself; the writer makes choices in words and sentence structure that accumulate to create a dominant impression on the audience. With what I've said in mind, describe in as much detail as possible (and/or draw a picture of) the created persona in the text you're exploring. As usual, make sure you cite evidence from each text to support your judgments.

DEVELOPMENT   As I said earlier, development in process writing is influenced by the cause/effect relationships present in the process; part of the developmental material included in any process text is material that explains operations within the process and the results of those operations. Working collaboratively, identify as many passages in the text as you can where the writer is explaining cause/effect relationships.

In addition, the more openly argumentative the text is, the more the writer will also include evidence-supported positive or negative judgments about operations within the process or about the process as a whole. With this in mind, identify those places in the text where the writer makes negative or positive judgments about part or all of the processes he or she is describing and analyzing.

ARRANGEMENT   All of the selections in this chapter are chronologically ordered to one degree or another. Processes do, after all, proceed through time. However, although the operations within processes are causally connected, they aren't necessarily fixed in their order. Just as writing and critical reading are recursive processes, a great many other processes are also recursive. In

continued on page 220

continued from page 219
addition, some of the texts included here (like a great many process texts) describe and analyze more than one process.

Working collaboratively, do a paragraph outline of the essay. (Part Six provides more information about outlining.) Then consider the reasons behind the writer's choices in arrangement. If more than one process is explained, why might the writer have chosen to explain one before the other? If the process is recursive, where in the text does the writer introduce a particular operation that is later reintroduced and further explored? Why might the writer have chosen to introduce it where he or she did? Why might the writer have chosen to further explore it where he or she did?

RESPOND—DEVELOP A PERSPECTIVE THROUGH WRITING

It's almost time for you to respond to a process by writing. However, before you do, read how two other student writers responded to complex processes.

Marci Wayman

BRINGING HOME THE RED LANTERN

The following process text by French major, cross-country runner, and dogsled racer Marci Wayman was written for a freshman composition class in 1994. Marci's comment on writing: "I may not be the most naturally talented writer, but I'm coachable."

When I take to the trail dog mushing, I always feel a mixture of excitement and fear. I guess it's the danger and unpredictability that make the sport so invigorating for me. My dogs are my best friends out there, and if I get lost I have to depend on their natural instincts to get me back home safely, or I could end up dead.

continued to next page

Like any race or competition, you and your teammates have to be mentally and physically prepared. It's not just the night before, or even the week before that counts. My dogs are like my teammates, and we all have to be rearing to go. Like a coach, I have to decide if my dogs are healthy and where to put each one. Justy and Rolf are my two lead dogs because they are smart and half the time seem to know what I'm thinking. They help keep the slack tight, the team in control and in line.

Although there's lots of preparation in demand before any race, just exactly how you prepare depends on weather, the length of the course and the condition of the trail. My average race is a six mile run, but I've raced forty-four miles and farther. For the longer races, I need to bring food, snacks and water for the dogs to replenish their energy.

If it is extremely cold outside, the dogs need extra fat to keep them warm. I feed them chunks of moose and reindeer fat and scraps we've saved from the hunting season. Sometimes my dad takes me ice fishing on the Bering Sea for tom cod to feed to the dogs for snacks. I also buy huge chunks of chicken and chop them up for treats. During racing season, I feed the dogs Kobuk 30/20 because it is high in energy. When it is mixed up, it looks like mud and smells like fish. Miki likes to stuff her head straight to the bottom of her pan. When she comes up, her whole face is covered with the repulsive looking food.

In Alaska, the weather can change in a matter of minutes, so you have to be prepared for all conditions. I lay my clothes out the night before to make sure I don't forget anything. I've made the mistake of not dressing properly for a run and paid for it. Once, I just wore two pairs of jeans with no snowpants because it was nice out. Unfortunately, I ended up coming home with a frostbit butt to uncomfortably sit and squirm on. Sometimes you have to learn your lesson yourself, but I could have ended up like my friend. Her hands got frostbit severely and she lost the tips of six fingers and thought she was going to lose more. So, now I take the extra precautions of having enough equipment to stay warm and always an extra pair of gloves in case I drop one. By the time I'm suited up, I have little or no skin exposed to the air.

After I decide who I'm taking out on the trail, the harnesses, tug lines, neck lines and tow line all need to be checked and laid

continued on page 222

continued from page 221

out properly. Rolf is longer in the body than Justy, so his tug line has to be shorter. Each dog has his or her own harness made to fit, and I need to make sure they get the right one. I cheat and write their names on them so other people helping me don't get confused. It is imperative that I check the line going to the ice hook and make sure the brake is secure. The ice hook is the main anchor that keeps the dogs from taking off without me. If anything comes loose on the trail, I could lose control and end up in a dog pile.

Sometimes I think that I spoil my dogs too much, but I'm not out there to win, only to have a good time. It makes me so mad when I see other mushers beating and yelling at their dogs just because they did not take a command right away. I can understand if the musher gets frustrated, but that is no reason to hit an animal.

Some mushers have huge dog lots with 50–300 dogs. I think there are more dogs in Nome than people. I only have six dogs, but I train them myself, and I know each and every one. Justy, Carroll, Rolf, Miki, Spud and Kiska are like my spoiled children, and I wouldn't have it any other way. I don't have to hire trainers to train and take care of my "budzer noodles" or "puppers." From time to time, I have to bribe my little sister to go out and feed the dogs, or hire a neighborhood boy if I go on vacation. The other mushers in the Nome Kennel Club realize that I am not able to just go out and choose the best dogs from my lot. So they awarded me with a Special Achievement Award at the end of the year.

The morning of the race, I get everything ready to go. All bundled up, I set the sled up with the quick release and the ice hook to keep the sled in place while I hook up the dogs. My puppers are all excited as I put their harnesses on them and hook them up to the sled. I always hook up Justy and Rolf first so they can hold the line out. The tug line goes from the main tow line to the backs of their harness, and the neck line to their collars. Everything is clamped together with a single Swedish clamp located just below the brush bow.

Carroll is my main wheel dog, closest to the sled because he is so strong. Alone, he has the strength to pull my two sisters, my

continued to next page

dad and me in the sled for a while. However, I can't put him with any other dog because he has the tendency to either fight or try to mount his partner whether it is male or female. Spud and Miki run smoothly together, so they run in swing, right behind the lead dogs. My puppy Kiska is just learning the role of being a good Alaskan mushing dog, so she hasn't been out on the trail yet.

Ramelle (Ramie) won't be on any more runs with the gang and me. My dad had to shoot her even though she was a great worker and my favorite. Ramie was a one person dog, though, and came off as mean to everyone else but me. She bit the oil man in the butt one day when she was loose. I've never seen a man run and jump onto our porch so fast. When mushers have to get rid of dogs, they usually take them out in the tundra, give them a bone and then shoot them in the back of the head. Well, Ramie wasn't dead the first time and came back to me, so my dad had to take her back out and shoot her again. That is the only time that I've ever seen my dad cry. But that's the way of life in Alaska, and we all have to deal with death first-hand in some way.

Before the race, each musher draws a number to see who goes out first. I never like going first because we don't have anyone to follow, and I don't like breaking the trail for the other mushers. The dogs are so eager to run that they are barking and jumping and only being held back by the strength of the starters. My adrenalin is going and the dogs are more than ready to go. Once you're off, the best part is in front of you.

I pump my feet in a rhythm with one foot on a runner and the other pushing the trail behind us. To help out the dogs, I get out and run alongside the sled on the uphill. Going down the hills, I have to brake so the sled won't hit Carroll in the behind. Some people might think that I'm crazy, but I sing to my dogs while we're out on the run. It seems to make them go faster and be happier. It doesn't matter what I sing; usually I just make something up.

Out on the trail, the language I use is totally different than the language I speak in everyday life. GEE is turn to the right; HAW is to the left; GEE GEE is a sharp right turn; HAW HAW is a sharp turn; COME GEE is the cue to turn around to the right and go back the same way; COME HAW is the same, but to the left; HIKE is let's get the heck out of here; GIT UP is the same as

continued on page 224

continued from page 223

hike; CHIGGEAH is just a word of encouragement; GIDDEAH is the same as the last one; XOPOKO means good job; and whatever else I feel like saying because out on the trail, there is no one to tell me what I can or can't say. If Rolf is slacking, all I have to do is click my tongue, and he immediately knows to pick up the pace. Singing to them calms them down and keeps them in rhythm.

When they run, all of them gallop in a synchronized manner. It's like they're all pushing off at the same time and jumping over a barrel. It's so smooth the way they run with their tongues flapping to the side. Occasionally, one will reach down and scoop up some snow with their teeth and keep on going.

If you were wondering how the dogs go to the bathroom during the race, or during regular training runs, I'll tell you. We never stop unless I have to fix something. They just poop on the run. If I have to go, then I'm pretty much out of luck in the short races. In longer races, there are checkpoints to stop at, most likely with honeybuckets. In the winter, they don't smell that bad due to the fact that everything is frozen, but watch out for them when you're camping in the summer time.

Passing other teams can sometimes be a problem. This is where it is important to have a good lead dog to hold the other dogs in place. This is where dog piles happen the most, when the teams intermingle for a huge dog fight; and sometimes all you can do is freak out and yell while your babies are being torn apart. Also, this is when the lines can be broken and need to be replaced. That's why I always bring extras of everything just in case something happens. Sometimes a dog is injured in the fight and needs to be carried in the basket of the sled.

There are other troubles out on the trail, and Justy and Rolf have saved my butt many times. Many times in training when I was lost, they brought me back home. I just let them lead the way. There is a certain trust that you have to have in your dogs.

I remember one time, however, where I wasn't so fortunate. We were going pretty fast down a hill onto some ice, and I didn't see it in time to break soon enough. To add to my troubles, there was a ninety degree angle turn to the left at the bottom of the hill with a bush right in front of me. I yelled "HAW" and they took

continued to next page

the command and turned to the left. The sled went out of control and I was dragged with the ice scraping my stomach and was then thrown into the bush. With a much lighter load, the dogs took off without me. I started running after the twerps and lucky for me, another musher had caught my runaway team and set the icehook. Reunited with my puppers, I went on with my race without singing my little songs, just wanting to finish.

Every normal race has some difficulties, but that is what makes it fun and challenging. Imagine being outside with no one except you and your budzer noodles among the clear tundra, hills, wildlife and snow. That is where I'd choose to be any day over people who only have to worry about themselves.

After every race, all the mushers pile into their trucks and head to Nachos, a local restaurant in Nome, Alaska, to eat Delilah's wonderful food, get their awards and tell their mushing stories. One gets the first place trophy and money, while one (and it has often been me) brings home the red lantern for last place.

Brian T. Ricker and T. Anthony Pollner

GETTING INTO BOB WEIR HOT SPRINGS

Brian Ricker and Anthony Pollner met in a composition class at The University of Montana. Very quickly, they went from being mere workshop partners to being nearly inseparable friends. These days, you can often see them driving the mountain roads above Missoula, Montana, in Anthony's increasingly dented green Subaru station wagon. The transcript of a conversation I had with them follows this essay, which was written for a composition class in 1995.

As freshmen at The University of Montana, we were introduced to quite a revealing experience. Nestled deep within the Idaho wilderness, 75 miles southwest of Missoula, lie the enchanted Bob Weir Hot Springs. These calcium fortified "pots," as they're called by regulars, help heal and cleanse the body like

continued on page 226

continued from page 225

nothing else. From deep within the earth's crust boiling water is forced to the surface where it collects and cools to a comfortable, soothing 100–110 degrees Fahrenheit—the perfect temperature for total muscle relaxation. These glorious springs are tucked away up on the bank of a creek, constantly releasing steam that blankets the rocks in which the pools have formed. Luckily, the springs are a good mile from the road, making them quite secluded. The ideal time at the hot spring would be spent alone, but usually this is not the case. Sometimes friends from school accompany us, or there are people already there in the water when we arrive. Either way, alone or not, a similar conflict within all of us is revealed upon visiting the springs.

On one particular occasion earlier on in the year, we brought a sizable group of new friends from school who hadn't been fully acquainted yet and were first time visitors to the springs. During the drive, the subject of swimming attire was raised. "Is there a place to change?" asked Estee. Lulu echoed a similar question: "Are there going to be a lot of people there?" Obviously they were not aware that bathing nude was customary, and had brought their swim suits.

When we finally arrived at the springs, the sun was still several hours from the horizon, so visibility was still good. The group, other than the two of us, suddenly became preoccupied with avoiding the inevitable: getting undressed. "I have to go to the bathroom," claimed one of the three girls. This set off a chain reaction and pretty soon everybody was off in the woods or smoking a cigarette in an effort to stall. In an attempt to lure the others into the pots we disrobed, and showing little hesitation, hopped in. "Come on in, it's lovely!" we yelled; as Lulu peered around the rocks at the naturally formed gnarled root staircase, she knew she must descend. From our view, she looked fully clothed but upon her stepping out from behind a boulder, we discovered she was dressed in only a t-shirt. Avoiding eye contact, she quickly descended the stairs and sat on the edge of the pool. In the blink of an eye, she had shed her shirt and plunged into the water. Looking around, we noticed that two of the girls that had scampered away earlier were now standing at the edge of the woods, with towels draped around them. They weren't going to be

continued to next page

caught dead in their b-day suits. Lulu, who had regained her composure because she was out of the spotlight, yelled to them, "C'mon, the water's great." Cindy took a step forward, hesitated, then took another. Estee followed suit, and soon they were at the edge of the pool. One problem still remained and it plagued them. How to take off the towels and get in the pool without exposing themselves. Estee flung her towel to the side, and with arms crossed, she slipped into the pool's warm water. Surprisingly, Cindy had accepted her fate and dropped her towel, marching boldly down into the spring. As Cindy was getting comfortable on the rocky bottom, Mike, the only dry one, began untying his boots. "This is kind of like being in an elevator with a bunch of people you don't know," he said, removing his watch. In agreement we all snickered. "You know how everyone stares blankly at the walls or at the light above the door," he continued, now tying up his hair. Upon stepping into the water his foot lost its grip on green moss and he went sprawling through the air and landed on the edge of the spring, half in half out. The conversation ceased and everyone, including Mike, began to laugh, as he sank slowly into the water.

By this time, the sun was almost completely gone, leaving a red glow across the sky. The subject soon changed to the weather, and before long, we were entirely relaxed. Any previous inhibitions were now gone, because everyone was covered.

Not long after, we saw the glow of two distant flashlights through the trees, down stream fifty feet. A hush settled over the group. A couple ascended the trail to the springs, saw our group, and said hello. They asked, "Is there room in that there pot for us?" We unselfishly replied that there was and invited them to join us. In the pool, we had quit speaking and some of the girls were staring. The man undressed without even thinking about it. The woman was tying up her Cocker puppy as the man awaited her. She too disrobed without hesitation. Everyone in the pool began shifting positions to make room for the couple. "Actually, we'll just go to the other one up there," the man said, while pointing up the hill. No one replied but we all gave a little sigh of relief. When the couple fell out of sight Mike exclaimed, "I'm glad they didn't come in. I'd have been uncomf with strangers." We all agreed and sat back to soak up some of the water. "Ahh, this is

continued on page 228

continued from page 227

the life," said Cindy, "sitting here surrounded by trees, naked, in a hot spring."

The night went on and as it did we became more comfortable with each other's company and forgot about our nudity. The hot springs seem more enjoyable that way. Even when we got out to put our clothes back on there was very little tension, but then again it was dark by that point.

Since then, we've gone back a dozen times, and although the people with us are different, the reaction is always the same. At first everyone (including us) is rendered defenseless without clothing, but eventually we all become accustomed to the nakedness. Clothing seems to act as a protectant and we don't mean from the weather. A barrier of some sort, and without it we feel overly self-conscious. Although some may think that this is due to society's conservative view on nudity, in reality it is the individual's obsession with personal vanity that creates these feelings of self-doubt. It is a shame that we are not more comfortable without clothing. The body itself is beautiful, not what hides it from view. In other words, you're born with what you get and you can't do anything about it, so why worry.

TWO STUDENT WRITERS TALK
ABOUT COLLABORATIVE WRITING

J. S.: What motivated you to write collaboratively?

B. R.: You were always talking about collaboration, so we decided why not give it a try.

A. P.: It was also because we had the same experience. I mean, we were going to the hot springs all the time, and when we got the process assignment, we talked about it, and we both wanted to write about it. It was a competition thing, too. I thought, why compete with Brian?

B. R.: Development was in there too. We were already prewriting by talking, and we thought it would be easier to develop the paper collaboratively.

continued to next page

A. P.: Right. It was like we had already begun to write by talking, and instead of fighting about who owned the topic, we thought it might be neat to write it together. I mean, we'd been there together. It was a shared experience. Why not write it together?

B. R.: So we came and asked you what you thought. Even though you kept talking about collaboration, it was hard for us to believe you'd actually let us do it.

J. S.: How come?

A. P.: It seemed like cheating. It wasn't something that was ever allowed at any school I ever went to. Also, the topic wasn't something that would have been allowed in high school.

J. S.: When you actually started writing, was developing the paper easier?

B. R.: Much. We'd just talked about it for so long, even before we got the process assignment. You know—the why's— why are people so self-conscious?

A. P.: It started out as just fun, but the more we worked at it, the more serious it began to be. Just the idea that going to the hot springs was research, because although we'd been a lot of times, we really had to go back and do a more purposeful observation. It was fun to sit there in the hot water and think, this is actually research.

B. R.: Yeah. In some ways it started out as a joke—you know—let's be outrageous; let's see what she does with this one; and then the better the paper got, the less of a joke it became.

J. S.: What was hard about collaborating?

A. P.: Voice was the hard part. We fought about words the whole time.

B. R.: You know, this thing went through several drafts. We'd bring a draft to you and you'd question a word, and it would be one of Anthony's choices, and I'd say, ''You see?'' and we'd start arguing.

A. P.: We both have pretty strong personal voices. I think Brian's is stronger, and he thinks mine is. It's amazing how just the smallest change in a word or in the order of words can be so irritating.

RESPONSIVE WRITING ASSIGNMENT

Write an essay in response to a process. After familiarizing yourself with the process by researching or exploring it thoroughly, construct a text in which you explain and analyze that process.

RESPONDING TO PROCESSES: A GUIDE TO THE PROCESS

Assess Your Past Performance
Explore the Writing Situation
Prewrite
Draft
Rewrite

ASSESS YOUR PAST PERFORMANCE

As you work through this assignment, continue to **assess** how you think and write, **learn** from your previous experience, and **respond by revising** your personal writing process. Read over your assessment of your performance from your last assignment, and consider your writing strengths and weaknesses. Identify the choice categories with which you had trouble. Then analyze why you had trouble, and focus on ways you might better employ the writing process to avoid repeating your mistakes. For example, if the last text you constructed was written in a voice that was unclear and awkward, think about why. Was it because you were trying to sound "professorial," and in so doing forgot to focus on the *meaning* of what you were writing? To improve your performance, you'll have to reword as you draft, focusing on meaning instead of sound.

EXPLORE THE WRITING SITUATION

To find an initial direction for your essay, actively explore the choices and constraints of the writing situation.

PG 190

Act. Notes

SUBJECT   The subject of your essay is constrained only in one way—you must respond to a **process** by constructing an explanatory, analytical text. The process you choose to write about may be one you've encountered in an academic discipline, or it may be one you've participated in during your personal life. Consider the examples cited earlier in this chapter and the process texts that you've read critically; they may help trigger tentative choices of subject.

Explore your notes from other classes, and make a list of possible subjects for writing. In addition, make a list of processes you've encountered or reencountered beyond the academic community. Focus on activities you engage in. Focus also on your job and on your personal history. This assignment is designed to help you sharpen your critical thinking skills, so challenge yourself to *analyze* the implications or significance of the process. A simple explanatory "how to" paper will bore you as well as your audience. Keep in mind that you will write more effectively if your subject interests and engages you.

AUDIENCE   Although your choice of audience is to some extent open in this assignment, there wouldn't be much point in explaining and analyzing a process for an audience already familiar with the process and/or your analysis.

PURPOSE   Although one of your general purposes for writing will be to **explain,** you are free to write for any additional writer or audience-based purpose or purposes. If you're writing to an outside audience, you might **persuade, entertain,** or **inform** as you're explaining. If you're writing for yourself as well as others, you might write to **learn** and **remember.**

Your specific purpose (the change you want in your audience) is up to you. As soon as you've decided on a subject, begin considering possible ways that encountering your perspective on the process might change other people. Do you want others to think differently, to act differently, to become advocates for your view of the process?

Keep in mind also that you are constructing an *essay.* A set of instructions with no message won't fulfill this assignment; the text you construct must *analyze* the implications or significance of a process, not simply describe that process.

THE WRITER   The person you are will have a great deal to do with the process you choose to write about and the way you analyze that process. All the writers whose selections are included in this chapter chose to write about processes that were significant to them. Think critically about your responses to the subject you choose, and consider what in your personal and educational histories makes that subject significant to you.

In process writing, critical thinking skills and knowledge of the subject are crucial. To effectively explain and analyze your subject, you'll have to become an "expert" on it by engaging in thorough research or exploration. However, the ability to effectively construct a process text also involves being continually aware of your audience. This is particularly true if your subject is controversial or so familiar that it's become second nature to you. We've all been confused at one time or another by an ineffective process text written by an expert who didn't take our knowledge or perspective into consideration. If you want your readers to follow and understand your description and analysis of a complex process, you'll have to think critically every step of the way about what your audience knows, and what they need to know.

TIME   Consider the time allowed you and the work you'll have to do to complete your project. Will extensive research be necessary? If so, what kind of research activities might you most likely engage in? How much time will you need for research? For thinking? For drafting and rewriting? Plan your time, and make a mental work schedule.

If your exploration of the writing situation hasn't triggered a choice of subject, choose the subject from your list of tentatives that you find most interesting and explore it by prewriting.

PREWRITE

RESEARCH OPPORTUNITY

Even if at first you think that you're an absolute expert on the process you've chosen as a subject, consider ways that research might enhance your essay. Remember that although thorough knowledge of the process is crucial here, your audience's knowledge and perspective also come into play. Search beyond yourself for other and deeper ways of viewing the process.

Either on your own or with one or more collaborative partners, **brainstorm** a list of possible research activities. If, like Hubble and Wayman, you've chosen a physical process as the subject of your writing, **observe** the process firsthand to increase your

continued to next page

knowledge and understanding. On the other hand, if your chosen process has abstract elements, as the trend toward high-tech farming does, a **library search** or an **interview** with an expert might lead you to new ways of viewing your subject. After following up on several sources, reconsider your subject. Has your knowledge of and perspective on the process changed? If so, explore in evidence-supported writing the why's behind the changes.

RESPONSIVE PREWRITING EXERCISE

As with a great many processes, the chosen order of the following strategies isn't necessarily fixed. Read over the entire set, and begin with the operation that seems to you the most logical starting place.

1. Write out in as close to chronological order as possible the actions or operations that make up the process. This may be harder to do than you think. You may find that you have to act out and actually go through the motions of physical processes to recall them accurately. Abstract processes may be even more difficult to recall accurately. If the process you're explaining is abstract, give yourself plenty of time, and put critical pressure on each operation as you write it down. Question yourself about the respective order and completeness of each operation.

2. Identify any causally related actions or operations. Then explore in evidence-supported writing *how* they're related and *why*.

3. Study the relationship each action or operation has to the process as a whole. If the action or operation were changed or omitted, would the result of the process be changed? If so, explore in evidence-supported writing the possible changes or effects.

4. Make a judgment about which actions or operations are most crucial. Then explore in evidence-supported writing the why's and how's behind your judgments.

5. Reread the chronology you laid out in step one. Is the order you wrote down necessary? Could the process be ordered differently? If it could, explore in writing *how* it could be re-ordered and *why* re-ordering wouldn't change the result of the process.

continued on page 234

continued from page 233
6. Identify those actions and operations in the process that a person who is totally unfamiliar with the process would need to know and understand.

FOCUS ON PURPOSE AND AUDIENCE

After studying the results of your prewriting up to this point, focus on your possible choices of purpose and audience. Since the text you create in this assignment will most likely have more than one general purpose, I've deviated from the usual audience–purpose ordering in this chapter. Exploring additional general purposes for writing first will probably make your choices of audience and specific purpose easier.

One of your general purposes is, of course, to explain. But what else do you want to do? Do you want to entertain others with a story of adventure, as Wayman does? Do you want to inform and persuade others, as Kramer does? Or do you want to learn about and come to an understanding of a process by writing about it? To decide on additional general purposes for writing, consider the process you've chosen to write about. If it's controversial, you may want to **persuade** others by writing an argumentative essay. (Chapter Nine, "Responding to Controversial Issues," provides additional information about argumentative writing.) If it's an interesting, esoteric process that you have the luck to be an expert on, you may want to **entertain** others or **explore** the process with others by writing a personal experience essay. (Chapter Seven, "Responding to Personal Experiences," can help here.) If it's something you want to know more about, you may want to write primarily for yourself in order to **learn** and **remember.**

AUDIENCE   With your general purposes in mind, focus on choosing your audience. Make a list of possible audience types who might be interested in knowing more about the process or your analysis of it. Focus on one or two from your list that you would like to converse with by writing. Then write a profile of each one. What are their interests? Their educational level? What are they likely to know about the process? What is their perspective on it likely to be? After you've written out your profiles, look back at the results of your prewriting and focus on what your possible audiences know about the process and what they need to know.

SPECIFIC PURPOSE   Once you've decided on an audience, focus on a specific purpose. How do you want to change your audience? What specific change in knowledge, thought, or action do you desire from that audience?

FOCUS ON A WORKING MESSAGE

Although not all the process texts that you read or write in your lifetime will have messages, the one that you're presently in the process of constructing requires a message. The message of your text will have a lot to do with your additional general purposes for writing. If your essay is persuasive, see Chapter Nine for more information about formulating messages in argumentative writing.

If your text isn't argumentative, the message you send may be more like a dominant impression than a main idea. To focus on a subtle message, consider the impact the process has on you, and explore that impact in writing. Why is the process important to you, and why should it be important to your audience? Looking over your determinations of message for the essays in this chapter might help here. As an example, for Malcolm X, why was learning to read significant?

If you haven't yet chosen a working message, don't be overly concerned. You may actually have to begin drafting (or even complete an entire draft) before your attitudes about the subject of your writing coalesce into a working message. However, if at this point you've decided on one, write it down in as few words as possible.

If you haven't made firm choices of general or specific purpose or of audience by this point, make tentative choices and continue to explore them as you draft.

DRAFT

DRAFT TO REVISE

The **revision** you engage in as you draft gives you the opportunity to expand on old ideas and formulate new ones. **Read** and **reread** your draft as you rewrite, and look for new ways of viewing your subject. Pay particular attention to those areas that have given you trouble in previous writing assignments, and **revise** as you draft by **cutting, adding, rearranging,** and **rewording.**

In process writing, audience awareness is a crucial factor. With only the words you put down on the page as a guide, your audience has to be able to mentally recreate an interrelated series of actions and operations with which they may be totally unfamiliar. As you draft, keep your audience profile close by and imaginatively put yourself into your audience's position. Ask yourself, "If I had the knowledge and perspective of this audience, what would I need to know to understand what's going on here?"

FOCUS ON YOUR CHOICES

VOICE   To write in an appropriate voice, consider your conclusive judgments about your subject (your attitudes). Consider also your emotional responses. However, keep in mind that the voice you choose to write in will have its roots in your purposes for writing. If your essay is persuasive, your voice should reflect your attitude toward the subject; however, it should also be a means of establishing credibility with your audience. For example, Kramer, writing to an audience of well-educated, socially conscious urbanites who aren't experts in farming, creates a voice that is both ominous (reflecting his attitude) and authoritative (establishing his credibility).

If you're writing a personal essay to entertain your audience or explore a process with them, your voice will be a detail of development that reveals your attitudes and feelings about the subject to your audience. Hubbell, whose essay originally appeared in the "Hers" column in the *New York Times* and was read by an audience interested in perspectives on gender, creates a wonderful, close to mythic, female persona on the page. The voice in her piece is knowledgeable, in charge, and, at the same time, powerfully sensual.

With your audience in mind, write a detailed description (or draw a detailed picture) of the voice you believe will most likely achieve your writer's purpose. Then, as you draft, read your emerging text aloud, and **reword** with your audience's responses in mind.

DEVELOPMENT   Although part of the developmental material in your essay will center on explaining the workings of your chosen process to your audience, some of your developmental material must focus on *analyzing* the process. Analyzing will require making evidence-supported judgments about the significance or implications of operations within the process and about the process as a whole. And the judgments that you make must all in some way relate back to your message. Look for ways to **cut** material that might lead your audience away from your focus. In addition, look for ways to **add** material that will clarify the steps of the process for your readers.

In "The Ruination of the Tomato," Kramer's judgments all center on the ways in which "technology, finances, personnel, and business systems" all interrelate to create a bland, tasteless product—the modern tomato. The judgment that he makes on the process as a whole is a negative one. But he also makes negative judgments about the actions and operations within the process, and all those judgments focus on technology taking over life, dehumanizing it, and making it bland. For example, in paragraph nine: "The few workers still needed at harvest time have learned not to fight the machine. They speak under, rather than over, the din of the harvest. They chat, and their hands stay constantly in fast motion. . . . Just a few years ago, when harvesting of cannery tomatoes was still being done by hand, ten times the labor was required on the same acreage to handle a harvest that yielded only a third of what growers expect these days."

The judgments Hubbell makes in "The Beekeeper" are more subtle and implicit than the judgments Kramer makes. They're impressionistic "attitudes" rather than openly negative (or positive) argumentative points, and added together they create a dominant impression on the audience. As she explains the processes of beekeeping and desensitizing the "strong young man" who works for her against bee stings, Hubbell keeps nudging us with slow, sensual (and sometimes sexual) language toward the subtle message of her text.

ARRANGEMENT   Like all the selections included in this chapter, your process essay will to some extent be chronologically ordered. However, since most complex processes aren't totally fixed, some amount of choice will be open to you. Consider your audience as you make the choices allowed to you. Are there some operations that your audience might need to understand before they can grasp others? For example, before Hubbell could get to the initiation of David that is at the heart of her essay, she first had to give us an overview of the process of beekeeping.

As you draft, **rearrange** the order of sentences or paragraphs or sections of your text with your audience response in mind. If you draft on the computer, use the block and move functions to rearrange. If you type or draft longhand, write on only one side of the page so that you can cut sections apart and rearrange them.

DRAFTING IS ACTIVE AND RECURSIVE

Continue to consider your audience as you draft. What do they need to know? Where are they most likely to have difficulties following the process? Since most processes have some recursive elements, expect to have to go back and fill things in as you discover gaps in your explanation and analysis.

REWRITE

Processes that we know well can often be harder to successfully explain and analyze than processes we're less familiar with. When a process becomes second nature to us, it's easy to forget the tricky elements that might escape the uninitiated. To test the effectiveness of your explanation and analysis, **workshop** your essay in a collaborative group. (Part Six provides strategies for peer editing and workshops.) Ask your workshop partners to read your essay carefully and to determine what your message is and what your general and specific purposes are. Then ask them if there are any gaps in your explanation and analysis.

ACTIVE REWRITING

Remember, be *active*. Focus on voice, development, and arrangement. Don't just change a word here and there. Leave yourself open to discovery as you revise. Consider your workshop partners' criticisms, your habitual writing weaknesses, and the techniques for responding to processes. Put yourself in your audience's position. Read your text critically, focusing on the following checklist, and continue to **cut, add, rearrange,** and **reword.**

- Is the process complete and understandable as you've developed it in your essay?
- Have you *analyzed* the actions and operations that make up the process by developing judgments about their significance or about their implications to one another and/or to the process as a whole?
- If your essay is argumentative, do you have a clear and focused message—a general reason *why* your audience should take the position you advocate?
- If your essay is not argumentative, do you at least communicate a dominant impression about the process?
- If your essay is argumentative, does your created voice establish your credibility with your audience, and does it also reflect your attitude toward the subject?
- If your essay is not argumentative, is your created voice appropriate to your message and purposes?
- Is your text correct in terms of mechanics (spelling, punctuation, sentence structure, and diction)?

EDIT TO FINAL FORM

Polish your text as you write the final draft. Focus on paragraphing, transitions, and any habitual problems with spelling, punctuation, and sentence structure. Part Six provides specific information and strategies.

PROOFREAD

If possible, put your response aside for at least a couple of hours before you proofread. Proofread for small careless errors by reading your text aloud, preferably to another person.

ASSESS YOUR PERFORMANCE BY WRITING CRITICALLY

The process of writing your process essay is not completed until you've assessed your performance. Study your evaluators' comments, and focus on **voice, arrangement, development,** and **usage.** (Part Six provides detailed strategies for assessing your writing weaknesses and learning through self-criticism.) With which choice category did you mainly have trouble? Write a page explaining why you think you had trouble with that particular category. Then write a second page in which you explain what you might have done to correct the problem.

CHAPTER NINE

RESPONDING TO CONTROVERSIAL ISSUES

THE WRITER'S SCENARIO

A writer encounters a controversial issue. The writer listens to arguments from both sides, studies the situation for a while, and then takes a postion in the context of the controversy. Finally, the writer is compelled by commitment to respond in the form of a written argument.

Controversial issues are situations that are marked by dispute. Controversial issues are complex; if they were simple, there would be only one way of interpreting their implications, and they wouldn't be surrounded by debate and marked by disagreement. But even more significant than being complex, controversial issues almost always suggest the need for change. Whether the situation is social, academic, or personal, controversy arises when old ideas and ways of doing things are challenged by new interpretations and perspectives. Think about the times in your life when a fomerly stable relationship suddenly became charged with conflict, and you'll realize that a challenge to change was involved. Teenagers suddenly come into conflict with their parents as they attempt to change and redefine the parent–child relationship. Formerly agreeable employers suddenly argue angrily when their employees demand higher wages; previously placid roommates suddenly become contentious when they're asked to clean up after themselves. Because controversies are both complex and marked by a challenge to previously held ways of viewing things, proponents on either side often are not only intellectually engaged but emotionally and morally engaged as well.

When you hear the word *controversy*, you usually think of those social controversies familiar through public debate; gun control involves social controversy, and so do abortion and euthanasia. But controversy isn't limited to social issues. All academic disciplines have their areas of controversy. Like social controversies, academic controversies center on the meaning and implications of complex situations.

Perhaps the most interesting thing about social and academic controversies is that no matter how heated they may get, in the long run they tend to be resolved. Looking back at the beginning of the twentieth century it's hard to believe that the social controversies that were then raging (disputes about women's suffrage, for example, or child labor) could actually have been the cause of so much public uproar. And this same tendency toward resolution is true of twentieth-century academic controversies.

About twenty years ago I read a book called *Continents in Motion* about the then radical and hotly debated theory of plate tectonics (the idea that the earth's crust is divided into "plates" that are in constant motion relative to each other). In the book's first chapter the author described an emotionally charged conference session where the theory's greatest proponent was publicly attacked by furious colleagues. Some of the attending geologists merely stalked out of the room, but others laughed or angrily shouted insults. This highly emotional response from a group of supposedly rational scientists might seem out of character, but scientists—like the rest of us humans—resist having their long-held views suddenly turned upside-down by radical change. Clearly, though, those angry geologists were eventually persuaded by the evidence to let go of their original positions in the controversy, because the theory of plate tectonics is generally accepted today.

Unlike a lot of personal disagreements, few social or academic controversies end in total stalemate. Generally, the pattern of resolution is a gradual refinement of argument. The debate will start with crude, extreme arguments that are improved and made more credible not only by more (and in some cases increasingly available) evidence but by the critical pressure put on each side by dialogue with the other. As the back-and-forth exchange of perspectives unfolds, each side discovers the holes in its own argument and then rushes to plug them.

There just may be a personal lesson to be learned from all this. Perhaps the reason that social and academic controversies are more likely to be resolved than personal arguments is that social and academic controversies take place in the context of a community. In the context of a large community, we're more likely to watch what we say and make sure it's credible because of the presence of so many and varied witnesses. In our one-on-one fights with friends and relatives, we can slide out of rationality into whining or bullying in order to get the change we want. Credibility becomes irrelevant; all we want is for the other side to give in. But in writing responses to controversial issues, credibility is not beside the point. In fact, credibility is everything.

A great deal of the writing you'll do in college will be in response to academic issues that are open to debate. In fact, most higher level academic writing—whether it be in the humanities, social sciences, or sciences—focuses on subjects that are open to dispute. To read and write effectively in the academic community, you'll have to become a critical reader and writer of argumentative prose. You'll have to be able to read other people's arguments and evaluate them, and you'll have to be formulate your own arguments and defend them reasonably. And that leads to the techniques for responding to controversial issues.

TECHNIQUES FOR RESPONDING TO CONTROVERSIAL ISSUES

1. Research or understand the issue thoroughly.
2. Develop a committed argumentative position within the context of the controversy.
3. Make the best choice of audience within the constraints of the writing situation.
4. Analyze your audience to determine what they know about the controversy and what their position is.
5. Present a credible argument for your position (and against your opponent's) with your audience analysis in mind.

RESPONDING TO CONTROVERSIAL ISSUES: PROFESSIONAL WRITING

PREREAD

To familiarize yourself with one or more of the following selections, preread. **Read the first three paragraphs** slowly, focusing on those things you understand. When you finish reading the third paragraph, stop and take stock. **Summarize** what's gone on in the text so far. If you're confused, go back and focus on the sentences you don't understand and **reread** them. Then **predict** the direction you think the text will take next. As you continue reading, compare your predictions with what unfolds on the page. After each of the paragraphs that remain, pause again to **summarize, reread** if necessary, and **predict.**

FORESTRY: ONLY GOD CAN MAKE A TREE, BUT . . . .

Michael Frome

Michael Frome is a writer and an environmentalist. The selection that follows is from his book Conscience of a Conservationist *published in 1989.*

The practice of clearcutting timber on public and private forests has become the subject of heated debate, both nationally and in various regions of the country—as well it should, considering the high stakes in economics, ecology, and esthetics. Controversies have arisen over the management of the California redwoods, the Douglas fir forests of the Pacific Northwest, spruce forests of southeast Alaska, lodgepole and ponderosa pine forests of the Rocky Mountains, the hardwood forests of the Northeast, and the mixed hardwood-pine forests of Appalachia and the South. Within the past three years, hearings on clearcutting have been conducted before committees of both houses of Congress. Reports and studies have been made by the Council on Environmental Quality, the United States Forest Service, deans of forestry schools, and concerned citizen groups. Yet there is still no resolution of the debate.

What is clearcutting? In an editorial appearing in its April 1972 issue, the magazine *Field & Stream* presented this blunt appraisal of the practice:

"It is a method of harvesting trees which causes complete devastation. It is more harmful than a forest fire. The land is churned up over vast areas by big machinery. *Every* tree is cut down and most of the surface plants are killed. Until grasses and shrubs can get started again, the land is wide open to extreme erosion. Timber companies prefer this method of harvest because it is cheaper than cutting selected mature trees and leaving the remainder unharmed and because having once destroyed a mixture of kinds of trees on a certain tract they can plant one type of tree, which they prefer. These trees are planted in neat little rows, all standing at the same height and all reaching maturity at the same time for another cutting. But it is no longer a forest any more than an orchard is a forest. There are no open grassy glens, no

continued on page 244

continued from page 243

bushes, no aspen or alders. Everything is crowded and shaded out by the trees, and for the major part of the growth years of the trees there is little food for animals or birds. It is a sterile sort of forest designed by a computer."

Quite different descriptions of clearcutting are offered by its advocates, who include, in addition to most of the forestry profession, large corporations, holding investments in timber lands or in mills.

5   "It is efficient, economic, and in general produces forest products and resources useful to man," declared Dr. Kenneth P. Davis of Yale University, president of the Society of American Foresters, while testifying before a Senate committee in 1970. The immediate consideration was a proposed moratorium on clearcutting in the national forests, as urged by citizen conversationists. To halt clearcutting, he warned, "would place an unwarranted and disruptive restriction on using a proper and, in many situations, necessary method of managing forest lands."

Edward P. Cliff, Chief of the Forest Service, addressing the National Council of State Garden Clubs in May 1965, declared that the practice "is something like an urban renewal project, a necessary violent prelude to a new housing development. When we harvest overmature, defective timber that would otherwise be wasted, there is bound to be a temporary loss of natural beauty. But there is also the promise of what is to come: a thrifty new forest replacing the old. The point is that there often must be a drastic, even violent upheaval to create new forests. It can come naturally—and wastefully—without rhyme or reason as it has in the past, through fires, hurricanes, insects, and other destructive agents. Or it can take place on a planned, purposeful, and productive basis."

Mr. Cliff served as Chief Forester from 1962 to 1972. Under his aegis clearcutting came of age; he defended and promoted it with fervor. "For the young 'citified,' articulate part of our citizenry," he declared before the Pacific Logging Congress of 1966, "it is especially easy and natural to get stirred up about outdoor beauty, recreation, wilderness, vanishing wildlife species and environmental pollution. It is not likely that very many know or even particularly care much about how timber is grown, har-

continued to next page

vested and used to meet their needs." The Chief likened acceler-ated timber cutting through modern technology to gardening, or farming of field crops. "Wild old stands have pristine beauty which is instantly felt and appreciated," he wrote in the 1967 *Year-book of Agriculture*. "But a newer forest, man-planned and man-aged and coming up sturdily where century-old giants formerly stood, also has its brand of beauty—similar in its way to the ter-raced contours and the orderly vegetative growth upon well-managed farmlands."

The clearcutting concept, as enunciated by Dr. Davis and Mr. Cliff, plainly emphasizes the anthropocentric—the design of na-ture for the use of man; it rejects the notion that resource man-agers must "think in ecosystems"—that they must relate every decision and every action to the entire complex picture rather than to an isolated component of the ecosystem, let alone to consid-erations of expediency or short-term economic returns. It denies the principles evoked by Aldo Leopold, forester of another gen-eration and yet a pioneer of today's ecological movement, who wrote: "The land is one organism. Its parts, like our own parts, compete with each other and cooperate with each other. The competitions are as much a part of the inner workings as the cooperations."

Clearcutting's bias toward commodity production in the short run, rather than toward protection of the resource in all its aspects for the long run, is often the main basis of attack in the media. Strong criticisms along these lines in *Field & Stream* and other publications (notably the *New York Times, Reader's Digest, Atlantic Monthly, Des Moines Register and Tribune* and *Montana Daily Missoulian*) have been summarily dismissed by spokesmen for the timber industry, the forestry profession, and the Forest Service with such epithets as "sensationalism," "hit-and-run re-porting," and "yellow journalism." In a speech on "The Nature of Public Reaction to Clearcutting," delivered in February 1972, an official of the Forest Service, John R. Castles, declared: "Prob-ably the most frustrating and insidious form of pressure is that generated by irresponsible or ill-informed news media people who seize an unsubstantiated reports, half-truth rumors, misinformation, or outright distortions without checking them further."

continued on page 246

continued from page 245

10   But the evidence, even from timber-forestry witnesses, appears to substantiate charges that clearcutting is environmentally pollutive and ecologically disruptive, as well as designed principally for immediate profit. In an article in the February 1972 issue of the *Journal of Forestry,* for instance, Dr. David M. Smith, professor of silviculture at Yale, described the emergence of the new synthetic forest: "Combinations of herbicides, prescribed burning, and powerful site-preparation machinery made it possible, almost for the first time, to start new stands entirely free of the competition of preestablished vegetation. In some localities, it has become possible to contemplate deliberate efforts to eliminate natural populations and replace them with the planted products of conscious genetic selection. . . . It takes no great wit to see that within this frame of reference, the optimum cutting practice will be that which removes nearly everything that will pay its way out of the woods. The future benefits which might be derived from growth on reserved merchantable trees are quite intangible from this point of view."

Professor Smith went further, joining the critics in their concern over damage done by heavy machinery used in logging and site preparation. "The vegetation can be swiftly repaired," he wrote, "but it may take centuries or millennia to repair the kind of damage to the soil that can result from deep gouging or scraping action. It is time there was more concern for adapting the machinery to the silviculture and less resignation to the idea that soil damage is an inevitable consequence of practical forest operation."

John McGuire, who succeeded Mr. Cliff as Chief of the Forest Service, also conceded, in an interview published in *American Forests* magazine of October 1972, that: "Roads have been cut where they shouldn't have been permitted. Erosions have followed that make it impossible to get a forest of quality, or even any forest, in that area again." But instead of talking about eliminating roads in order to regain protection of the natural resource, he proposed construction of an additional 100,000 to 150,000 miles of highway in the national forests, thus tending to give credence to charges that the Forest Service is the handmaiden of special economic interests. Or, as Justice William O. Douglas declared in his dissent in the *Mineral King* case (Sierra Club v. Morton), issued April 19,

continued to next page

1972: "The Forest Service—one of the federal agencies behind the scheme to despoil Mineral King—has been notorious for its alignment with lumber companies, although its mandate from Congress directs it to consider the various aspects of multiple use in its supervision of the national forests." In the same message, Justice Douglas likened clearcutting to strip mining.

The most dangerous kinds of chemical poisons, poured into the soil and seeping into streams, are implicit tools of clearcutting. Entomologists warn that a pure stand of timber forms an ideal situation for damage from insects and disease; infection is rapid from tree to tree, and if one species is destroyed, there is nothing left. A monoculturally managed forest, therefore, creates the need for pesticides and herbicides. Ultimately these chemicals do more harm than good, for the biotic diversity is destroyed. Nevertheless, the Forest Service has poisoned millions of acres of public land, encouraged the use of ecologically crude poisons on millions of additional acres, and ignored pleas and protests.

The general fear among environmentalists is that more wood is being cut than grown on both public and private forests. The timber industry called for increased logging of the national forests—even though three-quarters of commercial forest land is in private hands—and the Forest Service responded by trebling its cutting of timber in the period from 1950 to 1970. Still, the industry wants the Forest Service to increase production by accelerated cutting of old-growth forests and by ecologically questionable programs of thinning and fertilizing. It fought enactment of the Wilderness Act of 1964 and now opposes establishment of additional inviolate wilderness, although such areas stabilize soil and watersheds, provide habitat for a variety of wildlife species, and are cherished for recreational pursuits.

Justification of clearcutting is repeatedly attempted on grounds that it produces more game. "Actually, this is the strongest argument for clearcutting, because artificial openings in the forest are a boon to wildlife," wrote William E. Towell, executive vice-president of the American Forestry Association.

It is true that clearcuts produce quail habitat, often where nonexistent before, and that an abundance of deer browse is produced on many clearcut areas. Biologists note that these benefits are temporary, however; before many years, quail habitat and deer browse decline. Within ten years following planting the pine

15

continued on page 248

continued from page 247

canopy can be expected to close; until thinning, this clearcut is of use only as cover to wildlife. With increasingly short cutting rotations, it is difficult to anticipate how "mast" (foods such as berries and nuts) will be provided in the future for turkeys, squirrels, and deer. Removal of mast trees and cover is now destroying prime squirrel and turkey habitat, and lack of mast may reduce the carrying capacity for deer after a relatively few years. In the sequence of events, the clearing and conversion to pine in natural pine-hardwood areas, or hardwood areas with high deer populations, sometimes induces destruction of planted pines by deer, with the accompanying demand for hunters to "bring the deer population into balance."

Even though logging many improve deer habitat, serious disturbance eliminates such species as spotted owls and pine martens, which require old growth conifers for survival. Birds actually furnish the most efficient and least costly form of insect control in the forest. It is their definitive function in providing balance to the ecosystem. A single woodpecker, for example, has been estimated to be able to consume the larvae of 13,675 highly destructive wood-boring beetles per year. It is fair to generalize that the more numerous and varied the bird population of a forest, the broader the spectrum of natural insect control. John Smail, executive director of the Point Reyes Bird Observatory, a California research organization focusing on the ecology of nongame species, has reported on an analysis of nine breeding-bird censuses in coniferous forests in California, Colorado, and South Dakota. The analysis showed that 25 percent of the total number of birds using these forests are of species that nest in holes. These hole-nesters require older trees with some decayed portions in order to breed successfully (and feed large broods of young on destructive insects), although they forage on trees of various ages. "Any forestry practice producing solid stands of trees the same age reduces the diversity of bird species able to breed, and this in turn severely reduces possible insect control," according to Mr. Smail. "Clearcutting is the most drastic example."

The South is perhaps being hit harder by clearcutting than any other section of the country. Vast areas that once supported mixed forests have been reduced to even-aged stands of pine, like

continued to next page

apple orchards or orange groves. The sole purpose in transforming forests into farm lots is to provide pulp and paper for an affluent, throw-away society. "For a paper company, the obvious objective of pine management is to produce the largest volume of usable wood fiber per acre," wrote Henry Clepper in the August 1971 issues of *American Forests,* in describing the operations of International Paper Co., a timberland giant which owns 8 million acres in the United States and Canada—including 5 million acres of the South—and controls an additional 15 million acres under long-term lease from the Canadian government. "To attain this goal, foresters must control the site, which is to say the forest environment."

The *Louisiana Conservationist* in 1971 described how this is achieved. Under a headline, "Flourishing Forests Threaten Wildlife," this state publication noted: "When the stand reaches the desired stage of maturity the entire timber crop will be cut and the whole process repeated. To complete this cycle anywhere from 15 to 80 years may be required, depending upon the wood products desired. Already thousands of acres in blocks, ranging from 160 to well over 1,000 acres, have been stripped of existing timber, bulldozed, chopped, or burned clean, and then seeded or planted with pine. The small stream bottoms which have historically supported hardwoods are now the main targets. They provide a last and most critical retreat for game within the great sea of pine."

The industry's design to transform the rural South into a man-dominated forest, or massive pine factory, is embodied in a highly publicized campaign called "The Third Forest." According to the industry's report, titled *The South's Third Forest—How It Can Meet Future Needs,* there are now 24 billion cubic feet of "cull" trees—unwanted hardwoods—which take space needed for "better" trees. The removal of cull trees in order to provide for future growing stock would constitute the bulk of timber stand improvement on no less than 90 million acres. Dr. George Cornwell, professor of wildlife ecology at the University of Florida, commented on this proposal as follows:

"As wildlife habitat, cull trees usually mean food (mast) and housing (den and nest). In terms of natural beauty, most culls would be more highly valued by the forest recreationist than

20

continued on page 250

continued from page 249

the 'better' trees planted in their places. Imagine my disappointment on learning that, after several decades of wildlife managers' pleading with forest managers to retain these den, nest, and mast-producing trees for wildlife use, a major Southern forest policy plan would call for their removal throughout the Third Forest. This approach to the cull tree is symptomatic of the recommended silvicultural practices in the South's Third Forest and would appear to reflect a nearly total contempt for non-timber values."

Until the upsurge of recent years, clearcutting had been accepted as a silvicultural practice only in certain short-lived forest types which reproduce easily, such as aspen, jack pine, lodgepole pine, and some southern pines. But it always had been applied in small patches, so that surrounding trees deterred hot, dry winds from desiccating the forest soil, and were close enough to supply the openings with seed for regeneration while providing shade cover for young seedlings. The more prevalent system of silviculture was selective logging, or "selection-cutting." Essentially, this system is designed to follow and fit into nature's pattern of growth, maturity, and decline by selecting individual trees, or very small groups of trees, in order to favor species tolerant of shade, or larger groups up to quarter-acre clearings to favor species intolerant of shade.

With the advent of large machinery, however, clearcutting became a habit. It began in the Pacific Northwest, on the basis of assertions that Douglas fir, the most profitable—and hence most desirable—species, reproduces only in full sunlight. Since then clearcutting has spread to cover nearly all forest types.

What alternatives are there to clearcutting? Dr. Leon Minckler, professor of forestry at Syracuse University, who spent twenty years in research for the Forest Service, insists that clearcutting is not the way to go, that Eastern hardwood trees do regenerate better through other techniques. Other forest technicians are now challenging the idea that Douglas fir must be cut in large blocks. In an article in the *Journal of Forestry* for January 1972 Dr. Minckler wrote:

"For integrated uses (such as timber, wildlife, watershed, recreation, and esthetics), management should aim toward maximum diversity and minimum damage to the environment. This can be accomplished by single tree selection, group selection,

continued to next page

25

small patch cutting of a few acres, or a combination of these. Clearcutting, on the other hand, tends to minimize diversity and makes it almost impossible to avoid damage to the site, to streams, and to esthetic qualities. Most of all, it eliminates the forested character of a particular area for a long time. Ecologically it is a major disturbance. When harvesting mature stands, clearcutting is a cheap and effective way of extracting timber, but the sacrifice of other values may be a poor trade-off for cheap timber harvesting. In immature or partially mature stands, clearcutting may not even be the cheapest way of harvesting timber."

According to Gordon Robinson, a veteran California forester and consultant to the Sierra Club, good forestry consists of growing timber on long rotations, generally from 100 to 200 years, depending on the species and quality of the soil, but invariably allowing trees to reach full maturity before being cut. "It is not enough to have orderly fields of young trees varying in age from patch to patch," he declares. "In looking at a well-managed forest one will observe that the land is growing all the timber it can and that most of the growth consists of high-quality, highly valuable material in the lower portions of the large older trees. It will be evident that no erosion is taking place."

In short, while the corporate forester or timberman may insist that trees can be harvested and cultivated like any farm crop, in a genuine balanced-use forest immediate values must be integrated with long-range protection of soil, water, wildlife, wilderness, and scenery, and with assurances that harvested areas will grow more trees for future timber needs.

Business has a natural and understandable tendency to stress economics rather than ecology when thinking about resources. But land is an integral part of all life, and its resources remain part of the environment. In dealing with them, business needs to blend ecology and economics in its thinking. No landowner, large or small, should be able to control land use entirely for his own benefit without regard for what his actions do to others. Ownership is a trust which must be exercised in the interest of all—andone of the prime ingredients of that interest is the quality of the environment.

Dealing as we do with a complex earth mechanism which we only partially understand, we should be cautious in tampering with natural forces. Clearcutting has been subject to so many

continued on page 252

continued from page 251

challenges and criticisms, and may do such serious long-range damage to soils and streams of the nation, that it needs to be curbed at once and restricted to experimental uses only, until answers are fully known.

30   Certainly any system of conservation based solely on commodity production or economic self-interest is hopelessly lopsided. It tends to ignore, and thus to eliminate, elements in the life-community of the land that lack commercial value, but which are essential to its well-being; if the land mechanism as a whole is good, then every part is good, whether we understand it or not. Perhaps the first rule to guide those who use and administer the land should be that economic parts of the biotic clock will not function without the uneconomic parts. Once that rule is learned and applied, then and only then can we sustain healthy, productive forests for the long-term future.

GAYS IN ARMS
Jacob Weisberg

The following text by Jacob Weisberg was originally published in the New Republic *in February 1990.*

The Air Force is looking for a few gay men. To be exact, it's been looking for 18 of them at its Carswell base in Tarrant County, Texas. This is the number of non-commissioned officers who have been implicated in "homosexual activity" in the past two months. Twelve have been discharged, and six more are currently "under investigation," according to Capt. Barbara Carr, a public affairs officer.

At a news conference last month in Fort Worth, one of the 12 described the hunt for the wicked witches of west Texas. In December 1989 an officer of the Air Force's Office of Special Investigations informed him that he had been named as part of a gay ring. His honorable discharge papers were already prepared and would be signed if he cooperated by naming other homosexuals.

continued to next page

Otherwise, he would be court-martialed. After six hours of intermittent interrogation in a broom closet with a two-way mirror, the anonymous airman yielded five names, and ended his military career.

The outburst at Carswell is typical of the military's sporadic persecution of gays. For the most part enlisted homosexuals keep quiet, and although friends and commanding officers often know they are gay, most pass through the services without trouble. "Ninety-nine percent go through and do very well," says Sandra Lowe, an attorney with the Lambda Legal Defense and Education Fund. But now and again, either because someone proclaims his or her homosexuality openly or because an officer wants a purge, a dozen or so are exposed and quickly "released," as the Pentagon prefers to euphemize it. According to Department of Defense figures, about 1,400 are expelled in any given year, at a cost of some tens of millions of dollars in lost training.

Women are dismissed for homosexuality three times as often as men are, eight times as often in the Marine Corps. In 1988 agents of what columnist Jack Anderson calls the "notoriously overzealous" Naval Investigative Service (NIS) persuaded one female Marine to give them the names of 70 lesbians at the Parris Island, South Carolina, boot camp. Fourteen members of what the NIS calls a "nest" were discharged. Three who wouldn't name names did time in the brig for sodomy and "indecent acts."

One of those prosecuted at Parris Island was Capt. Judy Mead, a 12-year veteran of the Marines. Mead was brought before a board of officers on charges of conduct unbecoming an officer for having a "long-term personal relationship with a known lesbian." Although Mead was not charged with being gay herself, she once allegedly slept "in the same bed" with a civilian lesbian and was, on another occasion, "in the presence" of persons suspected to be lesbians. Mead protested she didn't know her friends were gay. One of the officers answered that her antenna should have gone up because her friends played softball and "looked homosexual." The panel recommended Mead for a less than honorable discharge. After a year of hearings and $16,000 in legal bills she was reinstated by a review board, but soon afterward she was passed over for a routine promotion despite her otherwise excellent service record.

5

continued on page 254

continued from page 253

Mead was acquitted because DOD policy doesn't explicitly prohibit association with homosexuals. That's about the only loophole. Under the Uniform Code of Military Justice, any homosexual act on or off duty is sufficient cause to warrant dismissal. Deeming even that too loose, the Pentagon issued a directive in 1982 that broadened the definition of homosexuality to include "a person, regardless of sex, who engages in, desires to engage in, or intends to engage in homosexual acts"—even if "acts" are never committed. This gives the armed forces the authority to terminate service persons at whim, on the flimsiest of evidence, for what are in essence thought-crimes. The most celebrated case of the moment is that of Joe Steffan, a naval cadet who stood near the top of his Annapolis class before he was expelled in 1987, two months before graduation, for telling friends he was gay. To date, the Navy has presented no evidence that Steffan ever practiced his preference.

In the wake of the Panama invasion, Americans are conducting a lively public debate on the difficult question of whether women should serve in combat. Opponents of letting women fight offer objections that are at least plausible. Most women do not meet objective standards of strength and endurance. There are reasons to suspect that sexually integrated units would not perform as effectively as traditional all-male ones. And so on. That is not to say that these objections are fully persuasive; women have never had a chance to disprove them in the U.S. armed services. Simply out of habit and prejudice, they are also denied many positions they could fill as well as men. In the case of homosexuals, however, the common justifications offered by defenders of the status quo do not make any practical or moral sense.

The arguments against letting gays serve are seldom stated. This is Pentagon policy: no official is allowed to defend the rules on the record. Spokesman Maj. Dave Super is only permitted to quote from an official statement that says "homosexuality is incompatible with military service." Beyond that he repeats that "the policy is the policy." A few months ago "Nightline" did a program on the Steffan case. Since the Navy was unwilling to

continued to next page

provide a spokesperson, ABC had to settle for Representative Robert K. Dornan, who raved about sodomy and called homosexuality a mental illness. With supporters like Dornan, the DOD doesn't need opponents.

The last time the Pentagon elaborated its rules on homosexuals was in 1982, when the office of Secretary of Defense Caspar Weinberger promulgated this rationale:

> Homosexuality is incompatible with military service. The presence of such members adversely affects the ability of the Armed Forces to maintain discipline, good order, and morale; to foster mutual trust and confidence among the members; to ensure the integrity of the system of rank and command; to facilitate assignment and worldwide deployment of members who frequently must live and work under close conditions affording minimal privacy; to recruit and retain members of the military services; to maintain the public acceptability of military services; and, in certain circumstances, to prevent breaches of security.

This is a jambalaya justification, which tosses every remotely palatable argument in the pot. Consumed in a hurry, it almost tastes OK, but later proves indigestible.

Weinberger's last argument, that homosexuals are a security risk, is the most familiar. It is also the least convincing. As the Navy's suppressed Crittenden report noted as far back as 1957: "The concept that homosexuals pose a security risk is unsupported by any factual data. Homosexuals are no more of a security risk, and in many cases are much less of a security risk, than alcoholics and those people with marked feelings of inferiority who must brag of their knowledge of secret information and disclose it to gain stature." Even if homosexuals were common targets for blackmail, the threat could be elmininated by allowing them out of the closet.

It is the Navy that is most preoccupied with the nexus of homosexuality and disloyalty. During its investigation of the exploded gun turret aboard the *USS Iowa* last year, the NIS put out a lurid story that Clayton Hartwig, one of 47 sailors who died in the explosion, had a "special relationship" with Kendall Truitt,

continued on page 256

10

continued from page 255

who was the beneficiary of his $100,000 life insurance policy. There was simply not any evidence for this accusation against the two petty officers. A Congressional hearing later discovered a far more likely reason for the accident: gunpowder used in the 16-inch gun that blew up had destabilized after being stored under improper conditions. The NIS may also have been responsible for the rumor that John Walker, of the Walker family spy ring, and Jerry Whitworth, another convicted Navy spy, were, in military parlance, "asshole buddies." There was no evidence that the two ever met.

Working backward through Weinberger's laundry list, the "public acceptability" argument is probably as close as the DOD comes to a legitimate worry. The fear is that some young men would be discouraged from volunteering if they knew they would be serving alongside homosexuals, and that parents would object to their boys serving in an unwholesome environment. The same line was taken against racial integration of the services before Harry S. Truman accomplished it by executive order in 1948. In that case fears were largely unrealized, and there is every reason to think they are exaggerated today. Public tolerance for homosexuals is now higher than support for racial integration was 40 years ago. According to a recent Gallup Poll, 60 percent of the public believes that gays should be allowed in the military.

The public acceptability argument goes in a particularly vicious circle: gays are unacceptable because they are unacceptable. Straight soldiers will continue to fear and scorn homosexuals until they are forced to become acquainted with them on a routine basis. Of course, the admission of gays will no more eliminate homophobia than the integration of blacks cured racism. But irrational prejudices are bound to diminish over time if the isolation and ignorance they feed upon is ended.

The privacy argument is one that is viscerally felt by many who have served in the military. Soldiers and sailors say they don't want to be regarded with sexual interest when they are naked in common showers or asleep in common barracks. On "Nightline" Dornan compared allowing a homosexual in a barracks to "putting a man in a harem." The truth is that there are plenty of gays in the showers now. Most estimates put the number

continued to next page

of male and female homosexuals in the branches of service at ten percent, mirroring the proportion in society at large. Denying this reality may make some straights more comfortable, but it doesn't make them invisible to those who may enjoy gazing at them. The unstated fear of some straights is that acknowledging the presence of homosexuals would free them to stare and proposition more openly and aggressively. But no one proposes to change rules about harassment or fraternization, which prohibit sexual advances and activity on duty.

When Weinberger notes the need to "ensure the integrity of the system of rank and command," he raises the specter that straights would refuse to take orders from homosexual commanders. This argument is again familiar from the time before racial integration. It was asserted then that no white soldier would take orders from a black commander. Some would not, and there were a few courts-martial for insubordination. But the overwhelming majority of whites faced the fact that even if they didn't like taking orders from blacks, they no longer had any choice about it. The same would happen with gays.

It is unclear why the Pentagon believes "mutual trust and confidence" would be undermined by homosexuals. One possible implication is that gays would be worried about personal relationships rather than about fighting, and would be less willing to make sacrifices for the group. But common sense and the example of ancient Greece suggest that male affection doesn't have to be Platonic to impel heroic deeds. Nor do mutual trust and confidence appear to have been shaken in West Germany, Italy, Sweden, Norway, Denmark, or the Netherlands, countries that allow gays to serve in their armies.

The argument heard most often today is that "discipline, good order, and morale" would suffer if homosexuals were allowed to fight alongside heteros. What's meant here is that the presence of sexual feelings would diminish the dynamic that binds men together and spurs them to fight and die. To be fair, the temper of a platoon that included open homosexuals would probably be different from that of one that didn't. But there is no reason to believe that it would be worse, that unit cohesion would suffer, or that the intangible but all-important process of bonding would fail to occur. The real fear, as Allan Berube, (in) *Coming*

15

continued on page 258

continued from page 257
Out Under Fire: Gay Men and Women in World War II . . . puts it, is that "gays would taint bonding and camaraderie with homosexual overtones." Military units are rife with homosexual anxieties in the first place. Like those who make the shower argument, those who make the morale case seem to feel the heterosexual nature of exclusively male activities and situations can't be called into question. The open presence of gays would make the homoerotic elements of bonding undeniable. As Berube puts it: "There's a safety to their not being named."

Many of these points have been made by internal investigations that the Pentagon feels obliged to cover up. The most famous example is the Crittendon report. Though it recommended that the military continue to exclude homosexuals, the study's debunking of the security risk myth and its conclusion that homosexuals perform their duties as well as heterosexuals were enough to get it buried for 20 years, until it was subpoenaed in a court case in 1977.

The story replayed itself just last year, when a report titled "Nonconforming Sexual Orientations and Military Suitability" was mailed anonymously to the House Armed Services Committee. Written by Theodore Sarbin, a psychology professor at the University of California, Santa Cruz, and Capt. Kenneth Karols, a Navy doctor, for the DOD's Personnel Security Research and Education Center (PERSEREC) in Monterey, California, the study asserts that "the military cannot indefinitely isolate itself from the changes occurring in the wider society." It argues that the forces should view homosexuals as a non-ethnic minority group, rather than as deviants or criminals, and should do research to test the hypothesis that gays "can function appropriately in military units."

20   After receiving the report from Armed Services, Representatives Gerry Studds and Pat Schroeder summoned Sarbin to a meeting on the Hill. They also invited Maynard Anderson, the Pentagon official who oversees PERSEREC. Anderson criticized the draft and said it was not ready to be released. Studds, who is gay, defended it. "When Gerry said he'd read it, Anderson went pale," Studds staffer Kate Dyer said. "Then he said I have a copy, and Anderson went paler. Then Gerry said he was going to release it to the press and Anderson went white."

continued to next page

Schroeder then asked if there were any other reports in the works bearing on the question of homosexuality. Anderson assured her there were not. A week later another document arrived in a plain wrapper: a PERSEREC report titled "Preservice Adjustment of Homosexual Military Accessions: Implications for Security Clearance Suitability." Its conclusion is that "homosexuals show preservice suitability-related adjustment that is as good or better than the average heterosexual." The report noted that its results "appear to be in conflict with the conceptions of homosexuals as unstable, maladjusted persons."

DOD's position is that neither report is finished. The Sarbin-Karols study was never even commissioned. The Pentagon says it asked for a report on whether homosexuals were reliable. Sarbin and Karols overstepped the bounds of their assignment by answering that they were *suitable*. "The entire effort, at least to date, is unfortunate," wrote Craig Alderman, Jr., Deputy Undersecretary of Defense for policy, in a memo to PERSEREC director Carson Eoyang. "Wholly aside from PERSEREC's lack of authority to conduct research into the military suitability area, we found (the report) to be technically flawed, to contain subject matter (Judeo-Christian precepts) which has no place in a Department of Defense publication." Eoyang memoed back that Alderman would not have objected if the report's conclusion had affirmed current policy. Sarbin has since rewritten the study limiting himself to the narrow question of security clearances. He said in a telephone interview that the report has been cleared for official release. But the Pentagon was unable to answer questions about its status.

Within the armed services, support for the policy appears to be weakening. Michael McIntyre, who interviewed officers for a 1980 thesis at the Naval Postgraduate School in Monterey, found that 92 percent of those he talked to did not think homosexuality should be grounds for discharge so long as it did not interfere with job performance. Still, the Joint Chiefs are not about to change their own accord. "Don't expect them to come forward," says Lawrence Korb, a former Defense official now at the Brookings Institution. "The armed forces is not a social experiment."

Korb thinks the change eventually will be accomplished by legislative or executive action. But both avenues seem closed for the present. Studds says it would be counterproductive to press

continued on page 260

continued from page 259
a bill in the House now, since it would have no chance of passage. "There is no way on earth Congress is going to take the initiative on this," he says. Of course, the simplest way to change the rules on gays would be by Presidential fiat, the way Harry Truman integrated the services in 1948. But then, George Bush is no Harry Truman.

HIV TESTING: VOLUNTARY, MANDATORY, OR ROUTINE?

Theresa L. Crenshaw

The following text by writer and lecturer Theresa Crenshaw first appeared in the Humanist *in 1988.*

The AIDS virus is formidable. For a preventable disease, it continues to spread at an alarming rate. As long as 90 percent of those who are infected—1.5 million people or more in the United States—don't know it and continue to spread it to others, we have little hope of controlling this epidemic.

Yet, there are many dilemmas and questions that face us as individuals and as a society. Isn't it better for a person who is infected not to know? How can one expect an infected person to stop having sex when he or she is already suffering more than a human being can bear? Are condoms sufficient protection? Is testing dependable? How can we protect the civil rights of the ill and the civil rights of the healthy?

There is no simple solution. Testing alone is not enough. We need all of our resources: common sense, sexual integrity, compassion, love, exclusivity, education, discipline, testing, condoms, and spermicides—to name just a few. We also need an emphatic, positive message that promotes *quality* sex rather than *quantity* sex. Multiple partners and casual sex are not in the best interest of health, but within an exclusive relationship quality sex can thrive.

In this context, perhaps we could take an in-depth look at the controversial issue of HIV-testing. Widespread voluntary testing,

continued to next page

if encouraged by health officials and physicians, will most probably be successful, making widespread mandatory testing unnecessary. The general population will cooperate. However, under certain circumstances, required or routine testing might be considered and could be implemented whenever common sense dictates without the feared repercussions of quarantine and discrimination. Regardless of whether testing is voluntary, required, or routine, maintaining confidentiality is critical. It is vitally important to understand that public health officials are trained to maintain confidentiality in all cases; they do not put advertisements in the newspaper or call a person's employer.

Confidentiality is nonetheless a genuine concern. Lists of infected persons have been stolen. There is probably no way humanly possible to ensure against any and all breaches of confidentiality throughout the United States and the world. It would be unrealistic to falsely assure individuals that confidentiality would be 100 percent secure. On the other hand, we must do everything within our power to come as close as possible to 100 percent confidentiality and to assure those who are concerned that these efforts are being made. There are many things we can do to improve our recording and to improve confidentiality systems. These aspects are being investigated and will hopefully be implemented by federal, state, and local authorities.

An encouraging point is that in Colorado, where HIV-positive status is reportable and contact tracing is routine, *there has not been one episode of breach of confidentiality*, demonstrating that when extra care is taken there can be great success. Often forgotten is the fact that confidentiality is equally important for voluntary, required, and routine testing. It must be applied to *all* forms of testing, and it must not be used to distinguish between them.

Mandatory testing brings to mind visions of concentration camps and human beings subjected to arbitrary and insensitive pubic health tactics. In practice, however, nothing could be further from the truth. Urine tests and blood counts are routinely required upon hospital admission. If a patient refuses, he or she will generally not be accepted by the hospital and certainly won't be allowed to undergo surgery. That's mandatory testing, but we take it in stride. And it has no hint of repressiveness; it is simply

5

continued on page 262

continued from page 261
a reasonable measure for the protection and well-being of both the patient and the hospital.

Likewise, tests for syphilis are mandatory in many states. In many countries, certain tests and inoculations are required before one can travel. In the not-so-distant past, health cards had to be carried by travelers along with their passports, proving that they had had certain immunizations. There is also required testing of schoolchildren for childhood diseases, which includes the tuberculin skin test, and various inoculations, without which they are not permitted to enter school. These are just a few examples of mandatory testing or treatments that are routine in our everyday lives—and that do not compromise our civil rights. However, since the term *mandatory* is emotionally charged, substituting the term *required* might more accurately reflect the intent.

Our society takes in stride sensible, necessary tests and treatments which in many circumstances are required in order to travel abroad or to perform certain jobs. However, strenuous arguments against any form of required testing for AIDS persist. The following are some of the issues most commonly raised by opponents of mandatory testing. I have attempted to analyze each argument.

10   *Mandatory testing will drive infected individuals underground. They will hide out and refuse to be tested.*

Since 90 percent of the 1.5 million or more individuals who are infected within the United States don't even know it, *they are already underground.* While certain numbers of people may use creative methods to avoid testing procedures, we would be able to reduce that percentage of people who do not know their HIV status to 10 percent instead of 90 percent, because most people would cooperate voluntarily.

Testing would cause more problems than it solves because huge numbers of people would receive false positive test results. Their lives would be destroyed by such test results.

The enzyme linked immunosorbent assay, or ELISA test, does have a high percentage of false positives, just as the tuberculin skin test has a high percentage of false positives. *That does not mean it is without value.* Whenever a test such as this is performed,

continued to next page

a physician never stops at screening tests. Follow-up studies are required to confirm a positive test result. For example, with tuberculosis, chest X-rays and sputum cultures are performed until a positive diagnosis of tuberculosis can be made. The tuberculin skin test is used to determine whether there are indications for further studies. The AIDS antibody test is used in the same fashion. If the ELISA is positive, it should be repeated again and the Western Blot test performed. If these are all positive, the likelihood of the result being a false positive approaches zero (per 400,000, according to Dr. James Curran of the Centers for Disease Control). Immune system studies can then be done and, although it is expensive and somewhat logistically difficult, a patient who wants additional proof of infection can request actual viral cultures. Since recent research demonstrates that there can be a year or more during which the virus is present but antibodies have not yet developed—the so-called window in time—the far greater problem with testing is the high number of false negatives that still will be missed. Another study by A. Ranki et al., in the September 12, 1987, issue of *Lancet*, indicates that up to 36 percent of ELISAs are false negatives in those individuals who have had sex with an infected person. As you see, the screening test is not perfect. There will be false negatives that escape detection, so that test should be repeated periodically. All false positives would be followed up with additional tests until a confirmed positive result can be established. In the near future, we will have a test for the virus itself, solving some of the problems we now face, especially the "window in time" between infection and antibody development.

There is no point in having yourself tested because there is no cure.

Although there is no cure, and indeed *because* there is no cure, it is even more essential to be tested and to know what your antibody status is, because, if you test positive, you must take every precaution not to infect another person. If this disease were curable, perhaps we could be more cavalier. But since we must protect individuals in society from it, we must motivate those who are already infected not to infect anyone else. To assume that everyone should and will behave as though they were infected is optimistic and unreasonable, although I think many can achieve this end. It is unlikely, however, for an individual to take

15

continued on page 264

continued from page 263
complete responsibility for his or her actions without definitive knowledge of infection. Even then it is a challenge.

There are other reasons for being tested. Someone who tests positive will live longer if counseled not to become exposed unnecessarily to other infections by visiting sick friends at home or in the hospital or by traveling extensively to countries where foreign organisms can cause unusual infections. Additional health counseling can lead to a healthier life-style, the avoidance of other opportunistic infections or cofactors, improved nutrition, and planning for the future—which includes estate planning, a will, and making other practical arrangements as indicated.

Perhaps the most important reason for being tested early is that many of the treatments becoming available are more effective the earlier they are instituted. If you know you are HIV-positive, you can apply for research projects for experimental protocols or arrange to take AZT (which is now available) or other similar drugs when they become approved for clinical use. In short, the reasons for being tested far outweigh the reasons for not being tested.

Testing is undesirable for many individuals who are unable to cope with the knowledge that they are infected. These people are better off not being tested.

Anyone who is asked whether or not they think they will be able to cope with the news of an HIV-positive test result would ordinarily say no. It is normal not to be able to cope well with a deadly, incurable disease. Most people who are tested receive pretest counseling. Often pretest counseling, advertently or inadvertently, dissuades individuals from being tested. At a recent conference in New York cosponsored by the American Medical Association and the Centers for Disease Control, one physician said that, with just three minutes on the telephone with someone inquiring about being tested, he succeeds in talking 57 percent of potential patients out of being tested. In the anonymous testing centers, we need only look at the numbers of people who show up for testing compared to those who leave without being tested to assess the effectiveness of some counseling in discouraging testing.

continued to next page

Yet, imagine an analogous situation for a woman needing a breast biopsy. If the physician asked, "Are you sure you want this biopsy? Do you realize that the results could show that you have cancer? Are you prepared to live with that? If the biopsy is positive, you'll need to have your breast removed. Do you think you can cope? How do you think your husband will feel about you sexually? What if the cancer is incurable and you're given a short time to live? Do you think you can handle that?" Of course, the answer to most of these questions would be "no," and many women needing breast biopsies would not pursue them. Instead, doctors help a women confront the need for the biopsy. They support her in helping her to deal with the natural reluctance and fear involved and help her to find the courage and determination to proceed.

We must do the same with AIDS testing. Instead of asking, "Are you sure you want this test?" and "Do you think you can cope?" the physician, psychologist, or therapist must take the same kind of approach they do with other necessary or valuable medical procedures. Assume it is a good idea to be tested. Compliment the person for his or her courage and self-responsibility in pursuing the test. Let each person know that you intend to help him or her get through some of the difficulties and will be there to talk in detail about the issues should that person's test turn out to be positive. Let patients know that you appreciate the courage it takes for them to proceed with the test. Emphasize that the test will be of value to them whether it turns out to be negative or positive. By taking the approach that it is valuable and worthwhile to be tested, counselors can help patients deal with their fear and discomfort rather than contribute to it. Many counseling centers are beginning to change to this approach, but too many still follow the one that effectively discourages testing.

Testing isn't cost-effective except in high-risk populations. Required testing will simply waste a lot of money getting nothing but negative results.

A negative result is exceedingly valuable and can be utilized to maintain health. Any individual who tests negative should be given written, taped, or individual information on how to remain uninfected so that they are motivated to protect that fortunate

continued on page 266

20

continued from page 265

status. Some studies have found that an HIV-negative result alone is sometimes not sufficient to motivate a change in sexual behavior. It is exceedingly worthwhile to test negative, especially if it can be combined with some information or counseling so that the individual can be given an opportunity to remain HIV-negative for life.

The cost of testing the entire population and counseling those who are HIV-positive on how not to spread the disease is a fraction of the cost that would be required to care for those who would otherwise become infected.

25   *Testing is no good. The day after someone has the test they could become infected. That's why safe-sex cards don't work.*

It is true that moments after blood has been drawn for an AIDS test the person could have sex and become infected. There is no question that the test is only as good as the behavior that follows it. On the other hand, if a person gets tested fairly regularly (every six months or once a year) and you meet that person five years after their first test and learn that that person has had the discipline and the concern about his or her health to remain negative for that period of time, it tells you something about the person's judgment and health status. One test may not carry a great deal of meaning, except to the individual who knows whether or not his or her behavior has been risky since the last test. On the other hand, a series of tests that are negative makes a statement of great importance.

It is also important to emphasize that testing is not enough. I do not support safe-sex cards if they are used in singles clubs with the recommendation that anyone who tests negative and carries a card can have sex with anyone else holding a similar card. Multiple partners multiplies the possible error. On the other hand, I think that one or more tests are very valuable if used as a prerequisite to a monogamous relationship and if condoms and spermicide are also used until at least a year has passed to protect against the window in time mentioned earlier.

If you institute mandatory testing, what are you going to do with the individuals who test positive? Isolate them? Quarantine them?

Society will do the same thing with individuals who test HIV-

continued to next page

positive on mandatory testing that they will do with any individuals who test HIV-positive on widespread voluntary testing. Most people who are fighting mandatory testing are actually fighting quarantine, afraid that one will lead to the other. I would much prefer that they support the valuable and meaningful step of testing and fight the issue of quarantine, rather than fight step two to avoid step three.

You should not test because some people will panic when they are told of a positive result and commit suicide.

30

This is one of the most worrisome consequences of testing. It is understandable that someone who tests positive would fleetingly consider taking his or her own life, and some individuals might progress to actually doing so. This is one of the reasons a positive test result should never be given by phone. A patient should be called to see his or her physician or counselor or to the anonymous testing center so that he or she can be counseled extensively at that moment.

There are no guarantees that will ensure that someone would not commit suicide, but we must do everything humanly possible to prevent it—short of not testing. The reason for this is simple: If that person were not tested and did not know that he or she were HIV-positive, the odds are good that that person would take someone else's life unknowingly through continued sexual activity. So, even in this case, informing and counseling the individual are preferable to allowing that person to remain ignorant and perhaps infect not one but many others, thereby sentencing them to death.

Contact tracing is of no value, requires too much manpower, and violates privacy.

Contract tracing is *always* voluntary. A patient must be willing to identify sexual partners for it to be successful. When the public health department performs contact tracing, it contacts the sexual partner without giving him or her the name of the person involved. Instead, health officials say, "It has come to our attention that you have been exposed to the AIDS virus, and it is important that you be tested in order to determine whether you have become infected." It is true that if the individual has had only one sexual partner in his or her entire life he or she will be able to

continued on page 268

continued from page 267

deduce who the person was. Since this is the exception rather than the general rule, and since the incubation period of this disease might go back a decade or more, in most cases it would be very difficult to identify the other individual involved.

35

Under what circumstances could required testing be instituted, and what rationale would justify implementing this system?

Hospital admission is an important opportunity for mandatory or required testing. In order to give the best care to a patient who is HIV-positive, a physician must know the patient's antibody status. A physician would treat a postoperative infection or any other infection far more aggressively with antibiotics in a patient that the physician knew to be HIV-positive than in one who did not have the potential for immune system compromise. Anyone admitted with an infection would be watched more closely if HIV-positive and would probably be treated earlier than someone whose immune system was more dependable.

Many argue that the doctor should use his or her discretion on whom to test. I argue that that feeds into a discriminatory bias suggesting that one can prejudge who might be suspiciously gay. There are no indicators in the healthy HIV-positive person to cause a physician to suspect which person needs testing.

One case history was particularly convincing that physicians need the test to help make a proper diagnosis. A women called a television program in San Francisco. She said that she had AIDS. Several months before, she had flown to San Diego to donate blood for her mother's elective surgery. Subsequently, she returned to San Francisco, had several additional sexual partners, and eventually was admitted to San Francisco General Hospital for acute respiratory distress. She was treated for allergies and asthma but almost died. During the time that she was in the hospital, she received a letter from the blood bank informing her that her blood had tested HIV-positive. She asked her roommate to open the letter. The doctors then made the diagnosis of Pneumocystic pneumonia, treated her, and she was discharged from the hospital a few days later.

San Francisco General is one of the hospitals that has the most experience in diagnosing and dealing with the AIDS virus. They missed this diagnosis and might not have made it without the aid

continued to next page

of the mandatory AIDS test performed by the blood bank. The patient would have died without a change in treatment approach. It seems to me that if such a sophisticated treatment center can miss the diagnosis it would be common in less-experienced hospitals. Physicians need the assistance of this kind of testing to guide them.

This also pertains to mental hospital admissions. AIDS dementia and central nervous system infection are proving to be more common than uncommon. Some researchers believe that over 90 percent of those infected manifest some degree of central nervous system involvement. Most psychologists and psychiatrists would still not suspect organic disease due to AIDS when a patient manifests acute or chronic depression, psychoses, schizophrenia, sociopathy, or aggressive or violent behavior. The virus can infect any part of the brain and, depending upon the location of infection, the resultant behavioral changes can be quite varied.

Should HIV testing be required for any special jobs?

Another challenging aspect of HIV infection not yet confronted by our society is the otherwise asymptomatic individual who has extensive central nervous system or brain infection causing impaired judgment and interference with fine motor coordination. Pilots, air traffic controllers, and those in similar professions could be affected. Testing for the AIDS virus under these circumstances is common sense, not discrimination.

Mandatory or routine testing has been suggested for many other situations and occupations. Testing is already common in the military, prisons, and during immigration. Other situations becoming more common opportunities for testing are during prenatal examinations and in substance abuse programs. Other situations being heatedly debated are premarital testing and testing for food handlers, teachers, health-care workers, and business travelers. . . .

Having reviewed the common arguments against mandatory or required testing, we have only to devise methods that will alleviate the concerns of those who oppose mandatory testing. The two greater obstacles are concerns about confidentiality and fear of quarantine. Everything possible must be done to improve the security of our record-keeping systems. Simultaneously,

continued on page 270

40

continued from page 269

society must be taught that everyone who is ill deserves our compassion, care, and respect, regardless of the source of infection.

45   The issue of testing must be separated from the issue of quarantine. We have tested and reported people with AIDS to the public health department for many years, and there has been no hint of quarantining unless violent or aggressive behavior puts others in danger. The issue of quarantining is independent, but related, and should be fought on a different front.

Mandatory, or preferably "required," testing under certain circumstances incorporates all the virtues of voluntary testing without the drawbacks. We do not now have widespread compliance with voluntary testing. Many individuals still prefer not to know. If only one person's health were at stake, this privilege could persist. However, the ostrich approach has never demonstrated itself to be of much value. In order to deal with reality, one must face it. Self-responsibility and responsibility to others requires it.

There would be widespread voluntary compliance with required testing just as there is for blood counts and tuberculin tests once it becomes widely recognized as a matter of common sense for health—for the benefit of every individual—and not an issue of coercion.

Voluntary testing is ideal but unrealistic in many situations. Required testing under certain circumstances is best for all concerned if handled with confidentiality and consideration. Routine testing in other circumstances will naturally evolve out of the preceding two. Should these trends materialize, being tested for AIDS will become a way of life. The challenge then becomes how to preserve the quality of life for everyone—the healthy and the ill.

ENCOUNTER THE SUBJECT

These three writers lived in the world long before the situations they chose to write about became controversial issues. And while they were living, they were learning from experience and from reading, and they were formulating judgments about what they experienced. When these writers finally came face to face with the controversies they later chose to write about, they were intellectually and morally predisposed—even if they didn't instantly make up their minds which side they were on—to view the controversies they encountered from the sum total of their knowledge and experience. I don't want you to get the idea that I'm being totally deterministic here. It wasn't so much the side of the issue that each writer was predisposed to as it was the way of viewing the issue. We are all individuals, and as we grow and evolve intellectually and personally, we find ourselves developing a world view. Particular principles and concerns become more important than others, and we focus again and again on the same concerns in the situations we encounter.

Consider your own major concerns. Think about your encounters with the controversial subjects of these essays. How might your prior experiences and knowledge have primed you to view the subject of gays in the military, HIV testing, or the clearcutting of timber? What is your first response when you think about each of these issues? Is there one concern common to your responses to all three?

RESEARCH OPPORTUNITY

To expand your encounter with one of these texts, **research** its subject. You might **interview** a credible expert on either side of the issue. Or you might do a **library search** with the purpose of finding and reading arguments that voice an opposing view to the essay you've chosen as your research focus. In addition, you might research recent developments in the controversy. For example, you might focus on how the status of gays in the military has changed (or not changed) since Weisberg wrote his piece during George Bush's presidency.

RESPONSIVE JOURNAL WRITING

Respond to the results of your research activities in the form of an exploratory journal entry. In what ways has your perspective on the issue you researched changed? In what ways has it remained the same?

LISTEN—READ CAREFULLY FOR MEANING

COLLABORATIVE WRITING ASSIGNMENT

Explore the meaning of at least one of the professional essays in this chapter in collaboration with your classmates. This collaboration can be done in the classroom or in small study and research groups beyond the classroom. Start the collaboration in groups of three or four. As you work, have one member of your group record your collaborative conclusions. After concentrated group work, open the discussion up to full-class conversation. Remember, reading is an interactive art. Expect to have disagreements with your collaborative reading partners.

RESEARCH UNKNOWNS.   Thorough knowledge of the subject is crucial to effective argumentative writing. Simply put, to develop and defend a committed position, writers have to know what they're talking about. For this reason, argumentative texts often contain much information and many references that are totally new to the reader. With this in mind, what references in the text leave you with questions?

ANALYZE THE SPEAKER.   Here you're going to start digging into the developmental material in the text. Your evidence-supported judgments about each speaker will lead you into the details that support his or her argumentative position.

Facts
From your reading, what factual information can you gather about the speaker? Make sure that you cite specific passages from the text to support your judgments. In addition, what information can you gather about the speaker from research?

Emotions
Where in the text does the speaker reveal his or her emotional reaction to the subject? Keep in mind that emotions can be revealed through language choices as well as developmental choices. Have you ever experienced similar emotions? If so, you might describe the circumstances and your responsive feelings to your collaborative partners.

continued to next page

Attitudes

Where in the text does the speaker draw conclusive judgments about the subject, and what are those judgments?

DETERMINE THE MESSAGE.   In argumentative writing the writer's message isn't an overall judgment on the controversy; it's not a blatant "pro" or "con." Instead, it's the general "why" behind the argument the writer is putting forward. For example, Weisberg doesn't just argue that gay men and lesbian women should be openly admitted to the military. Instead, his evidence is focused on a particular reason *why* gay men and lesbian women should be openly admitted to the armed forces. With this in mind, write down in as few words as possible the message (main idea or thesis) of the text.

DETERMINE THE AUDIENCE.   Making sure that you provide evidence from the text to support your judgments, describe the audience to whom the text is directed. For example, is Weisberg writing to the military community? Is he writing to the gay community? To another community entirely? What language or developmental material in Weisberg's text can you cite as evidence for your judgment?

DETERMINE THE PURPOSE.   Argumentative writing is the most openly persuasive of all writing. More often than not, the writer not only wants to change your thinking, but also wants you to become an advocate for his or her view of things. With this in mind, what specific change in thought or action does the speaker desire from the audience?

RESPONSIVE JOURNAL WRITING

Assess the effect of the critical reading process by journal writing. If your perspective on the subject of the text was changed in any way by the critical reading process, write at least a page in which you explain the changes. If your perspective wasn't changed, write at least a page explaining why it wasn't.

RESEARCH OPPORTUNITY

Now that you've read the texts carefully, you may be left with questions about the writers' interpretations or evidence. Focus on your questions, and brainstorm research activities that might lead you to answers. Then pursue one or more of the research activities that came out of your brainstorming. See the research chapters and Part Six for more information about brainstorming.

RESPONSIVE JOURNAL WRITING

Respond to your research by exploring your findings in a journal entry.

LEARN—READ WITH AN EYE TO THE WRITER'S CRAFT

FOCUS ON RESEARCH IN RESPONSES TO CONTROVERSY

All three of these writers speak with authority about the subjects of their writing. And, more than in any other way, they've achieved that authority by thoroughly researching the controversial situations to which they're responding. As you proceed to study the text you're exploring, focus your attention on the developmental material that came from sources beyond the writer's own experience.

FOCUS ON PERSUASION IN RESPONSES TO CONTROVERSY

Writing that takes a committed position in the context of a controversy is the most highly persuasive of all kinds of writing. The writer isn't just sharing a perspective; the writer is trying to enlist you as an advocate. And because responses to controversy are bent on enlisting you, you should be particularly critical of the persuasive techniques employed in them.

LOGOS, PERSUADING WITH REASON   All responses to controversy rely heavily on appeals to the reader's reason. We humans are by nature rational creatures; we gather evidence and draw conclusions, so we find it appealing when things make sense to us. However, things that make sense to us aren't necessarily *true;* they're just plausible—they could, under the right circumstances, be true. For example, take the first sentence of paragraph six of Crenshaw's essay on HIV testing:

> An encouraging point is that in Colorado, where HIV-positive status is reportable and contact tracing is routine, *there has not been one episode of breach of confidentiality,* demonstrating that when extra care is taken there can be great success.

Crenshaw gives us an example of a specific situation in which the confidentiality of HIV testing holds up, hoping that we'll conclude that—in general—the confidentiality of HIV testing won't be breached. Crenshaw isn't presenting us with an absolute truth; she's presenting us with a proven example (evidence) and inviting us to extend that example into other situations.

Frome uses a similar tactic in paragraph seventeen of his essay:

> Even though logging may improve deer habitat, serious disturbance eliminates such species as spotted owls and pine martens, which require old growth conifers for survival. Birds actually furnish the most efficient and least costly form of insect control in the forest. It is their definitive function in providing balance to the ecosystem. A single woodpecker, for example, has been estimated to be able to consume the larvae of 13, 675 highly destructive wood-boring beetles per year. It is fair to generalize that the more numerous and varied the bird population of a forest, the broader the spectrum of natural insect control.

Whether you're reading someone else's argument or building your own, the important thing to remember about appeals to reason is that you have to test them critically by challenging them. Although appeals to reason don't have to be absolutely *true,* they do have to stand up to critical pressure. They have to make more than just immediate sense; they have to continue to make sense when you extend them into other situations. So when you come across an appeal to reason, scrutinize it carefully. Has the writer (or you, if you're the writer) given enough examples to justify the generalization? Can the generalization actually be made? Perhaps the situations to which you're being invited to extend the example contain elements that will interfere with the neatness of the extension.

PATHOS, PERSUADING WITH EMOTION   Just as we humans are rational creatures, we're also creatures of emotion. We're moved not only by logic but by how we feel about things. As I've said before, appeals to emotion are not necessarily weaker or more suspect than appeals to reason. Appeals to emotion are used widely in responses to social controversies because social controversies are usually emotionally charged situations. In addition, because research is so crucial in responses to controversy, the writer will often add to his or her credibility by taking an emotional appeal from an outside source. For example, in paragraph three of his essay, Frome quotes an emotional appeal from a *Field & Stream* editorial as a way of supporting his own position against clearcutting:

> These trees are planted in neat little rows, all standing at the same height and all reaching maturity at the same time for another cutting. But it is no longer a forest any more than an orchard is a forest. There are no open grassy glens, no bushes, no aspen or alders. Everything is crowded and shaded out by the trees, and for the major part of the growth years of the trees there is little food for animals or birds. It is a sterile sort of forest designed by a computer.

Appeals to emotion should be tested critically. What's important to remember when you're evaluating emotional appeals is that they should be logically connected to the subject being written about. Even an appeal to an emotion as strong as fear can be valid as long as it's logically connected to the subject at hand. For example, the campaign against cigarette smoking appeals to the fear of cancer in potential smokers by citing lung cancer statistics in heavy smokers. On the other hand, advertisements often appeal to our emotions dishonestly, when they suggest (against fact and logic) that buying a particular product will make us beautiful, popular, or happy.

ETHOS, PERSUADING BY ESTABLISHING CREDIBILITY   Although the general credibility of writers depends to a large extent on the solidity of their reasonable and emotional appeals, there are other factors that affect just how much we trust a given writer. One significant factor is the writer's reputation in the world. For example, we're more likely to trust a well-known expert in a field over a person who has no credentials. In addition, sometimes just the fame of a person can lend her or him an unreasonable ''expert'' status; we see this ''credibility of fame'' at work every day in celebrities' endorsements of commercial products and political causes. When actor Robert Redford writes about environmental is-sues, we might be likely to find his opinions more credible because he plays honest, idealistic characters in his films.

Writers can also enhance their credibility by citing statistics or quoting agreeing authorities, by quoting disreputable sources with whom they disagree, or even by discrediting disagreeing authorities. Frome estab-lishes a skillful mixture of ''borrowing'' credibility and discrediting when he juxtaposes the emotional appeal from *Field & Stream* that describes reforestation after clearcutting as ''a sterile sort of forest designed by a computer'' with the quotation from former Chief Forester Edward P. Cliff, whose point of view Frome disagrees with:

> But a newer forest, man-planned and managed and coming up sturdily where century-old giants formerly stood, also has its brand of beauty—similar in its way to the terraced contours and the orderly vegetative growth upon well-managed farmlands.

One of the most powerful vehicles for credibility is the writer's created voice. The persona created on the page reveals the writer's attitude toward the audience as well as toward the subject. And once the audience begins to distrust the created voice, the writer's credibility is lost. Crenshaw, arguing for ''required'' HIV testing under some circumstances, creates a rational and compassionate persona in her essay. Here's an example from her introduction in which by naming the resources ''we need'' she sets herself up as being reasonable and caring:

> There is no simple solution. Testing alone is not enough. We need all of our resources: common sense, sexual integrity, compassion, love, exclusivity, education, discipline, testing, condoms, and spermicides—to name just a few. We also need an emphatic, pos-itive message that promotes *quality* sex instead of *quantity* sex. Multiple partners and casual sex are not in the best interest of health, but within an exclusive relationship quality sex can thrive.

Notice that the subject of her essay, HIV testing, comes late in her list of resources. The resources she names first are human qualities. By naming them first she implies that she not only possesses those qualities but acts in accordance with them when she supports required testing.

Just as you have to critically test appeals to reason and emotion, you also have to test appeals to credibility. A biased authority—whether that authority is yourself or an outside source—has no actual authority at all. As the reader, put critical pressure on the conclusions in the text. If you're the writer, test your own conclusions by thinking critically. Explore your personal and educational history, and question whether you actually have the experience and knowledge to be an authority on the subject. If you don't, find out more by researching your subject. Whether you're the reader or the writer, check the credibility of outside sources by researching them. Explore various sources and test their perspectives by **comparing and contrasting** them.

Each of these writers wanted to effect change. Behind all their choices was their desire to resolve the controversies they were writing about by moving as many people as possible away from their opposition's position and toward their own. In argument, more than in any other kind of writing, the writer's choices are delicate and audience-based.

COLLABORATIVE WRITING ASSIGNMENT

In collaborative groups, comparatively study the writer's choices in at least one of these three essays with an eye to improving your own argumentative writing and thinking. As you focus on each of the choice categories, keep in mind the determination you made of the essay's target audience. What's important here is not whether you were convinced by the writer's arguments, but rather whether the writer's chosen audience was likely to have been convinced.

VOICE   Created voice is a powerful factor in argumentative writing. The writer's credibility rests to a great extent on the trustworthiness of the persona he or she creates on the page. With this in mind, describe in as much detail as possible the created persona in the text you're exploring. As usual, make sure you cite evidence from the text to support your judgments.

DEVELOPMENT   Writers don't only argue *for* their side of things when they develop arguments; they also often argue directly *against* specific points raised previously by the opposition. The argumentative writing done in the context of social and academic controversies is a back-and-forth unfolding and refinement of perspectives. Each of these three writers responds directly to argumentative points raised by the opposition to develop his or her own interpretative conclusions. Working collaboratively,

continued to next page

identify as many of these directly responsive argumentative points in the text as you can.

Because argumentative writing is largely based on appeals to reason, writers of arguments usually rely heavily on secondary **research as a way of persuading** their audiences. All three of these writers partially establish their credibility by citing detailed evidence from outside sources. Working collaboratively, mark the passages in the text that come from outside sources. What's the rough percentage in the text of cited material?

In addition to appealing to reason and credibility, writers also argue by appealing to the emotions of their audiences. What emotional responses does the writer attempt to elicit from the audience?

ARRANGEMENT   All three of these texts contain similar elements. They all have introductions in which the writer establishes his or her credibility and provides background information that justifies his or her committed position. They all contain arguments both for their position and against the opposition's position. In addition, they all have conclusions where the writer discusses the implications of viewing the controversy from his or her perspective.

Working collaboratively, outline the essay you're exploring and respond to the following questions. Where in the essay is the writer's committed position first openly stated? What kind of developmental material does the writer present prior to stating his or her position? Why might the writer have chosen to present that material before stating his or her position? What is the argumentative emphasis in the essay? Does the writer mainly present arguments *for* his or her position or *against* the opposition? Considering the audience and purpose, why might the writer have chosen this emphasis?

RESPOND—DEVELOP A PERSPECTIVE THROUGH WRITING

You're almost ready to respond to a controversial issue by writing. However, before you do, read how two other student writers responded to controversy.

Grady Gadbow

THE POLITICS OF PROHIBITION AND THE DEATH OF THE AMERICAN DREAM

Grady Gadbow is a rock musician, fisher, hunter, and student. He wrote the following essay for a composition class in 1995.

It could be that at one time the United States was the land of the free and the home of the brave. I suppose, in comparison to some other countries in the world, we do have a few tasty morsels of so-called freedom, although I can't think of any aspect of our culture, or lack thereof, that reflects any particular bravery. Although freedom has always been a favorite word of politicians, the vast majority of government action only decreases actual freedom in the name of mob morality and politics itself.

Already America has the highest drinking age in the world, some of the stiffest restrictions on media broadcasting, drug laws so ridiculous they can barely be enforced, and with every passing decade an increasing prohibition on weaponry.

The new gun laws have been justified by their supporters as attempts to combat America's problem of violent crime. And attempts indeed they are, although there is a remarkable lack of any evidence that they are effective. For instance, fully automatic weapons have always been illegal, and although you may not be able to buy one at K-Mart, they're still out there and everyone knows it. Also, if you're an enterprising capitalist and gun savvy, you make a fully automatic weapon, and a lot of people do. There's good money in running illegal weapons if you know the right people. Last I heard, a full-auto AK-47, the world's most popular assault rifle, ran about eight hundred dollars. The legal semi-auto versions only cost about four hundred. With the most recent gun legislation, the importation of weaponry, including the AK from China, has been banned along with the production of high capacity magazines commonly attached to them. So far these laws have resulted in a dramatic upswing in gun sales; and when the stockpiles finally start to dwindle, we'll undoubtedly see a proliferation of these weapons on the private market at slightly higher prices. At all levels of commerce the prohibition of weaponry seems to mean that more people will own weapons.

continued to next page

Another measure connected with the crime bill was an increase in the price of a Federal Firearms License (FFL) from thirty dollars a year to two hundred dollars. The FFL allows the licensee to ship firearms out of state, and purchase them from factories at wholesale prices. It also makes the license holder an official gun dealer required to send in a form to the federal government containing the complete identity of the buyer of any weapon sold. Many small-time dealers who work gun shows or trade in firearms out of their homes simply won't bother to renew their FFLs, and all their transactions from then on will be what is known in the trade as private-owner deals. No registration forms will be sent in, and the weapons sold will be completely untraceable to their owners, should they be recovered at the scene of a crime. Legally, a private-owner dealer doesn't even have to know the name of someone he sells a gun to, and, thus, the whole registration process is circumvented. Yet another example of gun restriction measures backfiring.

Supposedly the idea behind gun control is to insure that bad guys don't get guns. However, seriously, is that realistic? Do our law enforcement agencies really keep control on us so tightly that black market hardware could be eliminated? In a country where there are already more guns than people, would our tax dollars spent on enforcement of more prohibitive baby-sitting laws really make a difference in the number of people getting shot? I think not.

The latest batch of gun laws have come in response to political pressure on the Clinton administration to do something about the proliferation of violent crime. With the perhaps deliberate short sightedness typical of professional politicians, our law makers took action, not against the causes of violence such as poverty, unemployment, decrepit educational systems, et cetera, but merely made a token denunciation of the tools of the trade. A more intensive look at violent crime was politically too dangerous.

Undeniably a huge percentage of violence in urban America is connected to the drug trade: violence between gangs fighting over control of the local drug market or between drug people and police. If the president had publicly addressed this problem on any serious level, it might have meant massive reexamination of

continued on page 282

continued from page 281

the Drug War. This war being fought constantly by our government against our own people results in staggering numbers of deaths and injuries. To really address the problem of violence, the president might have had to call the whole thing off, and Washington has never liked policy reversals. A massive, "Sorry about all the bloodshed, and long prison terms, we were wrong," wouldn't look so good. After all, a lot of people are kept comfortably employed fighting the Drug War. So the attack on violence was redirected on hardware. It's always safer for a politician to brag up a policy that makes no difference than to really shake up the system to make things better.

With shooting irons as the scapegoats of reluctant reformists, the legitimate sportsman is left with no real allies in the two party system. While the powerful NRA lobby steadfastly opposes any form of gun regulation, it supports only far right-wing political candidates. These are the same forces working to sell our public lands out from under us. Although figures like Montana Senator Conrad Burns claim to be on the side of hunters by opposing gun legislation, it just doesn't hold up in light of his support for privatization and development of public lands. If the NRA had their way, we could have all the guns we wanted but no place to shoot them.

Inevitably gun control supporters cite the example of Canada's low crime rate and make the shaky correlation to Canada's gun policies. What is less commonly mentioned is Canada's better developed health and welfare programs. An example of a different kind is Australia, where there has been hardly any gun control coupled with hardly any crime. Another point in the Australian's favor is the policy of fewer laws in general. As America has demonstrated more than once with prohibition laws, the more laws you make, the more crime you get. There is no reason to think that prohibiting guns will be any different than prohibiting alcohol or drugs. In a country with such a well established illegal gun market, it may prove a very dangerous move to broaden in any way the definition of illegal guns.

When laws were invented, they weren't designed to protect people from themselves or inhibit people's personal business. The reason we have laws is to protect our individual well-being from

continued to next page

deliberate harm inflicted by others. In that department, we pretty well cover misuse of weaponry with laws against theft, assault and murder. Realistically, nobody's well being is protected by laws against what people can own, what books we want to read, or even what drugs we want to take. These prohibitive laws are used by political strategists to skirt the real issues, to split political masses, to create single issue factions and special interest groups that can be roped into voting for people who actually act against them on all other issues. Not only does prohibition create crime, but it creates the confusion that poisons the American dream.

Hadley Skinner
IN DEFENSE OF AMERICAN EDUCATION*

Hadley Skinner is a music performance major at The University of Montana. Although Hadley has spent most of her nineteen years in Missoula, Montana, she has also lived in New York City, Japan and Slovakia.

Critics of the American school system view the Japanese school system as superior to ours. They base their opinions on comparative achievement-test scores, such as those from the Center for Education Statistics, which show Japan ranking first and the United States twelfth among twenty countries (OERI Bulletin 45). The figures appear to corroborate the superiority of the Japanese educational system. However, having attended schools in both systems, I would like to respond to these critics. I believe the Japanese system emphasizes memorization of facts and rote learning, which produce dependent learners. On the other hand, the American system encourages students to apply, analyze and evaluate facts and information. This makes them more self-sufficient learners and independent thinkers.

At the age of thirteen, I became acquainted with Japanese schools, which I attended for two years. I remember feeling very nervous because I couldn't speak the language, and I had also read articles about the difficulty of succeeding academically in Japan. The articles suggested that the Japanese schools covered more advanced subject matter over a shorter time than their

continued on page 284

---

*The writer of this essay has used the documentation style of the MLA Manual, 4 ed.

continued from page 283

American counterparts. I had even studied with a math tutor all summer to reach the math level of my Japanese peers.

The first few months in Japan seemed to support my preconceptions. The students worked hard and were constantly under pressure. They never took a break from their studies or went out with their friends or family because the minute they came home from school, they started to study. As Kay McKinney writes in "A Look at Japanese Education Today," there is so much expected of these students that "PTA newsletters sometimes suggest to parents when their children should get up and go to bed as well as the hours they should study and play during vacations" (28). In addition to the regular academic day, many of the students are expected to attend a cram school after school which drills them further on what their learning in school and prepares them for entrance exams into high school. These exams are important because if the students don't pass, they will never get into a high school, and their education effectively is over.

I, too, experienced these pressures. I became accustomed to monthly exams which covered new material and material from months and even years before. The Japanese system also required teachers to place the grades on a bell curve. So, only eleven students out of the two hundred in my class would receive an "A" for a course, and the same number would always receive an "F," no matter how hard they tried.

There is ample scholarly support to back up my personal experience. As Benjamin C. Duke writes in *Education and Leadership for the Twenty-First Century*, "Although undoubtedly cognizant that they sit at the pinnacle of the educational ladder at the secondary school level, the conditions under which they experience daily life, both at home and school and in between, cannot be described as very pleasant or accommodating. The academic pressure is severe, the classrooms crowded, the family expectations very high, the homes and apartments often times small and crowded, the commuting trains suffocating, and leisure facilities available at a grossly distorted premium" (113).

Duke also asked both Japanese and American students whether they were satisfied with their lives today. The results (141) were:

continued to next page

	Americans	Japanese
Very well satisfied	27.4%	5.3%
Satisfied	56.9	45.1
Dissatisfied	12.5	37.7
Very dissatisfied	1.9	10.6

Moreover, a study in the *1995 Japan Almanac* showed a dramatic increase in the number of students in secondary education who refused to attend school. In junior high school the number of students who didn't attend school rose from 13,536 in 1980, to 43,711 in 1991 (242).

I also noticed the program caused anger and competition among my classmates. It disturbed me to see my friends compete for the higher scores so that they could be one of the eleven selected to have an "A" stamped on their transcript. I began to see the discrimination against the people who didn't succeed in school. If students didn't do well, they were shunned by their teachers and other classmates.

I feel sorry for these students because they receive no help in school, such as remediation or special tutoring. McKinney did a study in one large Japanese city on first and fifth graders' ability to read, and found that "most children enter first grade well prepared in reading. However, by the fifth grade, many fall seriously behind" (34). I remember a student in my class who couldn't read past fourth-grade level, and because he never got help with this disability, he didn't have a chance at continuing his education at high school or college. (When I went back to Japan four years later, I saw him working at a grocery store, which is probably the only job he could qualify for.)

As I further learned the language and could participate more, I realized that Japanese students learn things in a different order than American students, making it appear as if they are farther ahead. For example, in the United States we take algebra for a year, then geometry for a year, then advanced algebra and finally pre-calculus. In the Japanese system, the students are given a little bit of algebra, geometry, and pre-calculus all in one year, so it appears as if they are learning harder material before we are. In

continued on page 286

continued from page 285

the end it evens out, and we all have the same information. So, when people read statistics such as those of the Center for Education Statistics, they ought to take them with a grain of salt. While these thirteen-year-old Japanese students are dabbling in lots of math subjects at once, the American students are spending a year mastering one mathematical subject before they can go on to the next. Thus, it's unfair to compare the Japanese with the Americans at such an early age.

After moving back to the United States, I realized I had overestimated the strengths of Japanese education. The Japanese system had made me so timid that I was afraid to speak up in class. I'd lost my self-confidence. In history, for example, I found that my American teachers wanted me to participate in discussions, and to articulate my thoughts on various issues. But my Japanese experience had taught me to learn by memorization instead of analyzing and synthesizing information. When Japanese teachers complete a lecture, no one ever asks questions. The students go home and memorize all the facts in the lecture. In class the next day teachers will drill them on the contents of the lecture. This way of learning never allows them to express their opinions. They get so wrapped up in memorizing facts that they never take time to discuss the issues.

I realize there are many people talking about the great Japanese system that produces so many "smart" people, but they should give some thought to how they're defining "smart." Japanese schools are like factories that create the same product over and over again. I would hope that more people realize that our system creates individuals and thinkers. I'm very thankful for the American teachers that taught me one of the most important skills of life—to think for myself.

WORKS CITED

Duke, Benjamin C. *Education and Leadership for the Twenty-First Century: Japan America and Britain*. New York: Prager Publishers, 1991.

"Education Problems." *Japan Almanac*. Tokyo: Asahi Shinbun. 1995.

McKinney, Kay. "A Look at Japanese Education Today," *Research in Brief*. Washington, D.C.: U.S. Department of Education, Office of Instruc-

continued to next page

tional Research and Improvement, Educational Resources Information and Research Center, 1987.

"Time Spent on Mathematics Instruction and Homework by Japanese and U.S. 13-Year-Old Students," *OERI Bulletin*. Washington, D.C.: U.S. Office of Education Research and Improvement, Center for Education Statistics, December 1986.

RESPONSIVE WRITING ASSIGNMENT

Write an essay in response to a controversial issue. After thoroughly analyzing or researching the issue, develop a reasonable argument that supports your position in the controversy.

RESPONDING TO CONTROVERSIAL ISSUES: A GUIDE TO THE PROCESS

Assess Your Past Performance
Explore the Writing Situation
Prewrite
Draft
Rewrite

ASSESS YOUR PAST PERFORMANCE

As you work through this assignment, continue to **analyze** how you think and write, **learn** from your previous experience, and **respond by revising** your personal writing process. Read over your assessment of your performance from your last assignment, and consider your writing strengths and weaknesses. Identify the categories with which you had trouble. Then analyze why you had trouble, and focus on ways you might better employ the writing process to avoid repeating your mistakes. For example, if the last text you constructed was underdeveloped, analyze why. Was it because you didn't give yourself enough time to **research** your subject thoroughly? To improve your performance, you'll have to budget time for more researching. Part Six provides detailed process-based revision strategies that will help you employ the writing process more effectively.

EXPLORE THE WRITING SITUATION

To find an initial direction for your essay, actively explore the **choices** and **constraints** of the writing situation.

SUBJECT   The subject of this essay is constrained only in one way— you must respond to a controversial issue by taking a committed position. The issue you choose to write about may be social, academic, or even personal. Consider the communities that you're a member of—your classes, campus, city, state, nation, or even your family. List the controversies that are currently topics of dispute in these communities. Of the controversies you've listed, choose a few that interest you—a few that you know something about and that are related to your experience. Remember, the position you take should be a committed one, and the best way to maintain that commitment is to choose a subject that relates to you personally. Explore your initial responses to the issues you've listed in a conversation with a classmate, friend, or instructor.

AUDIENCE   In argumentative writing, the choice of audience is up to you. What you have to keep in mind is that you're writing to move the controversy toward resolution. Change is what you're after; there's not much sense in writing to an audience that can't effect that change. Explore the possible audiences to whom you might write. Do you have any chance of changing the direct opposition, or might it be a better strategy to change to a more neutral audience? Consider your determinations of audience for the essay you chose to examine earlier in this chapter. Why might the writer have selected the audience he or she did?

PURPOSE   The general purpose in argumentative writing is given: persuade the audience that your point of view is the one they should also hold. But your specific purpose is less constrained. Just what is it that you want your audience to do once you've convinced them to agree with your message? Do you want them to think differently, to act differently, to become an advocate for your position?

THE WRITER   In argumentative writing, **self-criticism** is crucial. To be a convincing advocate you have to be as critical of your position as the opposition would be. Although personal investment is important in argument, rationality is absolutely necessary. Explore the why's behind your initial responses to the tentative subjects you've chosen. What in your experience makes these issues compelling? How might each controversy's resolution affect your life? Then consider the opposition in each controversy. What in their prior experiences might make them advocates for an opposing point of view? How might the controversy's resolution affect their lives? Outside of your personal investment, do you have more compelling reasons for your position than your opposition has for their position?

TIME   Since in most cases research is necessary in argumentative writing, you'll need plenty of time for this assignment. Consider the type of research necessary for each of your tentative subjects, and budget your time accordingly. Although library research can be time-consuming, primary research, such as interviews and questionnaires, can be even more so. If you believe that you don't have enough time to do the necessary research for a particular subject, you might have to choose another.

If your exploration has triggered your choices of subject and audience, further explore your audience's knowledge of the subject and position in the context of the controversy. If you haven't made a choice of subject and audience by this point, choose from your list of "tentatives" the subject that seems most appealing and explore it by prewriting.

PREWRITE

RESEARCH OPPORTUNITY

Thorough knowledge of the entire context of the controversy is vitally important in argumentative writing. If possible, choose a collaborative **research partner** (or form a research team); then **brainstorm** (either on your own or with your partners) a list of possible research techniques and sources for your subject. Refer to Chapters Five and Six for advice on **primary and secondary research techniques.** A good first step in researching argument is to seek out two credible experts in the field—one on either side of the issue—for preliminary **interviews.** Conflicting experts can help you understand the entire context of the controversy, and they can also point you toward other research sources. After following up as many sources as possible, reconsider your subject and audience. Has your perspective on the issue changed? If so, in what ways?

RESPONSIVE PREWRITING EXERCISES

1. Defining the controversy can help you make a final choice of audience as well as make initial choices in development. With this in mind, define the issue by analyzing it in the following ways.

   a. Who are the **active participants** in the situation? List the individuals or groups. For example, Weisberg would probably have listed gay men and lesbian women, the United States military establishment, and American society as a whole as active participants.

   b. Now explore the **causes and effects** of the controversy by **mapping** their **implications.** (See Part Six for more information on using cause/effect as a prewriting strategy.) List the **actions** of the participants in the controversy and the possible **motives** behind these actions. Then list the **consequences** of the participants' actions. Finally, speculate about ways the controversy might be **resolved.**

2. Explore the pros and cons of the issue by **comparing and contrasting** the reasons each side has for advocating its position. First, list each side's reasons. Then critically test the reasons by comparing and contrasting them.

3. Seek out a person who has an opposing viewpoint on the issue you've chosen to write about, and explore the subject in conversation. When the conversation is over, freewrite (write nonstop) about the issue for ten minutes.

FOCUS ON A TENTATIVE POSITION

Look back over the results of your explorations, and make a decision about where you stand on the issue. Consider the three model essays in this chapter as examples: Weisberg's essay is written from his position of support *for* admitting gays and lesbians into the military forces; Crenshaw's essay is written from her position *for* mandatory HIV testing; Frome's essay is written from his position *against* the practice of clearcutting.

FOCUS ON AUDIENCE AND PURPOSE

After deciding on a tentative position, focus on your possible choices of audience and purpose.

AUDIENCE   Since changing the status of the controversy is your goal, list and then evaluate the groups that you might possibly change with your argument. For example, Weisberg's list of "changeable groups" would probably have included gays and lesbians, the military establishment, and the American public; Crenshaw's list would probably have included individuals who are HIV-positive, people who are uninformed about the issue, and people who to one degree or another oppose mandatory testing; Frome's list would probably have included the foresters and corporations who support clearcutting, informed environmentalists who oppose clearcutting, and uniformed individuals who have an environmentalist bent.

Each of these writers focused on possible audiences and then went on to evaluate those audiences, keeping in mind the goal of moving the controversy toward resolution. The audience choices they made were delicate and specific, and those choices affected all the other choices they made in the process of writing. Weisberg decided not to write to the direct opposition, the military establishment, most likely because he felt he wouldn't be able to change them; instead, he chose to write to a particular segment of the American public. If you did a thorough job of evaluating Weisberg's language and development, you should have a relatively clear picture of his audience's values and concerns. Like Weisberg, Frome chose not to write to the direct opposition, but chose to write to an audience that was environmentally sensitive but uninformed about the issue. On the other hand, Crenshaw chose to write to the widest possible audience, including individuals likely to oppose mandatory testing.

The one thing all of these chosen audiences have in common is their ability to effect change once they've been convinced by the writer's argument. As concerned citizens, Weisberg's audience could put pressure on the government to admit gays to military service; as voters and activists, Frome's audience could oppose clearcutting; as informed citizens and health care providers, Crenshaw's audience could speak in favor of required testing.

Consider your possible choices of audience, and evaluate them carefully. Your aim is to change the status of the controversy by moving as many people as you can toward your position. Choosing an audience that can't be changed is pointless, but so is choosing an audience that has no power to effect change. Which group from your list of "possibles" are you most likely to change? How far might the controversy be moved toward resolution by changing that group?

If you haven't made a choice of audience by this point, make a tentative decision and explore it further as you complete the prewriting process.

PURPOSE   Once you've made a choice of audience, consider the change you desire in that audience. Do you want to make them advocates for your position? If so, what kind of action do you want them to undertake?

FOCUS ON A WORKING MESSAGE

Remember, in argumentative writing, the writer's message isn't a simple pro or con statement of position. Instead, the message focuses on a general reason *why* that position is taken by the writer and should be taken by the audience. According to Frome's text, for example, clearcutting should be opposed because it is "environmentally pollutive and ecologically disruptive, as well as designed principally for immediate profit." Look over your determinations of message for other essays in this chapter. Then, in as few words as possible, write down the general reason *why* your audience should agree with your position.

DRAFT

DRAFT TO REVISE

The **revision** you engage in as you draft gives you the opportunity to expand on old ideas and formulate new ones. **Read** and **reread** your draft as you write, and look for new ways of viewing your subject. Pay particular attention to those areas that have given you trouble in the past, and revise as you draft by **cutting, adding, rearranging,** and **rewording.**

In argumentative writing, credibility is of utmost importance. To agree with your message and be changed, your audience has to trust the authority of your voice and believe that your arguments are reasonable. And the only way that you'll achieve the credibility that's necessary to change your audience is by being actively **self-critical.** Before you begin drafting, evaluate the thinking you've done up to this point. Look back over your written responses to the prewriting strategies, and mark the material from your prewriting that might be likely to get the audience change you want. Then put critical pressure on the material you've underlined. Is there enough material to get the change you want from your audience? Which arguments are strongest? Do you have sufficient, quality evidence to support your arguments? Can you anticipate counterarguments from the opposition to any of your argumentative points? If so, can you expand your argument and make it sound? If self-criticism has revealed weaknesses in your position, you may want to do further research or choose another issue. If you believe your arguments are sound, continue to be self-critical as you draft.

FOCUS ON YOUR CHOICES

VOICE   The persona you create on the page will help to establish your credibility with your audience. Consider the kind of person your audience would be most likely to trust. For example, Crenshaw chose to write in a reasonable and empathetic voice because she was writing to an audience that contained members of the direct opposition. Some of the people she wrote to were concerned about the privacy issue raised by mandatory HIV testing, and she had to present herself as being as sensitive to that concern as they were. On the other hand, the audience that Weisberg wrote to wasn't his direct opposition. Although Weisberg developed his arguments reasonably, his choice of audience allowed him to be ironic and even at times sarcastic about the United States military establishment's position on admitting gays and lesbians to the armed forces.

With your audience in mind, write a detailed description (or draw a detailed picture) of the voice that you believe will most likely achieve your writer's purpose. Then, as you draft, read your emerging text aloud, and **reword** it with your audience's responses in mind.

DEVELOPMENT   Focus your attention on the three appeals (appeals based on **reason,** appeals based on **emotion,** appeals based on **credibility**) as you develop the points of your argument. However, whether you're appealing to reason, emotion, or credibility, to keep your argument focused, make sure that all the points of your argument are in some way related to your message. For example, all of Frome's argumentative points are aimed at demonstrating that clearcutting "is environmentally pollutive and ecologically disruptive, as well as designed principally for immediate profit." Test your points by comparing them with your focus, and **cut** those points that might lead your audience on an irrelevant tangent.

When you're appealing to the **reason** of your audience, look for ways to **add** detailed information and examples. Your purpose isn't to report what you believe about the controversy, but to convince your audience to take the position you hold. For example, Frome doesn't just state that clearcutting interferes with wildlife habitat; he goes on to give examples in the form of statistics and quoted material to support his assertion. Test the examples you include by making sure they hold up when extended to other situations.

Remember that appeals to **emotion** should be used only when they're logically connected to the subject at hand. Test your emotional appeals by looking for valid causal connections. Then **cut** emotional appeals if they don't stand up under critical pressure.

Finally, when you're making an appeal based on **credibility** by citing outside sources, don't rely too heavily on a single source. Most critical readers are suspicious of essays with a single research source. Not only can using many and varied sources add to your credibility, but it can also open up your thinking by forcing you to view the issue from different perspectives.

Keep in mind as well that how you establish your credibility is dependent on your audience. For example, Crenshaw establishes credibility with the direct opposition in her audience by going out of her way to present opposing arguments fairly. On the other hand, Frome and Weisberg, writing to neutral audiences, openly discredit their oppositions.

ARRANGEMENT　　How you choose to arrange your argument will depend to a large degree on your audience. If your audience contains members of the direct opposition, as Crenshaw's chosen audience does, you'll have to establish your credibility by convincing your audience that you have the same concerns they have. Having members of the direct opposition in your audience will also influence where and how you address opposing arguments. Since a disagreeing audience will be primed to object to your view of things, you'll have to begin dealing with opposing arguments as soon as possible.

How much your audience knows about the issue will have an additional effect on your arrangement choices. If your audience knows little about the subject, you may need to thoroughly define the controversy first off, as Frome does at the beginning of his essay. On the other hand, if your audience is familiar with the issue, you may be able to launch right into the points of your argument, the way Weisberg does.

As you draft, **rearrange** the order of sentences, paragraphs, or sections of your text with your audience's responses in mind. If you draft on the computer, use block and move functions to rearrange. If you type or draft longhand, write on only one side of the page so that you can cut sections apart and rearrange them.

DRAFTING IS ACTIVE AND RECURSIVE

Continue to be self-critical throughout the process of drafting your argument. Change is what you're after, and the only way you'll get that change is by being actively aware of your audience's concerns.

REWRITE

To argue effectively, you have to maintain a balance between audience awareness and personal commitment. Argument is the most audience-based of all the kinds of writing. When you write an argumentative essay, you're openly and admittedly trying to change other people's way of thinking. However, when you argue you're also personally invested in your writing; you've committed yourself to a particular position. And when we're personally committed, maintaining audience awareness is often difficult. Our strong feelings about an issue can often block our ability to see the flaws in our own argument. Test your draft by **workshopping** it in an informal collaborative group. (Part Six provides strategies for peer editing and workshops.) Ask your workshop partners to read your essay carefully and to determine who your audience is and what your message and purpose are. Then ask them to be as critical as possible of your argumentative points and the evidence that supports those points.

ACTIVE REWRITING

The key word here is *active*. Don't just make cosmetic style changes. Leave yourself open to new discoveries as you revise. Consider your workshop partners' criticisms, your habitual writing weaknesses, and the techniques for responding to controversial issues. Try to put yourself in your audience's position as you read your text critically and revise. Read your response critically, focusing on the following checklist, and continue to **cut, add, rearrange,** and **reword** with your audience's responses in mind.

- Considering your audience, are they likely to trust your created voice and find it credible?
- If your audience is uninformed about the issue, have you defined it for them and given them sufficient background information?
- If your audience contains members of the direct opposition, have you established a common ground with them by demonstrating that you understand and share their concerns? In addition, have you presented the opposition's arguments fairly, and have you begun to deal with those arguments early on in your text?
- Do you have a clear and focused message—a general reason *why* your audience should take the position you advocate?
- Do your argumentative points relate to your message?
- Do you have sufficient critically tested, credible evidence to support each point of your argument?

- If you've employed emotional appeals, are they relevant and logically connected to the issue?
- Is your text correct in terms of mechanics (spelling, punctuation, sentence structure, and diction)?

EDIT TO FINAL FORM

Polish your text as you write the final draft. Focus on paragraphing, transitions, and any habitual problems you may have with spelling, punctuation, and sentence structure. Part Six provides specific information and strategies.

PROOFREAD

If possible, put your response aside for at least a couple of hours before you proofread. Proofread for small, careless errors by reading your text aloud, preferably to another person.

ASSESS YOUR PERFORMANCE BY WRITING CRITICALLY

The writing process isn't completed until you've assessed your performance. Study your evaluator's comments, and focus on **voice, arrangement, development,** and **mechanics.** (Part Six provides detailed strategies for analyzing your writing weaknesses and learning through self-criticism.) With which category did you mainly have trouble? Write a page explaining why you think you had trouble with that particular category. Then write a second page in which you explain what you might have done to correct the problem.

PART
FOUR

RESPONDING

TO

TEXTS

Essay are

1) focused, specific

2) Personal - writer P.O.V

3) interpretive - arrive @ judgment (support)

4) analytical - take apart subject

CHAPTER
TEN
RESPONDING TO ESSAYS

THE ESSAY WRITER'S SCENARIO

A writer encounters a subject. The subject might be a text—a novel or short story, an essay or a poem, a film or painting, or even an advertisement; the subject might be a situation that exists in the world—homelessness or racism, divorce or marriage, or even something as personal as the writer's relationship with his or her father. Then the writer continues the encounter by **responding** in the form of a brief analytical, interpretative text. The **analysis** means the writer is taking apart the subject being written about in order to know it thoroughly. The **interpretation** means the writer is making evidence-supported judgments about the significance or meaning of that subject.

Essays are more personal than reports or articles; they're openly **interpretative,** rather than merely informative. This doesn't mean that essays are necessarily about subjects that are personal, nor does it mean that essays are necessarily written in a personal voice. In essays the writer is present, and although the writer may cite statistical evidence or even other people's conclusions to support interpretations, those interpretations will always have a personal twist to them. Because essays are more personal than articles and reports, essay writers have more choices open to them in the process of writing. Essay writers are usually compelled to write about their subjects because of their own interest and then choose specific audiences, purposes, and messages out of a desire to probe and communicate their interpretative judgments.

In addition, essays are short pieces of writing, usually no longer than twenty pages. Because of their brevity, their scope is highly focused, and they more often than not deal with a single aspect of a subject. A lot of the writing you'll do at your college or university will be done in response to brief, analytical, interpretative texts—formal essays or chapters in book-length works that focus on a single aspect of a subject. When you're asked to respond to an essay in writing, you'll often be writing an essay yourself. You'll be analyzing and interpreting another writer's analysis and interpretation of a subject. And to do that effectively, you'll have to critically encounter both the essay you're responding to and the subject behind that essay.

TECHNIQUES FOR RESPONDING TO ESSAYS

1. Read the essay carefully for meaning and craft.
2. Research the subject of the essay.
3. Analyze your audience to determine what they know about the subject and what their possible point of view might be.
4. Present an evidence-supported judgment about both the essay and its subject with your audience analysis in mind.

RESPONDING TO ESSAYS: PROFESSIONAL WRITING

The following pair of readings contains an essay written in response to a situation and a second essay written in response to the first. The writer of the first essay, Edward I. Koch, encountered a situation that exists in the world (crime and punishment in American society). After thinking about the subject for a while, Koch wrote an essay expressing his judgments about it. While all of this was going on, another man (David Bruck) was also **encountering** the subject and then **thinking** about it. When Koch's essay was published, Bruck read it and then decided to express his disagreements with Koch's judgments by **writing** a second essay.

PREREAD

To familiarize yourself with the subjects of the following selections, preread each of them. **Read the first three paragraphs** slowly, focusing on those things you understand. When you get to the end of the third paragraph, stop and take stock; **summarize** what has gone on so far. What do you know about the subject of the text? If you're confused, go back and focus on the sentences you don't understand and **reread** them, searching for meaning. Then **predict** what direction the text will take next. As you continue to read, compare your predictions with what unfolds on the page. After each of the remaining paragraphs, pause again to **summarize, reread** if necessary, and predict.

DEATH AND JUSTICE: HOW CAPITAL PUNISHMENT AFFIRMS LIFE
Edward I. Koch

Edward I. Koch is a former mayor of New York City. This selection originally appeared in the New Republic *in March 1985.*

Last December a man named Robert Lee Willie, who had been convicted of raping and murdering an 18-year-old woman, was executed in the Louisiana state prison. In a statement issued several minutes before his death, Mr. Willie said: "Killing people is wrong. . . . It makes no difference whether it's citizens, countries, or governments. Killing is wrong." Two weeks later in South Carolina, an admitted killer named Joseph Carl Shaw was put to death for murdering two teenagers. In an appeal to the governor for clemency, Mr. Shaw wrote: "Killing is wrong when I did it. Killing is wrong when you do it. I hope you have the courage and moral strength to stop the killing."

It is a curiosity of modern life that we find ourselves being lectured on morality by cold-blooded killers. Mr. Willie previously had been convicted of aggravated rape, aggravated kidnapping, and the murders of a Louisiana deputy and a man from Missouri. Mr. Shaw committed another murder a week before the two for which he was executed, and admitted mutilating the body of the 14-year-old girl he killed. I can't help wondering what prompted these murderers to speak out against killing as they entered the deathhouse door. Did their newfound reverence for life stem from the realization that they were about to lose their own?

Life is indeed precious, and I believe the death penalty helps to affirm this fact. Had the death penalty been a real possibility in the minds of these murderers, they might well have stayed their hand. They might have shown moral awareness before their victims died, and not after. Consider the tragic death of Rosa Velez, who happened to be home when a man named Luis Vera burglarized her apartment in Brooklyn. "Yeah, I shot her," Vera admitted. "She knew me, and I knew I wouldn't go to the chair."

During my twenty-two years in public service, I have heard the pros and cons of capital punishment expressed with special

continued on page 304

continued from page 303

intensity. As a district leader, councilman, congressman, and mayor, I have represented constituencies generally thought of as liberal. Because I support the death penalty for heinous crimes of murder, I have sometimes been the subject of emotional and outraged attacks by voters who find my position reprehensible or worse. I have listened to their ideas. I have weighed their objections carefully. I still support the death penalty. The reasons I maintain my position can be best understood by examining the arguments most frequently heard in opposition.

5   *1. The death penalty is "barbaric."* Sometimes opponents of capital punishment horrify with tales of lingering death on the gallows, of faulty electric chairs, or of agony in the gas chamber. Partly in response to such protests, several states such as North Carolina and Texas switched to execution by lethal injection. The condemned person is put to death painlessly, without ropes, voltage, bullets, or gas. Did this answer the objections of death penalty opponents? Of course not. On June 22, 1984, the *New York Times* published an editorial that sarcastically attacked the new "hygienic" method of death by injection, and stated that "execution can never be made humane through science." So it's not the method that really troubles opponents. It's the death itself they consider barbaric.

   Admittedly, capital punishment is not a pleasant topic. However, one does not have to like the death penalty in order to support it any more than one must like radical surgery, radiation, or chemotherapy in order to find necessary these attempts at curing cancer. Ultimately we may learn how to cure cancer with a simple pill. Unfortunately, that day has not yet arrived. Today we are faced with the choice of letting the cancer spread or trying to cure it with the methods available, methods that one day will almost certainly be considered barbaric. But to give up and do nothing would be far more barbaric and would certainly delay the discovery of an eventual cure. The analogy between cancer and murder is imperfect, because murder is not the "disease" we are trying to cure. The disease is injustice. We may not like the death penalty, but it must be available to punish crimes of cold-blooded murder, cases in which any other form of punishment would be inadequate and, therefore, unjust. If we create a society in which

continued to next page

injustice is not tolerated, incidents of murder—the most flagrant form of injustice—will diminish.

2. No other major democracy uses the death penalty. No other major democracy—in fact, few other countries of any description—are plagued by a murder rate such as that in the United States. Fewer and fewer Americans can remember the days when unlocked doors were the norm and murder was a rare and terrible offense. In America the murder rate climbed 122 percent between 1963 and 1980. During that same period, the murder rate in New York City increased by almost 400 percent, and the statistics are even worse in many other cities. A study at M.I.T. showed that based on 1970 homicide rates a person who lived in a large American city ran a greater risk of being murdered than an American soldier in World War II ran of being killed in combat. It is not surprising that the laws of each country differ according to differing conditions and traditions. If other countries had our murder problem, the cry for capital punishment would be just as loud as it is here. And I daresay that any other major democracy where 75 percent of the people supported the death penalty would soon enact it into law.

3. An innocent person might be executed by mistake. Consider the work of Hugo Adam Bedau, one of the most implacable foes of capital punishment in this country. According to Mr. Bedau, it is "false sentimentality to argue that the death penalty should be abolished because of the abstract possibility that an innocent person might be executed." He cites a study of the 7,000 executions in this country from 1893 to 1971, and concludes that the record fails to show that such cases occur. The main point, however, is this. If government functioned only when the possibility of error didn't exist, government wouldn't function at all. Human life deserves special protection, and one of the best ways to guarantee that protection is to assure that convicted murderers do not kill again. Only the death penalty can accomplish this end. In a recent case in New Jersey, a man named Richard Biegenwald was freed from prison after serving 18 years for murder; since his release he has been convicted of committing four murders. A prisoner named Lemuel Smith, who, while serving four life sentences for murder (plus two life sentences for kidnapping and robbery) in New York's Green Haven Prison, lured a woman corrections

continued on page 306

continued from page 305

officer into the chaplain's office and strangled her. He then mutilated and dismembered her body. An additional life sentence for Smith is meaningless. Because New York has no death penalty statute, Smith has effectively been given a license to kill.

But the problem of multiple murder is not confined to the nation's penitentiaries. In 1981, 91 police officers were killed in the line of duty in this country. Seven percent of those arrested in the cases that have been solved had a previous arrest for murder. In New York City in 1976 and 1977, 85 persons arrested for homicide had a previous arrest for murder. Six of these individuals had two previous arrests for murder, and one had four previous murder arrests. During those two years the New York police were arresting for murder persons with a previous arrest for murder on the average of one every 8.5 days. This is not surprising when we learn that in 1975, for example, the median time served in Massachusetts for homicide was less than two and a half years. In 1976 a study sponsored by the Twentieth Century Fund found that the average time served in the United States for first-degree murder is ten years. The median time served may be considerably lower.

10

4. *Capital punishment cheapens the value of human life.* On the contrary, it can be easily demonstrated that the death penalty strengthens the value of human life. If the penalty for rape were lowered, clearly it would signal a lessened regard for the victims' suffering, humiliation, and personal integrity. It would cheapen their horrible experience, and expose them to an increased danger of recurrence. When we lower the penalty for murder, it signals a lessened regard for the value of the victim's life. Some critics of capital punishment, such as columnist Jimmy Breslin, have suggested that a life sentence is actually a harsher penalty for murder than death. This is sophistic nonsense. A few killers may decide not to appeal a death sentence, but the overwhelming majority make every effort to stay alive. It is by exacting the highest penalty for the taking of human life that we affirm the highest value of human life.

5. *The death penalty is applied in a discriminatory manner.* This factor no longer seems to be the problem it once was. The appeals process for a condemned prisoner is lengthy and painstaking.

continued to next page

Every effort is made to see that the verdict and sentence were fairly arrived at. However, assertions of discrimination are not an argument for ending the death penalty but for extending it. It is not justice to exclude everyone from the penalty of the law if a few are found to be so favored. Justice requires that the law be applied equally to all.

6. *Thou Shalt Not Kill.* The Bible is our greatest source of moral inspiration. Opponents of the death penalty frequently cite the sixth of the Ten Commandments in an attempt to prove that capital punishment is divinely proscribed. In the original Hebrew, however, the Sixth Commandment reads "Thou Shalt Not Commit Murder," and the Torah specifies capital punishment for a variety of offenses. The biblical viewpoint has been upheld by philosophers throughout history. The greatest thinkers of the 19th century—Kant, Locke, Hobbes, Rousseau, Montesquieu, and Mill—agreed that natural law properly authorizes the sovereign to take life in order to vindicate justice. Only Jeremy Bentham was ambivalent. Washington, Jefferson, and Franklin endorsed it. Abraham Lincoln authorized executions for deserters in wartime. Alexis de Tocqueville, who expressed profound respect for American institutions, believed that the death penalty was indispensable to the support of social order. The United States Constitution, widely admired as one of the seminal achievements in the history of humanity, condemns cruel and inhuman punishment, but does not condemn capital punishment.

7. *The death penalty is state-sanctioned murder.* This is the defense with which Messrs. Willie and Shaw hoped to soften the resolve of those who sentenced them to death. By saying in effect, "You're no better than I am," the murderer seeks to bring his accusers down to his own level. It is also a popular argument among opponents of capital punishment, but a transparently false one. Simply put, the state has rights that the private individual does not. In a democracy, those rights are given to the state by the electorate. The execution of a lawfully condemned killer is no more an act of murder than is legal imprisonment an act of kidnapping. If an individual forces a neighbor to pay him money under threat of punishment, it's call extortion. If the state does it, it's called taxation. Rights and responsibilities surrendered by the individual are what give the state its power to govern. This contract is the foundation of civilization itself.

continued on page 308

continued from page 307

Everyone wants his or her rights, and will defend them jealously. Not everyone, however, wants responsibilities, especially the painful responsibilities that come with law enforcement. Twenty-one years ago a woman named Kitty Genovese was assaulted and murdered on a street in New York. Dozens of neighbors heard her cries for help but did nothing to assist her. They didn't even call the police. In such a climate the criminal understandably grows bolder. In the presence of moral cowardice, he lectures us on our supposed failings and tries to equate his crimes with our quest for justice.

15   The death of anyone—even a convicted killer—diminishes us all. But we are diminished even more by a justice system that fails to function. It is an illusion to let ourselves believe that doing away with capital punishment removes the murderer's deed from our conscience. The rights of society are paramount. When we protect guilty lives, we give up innocent lives in exchange. When opponents of capital punishment say to the state, "I will not let you kill in my name," they are also saying to murderers: "You can kill in your *own* name as long as I have an excuse for not getting involved."

It is hard to imagine anything worse than being murdered while neighbors do nothing. But something worse exists. When those same neighbors shrink back from justly punishing the murderer, the victim dies twice.

THE DEATH PENALTY
David Bruck

David Bruck is a lawyer in the South Carolina Office of Appellate Defense. This response to Koch's essay was published in the National Review *in April 1985.*

Mayor Ed Koch contends that the death penalty "affirms life." By failing to execute murders, he says, we "signal a lessened regard for the value of the victim's life." Koch suggests that people who

continued to next page

oppose the death penalty are like Kitty Genovese's neighbors, who heard her cries for help but did nothing while an attacker stabbed her to death.

This is the standard "moral" defense of death as punishment: even if executions don't deter violent crime any more effectively than imprisonment, they are still required as the only means we have of doing justice in response to the worst of crimes.

Until recently, this "moral" argument had to be considered in the abstract, since no one was being executed in the United States. But the death penalty is back now, at least in the southern states, where every one of the more than 30 executions carried out over the last two years has taken place. Those of us who live in those states are getting to see the difference between the death penalty in theory, and what happens when you actually try to use it.

South Carolina resumed executing prisoners in January with the electrocution of Joseph Carl Shaw. Shaw was condemned to death for helping to murder two teenagers while he was serving as a military policeman at Fort Jackson, South Carolina. His crime, propelled by mental illness and PCP, was one of terrible brutality. It is Shaw's last words ("Killing was wrong when I did it. It is wrong when you do it . . .") that so outraged Mayor Koch: he finds it "a curiosity of modern life that we are being lectured on morality by cold-blooded killers." And so it is.

But it was not "modern life" that brought this curiosity into being. It was capital punishment. The electric chair was J. C. Shaw's platform. (The mayor mistakenly writes that Shaw's statement came in the form of a plea to the governor for clemency: actually Shaw made it only seconds before his death, as he waited, shaved and strapped into the chair, for the switch to be thrown.) It was the chair that provided Shaw with celebrity and an opportunity to lecture us on right and wrong. What made this weird moral reversal even worse is that J. C. Shaw faced his own death with undeniable dignity and courage. And while Shaw died, the TV crews recorded another "curiosity" of the death penalty—the crowd gathered outside the deathhouse to cheer on the executioner. Whoops of elation greeted the announcement of Shaw's death. Waiting at the penitentiary gates for the appearance of the

5

continued on page 310

continued from page 309

hearse bearing Shaw's remains, one demonstrator started yelling, "Where's the beef?"

For those who had to see the execution of J. C. Shaw, it wasn't easy to keep in mind that the purpose of the whole spectacle was to affirm life. It will be harder still when Florida executes a cop-killer named Alvin Ford. Ford has lost his mind during his years of death-row confinement, and now spends his days trembling, rocking back and forth, and muttering unintelligible prayers. This has led to litigation over whether Ford meets a centuries-old legal standard for mental competency. Since the Middle Ages, the Anglo-American legal system has generally prohibited the execution of anyone who is too mentally ill to understand what is about to be done to him and why. If Florida wins its case, it will have earned the right to electrocute Ford in his present condition. If it loses, he will not be executed until the state has first nursed him back to some semblance of mental health.

We can at least be thankful that this demoralizing spectacle involves a prisoner who is actually guilty of murder. But this may not always be so. The ordeal of Lenell Jeter—the young black engineer who recently served more than a year of a life sentence for a Texas armed robbery that he didn't commit—should remind us that the system is quite capable of making the very worst sort of mistake. That Jeter was eventually cleared is a fluke. If the robbery had occurred at 7 P.M. rather than 3 P.M., he'd have had no alibi, and would still be in prison today. And if someone had been killed in that robbery, Jeter probably would have been sentenced to death. We'd have seen the usual execution-day interviews with state officials and the victim's relatives, all complaining that Jeter's appeals took too long. And Jeter's last words from the gurney would have taken their place among the growing literature of death-house oration that so irritates the mayor.

Koch quotes Hugo Adam Bedau, a prominent abolitionist, to the effect that the record fails to establish that innocent defendants have been executed in the past. But this doesn't mean, as Koch implies, that it hasn't happened. All Bedau was saying was that doubts concerning executed prisoners' guilt are almost never

continued to next page

resolved. Bedau is at work now on an effort to determine how many wrongful death sentences may have been imposed: his list of murder convictions since 1900 in which the state eventually *admitted* error is some 400 cases long. Of course, very few of these cases involved actual executions: the mistakes that Bedau documents were uncovered precisely because the prisoner was alive and able to fight for his vindication. The cases where someone is executed are the very cases in which we're least likely to learn that we got the wrong man.

I don't claim that executions of entirely innocent people will occur very often. But they will occur. And other sorts of mistakes already have. Roosevelt Green was executed in Georgia two days before J. C. Shaw. Green and an accomplice kidnapped a young woman. Green swore that his companion shot her to death after Green had left, and that he knew nothing about the murder. Green's claim was supported by a statement that his accomplice made to a witness after the crime. The jury never resolved whether Green was telling the truth, and when he tried to take a polygraph examination a few days before his scheduled execution, the state of Georgia refused to allow the examiner into the prison. As the pressure for symbolic retribution mounts, the courts, like the public, are losing patience with such details. Green was electrocuted on January 9, while members of the Ku Klux Klan rallied outside the prison.

Then there is another sort of arbitrariness that happens all the time. Last October, Louisiana executed a man named Ernest Knighton. Knighton had killed a gas station owner during a robbery. Like any murder, this was a terrible crime. But it was not premeditated, and is the sort of crime that very rarely results in a death sentence. Why was Knighton electrocuted when almost everyone else who committed the same offense was not? Was it because he was black? Was it because his victim and all 12 members of the jury that sentenced him were white? Was it because Knighton's court-appointed lawyer presented no evidence on his behalf at his sentencing hearing? Or maybe there's no reason except bad luck. One thing is clear: Ernest Knighton was picked out to die the way a fisherman takes a cricket out of a bait jar. No one cares which cricket gets impaled on the hook.

10

continued on page 312

continued from page 311

Not every prisoner executed recently was chosen that randomly. But many were. And having selected these men so casually, so blindly, the death penalty systems asks us to accept that the purpose of killing each of them is to affirm the sanctity of human life.

The death penalty states are also learning that the death penalty is easier to advocate than it is to administer. In Florida, where executions have become almost routine, the governor reports that nearly a third of his time is spent reviewing the clemency requests of condemned prisoners. The Florida Supreme Court is hopelessly backlogged with death cases. Some have taken five years to decide, and the rest of the Court's work waits in line behind the death appeals. Florida's death row currently holds more than 230 prisoners. State officials are reportedly considering building a special "death prison" devoted entirely to the isolation and electrocution of the condemned. The state is also considering the creation of a special public defender unit that will do nothing else but handle death penalty appeals. The death penalty, in short, is spawning death agencies.

And what is Florida getting for all of this? The state went through almost all of 1983 without executing anyone: its rate of intentional homicide declined by 17 percent. Last year Florida executed eight people—the most of any state, and the sixth highest total for any year since Florida started electrocuting people back in 1924. Elsewhere in the U.S. last year, the homicide rate continued to decline. But in Florida, it actually rose by 5.1 percent.

But these are just the tiresome facts. The electric chair has been a centerpiece of each of Koch's recent political campaigns, and he knows better than anyone how little the facts have to do with the public's support for capital punishment. What really fuels the death penalty is the justifiable frustration and rage of people who see that the government is not coping with violent crime. So what if the death penalty doesn't work? At least it gives us the satisfaction of knowing that we got one or two of the sons of bitches.

15   Perhaps we want retribution on the flesh and bone of a handful of convicted murderers so badly that we're willing to close our eyes to all of the demoralization and danger that come with it. A lot of politicians think so, and they may be right. But if they

continued to next page

are, then let's at least look honestly at what we're doing. This lottery of death both comes from and encourages an attitude toward human life that is not reverent, but reckless.

And that is why the mayor is dead wrong when he confuses such fury with justice. He suggests that we trivialize murder unless we kill murderers. By that logic, we also trivialize rape unless we sodomize rapists. The sin of Kitty Genovese's neighbors wasn't that they failed to stab her attacker to death. Justice does demand that murderers be punished. And common sense demands that society be protected from them. But neither justice nor self-preservation demands that we kill men whom we have already imprisoned.

The electric chair in which J. C. Shaw died earlier this year was built in 1912 at the suggestion of South Carolina's governor at the time, Cole Blease. Governor Blease's other criminal justice initiative was an impassioned crusade in favor of lynch law. Any lesser response, the governor insisted, trivialized the loathsome crimes of interracial rape and murder. In 1912 a lot of people agreed with Governor Blease that a proper regard for justice required both lynching and the electric chair. Eventually we are going to learn that justice requires neither.

ENCOUNTER THE SUBJECT

Before either of these writers could write about their subject, they had to have encountered it. **Encountering** is the stage of the writing process where **writer** comes face to face with **subject.** In this stage Koch and Bruck began to gather information about the situation they would later respond to by writing. Most likely, each of these writers encountered the subject over a period of many years, and the information that each gathered came both from firsthand experience and from reading. In addition, each encounter was shaped by a unique set of personal experiences—by each man's educational, social, and family backgrounds.

Think about your own encounter with the subject—crime and punishment in American society. When did that encounter begin? Did it come from firsthand experience? From reading? From family conversations? How might your educational, social, and family backgrounds have shaped your encounter with the subject? What judgments have you already framed about the subject?

The important thing to remember about the writer's encounter with subject is that it doesn't happen in isolation. In college-level writing, it happens in the context of a particular class, and this means that other things you learn in that class will affect your encounter. But it also happens in the context of the many communities of which you're a member. Some of the subjects that you'll encounter at your college or university will be totally new to you, but a great many won't. Often you'll already have begun your encounter, sometimes without actually being aware of it, and if you have, it's important to be critical of the information you've learned and the judgments you've already framed about that information.

For example, some of you who are reading this have already framed powerful judgments about the subject of crime and punishment in American society. Perhaps you believe, as Edward Koch does, that capital punishment is just and necessary. On the other hand, you may have come to the same conclusion about the death penalty as did David Bruck—that it is demoralizing and dangerous. Or you may have come up with a conclusion different from that of either Koch or Bruck.

RESEARCH OPPORTUNITY

Either on your own or with a research team made up of members of your class, **research** the subject of crime and punishment in American society. You might engage in **field research** by **interviewing** law enforcement personnel or prison inmates in your community, or by **observing** a court case or a parole board meeting. You might engage in **library research** by gathering information from **books, periodicals,** or a **specialized library.**

RESPONSIVE JOURNAL WRITING

After engaging in one or more research activities, explore your perspective on crime and punishment in American society. How has doing research into the subject changed your perspective?

LISTEN—READ CAREFULLY FOR MEANING

COLLABORATIVE WRITING ASSIGNMENT

Explore the meaning of both of these essays in collaboration with your classmates. This collaboration can be done in the classroom or in small study and research groups beyond the classroom. Start the collaboration in groups or three or four. As you work, have one member of your group record your analytic conclusions. When each group has gone all the way through the process and has reached either consensus or impasse, open the discussion up for full-class conversation.

RESEARCH UNKNOWNS.   None of us can read a challenging text without running into material that is unfamiliar. With this in mind, what material in the above essays is unknown to you? If you find you have questions about anything, whether if be language or evidence cited from an outside source, use the resources at your college or university to find answers to your questions.

ANALYZE THE SPEAKERS.   Here you're actually going to get into the developmental materials in the texts. Your evidence-supported judgments about each speaker will lead you into the details that support his persuasive position.

Facts
From your reading, what factual information can you glean about each speaker? Make sure that you cite specific passages from the text to support your assertions. What additional information can you gather about each speaker through research?

Emotions
Where in each text does the speaker reveal his own or another's emotional reactions to the subject? Again, make sure you cite specific passages to support your judgments. Have you ever felt similar emotional reactions? If so, write a brief description of the circumstances and your own responsive feelings.

Attitudes
Where in each text does the speaker voice conclusive judgments about the subject, and what are those judgments?

continued on page 316

continued from page 315

DETERMINE THE MESSAGE.   Write down in as few words as possible what the main idea or thesis of each text is. As always, provide specific evidence to support your judgment.

DETERMINE THE AUDIENCE.   Making sure that you provide evidence from the texts to support your judgments, describe in as much detail as possible the audience to whom each text is directed.

DETERMINE THE PURPOSE.   What change in knowledge, thought, or action does each speaker hope for from his audience?

RESPONSIVE JOURNAL WRITING

Assess the effect of the critical reading process by journal writing. If your perspective on the subject of these two texts was changed in any way by the critical reading process, write at least a page in which you explain the changes. If your perspective wasn't changed, write at least a page explaining why it wasn't.

A BRIEF ANTHOLOGY OF ESSAYS

DANGEROUS PARTIES
Paul Keegan

Paul Keegan is a contributing editor for Philadelphia Magazine.

I love the University of New Hampshire, its green lawns, its beautiful turn-of-the-century structures, the little paths that snake through the woods to classroom buildings hidden in the trees. I went to college here from 1976 to 1980. It's Everyman's school,

continued to next page

ten thousand kids on two hundred acres, cheap and easy to get into for New Hampshire students, expensive and more prestigious for the thirty-nine percent from out of state. Almost everyone can find their niche here, as I eventually did.

But it's the darker side of college life that took me back recently, the side that can emerge at a place like UNH after a night of partying at a bar like the Wildcat. The Wildcat is a pizza-and-beer joint in Durham, a small town that for nine months of the year is overrun by students. Steve Karavasilis, the owner, will pour you a draft beer for a dollar or a pitcher for $3.75. The Wildcat's signature is a wall of windowpanes that creates a huge, moving mosaic of Main Street. That's where the guys sit down with a pitcher to watch girls.

Steve has hung a sign clearly stating that you can't be served unless you are at least twenty-one. But somehow, last February 19, on a cold and clear Thursday night, two twenty-year-old sophomores named Chris and Jon, and a nineteen-year-old sophomore named Gordon, sat here and shared several pitchers of beer with a group of friends. The three were buddies who lived on the fourth floor of UNH's Stoke Hall. They were happy-go-lucky guys with a boyish charm and a bag of fraternity pranks. Jon and Gordon had recently become brothers at Sigma Alpha Epsilon. Jon, from Manchester, New Hampshire, was the character of the bunch, a slick talker who always wore his SAE hat, even when he walked to the shower carrying his soap and shaving cream in a six-pack carton. Gordon was tall and good-looking, a little moody, some thought. He was from Rochester, New York. And Chris, of Lexington, Massachusetts, was not a fraternity brother, but he had lots of friends at SAE.

The boys arrived at the Wildcat that Thursday night sometime between nine-thirty and ten o'clock and drank about six beers apiece. At about twelve-fifteen, they went out into the freezing night and headed back to their dorm, where they encountered an eighteen-year-old freshman named Sara who had been drinking heavily at a fraternity party. One by one, each of the three boys had sex with her. As the incident proceeded, witnesses said, Jon bragged in the hallway that he had a "train" going in his room and then gave his friends high fives, as a football player might do after scoring a touchdown.

continued on page 318

continued from page 317

3   Sexual assault, if that is what happened here, goes on at every college in America. About one woman student in eight is raped, according to a government survey. Ninety percent of these are victims of "acquaintance rape," defined as "forced, manipulated, or coerced sexual intercourse by a 'friend' or an acquaintance." Its most repugnant extreme is gang rape. Bernice Sandler of the Association of American Colleges says she has documented evidence of more than seventy incidents of this nationwide in the past four or five years. They usually involve fraternities and drugs or alcohol, she says, and the men nearly always contend that it wasn't rape, that they were merely engaged in group sex with a willing partner.

That was precisely the defense used by the UNH boys when they were arrested five days later. Jon and Chris were charged with aggravated felonious sexual assault, punishable by a maximum of seven and a half to fifteen years in prison, and Gordon with misdemeanor sexual assault. All three pleaded innocent, claiming Sara was a willing and active participant in everything that went on. Sara says she had a lot to drink and does not remember what happened.

Like friends of mine who went to other schools, I remember hearing vague tales about such incidents. What makes this case unique is that everyone on campus soon learned the details of what happened that night, and the turmoil that exploded was unlike anything UNH has experienced since the late sixties.

Four days after *Foster's Daily Democrat*, in nearby Dover, mistakenly reported that the boys had confessed to the crime, three life-sized male effigies were hung from a ledge at UNH's Hamilton Smith Hall along with a huge banner that read BEWARE BOYS, RAPE WILL NOT BE TOLERATED. When the accused were allowed to stay on in Stoke Hall, someone sprayed a graffiti message to UNH President Gordon Haaland on the walkway leading to his office: GORDON, WHY DO YOU ALLOW RAPISTS TO STAY ON CAMPUS? And senior Terry Ollila was barred from taking part in the university's judicial proceedings against the three because she was overheard saying, "I want to see these guys strung up by their balls."

continued to next page

Room 127 of Hamilton Smith Hall, where I struggled through Psychology 401, can feel claustrophobic when all of its 170 seats are full. It was here, in late spring, that the controversy, after simmering for months, began to heat up again. Thanks to a shrewd defense lawyer trying to reverse the tide of opinion running against his clients, the normally private student disciplinary hearings were held in public.

Jon, Chris, Gordon, and eleven other witnesses had their backs to the audience as they testified to the five Judicial Board members facing them across a large table. But they could feel the crowd close behind, hear the shuffling of feet, the coughing, the whispering. For four extraordinary evenings, witnesses nervously described what they had seen and heard, and the hearings soon became the hottest show in town. When sophomore John Prescott described how he had interrupted the alleged assault, he could hear women behind him whispering encouragement: "Yeah, good answer." When the testimony became graphic, the crowd gasped. At one point, when the defense began asking about the alleged victim's previous sex life, Sara's father leapt to his feet shouting.

Finally, in the early morning hours of May 7, the board found all three boys not guilty of sexual assault. Gordon, cleared of all charges, wept with relief. Jon and Chris were suspended for the summer and fall terms for violating a university rule entitled "Respect for Others."

It was at this point that the campus, poised at the precipice for months, went over the edge. Four days later, a hundred people, including Sara, turned out for an "educational forum" that turned into a shouting match and led Dan Garvey, the normally easygoing associate dean of students, to storm out of the room. The next day more than two hundred people showed up at a protest demonstration that was crashed by a group of about twenty fraternity members and boys from the fourth floor of Stoke. "Dykes!" they yelled. "Lesbians! Manhaters!" Then it got much uglier. "Look out, we're gonna rape *you* next!" shouted one. "I had Sara last night!" cried another.

Unrattled, the protesters acted out a satire of a rape trial and read a list of demands: the university should nullify the hearings,

10

continued on page 320

continued from page 319

make a public apology to Sara, and expel all three boys. As the group began marching to the office of Dean of Student Affairs J. Gregg Sanborn, they encountered Sanborn on the sidewalk. More than a dozen of them surrounded him, linked arms, and said they wouldn't let him go until he promised to respond to their demands.

Sanborn agreed, but in his response he defended the university's handling of the affair. Demonstrators marched to his office, announced they were relieving him of his duties, and hung a HELP WANTED sign from the flagpole. After a weekend of altercations between demonstrators, fraternity members, and other students, campus police arrested eleven protesters for criminal trespass. As the semester ended, a shaken President Haaland wrote an open letter advising everyone to return to UNH next fall "ready to examine our moral behavior."

15   Until then, I had followed the public agonies of my school from a distance. Incidents like the one in Stoke Hall were rare, I knew, and most nights at UNH were probably filled with the warm times among good friends that I remembered so vividly. Still, each new development also triggered less pleasant memories about college life, until finally I decided that I had to go back and find out exactly what was going on at my old school—or, for that matter, at virtually every school. In truth, though, I suspected I already knew.

When I moved into Stoke Hall as a freshman, in the fall of 1976, the place terrified me. It is a hulking, Y-shaped, eight-story monster, made of brick and concrete, crammed with 680 students. We called it The Zoo. It was named after Harold W. Stoke, president of UNH during the baby-boom-years that made high-rise dorms necessary on campuses across America. After a tearful good-bye to my parents, I introduced myself to my roommate, who was stoned, and then I ventured into the hallway to meet my new neighbors. They seemed much older than I, standing in front of their open doors bragging to each other about how much beer they'd drunk last night and how many times they'd gotten laid.

I lasted about two weeks in Stoke, then found an opening in another dorm. My new roommate was Ed, a born-again Christian

continued to next page

with a terrible sinus condition who would sit on the edge of his bed and play his guitar, accompanying himself by wheezing through his nose. He was engaged in this favorite hobby the cold January afternoon I returned from the holidays with four friends. My buddies pushed me into the room, laughing and screaming and dancing and tackling each other. Devout Ed looked up from his guitar in disgust and amazement, wheezed, and said, "What happened to *you?*"

What was happening to me, dear Ed, wherever you are, is that I was learning to drink, one of the two major components of a college education. The other, of course, is sex, and soon enough I learned about that, too.

When I returned to Durham last fall, I wasn't surprised to discover that some things don't change. Drinking is still the number one social activity, and beer the beverage of choice. As for sex, you want to try it but you're scared of it, so you usually get drunk before deciding anything. Thus, it's common to get drunk without having sex, but rare to have sex without getting drunk.

Drinking remains a sure fire way of getting to know someone in a hurry. This is necessary partly because of the tendency of college kids to travel in packs. Everybody goes to parties, not on dates, to get to know people, and at that age, the last thing you want to be is different. There are also practical considerations: hardly anyone has a car. The students' universe is Durham and the campus, for at least the first two years. And on weekends, there isn't anything to do on campus but party.

What has changed dramatically, however, is where the kids party. Today's students were incredulous at my stories about the huge keg blowouts in our dorms. UNH banned kegs from dorms in 1979, my senior year, when New Hampshire raised the drinking age. Then, in 1986, the university stopped serving alcohol at the student union pub when it found itself in the embarrassing position of selling liquor to minors that it couldn't seem to keep out. This leaves just two options for freshmen and sophomores who aren't lucky enough to know an upperclassman with an apartment: they can drink in their rooms with the door shut, or they can go to fraternity parties.

Frats were decidedly uncool in the sixties but began to come back in the mid-seventies. During my visit I couldn't help but

20

continued on page 322

continued from page 321

notice all the new frat houses that had popped up. Today, UNH has fourteen frats with twelve hundred members. "All the drinking has gone underground," Paul Gowen, chief of the Durham police, told me. "At least bars are controlled environments where they're obligated to cut you off if you have had too much to drink. But wearing a headband and marking it every time you chugalug a sixteen-ounce beer is not exactly what I would call a controlled environment."

Madbury Road, also known as Fraternity Row, looks exactly as you might expect: aristocratic old houses line one side of the street, set back from the road on small hills, with wide lawns stretching in front. Several frat members told me that a spate of bad publicity in the last few years over the usual offenses—alcohol poisonings, vandalism—had made this a period of retrenchment for the Greeks. Parties are now smaller and more exclusive. Posted outside the door are signs that say BROTHERS AND INVITED GUESTS ONLY. "Invited guests" means girls, preferably freshmen. The logic is circular: girls go to frat parties because they're the only place to drink and meet boys, who in turn, joined the frat because that's where the parties are where you drink and meet girls.

Fraternity Row is only a half a block up the hill from Stoke Hall. Forty percent of Stoke's residents last spring were freshman girls—250 of them—which makes the dorm an integral, if unofficial, part of the Greek system. Just out of high school, freshman girls are not yet wise to the ways of fraternity boys. On any Thursday, Friday or Saturday night on Madbury Road, after about ten o'clock, you'll see clusters of girls marching up from Stoke and the other dorms beyond, toward whichever houses are having parties that night.

25

There they find the beer, and the boys. Because the fraternity houses stand on private property, police can't go into a frat without probable cause. To protect themselves from the occasional sting operation, most frats now post at the door an enormous boy-man with a thick neck who, with deadly seriousness, asks every girl who enters the same question: "Are you affiliated with or related to anyone affiliated with the liquor commission or any

continued to next page

other law enforcement agency?" The girls will either say "No" or "Jeez, you've asked me that *three* times" before he lets them through.

One Friday night last fall I asked a fraternity member to take me to a party, and he agreed on the condition that I not identify him or the fraternity. We met at about eleven o'clock and walked to the frat house for what is known, without a trace of irony, as a Ladies' Tea. We squeezed past about eight guys standing near the door and descended a flight of stairs into the darkness. My first sensation was the overpowering stench of stale beer, and when we reached the bottom, I could see its source. Enormous puddles covered most of the basement floor. Standing in it were a couple of hundred kids jammed into a room the size of a two-car garage, picking up their feet and dropping them into the puddles—dancing—as rock blasted from two enormous speakers. The only illumination came from two flashing lights, one blue, the other yellow.

We pushed our way toward a long wooden bar with a line of frat boys behind it. They stood watching a wave of girls surging toward the corner where the beer was being poured, each girl holding an empty plastic cup in her outstretched hand. Two boys were pouring beer as fast as they could. My guide fetched two beers and told me one hundred tickets to the party were sold to girls, at three dollars apiece. Adding in girlfriends and sorority girls, he said, there were probably between one hundred fifty and two hundred girls in the house. "How many guys?" I shouted. "Oh, probably about seventy."

I asked how many kegs they'd bought tonight, and he led me behind the bar, past the sign that said BROTHERS ONLY BEHIND BAR—NO EXCEPTIONS. In the corner stood a walk-in wooden refrigerator with a "Bud Man" cartoon character painted on the door. Twelve empty kegs were stacked outside it. We opened the refrigerator and found fourteen more fresh kegs of Busch, their blue seals unbroken. Two others were hooked up to hoses that ran out to the bar. My host told me that Anheuser-Busch has student representatives on campus who take the orders, and the local distributor's truck pulls right up to the back door to drop the kegs off. A guy pouring beer said they'd probably go through twenty kegs tonight.

continued on page 324

continued from page 323

I asked a stocky senior whose shirt was unbuttoned to the middle of a hairless chest whether his frat gets into much trouble. "Oh, once in a while there will be some problems," he said. "You know, if somebody rapes somebody or if there's an alcohol thing." When I asked about the rape controversy he started to get angry.

30 "Everybody's singling fraternity guys out," he said, "I took a women's studies class last spring because I heard it would be easy. Ha. There were about twenty-five girls and three guys. They started giving me all this shit just because I was in a fraternity. What was I going to say? 'Yes, I think rape is a good thing'? I don't need that shit. So I dropped it and took Introduction to Film," he concluded. "All I had to do for it was sit there and watch movies."

I asked if he thought the rape issue was mostly about girls having sex and then changing their minds the next day. "Absolutely," he said. "I'll bet you guys twenty dollars each I could get laid tonight, no problem. But you know what? If I'm in bed with a girl and she says, 'I'm tired,' and then goes to sleep, you know what I'm thinking? I'm thinking handcuffs."

We walked back into the crowd and I asked where the bathroom was. My guide pointed to a door in a dark corner. When I pushed it open, I was assaulted by the stench of urine, and realized I was standing in a shower. Bits of soap were scattered around. A boy stood peeing on the tile floor. "So this is the urinal," I said, trying not to breathe. "Yep," he said, zipping up his pants, "just aim into the drain."

Later, at around one-thirty, I counted five couples on the dance floor making out. "You've Got to Give It to Me" by J. Geils was playing. Just before I left, I noticed a boy dancing with a very attractive girl. They were bathed in yellow light, circling a beer puddle. Her back was to me, but he saw that I was looking at her. The boy smiled broadly at me, knowingly, then looked at the girl, then back at me. It was all he could do to keep from giving me the thumbs-up sign.

That was a typical weekend night; what happened on the traumatic night of February 19, 1987, I pieced together from police

continued to next page

records, the testimony of witnesses, and conversations with most of the participants.

On that night, a freshman named Karen decided she was not in the mood to party with the other girls on the fourth floor of Stoke Hall. She was still upset about her grandfather, who had died in the fall. Also, a boy she liked was not treating her well. Karen told the others she'd rather just stay in her room and study. Her friend Sara, however, would have none of it. "Come on," she told Karen. "You never have any fun. What you need is to go out with your friends and have a good time."

This was typical Sara. She was popular, cute, fun-loving, and smart—she'd had a 3.9 grade point average the previous semester. She planned to be a biology major, and her friends marveled at how easily subjects like botany and chemistry came to her. But Sara was also a real partyer. It was not unusual for her to get everybody else on the floor psyched up to go out. And that night, excitement on the fourth floor was running high. There was a Ladies' Tea at Pi Kappa Alpha, a fraternity behind Stoke. The mood was infectious. Finally, Karen smiled and gave in.

Sara was in her room with her best friend, Michele drinking rum and Cokes and listening to Steve Winwood. By the time they left for the party forty minutes later, Sara had consumed two rum and Cokes, and had finished up with a straight shot. Finally, a little after ten, Karen and two other girls, Noelle and Tracy, were ready, and all five headed out into the cold night. The temperature was hovering around zero as they walked to the three-story frat house they called Pike.

The basement wasn't yet crowded. Sara and Karen squeezed up to the small curved bar. Each grabbed a plastic cup of beer and challenged the other to a chugging contest. Karen won. They laughed and went back for another. As the night wore on, Sara became preoccupied with a Pike brother named Hal who was pouring beer. Michele noticed Sara was drinking fast so she'd have an excuse to return and talk with him. But Hal acted cold, which hurt Sara's feelings.

Within an hour, Michele saw Sara dancing wildly. Later, she saw her leaning against a post, looking very spaced out. When Michele asked her something, Sara didn't seem to hear her. Linda, a freshman who also lived at Stoke, was looking for a friend when

continued on page 326

35

continued from page 325

she noticed Sara leaning against the wall. "Where's Rachel?" Linda shouted. When Sara didn't respond, Linda repeated the question, this time louder. Sara merely stared straight ahead. Finally, Linda shook her and screamed, *"Where is she?"* This elicited only a mumble, so Linda gave up.

40   At about twelve-thirty, Michele, Noelle, and Tracy decided to leave, but Sara said she wanted to stay longer. Karen and Sara agreed there was no reason to leave, since they were both having a good time. They assumed they'd go back together later. At length, Karen staggered upstairs, threw up, and passed out. When she awakened she was lying on the floor near the bathroom. By then, the party was over and Sara was gone.

At about twelve-thirty that night, Jon, Chris, and Gordon were returning to Stoke after their night at the Wildcat. The three sophomores were probably legally intoxicated but not out of control. Chris decided to go up to the fifth floor, while Jon and Gordon went to the fourth, where all three lived. They headed to one of the girls' wings, and on the way, dropped their pants around their ankles and raced down the hall, a favorite prank. They stopped to visit Laura, a dark-haired freshman who used to date Jon, and her roommate, Linda, who tried to talk to Sara at the party. No one was in, so they left a note: "We came to see you in our boxer shorts—Jon and Chris."

    On the way back to their wing, the two boys saw a girl in the hallway. She was looking for Scott, she said. Noticing her shirttail sticking our of the zipper of her pants, Gordon tugged on it playfully and said. "What's this?" Both boys laughed.

    Before going into his room, Jon asked the girl if he could have a good-night hug, which, he says, she gave him. He then asked for a good-night kiss, and she complied. When the couple backed toward the door, Gordon decided to leave the two of them alone. Without exchanging a word with her, Jon had sex with the girl in his room, where Gordon was already in bed. "I just did it with a girl; she's really horny," Jon told him. Still in his underwear, Gordon decided to check out what was happening. He says he entered Jon's room out of curiosity, without any sexual intentions. But once inside, he changed his mind.

continued to next page

Meanwhile, Jon raced up to the fifth floor to tell his room-mate, Chris, what was going on. The two went downstairs to their room. When they reached the door, the boys were surprised to see Linda and Laura, the girls they had left the note for about an hour earlier.

Wordlessly, Chris slipped into the room while Jon, in jeans and T-shirt, stayed outside with the girls, casually discussing the night's partying. The girls saw nothing unusual about Chris going into his own room at one-thirty in the morning, and Jon was being his normal smooth-talking self. But when they drifted near the door, according to the girl's account, Jon said, "Don't go in. Gordy's in there doing bad things with a drunk girl." (Jon denies using the words *bad things* and *drunk*.)

Oh, *really?* the girls said. "We were kidding around with Jon," recalls Laura. "It wasn't like, 'Oh my God, that's awful.' Usually, if you're in someone's room, it's because you want to be." Even though Chris was in the room, too, it's not terribly unusual to go to bed while two people are having sex in the bunk below you. What the girls didn't know was that it was Chris having sex with the girl while Gordon (whose activities with her had not included actual penetration) waited inside for them to leave so he could sneak back to his own room.

Soon Laura and Linda said good-night to Jon. As they passed John Prescott's room, they saw that the sophomore resident assistant was at his desk studying. Laura was a good friend of his, so they stopped in. After some small talk, the girls half-jokingly asked him how he could let such wild stuff go on in his wing and told him about Gordon and the drunk girl.

"It's not my job to monitor people's sex lives," Prescott told them. "But I'll look into it anyway, out of the goodness of my heart."

Prescott, a hotel administration and economics major from Hudson, New Hampshire, went to the room and knocked. When no one answered, he opened the door and saw two figures silhouetted on a bed. (He would later learn it was Jon, having a second round with the girl.) Prescott also saw Chris, sitting on a couch next to the bed, watching. (Chris maintains he was simply getting dressed.) According to Prescott, Chris looked up laughing and whispered, "Get out," waving him away. After telling Chris

45

continued on page 328

continued from page 327

several times to come out into the hall and being told to go away, Prescott barked, "Get out here *now*." Chris at last obeyed. "I was tense and nervous," Prescott remembers. "You don't confront your friends like that all the time."

50   Prescott asked if the girl had passed out, and Chris said no. "I want that girl out of the room," Prescott said.

"Oh, come on," Chris replied.

"Is she really drunk?" Prescott asked.

Chris nodded and laughed, Prescott says, although Chris denies this.

"Do you know that what you're doing could be considered rape?" Prescott said.

"No, it's not," Chris answered.

55   "You guys are going to learn one of these days that someone is going to wake up the next day and think that what happened was wrong, even if she wanted to be in there," Prescott said. "I want that girl out of the room." Chris finally agreed, but said he had to talk to her first.

Despite his role as the enforcer and voice of reason, Prescott nonetheless thought the events on his floor were entertaining— so much so that he went to see two of his friends and told them what had happened. " 'Wow! No way! Unbelievable!' " Prescott remembers them saying. "We were all laughing. It was funny, in a sick kind of way."

As Prescott and his friends went out into the hallway, Jon emerged from the room and walked toward them. When he reached the group, two of the boys said, he gave Prescott's friends high fives. Then he continued past them, slapping the air at knee level, giving low fives to other members of the imaginary team.

Prescott says Jon proceeded to tell the three of them in great detail what he had done with the girl and how he had gone to get Gordon and Chris. All three remember that during this conversation Jon told them he had a "train" going in his room. (Jon denies both the high fives and the train reference.) As the boys were talking, Linda and Laura returned, "not because we were worried about what had happened," Laura remembers. "We were still just hanging out." Then Joe, another freshman on the

continued to next page

floor, joined the group. A discussion ensued between the five boys and two girls about whether the boys' behavior was wrong. "Someone said, 'Hey, a drunk girl is fair game,' " Laura recalls, "which made Linda and me a little defensive, obviously." One of the boys suggested that maybe Joe could "get lucky, too." Joe walked toward the door—just to see what was happening, he says.

Inside, Chris was now alone with the girl. She got dressed, and for the first time there was verbal communication: Chris told her a lot of people were in the hallway talking about them and watching the door. He carefully explained how she could avoid them. Just as Joe reached the room, the door opened and the crowd saw a girl walk out, her shirt untucked. Without looking up, she disappeared into the stairwell.

To their astonishment, everyone recognized Sara, the girl who lived on the same floor. They had all assumed it was someone they didn't know, maybe a high school girl. Suddenly the atmosphere in the hallway changed. Linda and Laura were outraged. "You *assholes!*" one of them screamed. "How could you *do* such a thing?" No one was more shocked than Jon: "You mean you *know* her?" It was at that moment that Jon and Chris heard her name for the first time.

By now there were six witnesses, two of them girls who didn't seem to understand the boys' point of view. This was trouble. Chris and Jon decided to talk to Sara to forestall misunderstanding.

When Giselle, Sara's roommate, heard voices calling "Sara, Sara, Sara," she thought she was dreaming. But when she looked up from her bed, she saw two boys bent over her roommate's bed, shaking Sara's shoulder. "What the hell are you doing in here?" she demanded.

"We have to talk to Sara," they said. "It's very important."

Giselle got up. Sara was lying on her side with a nightshirt on. "You okay?" Giselle asked, shaking her gently. Sara nodded. "Do you want to get up?" she asked. Sara shook her head: no. "I don't think she should get up," Giselle said.

But they pleaded with her, so Giselle shrugged and went back to bed. A moment later, she saw Sara standing in the middle of

continued on page 330

60

65

continued from page 329

the room, wrapping herself in a blanket. One of the boys held her left arm with his right arm. This must have been, Giselle thought later, to prevent her from falling back into bed.

When the three were out in the hallway, Chris and Jon say, they all agreed on what had happened so there could be no misunderstanding later. Chris then suggested that Jon leave so he could talk to Sara more easily. Alone, they began kissing. They walked a few steps and opened the stairwell door. Then, at some time between three and four in the morning, beneath a window through which a slice of Pi Kappa Alpha was visible, near a heating vent painted the same blue as the walls around them, Chris and Sara got down on the landing and had sex again.

What is most puzzling about the way the kids in Stoke reacted to the incident is that for at least three days, until Sara first spoke with a counselor, no one called it rape. Even Prescott, who had used the term when he talked to Chris outside the room, insists that his main concern was the *perception* that it was rape, not whether it actually was. "These guys were my friends. My concern was *not* for the woman in that room. My concern was for the men. But look where it got me. Now when I see Gordon and say hi, he just gives me a blank look."

Prescott is thin and earnest-looking, with short blond hair and an angular face. Clearly, the incident has taken its toll on him, yet he talks about it willingly. Over the weekend, he told a friend what had happened, setting off the chain reaction of gossip that eventually led to Sara herself; only then did she go to the police. But Prescott's motives, he freely admits, were entirely base. "You know why I told him?" Prescott says today, "I wanted to astonish him."

70

But why didn't Prescott consider the possibility that the girl in the room was raped? "I just assumed she was willing, since I didn't know any differently," he says. "I saw her walk out of the room. Look, that's how sex happens here. Most scoops happen after parties, and guys go to parties to scoop."

But *three* guys?" "It doesn't surprise me that much," he says. "You hear stories about that kind of thing all the time. I don't expect it to happen, but I'm not ignorant that it goes on. I'm not

continued to next page

naive. My fault was in not going to see her *right* away, when she walked back to her room. Then there would be no question. I keep asking myself why I didn't. I don't know. I was like a pendulum swinging back and forth, and finally I just had to try to look at this objectively and make a judgment." He stares into space. "You know, I still can't make one."

Linda, who was one of the witnesses who recognized Sara when she emerged from the room, is transferring to another school. Last spring she took one look at the huge crowds at the Judicial Board hearings and walked away. The next day she was convinced that telling her story was the right thing to do; now she's not so sure. Fraternity members are mad at her, and she's disillusioned about the social life at UNH. "I guess rape happens all the time here," she says, sitting on the bed in her dorm room, wearing shorts and a UNH sweatshirt. "You know, at home, I'd get really drunk and black out and wake up at my boyfriend's house. It wouldn't matter because I was with friends. When I came to school here, people would tell me, 'Linda, don't get so drunk. You're a pretty girl. People may want to take advantage of you.' " She looks down at her hands in her lap and says softly, "I didn't believe that anyone would do something like that. But it's true, they will."

It was a brilliant September day, warm and sunny, when I at last began to feel good about my old school again. President Haaland had called a special convocation to undertake the moral re-examination he had promised in the spring. Sara had transferred to another school; Jon and Chris would soon plead guilty to misdemeanor sexual assault, for which they would each serve two months in prison. The court would also compel them to write a letter of apology to Sara. The misdemeanor charge against Gordon would be dropped altogether.

"Universities have thrived because they are driven by a core set of values," Haaland told the crowd of three thousand. "These shared values are free inquiry, intellectual honesty, personal integrity, and respect for human dignity." Then he announced a series of concrete steps: to make the job of coordinating the sexual-assault program a full-time position; to publicize sexual assault cases; to improve lighting, continue the escort service for women,

continued on page 332

continued from page 331

hire a full-time coordinator for the Greek system, and improve conditions in Stoke Hall. At the end, everybody sang the UNH alma mater: "New Hampshire, alma mater/All hail, all hail to thee!"

75   At the outdoor reception following the convocation some of the demonstrators who had trapped him on the sidewalk now chatted amiably with Dean Sanborn. "It just floored me that the administration got up there and actually said the word *rape*," said one. "Last year we couldn't even get them to say the word *woman*." The demonstrators, Sanborn told me, "deserve some credit for the change that's occurring."

    I wish I could end the story there, when the sky was blue and everything seemed fine again. But then I made one last trip to Durham. Rape crisis programs and well-lit pathways are important, of course, but they don't answer the questions that occurred to me when I met some of this year's freshman class.

    Ogre, as his friends call him, is a short, compact freshman whose boxers stick out from beneath his gray football shorts. On the door of his room is a sign that says Fish Defense HQ, and if you ask him about it he'll tell you with a deadpan look that mutant radioactive fish with lungs are attacking us all, that they've already got Peter Tosh and John F. Kennedy. If it weren't for Ogre's regiment, consisting of Opus and Garfield, his stuffed dolls, they'd probably have gotten him, too. Ogre is a funny kid.

    While I chatted with Ogre in his room, we were joined by a thin fellow with a blond crewcut, wearing a T-shirt with Butt-hole Surfers silk-screened across three identical images of a bloated African belly with a tiny penis below it. His eyelids drooped: our visitor was zonked. I asked him who the Butthole Surfers were, and he explained they were punk musicians, "not hard-core punk, but definitely influenced by hard-core, for sure." The subject soon turned to acquaintance rape, and the Butthole Surferite said he'd never heard of it. Ogre had. "You know, those notices we've been getting in our mailbox about rape, with the phony scene where she says no and he says yes," Ogre explained. "Oh, yeah," the kid nodded.

    Then Ogre summed up what he'd learned from the incident last spring: "You don't shit where you sleep," he said. "You don't

continued to next page

have sex with someone in your dorm. It causes too many problems. You've got to face them the next day."

Ogre had been in college only two weeks when he made those 80 remarks, so there's hope that eventually he'll grow up. Perhaps he will even think of other metaphors for making love. For my old school—and, I'd guess, for far too many others—the question is, What will he do in the meantime?

MARRIAGE AND LOVE
Emma Goldman

Emma Goldman was a social commentator. She died in 1940 at the age of seventy-one.

The popular notion about marriage and love is that they are synonymous, that they spring from the same motives, and cover the same human needs. Like most popular notions this also rests not on actual facts, but on superstition.

Marriage and love have nothing in common; they are as far apart as the poles; are, in fact, antagonistic to each other. No doubt some marriages have been the result of love. Not, however, because love could assert itself only in marriage; much rather is it because few people can completely outgrow a convention. There are today large numbers of men and women to whom marriage is naught but a farce, but who submit to it for the sake of public opinion. At any rate, while it is true that some marriages are based on love, and while it is equally true that in some cases love continues in married life, I maintain that it does so regardless of marriage, and not because of it.

On the other hand, it is utterly false that love results from marriage. On rare occasions one does hear of a miraculous case of a married couple falling in love after marriage, but on close examination it will be found that it is a mere adjustment to the inevitable. Certainly the growing-used to each other is far away from the spontaneity, the intensity, and beauty of love, without which the intimacy of marriage must prove degrading to both the woman and the man.

continued on page 334

continued from page 333

Marriage is primarily an economic arrangement, an insurance pact. It differs from the ordinary life insurance agreement only in that it is more binding, more exacting. Its returns are insignificantly small compared with the investments. In taking out an insurance policy one pays for it in dollars and cents, always at liberty to discontinue payments. If, however, woman's premium is a husband, she pays for it with her name, her privacy, her self-respect, her very life "until death doth part." Moreover, the marriage insurance condemns her to life-long dependency, to parasitism, to complete uselessness, individual as well as social. Man, too, pays his toll, but as his sphere is wider, marriage does not limit him as much as woman. He feels his chains more in an economic sense.

5   Thus Dante's motto over Inferno applies with equal force to marriage: "Ye who enter here leave all hope behind."

That marriage is a failure none but the very stupid will deny. One has but to glance over the statistics of divorce to realize how bitter a failure marriage really is. Nor will the stereotyped Philistine argument that the laxity of divorce laws and the growing looseness of women account for the fact that: first, every twelfth marriage ends in divorce; second, that since 1870 divorces have increased from 28 to 73 for every hundred thousand population; third, that adultery, since 1867, as ground for divorce, has increased 270.8 per cent; fourth, that desertion increased 369.8 per cent.

Added to these starling figures is a vast amount of material, dramatic and literary, further elucidating this subject. Robert Herrick, in *Together*; Pinero, in *Mid-Channel*; Eugene Walker, in *Paid in Full*, and scores of other writers are discussing the barrenness, the monotony, the sordidness, the inadequacy of marriage as a factor for harmony and understanding.

The thoughtful social student will not content himself with the popular superficial excuse for this phenomenon. He will have to dig down deeper into the very life of the sexes to know why marriage proves so disastrous.

Edward Carpenter says that behind every marriage stands the life-long environment of the two sexes; an environment so different from each other that man and woman must remain

continued to next page

strangers. Separated by an insurmountable wall of superstition, custom, and habit, marriage has not the potentiality of developing knowledge of, and respect of, each other, without which every union is doomed to failure.

Henrik Ibsen, the hater of all social shams, was probably the first to realize this great truth. Nora leaves her husband, not—as the stupid critic would have it—because she is tired of her responsibilities or feels the need of woman's rights, but because she has come to know that for eight years she had lived with a stranger and borne him children. Can there be anything more humiliating, more degrading than a life-long proximity between two strangers? No need for the woman to know anything of the man, save his income. As to the knowledge of the woman—what is there to know except that she has a pleasing appearance? We have not yet outgrown the theologic myth that woman has no soul, that she is a mere appendix to man, made out of his rib just for the convenience of the gentleman who was so strong that he was afraid of his own shadow.

Perchance the poor quality of the material whence woman comes is responsible for her inferiority. At any rate, woman has no soul—what is there to know about her? Besides, the less soul a woman has the greater her asset as a wife, the more readily will she absorb herself in her husband. It is this slavish acquiescence to man's superiority that has kept the marriage institution seemingly intact for so long a period. Now that woman is coming into her own, now that she is actually growing aware of herself as a being outside of the master's grace, the sacred institution of marriage is gradually being undermined, and no amount of sentimental lamentation can stay it.

From infancy, almost the average girl is told that marriage is her ultimate goal; therefore her training and education must be directed toward that end. Like the mute beast fattened for slaughter, she is prepared for that. Yet, strange to say, she is allowed to know much less about her function as wife and mother than the ordinary artisan of his trade. It is indecent and filthy for a respectable girl to know anything of the marital relation. Oh, for the inconsistency of respectability, that needs the marriage vow to turn something which is filthy into the purest and most sacred arrangement that none dare question or criticize. Yet that is

continued on page 336

continued from page 335

exactly the attitude of the average upholder of marriage. The pro-spective wife and mother is kept in complete ignorance of her only asset in the competitive field—sex. Thus she enters into life-long relations with a man only to find herself shocked, repelled, outraged beyond measure by the most natural and healthy in-stinct, sex. It is safe to say that a large percentage of the unhap-piness, misery, distress, and physical suffering of matrimony is due to the criminal ignorance in sex matters that is being extolled as a great virtue. Nor is it at all an exaggeration when I say that more than one home has been broken up because of this deplor-able fact.

If, however, woman is free and big enough to learn the mys-tery of sex without the sanction of State or Church, she will stand condemned as utterly unfit to become the wife of a "good" man, his goodness consisting of an empty head and plenty of money. Can there by anything more outrageous than the idea that a healthy, grown woman, full of life and passion, must deny na-ture's demand, must subdue her most intense craving, undermine her health and break her spirit, must stunt her vision, abstain from the depth and glory of sex experience until a "good" man comes along to take her unto himself as a wife? That is precisely what marriage means. How can such an arrangement end except in failure? This is one, though not the least important, factor of mar-riage, which differentiates if from love.

Ours is a practical age. The time when Romeo and Juliet risked the wrath of their fathers for love, when Gretchen exposed herself to gossip of her neighbors for love, is no more. If, on rare occasions, young people allow themselves the luxury of romance, they are taken in care by the elders, drilled and pounded until they become "sensible."

The moral lesson instilled in the girl is not whether the man has aroused her love, but rather is it, "How much?" The impor-tant and only God of practical American life: Can the man make a living? Can he support a wife? That is the only thing that justifies marriage. Gradually this saturates every thought of the girl; her dreams are not of moonlight and kisses, of laughter and tears; she dreams of shopping tours and bargain counters. This soul-

continued to next page

poverty and sordidness are the elements inherent in the marriage institution. The State and the Church approve of no other ideal, simply because it is the one that necessitates the State and Church control of men and women.

Doubtless there are people who continue to consider love above dollars and cents. Particularly is this true of that class whom economic necessity has forced to become self-supporting. The tremendous change in woman's position, wrought by that mighty factor, is indeed phenomenal when we reflect that it is but a short time since she has entered the industrial arena. Six million women wage-earners; six million women, who have the equal right with men to be exploited, to be robbed, to go on strike; aye, to starve even. Anything more, my lord? Yes, six million wage-workers in every walk of life, from the highest brain work to the most difficult menial labor in the mines and on the railroad tracks; yes, even detectives and policemen. Surely the emancipation is complete.

Yet with all that, but a very small number of the vast army of women wage-workers look upon work as a permanent issue, in the same light as does man. No matter how decrepit the latter, he has been taught to be independent, self-supporting. Oh, I know that no one is really independent in our economic treadmill; still, the poorest specimen of a man hates to be a parasite; to be known as such, at any rate.

The woman considers her position as worker transitory, to be thrown aside for the first bidder. That is why it is infinitely harder to organize women than men. "Why should I join a union? I am going to get married, to have a home." Has she not been taught from infancy to look upon that as her ultimate calling? She learns soon enough that the home, though not so large a prison as the factory, has more solid doors and bars. It has a keeper so faithful that naught can escape him. The most tragic part, however, is that the home no longer frees her from wage-slavery; it only increases her task.

According to the latest statistics submitted before a Committee "on labor and wages, and congestion of population," ten per cent of the wage workers in New York City alone are married, yet they must continue to work at the most poorly paid labor in the world. Add to this horrible aspect the drudgery of housework,

continued on page 338

continued from page 337

and what remains of the protection and glory of the home? As a matter of fact, even the middle-class girl in marriage can not speak of her home, since it is the man who creates her sphere. It is not important whether the husband is a brute or a darling. What I wish to prove is that marriage guarantees woman a home only by the grace of her husband. There she moves about in *his* home, year after year, until her aspect of life and human affairs becomes as flat, narrow, and drab as her surroundings. Small wonder if she becomes a nag, petty, quarrelsome, gossipy, unbearable, thus driving the man from the house. She could not go, if she wanted to; there is no place to go. Besides, a short period of married life, of complete surrender of all faculties, absolutely incapacitates the average woman for the outside world. She becomes reckless in appearance, clumsy in her movements, dependent in her decisions, cowardly in her judgment, a weight and a bore, which most men grow to hate and despise. Wonderfully inspiring atmosphere for the bearing of life, is it not?

20 But the child, how is it be protected, if not for marriage? After all, is not that the most important consideration? The sham, the hypocrisy of it! Marriage protecting the child, yet thousands of children destitute and homeless. Marriage protecting the child, yet orphan asylums and reformatories overcrowded, the Society for the Prevention of Cruelty to Children keeping busy in rescuing the little victims from "loving parents," to place them under more loving care, the Gerry Society. Oh, the mockery of it!

Marriage may have the power to "bring the horse to water," but has it ever made him drink? The law will place the father under arrest, and put him in convict's clothes; but has that ever stilled the hunger of the child? If the parent has no work, or if he hides his identity, what does marriage do then? It invokes the law to bring the man to "justice," to put him safely behind closed doors; his labor, however, goes not to the child, but to the State. The child receives but a blighted memory of its father's stripes.

As to the protection of the woman,—therein lies the curse of marriage. Not that it really protects her, but the very idea is so revolting, such an outrage and insult on life, so degrading to human dignity, as to forever condemn this parasitic institution.

continued to next page

It is like that other parental arrangement—capitalism. It robs man of his birthright, stunts his growth, poisons his body, keeps him in ignorance, in poverty and dependence, and then institutes charities that thrive on the last vestige of man's self-respect.

The institution of marriage makes a parasite of woman, an absolute dependent. It incapacitates her for life's struggle, annihilates her social consciousness, paralyzes her imagination, and then imposes its gracious protection, which is in reality a snare, a travesty on human character.

—If motherhood is the highest fulfillment of woman's nature, what other protection does it need save love and freedom? Marriage but defiles, outrages and corrupts her fulfillment. Does it not say to woman, Only when you follow me shall you bring forth life? Does it not condemn her to the block, does it not degrade and shame her if she refuses to buy her right to motherhood by selling herself? Does not marriage only sanction motherhood, even though conceived in hatred, in compulsion? Yet, if motherhood be of free choice, of love, of ecstasy, of defiant passion, does it not place a crown of thorns upon an innocent head and carve in letters or blood the hideous epithet, Bastard? Were marriage to contain all the virtues claimed for it, its crimes against motherhood would exclude it forever from the realm of love.

Love, the strongest and deepest element in life, the harbinger of hope, of joy, of ecstasy; love, the defier of all laws, of all conventions; love, the freest, the most powerful moulder of human destiny; how can such an all-compelling force be synonymous with that poor little State and Church-begotten weed, marriage?

Free love? As if love is anything but free! Man has bought brains, but all the millions in the world have failed to buy love. Man has subdued bodies, but all the power on earth has been unable to subdue love. Man has conquered whole nations, but all his armies could not conquer love. Man has chained and fettered the spirit, but he has been utterly helpless before love. High on a throne, with all the splendor and pomp his gold can command, man is yet poor and desolate, if love passes him by. And if it stays, the poorest hovel is radiant with warmth, with life and color. Thus love has the magic power to make of a beggar a king. Yes, love is free; it can dwell in no other atmosphere. In freedom it

continued on page 340

25

continued from page 339

gives itself unreservedly, abundantly, completely. All the laws on the statutes, all the courts in the universe, cannot tear it from the soil, once love has taken root. If, however, the soil is sterile, how can marriage make it bear fruit? It is like the last desperate struggle of fleeting life against death.

Love needs no protection; it is its own protection. So long as love begets life no child is deserted, or hungry, or famished for the want of affection. I know this to be true. I know women who became mothers in freedom by the men they loved. Few children in wedlock enjoy the care, the protection, the devotion free motherhood is capable of bestowing.

The defenders of authority dread the advent of a free motherhood, lest it will rob them of their prey. Who would fight wars? Who would create wealth? Who would make the policeman, the jailer, if woman were to refuse the indiscriminate breeding of children? The race, the race! shouts the king, the president, the capitalist, the priest. The race must be preserved, though woman be degraded to a mere machine—and the marriage institution is our only safety valve against the pernicious sex-awakening of woman. But in vain these frantic efforts to maintain a state of bondage. In vain, too, the edicts of the Church, the mad attacks of rulers, in vain even the arm of the law. Woman no longer wants to be a party to the production of a race of sickly, feeble, decrepit, wretched human beings, who have neither the strength nor moral courage to throw off the yoke of poverty and slavery. Instead she desires fewer and better children, begotten and reared in love and through free choice; not by compulsion, as marriage imposes. Our pseudo-moralists have yet to learn the deep sense of responsibility toward the child, that love in freedom has awakened in the breast of woman. Rather would she forego forever the glory of motherhood than bring forth life in an atmosphere that breathes only destruction and death. And if she does become a mother, it is to give to the child the deepest and best her being can yield. To grow with the child is her motto; she knows that in that matter alone can she help build true manhood and womanhood.

30   Ibsen must have had a vision of free mother, when, with a master stroke, he portrayed Mrs. Alving. She was the ideal

continued to next page

mother because she had outgrown marriage and all its horrors, because she had broken her chains, and set her spirit free to soar until it returned a personality, regenerated and strong. Alas, it was too late to rescue her life's joy, her Oswald; but not too late to realize that love in freedom is the only condition of a beautiful life. Those who, like Mrs. Alving, have paid with blood and tears for their spiritual awakening, repudiate marriage as an imposition, a shallow, empty mockery. They know, whether love last but one brief span of time or for eternity, it is the only creative, inspiring, elevating basis for a new race, a new world.

In our present pygmy state love is indeed a stranger to most people. Misunderstood and shunned, it rarely takes root; or if it does, it soon withers and dies. Its delicate fiber can not endure the stress and strain of the daily grind. Its soul is too complex to adjust itself to the slimy woof of our social fabric. It weeps and moans and suffers with those who have need of it, yet lack the capacity to rise to love's summit.

Some day, some day men and women will rise, they will reach the mountain peak, they will meet big and strong and free, ready to receive, to partake, and to bask in the golden rays of love. What fancy, what imagination, what poetic genius can foresee even approximately the potentialities of such a force in the life of men and women. If the world is ever to give birth to true companionship and oneness, not marriage, but love will be the parent.

THREE FACES OF GREED
Jane O'Reilly

Jane O'Reilly is a freelance writer. This selection originally appeared in Vogue *magazine.*

I saw some pictures in the newspaper of a kitchen that cost $100,000 to build. It belongs to a woman who does not cook. Ever. But she does entertain a lot. She serves crab meat, yam slices, unborn lamb, goat curry—all wheeled in, ready-to-eat, by the

continued on page 342

continued from page 341

caterers. This woman has constructed for herself a $100,000 warming oven. I call that greedy. She would probably call it success.

Greed is almost solipsistic. "Rivalry is 'look at ME, not at her.'" says New York City psychoanalyst Peter Neubauer, M.D. "Jealousy is a yearning for acceptance and love that is denied. Envy is wanting to gain something that can never be achieved, like being able to sing. But greed has to do with insatiability; because there is no gratification, the craving continues beyond satisfaction of the function. It is not, 'I want to have it because *you* have it.' It's I WANT IT."

Tolstoy wrote a short story, "How Much Land Does a Man Need?" in which a man is offered all the land he can run across in a day. He runs and runs, beyond any possibility of utility, across another stream, another meadow. And he drops dead. "That is greed," Dr. Neubauer says. "It is irrational, limitless, with no social component to give it grace."

A kind of avid acquisitiveness is going on these days, and it is something beyond mere showing off. *"I want, I want, I want"* is the mantra of the 'eighties. *People cannot get enough*—even the ones who already have everything that can be got in exchange for money. Their febrile mood is the social manifestation of a peculiar definition of "success" that has emerged as the overriding esthetic of the 'eighties. The word no longer describes a fluctuating process of life, such as "being happy," or "becoming depressed." No one needs to consider the question "success at what?" when success means only one thing: success at making money. The word no longer implies anything beyond itself, such as "hardworking" or "intelligent." Instead, it is used the way "kind" or "honest" or "generous" once were used, to describe a virtue. And the outward sign of grace indicating this modern attribute is wealth.

5

IDEAS OF THE 'EIGHTIES #1:   "They say life is a game, but you keep score in money."—former United States Senator George Smathers.

But, I keep asking, what is the social benefit of a $100,000 kitchen to someone who does not cook? In a city where an estimated forty thousand homeless people sleep in parks and door-

continued to next page

ways? Who exactly, in that city, will be helped by a twenty-eight story condo project next to the "21" Club, filled with one- and two-bedroom units "designed for corporate ownership and part-time New York residents"? The point is that there is no social benefit. The point is that money will be spent and money will be made. It is a system American novelist Frank Norris and British economic historian Richard H. Tawney as well as Friedrich Engels and Thorstein Veblen have been trying to explain for the last hundred years. The new and frightening thing about our extravagant tunnel vision is that nowadays the getting and the spending are ends in themselves. Even the kitchen and the condos are incidental.

IDEAS OF THE 'EIGHTIES #2:   "He who dies with the most toys *wins*."—motto on brass plaque advertised in *The Robb Report*. The same issue of this journal for big spenders carried an ad for a recovery hotline: 1-800-COCAINE. Spending frenzy is part of the short-circuited sensibility of the cocaine age.

Addicted is another word that explains today's idea of success. Spending and/or getting can become uncontrollable habits. I went through a short bout of aerobic spending last winter, and after a week or two, I edged up on a great insight: it would never have an end. One day, I spent a preposterous fortune on a knitted cap designed with a Scottie dog. Outside the store, I saw the same cap on a three-year-old Yuppie tot. I retired from the field and redirected my yearnings toward chocolate. Some people choose alcohol, or drugs, or gambling, or sex. Even earning money is addictive. Who knows if the M.B.A. doing conspicuous leisure with two weeks of helicopter skiing is working to support his spending, or spending to justify his earning? The one sure thing is that none of these fixes satisfies our undefined longings. Whatever it is we want, we cannot name it, and we cannot buy it.

IDEAS OF THE 'EIGHTIES #3:   "Without children I would be comfortable with $200,000 a year. Money means a lot to my happiness."—Laurie Gilbert, twenty-eight, a lawyer, in *Newsweek's* story on Yuppies.

continued on page 344

continued from page 343

10 It is a commonplace that capitalism makes greed supreme. Its demand that we accept the making of money as the basic good of society corrupts everything: religion, art, individual integrity. Nothing is worth doing for the satisfaction of doing it, or because it needs doing. There are no higher goals or larger responsibilities. For example:

IDEAS OF THE 'EIGHTIES #4: "I don't think you can say someone has too much if he's worked for it. If he's earned it, well, it's his to do with as he pleases."—William Kennedy, Pawtucket, Rhode Island, businessman, reacting to a letter from the American Catholic bishops urging changes in the economy to help the poor.

IDEAS OF THE 'EIGHTIES #5: "Medical school would be a poor return on my investment."—Marion Ryder, honors senior at Bowdoin College, in *The New York Times.*

IDEAS OF THE 'EIGHTIES #6: "It means millions."—Bill Johnson, first American gold medalist in Alpine downhill skiing, when asked what the medal meant to him.

We are watching capitalism cannibalize itself. The middle class—the foundation of a stable economy—is being devoured as more and more money goes to the rich. Downward mobility is the real trend behind the Yuppie flash: the median income for young families fell 14 percent in the last five years. And at the same time the people who are supposed to be giants of industry and commerce are nibbling at their own noses and fingertips. Take, for example, the Hunt brothers, two of the richest men in the world. They had an insatiable craving for silver. And they nearly brought down the banking system.

15 Consider also the corporate raiders: it is hard to find their productive contribution to society. T. Boone Pickens and Carl Icahn make their millions and millions by simply threatening to take over the management of companies. After an hysterical flurry in which defensive chief executive officers protect their perks, bonuses, and golden parachutes, the stockholders and such people that care about the actual stated purpose or product of the company are left with the bill. Icahn, for example, in just one of

continued to next page

his deals, was left with a $33 million profit after he *failed* to take over Marshall Field's in 1982. This kind of paper chase is not an industry, it is an activity: self-propelling, functionless, and—apparently—addictive.

David Riesman, author of *The Lonely Crowd*, once summed up the momentum of human behavior by offering a rule: "The more, the more." But consider—if you dare—the arms race, and you begin to get an idea of where it will all end. In a mushroom cloud. No theories of security or power make rational the obliteration of our resources by the military budget. The arms race has an insatiable life of its own, and its greedy appetite will eventually want to be fed by a war, or two.

This present period of graceless extravagance is not new. It echoes the Gilded Age (which inspired Veblen's ever-fresh term "conspicuous consumption" in 1899), the Jazz Age, and the 'fifties. The more altruistic 'thirties and 'sixties followed the latter eras of excess—not, perhaps, because of virtue, or even because greed became boring, but because of necessity. Nonetheless, the cycle turned. The 'nineties, if history is our guide, will be an improvement on the 'eighties. If we live that long.

RESPOND—EXPLORE YOUR PERSPECTIVE BY WRITING

It's almost time for you to respond to an essay by constructing one of your own. However, before you do, read how two other student writers responded to Emma Goldman's "Marriage and Love."

MARRIAGE AND LOVE

The author of this piece is a pre-law major at The University of Montana.

Emma Goldman's essay on love and marriage exposed feelings in me that I would have rather not faced. I had convinced myself that I truly believed in finding the man of my dreams, marrying him and living happily ever after. It was disturbing to be told that the link between love and marriage is just a myth, that in fact, they cannot exist together. My first response to

continued on page 346

continued from page 345

Goldman's radical opinions was to disregard them as garbage. But, as I began to examine my own opinions and experiences, I realized that there was some truth in what she was saying.

My exposure to the institution of marriage has not been a positive one. Most everyone in my family has been divorced at one time, except my parents. Why my parents have stayed together, however, is a mystery to all who know them. For years they have made each other extremely unhappy. They haven't slept in the same room for years, and they will barely ride in the same car. Somehow through the years, the feelings they once shared for each other were lost. Ideally, love grows and deepens in marriage. The exact opposite happened in my parent's case. I feel the reason for their failed marriage is evidence supporting Goldman's ideas on the economics of marriage.

My parents were married in college. My father graduated from Montana State with a degree in Film and Television. His dream was to become a successful film producer. Unfortunately, Montana isn't the best market for film work. The bigger markets are in places like California or New York. My mother wouldn't even consider moving to a big city. She wanted a family and they both knew that Montana was the best place to settle down. My father, feeling the pressure of supporting a family, decided to give up producing films and get a more stable job. He became an insurance salesman.

This was quite an adjustment for him. As the years went by my father became more and more bitter about his job. He hated being tied down to a desk. He missed working with films and the free lifestyle that went along with it. Eventually his feeling became very evident and he began to take out his unhappiness on the rest of the family.

The financial strain that both my parents felt didn't help matters either. They had struggled for years and could never seem to get ahead. Most of their arguments were about money, making our economic situation extremely obvious to my brother and me. I don't remember a time when money wasn't a concern. As a child I worried about money constantly. I was concerned about bills to next page and canceled health insurance while other kids my age didn't have a worry in the world about money.

continued to next page

My father finally decided that he couldn't stand another day at a job he hated. He quit the insurance business and tried to get back into film work. This was a major turning point in my parents' relationship. My father was angry and bitter that he had compromised his dream occupation and taken a job that he hated in order to support a family. The years of insurance sales had changed him considerably and he blamed my mother for holding him back because she has refused to move out of state. My mother was angry because my father was putting the whole family in financial jeopardy by pursuing a potentially dead end job.

Many times I have asked my mother why she stays with my father if she is so unhappy. She has had various excuses in the past: "For the kids' sake," or "I have a job and a life here." But recently she admitted the real reason. She has no money and nowhere to go. She can't afford to leave. As unhappy as she is, she is forced to stay because she doesn't have the money to be happy.

I hate to admit it, but my parents seem to be a perfect example supporting Goldman's ideas. Man is bound by financial obligation. Woman becomes dependent on the man as a provider. Man becomes bitter and is driven out of the house. Woman is trapped because she is dependent. This evidence makes it hard for me to deny Goldman's opinions.

As I explore my own feelings, I realize that witnessing my parents has had a huge effect on the person I am today. I seem to be extremely preoccupied with money. As soon as I was old enough, I got a job and began to support myself to a point. I hardly ever asked my parents for gas or spending money. I knew they couldn't afford to give me money, so I earned my own.

I also became incredibly stressed out over money matters. When applying for college aid, I about went crazy. My parents reassured me that everything would work out, but I still came unglued at the slightest setback or problem. When it comes to money matters, I lose my patience very easily and give myself ulcers worrying.

Now that I am at college, I have began to choose an occupation to pursue. I seem to consider only those occupations which are lucrative. As of now, I plan on attending law school. I feel that this would be a job that I would enjoy, but I can't help but wonder if I am choosing law for the financial gains. I guess I'm just afraid of becoming dependent on someone else.

continued on page 348

continued from page 347

My personal life has also been extremely affected by growing up in a bad marriage. At age 18, marriage should be the last thing on my mind, yet it seems to cross my mind frequently. When I begin to date someone, I automatically question myself about what kind of provider this guy would be. Could he support a family? Often these thoughts keep me from completely letting down my guard or taking a risk on someone who might not make a "good husband." When I should be thinking about having fun, I'm thinking about my future as half of a married couple. It scares me to death to think I might marry the wrong person and end up like my parents. That is my worst nightmare. I know that people always say that money can't buy happiness. But I do believe that not having any money can destroy the happiness that a couple might have. Financial stress can ruin even the strongest of relationships. This idea may sound shallow and materialistic, but I have witnessed it first hand. There are enough problems to deal with in marriage without having to worry about money all the time. If I could eliminate money as a problem either through my own career or through marriage, then it would be one less obstacle to overcome.

Admitting that I fit into Goldman's stereotype about marriage breaks my heart. I would love to believe that I could survive on passionate love alone, but the rational side of me knows that it is not possible. If given the choice between passionate, all-consuming love and a more stable, financially secure love, I would probably pick the more stable love. This choice might make me miserable, but my experiences have taught me that passionate love may not withstand the obstacles in life. I hope with all my heart that someday Goldman will be proved wrong. Unfortunately, I'm afraid, it won't be me that does the proving.

Lance Hummel

*MARRIAGE AND LOVE**

Lance Hummel earned a degree in forestry from The University of Montana in the early seventies. When the lumber mill Hummel

continued to next page

*The writer of this essay has used the documentation style of the APA Manual, 4 ed.

worked for shut down, he returned to school to study physical therapy.

Emma Goldman asserts that love and marriage have nothing in common, and that marriages are, in fact, based on wrong motives such as the man's money or the woman's appearance. She claims that marriage enslaves women, making them dependent on men, parasitic, petty, nagging, and quarrelsome. Goldman also contends that this unhappy home environment drives men from their own homes, causes failed marriages, and contributes to the neglect and abandonment of children. Furthermore, she believes the children would be best cared for in a non-marriage environment, an environment filled with the free, unreserved love of the single parent.

Although entertaining, Goldman's analysis of marriage is clouded by her unrealistic idealization of love and her narrow, cynical view of marriage. She largely fails to substantiate her opinions, or to offer the persuasive convincing evidence necessary for the reader to accept such radical ideas. I believe little evidence exists which affirms her views. In fact, when one examines the bulk of the facts surrounding marriage, the opposite views are supported.

Love has much to do with marriage, and is by far its greatest motivation. A 1991 national survey conducted by sociologists Patterson and Kim showed that "love" was the overwhelmingly favorite incentive for marriage among young adults. Interestingly, "love" was cited as the reason for marriage seven times more often then "money," and eleven times more often than "financial security." Another poll conducted by the Roper Organization showed "being in love" to be the most important consideration in a good marriage, leading all other considerations by a large margin (Benokraitis, 1993, p. 242). Marriage is not as Goldman asserts, principally motivated by money and financial security. Love is the predominant consideration, the driving force in marriage, and I believe this to be as true now as it was in Goldman's time.

Consider the opposite end of the marital spectrum—divorce. Divorce is much more common today than at any time in history, affecting one of every two marriages (Benokraitis, 1993, p. 426). If one were to believe Goldman, this epidemic of marriage failures should be attributed to loveless marriages and unhappy home environments. This is not the case. A recent survey ranked "falling

continued on page 350

continued from page 349

out of love'' low on the list of reasons for divorce, well below other reasons such as communication problems, infidelity, constant fighting, and emotional abuse (Benokraitis, 1993, p. 435). These results indicate that other factors such as communication problems or infidelity are more significant causes of divorce than "falling out of love." So I believe the results of these surveys to show that love is indeed present in marriage, but when other problems are allowed to overshadow that love, then divorce may follow.

This view of love and marriage is much more realistic than that of Goldman, and can be borne out in my own marriage. In fourteen years of marriage, my wife and I have found our own relationship to be somewhat fragile, dynamic, and in need of constant maintenance. Over that span of time, we've had to constantly adjust and readjust to the demands of new situations such as changing careers, having and raising children, and increasing financial burdens. Although at times we disagree, argue, or even become furious with one another, our mutual love is never compromised. Our love remains intact and is the foundation from which we grapple with our changing situations as well as with our personal problems. We've learned the need to be constantly aware of these problems and to be diligent in preventing them from undermining our relationship. If these problems were allowed to build up and threaten our marriage, it would be because we had failed to adequately deal with them, not because we had ceased loving each other.

Goldman paints a bleak, unhappy picture of the marital home environment, describing the woman as parasitic, petty, nagging, and quarrelsome, who drives the man from his own home. Although an unhappy, loveless environment may be characteristic of a relatively small number of marriages, Goldman's claim is absolutely false when one considers marriages as a whole. A number of social scientists have found married people to be healthier and happier than those who are single, divorced, or widowed (Benokraitis, 1993, p. 250). Furthermore, married people have substantially lower rates of suicide, depression, disease, and psychological problems than the non-married groups. So, rather than causing misery and unhappiness, studies show that marriage, in fact, promotes health, happiness, and psychological well-being.

continued to next page

Accordingly, the children of intact, married-couple families have been shown to suffer fewer behavioral, emotional, and psychological problems than children of single parents. A study by the National Institute of Mental Health showed that children of divorced and single parents were three times more likely to receive psychological counseling, five times more likely to be expelled from school, and were more likely to be involved in truancy, larceny, and drug use than children from intact, married-couple families (Benokraitis, 1993, p. 442). Instead of harming and abandoning children, as Goldman supposes, marriage actually protects them from behavioral and psychological problems, as well as crime, school problems, and drug use.

Goldman unrealistically glorifies the free, unconquered, and unfettered spirit of love. She exalts the power of love to make a beggar a king, to defy all laws, to make a hovel a home, and to feed and protect children. Although some of these lofty qualities do exist in love, they need a generous dose of reality in order to be successfully applied to real-world situations.

Love cannot pay the bills, supervise children, cook meals, wash dishes, clean house, or change diapers. People do these things. These are real-world problems or situations that need to be solved in order to provide a home environment in which love can thrive. And I believe that there is no substitute for a loving, cooperative marriage in providing for the solutions to real-world problems and for the needs of children. I realize that on my own, I could never adequately provide for the needs of our children; I need the support of my wife just as she needs mine. We each bring our own abilities and gifts to the relationship, and the combination of these abilities makes the home into a more loving, caring environment for our children than we could provide individually. In this way, I believe the combined abilities of the husband and wife to exceed the sum of their individual abilities. And when these mutual abilities are united with a cooperative, loving home environment, there is no better place for the caring and nurturing of the child.

REFERENCE

Benokraitis, N. V. (1993). *Marriages and families.* Englewood Cliffs, New Jersey: Prentice Hall.

RESPONSIVE WRITING ASSIGNMENT

After **exploring** the essays included in this chapter's anthology of essays (or at least three from another source) by **prereading** them, choose one and **read** it for both meaning and craft. Then, using your chosen essay as a starting place, **respond** to the same subject by writing an essay of your own. Since reading and writing are enhanced by collaboration, you may want to choose a partner from your class as a collaborator for the critical reading process or even for the entire writing process.

WRITING IN RESPONSE TO ESSAYS: A GUIDE TO THE PROCESS

Assess Your Past Performance
Explore the Writing Situation
Prewrite
Draft
Rewrite

ASSESS YOUR PAST PERFORMANCE

As you work through this assignment, continue to **assess** how you think and write, **learn** from your previous experience, and **respond by revising** your personal writing process. Read over your assessment of your performance from your last assignment, and consider your writing strengths and weaknesses. Identify the categories with which you had trouble. Then analyze why you had trouble, and focus on ways you might better employ the process to avoid repeating your mistakes.

EXPLORE THE WRITING SITUATION

Now that you've been given an assignment, it's time to explore the **choices** and **constraints** of the writing situation. One of the positive aspects of responding to an essay is that the constraints of the writing situation can make your available choices that much easier. And the biggest constraint you'll be operating under will be your own engagement with the subject. Because essays are personal and interpretative, it's vitally important to start with a subject that intrigues you. With the importance of personal engagement in mind, open yourself to the following passages and see if they trigger any responsive choices from you.

SUBJECT   If one of the essays you've explored in your search for a topic has authentically engaged you (either by enraging you or by pleasing you), it might be the essay to which you want to respond. Your choice of subject is open in this assignment, so explore thoroughly; look for a subject that will really engage you.

AUDIENCE   Your choice of audience is even more open than your choice of subject. You might write to the author of one of the essays or to the same audience that author was writing to. You might write to someone within the community of your class or to someone beyond the classroom who hasn't read the essay to which you decide to respond. Weigh your possible choices of audience in light of your interest; writing to an agreeing audience will lead you one way with your topic; writing to a disagreeing audience may lead you in an entirely different direction.

PURPOSE   Your general purpose here is also open. In the assignment you're told only to "respond." Just how you respond is up to you. For example, you might respond to an essay written to *entertain* by *explaining* or *informing*. However, keep in mind that since essays are by their nature **interpretative,** all essays have a powerfully **persuasive** element to them.

WRITER   Test your preconceived ideas by exploring your prior encounters with the subject. Put critical pressure on the conclusions you've drawn, and be open to amending your own perspectives. Just when did your own encounters with the subjects of the essays begin? How might your personal and educational histories have influenced your encounters?

TIME   If you've chosen an essay to respond to at this point, consider your time constraints. Do you need time for researching your subject? Outside reading or setting up interviews can take time, so schedule accordingly. Or you many need more thinking time for this assignment; because essays are personal, interpretative pieces of writing, they're by nature "think pieces."

RESEARCH OPPORTUNITY

To **expand your encounter** with the subject of your chosen essay, explore the topic by researching it either on your own or in a collaborative research team. For example, if you've decided to **respond** to Goldman's essay you might **explore** the change in societal attitudes towards marriage and love in America since the 1920s by doing **library research** or developing a **questionnaire** for comparative groups. Or if it's Keegan's essay you're responding to, you might explore acquaintance rape on your own campus by **interviewing** a campus sexual assault counselor.

If at this point you've chosen an essay to respond to, then go on to the reading for meaning process. If not, choose the essay that has so far intrigued you most, and encounter it critically by reading if for meaning.

READ THE ESSAY FOR MEANING

Reading an essay for meaning is almost always enhanced by collaboration. If you mainly agree with your collaborators, they can provide you with additional evidence to support your position. If your collaborators in the reading process disagree with you, all the better. Having to defend your ideas about what you think the essay essentially means can challenge you to expand or change your thinking. If necessary, go beyond the community of the class to find a partner for reading and conversation—a close friend with whom you regularly share ideas and perspectives is a natural choice.

RESEARCH UNKNOWNS.   Research any unknown elements in the essay.

ANALYZE THE SPEAKER

Facts
What facts can you glean about the speaker from the text? From research?

Emotions
Where in the text does the speaker describe his or her own or another's emotional reactions? Have you ever experienced similar emotional reactions?

Attitudes
Identify those passages in the text where the speaker voices his or her conclusive attitudes about the subject.

DETERMINE THE MESSAGE.   Write down in as few words as possible what you think the speaker's message is. Support your judgment with evidence from the text.

DETERMINE THE AUDIENCE.   Using language and developmental material as a source of clues, describe in as much detail as possible the audience to whom the text is directed. For example, what do you think the values of the audience are? What is their educational level? Their social or economic background? Their gender? Provide evidence from the text to support your determinations.

DETERMINE THE PURPOSE.   In your judgment, what ultimate change in knowledge, thought, or action does the speaker seek from his or her audience? In addition, what is the writer's general audience-based purpose (or purposes)? Is the writer writing to entertain? To inform? To explore? To persuade? Is there a mixture of purposes?

READ WITH AN EYE TO THE WRITER'S CRAFT

Perhaps the best way for you to really know what essays are is to become familiar with the genre through reading. The more essays you read, the more natural the form will become to you. So don't just read one essay in preparing to write your own. Choose a few and study the craft of the masters.

FOCUS ON PERSUASION IN ESSAY WRITING

Because essays are analytical and interpretative texts, they invariably contain a powerfully persuasive element. However, just which of the persuasive techniques an essay writer employs most often in a particular essay will depend on the subject being written about, the audience being addressed, and the purpose for writing.

VOICE   Although all essays are personal interpretations of experience, they can be written in voices that range from the highly personal to the most formal and distant. With this in mind, describe in as much detail as possible (or draw a detailed picture of) the created persona in the text you're exploring. Then consider the last two of the three persuasive techniques (**pathos** and **ethos**), and make a judgment about why you think the writer created that particular persona. Was it to persuade with emotion? Was it to establish credibility?

DEVELOPMENT   Just as writers reveal their attitudes through language choices, they also reveal their attitudes through their developmental choices. Identify those places in the text where the audience is being persuaded with reason. Then identify those places in the essay where the writer is persuading the audience by appealing to emotions. In addition, identify those places where the writer is persuading by establishing credibility. Finally, what kind of research do you think went into the writing of the essay?

ARRANGEMENT   Arrangement is closely connected to development. In fact, there's a kind of chicken-and-egg quality to their relationship; it is difficult even for the writer to determine which choice was made first. Since essays are by definition brief, and therefore highly focused, the chosen pattern of arrangement in any essay is usually tightly centered around a particular category of evidence. Essay writers don't have room to say everything they may know and think about their subjects; they have to limit their scope, and in the process of limiting, the main pattern of arrangement often emerges. Write a paragraph outline for the essay you're exploring. Around what category of evidence is the chosen pattern of arrangement mainly centered?

The chosen category of **evidence** makes up the **body** of the essay; in the body the writer provides the bulk of the developmental material that is intended to move you to agree with the text's message. But essays also have to give the reader background information so that the details in the body will be relevant in the real-world context. The **introduction** of the essay is the place where writers provide this **background** information— where they answer the reader's implicit question, "Why should I be as engaged by this subject as the writer is?" But the introduction is also the place where writers greet their audiences and establish a bond of trust with the people to whom they're writing. With this in mind, where does the introduction of your chosen essay end and its body begin? In addition, what kind of developmental material (descriptive, informational, conceptual, or emotional) is included in the essay's introduction?

Essays also have **conclusions.** And in spite of what you may have heard, an essay's conclusion isn't usually a single paragraph. In conclusions, writers explore with their readers the **implications** of the messages they're trying to communicate. In the conclusion of an essay the writer is saying, "You've seen the evidence; now here's why you should agree with my perspective." With this in mind, identify the conclusion of the essay.

Finally, and most importantly, writers choose to order and group their developmental material with their **audience** and **purpose** in mind. The ordering of material creates a movement of meaning. Writers choose to place one thing before another and to bundle bits of material together because they believe it will be easier for their audience to understand their position if they do. Focus on the order and grouping of the developmental material in your chosen essay, and look for audience and purpose-based choices in arrangement.

Now that you've thoroughly explored an essay by reading it for meaning and studying it with an eye to improving your own technique, it's time to begin writing your response.

PREWRITE

In writing your own responsive essay you'll be responding to two en-counters—your encounter with the subject of your chosen essay and your encounter with the essay itself. With this in mind, consider the following strategies. One piece of advice, though: as you work through these strat-egies, don't let the essay you're responding to totally dominate your think-ing. The essay you're in the process of writing is your own interpretation of experience, and although you should certainly put critical pressure on your interpretative position, both your judgments and the evidence that you choose to support your judgments should go beyond the essay to which you're responding into your own experience and knowledge.

RESPONSIVE PREWRITING EXERCISES

1. Test your preconceived ideas about the subject by exploring changes in your thinking that have resulted from critical reading. Write a brief analysis of your prior encounter with the subject of the text:

When did your encounter begin?
What judgments had you formed about the subject before you read the essay you're responding to?
Has your reading of the essay changed your prior judgments in any way? If so, explain how and why.

continued on page 358

continued from page 357

2. If you've done research on the subject of your essay, explore in writing how what you've learned from researching has affected your previously held ideas about the subject.

3. If your subject is a situation, make a judgment of who the **active participants** are. Then, in as much detail as possible, explore in writing the **actions** of the active participants, the **motives** behind those actions, and the actions' **consequences.** For example, if you've chosen the Keegan essay about acquaintance rape,

> Who do you think is responsible for the situation? Men? Women? Society as a whole? All three?
> What actions by those involved cause or have caused the situation to exist?
> What possible motives might the active participants have had for their actions?
> What are the consequences of those actions?

4. Since your choice of subject in this assignment should be compelled by your interest or belief, explore in writing the possible reasons for your interest in the subject. What experiences in your life might have made this subject compelling to you?

FOCUS ON AUDIENCE AND PURPOSE

After trying one or more of the above strategies, consider your personal perspective on the subject. Then focus on the choices and constraints of the writing situation, and answer the following questions. If necessary, choose an experimental audience and purpose to explore as you draft.

AUDIENCE   Who would you most like to change by writing your essay? In other words, who is your chosen audience? Briefly analyze your audience in writing. What are their values? What is their possible perspective on the subject? Why, in your judgment, do they have the perspective they do?

PURPOSE   What change in knowledge, thought, or action do you desire from your audience?

FOCUS ON A POSSIBLE MESSAGE

Read over the results of your prewriting. Based on what you've gotten down so far, write out in as few sentences as possible your summary judgment on the subject. Then check your judgment against your encounters with both the essay and the situation. Is there any evidence that refutes or weakens your position? If there is, you may need to adjust your judgment or do further research on the subject. Looking over your determinations for message in the essays you've read in this chapter might help here.

DRAFT

DRAFT TO REVISE

The revision you engage in as you draft gives you the opportunity to expand on old ideas and formulate new ones. **Read** and **reread** your draft as you write, and look for new ways of viewing your subject. Pay particular attention to those areas that have given you trouble in the past, and **revise** as you draft by **cutting, adding, rearranging,** and **rewording.**

Because of their personal nature, essays are more openly conversational than any other prose genre. The very origin of the word *essay* (from the French *essai,* originally meaning "a trial, a testing, an experiment") suggests the trying out of your own personal perspective on an audience of "others." Your essay is your personal, interpretative response. It's your turn now to probe the subject and draw conclusions. But, because it is your turn and no one else's, you have to take full responsibility. So use your mind to its full capacity. Test your judgments and assertions. Converse with yourself. Be your own most demanding critic. But also remember as you draft to consider your **audience, purpose,** and **message.**

FOCUS ON YOUR CHOICES

VOICE   To choose an appropriate voice, keep in mind that your created voice is the facet of personality, the persona, through which your audiences will hopefully come to trust you and find you **credible.** Write out a detailed description (or draw a detailed picture) of the persona you want your audience to come to know. Then, as you draft, read your emerging text aloud, and **reword** with your audience's responses in mind.

If we compare the two essays at the beginning of this chapter, we'll see that in Koch's essay the voice is more openly conversational than the voice in Bruck's piece; the persona Koch creates on the page is that of a thoughtful, responsible, experienced man who has carefully weighed the arguments on both sides of the issue. Where Bruck uses the pronoun *I* only once in his essay (interestingly, to make a disclaimer), Koch uses it repeatedly in his introduction both to establish his **credibility** as an experienced civil servant and to acknowledge his personal responsibility in deciding that capital punishment is just. Bruck takes another tack; the pronoun he uses repeatedly is *we*. Bruck's created persona is a much more distant figure. He's trying to focus the audience's attention not on himself but on itself. By using *we* and remaining distant, he's forcing his audience to take responsibility for, as he writes, "kill[ing] men whom we have already imprisoned."

Both writers carefully chose the voices they employed in their pieces with their audience and purpose in mind. Koch knew that many of the people in his audience would come to his text feeling that capital punishment was inhumane, and he decided that creating the persona of a responsible, thoughtful man making an admittedly difficult decision was the best way to establish his **credibility** and **persuade** his audience. Bruck, writing in response to Koch, wanted to win back any members of the audience who had been swayed by Koch's argument, so he chose to focus the audience's attention back on its own personal responsibility.

In essay writing, voice may just be the most important category of choice. Although essays are personal interpretations of experience, the created voice in any particular essay can range from the most personal and familiar to the most formal and reserved. And the choice that you as a writer make in this area should have everything to do with audience. The words that you choose and the sentence structures that you use to frame those words should certainly reflect your attitude toward your subject, but your choices should also be aimed at getting the change you want in your reader. Remember, your writing in this assignment is driven by the conclusive judgments you've drawn about experience (your attitudes). Your attitudes are very close to you, and it will be very easy for you to forget about your audience as you draft and begin writing only for yourself. Just keep in mind that you're not writing to express interpretations; you're writing to convince someone else that your interpretations are credible.

DEVELOPMENT   To convince your audience, justify your conclusive judgments by supplying sufficient experiential or researched evidence. "Sufficient" here doesn't just refer to *quantity;* in terms of evidence, *quality* is as important as quantity. Quality evidence is evidence that has been critically tested. If you want to convince your audience, you have to test your evidence by imaginatively putting yourself in the audience's position; you have to say, "If I were my audience, would this bit of evidence convince me?"

Koch, out of his stance as a thoughtful and responsible man, has chosen to use evidence that appeals to the **reason** of his audience and establishes his **credibility;** he cites statistics and the opinions of authoritative figures (philosophers and statesmen), duplicating for the reader his own process of reasonably coming to the conclusion that the death penalty, even though it "diminishes us all," is "just and necessary." On the other hand, Bruck wants to confront his audience with the personal responsibility of taking a human life. Again and again he appeals to this audience's **emotions** by citing specific cases of real people wrongly convicted.

As you draft, look for opportunities to **add** relevant developmental material and **cut** material that might lead your audience away from your focus.

ARRANGEMENT   Take into consideration your audience's perspective and knowledge as you draft, and order and group the developmental material accordingly. What does your audience need to know first off? Keep in mind the function of each of the parts of your essay. The **introduction** greets the audience and gives them the background information they need; it's also the place where your message is initially brought into focus. Your audience doesn't necessarily need to have the message of the essay stated in a single sentence in the introduction, but your audience will have to begin to know the general direction in which the essay is headed. In both the Koch essay and the Bruck essay, we know in the first few paragraphs the stance that the writer has taken. In addition, each writer makes the subject relevant to his readers by putting it in a real-life context. Koch does this by narrating in quick succession three stories that suggest that capital punishment might deter murderers. Bruck brings capital punishment out of the realm of abstract "theory" into the context of everyday life.

The **body** of the essay is where the bulk of your evidence will be presented. Consider what your audience needs to be shown in order to be convinced. The body is also the place where you'll voice your conclusive attitudes about the bits of evidence within your chosen overall category. In addition, there should be a movement of meaning, a logical progression, in the way you choose to sequence the bits of evidence that make up the body. There are no hard and fast rules to this sequencing, but the sequence you choose should have a rationale behind it. After an anecdotal introduction, Koch chose to **divide** his argument into clearly marked oppositional points, the last of which (that capital punishment is "state-sanctioned murder") was at the heart of his audience's possible opposition. Bruck also **divided** his argument into points, but then he went on to **illustrate** each point with a specific anecdote.

The **conclusion** is where you'll voice your overall, compelling judgment on the evidence you've presented so far in your essay. Your conclusion is your opportunity to look back with your audience on your interpretation of experience and to explore its implications. Your conclusion is also your final opportunity to nudge your **audience** to move the way your want them to move. So as you write your conclusion, think hard about your specific **purpose.** Koch, who was writing to an audience that was ambivalent about his subject, chose to conclude his essay by focusing on a victim of a specific murder in order to suggest that not favoring capital punishment was morally irresponsible. Bruck, who was writing to recapture anyone who might have been swayed by Koch, chose not only to discredit Koch by suggesting his stance might be politically motivated, but also chose to focus his audience's attention on their personal accountability.

Rearrange the order of sentences, paragraphs, or sections of your text with your audience responses in mind. If you draft on the computer, use the block and move functions to rearrange. If you type or write longhand, write on only one side of the page so that you can cut sections apart and rearrange them.

WRITING IS ACTIVE AND RECURSIVE

Remember, writing is recursive. Drafting is an opportunity to put pressure on the conclusions you've drawn about the subject in earlier stages of the process. As you draft, actively test the results of your prewriting by rethinking each assertion you make. Search for new ways of viewing the subject, and be ready to change your prior assertions if they don't hold up under the pressure of self-criticism.

REWRITE

Test your essay in a collaborative **workshop.** Come prepared with any questions that may have occurred to you about your work during the drafting process. Part Six offers suggestions and strategies for workshops.

REWRITE ACTIVELY

The key word here is *active.* Don't just make cosmetic style changes. There is no way that you can take revision too far. Leave yourself open for new discoveries as you revise. Imagine yourself as your chosen audience. Read your essay critically, focusing on the following checklist, and continue to **cut, add, rearrange,** and **reword** with your audience's responses in mind.

- Have you written with a specific purpose in mind?
- Has your working message been clarified into a focused message?
- Does your voice accurately convey the meaning that you want it to convey? Are your word choice and sentence structure correct?
- Have you given your audience sufficient background information in your introduction, and is your intended message at least suggested?
- Have you supplied enough detailed evidence to convince your audience to agree with your message?
- Have you connected your evidence to your message by making conclusive interpretative judgments about the bits of evidence you supply in the body of your essay?
- Have you arranged the evidence within the body of your essay effectively? Is there a logical and recognizable movement of meaning?
- Does your conclusion contain a summary judgment that connects your message with all the evidence you have supplied?
- Is your text correct in terms of mechanics (spelling and punctuation)?

EDIT TO FINAL FORM

Polish your text as you write the final draft. Focus on paragraphing, transitions, and any habitual problems you may have with spelling, punctuation, and sentence structure. Part Six provides specific information and strategies.

PROOFREAD

If possible, put your response aside for at least a couple of hours before you proofread. Proofread for small, careless errors by reading your text aloud, preferably to another person.

ASSESS YOUR PERFORMANCE BY WRITING CRITICALLY

The process isn't completed until you've assessed your performance. Study your evaluators' comments; and focus on **voice,**

continued on page 364

continued from page 363

arrangement, development, and **mechanics.** Part Six provides strategies for analyzing evaluators' comments and mapping your own patterns of writing weakness. With which category did you mainly have trouble? Write a page explaining why you think you had trouble with that particular category. Then write a second page in which you explain what you might do to correct the problem.

CHAPTER
ELEVEN
RESPONDING TO FICTION
AND FILM

THE WRITER'S SCENARIO

A writer encounters a work of fiction or a film. The work of fiction might be a novel, short story, or a play. The film might be a contemporary one or a "classic." The writer reads the work of fiction closely or views the film carefully, searching for meaning in it. The writer studies the language and dialogue in the work, examines the physical settings described or depicted in it, and empathizes with the characters, comparing and contrasting their experiences with his or her own experiences. Finally, after thinking (and, optimally, after researching what other writers have written about the work and discussing the work with others), the writer responds by constructing a written text that argues for a particular interpretation of the work's meaning.

Fictional works focus on **characters** and on their **actions** in particular **places** and **times.** What all works of fiction have in common is that they contain some **dramatic** element. Something happens in them that **challenges characters to change.** Works of fiction have been around almost as long as people have. Long before any written language was developed, people passed on the stories that were significant in their cultures by speaking them, singing them, and physically recreating them in rituals and dances.

And for as long as works of fiction have been part of human culture, people have been **interpreting** them by making judgments about their meaning. In cultures with oral traditions, the singers and speakers of stories don't merely deliver those stories to their listening audiences; they interpret them by using body language, inflection, and emphasis. Likewise, on the modern stage, actors don't merely memorize lines and recite them. They read the texts of the plays they perform carefully and critically, and they develop interpretive positions about the characters they portray. One actor's interpretive "reading" of a character will be very different from another actor's "reading" of that same character. The words the actors speak may be the same, but the way those words are spoken can radically change the way that the character is presented on the stage.

And just as speakers and singers in oral cultures and actors on the modern stage interpret the stories and characters they present, you as a reader of fiction and a viewer of film also interpret. You imaginatively enter the world created in the work, and you make judgments about that world and about the characters you encounter in it. You find the created world you enter disturbing, exciting, or wonderfully pleasant; you identify with one character and dislike another. Think about your recent experiences as a reader and viewer of fictional works. You may have read a novel and felt let down when you finished it—not because you were disappointed in the way it ended, but because you were sorry to have left the world created in it. Or you may have seen a film and been moved by the heroism of a particular character or by that character's similarity to yourself or someone close to you. You may even have talked about the book or film to a friend who had also encountered it, and discovered in your conversation that your friend had drawn conclusions about the work very different from the conclusions you'd drawn. For example, you may have found a particular film terrifying, while your friend thought the same film was funny, or you may have understood and approved of the actions of a particular character, while your friend found those actions puzzling.

The interpretive conclusions that you draw about fictional works have a great deal to do with your personal and educational histories. If you've experienced a situation in your life and then encounter a character in a similar situation in a film, you're more likely to be moved than someone who hasn't experienced a similar situation. Likewise, if you've studied a historical period and then read a novel set in that period, your knowledge of the events and social forces of that period will affect the interpretive conclusions you draw. What you know and believe profoundly influences the judgments you make about all the texts and situations you encounter in the world. However, since the best fictional works take as their subjects those things in life that are emotionally charged and provocative, reading and writing about fictional works requires working hard to maintain a balance between emotional and rational understanding. Sometimes a work of fiction will show you things about yourself and the world that you don't want to see, and your initial reading can be so charged with negative emotions that you may want to dismiss the work as worthless.

The ability to critically read and effectively interpret works of fiction is important in the academic community and in the world at large. Fictional works are a large part of the record of human existence, and writing about them can help you understand the ways that human thought has changed and evolved. In addition, interpreting fictional works will encourage you to reflect on your life and challenge you to grow and change.

To effectively read and then write critically about works of fiction, consider the following techniques.

TECHNIQUES FOR RESPONDING TO FICTION AND FILM

1. Preread (or preview) the work and, if possible, research it thoroughly and discuss it with others who are familiar with it.
2. Reread (or re-view) the work, focusing on the dramatic activity in it. Explore in detail the *characters* in the text, the *significant actions* they engage in, the *motives* behind those actions, and the actions' *consequences*.
3. Explore physical setting, point of view, and tone in order to determine meaningful elements.
4. Develop an interpretive position about the work's meaning.
5. Analyze your audience to determine what they know about the work and what their possible interpretive position might be.
6. Present your evidence-supported interpretive position with your audience analysis in mind.

RESPONDING TO FICTION AND FILM: PRIMARY TEXTS

PREREAD FICTION

To familiarize yourself with Ernest Hemingway's short story "Hills Like White Elephants," preread. **Read** the first twenty-five lines, focusing on those things you understand. When you get to the end of the twenty-fifth line, stop and take stock. **Summarize** what's gone on in the text so far. If you're puzzled by anything, go back and focus on the passages you have questions about and **reread** them. Then **predict** the direction you think the text will take next. As you continue reading, compare your predictions with what unfolds on the page. After each twenty lines or so (or any time you're puzzled), pause again to **summarize, reread,** and **predict.**

HILLS LIKE WHITE ELEPHANTS
Ernest Hemingway

The hills across the valley of the Ebro were long and white. On this side there was no shade and no trees and the station was between two lines of rails in the sun. Close against the side of the station there was the warm shadow of the building and a curtain, made of strings of bamboo beads, hung across the open door into the bar, to keep out flies. The American and the girl with him sat at a table in the shade, outside the building. It was very hot and the express from Barcelona would come in forty minutes. It stopped at this junction for two minutes and went on to Madrid.

"What should we drink?" the girl asked. She had taken off her hat and put it on the table

"It's pretty hot," the man said.

"Let's drink beer."

"*Dos cervezas*," the man said into the curtain.

"Big ones?" a woman asked from the doorway.

"Yes. Two big ones."

The woman brought two glasses of beer and two felt pads. She put the felt pads and the beer glasses on the table and looked at the man and the girl. The girl was looking off at the line of hills. They were white in the sun and the country was brown and dry.

"They look like white elephants," she said.

"I've never seen one," the man drank his beer.

"No, you wouldn't have."

"I might have," the man said. "Just because you say I wouldn't have doesn't prove anything."

The girl looked at the bead curtain. "They've painted something on it," she said. "What does it say?"

"Anis del Toro. It's a drink."

"Could we try it?"

The man called "Listen" through the curtain. The woman came out from the bar.

"Four reales."

"We want two Anis del Toro."

"With water?"

continued to next page

"Do you want it with water?"

"I don't know," the girl said. "Is it good with water?"

"It's all right."

"You want them with water?" asked the woman.

"Yes, with water."

"It tastes like licorice," the girl said and put the glass down.

"That's the way with everything."

"Yes," said the girl. "Everything tastes of licorice. Especially all the things you've waited so long for, like absinthe."

"Oh, cut it out."

"You started it," the girl said. "I was being amused. I was having a fine time."

"Well, let's try and have a fine time."

"All right. I was trying. I said the mountains looked like white elephants. Wasn't that bright?"

"That was bright."

"I wanted to try this new drink: That's all we do, isn't it— look at things and try new drinks?"

"I guess so."

The girl looked across at the hills.

"They're lovely hills," she said. "They don't really look like white elephants. I just meant the coloring of their skin through the trees."

"Should we have another drink?"

"All right."

The warm wind blew the bead curtain against the table.

"The beer's nice and cool," the man said.

"It's lovely," the girl said.

"It's really an awfully simple operation, Jig," the man said. "It's not really an operation at all."

The girl looked at the ground the table legs rested on.

"I know you wouldn't mind it, Jig. It's really not anything. It's just to let the air in."

The girl did not say anything.

"I'll go with you and I'll stay with you all the time. They just let the air in and then it's all perfectly natural."

"Then what will we do afterward?"

"We'll be fine afterward. Just like we were before."

"What makes you think so?"

continued on page 370

continued from page 369

"That's the only thing that bothers us. It's the only thing that's made us unhappy."

The girl looked at the bead curtain, put her hand out and took hold of two of the strings of beads.

"And you think then we'll be all right and be happy."

"I know we will. You don't have to be afraid. I've known lots of people that have done it."

"So have I," said the girl. "And afterward they were all so happy."

"Well," the man said, "if you don't want to you don't have to. I wouldn't have you do it if you didn't want to. But I know it's perfectly simple."

"And you really want to?"

"I think it's the best thing to do. But I don't want you to do it if you don't really want to."

"And if I do it you'll be happy and things will be like they were and you'll love me?"

"I love you now. You know I love you."

"I know. But if I do it, then it will be nice again if I say things are like white elephants, and you'll like it?"

"I'll love it. I love it now but I just can't think about it. You know how I get when I worry."

"If I do it you won't ever worry?"

"I won't worry about that because it's perfectly simple."

"Then I'll do it. Because I don't care about me."

"What do you mean?"

"I don't care about me."

"Well, I care about you."

"Oh, yes. But I don't care about me. And I'll do it and then everything will be fine."

"I don't want you to do it if you feel that way."

The girl stood up and walked to the end of the station. Across, on the other side, were fields of grain and trees along the banks of the Ebro. Far away, beyond the river, were mountains. The shadow of a cloud moved across the field of grain and she saw the river through the trees.

"And we could have all this," she said. "And we could have everything and every day we make it more impossible."

continued to next page

"What did you say?"

"I said we could have everything."

"We can have everything."

"No, we can't."

"We can have the whole world."

"No, we can't."

"We can go everywhere."

"No, we can't. It isn't ours any more."

"It's ours."

"No, it isn't. And once they take it away, you never get it back."

"But they haven't taken it away."

"We'll wait and see."

"Come on back in the shade," he said. "You mustn't feel that way."

"I don't feel any way," the girl said. "I just know things."

"I don't want you to do anything that you don't want to do—"

"Nor that isn't good for me," she said. "I know. Could we have another beer?"

"All right. But you've got to realize—"

"I realize," the girl said. "Can't we maybe stop talking?"

They sat down at the table and the girl looked across at the hills on the dry side of the valley and the man looked at her and at the table.

"You've got to realize," he said, "that I don't want you to do it if you don't want to. I'm perfectly willing to go through with it if it means anything to you."

"Doesn't it mean anything to you? We could get along."

"Of course it does. But I don't want anybody but you. I don't want any one else. And I know it's perfectly simple."

"Yes, you know it's perfectly simple."

"It's all right for you to say that, but I do know it."

"Would you do something for me now?"

"I'd do anything for you."

"Would you please please please please please please please stop talking?"

He did not say anything but looked at the bags against the wall of the station. There were labels on them from all the hotels where they had spent nights.

continued on page 372

continued from page 371

"But I don't want you to," he said. "I don't care anything about it."

"I'll scream," the girl said.

The woman came out through the curtains with two glasses of beer and put them down on the damp felt pads. "The train comes in five minutes," she said.

"What did she say?" asked the girl.

"That the train is coming in five minutes."

The girl smiled brightly at the woman, to thank her.

"I'd better take the bags over to the other side of the station," the man said. She smiled at him.

"All right. Then come back and we'll finish the beer."

He picked up the two heavy bags and carried them around the station to the other tracks. He looked up the tracks but could not see the train. Coming back, he walked through the barroom, where people waiting for the train were drinking. He drank an Anis at the bar and looked at the people. They were all waiting reasonably for the train. He went out through the bead curtain. She was sitting at the table and smiled at him.

"Do you feel better?" he asked.

"I feel fine," she said. "There's nothing wrong with me. I feel fine."

PREVIEW FILM

To familiarize yourself with Clint Eastwood's *Unforgiven,* preview. First, arrange a viewing either on your own or as part of a group. If you preview on your own or in a small group, you'll be able to pause the video player when you need to re-view and take notes. However, if your preview takes place in a classroom or college viewing room, you'll have to be particularly attentive as you watch. Bring a pen and notebook to the viewing to jot down notes about puzzling elements in the film.

Focus on scenes as you preview. **Watch the first scene** carefully. At the end of the first scene, quickly **summarize** what's gone on so far. If you're confused by anything, **re-view** if possible, or make a brief written note (a word or two will do). Then **predict** the direction you think the film will take next. As you continue viewing, quickly focus your thinking after each scene, and **summarize, re-view** if possible, and **predict.**

LISTEN—ANALYZE FICTION AND FILM FOR MEANING

COLLABORATIVE WRITING ASSIGNMENT

Explore the meaning of one of these primary texts in collaboration with your classmates. If the focus of your study is "Hills Like White Elephants," this collaboration can be done in the classroom or in small study and research groups beyond the classroom. However, if *Unforgiven* is your focus, the collaboration will probably work best if your group has direct access to a VCR.

Start the collaboration in groups of three or four. Then, after concentrated group work, open the discussion up to full-class conversation. As you work, **annotate** your personal copy of the text by **marking** relevant passages and **noting** their significance in writing. (In terms of responding to the film, annotate the notes you took while viewing it.) In addition, have one member of your group record your collaborative conclusions or lasting differences in opinion.

READING FICTION AND FILM FOR MEANING:
A GUIDE TO THE PROCESS
    Know the Text Thoroughly
    Search for Meaning in the Text
    Consider Theme

KNOW THE TEXT

RESEARCH UNKNOWNS.   In works of fiction, words and references can often be loaded with meaning. To avoid missing the potential significance of details, research any words or references that leave you with questions. For example, in *Unforgiven* when English Bob refers to a newspaper headline and then goes on to comment on it, do you know precisely what he's talking about?

OUTLINE THE PLOT.   Before you can begin reading a fictional text for meaning, you have to have an overview of what's

continued on page 374

continued from page 373

actually going on in that text. Outline the actions that take place in the fictional work to have an accurate record of the work's chronology. See Part Six for a detailed explanation of outlining.

SEARCH FOR MEANING IN THE TEXT

The whole point of reading fictional works critically is to have your thinking about the world and yourself challenged and changed. And the only way that challenge and change can take place is if you personally enter and interact with the work. Although discussing the work with others can aid you in your search for meaning, the final conclusions you draw should be your own. Complex fictional works have many possible interpretations. Your goal here isn't to nail down the absolute "truth" of *Unforgiven* or "Hills Like White Elephants" but instead to study the work carefully and discuss it with others to develop **your own evidence-supported position** about its meaning. With this in mind, search for meaning in the following ways.

DISCERN AND ANALYZE EMOTIONAL POINTS. Since fictional works take as their subjects situations of conflict and crisis, discerning where in a text major characters respond emotionally can help you make judgments about individual characters and about the meaning of the text as a whole. For example, in "Hills Like White Elephants," the American responds emotionally to Jig's comment about the hills and begins the arguments that makes up the bulk of the story; in *Unforgiven*, Ned responds emotionally when he decides not to shoot the cowboys pinned down in the canyon. With these two examples in mind, determine and mark on your outline the emotional high points in the text you're examining.

In addition, to emotionally enter the world created in the text, try empathizing with the characters at this point. Have you ever experienced emotional responses like the ones you've discerned? For example, have you ever felt, as Jig does in "Hills Like White Elephants," that you desperately wanted someone to stop talking? If so, explore the circumstances under which you had the same responses as a specific character.

continued to next page

FOCUS ON THE DRAMATIC ACTIVITY OF CHARACTERS.
Fictional works focus on **characters,** their **actions,** and the **consequences** of those actions. The major characters in works of fiction are **changed** by their own actions and by the actions of others. Sometimes the actions that bring about change are highly dramatic, **physical actions** (the killing of Ned in *Unforgiven,* for example). However, sometimes these actions and the changes brought about by them are more subtle, like the American's and Jig's **conversational responses** in "Hills Like White Elephants." With this idea in mind, study the text carefully and identify the physical and conversational actions that bring about changes in the major characters.

The **motives** of characters in fictional works are perhaps even more significant than the actions those characters engage in. To fully interpret **changes** in characters, you'll have to make judgments about those characters' motives. To a large extent your interpretation of *Unforgiven* or "Hills Like White Elephants" will rest on your evidence-supported judgments about the main characters' motives. Consider **why** the characters you're exploring **act** and **react** in the ways they do, and identify and mark evidence in the text that supports the judgments you make. First, speculate about **general motives.** For example, why, in your judgment, is the American irritated with the girl? Is he selfish? Is he afraid? Or is there some other reason? Then speculate about the **motives behind particular important actions** (studying your determination of the emotional points in the work can help here). For example, why does Jig "smile brightly" at the end of Hemingway's story? Finally, study your determinations of motive, and make evidence-supported judgments about how the characters have changed during the course of the work.

Rather than change, the minor characters in fictional works **function.** They act to bring about changes in the major characters, or their presence in the work functions to reveal meaning. For example, in *Unforgiven* the prostitutes who pool their money to hire the assassins bring about change but don't change themselves. Likewise, in Hemingway's story the people "all waiting reasonably for the train" don't change but might function to reveal meaning. With this in mind, make a list of the minor

continued on page 376

continued from page 375
characters in the text you're studying, and explore their possible functions in the work.

In addition, look for the meaning in **similarities** and **differences** between characters. Often in fictional works one character functions to make us aware of the flaws or strengths in another. For example, in *Unforgiven* Ned can't shoot the cowboy, while Munny can and does. What might this contrast reveal about the character of Munny?

EXPLORE THE SETTING FOR MEANING.   Just as minor characters function to bring about meaning in fictional works, the physical settings—the times, places, and social and historical contexts—described and depicted also reveal meaning. First, examine the **general setting** of the work you're focusing on and search for meaning in it. For example, "Hills Like White Elephants" is set at a railway station in a rural area of Spain. What possible meanings might a railroad station convey? What might be meaningful in the landscape described in the story? And although *Unforgiven* is a fictional work, it's set in the historical (not the mythological) past. The film opens with the year printed on the screen, and real events and people of the time are referred to. What possible meaning might this historical context convey?

Then examine the settings in **specific scenes,** and consider their meaning. Consider also the **similarities** and **differences** between these specific settings. For example, in *Unforgiven* Ned's farm is very different from Munny's, and in "Hills Like White Elephants" the landscape on one side of the station contrasts sharply with the landscape on the other. What might be meaningful about these differences?

Finally, since in the best works of fiction even the smallest details are meaningful, examine **repeated small details.** In "Hills Like White Elephants," the beaded curtain hung across the entrance to the bar is referred to again and again. What might be meaningful in this repeated detail?

CONSIDER THE STRUCTURE.   In addition to giving you an overview of the movement in a work of fiction, outlining the plot

continued to next page

will help you look for potential meaning in the work's **structure**. In a great many fictional texts the structure itself is a conveyer of meaning. In "Hills Like White Elephants," the whole story takes place in the time the couple spends waiting for a train. What possible meaning might there be in this?

DETERMINE AND ANALYZE POINT OF VIEW.   Point of view in a fictional work is the position from which the unfolding action is observed or considered. Some works are told from a **first-person** narrative position; everything we see comes through the eyes and consciousness of a single character in the work. This character may be **reliable** (someone we come to trust as telling us the "real" story) or **unreliable** (someone we have reason to believe may not be telling us the whole "truth").

However, many works of fiction are **third-person omniscient** narratives; in these, we presumably see everything through the eyes of an all-knowing and all-seeing narrator. Some omniscient narrators are **intrusive;** they make judgments about what's going on in the story. Some omniscient narrators are **objective;** they report what's happening without comment.

In addition, some works **mix** narrative points of view. Some third-person fictional works limit their viewpoint to the consciousness of a single character; the narrator isn't an "I" guiding us through the story, but our access to the created world comes only through the mind and eyes of a particular character. Other works show us the created world through the eyes of more than one character. They may jump from one first-person viewpoint to another, or they may be mainly third-person omniscient and then suddenly show us the world through the eyes of a single character.

Determine the point of view in the work you're focusing on. Then, consider the **meaning** of that point of view by speculating about how the story might be changed if told from a different viewpoint. "Hills Like White Elephants" is told from an objective third-person omniscient point of view. How might the story be changed if the narrator were intrusive? How might the story be changed if either the American or Jig were the narrator? What might the chosen point of view reveal about the meaning of the story?

continued on page 378

continued from page 377

FOCUS ON TONE.   Tone is another conveyer of meaning in fiction and film. The tone of a fictional work is the **general created atmosphere.** This atmosphere is created by the use of language and imagery in novels and short stories, and by the additional uses of color and light in film. The **tone** of a particular short story or film is closely related to the **narrative point of view** in the work. Remember, narrative point of view is the position from which the action in a story is observed or considered, and that position is conveyed to a large extent through choices in language and imagery. For example, in a short story told from an objective position, the language will reflect that objectivity and be somewhat detached. Likewise, the atmosphere in a film presented from an objective position will be neutral, rather than being drenched with light or dark or weighted with symbolism.

Make an evidence-supported judgment about the tone of the work you're focusing on, and speculate about the possible meaning of that tone.

CONSIDER THEME

The theme of a fictional work is its general message or main idea. Simply put, a fictional work's theme is **what that work is about.** However, since the best works of fiction take as their subjects human interactions that are complex and charged with conflict, just exactly what a work of fiction is about is usually up for debate. In fact, the very thing that makes works of fiction so compelling is that they can have many meanings. Although discussing the work with others and reading other writer's interpretations can aid you in your search for meaning, the determination you make of a work's theme depends on your intellectual and emotional responses as a reader.

Since fictional works focus on how individuals are **challenged to change,** a good way to start considering theme is by re-examining character. First, look back over the results of your collaboration, and focus on your interpretive judgments of the main characters' **motives.** Then explore the ways in which the main characters have **changed** (or not changed) during the course of the work. For example, in what ways is William Munny different at the end of *Unforgiven* from the way he was at its beginning? In

continued to next page

what ways is he the same? Finally, test your conclusions by speculating about what you think would happen if the story continued to unfold. For example, if you're focusing on "Hills Like White Elephants," how do you believe the relationship between Jig and the American will continue to unfold? Will she have the abortion or not? Will their relationship continue? If so, what will be the nature of that relationship? If not, what will happen to each of them? Keep in mind that you must **locate** and **mark evidence** in the text to support each of your speculative judgments.

Put additional critical pressure on your judgments and predictions by considering your collaborative partners' conclusions. Then, after weighing the evidence, write down in as few words as possible your judgment of the work's theme.

RESPONDING TO FICTION AND FILM: SECONDARY RESPONSES

FOCUS ON THE CONVERSATIONAL NATURE OF INTERPRETIVE WRITING

The **secondary responses** included in this chapter reflect the **conversational nature** of most interpretive writing. The writers whose selections are included here have developed their **persuasive** positions not only by reading the **primary** text of the short story or film they're responding to, but also by reading and considering other writers' **interpretive positions.** Just as you conversed about the text you're studying with your collaborative partners, these writers "conversed" by reading and responding to other writers' interpretations. As you actively preread the **secondary** responses included here, focus on those places in the texts where the writers are agreeing or disagreeing with others' interpretations.

SECONDARY RESPONSES TO "HILLS LIKE WHITE ELEPHANTS"

If "Hills Like White Elephants" is the focus of your study, preread the three brief interpretive responses included below. All three were originally published in the *Explicator*, a quarterly that publishes only short interpretive responses. **Read** the first paragraph of each response slowly. When you get to the end of the first paragraph, stop and **summarize** what's gone on in the text so far. If you're confused, go back and focus on the sentences you don't understand and **reread** them. Then **predict** the direction the text will take next. As you continue reading, compare your predictions with what appears in the text. After each paragraph, pause again to **summarize, reread** if necessary, and **predict.**

HEMINGWAY'S "HILLS LIKE WHITE ELEPHANTS"

J. F. Kobler

The major symbolic importance of the hills themselves in Hemingway's "Hills Like White Elephants" may be part of the reason why a less imposing piece of the physical setting has so far escaped close critical analysis. Between the railroad station and the bar is "a curtain, made of strings of bamboo beads, hung across the open door into the bar, to keep out flies." After this first paragraph description of the thin curtain, Hemingway mentioned it seven more times in a story of only 1450 words.

For the bar waitress and for the man who wants his girl friend to have an abortion, the curtain is barely noticed or noticeable; it is an impediment to nothing. The man orders the first two beers "into the curtain." To get another drink later, he "called 'Listen' through the curtain." Bringing a round of drinks, "The woman came out through the curtains. . . ." Near the end of the story, the man finishes one last Anis del Toro in the bar and comes "out through the bead curtain" back into the station. In all these words and actions the man takes no personal notice of the curtain.

However, to the pregnant woman the curtain is much more important, even though she never passes through it or places orders through it. Rather, she looked directly at the bead curtain: "They've printed something on it" she said. "What does it say?" She forces him to see and read the curtain; he tells her it says " 'Anis del Toro. It's a drink.' " Later she again looks "at the bead curtain" and puts her hand out to take hold of "two of the strings of beads." This action comes shortly after Hemingway has written, "The warm wind blew the bead curtain against the table." The conjunction of her touching the curtain and its touching the table suggests that she is the one who notices its movement.

Of course, we may call the curtain a symbol. Or we may see it simply as another of those small facts which so often help to

continued to next page

produce the emotion in Hemingway's stories. Whatever we call the bead curtain, by not impinging directly upon the consciousness of the man and by being more important to the woman, it reflects their attitudes toward the never named central issue of the story: the abortion. Neither the curtain nor the abortion is important to him. Neither will obstruct his happy progress through life. A curtain is just a normal thing to hang in a doorway to keep out flies. An abortion is just a normal thing to have when an unmarried woman is pregnant. The proposed abortion separates the two of them in a way the curtain can never separate the bar and the station. Her direct visual and tactile responses to the curtain connote her much deeper response to the abortion. This simple bead curtain is the touchstone of their conflicting emotions.

When the man stops in the bar alone for one last drink of Anis, he "looks at the people. They were all waiting reasonably for the train." But on the other side of the curtain, which he walks through, still oblivious to it or to another's real feelings, sits that unreasonable woman.

To his selfish eye the reasonable people are all on his side of the flimsy partition. A simple little abortion should not keep them emotionally or physically apart; it is no more a solid separating device than is a curtain of bamboo beads. But there sits this woman, separated from him by strands no bigger around than an umbilical cord, uttering her final words, " 'I feel fine.' " By which she means that she feels fine in her pregnancy and intends to remain in that condition for her normal term.

HEMINGWAY'S "HILLS LIKE WHITE ELEPHANTS"
Gary D. Elliot

Ernest Hemingway's "Hills Like White Elephants" has received less attention than it has deserved, but of even more significance is the fact that the most effective symbol developed in the story has gone unnoticed. Truly, the young woman of the story is

continued on page 382

continued from page 381

reluctant to undergo an abortion because she fears what will happen to the couple's relationship, and the American man is selfish, and the title has symbolic importance. However, the underlying and significant reason for her reluctance about the abortion becomes clear when Hemingway's careful handling of religious symbolism receives attention.

By means of a carefully constructed opening paragraph, the reader is placed in the story's setting; and in that paragraph the narrator mentions "a curtain, made of strings of bamboo beads . . ." (Hemingway, *The Complete Short Stories*, p. 273). The bamboo beads are the key to the girl's lack of enthusiasm about her lover's urging an abortion because the bead curtain represents and functions as a rosary for this young woman who must certainly be a Catholic. She resists an abortion because her religious heritage adamantly opposes such action.

It is the girl who looks at the bead curtain and who sees that something has been printed on it and who asks " 'What does it say?' " (p. 273). The American man, however, sees only the name of a drink and calls through the curtain for additional drinks. The woman's curiosity about the curtain and fascination with it continues as "the warm wind blew the bead curtain against the table" (p. 274). While the man pressed for a decision about the abortion and becomes frustrated at her hesitancy, "the girl looked at the bead curtain, put her hand out and took hold of two of the strings of beads" (p. 275). The young lady resists abortion, she says, because she fears happiness will be lost and because she wants things to be as they were. However, her greatest resistance comes from the religious sensibilities resurrected by the presence of the bead curtain. After touching the beads, she seems to see clearly and to know certainly that the world " 'isn't ours any more' " (p. 276).

The bead curtain seems to be only a part of the setting until the woman looks at it, takes note of it, and finally touches it. The bead curtain as a symbol provides an effective key for a clear understanding of the young woman's feeling. Appropriately, the man feels uncomfortable in the woman's presence and goes "out through the bead curtain" (p. 278). The curtain hangs physically between them; however, it is the young girl's religion, symbolized by the beads, which actually separates them and makes it impossible for the couple to communicate.

HEMINGWAY'S "HILLS LIKE WHITE ELEPHANTS"
Mary Dell Fletcher

Most of the critical commentary on "Hills" has focused on the terse indirect language and its role in defining both character and conflict. Essential to understanding both the nature and depth of the conflict, however, is the story's setting, the significance of which has been mentioned by a few critics but fully treated by none. Even before we get a glimpse of the young man and woman in the railroad station, we are given a precise delineation of the landscape:

> The hills across the valley of the Ebro were long and white. On this side there was no shade and no trees and the station was between two lines of rails in the sun. Close against the side of the station there was the warm shadow of the building . . .

The train station, somewhere between Barcelona and Madrid, is located between two lines of rails, which in turn lie between "this side," a range of hills in "brown and dry" country, and "the other side," lush and fertile land with "fields of grain and trees along the banks of the Ebro." The station and the tracks, where the action occurs, serve as a dividing line between the hot, dry country and the fields of grain and trees. The couple's position in relation to the dry hills and the river is significant; they are close against "this side" of the station in a bar. The tension in setting is obvious and prepares the reader for the conflict between the lovers who have reached an impasse in their relationship. These dichotomous landscape images are noted by Reid Maynard who, in treating lietmotifs of "two" in the story, suggests they represent respectively, the couple's present "strained relationship" and their past "close relationship." (*University Review*, 37 [1971], 273–75.) I suggest that the latter image (trees, grain, river) represents the potential future, rather than the past, since details of the story imply that the couple's relationship has been purely physical with no spiritual dimension.

The couple's strained relationship is evident from the outset in their preoccupation with ordering drinks and in their attempts

continued on page 384

continued from page 383

at light conversation. Their talk is empty, meaningless. Jig's remark that the hills "look like white elephants" (whatever it means) fails to evoke the response she expects, fails to recapture a former time when their behavior was more spontaneous and inane remarks had private meaning. But despite the implied intimacy of their past, their relationship has been both superficial and tenuous, as is suggested in the description of the bags: "There were labels on them from all the hotels where they had spent nights." Now the intimacy has been removed by an urgent problem, Jig's pregnancy, which requires a commitment the man is unwilling to make and the girl unwilling to demand because pleasure has been the *summmum bonum* of their existence together. Jig therefore insists that she is having a "fine time" ("all right, I was trying") and agrees to have the "awfully simple operation" if "it will be fine afterwards."

In spite of the man's promise that the abortion will restore their former carefree relationship, Jig has doubts: "What makes you think so?" Unconsciously she reaches out and takes hold of the bead curtains in the makeshift bar. The touch of the beads gives form to her undefined fears. Her move is symbolic, as Gary D. Elliot suggests (*Explicator*, 35, No. 4 [1977], 22); at this point her Catholic sensibility asserts itself and she begins to realize the magnitude of her contemplated act. Ultimately, however, fear of losing her man triumphs and she surrenders, knowing instinctively that "the world is lost." As she looks across to "the other side" where she sees the grain, trees, and river, she realizes the terrible irony of their choice: "And we could have all this. . . . And we could have everything and every day makes it more impossible." The life-giving landscape ("everything") is now associated in Jig's mind with "the whole world," that is, a fruitful life where natural relations culminate in new life and spiritual fulfillment, not in barrenness and sterility, as represented by the dry hills.

Since the conflict is illuminated by the landscape on each side of the track, it is tempting to tie the resolution in with the two sets of tracks—one set associated with the dry hills and the other with the fertile valley. When it is announced that the train is coming, the man carries the bags "around the station to the *other* tracks." (italics mine). In terms of the symbolism already imbued

continued to next page

the two sides, the movement toward "the other side" suggests a positive ending. So does the girl's smile which occurs for the first time and is mentioned twice in the final paragraph. The facts, however, cause hesitation in extending the symbolism that far. From the outset the couple has planned to board the express from Barcelona to Madrid, where the abortion will be performed. Therefore, when the man carries the bags to "the other side," he is not necessarily reversing his decision, as the symbolism suggests. Quite likely "this side" is a switch line (or siding) and "the other side" a main line and boarding place for trains going either direction.

Although the symbolism, in objectifying the two ways open to the couple, applies more to conflict than to resolution, it is central to the meaning of the story; that is, it is less important that we know the course chosen than the significance of the two choices. The rootless barren life, devoid of responsibility, is represented by the dry hills, the side the couple is already on. Their stilted conversation, their lack of spontaneity, indicate their denial of life; but Jill believes they can forego the abortion, accept the responsibility of parenthood, and inherit "the other side."

ENCOUNTER THE SUBJECT

Each of these three writers came to the reading of Hemingway's story with unique personal and educational histories. The interpretive conclusions these writers developed were influenced by their prior knowledge and experience. Consider your own experiences with abortion and male/female relationships. How might these experiences have influenced your interpretive judgments about the story?

RESEARCH OPPORTUNITY

To expand your encounter with Hemingway's story, you might locate and critically read responses to "Hills Like White Elephants" that were written shortly after its publication in 1927, and then compare those early responses to the secondary responses included here.

RESPONSIVE JOURNAL WRITING

Respond to the results of your research in the form of an exploratory journal entry. In what ways has your perspective of "Hills Like White Elephants" changed? In what ways has it remained the same?

A SECONDARY RESPONSE TO *UNFORGIVEN*

If *Unforgiven* is the focus of your study, **preread** the secondary response written to it. **Read** the first five paragraphs slowly, focusing on those things you understand. When you finish reading paragraph five, stop and take stock. If you're confused, go back and **reread** the sentences you don't understand. Then **predict** the direction you think the text will take next. As you continue reading, compare your predictions with what unfolds on the page. After each of the paragraphs that remain, pause to **summarize, reread** if necessary, and **predict.**

CLINT EASTWOOD AND THE MACHINERY OF VIOLENCE

John C. Tibbetts

Thunder prowls outside the grimy barroom of Big Whiskey, Wyoming. Through the swinging doors enters a haggard stranger in tattered clothes. He levels a shotgun at the town sheriff.

"You be William Munny out of Missouri," says Sheriff "Little Bill" Daggett, addressing the gunman.

"That's right," the lanky intruder answers. "I've killed women and children. Killed about just everything that walks or crawls at one time or another. And I'm here to kill you, Little Bill."

After a few moments, Munny sights along the barrel, his opponent standing motionless at pointblank range. He pauses a long moment—then fires. Turning about, almost as an afterthought, he guns down at close range an innocent bystander before disappearing out the door.

continued to next page

The conclusion to Clint Eastwood's *Unforgiven*, his tenth western, comes as a shock. When Eastwood, as bounty hunter Will Munny, blows away Gene Hackman, as Sheriff Daggett, we don't experience the nervous thrill we have felt over the years at the gun-toting exploits of Eastwood's spaghetti westerns or his Dirty Harry pictures. Gone, too, is the relief, the catharsis of a conflict between good and evil resolved by a violent action. Although Eastwood is on a mission of vengeance, his killing is cold, calculating, and ruthless. The scene violates the cardinal rule of all westerns—the good guy (no matter how provoked) can't just shoot a man in cold blood. A queasy disquiet, an unease gathers in a lump in our stomach.

"You know," says Eastwood, commenting on the scene in an interview with this writer. "Violence has been glamorized since literature began. People have always tried to make the West heroic. But it wasn't very heroic at all. Little Bill was a sheriff, but he was really just a killer who happened to have the law on his side. Will Munny was also a killer, and in the showdown he wasn't going to do any of this 'you draw first' stuff. He'd reverted to his violent ways. He'd thrown a switch or something and now a kind of machinery was back in action, a 'machinery of violence,' I guess you could say. No, it wasn't glamorous at all."

Although Clint Eastwood is best known—in many cases critically reviled—for the graphic violence of his pictures, he seems lately to be reconsidering the excesses of his youth. *Unforgiven*, in particular, belongs to a handful of westerns that question the cherished formulas and conditions of the genre. In his classic 1954 essay on the western genre, "Movie Chronicle: The Westerner," Robert Warshow had defined the form of the western—as it had evolved from the dime novelists of the 19th century, the paintings of Frederic Remington, and the genteel novels of Owen Wister—as "the free movement of men on horses," a kind of story-telling formula that depicts the western hero as "the last gentleman" who, paradoxically, must resort to the violence of the gun to resolve moral ambiguities; the last art form, moreover, "in which the concept of honor retains its strength." However, Warshow had also predicted that westerns were beginning to show signs of degeneration; that "the celebration of acts of violence" were "left more and more to the irresponsible."

continued on page 388

continued from page 387

Arguably, Raoul Walsh's *Pursued* (1947), Nicholas Ray's *Johnny Guitar* (1953), Arthur Penn's *The Left-Handed Gun* (1958), Robert Benton's *Bad Company* (1971), Robert Altman's *McCabe and Mrs. Miller* (1971) and *Buffalo Bill and the Indians* (1976), and Sam Peckinpah's *The Wild Bunch* (1969) and *Pat Garrett and Billy the Kid* (1973)—to name just a few that have preceeded *Unforgiven*—prove the point. Consider the following examples:

1) Violence.   The acts of violence that were necessary to settle disputes and impose frontier justice in Gary Cooper's *The Virginian* (1929) and William Wellman's *The Ox-Bow Incident* (1943) have either become gratuitous and/or sadistic in *Bad Company* or poeticized into the choreographed slow motion aesthetic of *The Wild Bunch*.

2) The gun duel.   That most hallowed convention of the classic western, the showdown and the fast draw, as exemplified in Fred Zinnemann's *High Noon* (1952)—where the hero draws his gun only after being threatened by the villain—is replaced by heroes who shoot first and ask questions later (if they ask them at all). Now, the hero-gunfighter may be neurotic or cowardly (*The Left-Handed Gun* and *Pursued*) or, in the case of *Johnny Guitar*, left out of the final showdown entirely (the two combatants are women, Mercedes McCambridge and Joan Crawford). In *The Wild Bunch* the heroic "last stand" of the Bunch is suicidal, and, ultimately, pointless.

3) The myth of the West.   The fabulous legends of Buffalo Bill, Wyatt Earp, and Billy the Kid, as exemplified by countless William Wellman and John Ford pictures, are exposed as nothing more than the hysterical machinations of hack journalists and media exploiters in *Buffalo Bill and the Indians*. The "West" is a purely commercial terrain, useful only for marketing a product.

4) The landscape.   Those rejuvenating vistas and terrains of John Ford's Monument Valley locations of the 1940s (*My Darling Clementine, She Wore a Yellow Ribbon*) have been replaced by the inhospitable, blasted landscapes of *Bad Company*. The land is now only a threat, diminishing its inhabitants, driving them to drink, to lawlessness, insanity, and early deaths.

Unforgiven seems to participate in all this revisionary mayhem, too. Its violence, though not inordinately graphic, is none-

continued to next page

theless obvious, brutal, and apparently gratuitous. It opens with an attempted rape and the vicious knife-slashing of a prostitute's face. Among the subsequent incidents, one man is beaten and kicked to a pulp, another tortured to death, and another murdered while sitting in an outhouse. Hero/villain roles are reversed: the "good guys" are all bounty hunters who kill simply for money; and the "bad guy" is the sheriff trying to protect his town. There's even a dime novelist on hand to observe with wide eyes the sleazy reality behind the legends he has been purveying. As for the climactic "showdown," that, as has been shown, is nothing more than a cold-blooded assassination.

Yet it can be argued that *Unforgiven*, far from being one more nail in the coffin of the presumably deceased western genre, in some ways marks a return to some of the more elemental propositions of the classic form. It raises troubling questions about the very nature and consequences of violence in our society. The casting of Eastwood, Gene Hackman, and Richard Harris does indeed exploit their reputations for macho violence, but it's a resonance that also conveys a profound rejection (or at least reconsideration) of that reputation.

No mistaking it—Eastwood, Hackman, and Harris have appeared in some of the most violent movies in the past forty years. Eastwood served his apprenticeship with two of the top directors in the business, both noted for the graphic, choreographed violence of their pictures, Sergio Leone and Don Siegel. For Leone during his years in Italy, Eastwood made the "Man With No Name" series, *A Fistful of Dollars* (1964), *For a Few Dollars More* (1965), and *The Good, the Bad and the Ugly* (1967). These "spaghetti westerns," as they were dubbed by a derisive press, were all marked by a deliberate, highly stylized tension punctuated by episodes of explosively graphic carnage. Their international success thrust him into the front rank of western stars. Back in America he teamed up with veteran director, Don Siegel, whose *Riot in Cell Block 11* (1954), *Invasion of the Body Snatchers* (1956), and *The Killers* (1964) were already landmarks in cinematic mayhem. Together, Eastwood and Siegel made some of the enduring classic action films, the stylishly gory grand "guignol" *The Beguiled* (1971), *Dirty Harry* (1971), first and best of the Harry Callahan films—"A wall-to-wall carpet of violence," said Siegel—and the

continued on page 390

continued from page 389

gritty *Escape from Alcatraz* (1979). "[Clint] is a tarnished super-hero, actually an anti-hero," said Don Siegel in 1974. "You can poke at a character like that. He makes mistakes, does things in questionable taste, is vulnerable. He's not a white knight rescuing the girl; he seduces her."

Leone and Siegel were to have a great impact on Eastwood's own directorial career, which began with a sensational horror film, *Play Misty for Me* (1971) and continued through the comic misadventures of such diverse films as *Every Which Way but Loose* (1978), the western adventures of *The Outlaw Josey Wales* (1976), and the mordant biopics, *Bird* (1988) and *White Hunter, Black Heart* (1990). From Leone he seems to have inherited a sense of the grotesquely absurd (an attitude that sees the world as a series of what commentator Stuart M. Kaminsky has called "comic nightmares of existence"); and from Siegel the use of protagonists who are flawed—or, as film scholar Andrew Tudor typifies them, "emotionally crippled heroes." As both director and actor for his Malpaso Productions, his movie company founded in 1968, Eastwood maintains a detachment from his grim, even shabby material. There are no false codes of chivalry, religion, or romance to buffer a man against the brutal realities of life, what critic Manny Farber described as "middle-aged, middle-class sordidness." His worth can be measured only by his survival; if he dies, he's a loser. In this sense, Eastwood is the heir apparent to the American director who was so admired by both Leone and Siegel, Howard Hawks.

Gene Hackman was once described by Warren Beatty as "the best actor in the movies," who's been nominated for an Oscar four times. However, his reputation as a tough guy was consolidated by his Best Actor Oscar in 1971 for his performance as the pugnacious cop, Popeye Doyle, in *The French Connection*. The ex-Marine had already stunned audiences as Buck Barrow in the notorious death scene in Arthur Penn's benchmark essay in graphic violence, *Bonnie and Clyde* (1967). Although for the next twenty years he would appear in several films distinguished for their quietly gentle, if disturbing sensitivity—notably, *I Never Sang for My Father* (1970) and *The Conversation* (1971), and a comedy or two—witness his turns as Lex Luthor in the first two "Superman" movies and the winning goofy inventor in *All Night Long*

continued to next page

(1981)—it was his edgy, explosive portrayals as a trigger-happy panhandler in *Scarecrow* (1971) and the dangerous FBI agent in *Mississippi Burning* (1988) that were most memorable.

Although trained at the London Academy of Music and Dramatic Art, and cast member of several well-known movies, including *The Wreck of the Mary Deare* (1959) and *Mutiny on the Bounty* (1962), Richard Harris had to wait for international stardom with *This Sporting Life* (1963). Harris won Best Actor at Cannes for his portrayal of Frank Machin, a brawling coal miner whose violent nature wins him celebrity on the rugby field and disaster in his personal life. The movie came at the crest of the "Free Cinema" movement in England, 1959–1964, when films about "angry young men" were all the rage. A "motif of force," as director Lindsay Anderson described it, dominated the brutal rugby sequences and the chilling, dehumanized sex scenes with co-star Rachel Roberts. "There was a hard, intransigent, ruthless quality about it," opined filmmaker Karel Reisz. "Here pain is called pain," wrote a critic; "and the feeling is one of liberation." Excepting a long stage stint as King Arthur in the musical, *Camelot*, and a handful of fine, relatively non-violent pictures, such as *Juggernaut* (1974) and *Robin and Marian* (1976), Harris continued to win his widest audiences with the graphically visceral horrors of the Sioux' tribal induction ceremony in *A Man Called Horse* (1970) and its sequel, *The Return of a Man Called Horse* (1976), and a gruesome mauling by a bear in *Man in the Wilderness* (1971).

In the parlance of *Unforgiven*, the excesses of the past have been catching up with these three actors (which is precisely to the point). Eastwood, particularly, has been a constant target for critical scorn and invective. Pauline Kael's attacks have been especially devastating. She wrote in 1981: "In a Clint Eastwood film, Eastwood can't go into a diner and ask for a glass of water without someone's picking a fight with him. Action movies say that the world is always threatening your manhood every minute of the day." Three years later in a review of *Tightrope*, one of Eastwood's darker essays into his flawed hero persona (Homicide Inspector Wes Block), she acknowledged that while he's the only person these days who makes movies "about how tough it is to be a man," he was nothing more than a "trash filmmaker" whose work was "primitive" and whose screen persona was full of a

continued on page 392

continued from page 391

"stone-faced hokum." She concluded her diatribe: "The world is set up as a jungle, and you're one of the beasts in it, and so is he." Kael sniffed at those critics who greeted these movies as returns to Hollywood's classic genre formulas. "I didn't go to the movies to see car crashes or galloping horses or gangsters shooting each other. . . . I went because I wanted to 'see the picture'—to become involved in the characters' intertwined lives and to experience the worlds that all the hacks and craftsmen and artists who worked in the movies could bring into being." Nonetheless, in recent years, Eastwood's directorial efforts like *Bronco Billy* and *Bird* have been acclaimed by the Cinemateque in Paris, the British Film Institute and the Cannes Film Festival.

Now in their sixties, Eastwood, Hackman and Harris are reviewing their past sins. Despite Kael's charges, Eastwood is defensive about his purported nonsensitivity to women's roles in his pictures. In a 1988 interview in American Film he referred to himself as "a feminist director." Two years later, in another interview, Eastwood signalled the end of Harry Callahan. He had defended Harry against charges of right-wing fascism ("You can certainly interpret Dirty Harry as an individual going against the system"), but now he made a startling prediction: "Harry's a strong character, and I enjoy playing him. But . . . at a certain point I said to myself, 'You can't just go around blowing people away with a .44.' " Dirty Harry would be heard from no more. Was Eastwood searching for a new definition of macho? "Macho is probably one of the most misused words in the language. The most macho guys on the screen were very sensitive people." The year 1991 passed without an Eastwood release—an unusual lapse in his otherwise consistently prolific career.

Hackman had angioplasty surgery in 1991 after complaining of a cruel schedule that had kept him one of the busiest actors in the business. He himself admits that there were some real clinkers among his many projects, including Dan Aykroyd's police partner in *Loose Cannons* and a boxing trainer in *Split Decisions*. In an interview in *Premiere* magazine in 1991, he admitted he particularly doesn't like his action/violence roles: "It really has nothing to do with what you're trained for. I much prefer to do what I know how to do, which is work in controlled situations—like theater." He has even grown weary of watching his own movies.

continued to next page

"I rarely watch them in a theater where the civilian audiences are. I'll see a film once in a while in a rough state just before I loop in postproduction. . . . But it really costs me a lot emotionally to watch myself on screen. I don't enjoy it. . . . I think of myself— and feel—like I'm quite young, and then I look at this old man with the baggy chins and the tired eyes and the receding hairline and all that." Although he has always loved the theater, his most recent Broadway outing, *Death and the Maiden* (co-starring Richard Dreyfus and Glenn Close) was a critical disaster.

Since his success in *Camelot* on stage and screen, Richard Harris's film career had been in relative eclipse. He had not had a hit movie until his maniacal performance in *The Field* (1991) won him a Best Actor Oscar nomination. When he appeared in London's West End last year as the title character in Pirandello's *Henry IV*, he declared then it would be his farewell to the stage. So disenchanted had he become, meanwhile, with the general run of movie roles offered him, that he hesitated before taking on the role of the tough Irish patriot, Paddy O'Neil, in *Patriot Games*. His decision to take it on may come as a surprise: "I read it and decided that if Hollywood is going to do something on the situation in Ireland, I would do it only if I could play the one guy who truly represents that movement in Ireland which stands for a united Ireland, but which pursues those ends through elections— the republican point of view—not the violence. I don't approve of the violence whatsoever. I am passionate about a united Ireland, but I approve of doing it by political means. I wanted to make sure that whoever did that part wasn't a Hollywood actor or a bit player. That's why I did it."

Harris is speaking to a small group of journalists gathered at Suite 1825 in the Regency Hotel in late July of 1992 for interviews about *Unforgiven*. In a few moments he is joined by Gene Hackman and Clint Eastwood. At first you find it a rather awesome occasion. You can't help thinking, "Here they are, three very tough guys, together in this room—three of the most celebrated (or notorious) exemplars of the best (or the worst) in screen action and violence, unrivalled purveyors of gore and mayhem—here in this room at this one time!" Instinctively, you look over your shoulder—say, who's *directing* this thing, Sam Peckinpah?

But, after all, it's just a hot day and these are just three guys tired out after a long day of interviews before the television

continued on page 394

continued from page 393

cameras. Hours of three-minute interviews and soundbites. Now, they're ready to just lay back and relax. Study them a moment and they present a study in contrasts: Harris's white hair tumbles to his shoulders; he's dressed in a rugby sweater, white slacks and an ankle-length black coat; he's a volatile collection of twists and turns, his speech peppered with flamboyant pantomime. Hackman is attired in conservative browns; he's moody and quiet; he answers questions succinctly—no excessive verbiage here. Then there's Eastwood, nattily attired in creased white trousers, open-necked polo shirt, and grey-green coat. His hair is close cropped and he's entirely at ease, surveying us with an almost patrician nonchalance.

Yet, oddly, they really do seem like their characters in *Unforgiven*—reunited, each brought here by commercial circumstances and the lure of a sizeable "bounty." So different are they that, as they talk, you half expect to hear tales of difficulties and tensions on the set.

Not so. They all agree that the *Unforgiven* shoot was a generally agreeable project.

"Making a film can be a nightmare," explains Eastwood. "Because you bring a whole company into a certain area (in this case, locations in Alberta, Canada) and you've got all your stuff with you. You've got shops and trucks and you've got all kinds of stuff. You can make anything. And it can become very tense; and if it's tense at the top, it's going to be tense all the way through. If I'm not ready to go, I can't expect anyone else to be ready to go."

Harris interjects suddenly—"Listen," he says. There's a pause. Only the humming of the air conditioner is heard. He resumes: "That's what you heard on the set on any given day. Eastwood is so organized. It's almost unbearable, he's so organized. And the crew—they've all been around him for years. One guy works in wardrobe—and he's been with him since the *Rawhide* days. And they all know what he wants. Nobody has to raise their voice. He doesn't like that. He doesn't like aggravation, he doesn't like temperament. He knows exactly what's coming into the lens. It's one of the best experiences I've had in my entire life."

We all wonder at this—doesn't Eastwood *ever* raise his voice?

continued to next page

For the first time Eastwood stirs restlessly. "I'm not by nature somebody who likes to shout and all that stuff," he says after apause. "But I'm capable of it. Stand outside my window sometime. But my nature is to be more, well, *within,* I think. That's sometimes an advantage and sometimes not. Besides, with Harris on the set, you don't need any more distractions!" He laughs while Harris tosses his long white hair in mock exasperation.

Then Eastwood begins to talk about *Unforgiven.* He rarely does interviews these days. He doesn't have to. But he's obviously delighted when asked about the unusually stark "look" of the photography, executed in mostly muted colors and available light.

"I remember those high-glass Technicolor westerns I saw as a kid," he explains. "All that light and those saturated colors. I never liked it. Some of them are called 'classics' but they were too artificial and unreal. My approach to *Unforgiven*—and to *Pale Rider* and *Bird* before it—was to forget that we're shooting in color. It's as if we're shooting in black and white and getting the kind of look you saw in something like John Ford's *My Darling Clementine* (1947). I told the production designer and the set decorator and the costume people to keep muted tones to everything. Not everybody likes that, but that's the way I want it."

It's suggested that this kind of indulgence may account for the relative box office failure of his last few pictures.

Eastwood smiles, but he pauses a few beats before answering. "If I have to succumb to the commercial pressures, I think that would be the end of it being enjoyable. If I had to—well, if somebody said to go back and repeat yourself—let's go back and see if we can create as much mayhem as Arnold and Sylvester—that would be not right for me anymore, I don't think. It would show through that I was just repeating myself. To repeat a genre like the western is fun, but to repeat the same character is not fun. I must say, I'm in a stage in life where if it's not enjoyable, I don't want to do it at all.

"Take those things I did with Sergio [Leone]; if you analyze the stories, there wasn't a whole lot said in them. They were great fun but more or less operas, you know? They had a lot of shooting and crazy one-upmanship, but. . . ." His voice trails off, his still handsome face crinkled into a rueful smile. He speaks slowly,

continued on page 396

continued from page 395

carefully choosing his words. "I began to get real tired of those famous lines everybody was always asking me to repeat," he added. "In the early 1970s it was 'Give me that line about "Do you feel lucky, punk?' "; and then it was 'Make my day!" I thought, that's fun; we've got a line everybody seems to be quoting. But years later, I must say, I'm tired of it. I mean, *it's only a line in a movie. . . .*" He spreads his arms gently, his movements always measured and deliberate.

"There's nothing funny about the violence in *Unforgiven.* Now, I'm certainly not doing any penance for any of the mayhem I've presented on the screen over the years. I grew up with *White Heat* and *Public Enemy* and all those Jimmy Cagney films shooting people in the trunks of cars and all kinds of craziness. But it never made us into criminals and we didn't go out and start blowing people away because we saw it on the screen. You always realized it was just a movie. Like my movies.

"But at the same token, I think it's a time in my life and a time in history that maybe violence should not be such a humorous thing. Or that it should be portrayed without its consequences. Look at the communications industry. With so much competition now in the news casts, they're all trying to see who can cut to the bloodiest accident on the highway. In *Unforgiven* I wanted to show *consequences* to the violence. Maybe there's consequences to both the perpetrator as well as the victim. That was a message I had to get across to Gene. I know when I tried to get him to play Little Bill Daggett, he said he didn't want to do any more films with a lot of violence."

Hackman agrees. "Even my kids have been asking me to stop doing those kinds of pictures. I have a lot of feelings about films I've done. Not regrets so much. But there are more than a couple of films I probably shouldn't have done. But, you know, you take what's offered to you early in your career. And, unfortunately, you establish yourself as being able to do certain kinds of things, like Popeye Doyle's violent edge, or something. And so you continue on that level. It's very difficult to break out of that mode in film making, because they cast so close to type."

Eastwood fills in the temporary pause. "Gene just felt that there was enough of that stuff going around. I guess he was dis-

continued to next page

enchanted with movies that were just a 'Can you top this?' kind of thing—how many ways you can dismember and do away with people. But I said to him, would you at least read it? I think we have an opportunity to make a statement about violence and the moral issue of it. Because there is a concern, a concern for the characters: that everything that has happened and they have done is having repercussions."

"Yeah," responds Hackman. "This doesn't appeal to our baser instincts about violence. I really believe that. It doesn't make us feel we want to be involved in that kind of thing. Here, we see the *aftermath* of violence."

True enough. All the characters in the movie are confronted with their past misdeeds. Hackman's Little Bill has gone "straight" and become the sheriff of the Wyoming town of Big Whiskey. He has a passion for law and order and gun control. But when the bounty hunters arrive, they trigger in him not only unpleasant reminders of his past, but that "machinery of violence" of which Eastwood spoke. Now, Daggett's passion for law and order turns perverse and he becomes a fascist tyrant who brutally humiliates, tortures, and kills the invaders. "I tried to make him human and a monster at the same time," Hackman says. Harris's English Bob, seen at first as an elegant, if arrogant gentleman in fancy clothes with an aristocratic turn of phrase and accent, is in turn exposed by Daggett as the common bully he really is. "I knew Englishmen like that when I was growing up in Limerick, Ireland," says Harris. "He's all bluster and fraud. I especially like the moment when Bob's humiliated by Daggett. Listen closely and you'll hear me reverting to a cockney accent. My character is just a common bully." Eastwood's Will Munny and Morgan Freeman's Ned Logan have tried to put their past aside to become farmers. Yet, when the lure of the $1,000 bounty presents itself, both leave their families and ride north. Logan, who is the most humane and gentle of the outlaws, realizes at last he's no longer capable of killing. But when he tries to leave Big Whiskey, he's captured and tortured by Daggett. Eastwood, on the other hand, after protesting constantly that he's "not that kind of killer" any more, finds in the moment of confrontation with Daggett that the old "machinery of violence" kicks in easily. He coldly murders Daggett at pointblank range and shoots some

continued on page 398

continued from page 397

bystanders with no more compunction than someone would show swatting a fly. ''Munny has been protesting all the time that he's changed,'' says Eastwood. ''But maybe he's been protesting too much. . . .''

Like Will Munny, Eastwood himself has survived in a tough business by wits and skill. Like Will, he knows the years are gaining on him. The recent deaths, particularly, of Eastwood's two mentors, Sergio Leone and Don Siegel, are very much on his mind these days. ''Both of those gentlemen unfortunately passed away in the last two years,'' he says. ''Sergio, I had the pleasure of spending some time with in Rome just prior to his death. I hadn't seen him in many years. Then, when I returned to the States, Don was ailing; and then he passed away. It was sad. There's a certain stage in life where everyone starts losing friends and associates. And it happened to me at a very young age. First it was Inger Stevens and Jean Seberg. Now Don and Sergio. After a lifetime of this, you start thinking—that was a nice moment in life. But you go on. Now, someday, somebody might say, 'Hey Eastwood, I remember him.' ''

Unmistakably, *Unforgiven* is redolent with this elegiac mood, even fatalistic resignation about life and death. ''We all have it comin', kid,'' Munny says at one point to the erstwhile gunslinger who rides with him. Even the violence has nothing sensational or glamorous about it. It's just the necessary consequence of people who have become enmired in violent lives. They will live by it and they will die by it. Nothing could be more central to the traditional western. We are reminded again of Robert Warshow's words about the genre's ''moral ambiguity''; the western hero, for all his virtues, *is nonetheless ''a killer of men.''* The gunslinging high jinks of the ''Dollars'' movies, for all their carnage, had evaded that troubling truth. Killing was a game, not a reality. Whatever Munny's justifications for killing—and he is, after all, avenging the cruel torture and murder of his best friend—he does it with ruthless, cold-blooded precision. And he does it with no mercy, compassion, or remorse whatever. Just as Warshow had also said that ''it is not violence at all which is the 'point' of the Western movie, but a certain image of man, a style, which expresses itself most clearly in violence,'' William Munny at last reverts to that

continued to next page

efficient killing machine he had been. It is an image as beautiful in its graceful precision as it is deadly in its horrible finality. "You'll notice," affirms Eastwood, "that Munny is no longer the clumsy has-been you've seen throughout the film—falling from his horse, missing things at target practice, getting beaten up. For the first time, he's back now in full charge of his abilities."

Left without the solace of a glamorous, chivalrous, or even cathartic denouement, we are allowed only the satisfaction that Munny, apparently, has survived. In the film's quiet epilogue we see a shot of the Munny farm, now deserted, starkly outlined against the sky. The words crawling upward across the screen tell us that he left the place with his two children, and that his destination remains unknown. Has he at last put his past behind him; or has his violent nature, that relentless "machinery of violence" again subsided only temporarily into a subterranean whisper? Is he a hero, or is he merely again a fugitive from the justice that surely will overtake him at last? At the very least, Munny is obeying at least one hidebound tenet of the western—he must vanish, or go away in the face of the civilization that endangers his very existence.

Eastwood himself is content to leave the ambiguity intact. "We all hope we change for the good," he says, "and we hope Will Munny at last has changed for the good. But sometimes you wonder if we aren't really just going in circles, chasing our tails. And Munny *does* at the end revert back to what he's been, doesn't he? Maybe he hasn't really learned anything."

And what about Eastwood's own westerns? When I ask him if *Unforgiven* is the last western he'll make, he just smiles and replies, again enigmatically: "Maybe or maybe not. Whether it's my last western remains to be seen, but if I was going to do a last western, it seems it would be a good one!"

ENCOUNTER THE SUBJECT

Tibbetts encountered violence in society and Western movies long before he ever saw *Unforgiven,* and those prior encounters influenced the interpretive conclusions he drew about the film. Consider your own experiences with violence in society and Western movies. How might your past experiences with these subjects have influenced your interpretive judgments about *Unforgiven?*

RESEARCH OPPORTUNITY

To **expand your encounter** with *Unforgiven,* you might do a **library search** to locate and **critically read** the Pauline Kael comments referred to by Tibbetts.

RESPONSIVE JOURNAL WRITING

Respond to the results of your research in the form of an exploratory journal entry. In what ways has your research changed your perspective on the film? In what ways has your perspective remained the same?

LISTEN—READ RESPONSES TO FICTION AND FILM CAREFULLY FOR MEANING

CONSIDER COMMUNITY WHEN READING INTERPRETIVE RESPONSES

More often than not, an interpretive response is written in the context of a particular community of readers and writers. For example, Tibbetts writes to an audience of film scholars and people interested in and knowledgeable about films (particularly Westerns). Since interpretive responses are often directed at audiences who are thoroughly familiar with the general field, you may find that reading them for meaning will be harder work than reading texts directed at more general audiences. You may find yourself astonished and intimidated by a particular writer's breadth of knowledge. You may have to look words up in a dictionary and research references to discern the meaning of the text. However, as you work to know more, keep in mind that even those writers who know a great deal started out (as we all do) with no knowledge of the subject.

In addition, since most interpretive texts are written in the context of communities, you'll find that they often follow the **writing conventions** of those communities. A convention is a **practice or procedure generally agreed upon by a particular community: a custom.** Like social customs, writing conventions follow the desires and concerns of the community and are subject to change. The writers whose responses are included in this chapter were aware of the conventions of the communities they were writing in and for, and those conventions influenced the choices they made as they constructed their texts. For example, all the responses included in this chapter are written from distant, authoritative positions. These writers don't seem to be speculating about what they think the primary texts mean; Kobler, for instance, doesn't write, "I *think* the girl will keep her baby" but, instead, "By which she means that she feels fine in her pregnancy and intends to remain in that condition for her normal term." The language Kobler employs (like the language all the writers included here employ) is direct and authoritative, and that language reflects a **convention** currently followed in most fiction and film interpretation. As you work through the following collaboration, focus on the writer's use of language as a means of establishing authority.

COLLABORATIVE WRITING EXERCISE

Explore the meaning of the relevant secondary texts included here in collaboration with your classmates. This collaboration can be done in the classroom or in small study and research groups beyond the classroom. Start the collaboration in groups of three or four. As you work, have one member of your group record your collaborative conclusions. After concentrated group work, open the discussion up to full-class conversation.

RESEARCH UNKNOWNS.   Most effective interpretive responses are written by people who have researched their subjects. For this reason, interpretive texts are likely to contain references to other secondary texts. In addition, since a great many interpretive texts are directed at audiences familiar with the field and subject being written about, they're likely to contain words and references that are new to you. For example, if you're reading Tibbetts' text, do you know what *guignol* means? Research any words or references that leave you with questions.

continued on page 402

continued from page 401

ANALYZE THE SPEAKER.   Here you're going to start digging into the developmental material in the text you're exploring. Your evidence-supported judgments about the speaker will lead you into the details that support his or her argumentative position. Since the interpretive responses in this chapter are written from distant, authoritative positions, you'll find that these writers don't often reveal facts about themselves, nor do they openly express their own emotions. However, keep in mind that interpreting a fictional work involves **emotional** as well as **rational interaction** with the text. Although these writers may not openly express how they feel, many of the judgments they make are based on emotional responses. For example, when Elliott agrees with other readers and states that "the American man is selfish," his judgment is based on his emotional response to the actions of the character. Likewise, Tibbetts' judgment of the final shootout in *Unforgiven* as "an image as beautiful in its graceful precision as it is deadly in its horrible finality" is based on an emotional response. As you analyze the speaker(s) here, consider possible connections between interpretive judgments and emotional responses.

Facts
From your reading, what factual information (if any) can you gather about the speaker? Make sure that you cite specific evidence from the text to support your judgments.

Emotions
Where in the text does the speaker reveal his or her emotional reactions to the primary text? Were your own emotional responses to the primary text similar, or were they different? For example, do you feel, as Elliott does, that the American in "Hills Like White Elephants" is selfish, or is your emotional response to the character different from Elliott's? How might your personal history have influenced your emotional reactions to the primary text?

Attitudes
Where in the text does the speaker draw conclusive judgments about the primary text, and what are those judgments?

continued to next page

DETERMINE THE MESSAGE. More often than not, in interpretive writing, the writer's message isn't just an overall judgment about the meaning of the primary text. Instead, the writer's message is usually a judgment about how the theme of the primary text is conveyed to the reader. Generally, interpretive texts focus on how one thing or one category of things in the work (character, setting, tone, point of view, or structure) conveys that work's theme. For example, Tibbetts doesn't only argue for a particular interpretation of *Unforgiven;* he attempts to show how the portrayal of violence in the film is evidence for his interpretation. Likewise, Fletcher doesn't only argue for a particular interpretation of "Hills Like White Elephants." Instead, she attempts to show how aspects of the story's setting are evidence for her interpretation of the work's theme. Often, the writer will convey the message in a single sentence, as Organ does in the first paragraph of his response. However, sometimes the message is conveyed in several key sentences, usually in the introductory and concluding paragraphs.

With this in mind, locate in the text (or write down in as few words as possible) the text's message.

DETERMINE THE AUDIENCE. Making sure that you provide evidence from the text to support your judgments, describe in as much detail as possible the audience to whom the text is directed.

DETERMINE THE PURPOSE. Most interpretive writing is **persuasive.** The writer has developed an **interpretive position** and is trying to **persuade** others that this position is **credible.** However, a great many interpretive texts **explain** or **inform** as they persuade. For example, in addition to persuading, Tibbetts' text also **informs** its audience about Western movies and Eastwood's career as a director, and it **explains** what Eastwood's position as a director entails. With this in mind, determine the additional general purposes of the text you're exploring.

The specific purpose of any interpretive text is tightly connected to the text's message. Writers of interpretation want to convince their audiences to agree that their positions are credible. Consider the message of the text you're exploring. Then make a judgment about whether that text has accomplished its purpose.

continued on page 404

continued from page 403
For example, if you're focusing on Elliott's response, has the text accomplished its purpose by making an adequate case that Jig's Catholicism, symbolized by the beaded curtain, causes the tension in her relationship with the American?

RESEARCH OPPORTUNITY

Now that you've read the text(s) carefully, you may be left with **questions** about the writer's (or writers') **interpretations** or **evidence.** Some of these questions may have to do with whether the writer is accurately reporting action or dialogue from the **primary text;** for example, you may **accurately** remember Jig as saying, "And we could have everything and every day we make it more impossible," while Fletcher **inaccurately** quotes Jig as saying, "And we could have everything and every day makes it more impossible." If at any time during your reading, you found yourself thinking "But that's not what happened in the story (or film)," go back and carefully reread the relevant passages (or re-view the relevant scenes) in the primary text. Although you may be tempted to let small inaccuracies pass, keep in mind that even the smallest detail in a work of fiction can be full of potential meaning. For example, an entire interpretation of "Hills Like White Elephants" might be built around Jig's assuming of responsibility by saying, "*we* make it more impossible" (italics mine), rather than "every day makes it more impossible." To test a secondary response for accuracy, compare the primary text with what's being reported in the response. Has the writer accurately described or quoted the material? If not, how might the inaccuracy affect the potential meaning of the primary text?

RESPONSIVE JOURNAL WRITING

Respond to your research by exploring your findings in a journal entry.

LEARN—READ RESPONSES TO FICTION AND FILM WITH AN EYE TO IMPROVING YOUR OWN TECHNIQUE

FOCUS ON PERSUASION IN INTERPRETING FICTION AND FILM

By definition, interpretive writing is highly **persuasive.** Each of the writers whose secondary text appears in this chapter was attempting to convince an audience that his or her interpretive position was credible. In addition, the writers were following the conventions of a particular community as they wrote. And one of the conventions of that community is to prefer appeals to reason **(logos)** and credibility **(ethos)** over appeals to emotion **(pathos).**

ETHOS. PERSUADING WITH REASON   The bulk of the developmental material in each of the secondary texts in this chapter attempts to persuade with reason. Each of the responses included here builds an evidence-supported argument for a particular interpretation of the primary text.

PATHOS. PERSUADING WITH EMOTION   I don't want you to get the idea that you won't find *any* emotional appeals in these texts; even though persuading with emotion is not preferred, the writers do (in some cases perhaps unconsciously) employ pathos. The truth is, it's difficult to keep emotional appeals out of an interpretive text, because we find the meaning of a work of fiction with our emotions as well as with our powers of reason.

ETHOS, PERSUADING BY ESTABLISHING CREDIBILITY   The conventions of the community also influence how these writers establish their credibility. Just their adherence to the conventions is a major way in which they persuade their audiences that they're credible.

COLLABORATIVE WRITING ASSIGNMENT

Either in the classroom or in small groups beyond the classroom, study the writer's choices in each relevant selection with an eye to improving your own skill at interpretive writing.

continued on page 406

continued from page 405

VOICE   Although all the responses to "Hills Like White Elephants" are written in voices that are to one degree or another distant and authoritative, you'll find that some are easier to read than others. If you're focusing on the **responses** to Hemingway's story, compare the texts that are easy to read with those that are difficult. Then describe in as much detail as possible (or draw a detailed picture of) the created personas in the four texts. Which voices seem more credible? Why? As usual, make sure you provide evidence from each text to support your judgments.

Perhaps because Tibbetts is responding to a text from popular culture, rather than a text that has been accepted as a work of art, the persona he creates is more relaxed than the professional responses to "Hills Like White Elephants." After carefully studying the language choices in Tibbett's text, describe in as much detail (or draw a detailed picture of) the created persona in his text.

DEVELOPMENT   In addition to arguing for their interpretation of elements in a primary text, writers also **respond** to what other writers have written about the text. Writers may argue directly *against* other writers' interpretations or even use other writers' interpretations as a starting place to build their own arguments. With this in mind, identify the directly responsive passages in the text(s) you're exploring.

Because writers' interpretive positions are largely based on **evidence** found in the primary text, responses to fictional works invariably contain quantities of material **directly quoted** or **cited** from those works. With this in mind, mark the direct quotations and/or the passages that summarize action in the text(s) you're exploring. For example, Kobler quotes Jig as saying, "I feel fine" at the end of "Hills Like White Elephants." Are any of the cited passages you identified inaccurately quoted?

However, writers don't merely quote; they also **interpret** elements in the primary text by making judgments about their meaning. Kobler doesn't merely quote Jig but goes on to interpret that quotation as meaning "she feels fine in her pregnancy and intends to remain in that condition for her normal term." With this in mind, mark those passages in each text where the writer

continued to next page

makes interpretive judgments about quoted material. Which judgments are you willing to accept as reasonable? Which judgments are you not willing to accept as reasonable?

In addition to agreeing and disagreeing with other writers' interpretations and using evidence from primary texts (both, in themselves, research activities), writers may support their interpretive positions with evidence they've gathered by engaging in other forms of **research.** Writers of interpretive responses often examine drafts of the primary text, or research the life of the primary text's writer or director. For example, Tibbetts, whose interpretation focuses on *how* Eastwood's vision shaped the text of *Unforgiven,* supports a large part of his argument with material gathered from **interviewing** Eastwood. With this in mind, identify any evidence that was gathered through additional forms of research.

ARRANGEMENT   All the responses to ''Hills Like White Elephants'' reprinted here contain similar elements. They all have **introductions** where the **primary text** and its **author** are **named** and where the element that will be explored for meaning is **identified.** Within the first few sentences of their responses, Kobler, Organ, and Elliott have all identified the bamboo curtain as the focus of their interpretation. Likewise, Fletcher almost immediately identifies the setting as the focus of her interpretation.

After naming the primary text and its author and identifying the focus of their interpretations, all four of these writers go on (with some minor variations) to present their **arguments** in an order that roughly follows the chronology of the story. Fletcher begins her argument with the quoted description of the valley that opens the story and ends it with the action of the American carrying the luggage to the other tracks. Most (but not all) interpretive texts follow the chronology of the primary text, not because any rule has been laid down that they must do so but because the elements in a fictional work gather meaning as the action of the work unfolds. The first time the beaded curtain and the contrasting landscape in ''Hills Like White Elephants'' are mentioned we hardly notice them, but as the story continues, they're mentioned again and again and become more and more meaningful. By following the chronology of the story as they

continued on page 408

continued from page 407

present their arguments, the writers of these responses are tracing the deepening significance of the elements on which they're focusing.

Tibbetts' text, being as much an interpretation of Eastwood's creative vision as it is of *Unforgiven,* follows more than one chronology, among them the chronology of Eastwood's career as a director and the chronology of the changes in Western movies in general.

Outline the texts (or text) you're exploring and examine how the writers have arranged their argumentative points.

RESPONDING TO FICTION: STUDENT RESPONSES

It's almost time for you to respond to a fictional work in writing. However, before you do, read how two student writers responded to Hemingway's "Hills Like White Elephants."

Tripp Green

HILLS LIKE WHITE ELEPHANTS: CRITICAL ANALYSIS

Tripp Green is a student at The University of Montana majoring in Liberal Studies. He wrote this response for a composition class in 1995.

In Ernest Hemingway's short story *Hills Like White Elephants,* the continuous use of alcohol by Jig and the American represents the discomfort and emptiness of their relationship. The couple relies on alcohol as a distraction from how unhappy they are together and from the startling realization of what they are about to do. The alcohol fills in for lost spontaneity in their lives. All they do is "look at things and try new drinks" (p. 212). To avoid having a meaningful conversation about the abortion they divert

continued to next page

their attention away from the subject by noting how "The beer's nice and cool" (p. 212) and whether they should " . . . have another drink." The alcohol, in effect, symbolizes the poisoning and dying of their happiness, just as the abortion will carry off the life of their unborn child.

Immediately after arriving at the train station, Jig asks "What should we drink?" (p. 211). She is trying to keep her mind off of the reason why they are there, to catch a train to Madrid where she is supposed to have an abortion. The man, just as eager to avoid having her make this realization, orders two big beers. Before they even finish their beers, the man orders two more drinks, Anis del Toros served with water. Alone, Anis del Toro is a green liquor but when served with water it becomes cloudy and murky. This represents the irreversible polluting that their relationship will have if Jig has the abortion. The clouding of the Anis also parallels the clouding of their minds as Jig grows apathetic and unemotional about her situation.

Jig's dreams of love and children slowly fade away as absinthe replaces them as the thing she has " . . . waited so long for" (p. 212). It is not the absinthe that Jig wants, however, but the nervous derangement, absinthism, that is caused from drinking too much of it. This clouding of her consciousness will be her only way to escape the misery she will have by aborting the baby she wants to keep so dearly.

Alcohol has become the life of the couple. Surface level talk about "new drinks" becomes the only thing they can discuss without argument. The man simply dismisses the awkwardness of their meaningless conversations by reminding her how he gets when he worries. Jig in her tipsy, disillusioned state plays along with the notion that after the abortion " . . . everything will be fine" (p. 213). The man continually reminds her that her pregnancy is the only thing that "bothers" them and makes them "unhappy." He implies that once "it" is gone they can continue to live their extravagant lives of looking at things and trying new drinks.

Just as the two of them have loved irresponsibly, they continue to live and drink irresponsibly. They continue to stay together despite their unhappiness. They are able to ignore their sad situation by drinking. By drinking they are able to avoid

continued on page 410

continued from page 409

talking and discovering that if they go through with the abortion they will never be happy. The more they drink, the easier it becomes to justify the abortion. Their excessive drinking not only leads to the inevitable failure of their relationship but to the death of their child.

As Jig and the American continue to live and drink irresponsibly, the terrible knowledge of what they are about to do is unable to surface. Afraid of facing the ugliness of their irresponsibility, they drink away all remnants of guilt and commitment. They temporarily convince themselves that things will be better after the abortion. What they fail to see is that by ignoring their sadness by drinking they are only leading themselves into more sadness. Aborting their baby will lead to the certain failure of their relationship. Their dependence on alcohol will ultimately lead to a sorrow they won't be able to ignore.

Lauren Davidson

HILLS LIKE WHITE ELEPHANTS

Lauren Davidson is a student at The University of Montana. She wrote this response for a composition class in 1995.

The outcome of the couple's relationship in Ernest Hemingway's short story "Hills Like White Elephants" is left open to the reader's interpretation. However, there is more evidence in the text that suggests that the girl capitulates to the man and has the abortion than not.

The man's dominance over the girl is introduced in the very first paragraph where it states, "The American and the girl with him . . ." Other signs of the man's dominant position are distributed throughout the story. As soon as the conversation starts, the man is ready to jump down the girl's throat. And again, and again, the girl caters to his irritability and defensiveness by falling silent or changing the subject after his comments.

continued to next page

At one point in the story, the "American" reminds the girl of his superiority by warning her. "You know how I get when I worry," he says, as if she should be worried that he is worrying. The man continually pressures the girl to have the abortion. He states that he knows that it is a "perfectly simple operation" but then says that he doesn't want her to do it if she doesn't want to. He not only wants to convince her to have the abortion, but he also wants her to believe that *she* has decided to have it. He goes back and forth throughout the story, pressuring her and then refusing to take responsibility; however, he never asks about her about *her* feelings on the matter.

The girl is obviously dependent on this man. She knows that if she decides to have the child, her life with him will terminate, and she is too dependent upon him to let that happen. She is afraid of losing her security. This is made clear to the reader when the girl asks the man, "And if I do it you'll be happy and things will be like they were and you'll love me?" She needs reassurance of his love because she obviously has doubts. She knows that their relationship is not stable, but she does not have the courage to give up what little she has.

Finally, she gives herself up, thinking that she cannot risk losing her only security. She states, "Then I'll do it. Because I don't care about me." At that moment she forfeits the last of her independence. After making the decision to have the abortion, she realizes that she has given up everything. She stands up and walks to the end of the station where she sees the shadow of a cloud move across the field of grain. The shadow represents the girl's future unhappiness, which she has resigned herself to. She expresses her resignation to the situation by looking at the fertile grain fields and saying, "And we could have all this. And we could have everything and every day we make it more impossible." At this point she has given up all hope of the fertile life she wanted with the man.

After she gives in, she becomes irritated when the man continues to press her to take full responsibility for the decision to have the abortion. She finally asks him forcefully to stop talking because she wants to be left alone. When he persists further, she threatens to scream in her frustration. The man then leaves to

continued on page 412

continued from page 411
carry the bags around to the other side of the station. On the way back he stops in the bar for a solitary drink, and looks at the "reasonable" people waiting for the train. To the man, the girl is unreasonable if she resists his will in any way; he wants her to have the abortion *and* take full responsibility for it.

When he goes back through the curtain to the girl, he asks her if she feels better. And the girl, who has given up everything, smiles at him. With her smile she signals her total capitulation. She tells him that there is nothing wrong with her; she feels "fine," meaning that in in order to save their relationship, she will have the "simple operation" and terminate her pregnancy.

Jonathan Meek

RESPONSE TO UNFORGIVEN

Jon Meek is a freshman Music Education major at The University of Montana.

He calls himself the Skofield Kid. The near-sighted, scruffy looking, blond haired young man wants to be a gunman, yet his mind is changed as he realizes what being a gunman really entails. His saga is played out on screen in Clint Eastwood's movie *Unforgiven*, but many viewers may not realize the significance of the fly-off-the-handle, wet-behind-the-ears, aspiring killer. The Kid is the viewer's stand-in throughout the movie. He represents each uncomprehending child who stares into the mirror, admiring the reflection of the young boy or girl posing with rifle in hand.

The Skofield Kid wants to be seen as a dangerous man with a gun, and he is given his chance to become one. He has idealized the life of a gunman in his own mind as is shown in his questioning of William Munny, a known killer. He eagerly asks the killer what killing people is like and intends to find out for himself. However, when the Kid finally does kill a man, it is no showdown at high noon. There is no face-off in the middle of town, no

continued to next page

glamour. The Kid blasts his victim at point blank range in an outhouse while the man's pants are down. He sees the man's every grimace and realizes his victim's helplessness. He has committed cold-blooded murder.

Later, at the meeting place outside Big Whiskey, the young murderer rambles crazily about his feat in an attempt to mask what really transpired, but he breaks down crying as remorse fills him. The viewers watch him do it, and each is given the chance to ponder what it really means to kill a fellow human being. The victim will "never breathe again and will be dead for a very long time," and the responsibility for the death falls on the perpetrator's shoulders. While the Skofield Kid must learn his lesson the hard way, the movie viewer can experience the emotional consequences of killing someone vicariously through him.

Clint Eastwood demonstrates through the Kid the coldness of murder without the traditional glamour that has come to be expected from Hollywood. No longer a would-be gunman, the Skofield Kid has learned for the benefit of each viewer what it really means to kill someone. No longer blind, he can see that it means to carry the mental picture of the victim's gruesome appearance forever, knowing that the responsibility of death falls on the murderer's shoulders. The viewer is given the chance to be purged without going beyond the mirror to commit a senseless, devastating act of violence.

RESPOND—DEVELOP A PERSPECTIVE THROUGH WRITING

RESPONSIVE WRITING ASSIGNMENT

Respond to a work of short fiction or a film. After reading (or viewing) a **primary text** for meaning in collaboration with your classmates and, if possible, engaging in **research,** construct a text in which you develop an **interpretive position** about the work's meaning.

> ## RESPONDING TO FICTION AND FILM: A GUIDE TO THE PROCESS
>
> Encounter a Primary Text
> Assess Your Past Performance
> Explore the Writing Situation
> Read the Primary Text for Meaning
> Prewrite
> Draft
> Rewrite

ENCOUNTER A PRIMARY TEXT

Preread (or preview) a primary text, either one from the anthology or list included here or one from another source.

A BRIEF ANTHOLOGY OF SHORT FICTION

GIRL
Jamaica Kincaid

Wash the white clothes on Monday and put them on the stone heap; wash the color clothes on Tuesday and put them on the clothesline to dry; don't walk barehead in the hot sun; cook pumpkin fritters in very hot sweet oil; soak your little cloths right after you take them off; when buying cotton to make yourself a nice blouse, be sure that it doesn't have gum on it, because that way it won't hold up well after a wash; soak salt fish overnight before you cook it; is it true that you sing benna[1] in Sunday school?; always eat your food in such a way that it won't turn someone else's stomach; on Sundays try to walk like a lady and not like the slut you are so bent on becoming; don't sing benna in Sunday school; you mustn't speak to wharf-rat boys, not even

___
[1]Calypso or rock and roll.

continued to next page

to give directions; don't eat fruits on the street—flies will follow you; *but I don't sing benna on Sundays at all and never in Sunday school*; this is how to sew on a button; this is how to make a buttonhole for the button you have just sewed on; this is how to hem a dress when you see the hem coming down and so to prevent yourself from looking like the slut I know you are so bent on becoming; this is how you iron your father's khaki shirt so that it doesn't have a crease; this is how you iron your father's khaki pants so that they don't have a crease; this is how you grow okra—far from the house, because okra tree harbors red ants; when you are growing dasheen, make sure it gets plenty of water or else it makes your throat itch when you are eating it; this is how you sweep a corner; this is how you sweep a whole house; this is how you sweep a yard; this is how you smile to someone you don't like too much; this is how you smile to someone you don't like at all; this is how you smile to someone you like completely; this is how you set a table for tea; this is how you set a table for dinner; this is how you set a table for dinner with an important guest; this is how you set a table for lunch; this is how you set a table for breakfast; this is how to behave in the presence of men who don't know you very well, and this way they won't recognize immediately the slut I have warned you against becoming; be sure to wash every day, even if it is with your own spit; don't squat down to play marbles—you are not a boy, you know; don't pick people's flowers—you might catch something; don't throw stones at blackbirds, because it might not be a blackbird at all; this is how to make a bread pudding; this is how to make doukona; this is how to make pepper pot; this is how to make a good medicine for a cold; this is how to make a good medicine to throw away a child before it even becomes a child; this is how to catch a fish; this is how to throw back a fish you don't like, and that way something bad won't fall on you; this is how to bully a man; this is how a man bullies you; this is how to love a man, and if this doesn't work there are other ways, and if they don't work don't feel too bad about giving up; this is how to spit up in the air if you feel like it, and this is how to move quick so that it doesn't fall on you; this is how to make ends meet; always squeeze bread to make sure it's fresh; *but what if the baker won't let me feel the bread?*; you mean to say that after all you are really going to be the kind of woman who the baker won't let near the bread?

CATHEDRAL
Raymond Carver

This blind man, an old friend of my wife's, he was on his way to spend the night. His wife had died. So he was visiting the dead wife's relatives in Connecticut. He called my wife from his in-laws'. Arrangements were made. He would come by train, a five-hour trip, and my wife would meet him at the station. She hadn't seen him since she worked for him one summer in Seattle ten years ago. But she and the blind man had kept in touch. They made tapes and mailed them back and forth. I wasn't enthusiastic about his visit. He was no one I knew. And his being blind bothered me. My idea of blindness came from the movies. In the movies, the blind moved slowly and never laughed. Sometimes they were led by seeing-eye dogs. A blind man in my house was not something I looked forward to.

That summer in Seattle she had needed a job. She didn't have any money. The man she was going to marry at the end of the summer was in officers' training school. He didn't have any money, either. But she was in love with the guy, and he was in love with her, etc. She'd seen something in the paper HELP WANTED—*Reading to Blind Man*, and a telephone number. She phoned and went over, was hired on the spot. She'd work with this blind man all summer. She read stuff to him, case studies, reports, that sort of thing. She helped him organize his little office in the county social-service department. They'd become good friends, my wife and the blind man. How do I know those things? She told me. And she told me something else. On her last day in the office, the blind man asked if he could touch her face. She agreed to this. She told me he touched his fingers to every part of her face, her nose—even her neck! She never forgot it. She even tried to write a poem about it. She was always trying to write a poem. She wrote a poem or two every year, usually after something really important had happened to her.

When we first started going out together, she showed me the poem. In the poem, she recalled his fingers and the way they had moved around over her face. In the poem, she talked about what she had felt at the time, about what went through her mind when

continued to next page

the blind man touched her nose and lips. I remember I didn't think much of the poem. Of course, I didn't tell her that. Maybe I just don't understand poetry. I admit it's not the first thing I reach for when I pick up something to read.

Anyway, this man who'd first enjoyed her favors, the officer-to-be, he'd been her childhood sweetheart. So okay. I'm saying that at the end of the summer she'd let the blind man run his hands over her face, said goodbye to him, married her childhood, etc., who was now a commissioned officer, and she moved away from Seattle. But they'd kept in touch, she and the blind man. She made the first contact after a year or so. She called him up one night from an Air Force base in Alabama. She wanted to talk. They talked. He asked her to send him a tape and tell him about her life. She did this. She sent the tape. On the tape, she told the blind man about her husband and about their life together in the military. She told the blind man that she loved her husband but she didn't like it where they lived and she didn't like it that he was a part of the military-industrial thing. She told the blind man she'd written a poem and he was in it. She told him that she was writing a poem about what it was like to be an Air Force officer's wife. The poem wasn't finished yet. She was still writing it. The blind man made a tape. He sent her the tape. She made a tape. This went on for years. My wife's officer was posted to one base and then another. She sent tapes from Moody AFB, McGuire, McConnell, and finally Travis, near Sacramento, where one night she got to feeling lonely and cut off from people she kept losing in that moving-around life. She got to feeling she couldn't go it another step. She went in and swallowed all the pills and capsules in the medicine chest and washed them down with a bottle of gin. Then she got into a hot bath and passed out.

But instead of dying, she got sick. She threw up. Her officer—why should he have a name? he was the childhood sweetheart, and what more does he want?—came home from somewhere, found her, and called the ambulance. In time, she put it all on a tape and sent the tape to the blind man. Over the years, she put all kinds of stuff on tapes and sent the tapes off lickety-split. Next to writing a poem every year, I think it was her chief means of recreation. On one tape, she told the blind man she'd decided to

continued on page 418

continued from page 417

live away from her officer for a time. On another tape, she told him about her divorce. She and I began going out, and of course she told her blind man about it. She told him everything, or so it seemed to me. This was a year ago. I was on the tape, she said. So I said, okay, I'd listen to it. I got us drinks and we settled down in the living room. We made ready to listen. First she inserted the tape into the player and adjusted a couple of dials. Then she pushed a lever. The tape squeaked and someone began to talk in this loud voice. She lowered the volume. After a few minutes of harmless chitchat, I heard my own name in the mouth of this stranger, this blind man I didn't even know! And then this: ''From all you've said about him, I can only conclude—'' But we were interrupted, a knock at the door, something, and we didn't ever get back to the tape. Maybe it was just as well. I'd heard all I wanted to.

Now this same blind man was coming to sleep in my house.

''Maybe I could take him bowling,'' I said to my wife. She was at the draining board doing scalloped potatoes. She put down the knife she was using and turned around.

''If you love me,'' she said, ''you can do this for me. If you don't love me, okay. But if you had a friend, any friend, and the friend came to visit, I'd make him feel comfortable.'' She wiped her hands with the dish towel.

''I don't have any blind friends,'' I said.

''You don't have *any* friends,'' she said. ''Period. Besides,'' she said, ''goddamn it, his wife's just died! Don't you understand that? The man's lost his wife!''

I didn't answer. She'd told me a little about the blind man's wife. Her name was Beulah. Beulah! That's a name for a colored woman.

''Was his wife a Negro?'' I asked.

''Are you crazy?'' my wife said. ''Have you just flipped or something?'' She picked up a potatato. I saw it hit the floor, then roll under the stove. ''What's wrong with you?'' she said. ''Are you drunk?''

''I'm just asking,'' I said.

Right then my wife filled me in with more detail than I cared to know. I made a drink and sat at the kitchen table to listen. Pieces of the story began to fall into place.

continued to next page

Beulah had gone to work for the blind man the summer after my wife had stopped working for him. Pretty soon Beulah and the blind man had themselves a church wedding. It was a little wedding—who'd want to go to such a wedding in the first place?—just the two of them, plus the minister and the minister's wife. But it was a church wedding just the same. It was what Beulah had wanted, he'd said. But even then Beulah must have been carrying the cancer in her glands. After they had been inseparable for eight years—my wife's word, *inseparable*—Beulah's health went into a rapid decline. She died in a Seattle hospital room, the blind man sitting beside the bed and holding on to her hand. They'd married, lived and worked together, slept together—had sex, sure—and then the blind man had to bury her. All this without his having even seen what the goddamned woman looked like. It was beyond my understanding. Hearing this, I felt sorry for the blind man for a little bit. And then I found myself thinking what a pitiful life this woman must have led. Imagine a woman who could never see herself as she was seen in the eyes of her loved one. A woman who could go on day after day and never receive the smallest compliment from her beloved. A woman whose husband could never read the expression on her face, be it misery or something better. Someone who could wear makeup or not—what difference to him? She could, if she wanted, wear green eye-shadow around one eye, a straight pin in her nostril, yellow slacks and purple shoes, no matter. And then to slip off into death, the blind man's hand on her hand, his blind eyes streaming tears—I'm imagining now—her last thought maybe this: that he never even knew what she looked like, and she on an express to the grave. Robert was left with a small insurance policy and half of a twenty-peso Mexican coin. The other half of the coin went into the box with her. Pathetic.

So when the time rolled around, my wife went to the depot to pick him up. With nothing to do but wait—sure, I blamed him for that—I was having a drink and watching the TV when I heard the car pull into the drive. I got up from the sofa with my drink and went to the window to have a look.

I saw my wife laughing as she parked the car. I saw her get out of the car and shut the door. She was still wearing a smile. Just amazing. She went around to the other side of the car to where the blind man was already starting to get out. This blind man,

continued on page 420

continued from page 419

feature this, he was wearing a full beard! A beard on a blind man! Too much, I say. The blind man reached into the back seat, and dragged out a suitcase. My wife took his arm, shut the car door, and, talking all the way, moved him down the drive and then up the steps to the front porch. I turned off the TV. I finished my drink, rinsed the glass, dried my hands. Then I went to the door.

My wife said, "I want you to meet Robert. Robert, this is my husband. I've told you all about him." She was beaming. She had this blind man by his coat sleeve.

The blind man let go of his suitcase and up came his hand.

I took it. He squeezed hard, held my hand, and then he let it go.

"I feel like we've already met," he boomed.

"Likewise," I said. I didn't know what else to say. Then I said, "Welcome. I've heard a lot about you." We began to move then, a little group, from the porch into the living room, my wife guiding him by the arm. The blind man was carrying his suitcase in his other hand. My wife said things like, "To your left here, Robert. That's right. Now watch it, there's a chair. That's it. Sit down right here. This is the sofa. We just bought this sofa two weeks ago."

I started to say something about the old sofa. I'd liked that old sofa. But I didn't say anything. Then I wanted to say something else, small-talk, about the scenic ride along the Hudson. How going *to* New York, you should sit on the right-hand side of the train, and coming *from* New York, the left-hand side.

"Did you have a good train ride?" I said. "Which side of the train did you sit on, by the way?"

"What a question, which side!" my wife said. "What's it matter which side?" she said.

"I just asked," I said.

"Right side," the blind man said. "I hadn't been on a train in nearly forty years. Not since I was a kid. With my folks. That's been a long time. I'd nearly forgotten the sensation. I have winter in my beard now," he said. "So I've been told, anyway. Do I look distinguished, my dear?" the blind man said to my wife.

"You look distinguished, Robert," she said. "Robert," she said. "Robert, it's just so good to see you."

continued to next page

My wife finally took her eyes off the blind man and looked at me. I had the feeling she didn't like what she saw. I shrugged.

I've never met, or personally known, anyone who was blind. This blind man was late forties, a heavy-set, balding man with stooped shoulders, as if he carried a great weight there. He wore brown slacks, brown shoes, a light-brown shirt, a tie, a sports coat. Spiffy. He also had this full beard. But he didn't use a cane and he didn't wear dark glasses. I'd always thought dark glasses were a must for the blind. Fact was, I wished he had a pair. At first glance, his eyes looked like anyone else's eyes. But if you looked close, there was something different about them. Too much white in the iris, for one thing, and the pupils seemed to move around in the sockets without his knowing it or being able to stop it. Creepy. As I stared at his face, I saw the left pupil turn in toward his nose while the other side made an effort to keep in one place. But it was only an effort, for that eye was on the roam without his knowing it or wanting it to be.

I said, "Let me get you a drink. What's your pleasure? We have a little of everything. It's one of our pastimes."

"Bub, I'm a Scotch man myself," he said fast enough in this big voice.

"Right," I said. Bub! "Sure you are. I knew it."

He let his fingers touch his suitcase, which was sitting alongside the sofa. He was taking his bearings. I didn't blame him for that.

"I'll move that up to your room," my wife said.

"No, that's fine," the blind man said loudly. "It can go up when I go up."

"A little water with the Scotch?" I said.

"Very little," he said.

"I knew it," I said.

He said, "Just a tad. The Irish actor, Barry Fitzgerald? I'm like that fellow. When I drink water, Fitzgerald said, I drink water. When I drink whiskey, I drink whiskey." My wife laughed. The blind man brought his hand up under his beard. He lifted his beard slowly and let it drop.

I did the drinks, three big glasses of Scotch with a splash of water in each. Then we made ourselves comfortable and talked about Robert's travels. First the long flight from the West Coast

continued on page 422

continued from page 421

to Connecticut, we covered that. Then from Connecticut up here by train. We had another drink concerning that leg of the trip.

I remembered having read somewhere that the blind didn't smoke because, as speculation had it, they couldn't see the smoke they exhaled. I thought I knew that much and that much only about blind people. But this blind man smoked his cigarettes down to the nubbin and then lit another one. This blind man filled his ashtray and my wife emptied it.

When we sat down at the table for dinner, we had another drink. My wife heaped Robert's plate with cube steak, scalloped potatoes, green beans. I buttered him up two slices of bread. I said, "Here's bread and butter for you." I swallowed some of my drink. "Now let us pray," I said, and the blind man lowered his head. My wife looked at me, her mouth agape. "Pray the phone won't ring and the food doesn't get cold," I said.

We dug in. We ate everything there was to eat on the table. We ate like there was no tomorrow. We didn't talk. We ate. We scarfed. We grazed that table. We were into serious eating. The blind man had right away located his foods, he knew just where everything was on his plate. I watched with admiration as he used his knife and fork on the meat. He'd cut two pieces of meat, fork the meat into his mouth, and then go all out for the scalloped potatoes, the beans next, and then he'd tear off a hunk of buttered bread and eat that. He'd follow this up with a big drink of milk. It didn't seem to bother him to use his fingers once in a while, either.

We finished everything, including half a strawberry pie. For a few moments, we sat as if stunned. Sweat beaded on our faces. Finally, we got up from the table and left the dirty plates. We didn't look back. We took ourselves into the living room and sank into our places again. Robert and my wife sat on the sofa. I took the big chair. We had us two or three more drinks while they talked about the major things that had come to pass for them in the past ten years. For the most part, I just listened. Now and then I joined in. I didn't want him to think I'd left the room, and I didn't want her to think I was feeling left out. They talked of things that had happened to them—to them—these past ten years. I waited in vain to hear my name on my wife's sweet lips. "And

continued to next page

then my dear husband came into my life"—something like that. But I heard nothing of the sort. More talk of Robert. Robert had done a little of everything, it seemed, a regular blind jack-of-all-trades. But most recently he and his wife had had an Amway distributorship, from which, I gathered, they'd earned their living, such as it was. The blind man was also a ham radio operator. He talked in his loud voice about conversations he'd had with fellow operators in Guam, in the Philippines, in Alaska, and even in Tahiti. He said he'd have a lot of friends there if he ever wanted to go visit those places. From time to time, he'd turn his blind face toward me, put his hand under his beard, ask me something. How long had I been in my present position? (Three years.) Did I like my work? (I didn't.) Was I going to stay with it? (What were the options?) Finally, when I thought he was beginning to run down, I got up and turned on the TV.

My wife looked at me with irritation. She was heading toward a boil. Then she looked at the blind man and said, "Robert, do you have a TV?"

The blind man said, "My dear, I have two TVs. I have a color set and a black-and-white thing, an old relic. It's funny, but if I turn the TV on, and I'm always turning it on, I turn on the color set. It's funny, don't you think?"

I didn't know what to say to that. I had absolutely nothing to say to that. No opinion. So I watched the news program and tried to listen to what the announcer was saying.

"This is a color TV," the blind man said. "Don't ask me how, but I can tell."

"We traded up a while ago," I said.

The blind man had another taste of his drink. He lifted his beard, sniffed it, and let it fall. He leaned forward on the sofa. He positioned his ashtray on the coffee table, then put the lighter to his cigarette. He leaned back on the sofa and crossed his legs at the ankles.

My wife covered her mouth, and then she yawned. She stretched. She said, "I think I'll go upstairs and put on my robe. I think I'll change into something else. Robert, you make yourself comfortable," she said.

"I'm comfortable," the blind man said.

"I want you to feel comfortable in this house," she said.

continued on page 424

continued from page 423
"I am comfortable," the blind man said.

After she'd left the room, he and I listened to the weather report and then to the sports roundup. By that time, she'd been gone so long I didn't know if she was going to come back. I thought she might have gone to bed. I wished she'd come back downstairs. I didn't want to be left alone with a blind man. I asked him if he wanted another drink, and he said sure. Then I asked if he wanted to smoke some dope with me. I said I'd just rolled a number. I hadn't, but I planned to do so in about two shakes.

"I'll try some with you," he said.

"Damn right," I said. "That's the stuff."

I got our drinks and sat down on the sofa with him. Then I rolled us two fat numbers. I lit one and passed it. I brought it to his fingers. He took it and inhaled.

"Hold it as long as you can," I said. I could tell he didn't know the first thing.

My wife came back downstairs wearing her pink robe and her pink slippers.

"What do I smell?" she said.

"We thought we'd have us some cannabis," I said.

My wife gave me a savage look. Then she looked at the blind man and said, "Robert, I didn't know you smoked."

He said, "I do now, my dear. There's a first time for everything. But I don't feel anything yet."

"This stuff is pretty mellow," I said. "This stuff is mild. It's dope you can reason with," I said. "It doesn't mess you up."

"Not much it doesn't, bub," he said, and laughed.

My wife sat on the sofa between the blind man and me. I passed her the number. She took it and toked and then passed it back to me. "Which way is this going?" she said. Then she said, "I shouldn't be smoking this. I can hardly keep my eyes open as it is. That dinner did me in. I shouldn't have eaten so much."

"It was the strawberry pie," the blind man said. "That's what did it," he said, and he laughed his big laugh. Then he shook his head.

"There's more strawberry pie," I said.

continued to next page

"Do you want some more, Robert?" my wife said.

"Maybe in a little while," he said.

We gave our attention to the TV. My wife yawned again. She said, "Your bed is made up when you feel like going to bed, Robert. I know you must have had a long day. When you're ready to go to bed, say so." She pulled his arm. "Robert?"

He came to and said, "I've had a real nice time. This beats tapes, doesn't it?"

I said, "Coming at you," and I put the number between his fingers. He inhaled, held the smoke, and then let it go. It was like he'd been doing it since he was nine years old.

"Thanks, bub," he said. "But I think this is all for me. I think I'm beginning to feel it," he said. He held the burning roach out for my wife.

"Same here," she said. "Ditto. Me, too." She took the roach and passed it to me. "I may just sit here for a while between you two guys with my eyes closed. But don't let me bother you, okay? Either one of you. If it bothers you, say so. Otherwise, I may just sit here with my eyes closed until you're ready to go to bed," she said. "Your bed's made up, Robert, when you're ready. It's right next to our room at the top of the stairs. We'll show you up when you're ready. You wake me up now, you guys, if I fall asleep." She said that and then she closed her eyes and went to sleep.

The news program ended. I got up and changed the channel. I sat back down on the sofa. I wished my wife hadn't pooped out. Her head lay across the back of the sofa, her mouth open. She'd turned so that her robe had slipped away from her legs, exposing a juicy thigh. I reached to draw her robe back over her, and it was then that I glanced at the blind man. What the hell! I flipped the robe open again.

"You say when you want some strawberry pie," I said.

"I will," he said.

I said, "Are you tired? Do you want me to take you up to your bed? Are you ready to hit the hay?"

"Not yet," he said. "No, I'll stay up with you, bub. If that's all right. I'll stay up until you're ready to turn in. We haven't had a chance to talk. Know what I mean? I feel like me and her

continued on page 426

continued from page 425

monopolized the evening." He lifted his beard and he let it fall. He picked up his cigarettes and his lighter.

"That's all right," I said. Then I said, "I'm glad for the company."

And I guess I was. Every night I smoked dope and stayed up as long as I could before I fell asleep. My wife and I hardly ever went to bed at the same time. When I did go to sleep, I had these dreams. Sometimes I'd wake up from one of them, my heart going crazy.

Something about the church and the Middle Ages was on the TV. Not your run-of-the-mill TV fare. I wanted to watch something else. I turned to the other channels. But there was nothing on them, either. So I turned back to the first channel and apologized.

"Bub, it's all right," the blind man said. "It's fine with me. Whatever you want to watch is okay. I'm always learning something. Learning never ends. It won't hurt me to learn something tonight. I got ears," he said.

We didn't say anything for a time. He was leaning forward with his head turned at me, his right ear aimed in the direction of the set. Very disconcerting. Now and then his eyelids drooped and then they snapped open again. Now and then he put his fingers into his beard and tugged, like he was thinking about something he was hearing on the television.

On the screen, a group of men wearing cowls was being set upon and tormented by men dressed in skeleton costumes and men dressed as devils. The men dressed as devils wore devil masks, horns, and long tails. This pageant was part of a procession. The Englishman who was narrating the thing said it took place in Spain once a year. I tried to explain to the blind man what was happening.

"Skeletons," he said. "I know about skeletons," he said, and he nodded.

The TV showed this one cathedral. Then there was a long, slow look at another one. Finally, the picture switched to the famous one in Paris, with its flying buttresses and its spires reaching

continued to next page

up to the clouds. The camera pulled away to show the whole of the cathedral rising above the skyline.

There were times when the Englishman who was telling the thing would shut up, would simply let the camera move around over the cathedrals. Or else the camera would tour the countryside, men in fields walking behind oxen. I waited as long as I could. Then I felt I had to say something. I said, "They're showing the outside of this cathedral now. Gargoyles. Little statues carved to look like monsters. Now I guess they're in Italy. Yeah, they're in Italy. There's paintings on the walls of this one church."

"Are those fresco paintings, bub?" he asked, and he sipped from his drink.

I reached for my glass. But it was empty. I tried to remember what I could remember. "You're asking me are those frescoes?" I said. "That's a good question. I don't know."

The camera moved to a cathedral outside Lisbon. The differences in the Portuguese cathedral compared with the French and Italian were not that great. But they were there. Mostly the interior stuff. Then something occurred to me, and I said, "Something has occurred to me. Do you have any idea what a cathedral is? What they look like, that is? Do you follow me? If somebody says cathedral to you, do you have any notion what they're talking about? Do you know the difference between that and a Baptist church, say?"

He let the smoke dribble from his mouth. "I know they took hundreds of workers fifty or a hundred years to build," he said. "I just heard the man say that, of course. I know generations of the same families worked on a cathedral. I heard him say that, too. The men who began their life's work on them, they never lived to see the completion of their work. In that wise, bub, they're no different from the rest of us, right?" He laughed. Then his eyelids drooped again. His head nodded. He seemed to be snoozing. Maybe he was imagining himself in Portugal. The TV was showing another cathedral now. This one was in Germany. The Englishman's voice droned on. "Cathedrals," the blind man said. He sat up and rolled his head back and forth. "If you want the truth, bub, that's about all I know. What I just said. What I heard him say. But maybe you could describe one to me? I wish

continued on page 428

continued from page 427

you'd do that. If you want to know, I really don't have a good idea."

I stared hard at the shot of the cathedral on the TV. How could I even begin to describe it? But say my life depended on it. Say my life was being threatened by an insane guy who said I had to do it or else.

I stared some more at the cathedral before the picture flipped off into the countryside. There was no use. I turned to the blind man and said, "To begin with, they're very tall." I was looking around the room for clues. "They reach way up. Up and up. Toward the sky. They're so big, some of them, they have to have these supports. To help hold them up, so to speak. These supports are called buttresses. They remind me of viaducts, for some reason. But maybe you don't know viaducts, either? Sometimes the cathedrals have devils and such carved into the front. Sometimes lords and ladies. Don't ask me why this is," I said.

He was nodding. The whole upper part of his body seemed to be moving back and forth.

"I'm not doing so good, am I?" I said.

He stopped nodding and leaned forward on the edge of the sofa. As he listened to me, he was running his fingers through his beard. I wasn't getting through to him, I could see that. But he waited for me to go on just the same. He nodded, like he was trying to encourage me. I tried to think what else to say. "They're really big," I said. "They're massive. They're built of stone. Marble, too, sometimes. In those olden days, when they built cathedrals, men wanted to be close to God. In those olden days, God was an important part of everyone's life. You could tell this from their cathedral-building. I'm sorry," I said, "but it looks like that's the best I can do for you. I'm just no good at it."

"That's all right, bub," the blind man said. "Hey, listen. I hope you don't mind my asking you. Can I ask you something? Let me ask you a simple question, yes or no. I'm just curious and there's no offense. You're my host. But let me ask if you are in any way religious? You don't mind my asking?"

I shook my head. He couldn't see that, though. A wink is the same as a nod to a blind man. "I guess I don't believe in it. In anything. Sometimes it's hard. You know what I'm saying?"

continued to next page

"Sure, I do," he said.

"Right," I said.

The Englishman was still holding forth. My wife sighed in her sleep. She drew a long breath and went on with her sleeping.

"You'll have to forgive me," I said. "But I can't tell you what a cathedral looks like. It just isn't in me to do it. I can't do any more than I've done."

The blind man sat very still, his head down, as he listened to me.

I said, "The truth is, cathedrals don't mean anything special to me. Nothing. Cathedrals. They're something to look at on late-night TV. That's all they are."

It was then that the blind man cleared his throat. He brought something up. He took a handkerchief from his back pocket. Then he said, "I get it, bub. It's okay. It happens. Don't worry about it," he said. "Hey, listen to me. Will you do me a favor? I got an idea. Why don't you find us some heavy paper? And a pen. We'll do something. We'll draw one together. Get us a pen and some heavy paper. Go on, bub, get the stuff," he said.

So I went upstairs. My legs felt like they didn't have much strength in them. They felt like they did after I'd done some running. In my wife's room, I looked around. I found some ballpoints in a little basket on her table. And then I tried to think where to look for the kind of paper he was talking about.

Downstairs, in the kitchen, I found a shopping bag with onion skins in the bottom of the bag. I emptied the bag and shook it. I brought it into the living room and sat down with it near his legs. I moved some things, smoothed the wrinkles from the bag, spread it out on the coffee table.

The blind man got down from the sofa and sat next to me on the carpet.

He ran his fingers over the paper. He went up and down the sides of the paper. The edges, even the edges. He fingered the corners.

"All right," he said. "All right, let's do her."

He found my hand, the hand with the pen. He closed his hand over my hand. "Go ahead, bub, draw," he said. "Draw. You'll see. I'll follow along with you. It'll be okay. Just begin now like I'm telling you. You'll see. Draw," the blind man said.

continued on page 430

continued from page 429

So I began. First I drew a box that looked like a house. It could have been the house I lived in. Then I put a roof on it. At either end of the roof, I drew spires. Crazy.

"Swell," he said. "Terrific. You're doing fine," he said. "Never thought anything like this could happen in your lifetime, did you, bub? Well, it's a strange life, we all know that. Go on now. Keep it up."

I put in windows with arches. I drew flying buttresses. I hung great doors. I couldn't stop. The TV station went off the air. I put down the pen and closed and opened my fingers. The blind man felt around over the paper. He moved the tips of his fingers over the paper, all over what I had drawn, and he nodded.

"Doing fine," the blind man said.

I took up the pen again, and he found my hand. I kept at it. I'm no artist. But I kept drawing just the same.

My wife opened up her eyes and gazed at us. She sat up on the sofa, her robe hanging open. She said, "What are you doing? Tell me, I want to know."

I didn't answer her.

The blind man said, "We're drawing a cathedral. Me and him are working on it. Press hard," he said to me. "That's right. That's good," he said. "Sure. You got it, bub. I can tell. You didn't think you could. But you can, can't you? You're cooking with gas now. You know what I'm saying? We're going to really have us something here in a minute. How's the old arm?" he said. "Put some people in there now. What's a cathedral without people?"

My wife said, "What's going on? Robert, what are you doing? What's going on?"

"It's all right," he said to her. "Close your eyes now," the blind man said to me.

I did it. I closed them just like he said.

"Are they closed?" he said. "Don't fudge."

"They're closed," I said.

"Keep them that way," he said. He said, "Don't stop now. Draw."

So we kept on with it. His fingers rode my fingers as my hand went over the paper. It was like nothing else in my life up to now.

continued to next page

Then he said, "I think that's it. I think you got it," he said. "Take a look. What do you think?"

But I had my eyes closed. I thought I'd keep them that way for a little longer. I thought it was something I ought to do.

"Well?" he said. "Are you looking?"

My eyes were still closed. I was in my house. I knew that. But I didn't feel like I was inside anything.

"It's really something," I said.

ROMAN FEVER
Edith Wharton

1

From the table at which they had been lunching two American ladies of ripe but well-cared-for middle age moved across the lofty terrace of the Roman restaurant and, leaning on its parapet, looked first at each other, and then down on the outspread glories of the Palatine and the Forum, with the same expression of vague but benevolent approval.

As they leaned there a girlish voice echoed up gaily from the stairs leading to the court below. "Well, come along, then," it cried, not to them but to an invisible companion, "and let's leave the young things to their knitting"; and a voice as fresh laughed back: "Oh, look here, Babs, not actually *knitting*—" "Well, I mean figuratively," rejoined the first. "After all, we haven't left our poor parents much else to do. . . ." and at that point the turn of the stairs engulfed the dialogue.

The two ladies looked at each other again, this time with a tingle of smiling embarrassment, and the smaller and paler one shook her head and colored slightly.

"Barbara!" she murmured, sending an unheard rebuke after the mocking voice in the stairway.

The other lady, who was fuller, and higher in color, with a small determined nose supported by vigorous black eyebrows,

continued on page 432

continued from page 431

gave a good-humored laugh. "That's what our daughters think of us!"

Her companion replied by a deprecating gesture. "Not of us individually. We must remember that. It's just the collective modern idea of Mothers. As you see—" Half-guiltily she drew from her handsomely mounted black handbag a twist of crimson silk run through by two fine knitting needles. "One never knows," she murmured. "The new system has certainly given us a good deal of time to kill; and sometimes I get tired just looking—even at this." Her gesture was now addressed to the stupendous scene at their feet.

The dark lady laughed again, and they both relapsed upon the view, contemplating it in silence, with a sort of diffused serenity which might have been borrowed from the spring effulgence of the Roman skies. The luncheon hour was long past, and the two had their end of the vast terrace to themselves. At its opposite extremity a few groups, detained by a lingering look at the outspread city, were gathering up guidebooks and fumbling for tips. The last of them scattered, and the two ladies were alone on the air-washed height.

"Well, I don't see why we shouldn't just stay here," said Mrs. Slade, the lady of the high color and energetic brows. Two derelict basket chairs stood near, and she pushed them into the angle of the parapet, and settled herself in one, her gaze upon the Palatine. "After all, it's still the most beautiful view in the world."

"It always will be, to me," assented her friend Mrs. Ansley, with no slight a stress on the "me" that Mrs. Slade, though she noticed it, wondered if it were not merely accidental, like the random underlinings of old-fashioned letter writers.

"Grace Ansley was always old-fashioned," she thought; and added aloud, with a retrospective smile: "It's a view we've both been familiar with for a good many years. When we first met here we were younger than our girls are now. You remember?"

"Oh, yes, I remember," murmured Mrs. Ansley, with the same undefinable stress. "There's that headwaiter wondering," she interpolated. She was evidently far less sure than her companion of herself and of her rights in the world.

continued to next page

"I'll cure him of wondering," said Mrs. Slade, stretching her hand toward a bag as discreetly opulent-looking as Mrs. Ansley's. Signing to the headwaiter, she explained that she and her friend were old lovers of Rome, and would like to spend the end of the afternoon looking down on the view—that is, if it did not disturb the service? The headwaiter, bowing over her gratuity, assured her that the ladies were most welcome, and would be still more so if they would condescend to remain for dinner. A full-moon night, they would remember. . . .

Mrs. Slade's black brows drew together, as though references to the moon were out of place and even unwelcome. But she smiled away her frown as the headwaiter retreated. "Well, why not? We might do worse. There's no knowing, I suppose, when the girls will be back. Do you even know back from *where*? I don't!"

Mrs. Ansley again colored slightly. "I think those young Italian aviators we met at the Embassy invited them to fly to Tarquinia for tea. I suppose they'll want to wait and fly back by moonlight."

"Moonlight—moonlight! What a part it still plays. Do you suppose they're as sentimental as we were?"

"I've come to the conclusion that I don't in the least know what they are," said Mrs. Ansley. "And perhaps we didn't know much more about each other."

"No; perhaps we didn't."

Her friend gave her a shy glance. "I never should have supposed you were sentimental, Alida."

"Well, perhaps I wasn't." Mrs Slade drew her lids together in retrospect; and for a few moments the two ladies, who had been intimate since childhood, reflected how little they knew each other. Each one, of course, had a label ready to attach to the other's name; Mrs. Delphin Slade, for instance, would have told herself, or anyone who asked her, that Mrs. Horace Ansley, twenty-five years ago, had been exquisitely lovely—no, you wouldn't believe it, would you? . . . though, of course, still charming, distinguished. . . . Well, as a girl she had been exquisite; far more beautiful than her daughter Barbara, though certainly Babs, according to the new standards at any rate, was more effective—had more

continued on page 434

continued from page 433

edge, as they say. Funny where she got it, with those two nullities as parents. Yes; Horace Ansley was—well, just the duplicate of his wife. Museum specimens of old New York. Good-looking, irreproachable, exemplary. Mrs. Slade and Mrs. Ansley had lived opposite each other—actually as well as figuratively—for years. When the drawing-room curtains in No. 20 East 73rd Street were renewed, No. 23, across the way, was always aware of it. And of all the movings, buyings, travels, anniversaries, illnesses—the tame chronicle of an estimable pair. Little of it escaped Mrs. Slade. But she had grown bored with it by the time her husband made his big *coup* in Wall Street, and when they bought in upper Park Avenue had already begun to think: "I'd rather live opposite a speakeasy for a change; at least one might see it raided." The idea of seeing Grace raided was so amusing that (before the move) she launched it at a woman's lunch. It made a hit, and went the rounds—she sometimes wondered if it had crossed the street, and reached Mrs. Ansley. She hoped not, but didn't much mind. Those were the days when respectability was at a discount, and it did the irreproachable no harm to laugh at them a little.

A few years later, and not many months apart, both ladies lost their husbands. There was an appropriate exchange of wreaths and condolences, and a brief renewal of intimacy in the half-shadow of their mourning; and now, after another interval, they had run across each other in Rome, at the same hotel, each of them the modest appendage of a salient daughter. The similarity of their lot had again drawn them together, lending itself to mild jokes, and the mutual confession that, if in old days it must have been tiring to "keep up" with daughters, it was not, at times, a little dull not to.

No doubt, Mrs. Slade reflected, she felt her unemployment more than poor Grace ever would. It was a big drop from being the wife of Delphin Slade to being his widow. She had always regarded herself (with a certain conjugal pride) as his equal in social gifts, as contributing her full share to the making of the exceptional couple they were: but the difference after his death was irremediable. As the wife of the famous corporation lawyer, always with an international case or two on hand, every day brought its exciting and unexpected obligation: the improptu

continued to next page

entertaining of eminent collegues from abroad, the hurried dashes on legal business to London, Paris or Rome, where the entertaining was so handsomely reciprocated; the amusement of hearing in her wake: "What, that handsome woman with the good clothes and the eyes is Mrs. Slade—*the* Slade's wife? Really? Generally the wives of celebrities are such frumps."

Yes; being *the* Slade's widow was a dullish business after that. In living up to such a husband all her faculties had been engaged; now she had only her daughter to live up to, for the son who seemed to have inherited his father's gifts had died suddenly in boyhood. She had fought through that agony because her husband was there, to be helped and to help; now, after the father's death, the thought of the boy had become unbearable. There was nothing left but to mother her daughter; and dear Jenny was such a perfect daughter that she needed no excessive mothering. "Now with Babs Ansley I don't know that I *should* be so quiet," Mrs. Slade sometimes half-enviously reflected; but Jenny, who was younger than her brilliant friend, was that rare accident, an extremely pretty girl who somehow made youth and prettiness seem as safe as their absence. It was all perplexing—and to Mrs. Slade a little boring. She wished that Jenny would fall in love—with the wrong man, even; that she might have to be watched, out-maneuvered, rescued. And instead, it was Jenny who watched her mother, kept her out of drafts, made sure that she had taken her tonic. . . .

Mrs. Ansley was much less articulate than her friend, and her mental portrait of Mrs. Slade was slighter, and drawn with fainter touches. "Alida Slade's awfully brilliant; but not as brilliant as she thinks," would have summed it up; though she would have added, for the enlightenment of strangers, that Mrs. Slade had been an extremely dashing girl; much more so than her daughter, who was pretty, of course, and clever in a way, but had none of her mother's—well, "vividness," someone had once called it. Mrs. Ansley would take up current words like this, and cite them in quotation marks, as unheard-of audacities. No; Jenny was not like her mother. Sometimes Mrs. Ansley thought Alida Slade was disappointed; on the whole she had had a sad life. Full of failures and mistakes; Mrs. Ansley had always been rather sorry for her. . . .

continued on page 436

continued from page 435

So these two ladies visualized each other, each through the wrong end of her little telescope.

2

For a long time they continued to sit side by side without speaking. It seemed as though, to both, there was a relief in laying down their somewhat futile activities in the presence of the vast Memento Mori which faced them. Mrs. Slade sat quite still, her eyes fixed on the golden slope of the Palace of the Caesars, and after a while Mrs. Ansley ceased to fidget with her bag, and she too sank into meditation. Like many intimate friends, the two ladies had never before had occasion to be silent together, and Mrs. Ansley was slightly embarrassed by what seemed, after so many years, a new stage in their intimacy, and one with which she did not yet know how to deal.

Suddenly the air was full of that deep clangor of bells which periodically covers Rome with a roof of silver. Mrs. Slade glanced at her wristwatch. "Five o'clock already," she said, as though surprised.

Mrs. Ansley suggested interrogatively: "There's bridge at the Embassy at five." For along time Mrs. Slade did not answer. She appeared to be lost in contemplation, and Mrs. Ansley thought the remark had escaped her. But after a while she said, as if speaking out of a dream: "Bridge, did you say? Not unless you want to. . . . But I don't think I will, you know."

"Oh, no," Mrs. Ansley hastened to assure her. "I don't care to at all. It's so lovely here; and so full of old memories, as you say." She settled herself in her chair, and almost furtively drew forth her knitting. Mrs. Slade took sideway note of this activity, but her own beautifully cared-for hands remained motionless on her knee.

"I was just thinking," she said slowly, "what different things Rome stands for to each generation of travelers. To our grandmothers, Roman fever; to our mothers, sentimental dangers—how we used to be guarded!—to our daughters, no more dangers than the middle of Main Street. They don't know it—but how much they're missing!"

continued to next page

The long golden light was beginning to pale, and Mrs. Ansley lifted her knitting a little closer to her eyes. "Yes; how we were guarded!"

"I always used to think," Mrs. Slade continued, "that our mothers had a much more difficult job than our grandmothers. When Roman fever stalked the streets it must have been comparatively easy to gather in the girls at the danger hour; but when you and I were young, with such beauty calling us, and the spice of disobedience thrown in, and no worse risk than catching cold during the cool hour after sunset, the mothers used to be put to it to keep us in—didn't they?"

She turned again toward Mrs. Ansley, but the latter had reached a delicate point in her knitting. "One, two, three—slip two; yes, they must have been." She assented, without looking up.

Mrs. Slade's eyes rested on her with a deepened attention. "She can knit—in the face of *this!* How like her. . . ."

Mrs. Slade leaned back, brooding, her eyes ranging from the ruins which faced her to the long green hollow of the Forum, the fading glow of the church fronts beyond it, and the outlying immensity of the Colosseum. Suddenly she thought: "It's all very well to say that our girls have done away with sentiment and moonlight. But if Babs Ansley isn't out to catch that young aviator—the one who's a Marchese—then I don't know anything. And Jenny has no chance beside her. I know that too. I wonder if that's why Grace Ansley likes the two girls to go everywhere together? My poor Jenny as a foil—!" Mrs. Slade gave a hardly audible laugh, and at the sound Mrs. Ansley droped her knitting.

"Yes—?"

"I—oh, nothing. I was only thinking how your Babs carries everything before her. That Campolieri boy is one of the best matches in Rome. Don't look so innocent, my dear—you know he is. And I was wondering, ever so respectfully, you understand . . . wondering how two such exemplary characters as you and Horace had managed to produce anything quite so dynamic." Mrs. Slade laughed again, with a touch of asperity.

Mrs. Ansley's hands lay inert across her needles. She looked straight out at the great accumulated wreckage of passion and

continued on page 438

continued from page 437

splendor at her feet. But her small profile was almost expression-less. At length she said: "I think you overrate Babs, my dear."

Mrs. Slade's tone grew easier. "No, I don't. I appreciate her. And perhaps envy you. Oh, my girl's perfect; if I were a chronic invalid I'd—well, I think I'd rather be in Jenny's hands. There must be times . . . but there! I always wanted a brilliant daughter . . . and never quite understood why I got an angel instead."

Mrs. Ansley echoed her laugh in a faint murmur. "Babs is an angel too."

"Of course—of course! But she's got rainbow wings. Well, they're wandering by the sea with their young men; and here we sit . . . and it all brings back the past a little too acutely."

Mrs. Ansley had resumed her knitting. One might almost have imagined (if one had known her less well, Mrs. Slade re-flected) that, for her also, too many memories rose from the lengthening shadows of those august ruins. But no; she was sim-ply absorbed in her work. What was there for her to worry about? She knew that Babs would almost certainly come back engaged to the extremely eligible Campolieri. "And she'll sell the New York house, and settle down near them in Rome, and never be in their way . . . she's much too tactful. But she'll have an excellent cook, and just the right people in for bridge and cocktails . . . and a perfectly peaceful old age among her grandchildren."

Mrs. Slade broke off this prophetic flight with a recoil of self-disgust. There was no one of whom she had less right to think unkindly than of Grace Ansley. Would she never cure herself of envying her? Perhaps she had begun too long ago.

She stood up and leaned against the parapet, filling her trou-bled eyes with the tranquilizing magic of the hour. But instead of tranquilizing her the sight seemed to increase her exasperation. Her gaze turned toward the Colosseum. Already its golden flank was drowned in purple shadow, and above it the sky curved crys-tal clear, without light or color. It was the moment when after-noon and evening hang balanced in mid-heaven.

Mrs. Slade turned back and laid her hand on her friend's arm. The gesture was so abrupt that Mrs. Ansley looked up, startled.

"The sun's set. You're not afraid, my dear?"

continued to next page

"Afraid—?"

"Of Roman fever or pneumonia? I remember how ill you were that winter. As a girl you had a very delicate throat, hadn't you?"

"Oh, we're all right up here. Down below, in the Forum, it does get deathly cold, all of a sudden . . . but not here."

"Ah, of course you know because you had to be so careful." Mrs. Slade turned back to the parapet. She thought: "I must make one more effort not to hate her." Aloud she said: "Whenever I look at the Forum from up here, I remember that story about a great-aunt of yours, wasn't she? A dreadfully wicked great-aunt?"

"Oh, yes; great-aunt Harriet. The one who was supposed to have sent her young sister out to the Forum after sunset to gather a night-blooming flower for her album. All our great-aunts and grandmothers used to have albums of dried flowers."

Mrs. Slade nodded. "But she really sent her because they were in love with the same man—"

"Well, that was the family tradition. They said Aunt Harriet confessed it years afterward. At any rate, the poor little sister caught the fever and died. Mother used to frighten us with the story when we were children."

"And you frightened *me* with it, that winter when you and I were here as girls. The winter I was engaged to Delphin."

Mrs. Ansley gave a faint laugh. "Oh, did I? Really frighten you? I don't believe you're easily frightened."

"Not often; but I was then. I was easily frightened because I was too happy. I wonder if you know what that means?"

"I—yes. . . ." Mrs. Ansley faltered.

"Well, I suppose that was why the story of your wicked aunt made such an impression on me. And I thought: 'There's no more Roman fever, but the Forum is deathly cold after sunset—especially after a hot day. And the Colosseum's even colder and damper.'"

"The Colosseum—?"

"Yes. It wasn't easy to get in, after the gates were locked for the night. Far from easy. Still, in those days it could be managed; it *was* managed, often. Lovers met there who couldn't meet elsewhere. You knew that?"

continued on page 440

continued from page 439

"I—I dare say. I don't remember."

"You don't remember? You don't remember going to visit some ruins or other one evening, just after dark, and catching a bad chill? You were supposed to have gone to see the moon rise. People always said that expedition was what caused your illness."

There was a moment's silence; then Mrs. Ansley rejoined: "Did they? It was all so long ago."

"Yes. And you got well again—so it didn't matter. But I suppose it struck your friends—the reason given for your illness, I mean—because everybody knew you were so prudent on account of your throat, and your mother took such care of you. . . . You *had* been out late sight-seeing, hadn't you, that night?"

"Perhaps I had. The most prudent girls aren't always prudent. What made you think of it now?"

Mrs. Slade seemed to have no answer ready. But after a moment she broke out: "Because I simply can't bear it any longer—!"

Mrs. Ansley lifted her head quickly. Her eyes were wide and very pale. "Can't bear what?"

"Why—your not knowing that I've always known why you went."

"Why I went—?"

"Yes. You think I'm bluffing, don't you? Well, you went to meet the man I was engaged to—and I can repeat every word of the letter that took you there."

While Mrs. Slade spoke Mrs. Ansley had risen unsteadily to her feet. Her bag, her knitting and gloves, slid in a panic-stricken heap to the ground. She looked at Mrs. Slade as though she were looking at a ghost.

"No, no—don't," she faltered out.

"Why not? Listen, if you don't believe me. 'My one darling, things can't go on like this. I must see you alone. Come to the Colosseum immediately afer dark tomorrow. There will be somebody to let you in. No one whom you need fear will suspect'— but perhaps you've forgotten what the letter said?"

Mrs. Ansley met the challenge with an unexpected composure. Steadying herself against the chair she looked at her friend, and replied: "No; I know it by heart too."

continued to next page

"And the signature? 'Only *your* D.S.' Was that it? I'm right, am I? That was the letter that took you out that evening after dark."

Mrs. Ansley was still looking at her. It seemed to Mrs. Slade that a slow struggle was going on behind the voluntarily controlled mask of her small quiet face. "I shouldn't have thought she had herself so well in hand," Mrs. Slade reflected, almost resentfully. But at this moment Mrs. Ansley spoke. "I don't know how you knew. I burnt that letter at once."

"Yes; you would, naturally—you're so prudent!" The sneer was open now. "And if you burnt the letter you're wondering how on earth I know what was in it. That's it, isn't it?"

Mrs. Slade waited, but Mrs. Ansley did not speak.

"Well, my dear, I know what was in that letter because I wrote it"

"You wrote it?"

"Yes."

The two women stood for a minute staring at each other in the last golden light. Then Mrs. Ansley dropped back into her chair. "Oh," she murmured, and covered her face with her hands.

Mrs. Slade waited nervously for another word or movement. None came, and at length she broke out: "I horrify you."

Mrs. Ansley's hands dropped to her knee. The face they uncovered was streaked with tears. "I wasn't thinking of you. I was thinking—it was the only letter I ever had from him!"

"And I wrote it. Yes; I wrote it! But I was the girl he was engaged to. Did you happen to remember that?"

Mrs. Ansley's head drooped again. "I'm not trying to excuse myself . . . I remembered. . . ."

"And still you went?"

"Still I went."

Mrs. Slade stood looking down on the small bowed figure at her side. The flame of her wrath had already sunk, and she wondered why she had ever thought there would be any satisfaction in inflicting so purposeless a wound on her friend. But she had to justify herself.

"You do understand? I'd found out—and I hated you, hated you. I knew you were in love with Delphin—and I was afraid; afraid of you, of your quiet ways, your sweetness . . . your . . . well, I wanted you out of the way, that's all. Just for a few weeks;

continued on page 442

continued from page 441

just till I was sure of him. So in a blind fury I wrote that letter . . . I don't know why I'm telling you now."

"I suppose," said Mrs. Ansley slowly, "it's because you've always gone on hating me."

"Perhaps. Or because I wanted to get the whole thing off my mind." She paused. "I'm glad you destroyed the letter. Of course I never thought you'd die."

Mrs. Ansley relapsed into silence, and Mrs. Slade, leaning above her, was conscious of a strange sense of isolation, of being cut off from the warm current of human communion. "You think me a monster!"

"I don't know. . . . It was the only letter I had, and you say he didn't write it?"

"Ah, how you care for him still!"

"I cared for that memory," said Mrs. Ansley.

Mrs. Slade continued to look down at her. She seemed physically reduced by the blow—as if, when she got up, the wind might scatter her like a puff of dust. Mrs. Slade's jealousy suddenly leapt up again at the sight. All these years the woman had been living on that letter. How she must have loved him, to treasure the mere memory of its ashes! The letter of the man her friend was engaged to. Wasn't it she who was the monster?

"You tried your best to get him away from me, didn't you? But you failed; and I kept him. That's all."

"Yes, That's all."

"I wish now I hadn't told you. I'd no idea you'd feel about it as you do; I thought you'd be amused. It all happened so long ago, as you say; and you must do me the justice to remember that I had no reason to think you'd ever taken it seriously. How could I, when you were married to Horace Ansley two months afterward? As soon as you could get out of bed your mother rushed you off to Florence and married you. People were rather surprised—they wondered at its being done so quickly; but I thought I knew. I had an idea you did it out of *pique*—to be able to say you'd got ahead of Delphin and me. Girls have such silly reasons for doing the most serious things. And your marrying so soon convinced me that you'd never really cared."

"Yes. I suppose it would," Mrs. Ansley assented.

continued to next page

The clear heaven overhead was emptied of all its gold. Dusk spread over it, abruptly darkening the Seven Hills. Here and there lights began to twinkle through the foilage at their feet. Steps were coming and going on the deserted terrace—waiters looking out of the doorway at the head of the stairs, then reappearing with trays and napkins and flasks of wine. Tables were moved, chairs straightened. A feeble string of electric lights flickered out. Some vases of faded flowers were carried away, and brought back replenished. A stout lady in a dust coat suddenly appeared, asking in broken Italian if anyone had seen the elastic band which held together her tattered Baedeker. She poked with her stick under the table at which she had lunched, the waiters assisting.

The corner where Mrs. Slade and Mrs. Ansley sat was still shadowy and deserted. For a long time neither of them spoke. At length Mrs. Slade began again: "I suppose I did it as a sort of joke—"

"A joke?"

"Well, girls are ferocious sometimes, you know. Girls in love especially. And I remember laughing to myself all that evening at the idea that you were waiting around there in the dark, dodging out of sight, listening for every sound, trying to get in—Of course I was upset when I heard you were so ill afterward."

Mrs. Ansley had not moved for a long time. But now she turned slowly toward her companion. "But I didn't wait. He'd arranged everything. He was there. We were let in at once," she said.

Mrs. Slade sprang up from her leaning position. "Delphin there? They let you in?—Ah, not you're lying" she burst out with violence.

Mrs. Ansley's voice grew clearer, and full of surprise. "But of course he was there. Naturally he came—"

"Came? How did he know he'd find you there? You must be raving!"

Mrs. Ansley hesitated, as though reflecting. "But I answered the letter. I told him I'd be there. So he came."

Mrs. Slade flung her hands up to her face. "Oh, God—you answered! I never thought of your answering. . . ."

"It's odd you never thought of it, if you wrote the letter."

"Yes. I was blind with rage."

continued on page 444

continued from page 443

Mrs. Ansley rose, and drew her fur scarf about her. "It is cold here. We'd better go. . . . I'm sorry for you," she said, as she clasped the fur about her throat.

The unexpected words sent a pang through Mrs. Slade. "Yes; we'd better go." She gathered up her bag and cloak. "I don't know why you should be sorry for me," she muttered.

Mrs. Ansley stood looking away from her toward the dusky secret mass of the Colosseum. "Well—because I didn't have to wait that night."

Mrs. Slade gave an unquiet laugh. "Yes; I was beaten there. But I oughtn't to begrudge it to you, I suppose. At the end of all these years. After all, I had everything; I had him for twenty-five years. And you had nothing but that one letter that he didn't write."

Mrs. Ansley was again silent. At length she turned toward the door of the terrace. She took a step, and turned back, facing her companion.

"I had Barbara," she said, and began to move ahead of Mrs. Slade toward the stairway.

A BRIEF LIST OF SUGGESTED FILMS

Bladerunner
The Remains of the Day
Six Degrees of Separation
The Hudsucker Proxy
Heavenly Creatures
The Crying Game
Clueless
The Piano
Wild Bill

ASSESS YOUR PAST PERFORMANCE

Just as writing is a recursive process, the continuing journey toward becoming a better writer is a recursive process. As you work through this assignment, continue to **assess** how you think and write, **learn** from your previous experience, and **respond by revising** your personal writing process. Read over your assessment of your performance from your last assignment, and consider your writing strengths and weaknesses. Identify the choice categories with which you had trouble. Did you have trouble with voice? Development? Arrangement? Mechanics? Then analyze why you had trouble, and focus on ways you might better employ the writing process to avoid repeating your mistakes. For example, if the last text you constructed was underdeveloped, think about why. Was it because you didn't consider what your **audience** might need to know? Was it because you didn't sufficiently explore your ideas and gather evidence by **pre-writing?** To improve your performance, you'll have to focus more attention in this assignment on audience analysis and on prewriting and research. Part Six provides detailed strategies for prewriting and process-based revision.

EXPLORE THE WRITING SITUATION

Now that you've been given an assignment, it's time to explore the **choices** and **constraints** of the writing situation. Just as the writers of the responses included in this chapter wrote in the context of particular communities, you'll be writing your response in the context of your classroom community. Listen carefully and thoughtfully to your classmates' emotional and intellectual responses to the primary text. Your agreements and disagreements with their judgments about the meaning of particular elements in the work will help you develop your own interpretive position.

SUBJECT   The subject of your response will be the **primary text,** the short story or film that was assigned by your instructor or chosen by the class community as the focus of your collaborative study. However, since the addition of **research** will almost certainly enhance this project, you may also be responding to a **secondary text,** as Tibbetts does when he builds his argument on his disagreement with Robert Warshow's prediction about the degeneration of Western movies.

AUDIENCE   Your audience should be the other members of your classroom community, so listen carefully to their responses as you collaboratively read the primary text for meaning.

PURPOSE   Although your most obvious general purpose for writing will be to **persuade** your audience that your **interpretation** of the primary text is **credible,** you may also write for additional general purposes. Like Tibbetts, for example, you might **inform** or **explain** as you persuade.

WRITER   Keep in mind that to effectively interpret a work of fiction you have to maintain a balance between **emotional** and **rational** understanding. Often a work of fiction will show you things about yourself and the world that you don't want to see. If you find yourself responding with anger when you initially read a text, analyze why. How might your personal and educational histories have influenced your emotional response? Keep in mind also that your interpretation is just that—an interpretation. Others in the class community are certain to interpret the text differently from the way you interpret it, so expect to have lasting disagreements.

TIME   Consider all the tasks this assignment will require, and budget your time accordingly. First, you'll have to encounter the primary text by reading it for meaning in collaboration with others. How many class (and/or small group) sessions will it take for you to adequately examine the text? Then you may have to expand on your encounter by engaging in research. How long might researching your subject take? Finally, you'll have to construct your response. How long has it taken you to complete other assignments in the course? Considering the discussion and research required, how much longer might it take you to complete this assignment?

READ THE PRIMARY TEXT FOR MEANING

COLLABORATIVE WRITING ASSIGNMENT

Follow the reading for meaning process outlined earlier in this chapter, and explore the meaning of a primary text in collaboration with your classmates.

This collaboration can be done in the classroom or in small study and research groups beyond the classroom. However, if a film is your focus, the collaboration will probably work best if your small group has direct access to a VCR.

Start the collaboration in groups of three or four. Then, after concentrated group work, open the discussion up to full-class conversation. As you work, **annotate** your personal copy of the text by **marking** relevant passages and **noting** their significance in writing (or by taking notes if you're viewing a film). In addition, have one member of your group record your collaborative conclusions or lasting differences in opinion.

PREWRITE

RESEARCH OPPORTUNITY

Expand your perspective on the primary text and on its author or director by consulting sources beyond the community of your class. Do a **library search:** locate and critically read responses to the work you're examining or texts written about its author or director. If you're responding to a film, the *Literature/Film Quarterly* and the *Film Quarterly* are excellent sources. Both of these journals include interpretive essays, as well as film reviews and interviews with directors. If you're responding to a short story, find out more about the author by consulting a biographical dictionary. In addition, if you're focusing on one of the stories included in the anthology in this chapter. *Contemporary Literary Criticism* and *Black Literature Criticism* might be useful. Both provide brief biographies of authors as well as interviews, interpretive essays, and reviews.

Use the following strategies for prewriting:

- **Summarize** the results of your collaborative reading. Start with your analysis of the **emotional points** in the text, and work through **dramatic activity, setting, structure, point of view,** and **tone.** Identify the judgments you made about the meaning of each element. Then explore each judgment by writing nonstop for ten minutes.
- **Test the credibility of your summary** by **rereading** the primary text. As you read, compare your judgments with the passages you annotated as you read for meaning, and look for and mark any supporting evidence you may have missed. In addition, compare your judgments with any additional information you may have gathered by **researching.**
- **Test your collaborators' judgments** by focusing on the passages in the text that support them. In addition, test your collaborators' judgments against any information you've gathered by **researching.** Then explain why you think each judgment is credible or weak.

- **Compare** your collaborators' most credible judgments with your own. Are your own judgments equally credible? Explain why or why not in writing.
- Finally, focus once more on your judgment of the work's **theme.** How is **your judgment** different from the judgments made by your collaborative partners or the writers of **researched sources?** How is your judgment similar? Considering the results of your prewriting so far, is your judgment of theme **credible?** If so, explain in writing why it is. If not, focus once again on character change and reconsider the theme.

FOCUS ON AUDIENCE AND PURPOSE

AUDIENCE   Since you've already discussed the primary text with members of your audience (your classmates), you should have a fairly good idea of your audience's knowledge and concerns. However, there may be people in the community you would particularly like to consider as you draft your text. Perhaps you've had an open disagreement with someone in your class and would like to develop that disagreement (as Tibbetts does when he disagrees with Warshow and Kael). Or you may have agreed with someone but would like to develop that person's judgment in a different direction (as Kobler does when he agrees with Elliott that the bead curtain in "Hills Like White Elephants" is significant). Focus once more on your collaborative partners' judgments. Which partner (or partners) is likely to be most critical of your interpretive judgments? Test the validity of criticisms by exploring in writing the reasons behind those criticisms.

PURPOSE   Although your most obvious **general purpose** for writing will be to **persuade,** what additional purposes might you have? If you've gathered information about the author or director, you might want to **inform** and **explain** as you persuade. The **specific purpose** of your text will be to convince your audience to agree that your message is credible. However, before you can focus on that purpose, you have to decide on a working message.

FOCUS ON A WORKING MESSAGE

In interpretive writing, the writer's message isn't merely an overall judgment about the meaning of the primary text but rather a judgment about *how* the work's meaning is conveyed to the reader. Each of the secondary tests included in this chapter focuses its study on a particular meaningful element in the primary text. Kobler and Elliott all focus on the beaded curtain; Fletcher focuses on the "dichotomous landscape images," and Tibbetts focuses on the portrayal of violence in *Unforgiven*. By focusing on a single element, these writers limited the scope of their interpretive studies. Each of these writers knew that there was no way to fully explore all the meaningful elements in the primary text in a brief response.

To decide on a working message, consider your judgment of the work's theme. Then look over your summary from the "strategies" section of this prewriting exercise. Explore those elements that seem particularly significant to you. For example, have you written extensively about a single repeated detail in language or imagery? After you've explored the possibilities, choose one element upon which to focus your study. Then, in as few words as possible, make a written judgment about the meaning of that element and how that meaning helps to convey the work's overall theme.

DRAFT

DRAFT TO REVISE

The **revision** you engage in as you draft gives you the opportunity to expand on old ideas and formulate new ones. **Read** and **reread** your draft as you write, and look for new ways of viewing your subject. Pay particular attention to those areas that have given you trouble in previous writing assignments, and revise as you draft by **cutting, adding, rearranging, and rewording.**

Your purpose here is to move your audience to agree that your response to the text is credible. However, the only way you'll achieve the credibility necessary to move your audience is by being actively **self-critical.** Before you begin drafting, evaluate the thinking you've done up to this point. Look back over your written responses to the prewriting strategies, and with the message of your response in mind, mark the material from your prewriting that might be likely to get the audience movement you want. Then put critical pressure on the material you've marked. Do you have sufficient, quality evidence to support your interpretive position? Can you anticipate criticism from any members of your class? If self-criticism has revealed any weaknesses in your interpretive position, you may want to choose another element as the focus of your study. If you believe your position can be effectively argued, continue to be self-critical as you draft.

FOCUS ON YOUR CHOICES

VOICE   The persona you create on the page will help to establish your credibility with your audience. Consider the context of your class community. What kind of created persona is your audience likely to find most credible? Look back over your judgments about the voices in the responses included in this chapter. Which responses did you and your collaborative partners find most readable? Which did you find least readable, and why? Although you may be tempted to imitate the voice of one of these writers, keep in mind that they were writing to communities quite different from your class community. Your goal in creating an appropriate voice isn't to sound "professorial" but instead to establish your credibility with the particular audience for whom you're writing.

With your audience in mind, write a detailed description (or draw a detailed picture) of the voice you believe will most likely achieve your writer's purpose. Then, as you draft, read your emerging text aloud, and **reword** with your audience's responses in mind.

DEVELOPMENT   As you read and reread, look also for ways to **cut** and **add** developmental material. Clarify your ideas by cutting material that might lead your audience away from your focus. In addition, put pressure on your interpretive points, and look for ways to expand your emerging position by adding. Consider that the developmental material contained in interpretive writing falls into three main categories. First, (and most important) there are the writer's evidence-supported judgments about the meaning of elements in the primary text. Second, there are the writer's agreements and disagreements with others' interpretations. And third, there is material gathered from additional research sources (interviews, drafts of the primary text, biographical or historical studies). Although your own judgments about the meaning of the text are most important here, those judgments will be strengthened if you incorporate others' responses and additional research into your argument. Think critically as you draft, and look for ways to connect your responses with the responses of others and with additional research sources you may have encountered. For example, if you disagreed with a classmate during discussion, you might use that disagreement as a starting place to build or amend a point in your argument. Likewise, if you've read an interview with the author or director of the primary text, consider ways in which material in the interview might support or undercut your position.

ARRANGEMENT   As you make choices in arrangement, consider what your audience needs to know to easily follow you argument. For example, the responses in this chapter to "Hills Like White Elephants" all begin with a clear presentation of the writers' interpretive positions. Then they all go on to trace the deepening meaning of a particular element in the story. They don't follow a similar arrangement pattern because there's a rule that dictates they must but rather because there's a logic to that arrangement pattern. Simply put, it's easier for an audience to follow an argument if they first know what direction that argument will take.

As you draft, **rearrange** the order of sentences, paragraphs, or sections of your text with your audience response in mind. If you draft on the computer, use the block and move functions to rearrange. If you type or draft longhand, write on only one side of the page so that you can cut sections apart and rearrange them.

REWRITE

To effectively interpret a work of fiction, you have to maintain a balance between emotional and rational understanding. Ultimately, your personal interaction with the text is what breathes life into it and makes it relevant to your life. However, to share your interpretation with others you'll have to convince them that the meaning you take from the text is credible. Test your draft by **workshopping** it with one or more partners. The Part Six section provides detailed strategies for peer editing and workshops. Ask your workshop partners to read your response carefully and to identify the message that defines the focus of your interpretation. Then ask them to be as critical as possible of your interpretive points and the evidence that supports those points.

ACTIVE REVISING

The key word here is *active*. Don't just make cosmetic changes in usage. Consider your workshop partners' criticism, your performance in previous assignments, and the techniques for responding to fiction and film. Try to put yourself in your audience's position as you read your text critically and revise. Read your response critically, focusing on the following checklist, and continue to **cut, add, rearrange,** and **reword** with your audience's responses in mind.

- Considering your audience's knowledge and perspective, are they likely to find your created voice appealing and credible?

- Do you have a clearly discernible message that focuses on *how* the meaning of the primary text is conveyed to the reader?
- Do your argumentative points relate to your message?
- Do you have sufficient critically tested, credible evidence to support each interpretive point that you make?
- Is your argument arranged in a way that makes it logical and easy to follow?
- Are your references to and quotations from the primary text accurate?
- If you cited outside sources, did you document them properly?
- Is your text correct in terms of mechanics (spelling, punctuation, sentence structure, and diction)?

EDIT TO FINAL FORM

Polish your text as you write the final draft. Focus on paragraphing, transitions, and any habitual problems you may have with spelling, punctuation, and sentence structure. See Part Six for specific information and strategies.

PROOFREAD

If possible, put your response aside for at least a couple of hours before you proofread. Proofread for small careless errors by reading your text aloud, preferably to another person.

THINK CRITICALLY ABOUT YOUR PERFORMANCE

The writing process isn't completed until you've analyzed your performance. Study your evaluator's comments, and focus on **voice, development, arrangement,** and **mechanics.** Part Six of this book provides detailed strategies for analyzing your writing weaknesses and learning through self-criticism. With which category did you mainly have trouble? Write a page explaining why you think you had trouble with that particular category. Then write a second page in which you explain what you might have done to correct the problem.

PART FIVE

STRATEGIES FOR WRITING IN THE ACADEMIC COMMUNITY

CHAPTER TWELVE

WRITING THE RESEARCH PAPER

THE WRITER'S SCENARIO

You, the writer, encounter any one of the Responsive Writing Assignments (or a writing assignment in another college class). The assignment you encounter might be a response to a work of fiction or a film, or it might be a response to a process or even a personal experience. As you explore the writing situation, you discover either that research is required or that you have unanswered questions. You may have begun to formulate opinions or ideas about the subject you're responding to, but a little voice in your head keeps telling you that your amorphous ideas might not be all that credible. On the other hand, you may be certain that your point of view makes sense, but your certainty is based on intuition or on personal experience, neither of which you believe to be particularly compelling to your instructor or classmates.

After thinking for a while, you decide that your present knowledge and experience aren't enough to answer your nagging questions or to confirm (or deny) your intuitive insights. To know enough to be credible to yourself or others, you have to reach beyond yourself; you have to engage in research.

SOME CONSIDERATIONS

CONSIDER TIME CONSTRAINTS.   Like other kinds of detective work, researching takes time. You'll have to sort through a great deal of information that's not relevant to find the pertinent information that will help you complete your project. So budget at least three times the amount of time it would normally take you to write a paper that doesn't include research.

PREWRITING WILL BE EXTENDED AND INTERRUPTED.   When you're writing a paper that involves research, the prewriting process will be extended because you'll be reaching beyond yourself to gather and evaluate information. Although you should spend much of your time actually writing, the time you spend with pen and paper or at the

---

COMPUTER TIP

Recording notes in a computer file can make drafting your text easier because you can work directly from your notes, rather than recopying them.

---

computer will be interrupted by trips out to talk with a **mentor** or expeditions to engage in **primary** or **secondary** research.

KEEP A RESEARCH JOURNAL.   Although note cards are a traditional way of recording the results of research, a good way to organize your project is by keeping a **research journal,** either in a notebook or in a computer file. A computer file is particularly useful for researching; in addition to using the file for prewriting, you can use it as a place to record your research notes.

PREWRITE TO EXPLORE
WHAT YOU KNOW AND BELIEVE

CONSIDER CONTEXT

When you write in the academic setting, you're usually *responding* to a subject you've encountered in the context of a class, so you're not starting the research process from ground zero. For example, if you're researching sexual assault on college campuses for a response to Paul Keegan's essay "Dangerous Parties" (Chapter Ten), you'll already know something about the subject from reading Keegan's essay; you may know additional things about the subject from some other source. Similarly, if you're researching Helmut Kohl for a paper you're writing in a class about contemporary Europe, you'll already know something about German politics.

FORMULATE A WORKING HYPOTHESIS

The *amount* you know about your subject will determine the initial steps you take to begin actively researching. If you already know a substantial amount about your subject at the start, you may be able to begin by formulating a **working hypothesis,** an **essential question** or **judgment** about your subject that will focus and guide your research. If your working hypothesis is a judgment, it may turn out to be the **message** of your finished text; if your working hypothesis is a question, the answer to it may turn out to be the message of your completed text. On the other hand, if you know little about your subject, you may have to do some preliminary research (**critical reading** or **interviewing**) before you formulate a working hypothesis. To decide if you're ready to formulate a working hypothesis, consider the following strategies.

1. Use one of the prewriting strategies from Part Six to explore what you know about the subject you've decided to research. Keep focused on factual information, and write until you've exhausted your knowledge of the subject.
2. Then use the same strategy to explore what you believe about the subject. Try to come up with at least one supporting reason or bit of evidence for each belief you record.
3. When you've run out of things to write, go back and evaluate what you've gotten down so far. Reread your prewriting carefully and slowly.
4. Formulate as many questions as you can about each bit of information and each belief that you've recorded.

At this point you may be ready to formulate a **working hypothesis,** an **essential question** or **judgment** about your subject that will focus and guide your research. However, keep in mind that the hypothesis you formulate is only a *working* one; expect to amend or change it completely as you learn more about your subject.

FORMULATE A WORKING HYPOTHESIS

Focus on a single aspect of the subject
Pose a question (hypothesis as question)
Consider evidence
Tentatively answer the question (hypothesis as judgment)

If you were responding to Paul Keegan's essay, for example, the single aspect you focus on might be the relationship between alcohol use and sexual assault on your campus—a general relationship Keegan refers to in paragraph five of his essay. The next step would be to pose a question about your narrowed subject, which in this case might be "Is alcohol use a significant factor in cases of sexual assault on our campus?" Then you would consider the evidence you've already explored by prewriting. If your prewriting doesn't suggest that you can answer the question at this point, your working hypothesis might be the **question** you've posed. However, if your prewriting suggests a **tentative answer** to the question, your working hypothesis would either be the **judgment** "Alcohol is a significant factor in cases of sexual assault on our campus" or the **judgment** "Alcohol is not a significant factor in cases of sexual assault on our campus."

RESEARCH TO INCREASE YOUR KNOWLEDGE AND UNDERSTANDING

CONFIRM OR DENY BY INTERVIEWING A MENTOR   Interviewing a credible expert is an efficient way of confirming or denying your initial questions or judgments about your subject. In addition, a credible expert can function as **research mentor** who will point you toward other credible sources—pertinent written texts or other experts. Your college's schedule of classes and the campus phone directory can help you find credible experts on campus. Off-campus experts can be found by consulting your city or regional phone directory.

If your subject is a controversial one, it's best to find two mentors with opposing viewpoints. Getting the viewpoints and an overview of the kinds of evidence that support those viewpoints can help you decide what you think about the subject, and it can also be an introduction to the exciting and sometimes blistering dialogue that is a part of most social and academic controversies. Often a subject that may seem not to be controversial is in fact a focus of hot debate. As part of your interview, it's a good idea to ask your mentor if the subject is a controversial one. For example, although you may not initially think sexual assault on campus is a controversial issue, you will probably find people with "expert" status on your campus who have deep disagreements about its causes or even its existence.

Come to the interview with your mentor prepared with your working hypothesis and the reasons and evidence you have for believing that your hypothesis is worth pursuing.

CONTINUE PREWRITING   Follow the suggestions for **interviewing** in the "Primary Research" chapter, and write up the results of your research in your **journal.** What has been confirmed? What has been denied? What evidence did your mentor supply to either confirm or deny? **Reevaluate** your **working hypothesis** by continuing your **prewriting.** If it seems no longer viable, consider a new focus. If it seems worth pursuing, return to your mentor for further conversation and advice about possible sources.

LOCATE PERTINENT SOURCES   You'll use the information you gather from secondary sources either to **inform** your audience about the your focused subject or as **evidence** to **support a persuasive hypothesis.** Keep these two essential purposes in mind as you proceed to locate, evaluate, and use research sources.

   With your hypothesis and what you've learned so far in mind, **brainstorm** a list of possible sources. (See Part Six for an explanation of brainstorming.) Consider the types of sources defined in the **primary** and **secondary** research chapters (Chapter Four and Chapter Five) of this book. The types of research that you engage in will depend to a large degree on your subject and on your hypothesis. Some subjects may demand mainly secondary research. For example, if you're researching to enhance a written response to Hemingway's "Hills Like White Elephants" and there is no Hemingway expert on your campus, you'll mainly engage in secondary research. On the other hand, some subjects may demand mainly primary research; if you're writing about sexual assault on your campus, the focus will be a local one, and you'll mainly engage in primary research by **interviewing** or by developing a **questionnaire.**

FINDING SECONDARY SOURCES   **Use the Card or Computerized Catalogue to Locate Pertinent Sources.** Although some libraries still use card catalogues that contain index cards listing all holdings, many libraries have converted to computerized systems. In a computerized system you gain access to the library's catalogue through a computer terminal. In a card catalogue every item in the library has at least three cards—a **subject** card, an **author** card, and a **title** card.

COMPUTER TIP

Computerized cataloging systems contain more information than print ones. Most computerized systems will tell you how many copies of the source are in the library and whether the source is currently available.

SUBJECT CARD

813.52 H488Zbe2	**HEMINGWAY, ERNEST** Benson, Jackson J., ed. New Critical Approaches to the Short Stories of Ernest Hemingway. – Durham: Duke University Press, c1990.

AUTHOR CARD

813.52 H488Zbe2	**Benson, Jackson J., ed.** New Critical Approaches to the Short Stories of Ernest Hemingway. – Durham: Duke University Press, c1990.

TITLE CARD

**New Critical Approaches to the Short Stories
of Ernest Hemingway**

813.52
H488Zbe2

> **Benson, Jackson J., ed.**
>
> New Critical Approaches to the Short
> Stories of Ernest Hemingway. –
> Durham: Duke University Press, c1990.

COMPUTER TIP

Computerized systems will give you the same kinds of information with less legwork, because while sitting at a computer terminal you can access information about several sources at one

continued to next page

> time. Most computerized catalogues will do **key word** searches as well as **subject, author,** and **title** searches. In addition, many computerized catalogues are connected to catalogues at other libraries, and most will print out a list of the sources you choose to investigate further.

Know Your Library's Particular Cataloguing System to Locate Sources in the Building. If your library uses the Dewey Decimal System, items will be categorized and housed according to the following numerical divisions:

Dewey Decimal System

000	General Works
100	Philosophy and Related Disciplines
200	Religion
300	Social Sciences
400	Language
500	Pure Sciences
600	Technology
700	The Arts
800	Literature
900	General Geography and History

If your library uses the Library of Congress Classification System, items will be categorized and housed according to the following divisions:

Library of Congress Classification System

A	General Works
B	Philosphy and Religion
C	Auxiliary Sciences of History
D	History: General and Old World
E–F	History: America
G	Geography. Maps. Anthropology
H–HJ	Economics and Business
HM–HX	Sociology
J	Political Science
K	Law (General)
L	Education
M	Music

N	Fine Arts
P	Language and Literature
Q	Science
R	Medicine
S	Agriculture
T	Technology
U	Military Science
V	Naval Science
Z	Bibliography. Library Science

Evaluating Secondary Sources

Secondary sources can be useful in different ways. First, they can supply you with information that is **pertinent** to your hypothesis—information that will either directly **inform** your audience about your subject or **support** or **oppose** your hypothesis. Second, secondary sources can supply you with **background information** that can help you understand the context of your subject. Finally, secondary sources can lead you to additional pertinent sources. To evaluate the usefulness of secondary sources, consider the following strategies (see also the secondary research chapter).

1. ***Read the table of contents and index with your subject and hypothesis in mind.*** A source's table of contents and index can point you toward pertinent and background information contained within the source itself. However, a source's table of contents and index can also lead you to additional sources. For example, an exploratory reading of the table of contents of Benson's *New Critical Approaches to the Short Stories of Ernest Hemingway* not only tells us that the book contains an article about ''Hills Like White Elephants,'' but it also tells us that the book contains a comprehensive checklist of texts written about Hemingway's work.

2. ***Search for the most current sources.*** Although in some fields only the most current information will be useful, there are many fields in which older sources are still pertinent. However, even in fields where older sources are still useful, finding the most current sources can help you understand your subject more thoroughly by letting you see how the conversation about your subject is unfolding in the field. For example, many of the responses to Ernest Hemingway's short story ''Hills Like White Elephants'' included in Chapter Eleven (''Responding to Fiction and Film'') contain references to other writers' interpretations. These references are evidence that the writers have kept up with and are actively participating in the ongoing conversation about Hemingway's work and this particular story.

3. ***Test credibility by noting citations.*** In every field there are people who have greater status than others. This status is usually

marked by greater productivity. The more knowledge and experience a person has in a field, the more likely you are to come across his or her name in catalogues, bibliographical material, and citations. As you explore sources for their usefulness, look for names that are repeated again and again. Then locate and explore the sources authored by these recognized experts.

Locating and Evaluating Primary Sources

Since the primary research you engage in will be self-directed, locating and evaluating sources is something you'll do simultaneously. Locate subjects for **interviews** by consulting your college catalogue and the campus and local phone directories. In addition, ask interview subjects to suggest additional sources. To decide on **observation** sites and on groups of subjects for **questionnaires,** consider your hypothesis and choose a site or group that can provide you with pertinent information.

GATHER AND ANALYZE THE RESULTS OF YOUR RESEARCH

Use the copying machine in your library to duplicate pertinent material from secondary sources so that you can mark and annotate each text. Record the full bibliographical information for secondary sources (call number, author, editor, title, date, publisher, and place of publication) at the top of each duplicated text.

Similarly, record the full biographical information for primary sources in your research notes (name and title of interview subject, description of questionnaire subject group or observation site, date and time of research contact).

As you analyze the results of your primary research or intensively read secondary sources, focus on the information in your sources that will either **inform** your audience about the focus of your subject or provide evidence to **support** your persuasive position. However, keep in mind that you can't ignore information that opposes your point of view. Since opposing information might undercut the credibility of your text, it must be analyzed and dealt with.

PRIMARY SOURCES

CONTINUE PREWRITING.   After following the suggestions for engaging in **primary research** in Chapter Five, "Primary Research," write up the results of your research in your **journal.** What additional **information** have you gathered about your subject? What has been **confirmed?** What has been **denied?** What evidence did your subjects supply to either confirm or deny? **Reevaluate** your **working hypothesis** and add to your emerging text by continuing your **prewriting.**

SECONDARY SOURCES

READ SECONDARY SOURCES CRITICALLY.   Once you've evaluated the usefulness of secondary sources, you'll be ready to read them intensively. If the source you're reading is persuasive or interpretive rather than purely informational, begin by following the critical reading model laid out in Chapter Two:

Preread
Reread the Text Carefully
Research Unknowns
Analyze the Speaker
    Facts
    Emotions
    Attitudes
Determine the Message
Determine the Audience
Determine the Purpose

As you read the text critically (or if the text is purely informational), consider the following annotative strategies:

1. **Circle unknowns,** and record the results of your research in the margins of the text.
2. **Bracket** and mark with an "A" or a "D" material that you **agree** or **disagree** with.
3. **Underline** material that you may want to **quote** or **paraphrase.**

CONTINUE PREWRITING.   After you've critically read each source, continue your prewriting by **recording** and **analyzing** the results of your research in your **journal.** What additional information have you gathered about your subject? What has been **confirmed?** What has been **denied?** What evidence did your source supply to either confirm or deny? **Reevaluate** your **working hypothesis,** and revise it if necessary. Then formulate a **working message.** Your working message will likely be your **revised hypothesis,** or a more focused version of it.

DRAFTING

To ensure that the text you create is your own, rather than a compilation of other people's ideas and opinions, it's a good idea to begin by writing a draft that doesn't contain any material from **secondary** sources. Writing an initial draft without including material from secondary sources will allow you to think independently and is more likely to lead you to new insights about the subject of your research. In addition, writing a draft of this kind will help you avoid **plagiarism.**

Consider the choices and constraints of the writing situations (subject, audience, writer, and purpose) before you begin your initial draft. If you're responding to one of the Responsive Writing Assignments in this book, follow the instructions for drafting and revising in the relevant chapter, and focus on choices in **voice, development,** and **arrangement.**

Although many instructors prefer a distant, formal voice for research papers, the particular writing situation may allow you to write in a personal voice, as student writer Lance Hummel does in his researched response to Emma Goldman's essay "Marriage and Love."

The developmental material in your initial draft should all in some way relate to your working message; it should include your own judgments or interpretations and any supportive evidence you've gathered from **primary research activities** (interviews, questionnaires, observations, and the critical reading of primary texts).

How you choose to arrange the material in your text will depend to a large degree on the choices and constraints of the writing situation. For more detailed strategies for arrangement, consult the appropriate Responsive Writing Assignments and Part Six.

AVOIDING PLAGIARISM

Plagiarism occurs when a writer appropriates and passes off as his or her own the ideas or writings of someone else. Intentional plagiarism is stealing. In the academic and professional writing communities, passing off someone else's intellectual or creative property as your own is an actionable offense. Similarly, at most colleges acts of intentional plagiarism are severely punished. A student who plagiarizes might receive a failing grade for the plagiarized paper or for the class in which the act of plagiarism took place. Or he or she might even be expelled from the college altogether.

Some student plagiarism is inadvertent. Often, beginning researchers unintentionally plagiarize because they're unfamiliar with the **conventions** of **documentation.** However, even students who inadvertently plagiarize by failing to properly acknowledge sources can be subject to disciplinary action. To ensure that you properly document sources, consider the section that follows. As you study the conventions, keep in mind that their purpose is an ethical one; the conventions exist to protect the integrity of individuals' ideas. Everything you take from a source that isn't

common knowledge (factual information found in many sources) should be documented.

USING AND DOCUMENTING SOURCES

QUOTING MATERIAL   Put quotation marks around passages, sentences, or groups of words shorter than four lines long that you quote from a source. However, quote material *sparingly*—only when you think the language of the quotation is particularly pertinent. Your goal is to use material from outside sources to *support* your own judgements, so quoted (or paraphrased) material shouldn't make up the bulk of your text.

PUNCTUATING QUOTED MATERIAL

If you quote a whole sentence from a source but integrate it into a sentence of your own, don't start the quoted sentence with a capital letter, but do bracket the letter that had been capitalized:

> John Tibbetts argues that "[t]he casting of Eastwood, Gene Hackman, and Richard Harris does indeed exploit their reputation for macho violence, but it's a resonance that also conveys a profound rejection (or at least reconsideration) of that reputation."

If you quote a whole sentence but separate it from the rest of the sentence with an introductory or concluding phrase, begin the quoted sentence with a capital letter and separate it from the rest of the sentence with a comma or a colon:

> John Tibbetts says, "The casting of Eastwood, Gene Hackman, and Richard Harris does indeed exploit their reputation for macho violence, but it's a resonance that also conveys a profound rejection (or at least reconsideration) of that reputation."

INDENT QUOTED MATERIAL MORE THAN FOUR LINES LONG. To avoid confusing your readers about what is quoted and what is your own, indent and single space long quoted passages. Notice the use of a colon in the following example.

> After appealing to the emotions of his audience in the first three paragraphs of his essay, in paragraph four Koch skillfully establishes his credibility as an experienced and thoughtful public servant:
>
> > As a district leader, councilman, congressmen, and mayor, I have represented constituencies generally thought of as liberal.

Because I support the death penalty for heinous crimes of murder, I have sometimes been the subject of emotional and outraged attacks by voters who find my position reprehensible or worse. I have listened to their ideas. I have weighed their objections carefully. I still support the death penalty.

USE ELLIPSIS POINTS TO SIGNAL DELETIONS.   To avoid being accused of quoting a source out of context, signal any deletions with ellipsis points (three periods with a space between each).

USE BRACKETS TO SIGNAL ADDITIONS OR CHANGES.   If you change or add language to a quotation to make it fit into a sentence of your own, signal the addition or change by bracketing it:

> Koch argues that "no other democracy . . . [is] plagued by a murder rate such as that in the United States."

USE SINGLE QUOTATION MARKS TO SET OFF A QUOTATION WITHIN A QUOTATION.

> Steele points out that "it is no crime to just 'hold on,' and it is hardly a practice limited to blacks."

PARAPHRASING MATERIAL

When you paraphrase, you put into *your own words* ideas or information from a source. To paraphase correctly you have to *accurately communicate* someone else's ideas, but you have to do it *without using* his or her *language.* To paraphrase correctly, follow the structure of the passage, but use your own language.

Original   On the contrary, it can easily be demonstrated that the death penalty strengthens the value of human life. If the penalty for rape were lowered, clearly it would signal a lessened regard for the victims' suffering, humiliation, and personal integrity. It would cheapen their horrible experience, and expose them to an increased danger of occurrence.

Paraphrase   Koch argues that capital punishment increases society's reverence for life, rather than diminishing it. To support his argument he uses rape as an example, claiming that punishing rapists less severely would indicate a lower level of respect for rape victims' pain. Decreasing the punishment for rape would make the victims' ordeal seem less consequential and would also increase their chances of being raped again.

STYLES OF DOCUMENTATION

In recent years styles of documentation have been simplified. The Modern Language Association **(MLA),** the American Psychological Association **(APA),** and most professional organizations in the sciences advocate parenthetical methods of acknowledging sources, where citations keyed to a list of works cited are placed in parentheses in the text. Although the documentation styles of different professional organizations differ, all include the **author,** the **title** of the work, the **publisher,** the **date** and **place** of publication, and the relevant **page number(s).**

The MLA style is used mainly in the humanities, and the APA style is used mainly in the social sciences. Each of the sciences has its own style, so if you're writing in a science class it's best to ask your instructor about the appropriate style of documentation. However, I will include here the style recommended in the *CBE Style Manual*, the publication manual of the American Council of Biology Editors.

For more information about documentation in particular disciplines, consult the **MLA Handbook for Writers of Research Papers,** Fourth Edition (1995), the **Publication Manual of the American Psychological Association,** Fourth Edition (1995), or the **CBE Style Manual,** revised Fifth Edition (1983).

CONVENTIONS FOR CITATIONS IN THE TEXT

The MLA and APA styles are similar but not identical. The following examples illustrate how to document a source when the author's name isn't used in the text.

MLA   Whaley's work has been described as "technically brilliant and intellectually elegant" (Gadbow 78).

APA   Whaley's work has been described as "technically brilliant and intellectually elegant" (Gadbow, 1990, p. 78).

You can see that the two styles supply basically the same information. The MLA style is more economical, containing only the author's name and the relevant page number. The APA style adds the date of publication and "p." before the relevant page number, and also uses commas to separate the author, date, and page number.

However, the CBE style is a bit different. Rather than citing the author's name in the text, the CBE style uses numbers that refer to a sequentially ordered list of cited works. If you were using the CBE style, you'd place a number one in parentheses after the first source you cited, a number two after the second, and so on. Then any time you referred to the same source again, you would repeat the originally assigned number.

CBE   Whaley's work has been described as "technically brilliant and in-
        tellectually elegant" (2).

The "2" in the above example would mean that the source being quoted was the second new source quoted in the text and would also refer to that source's position on the list of works cited at the end of the text.

However, if you use the author's name in the text, you would document in the following ways:

MLA   Gadbow describes Whaley's work as "technically brilliant and in-
        tellectually elegant" (78).
APA   Gadbow describes Whaley's work as "technically brilliant and in-
        tellectually elegant" (1990, p. 78).
CBE   Gadbow describes Whaley's work as "technically brilliant and in-
        tellectually elegant" (2).

If the source has more than one author, the MLA style uses the names of all the authors, unless there are more than three. If there are more than three, cite only the first author's name followed by *et al.* The APA style cites all the authors the first time the source is referred to, but only the first author's name plus *et al.* for later references. Since the CBE style of citation lists sources sequentially, a source with more than one author would be cited the same way as a source with a single author.

MLA   Scientific studies can be inaccurate because "the expectations of
        the observers often lead them to a biased reading of the data"
        (Prange, Goedicke, and Barrett 24).
APA   Scientific studies can be inaccurate because "the expectations of
        the observers often lead them to a biased reading of the data"
        (Prange et al., 1988, p. 24).
CBE   Scientific studies can be inaccurate because "the expectations of
        the observers often lead them to a biased reading of the data" (4).

When the names of the authors are used in the text, the MLA style cites only the relevant page number, but the APA style cites the date immediately following the authors' names and the page number immediately following the quoted or paraphrased information. The less-complicated CBE style cites the source's sequential number immediately following the authors' names.

MLA   In their discussion of inaccuracy in scientific studies, Prange, Goedicke, and Barrett state that "the expectations of the observers often lead them to a biased reading of the data" (24).

APA   In their discussion of inaccuracy in scientific studies, Prange, Goedicke, and Barrett (1988) state that "the expectations of the observers often lead them to a biased reading of the data" (p. 24).

CBE   In their discussion of inaccuracy in scientific studies, Prange, Goedicke, and Barrett (4) state that "the expectations of the observers often lead them to a biased reading of the data."

If you cite two or more sources by the same author or authors when using the MLA style, place a shortened form of the title before the page number. If you're following the APA style and you encounter multiple sources with the same author and date of publication, place a lowercase letter after the date. If you're following the CBE style, with its sequential form of documentation, just place the number of the source immediately after the quoted material or the name of the author, as shown above.

MLA   In their discussion of inaccuracy in scientific studies, Prange, Goedicke, and Barrett state that "the expectations of the observers often lead them to a biased reading of the data" (*Methods* 24).

APA   In their discussion of inaccuracy in scientific studies, Prange, Goedicke, and Barrett state that "the expectations of the observers often lead them to a biased reading of the data" (Prange et al., 1988a, p. 24).

If you quote material that is itself quoted in one of your sources, acknowledge the author(s) of the quotation in your text, but cite the source that quoted the material.

MLA   Patterson said that "the short story may be the greatest of all literary genres, but you can't get rich writing them" (qtd. in McNamer 11).

APA   Patterson said that "the short story may be the greatest of all literary genres, but you can't get rich writing them" (cited in McNamer 11).

CONVENTIONS FOR LISTS OF SOURCES

All styles of documentation include a list of the sources cited in the text. However, just what this list is called differs from one style of documentation to another. If you're following the MLA style, you'll title your list

"Works Cited"; if you're following APA style, the title of your list will be "References"; the CBE recommends "Literature Cited" or "References Cited." CBE reference lists are ordered sequentially, with the sources listed in the order they appear in the text. MLA and APA lists are alphabetically arranged. Keep in mind that only sources you have used and acknowledged in your text should be in your list of cited sources.

BOOKS

By One Author

MLA   Gadbow, Kathleen. *Cutbank Creek*. New York: Harper, 1995.
APA   Gadbow, K. (1995). *Cutbank creek*. New York: HarperCollins.
CBE   2. Gadbow, K. Cutbank creek. New York: HarperCollins; 1995: 38–40.

By More Than One Author

MLA   Prange, Marnie A., Patricia Goedicke, and Sharon Barrett. *Research Methodology*. New York: Macmillan, 1988.
APA   Prange, M.A., Goedicke, P., & Barrett, S. (1988). *Research methodology*. New York Macmillan.
CBE   1. Prange, M. A.; Goedicke, P; Barrett, S. Research methodology. New York: Macmillan; 1988: 24.

By an Unknown Author

MLA   *American Heritage College Dictionary*. 3rd ed. Boston: Houghton Mifflin, 1993.
APA   *American heritage college dictionary* (3rd ed.). (1993). Boston: Houghton Mifflin.
CBE   3. American heritage college dictionary. Boston: Houghton Mifflin; 1993: 280.

Edited, Rather Than Authored

MLA   Benson, Jackson J., ed. *New Critical Approaches to the Short Stories of Ernest Hemingway*. Durham, NC: Duke, 1990.
APA   Benson, J. J. (Ed.). (1990). *New critical approaches to the short stories of Ernest Hemingway*. Durham, NC: Duke University Press.
CBE   4. Benson, J. J. New critical approaches to the short stories of Ernest Hemingway. Durham, NC: Duke University Press; 1990: 158–9.

By an Association or Agency

MLA   Association for the Study of the Gray Wolf. *A Report on the Gray Wolf Population in Northern Montana*. New York: Augsberg, 1993.

APA   Association for the Study of the Gray Wolf. (1993). *A report on the gray wolf population in northern Montana*. New York: Augsberg Publishing.

CBE   5. Association for the Study of the Gray Wolf. A report on the gray wolf population in northern Montana. New York: Augsberg Publishing; 1993: 251–2.

In an Anthology

MLA   Henley, Patricia. "The Secret of Cartwheels." *Best American Short Stories 1990*. Ed. Richard Ford. Boston: Houghton Mifflin, 1990. 84–97.

APA   Henley, P. (1990). The secret of cartwheels. In R. Ford (ed.), *Best American short stories 1990* (pp. 84–97). Boston: Houghton Mifflin.

ARTICLES

From a Magazine

MLA   McCarthy, Michael. "The Luncheon Menu." *American Life* 8 January 1995: 6, 9.

APA   McCarthy, M. (1995, January 8). The luncheon menu. *American Life*, 6, 9.

CBE   1. McCarthy, M. The luncheon menu. Am. Life. 8 Jan: 6, 9; 1995.

From a Newspaper

MLA   Franz, Michael. "Mountain Flying Proves Hazardous." *Stevensburg Standard* 8 June 1994: 1, 8.

APA   Franz, M. (1994, June 8). Mountain flying proves hazardous. *The Stevensburg Standard*, pp. 1, 8.

CBE   7. Franz, M. Mountain flying proves hazardous. Stevensburg Standard. 8 June: 1, 8; 1994.

From a Scholarly Journal

MLA   Man, Glenn K. S. "The Third Man: Pulp Fiction and Art Film." *Film Literature Quarterly* 21 (1993): 171–77.

APA   Man, G. K. S. (1993) The Third Man: Pulp fiction and art film. *Film Literature Quarterly, 21,* 171–177.

CBE   1. Man, G. K. S. The Third Man: pulp fiction and art film. Film Lit. 21: 171–177; 1993.

With an Unknown Author

MLA   "Plane Crash in Boston." *New York Times* 17 Feb. 1995, sec. 1: 1.

APA   Plane crash in Boston. (1995, Feb. 17). *The New York Times,* section 1, p. 1.

CBE   4. Plane crash in Boston. New York Times. 17 Feb: sec. 1, 8; 1995.

An Editorial

MLA   "Education in Crisis." Editorial. *Newark News* 21 July 1994, pt. 2: 4.

APA   Education in crisis. (1994, July 21). (Editorial). *Newark News,* part 2, p. 4.

CBE   3. Education in crisis. Editorial, Newark News. 21 July: pt. 2, 4; 1994.

A Review

MLA   Park, Mary. "The Quest for Goodness." Rev. of *John Limon: Reckless Imposter,* by Rhian Ellis. *Widestate Review* 51. (1993): 303–05.

APA   Park, M. (1993). The quest for goodness. [Review of the book *John Limon: Reckless imposter*] *Widestate Review, 51,* pp. 303–305.

ELECTRONIC SOURCES   When you document electronic sources, in addition to author, title, and publication information, you also include the name of the electronic source and (when you use MLA documentation style) the date you accessed the information.

From a Computer Service

MLA   Fredrickson, Alicia. "Guilds Return to Rural America." *New York Times* 14 Feb. 1996: *New York Times Online.* Online. Nexis. 9 May 1996.

APA   Fredrickson, A. (1996, Feb. 14). *New York Times* [On-line]. Available: Nexis.

Through a Computer Network

Your entry for a source accessed through a computer network should include the document's number of pages or paragraphs. If you're using

MLA style and no number is given, write "n. pag." ("no pagination") after the publication information.

MLA Baldwin, Norma "Ghosts in Cyberspace." *NetJournal* 2.4 (10 Aug. 1995): 10 pp. Online. Internet. 23 Sept. 1995.

Brosman, Michael. "The Lusitania Revisited." *Counter Forum* 1.3 (1994): n. pag. Online. Internet. 10 May 1995.

APA Brosman, M. (1994). The Lusitania revisited. *Counter Forum* [On-line], *1.3*. Available: Internet.

An Electronic Text

A great many works of literature as well as government documents and other texts can be accessed on the Internet. However, anyone with the appropriate technology can put anything on the Internet, so it's important to make sure that the material you access is reliable by checking documentation or asking your instructor.

MLA Hardy, Thomas. *Far from the Madding Crowd*. Ed. Ronald Blythe. Harmondsworth: Penguin, 1978. Online. Oxford Text Archive. Internet. 5 Oct. 1995.

APA National Institute of Mental Health. (1995). *Clinical treatment in bi-polar disorder* [On-line]. Available: Internet.

OTHER SOURCES

Interviews

MLA Zapf, Nancy. "Nancy Zapf." With Allyson Goldin. *Midnight Review* 23 (1994): 78–90.

APA Zapf, N. (1994). [Interview with Allyson Goldin]. *Midnight Review*, 23, 78–90.

MLA Park, Mary. Personal interview. 9 Jan. 1995.

When you use the APA and CBE styles, acknowledge a personal interview source in your text by placing in parentheses the person's name followed by a comma, the words "personal communication," and the date of the interview.

Performances

MLA *The Fence*. By Mark Morris. Dir. Connie Poten. Victor Matthews Theater, London. 29 Aug. 1994.

APA Morris, M. (Playwright), & Poten, C. (Director). (1994, Aug. 29). The fence [play]. Victor Matthews Theater, London.

REWRITE

Keep in mind that the researched paper you are writing is your own paper. The sources you cite are only evidence to back up your own conclusive judgments. The most common mistake novice writers make is the knitting of other people's ideas together into an "edited" report rather than an authentically written researched essay. To avoid "editing" and actually write your own essay, follow the directions under the rubric "Rewrite" in the particular "Responsive Writing Assignment" you're working on. For example, if you're writing a researched essay in response to a controversial issue, following the "Rewrite" directions in Chapter Nine will help you focus on your own responses rather than on your sources' responses.

In addition, as you rewrite, pay particular attention to the material from outside sources in your text. Read sentences and paragraphs with quoted material aloud to check for smoothness and proper integration; make sure cited material is accurately quoted or paraphrased; and concentrate on following the proper conventions for punctuating and acknowledging sources.

A STUDENT WRITER WRITES AND TALKS ABOUT WRITING

Micha Silberman is a twenty-one-year-old from California, majoring in forestry at The University of Montana. In the last few months, after years of avoiding writing, Micha has begun to enjoy taking his writing seriously. Let's read a draft of Micha's paper and the final paper he produced and then explore with him the process of writing his very first researched paper.

The formal process of writing the paper started at the moment Micha was given an assignment (in room 205 of the Liberal Arts building on The University of Montana campus) to write in response to a controversial issue. With that assignment, Micha was faced with a **writing situation.** The only constraint he was operating under, outside of having to work under a deadline, was that he had respond to a controversy. His choice of **subject** was open, as were his choices of **audience** and **purpose.**

Beautiful Fire

Micha Silberman

Summer has come. The stress from school is over and you want to take a break from everyday life. Dust off the suitcases, pack up the car and head some-where--anywhere U.S.A. Perhaps you're driving through the corn fields of Nebraska or the Giant Sequoias of California. You take a deep breath to smell the clean air, and, suddenly, you smell smoke. Ahead of you a towering ash cloud rises, and fire burns through a delicate wind-swept field. As you get clos-er, you see Forest Service staff watching, letting the fire they've set spread until it engulfs shrubs along the field's edge. You came here to see the beauty of the natural world, and what you're looking at isn't beau-tiful. Stop. Don't look away. Although this burned and burning area may not look pretty to the uneducated eye, you must realize that this purposely set "pre-scribed burn" is part of a beautiful process of the whole.

try to work this quote in smoothly

You need a transition here.

"People who have only a limited understanding of the role of a fire in the development of a natural community see a newly burned forest (or grassland area) as land management at its worst" (Holochek 439). These people find bare ashen soil with only occa-sional bumps of charred wood profoundly disturbing and ugly. However, like a seeded field or ground newly cleared for a home, this disturbance is part of a creative process.

is this citation correct in format?

From the 1930's to the late 1940's Aldo Leopold was at the forefront of the conservation movement. Leopold once said, "our ability to perceive quality in nature begins, as in art, with the pretty. It proceeds through successive stages of the beautiful" (Leopold from Callicott pg. 240). "A thing is right when it tends to preserve the integrity, stability, and beauty of a biotic community. It is wrong when it tends otherwise" (Leopold 224-225).

ask the people in forestry for correct form

Again, you just drop these quotes in.

Why the space?

The confusion of prettiness and beauty is at the center of the basic misunderstanding between the public and land managers over the practice of prescribed burning. To understand the rightness of prescribed burning, we must come to understand the difference between prettiness and beauty. All ecosystem processes may not be pretty, but working together as a whole they create something beautiful. Pretty is the large, smooth rock carved by glaciers long ago. Pretty is the squirrel rummaging the forest floor. Pretty is the white-headed Bald Eagle soaring through the sky. Each individual aspect that you see may be pretty. But beauty is something more. Travel a mile straight up and look down at all the processes combined as a whole, and what you see is beautiful. Sit on one side of the Grand Canyon and look across and down, and that is beauty at its best.

A fire in a forest or a grassland may not be a pretty sight, but it's a beautiful process of the whole. We must realize that fire was here long before man and is a natural phenomenon. "Giant sequoias were subject to fires every 10 to 20 years before 1875, with individual trees experiencing fires at intervals of 3 to 35 years. Fires coursed through Ponderosa pine communities with even more frequency, averaging a fire every 6 to

Again, try to work quoted material in smoothly.

9 years" (Robinson 305, from Kilgore and Taylor '79). *Form?*
Many biological communities have adapted to the
natural process of fire. "Jack pines produce cones that
hang unopen for decades. When fires occur, the cones
open slowly in the heat, releasing winged seeds that
the wind spreads over short distances. The seeds
grow free of competition from the seedlings of other
kinds of trees" (Robinson 35). Longleaf pines have yet
another style of adapting to fire. They drop their seeds
and grow a small puff of needles on the forest floor.
Although these needles stay the same until there is a
fire, below them the seed grows an ever larger tap root *Is this*
that stores more and more nutrients. When the fire *yours?*
occurs the small top is lost, leaving the underground
taproot intact. With no other plant competition and its
store of nutrients, the longleaf pine taproot will grow
a tree three to five meters tall in a few short years.

This is chronologically confused.
    These fire-adaptive trees and many other plant
species were greatly diminished when people started
moving west, stopped, and settled down. Back then a
natural fire wasn't easily controlled, and scores of
people lost their lives fighting them. This early loss of
American life contributed to the huge public image
problem prescribed burning has today. "In the late *Again,*
1930's Walt Disney's Bambi and the U.S. Forest *work this in.*
Service's Smokey the Bear depicted a forest fire as a
terrifying enemy of wildlife. The campaign was very
effective, and the exclusion of fires became a basic
tenet of forest protection" (Robinson 325). This exclusion of fire caused many detrimental unnatural
processes that affected the diversity of plant and animal species in western ecosystems.

The beautiful process of any fire maintains diversity and removes dead wood, but also adds much more stability to the burned area. "After burning, regrowth of the same grasses is tender, usually enriched with protein" (Robinson 297). Also, the foliage and sprouting plants during the next growing season after a fire are very pretty (Holochek 439-440). After a fire, nutrients made highly accessible by the fire's process will create some of the most beautiful plant communities. Certain colorful plants only appear for a brief time during the short postfire recovery period (Holochek 439-440). "The nutritional quality of vegetation as food usually depends on soil fertility--that is on the abundance of nutrients in the soil" (Robinson 92). These accessible nutrients provide a more palatable substance for animals.

All quotes.

Not much of you in here.

Unfortunately, animals "tend to congregate on recent burns, largely because of accessibility of the tender, succulent new growth. Utilization of weeping lovegrass, for example, increased more than fifty per cent after a winter burn" (Holochek 438, from Klett '71). Wildlife will congregate in these freshly burned areas causing irreversible damage to the young plants and the soil by overgrazing. The congregating animals eat too much of the plant material in the area, allowing the possibility of less nutritious and sometimes noxious plants to take root. In addition, the weight of all the animals compacts the soil, thus making it difficult for water to infiltrate into the ground with the needed nutrients for plants to survive. However, unlike naturally occurring fires, prescribed burns can be distributed throughout the ecosystem, thus spread-

Is this yours?

ing out the animals, reducing any damage they could create by congregating in one area of new growth.

Another way in which prescribed burning may be more beneficial to an ecosystem than naturally occurring fire has to do with heat intensity. Fire exists in a two dimensional aspect which includes intensity and duration. These two components are of the utmost importance to control. One intense fire will burn hotter than many small fires. Soils exposed to the high temperatures of a long awaited natural fire "may develop resistance to wetting as a result of burning. The nonwettable character may last a year or more, and may be a prime factor in the typically high runoff and erosion rates following fires" (Holochek 437). A prescribed burn is created to be low in intensity and therefore leaves some material on the ground as protection from erosion. All fires will most likely release nutrients into the soil from burnt plant material. Nitrogen, phosphorus, and sulfur are the main nutrients, and of these three nitrogen is usually the most important. A prescribed burn allows these nutrients to get into the soil easier than an intense fire because there is less erosion and runoff. A less intense fire also vents fewer nutrients as smoke and ash. All of these details combined together will make it easier for the nutrients to enter the new plant material.

Again, work this in smoothly.

Although naturally occurring fires often burn out of control, the intensity and duration of prescribed burns can be easily controlled through the fire triangle. The fire triangle is made of three components: fuel, air and heat. Removing any one of these three components will immediately diminish the fire. In prescribed burning the fuel is given to us by mother nature. Fuel is all the plant species within the given burn area. We can't control how much fuel is present, but we can control the moisture of the fuel. The wetter the fuel is, the less intense the fire will be. The moisture of the fuel will vary according to the time of day. Fuel fired early in the morning will be wetter and will burn with less intensity than fuel fired later in the day.

Wind speed will affect the duration of a fire. The lower the wind speed, the slower the fire will move. A slower moving fire allows the intensity to maximize its output thus destroying more plant material. An optimum wind speed is 15 mph. The optimum combination of moisture and wind speed is controllable only by waiting. Sometimes burn managers will wait weeks for the optimum level to occur.

Heat is the most controllable aspect of the fire triangle. The intensity of a fire is how hot the fire is or the heat inside it. If you start a fire in just one spot the heat will stay about the same. When you start several fires the heat is expanded logarithmically when the fires make contact with one another. This creates a flare up or higher intensity fire in the small locations of contact, and more plant material will be destroyed in that flare up area.

Properly coordinated prescribed burns create the naturally appropriate environment for the plants and animals they are managed for. A controlled fire will have all the benefits of a natural fire plus a reduction in the over destructive force of a natural fire. Biologists, conservationists, foresters and their fire crews all work together to produce a properly coordinated prescribed burn. If you find a fire that is not being controlled, please contact the nearest fire service. The quicker someone can get to a natural fire, the less fuel or material it will destroy. Remember, a prescribed burn is used for the purpose of management. However, in the end it just might create something you would like to see. Now, knowing the difference between pretty and beautiful, go out into the world and enjoy what a prescribed burn just might have created for you.

HW

Micha,

Work the quoted material in. As it stands you don't get as much meaning out of the quoted material as you might because you just drop it in. Thinking about what you mean to communicate will also help with transitions and the chronologically confused paragraph on the third page.

Also — Ask your forestry professors about the proper documenttion style, and make sure you cite all sources.

Micha Silberman

BEAUTIFUL FIRE (FINAL)*

Summer has come. The stress from school is over and you want to take a break from everyday life. Dust off the suitcases, pack up the car and head somewhere—anywhere U.S.A. Perhaps you're driving through the corn fields of Nebraska or the giant sequoia forests of California. You take a deep breath to smell the clean air, and, suddenly, you smell smoke. Ahead of you a towering ash cloud rises, and fire burns through a delicate windswept field. As you get closer, you see Forest Service staff watching, letting the fire they've set spread until it engulfs shrubs along the field's edge. You came here to see the beauty of the natural world, and what you're looking at isn't beautiful. Stop. Don't look away. Although this burned and burning area may not look pretty to the uneducated eye, you must realize that this purposely set "prescribed burn" is part of a beautiful process of the whole.

To the educated eye of a land manager this prescribed burn is the first step in a process of renewal. However, "people who have only a limited understanding of the role of a fire in the development of a natural community see a newly burned forest (or grassland area) as land management at its worst" (1). These people find bare ashen soil with only occasional bumps of charred wood profoundly disturbing and ugly. Nevertheless, like a seeded field or ground newly cleared for a home, this disturbance is part of a creative process.

From the 1930's to the late 1940's Aldo Leopold was at the forefront of the conservation movement. Leopold once said, "our ability to perceive quality in nature begins, as in art, with the pretty. It proceeds through successive stages of the beautiful" (Leopold from 2). The confusion of prettiness and beauty is at the center of the basic misunderstanding between the public and land managers over the practice of prescribed burning. To understand the rightness of prescribed burning, we must come to understand the difference between prettiness and beauty. All ecosystem processes may not be pretty, but working together as a whole they create something beautiful. Pretty is the large, smooth rock carved by glaciers long ago. Pretty is the squirrel rummaging the forest

continued on page 486

*The writer of this essay has used the documentation style of the CBE Manual, 5 ed.

continued from page 485

floor. Pretty is the white-headed Bald Eagle soaring through the sky. Each individual aspect that you see may be pretty. But beauty is something more. Travel a mile straight up and look down at all the processes combined as a whole, and what you see is beautiful. Sit on one side of the Grand Canyon and look across and down, and that is beauty at its best.

A fire in a forest or a grassland may not be a pretty sight, but it's a beautiful process of the whole. We must realize that fire was here long before man and is a natural phenomenon. Before the settlement of the American west "giant sequoias were subject to fires every 10 to 20 years..., with individual trees experiencing fires at intervals of 3 to 35 years" (Robinson from 3). And in addition to being a natural phenomenon, fire is also a productive one. Many biological communities have adapted to the natural process of fire. "Jack pines [for example] produce cones that hang unopen for decades. When fires occur, the cones open slowly in the heat, releasing winged seeds that the wind spreads over short distances. The seeds grow free of competition from the seedlings of other kinds of trees" (4). Longleaf pines have yet another style of adapting to fire. They drop their seeds and grow a small puff of needles on the forest floor. Although these needles stay the same until there is a fire, below them the seed grows an ever larger tap root that stores more and more nutrients. When the fire occurs the small top is lost, leaving the underground taproot intact (5). With no other plant competition and its store of nutrients, the longleaf pine taproot will grow a tree three to five meters tall in a few short years.

These fire-adaptive trees and many other plant species were greatly diminished when people started moving west, stopped, and settled down. Back then a natural fire wasn't easily controlled, and scores of people lost their lives fighting them. This early loss of American life was a primary motivation for the adoption of fire suppression as a land management policy. Later, "Walt Disney's Bambi and the U.S. Forest Service's Smokey the Bear depicted a forest fire as a terrifying enemy of wildlife . . . , and the exclusion of fires became a basic tenet of forest protection" (4). However, this exclusion of fire caused many detrimental unnatural processes that affected the diversity of plant and animal

continued to next page

species in western ecosystems. When Aldo Leopold wrote "a thing is right when it tends to preserve the integrity, stability, and beauty of a biotic community . . . [and] wrong when it tends otherwise" (6), he got to the heart of what makes routine fire suppression an unsatisfactory land management policy. On the other hand, proscribed burning is right because it helps restore ecosystems to a more natural and stable state.

The beautiful process of any fire maintains diversity and removes dead wood, but also adds much more stability to the burned area. In the period after a fire, "regrowth of the same grasses is tender, usually enriched with protein" (4); nutrients made highly accessible by the fire's process will create some of the most beautiful plant communities. Certain colorful plants only appear for a brief time during the short postfire recovery period (1). In addition, the accessible nutrients contained in these plants provide a more palatable substance for animals.

Unfortunately, animals "tend to congregate on recent burns, largely because of accessibility of the tender, succulent new growth" (Holochek from 7). Wildlife will congregate in these freshly burned areas causing irreversible damage to the young plants and the soil by overgrazing. The congregating animals eat too much of the plant material in the area, allowing the possibility of less nutritious and sometimes noxious plants to take root. In addition, the weight of all the animals compacts the soil, thus making it difficult for water to infiltrate into the ground with the needed nutrients for plants to survive. However, unlike naturally occurring fires, prescribed burns can be distributed throughout the ecosystem, thus spreading out the animals, reducing any damage they could create by congregating in one area of new growth (8).

Another way in which prescribed burning may be more beneficial to an ecosystem than naturally occurring fire has to do with heat intensity. Fire exists in a two dimensional aspect which includes intensity and duration. These two components are of the utmost importance to control. One intense fire will burn hotter than many small fires. Soils exposed to the high temperatures of a long awaited natural fire "may develop [a] resistance to wetting as a result of burning. . . [that] may last a year or more, and may be a prime factor in the typically high runoff and erosion rates

continued on page 488

continued from page 487

following fires" (1). A prescribed burn is created to be low in intensity and therefore leaves some material on the ground as protection from erosion. All fires will most likely release nutrients into the soil from burnt plant material. Nitrogen, phosphorus, and sulfur are the main nutrients, and of these three nitrogen is usually the most important. A prescribed burn allows these nutrients to get into the soil easier than an intense fire because there is less erosion and runoff. A less intense fire also vents fewer nutrients as smoke and ash. All of these details combined together will make it easier for the nutrients to enter the new plant material.

Although naturally occurring fires often burn out of control, the intensity and duration of prescribed burns can be easily controlled through the fire triangle. The fire triangle is made of three components: fuel, air and heat. Removing any one of these three components will immediately diminish the fire. In prescribed burning the fuel is given to us by mother nature. Fuel is all the plant species within the given burn area. We can't control how much fuel is present, but we can control the moisture of the fuel. The wetter the fuel is, the less intense the fire will be. The moisture of the fuel will vary according to the time of day. Fuel fired early in the morning will be wetter and will burn with less intensity than fuel fired later in the day.

Wind speed will affect the duration of a fire. The lower the wind speed, the slower the fire will move. A slower moving fire allows the intensity to maximize its output thus destroying more plant material. An optimum wind speed is 15 mph. The optimum combination of moisture and wind speed is controllable only by waiting. Sometimes burn managers will wait weeks for the optimum level to occur.

Heat is the most controllable aspect of the fire triangle. The intensity of a fire is how hot the fire is or the heat inside it. If you start a fire in just one spot the heat will stay about the same. When you start several fires the heat is expanded logarithmically when the fires make contact with one another. This creates a flare up or higher intensity fire in the small locations of contact, and more plant material will be destroyed in that flare up area.

Properly coordinated prescribed burns create the naturally appropriate environment for the plants and animals they are

continued to next page

managed for. A controlled fire will have all the benefits of a natural fire plus a reduction in the over destructive force of a natural fire. Biologists, conservationists, foresters and their firecrews all work together to produce a properly coordinated prescribed burn. If you find a fire that is not being controlled, please contact the nearest fire service. The quicker someone can get to a natural fire the less fuel or material it will destroy. Remember, a prescribed burn is used for the purpose of management. However, in the end it just might create something you would like to see. Now, knowing the difference between pretty and beautiful, go out into the world and enjoy what a prescribed burn just might have created for you.

LITERATURE CITED

1. Holochek, J. L.; Pieper, R. D.; Herbel, C. H. Range management: principles and practices. Englewood Cliffs, NJ: Regents/Prentice Hall; 1989.

2. Callicott, J. B. In defense of the land ethic; essays in environmental philosophy. Albany, NY: State University of New York Press; 1989.

3. Kilgore, B. M.; Taylor, D. Fire history of a sequoia-mixed conifer forest. Ecol. 60: 129–142; 1979.

4. Robinson, W. L.; Bolen, E. G. Wildlife ecology and management. 2nd ed. New York: Macmillan Publishing Company; 1989.

5. Florence, M. Plant succession on prescribed burn sites in chamise chaparral. Rangelands 9: 119–122; 1987.

6. Leopold, A. A Sand County almanac and sketches here and there. New York: Oxford University Press; 1949.

7. Klett, W. E.; Hollingsworth, D.; Schuster, J. L. Increasing infiltration by burning. J. Range Managem't 24: 22–24; 1971.

8. Pase, C. R.; Lindenmuth, A. W. Effects of prescribed fire on vegetation and sediment in oak-mountain mahogany chaparral. J. For. 69: 800–805; 1971.

Now read this transcript of a conversation I had with Micha about how he writes and how he wrote this particular paper. Focus on those places in the transcript where Micha is being actively self-critical of his own writing and thinking.

J. S.:   Just when was it that you chose the subject of your paper?

M. S.:   As soon as you said we had to do research, I had my subject—prescribed burning—and I started working on it. I'm a wildlife biology major, and we'd discussed prescribed burning in some of my classes, and I wanted to know more about it.

J. S.:   How did you make your choice of audience?

M. S.:   That [audience] was one of the problems with my writing in the past. Because I didn't write to an audience. I just wrote. Now I was writing to the other students in the class. I had to think about what the context was. It was going to be a paper for other students, so I wanted to write it as informatively as I could, but still so that people outside of the field could understand it.

J. S.:   What was your purpose for writing?

M. S.:   I wanted the general public to understand why prescribed burning is important to the management of wildlife areas because there's been so much sentiment against it.

J. S.:   What about you, the writer? How did who you are and your personal and educational history affect the writing of the paper?

M. S.:   This was the first paper I ever took seriously. I feel a little bit more comfortable writing now. All through high school, we mostly read a lot and we didn't do much writing. And then here at the university, I just tried to avoid writing. The first few papers I wrote this semester were written with my usual sarcasm. I think it was because I didn't know any other way to write. I must have skipped the week in school when they taught us how to take things seriously.

J. S.:   Why did you stop being sarcastic?

M. S.:   I think it was the comments I got on my papers. I realized that if I wanted a good grade, I'd better change. Once I tried not being sarcastic, I liked it better. I concentrate and try to get down what I really mean. I was a horrible writer. I hated to write. It was because I never felt comfortable doing it. I think I was putting

continued to next page

thought to word without really thinking about what I was thinking or writing. It would come right out of my head onto the paper. If you're sarcastic, you don't have to worry about what other people think. I've always screwed around ninety-nine-point-nine percent of the time. I've tried not to take anything seriously, and that's probably why it was easier not to be serious. You could just go out on your own limb. You didn't have to think about it. But with the research paper it was different. I was interested. It [the subject, prescribed burning] came up in a lot of my classes. I really did want to get an understanding of it because it was important in my field. I wanted to know how prescribed burning worked. Once I got into it, I found it even more interesting, and I wanted to do it properly—write the paper properly.

J. S.: What about the possibility of being published?

M. S.: I guess it typifies how lucky I get sometimes. I wanted to do it because it was different.

J. S.: Different? A lot of things are different. I could hit you over the head with my cup, and that would be different.

M. S.: But that wouldn't be fun.

J. S.: What's fun about the idea of being published?

M. S.: Whacking my friends upside the head with it. Not my friends here. The people I knew when I was in high school. I think I became so sarcastic and off the wall in high school because no one took me seriously. My high school was very uppity-uppity and cliquish. Every one had to one-up everyone else. Actually knowing what I'm talking about has made me realize that people can take me seriously—that I can take myself seriously. In one way or another, I told most of the people in my high school to go fly a kite by my senior year. And now I can tell them to go fly a kite in a serious way by writing something serious.

J. S.: How did who you are as a person affect your choice of subject?

M. S.: My major, wildlife biology. I've always been an outdoorsy person. My dad suggested I go into Scouts even though I didn't want to. Then we went camping

continued on page 492

continued from page 491

and camping and camping, and I loved it. I'm an Eagle Scout. It was a pain, but it was well worth it. I got to get outdoors and experience other things besides being stuck in the city. I was born and raised in the city, and I guess I just like getting out of the cement forest. The city is just one small, pretty part of the picture, but I guess you have to experience something beyond that to understand the whole beauty of life.

J. S.:   Describe how you usually write and how you wrote the research paper in particular.

M. S.:   My best time to write is eleven P.M. to two A.M. I write sitting on my bed listening to Enya or Clannad— smooth, soothing Celtic music. I'll just sit there and write down ideas and then format how I want to write it—where I want to start, you know, how I want the ideas to flow. Then I go to bed and sleep on it, I guess. In the morning I formalize it into a draft, using the computer downstairs in the lab. I like to use the computer right off early in the morning. There aren't as many people in the lab, and I feel fresher. Writing is the first thing I'm going to do, and I wake up knowing that. Then I let someone else read it and watch it get shredded, and then I rewrite it. If I'm actually having trouble with it, I'll have Janet read it. She's a journalism major and has done editorial work for a few years. She lives down the hall, and I just knock on her door and say, "Help." If I'm not having trouble, I'll just ask the guys from first floor to read it to see if they have any ideas.

J. S.:   Have you always had people read your papers?

M. S.:   What papers? I never wrote a paper until this semester. There have to be papers in order for someone to read them.

J. S.:   Did you take the research paper to Janet or to the guys on the first floor?

M. S.:   Before I was finished, I had everyone take a look at it several times. I wanted to make sure I didn't make any scientific mistakes. After I had Janet and the guys read

continue to next page

it, I had two forestry professors read it. The first one wasn't an expert in the subject. He sent me to the guy in the state who's the big expert. He really shredded it. I'd trusted another student to give me information, and he turned out to be wrong. A lot of the major scientific points I'd made were incorrect, so I had to do more research. I was disappointed, but it was good to know the right stuff. I wanted to know the truth about it. This is my major, and the last thing I wanted was to get the facts wrong. The main problem I had before I wrote this paper was that I'd never actually gone out and gotten any facts at all. If you're writing a sarcastic paper, you don't need to have facts. If you don't care if people take you seriously in the first place, why bother to look something up?

CHAPTER THIRTEEN

STRATEGIES FOR RESPONDING TO ESSAY QUESTIONS

Essay exams are designed to **test your knowledge** of a particular subject, your ability to **think critically** about that subject, and your ability to **write** with clarity and precision. As you study this chapter, keep in mind that knowledge, thinking ability, and writing ability are equally important ingredients for writing successful essay exam responses.

LONG-TERM STUDY STRATEGIES

From the moment the syllabus is handed out in a class, you'll know if essay responses will be required. If they are, you'll have to employ study strategies aimed at guaranteeing you the critical thinking and writing practice that will enable you to write successful responses. Essay responses are rarely demanded in courses that are purely fact-based. That's why fact-based courses often have a large number of students in them. If students are learning only facts, they don't have to discuss concepts to understand them, and professors don't have to test the students' understanding with subjectively graded papers. Objective examinations are a much more efficient tool for testing students' knowledge of factual information. Therefore, the courses at your college or university in which you'll most likely be asked to write essay responses will be the courses that are conceptually oriented.

However, to successfully respond to essay questions, you'll have to examine and analyze the many different "texts" that make up the content of the course you're enrolled in by studying each one carefully for its content and meaning and for the evidence that supports that meaning. In conceptually oriented classes you'll have, first, the "text" of the classroom. The active speakers in that text will be your instructor and you and your classmates. Second, you will have written texts—textbooks and outside readings. You may also be asked to attend lectures or performances and to view films or nonverbal texts such as paintings or sculpture. In addition to studying each text individually, you should study them comparatively for areas of interaction, for overlap, and for agreements or disagreements.

Practicing critical thinking also requires being discerning and judgmental about your own responses. You are free to disagree with anything you read or hear, but your disagreements must be thoughtful and supported with tested evidence drawn from the content of the course and from your own knowledge and experience. To practice the critical thinking and writing necessary for writing successful essay responses, consider the following study strategies.

PRACTICE CRITICAL THINKING

ENGAGE IN CHALLENGING CONVERSATION.   Practice critical thinking skills by **conversing** with others about the texts and situations you encounter in your classes. The back-and-forth exchange of challenging dialogue exposes you to other people's knowledge and ways of thinking, and it also gives you the opportunity to test your conclusions.

LISTEN ACTIVELY.   Practice critical thinking by listening actively. Whether you're attending a classroom lecture or engaging in conversation with a friend about the content of a course, be an active listener: **listen carefully, consider** what the speaker has to say, and **frame judgments** about what you hear.

Discern your instructor's teaching style, and attend accordingly. Some instructors favor a question-and-answer style; others are lecturers. Discerning your instructor's style can help you "read" the "text" of the classroom more effectively for meaning.

Like speeches, lectures are formal spoken discussions of subjects delivered before audiences. However, unlike speeches, lectures aren't constructed as written texts and then read to audiences. Instead, lectures are spoken texts, constructed from notes *as* they're delivered. The very best lectures are more exciting than speeches; they're more openly conversational. The lecturer's mind is spurred on to new discoveries by the dynamic of the face-to-face meeting with an audience. Just as you come to understand more in the very best conversations (or during the process of writing when you converse with yourself), excellent lecturers discover more as they speak before live and responsive audiences. You may have already encountered or heard about an excellent lecturer. On any college or university campus there are instructors whose ability to lecture has made them well-known in the community. To get the most out of lectures, consider the following specific strategies.

TAKE THOROUGH, WELL-ORGANIZED NOTES.   Most lecturers work from outlined notes, which means that the lectures they deliver have discernible divisions. The lecturer will usually introduce a subject, explain its place in the context of the course content, and then go on to make a series of evidence-supported points about it. When you attend a class lecture, be prepared to listen for and record in your notes the movement from one division to another and the detailed points within each division. Listen for key phrases, and make sure that you take down all board writing.

READ YOUR NOTES CRITICALLY.   As soon as possible, read your notes and fill in any pertinent information that you may have left out. Consider how the subject of the lecture fits into the context of the class. What was the purpose of the lecture? Did the lecture have a specific message? If you have any questions, write them out.

RESEARCH ANY UNKNOWNS.   Use the resources available on your campus (the library, your instructor) to find answers to your questions.

APPLY CONCEPTS.   Practice critical thinking by applying the **general concepts** you learn to **specific texts and situations** you encounter in the academic community and the other communities of which you're a member.

SUPPLY EVIDENCE.   Practice critical thinking by mentally **supplying evidence** for the conclusions you draw about texts and situations that you encounter in your classes. Supplying evidence can help you test your conclusive judgments, and it can also lead you to new ideas.

PRACTICE CRITICAL READING

PREREAD.   Practice critical reading by familiarizing yourself with texts before you actively read them for meaning. **Read** the first few paragraphs slowly, focusing on those things you understand. Then **summarize, reread** (if necessary), and **predict.** In addition, use the predicting technique from prereading to get more out of lectures, question-and-answer sessions, and conversations.

READ CAREFULLY FOR MEANING.   Practice critical reading by analyzing texts carefully for meaning: **research** any **unknown** words or references; **analyze** the **speaker** to come to an understanding of his or her perspective; **determine** the **audience, message,** and **purpose;** and frame **judgments** about what you read.

PRACTICE CRITICAL WRITING

KEEP COURSE JOURNALS. Practice critical writing by keeping a **course journal** for each class in which you're enrolled (a computer file or even the notebook for the class will do). Since writing is a process of discovery and clarification, writing down your responses to the content of your classes will move you further along in knowledge and understanding of that content. Read the assigned texts in the class for their meaning, and record the results of your analysis in writing, complete with supporting evidence. Consider the **writer-based purposes** for writing; use your course journals to **remember** facts, to **record** observations, and to **explore** concepts in order to **understand** them. Use journals also to **express** your judgments about (and your emotional responses to) the subjects of your writing. After you have several journal entries, compare them, looking for areas of interaction. Then record your responses.

KEEP A PERSONAL JOURNAL. **Practice** critical writing by keeping a **personal journal.** Responding to the texts (films, books, articles) and situations (personal relationships, social controversies) that you encounter beyond the academic community will help you **make connections** between what you're learning in your classes and what's going on in your personal and cultural life.

STRATEGIES FOR STUDYING FOR EXAMS

EXPLORE THE WRITING SITUATION IN ADVANCE

The strategies that follow aren't last-minute approaches. Writing takes time; preparing to write an essay exam takes time; you can't cram and successfully write an essay response. Therefore, *a few days before the exam,* begin preparing by exploring the writing situation in advance. An essay question, like any writing situation, involves a **writer,** a **subject,** an **audience,** and a **purpose** for writing.

CONSIDER YOUR PAST PERFORMANCE. Remember that essay exams are designed to test your **knowledge,** your **thinking** ability, and your **writing** ability.

ANALYZE YOUR AUDIENCE. Instructors are human beings who have particular concerns and interests. To discern the interests and concerns of your audience, read over your notes and your course journals, and look for and mark recurring ideas and judgments. Then write out a detailed description of your audience. What are your instructor's major values and concerns about the **subject** matter of the class? What reasons does he or she repeatedly give for having these concerns? What judgments does he or she make about the texts and situations you've encountered in the class? For example, consider the course in which you use this book. What are your instructor's major concerns about critical reading and writing? Which parts of the two processes does he or she repeatedly emphasize?

FORMULATE POSSIBLE QUESTIONS.   There are a finite number of questions that your instructor can ask you about the subject matter. If you have already taken an essay exam in the class, study the exam and consider the kinds of questions your instructor asked. Then, preferably in collaboration with three or four classmates, formulate and write out at least five possible questions your instructor might ask on the exam. As you formulate your questions, focus on **key concepts** from the class and on the four audience-based **purposes** for writing most likely to be used in academic writing (persuade, inform, explain, explore). What in the course content might your instructor ask you to take and defend a position on? What concepts might your instructor ask you to explain and illustrate? What in the course content might your instructor ask you to explore or inform him or her about? For example, if you're preparing for an essay exam that will test your ability to critically read a text, what key concepts from the critical reading process might you be asked to explain and illustrate?

WRITE OUT THE ANSWERS TO THE QUESTIONS.   Writing out answers to the questions you've formulated will allow you to see gaps in your knowledge and understanding of the subject matter. And it will also give you practice writing about the subject in purposeful ways, using the vocabulary of the class. Even if your instructor doesn't ask you exactly the questions you've formulated and written out, the questions he or she does ask are bound to have some areas of correspondence.

POSE STUDY QUESTIONS.   Focus on gaps in your knowledge and understanding of the subject matter, and write out as many questions as you can.

FOCUS YOUR STUDY TO FILL IN GAPS.   Go back to journals, class notes, primary texts, classmates, and your instructor for further focused study and conversation. Don't feel reticent about approaching your instructor. However, don't wait until the last minute, and don't ask unfocused, superficial questions like "What will be on the exam?" or "Will the exam be hard?" Most instructors welcome specific questions about the subject matter, because such questions indicate student interest and engagement. I find that my estimation of a student automatically goes up a few notches when he or she stays after class to ask a question or visits my office for further conversation about what's going on in class.

REFORMULATE QUESTIONS AND REWRITE.   Continue to practice putting your knowledge and understanding of the subject matter in visible form on the page by reformulating your original questions and rewriting your answers.

MEMORIZE KEY ELEMENTS AND SPELLINGS.   Memorize important dates; short pertinent quotations; any formulas; and the spellings of key terms, pertinent names, or concepts.

STRATEGIES FOR TAKING EXAMS

READ OVER THE ENTIRE EXAM.   Get an overview, and critically read each question carefully. Often, students who have studied hard don't perform well on essay exams simply because they don't answer the *exact* question being asked. Each question on the exam will be a separate writing situation. Although the audience and the writer in each of these situations will be the same, the specific **subject** and **purpose** for writing in each will be different. Therefore, focus on the language in each question that defines subject and purpose. Underlining subject-defining words and key directional verbs (*describe, explain, compare, contrast, defend*) can help you discern and remember the focus of each question. Some questions will supply you with a judgment or message and ask you to defend or give evidence for it; others will demand that you formulate a judgment or message and then go on to illustrate it. In addition, some questions may have more than one part, and you must be sure to answer all parts. For example, a question in a exam testing your ability to read a text critically might ask you to first determine the message of a text and give evidence for your determination, and then ask you to state and support your agreements or disagreements with the text's message.

PROPORTION YOUR TIME.   Consider the time constraints, and proportion your time accordingly. You don't want to use all your time on one question. Consider how much time you have and how many points each question is worth. Most instructors will signal the point value in parentheses after each question. For example, if a question is worth twenty-five points out of a possible one hundred, allow yourself roughly a quarter of your total time to write that question. However, allow yourself a few minutes at the end of the exam to proofread for technical problems.

WRITE LEGIBLY AND CORRECTLY.   You will not have time to rewrite the exam, so write clearly. Ink is easier to read than pencil. Neatly cross out corrections, and generally focus on making your answers as easy to read as possible. In addition, keep in mind that spelling, sentence structure, and punctuation do count. As you finish writing each question, read it over silently to yourself, and mentally listen to the language. Check the spelling and punctuation. Then make any necessary corrections.

START WITH THE EASIEST QUESTION.   Writing the easiest question first will allow you to warm up your mind. As you write, information and ideas about the harder questions you've read will likely come to you. And when this happens, make notes in the margins of the exam as reminders.

SUPPLY SPECIFIC EXAMPLES, REASONS, AND EVIDENCE.   Keep in mind that your instructor is testing *your* knowledge and understanding. To a certain extent, the "professorial" audience is an artificial one; usually when we write to an audience who knows more than we do about a subject, we assume they know what we're talking about, and we tend to leave out convincing, supporting details. However, the "professorial" audience demands a thorough response to each question.

READ OVER THE EXAM AND MAKE CORRECTIONS.   When you've finished writing, read over each question once again and make any minor corrections needed.

RESPOND—PRACTICE THE CONCEPTS YOU'VE LEARNED BY WRITING

Practice the strategies for taking essay exams presented in this chapter by reading a text and responding to it. Read the text included here. Then consider the concepts you've learned, and respond to the collaborative and individual writing assignments that end this chapter.

BEING A MAN
Paul Theroux

Paul Theroux is a writer and teacher. This selection is excerpted from his book Sunrise with Seamonsters *(1985).*

There is a pathetic sentence in the chapter "Fetishism" in Dr. Norman Cameron's book *Personality Development and Psychopathology*. It goes, "Fetishists are nearly always men; and their commonest fetish is a woman's shoe." I cannot read that sentence without thinking that it is just one more awful thing about being a man—and perhaps it is an important thing to know about us.

I have always disliked being a man. The whole idea of manhood in America is pitiful, in my opinion. This version of masculinity is a little like having to wear an ill-fitting coat for one's entire life (by contrast, I imagine femininity to be an oppressive sense of nakedness). Even the expression "Be a man!" strikes me as insulting and abusive. It means: Be stupid, be unfeeling, obedient, soldierly, and stop thinking. And yet it is part of every man's life. It is a hideous and crippling lie; it not only insists on difference and connives at superiority, it is also by its very nature destructive—emotionally damaging and socially harmful.

The youth who is subverted, as most are, into believing in the masculine ideal is effectively separated from women and he spends the rest of his life finding women a riddle and a nuisance. Of course, there is a female version of this male affliction. It begins with mothers encouraging little girls to say (to other adults) "Do you like my new dress?" In a sense, little girls are traditionally urged to please adults with a kind of coquettishness, while boys are enjoined to behave like monkeys towards each other. The nine-year-old coquette proceeds to become womanish in a subtle power game in which she learns to be sexually indispensable, socially decorative and always alert to a man's sense of inadequacy.

Femininity—being lady-like—implies needing a man as witness and seducer; but masculinity celebrates the exclusive company of men. That is why it is so grotesque; and that is also why there is no manliness without inadequacy—because it denies the natural friendship of women.

COLLABORATIVE WRITING ASSIGNMENT

As I suggested earlier in this chapter, there are a finite number of questions that your instructor might ask you about the text you've read. Consider the kinds of questions your instructor might be likely to ask. Then, in collaboration with three or four classmates, formulate and write out at least three possible questions your instructor might ask about "Being a Man." As you formulate your questions, focus on **key concepts** from this book and on the four audience-based **purposes** for writing most likely to be used in academic writing (persuade, inform, explain, explore). What might your instructor ask you to take and defend a position on? What concepts might your instructor ask you to explain and illustrate? What might your instructor ask you to explore or inform him or her about? For example, since you're preparing for an essay exam that will test your ability to critically read a text, what key concepts from the critical reading process might you be asked to explain and illustrate?

RESPONSIVE WRITING ASSIGNMENT

Write out the answers to the questions you formulated in the collaborative writing assignment you engaged in above. If, during the process of writing, you find you have gaps in your knowledge of the text or in your understanding of the critical reading process, fill in those gaps by rereading the text, studying the critical reading model, or engaging in conversation with a classmate or your instructor. Keep writing, rereading, studying, and rewriting until your responses are as complete as possible.

ASSESS YOUR PERFORMANCE
BY WRITING CRITICALLY

Assess your skill at writing in response to essay questions by writing a page explaining what was most difficult about the Responsive Writing Assignment in this chapter. Then write a second page in which you explain what you learned from responding to the assignment.

PART SIX

STRATEGIES
FOR
ASSESSMENT
AND
PROCESS-BASED
REVISION

INTRODUCTION

My writing weaknesses have to do with the way I have a hard time getting my meaning across to the reader. All the little mistakes I make while writing—things like simple punctuation or wrong word selection—make a big difference to the reader.

—Jason Schyuler

When Jason wrote these two sentences on the first day of a composition class, he got to the heart of what makes following the conventions of writing important. Writing is a communicative act, and the "little mistakes" you make while writing affect the accuracy of the **meaning** you're trying to communicate. Writing conventions aren't arbitrary "rules"; instead, they're ways of communicating that are familiar and, therefore, easy to follow. In fact, no convention is a "rule" but only an agreement to accept certain actions or practices. For example, in much (but not all) of the world, driving a car on the right side of the road is the convention. Like most conventions, writing conventions change with time and circumstance. At the beginning of this century in the United States, the word that U.S. citizens spell today as "color" had the conventional spelling "colour." Writing conventions do indeed change, but the general spirit behind them remains the same: writing conventions exist to make the communication of meaning more accurate. Simply put, if you fail to follow the conventions, you risk confusing your audience about what you *mean*.

However, *recognizing* the mistakes you make in the conventions is difficult to do on your own. No working writer constructs a text without engaging in some form of **informal collaboration.** At your college or university you have many collaborative sources: classmates, instructors, and the writing center or writing lab can all be used to help at any stage of the process. However, the best way to use any of these sources is actively and critically. Don't just have someone proofread your final draft and "correct" your punctuation. If punctuation is major problem for you, use your collaborator as an assessor and teacher, not merely as a correcting device. The most effective collaborative relationships are ones that help you assess your writing weaknesses and help you revise your use of the writing process to overcome those weaknesses.

A GUIDE TO PROCESS-BASED REVISION

Collaborate to Assess Your Problem Areas
Employ Process-Based Strategies to Revise
Practice What You've Learned in Subsequent Assignments

COLLABORATE TO ASSESS YOUR PROBLEM AREAS.   The most efficient way to identify your problem areas is through **collaboration** in a **workshop** with peer writers or in an **editorial relationship** with a mentor. Collaborating with others to identify and analyze your writing weaknesses is perhaps the most valuable part of the lifelong process of becoming a better writer. In addition, reading other writers' texts and helping them devise strategies for revision will move you to a greater understanding of how the process of writing works for different writers and in different writing situations. The more you think and talk about how you and others write, the more likely you are to revise individual papers effectively and use the writing process in general. However, effective collaboration is an active process that requires having both interpersonal skills and a knowledge of the writing process.

As the critical reader or criticized writer in a collaborative relationship, you'll have to go beyond cosmetic correcting or passive listening. You'll have to learn to identify problem areas in your own and other people's writing, but you'll also have to analyze why you and your collaborative partners make the mistakes you do. Identifying habitual problems is the first step toward becoming a better writer. Writing weaknesses are writer-specific. You'll find that in assignment after assignment you or another writer will have the same habitual problems. However, behind every writing weakness there's a reason—a gap in knowledge or a habitual misuse of the process. The major areas in which to look for weaknesses are the following:

Voice
Development
Arrangement
Mechanics

PROBLEMS WITH VOICE

COLLABORATE TO ASSESS THE PROBLEM.   If your instructors or collaborative partners often write "awkward" or "unclear" or "wrong word" on your papers, you most likely have problems with voice. Voice, you'll remember, is made up of **word choice** and **sentence structure.** Voice is similar to competitive ice-skating in that it can be evaluated both on its artistic merit and on its technical correctness. An **"artistically meritorious"** voice is **unified** by the writer's attitude toward the subject and is also **appropriate** to the writer's audience and purpose. A **"technically correct"** voice is free of sentence structure and word choice errors. Artistic problems and technical problems with voice aren't mutually exclusive. In fact, artistic problems with voice are often the root cause of technical errors.

COMMON ARTISTIC PROBLEMS WITH VOICE

PRETENTIOUS VOICE

One of the major causes of awkward, unclear writing is pretentious language choice. The word *pretentious* comes from the Latin word *praetendere,* which means "to pretend." A *pretension* is a showy display meant to impress other people. For example, buying a fancy car just to impress your neighbors would be a pretension. In writing, pretentious voice occurs when the writer is more interested in impressing an **audience** with **inappropriate fancy language** than he or she is in conveying meaning. Pretentious word and sentence structure choices are problematic for two reasons: first, they often **obscure the meaning** the writer is trying to communicate; second, just like buying that fancy car, they affect the writer's **credibility** by making him or her seem silly rather than impressive. Problems with pretentious voice can range in seriousness from the occasional choice of an overblown word or phrase by a writer to whole papers in which the writer's desire to "sound" like an authority becomes an end in itself, and any attempt to communicate meaning goes out the window. Interestingly, writers who have problems with pretentious voice are usually intelligent people who love language; they just love language so much that they often strain to make impressive word and sentence structure choices and in the process forget that the point of writing is to **communicate meaning** as clearly as possible.

COLLABORATE TO IDENTIFY PRETENTIOUS VOICE.   If your collaborators comment that your writing is "flowery" or "overwritten" or contains "jargon," you may have problems with pretentious voice. Similarly, if the text you read in a workshop is so overloaded with fancy words and sentence structures that its meaning is clouded or that it seems silly rather than credible, your partner may be making pretentious language choices. Problems with pretentious voice often lead writers to make faulty choices in connotation and denotation (see definitions and strategies under "Technical Problems with Voice"). In the following sentence the writer tries so hard to impress us with big words that we have difficulty understanding his meaning:

Original   Imbued with a new sense of pride and self-assurance, I became more audacious in my perceived role as a unique individual.

PROCESS-BASED REVISION STRATEGY   Redirect your energy away from impressing and toward communicating meaning as simply as possible. Imagine you're writing for the least intimidating audience possible (your closest friend or yourself). Then **reword** with **appropriate, relaxed language,** aiming for **clear, direct meaning.** As you practice writing as simply as possible, you may worry that your language is too "plain." However, don't heed these worries. The "plain" language of writers with pretentious voice problems is usually much more elegant than the "impressive" language they strain to create on the page. In addition, try the long-term strategy of keeping a "plain language" personal journal. After you have a few entries, read what you've written. Writing only for yourself and reading what you've written will help you appreciate the elegance of your own personal voice.

Revised   Because I had developed a new sense of pride and self-assurance, I was free to be myself.

INCONSISTENT VOICE

Inconsistent voice occurs when the writer shifts from one created persona to another in a single piece of writing. The persona you create on the page should be **appropriate** to your **purpose** and should also reflect a **unified attitude** toward the **subject.** Just as a pretentious voice can make a writer seem silly rather than impressive, a voice that veers from formal to informal, or from dead serious to highly amusing, can make the writer seem out of control and undercut his or her credibility.

COLLABORATE TO IDENTIFY INCONSISTENT VOICE.   If your collaborators comment that particular words or phrases are ''jarring'' or ''inappropriate,'' you may have problems with voice unity. Likewise, if you read a partner's text in a workshop and the voice suddenly shifts from formal and distant language to conversational language, your partner may not be creating a unified voice. Shifting out of one voice into another can often be the cause of pronoun shifts (see the ''Technical'' section). In the following passage the writer loses authority by shifting suddenly in the last sentence from a distant voice to a personal, colloquial one:

Original   From the start of the story, the reader realizes that the girl is skeptical about having an abortion. Unlike the American, she is able to look into the future and understand that an abortion will not bring the couple assured happiness. The girl seeks reassurance from the man, asking him, ''And if I do it you'll be happy and things will be like they were and you'll love me?'' Instinct tells her that things won't be the same. In fact, I think if she goes through with it, there will be hell to pay!

PROCESS-BASED REVISION STRATEGY.   **Reread** your text aloud. As you read, listen to your language and consider your **purpose** and **audience.** Then **reword for appropriateness and consistency.**

Revised   From the start of the story, the reader realizes that the girl is skeptical about having an abortion. Unlike the American, she is able to look into the future and understand that an abortion will not bring the couple assured happiness. The girl seeks reassurance from the man, asking him, ''And if I do it you'll be happy and things will be like they were and you'll love me?'' Instinct tells her that things will not be the same; therefore, she must search for such reassurance.

CASUAL VOICE

Casual voice problems are at the opposite end of the voice spectrum from problems with pretentious language. Writers with informal voice problems don't strain to make impressive language choices; they just write the way they speak without considering the effect their **inappropriately casual language** will have on their **audience.** Although in some writing situations (for example, letters to friends or some personal essays) a casual voice may be appropriate, in most academic writing situations informal or overly conversational language will undercut the writer's credibility by making him or her sound like an amateur. In addition, problems with casual language often lead writers to make technical errors in sentence structure and word choice.

COLLABORATE TO IDENTIFY THE PROBLEM.   If your readers often comment that your language is "too informal" or "overly conversational," you may have habitual problems with casual voice. Likewise, if your workshop partners' papers are overloaded with informal language (e.g., "like," "then," "I think," "this," "I figure"), he or she likely has problems with casual voice. In the following passage the writer's use of inappropriately informal language undercuts his credibility and leads him to make technical errors:

Original   I strongly disagree with Emma Goldman's essay "Marriage and Love." All of Emma's views are so extremely pessimistic and never optimistic that they don't sound like reality. Like, in this instance following her last statement there, she uses a quote from Dante that is so cynical it hurts: "Ye who enter here leave all hope behind." I personally think that Emma is the most cynical woman in the world and that makes it hard for me to believe her.

PROCESS-BASED REVISION STRATEGY   Read aloud first a page from your own paper and then a page from the paper of one of your partners who doesn't have a problem with informal language. As you read, listen to the differences in language choices. Then read your own work aloud a second time and **cut unnecessary informal words** and **reword** others into more formal language as you go along. Don't be discouraged if you have to repeat this rereading, rewording process a few times. Because you've been writing informally for a long time, breaking the habit may take time. As a long-term strategy, try reading passages from the model essays in this book or from the newspaper aloud to yourself for ten minutes every day. Listening to the sound of appropriately formal language as you read will help you make more formal choices in your own writing.

Revised   I strongly disagree with the judgments in Emma Goldman's essay "Marriage and Love." Goldman's views seem to be driven by an extremely pessimistic attitude, rather than by much real evidence. Her use of Dante's "Ye who enter here leave all hope behind," equating marriage with hell, is evidence of her excessive cynicism. It's difficult to take Goldman seriously because her judgments are so extreme.

THINK CRITICALLY ABOUT YOUR PERFORMANCE—CONSIDER THE CONNECTION BETWEEN ARTISTIC AND TECHNICAL PROBLEMS WITH VOICE

As you've probably noticed, artistic problems with voice often go hand in hand with technical problems with voice. For example, writers for whom pretentious language is a problem will often strain to employ complicated sentence structures that they don't yet command; in the process they create awkward, technically incorrect sentences. Similarly, writers for whom casual voice is a problem will often construct unclear, fragmented sentences that wouldn't be problematic in the back-and-forth exchange of spoken conversation.

COMMON TECHNICAL PROBLEMS WITH VOICE

COLLABORATE TO ASSESS YOUR SPECIFIC PROBLEMS

MAP YOUR TECHNICAL ERRORS IN VOICE.   As with all writing weaknesses, technical errors in voice are habitual and writer-specific. No one writer will make all the technical errors possible, but those errors he or she does make will be repeated again and again. One writer may repeatedly create sentence fragments; another writer may repeatedly shift verb tense. The habitual errors you make in voice aren't mysterious and insurmountable; instead, they merely indicate gaps in your knowledge of the conventions. Filling in those gaps is simply a matter of identifying your specific problems and learning the proper conventions. If you have technical problems with voice, identify and analyze your specific areas of weakness by **mapping** them with the help of a collaborator (your instructor, a writing lab tutor, or a *knowledgeable* fellow student).

To map:

- Identify
- Determine Scope
- Prioritize
- Define
- Discuss
- Practice

1. Ask your collaborator to **identify the technical errors** in voice in your text by marking them.

2. **Determine the scope** of your problems by connecting similar mistakes with a continuous line. For example, with the help of your collaborator, locate the first sentence fragment in your text and draw a line from it to the second fragment, then to the third, and so on. Follow the same process with other specific errors.

3. **Prioritize** your problems. Concentrating on your problems one at a time will make overcoming them easier. For example, if you have problems with sentence fragments and parallel structure, use the list of Common Technical Problems with Voice that follows to determine which problem to concentrate on first, and write out **your priority list.**

4. Work through your priority list (give yourself a couple of days to **concentrate on each problem**). Pre-read and then read thoroughly the section that defines the problem and provides **strategies for solving it.**

5. Discuss the definition with your knowledgeable collaborator. Talking through the definition and your problem will clear up any misunderstandings you may have and help **set the proper use of the convention** in your mind.

6. Practice the correct use of the convention by revising the sentences identified in your text in step one. Have your priority list on hand whenever you write (even in your journal), and continue to **practice** the proper conventions.

COMMON TECHNICAL PROBLEMS WITH VOICE

Fragmented Sentences

Lack of Parallel Structure

Misplaced and Dangling Modifiers

Faulty Subject–Verb Agreement

Faulty Pronoun–Antecedent Agreement

Faulty Pronoun Reference

Shift in Person

Shift in Tense

Faulty Denotation and Inappropriate Connotation

FRAGMENTED SENTENCES

Fragmented sentences, like whole sentences, have a capital letter at the beginning and a period, exclamation point, or question mark at the end. However, fragmented sentences are only **parts of sentences;** they don't make complete sense when you read them in isolation. A fragment may be missing one or both of the elements that would make it a whole, meaningful sentence—a subject and a complete verb—or it may start with a word that makes its meaning dependent on another sentence. Fragments are a significant problem because they usually interfere with the meaning you're trying to communicate, forcing the reader to stop and figure things out. When you revise your own fragments or help a partner with revision, it's important to read the sentences before and after the fragment to ensure that the revision accurately communicates the intended meaning. A useful strategy for identifying fragments is to read the paragraphs in your (or your partner's) text backwards, starting at the last sentence and finishing with the first. When you read sentences in isolation, it's easy to see which sentences are complete and which ones aren't.

FRAGMENT MISSING SUBJECT

Incorrect   Theroux says most young men are forced to believe the ideal male needs only male companionship. And are therefore separated from women.

Revised   Theroux says most young men are forced to believe the ideal male needs only male companionship and are therefore separated from women.

FRAGMENT MISSING COMPLETE VERB

Incorrect   The girl had brought along four suitcases. Each of a different color.

Revised   The girl had brought along four suitcases. Each one was a different color.

FRAGMENT STARTING WITH A WORD THAT MAKES IT DEPENDENT

Incorrect   Theroux says most young men are forced to believe the ideal male needs only male companionship and are, therefore, separated from women. Considering them a "riddle and a nuisance."

Revised   Theroux says most young men are forced to believe the ideal male needs only male companionship and are, therefore, separated from women, considering them a "riddle and a nuisance."

EXERCISE FOR PRACTICE

Practice identifying and revising sentence fragments by revising the following passages. Then check your work by conferring with a knowledgeable collaborator.

The emphasis has been to extend a patient's life. With no worry about how much suffering a person endures along the way.

Just as the American and the girl have loved irresponsibly. They continue to drink irresponsibly.

Goldman argues that marriage enslaves women. And men as well.

The man was having a drink at the bar when he noticed them. The people. They were all "waiting reasonably for the train."

LACK OF PARALLEL STRUCTURE

For your readers to understand the meaning of sentences that list or compare elements or examples, the elements or examples you list or compare should have similar grammatical structures.

Incorrect   The American man in Hemingway's short story "Hills Like White Elephants" is selfish, wants to continue his carefree lifestyle, and insensitive to the girl's situation.

Revised   The American man in Hemingway's short story "Hills Like White Elephants" is selfish, insensitive, and interested only in continuing his carefree lifestyle.

EXERCISE FOR PRACTICE

Practice the proper convention by constructing three sentences with correct parallel elements. Then check the sentences you construct by conferring with a knowledgeable collaborator.

MISPLACED AND DANGLING MODIFIERS

Words, phrases, or clauses that are **too far away from the words they relate to** will leave your readers confused about the meaning you're trying to communicate.

MISPLACED MODIFIER

Incorrect   Rising like white elephants, the girl looked at the hills on the other side of the valley.

Revised   The girl looked at the hills, which rose like white elephants on the other side of the valley.

DANGLING MODIFIER

Incorrect   Hurrying to catch the train, their bags were left behind on the platform.

Revised   In their hurry to catch the train, they left their bags behind on the platform.

EXERCISE FOR PRACTICE

Practice the correct placement of modifiers by revising the following sentences. Then check your work by conferring with a knowledgeable collaborator.

Standing at the end of the station, her mind was made up.
Most critics think that the American man is selfish incorrectly.
Having decided not to have the baby, their relationship will not last very much longer.

FAULTY SUBJECT–VERB AGREEMENT

The subject and verb in a sentence **must agree in number.** Plural subjects must be accompanied by verbs with plural endings. For example, "The *man eats* toast every morning" but "The *men eat* toast every morning." Subject–verb agreement can be particularly problematic for non-native speakers of English or for people whose dialects don't follow the conventional rule. However, a common kind of faulty subject–verb agreement occurs when the sentence you're constructing contains more than one noun and you mistake the noun closest to the verb for the verb's subject.

Incorrect   Only a small percentage of college students graduates without going into debt.

Revised   Only a small percentage of college students graduate without going into debt.

EXERCISE FOR PRACTICE

Practice subject–verb agreement by constructing three sentences in which you use the convention correctly. Then check the sentences you construct by conferring with a knowledgeable collaborator.

FAULTY PRONOUN–ANTECEDENT AGREEMENT

To avoid awkwardness and for the sake of precision, the pronoun you use to replace a word you don't want to repeat **should agree in gender and number** with the word it refers to. For correct gender agreement, for example, you'd replace *the girl* with *she*. For correct number agreement, you'd replace the *the hills* with *they* and *the station* with *it*. Although most of the time correct agreement is obvious, there are three kinds of antecedents that cause many people problems. First, singular words such as *either, neither, one,* and *each* should take singular pronouns.

Faulty agreement   Neither of the women felt that they agreed with the text's message.

Revised   Neither of the women felt that she agreed with the text's message.

Second, collective nouns (*couple, audience, committee, jury,* and *crew*) are singular in form but can be viewed as plural. With collective nouns the correct pronoun choice depends on the precise meaning the writer is trying to communicate. If the group is acting as a whole, use a singular pronoun.

Faulty agreement   The jury handed down their verdict of guilty.
Revised   The jury handed down its verdict of guilty.

If the group is acting separately, use a plural pronoun.

Faulty agreement   The couple sipped its drinks and continued to argue.
Revised   The couple sipped their drinks and continued to argue.

EXERCISE FOR PRACTICE

Practice pronoun–antecedent agreement by constructing three sentences in which you use singular nouns and pronouns correctly and three sentences in which you use collective nouns and pronouns correctly. Then check the sentences you construct by conferring with a knowledgeable collaborator.

Finally, there are ungendered singular nouns (*student, anyone,* and *citizen*) that can lead writers into making sexist language choices. Although in the past, masculine pronouns (*he, him,* and *his*) were acceptable choices for replacing ungendered nouns, recently the generic *he* has come to be considered sexist. Although you should avoid using sexist language, don't use a plural pronoun when you should be using a singular one.

Faulty agreement   Each student handed in their assignment.

To avoid sexist pronoun choices without making agreement errors, do one of the following: Use both gendered pronouns—*he or she, his or hers.*

Revised example   Each student handed in his or her assignment.

Rewrite to delete the personal pronoun.

Revised example   Each student handed in the day's assignments.

Make the antecedent plural.

Revised example   The students handed in their assignments.

EXERCISE FOR PRACTICE

Practice pronoun–antecedent agreement by constructing three sentences in which you use ungendered singular nouns correctly. Then check the sentences you construct by conferring with a knowledgeable collaborator.

FAULTY PRONOUN REFERENCE

To **avoid confusing your readers** about *who* is actually doing *what* to *whom* in the texts you construct, it's important to **use pronouns precisely.** There are two common problems with faulty pronoun reference. The first happens when a writer uses a word like *this* or *it* to refer to a word that is implied but never stated.

Vague reference	The treaty ensured that an armed attack against any one NATO member nation would be considered by the United States as an attack against all member nations. This allowed the United States to extend the protection of its nuclear weapons capability into Western Europe.
Revised	The treaty ensured that an armed attack against any one NATO member nation would be considered by the United States as an attack against all member nations. The attack-one, attack-all nature of the treaty allowed the United States to extend the protection of its nuclear weapons capability into Western Europe.

EXERCISE FOR PRACTICE

Practice avoiding vague pronoun reference by constructing a paragraph in which you use the convention correctly. Then check your work by conferring with a knowledgeable collaborator.

The second problem occurs when the pronoun could possibly refer to more than one word.

Ambiguous reference	Camille told Allison that she got an "A" as a final grade.
Revised	Camille told Allison that Allison got an "A" as a final grade.

EXERCISE FOR PRACTICE

Practice avoiding ambiguous pronoun reference by constructing three sentences in which you use the convention correctly. Then check your work by conferring with a knowledgeable collaborator.

SHIFT IN PERSON

Unnecessary shifts from one person to another in a single text break the unity of your created voice and undermine your credibility. The most common pronoun shift—from *one* to *I* or *you*—usually happens when the writer is straining to maintain a pretentious voice.

Shift in person	If one agreed with Goldman, you would have to conclude that marriage should be outlawed for the good of society.
Revised	If you agreed with Goldman, you would have to conclude that marriage should be outlawed for the good of society.
Shift in person	When we consider that Germany had lost its sovereignty, military might, and industrial backbone, you can understand why the German government was so eager to negotiate.
Revised	When we consider that Germany had lost its sovereignty, military might, and industrial backbone, we can understand why the German government was so eager to negotiate.

EXERCISE FOR PRACTICE

Practice avoiding shift in person by constructing three sentences in which you use the convention correctly. Then check your work by conferring with a knowledgeable collaborator.

SHIFT IN TENSE

Shifting unnecessarily from the past to the present or from the present to the past in a single piece of writing is **awkward** and **confusing** to your readers. Unnecessary shifts in tense often occur in responses to literature and in personal experience writing. The current convention in literary analysis is to use the present tense when referring to the action in a literary work. The following passage about Hemingway's story "Hills Like White Elephants" is an example of a writer having problems with the present tense convention in literary analysis.

Shift in tense	On the other hand, the implications of the girl's pregnancy are regarded very differently by the man. To him, the pregnancy was an imposition on their lives, an unwelcome intrusion into their carefree traveling.
Revised	On the other hand, the implications of the girl's pregnancy are regarded very differently by the man. To him, the pregnancy is an imposition on their lives, an unwelcome intrusion into their carefree traveling.

In personal experience writing, the writer can get so caught up in the action that he or she inadvertently shifts out of past tense into the exciting immediacy of present tense.

Shift in tense	The Mount Olive road crested after a steady rise, and Nancy had to gear down just before the summit. She was just about to put the car in third, when the fox leaps up onto the low wall on the right side of the road. He stands there, and he turns his head around to watch the car as it passes.
Revised	The Mount Olive road crested after a steady rise, and Nancy had to gear down just before the summit. She was just about to put the car in third, when the fox leaped up onto the low wall on the right side of the road. He stood there, and he turned his head around to watch the car as it passed.

EXERCISE FOR PRACTICE

Practice avoiding shift in tense by constructing a paragraph in which the tense is unified. Then check your work by conferring with a knowledgeable collaborator.

FAULTY DENOTATION AND
INAPPROPRIATE CONNOTATION

Faulty denotation occurs when a writer chooses a word with a different specific, direct meaning than the meaning he or she wants to communicate. For example, using the word *racism* to describe gender bias would be faulty denotation because the literal meaning of racism is discrimination or prejudice based on *race,* not on *gender.*

Inappropriate connotation, however, is a subtler diction problem altogether. The connotation of a word is its associated or indirect meaning. For example, although the words *altercation, spat,* and *debate* all have roughly the same meaning, the associations they bring to mind are quite different, so the words aren't exactly interchangeable.

Both faulty denotation and inappropriate connotation can undercut your **credibility.** To avoid faulty denotation and inappropriate connotation, pay attention to how new words you hear or read are used, and consult your dictionary regularly. In addition, if you use a thesaurus, make sure you do so in conjunction with your dictionary. Although pressing the thesaurus key on your word processor may seem like a quick and easy way to elevate your vocabulary, checking the connotation of a word with a second source can keep you from making an inappropriate choice.

In fourteen years of marriage my wife and I have found our own (relationship/association) to be somewhat (fragile/flimsy), (dynamic/energetic), and in need of constant maintenance. Over that span of time, we've had to (interminably/constantly) adjust and readjust to the demands of new situations, such as changing careers, the having and raising of children, and increasing financial burdens. Although at times we disagree, (argue/altercate), or even become (angry/furious) with one another, our (bilateral/mutual) (infatuation/love) is never compromised. Our love remains intact and is the (substructure/foundation) from which we (tussle/grapple) with our changing situations as well as with our personal problems.

THINK CRITICALLY ABOUT YOUR PERFORMANCE—CONSIDER THE CONNECTION BETWEEN PROBLEMS WITH VOICE AND PROBLEMS WITH DEVELOPMENT

Since the voice you create on the page reflects your attitude toward your subject, an inappropriately chosen voice can often affect the choices you make in developing your text. If your voice is vague and casual, the developmental material you include is likely to be vague and casual as well. Similarly, if your voice is pretentious, you're likely to lose track of the *meaning* you should be communicating. The point is, don't let a badly chosen voice dominate your thinking. Consider your audience as well as your attitude toward your subject.

EXERCISE FOR PRACTICE

Practice appropriate connotation by choosing the more appropriate word in each set of parenthesis in the passage that follows. Then check your work by conferring with a knowledgeable collaborator.

PROBLEMS WITH DEVELOPMENT

COLLABORATE TO ASSESS PROBLEMS WITH DEVELOPMENT. If your instructors or peer evaluators often write comments like "expand on this," "provide examples," "give evidence," or "make a judgment," you may have habitual problems with development. Ideally, a well-developed text should contain sophisticated, logically sound **judgments** all unified under a single, clear **message,** and supporting **evidence, examples,** or **reasons** for every judgment.

*To **add** the evidence and/or interpretive judgments necessary for a text to be well-developed, employ process-based strategies: Read Critically, Research, and Prewrite.* One cause for problems with development has to do with evidence; you may not be providing sufficient evidence (quantity and/or quality) to back up your conclusive judgments. Another cause of problems with development may be that you're not interpreting the evidence you do supply by drawing conclusions; you're just knitting bits of evidence together without making judgments about the meaning or significance of the examples and evidence you provide. If you have habitual problems with development, analyze why, and go back to the step of the writing process where those problems have their root. You may need to spend more time engaging in **critical reading** or **research** to gather evidence, or more time **prewriting** to evaluate or interpret evidence.

COMMON PROBLEMS WITH DEVELOPMENT

Unfocused Message
Lack of Supporting Evidence, Reasons, or Examples
Lack of Writer-Based Judgments
Logically Unsound Writer-Based Judgments

STRATEGIES FOR PROCESS-BASED REVISION

CRITICAL READING AND RESEARCH

To construct a well-developed text, you have to know what you're writing about. All the intelligence and skill with language in the world won't make up for a lack of knowledge of your subject. To put critical reading and research at the top of your writing process, see Part Two, "Critical Reading, Research, and Writing," and Chapter Ten, "Writing the Researched Paper."

PREWRITING

Prewriting is thinking on paper (or on the computer screen). It's here that you begin to generate the judgments and evidence that will make up the developmental bulk of the text you're constructing. Prewriting is a highly personal thing. No two writers do it exactly the same way. The prewriting strategies laid out below are ones that are commonly employed. The best way to use them is by experimentation. Try using as many as work for you.

AVOIDING FALLACIOUS THINKING

However, as you prewrite, make sure you avoid fallacious thinking. A **fallacy** is an error in thinking or a conscious deception that results in a mistaken or false conclusion. However, because fallacies often *sound* reasonable, they can be accepted by uncritical audiences. To avoid making logically unsound judgments and to recognize them when you encounter them, think critically as you prewrite and read critically. Although the three kinds of fallacies discussed below are grouped to correspond with the persuasive techniques *logos* (persuading with reason), *pathos* (persuading with emotion), and *ethos* (persuading by establishing credibility), they are all the result of faulty or deceptive logic. **Logical fallacies** (logos) are errors in **reasoning; emotional fallacies** (pathos) are immoderate or logically unrelated appeals to **emotion; ethical fallacies** (ethos) are logically unrelated attempts to **discredit** an opponent.

LOGICAL FALLACIES

- In a **non sequitur,** which means "it does not follow" in Latin, the writer or speaker draws a conclusion that isn't causally related to its premises.

Example   Congressman Pat Williams is a liberal Democrat; therefore, he will vote for gun control legislation in Congress.

Just because Congressman Williams is a liberal Democrat doesn't
mean he will necessarily vote for gun control legislation.

- In a **post hoc** fallacy, which means "after this, therefore caused by
this," the writer or speaker suggests that because one event
happened *after* another event, the second event must have been
caused by the first.

Example   Another example of Clinton's success as a president was
the increase in new home construction after his election
in 1992.

Although new housing starts may have increased after Clinton's
election in 1992, there is no clear connection between his
administration's policies and the increase.

- When a writer or speaker **begs the question,** he or she implies
that something that is up for debate has already been accepted as
true.

Example   Because they're irresponsible and irrational by their very
nature, young people should not be allowed to consume
alcohol until they're twenty-one.

The writer suggests that all young people are irresponsible and
irrational; however, there are quite a few people who would
debate the conclusion.

- In a **hasty generalization** the writer or speaker draws a
conclusion based on too little evidence.

Example   Professor Smith gave Anne a lower grade than he gave
Paul. He obviously gives higher grades to male students
than he does to females.

Concluding that Professor Smith gives men higher grades than
women on the basis of such a small sample would be unfair and
irrational.

EMOTIONAL FALLACIES

- Writers and speakers may use **veiled threats** to frighten their
audiences into agreeing with a particular position or taking a
course of action.

Example   If I'm not reelected in November, taxes will be raised
and the economy will fail.

The writer isn't providing evidence for anything, but only
enumerating bad things that might happen if he or she isn't
elected.

- In a **false analogy** the writer or speaker attempts to move us
emotionally by comparing one situation with another situation
that isn't similar in all or in significant respects.

  Example   Just as the female black widow spider lures and con-
  sumes her mate, the female of the human species entraps
  and destroys the male.

Humans and spiders are significantly different.

- In the **bandwagon** fallacy a writer or speaker suggests that a
proposition should be accepted because everyone thinks it's
reasonable or true.

  Example   Ninety-five percent of the student body is behind the
  tuition increase. Shouldn't you support it too?

Ninety-five percent of the student body could be wrong.

ETHICAL FALLACIES

- In **ad hominem** (meaning "to the man") fallacies the writer or
speaker attacks an opponent's character instead of concentrating
on the issue.

  Example   President Clinton had a relationship with Gennifer
  Flowers; therefore, he can't be trusted to make the right
  decision about Bosnia.

Clinton's relationship with Flowers has nothing to do with his
foreign policy decisions.

- In **guilt by association** a writer or speaker tries to discredit an
opponent by connecting him or her with a person the audience
views as unsavory.

  Example   Don't vote for Kirsten Peterson for student council president; her roommate was arrested for shoplifting.

The roommate's activities have nothing to do with Peterson's qualifications.

EXERCISE FOR PRACTICE

Either in collaboration with others or on your own, practice recognizing the fallacies discussed above by constructing two examples of each type. Then check your work by conferring with a knowledgeable collaborator.

EARLY-STAGE PREWRITING STRATEGIES

FREEWRITING.   If you have problems with pretentious language or trouble getting started on writing projects in general, openly **exploring** your subject without worrying about your audience's responses may be a good way to free up your mind. To freewrite, **just write nonstop** about a subject until you've generated as much language as possible. Don't take your pen off the page (or your fingers off the keyboard). If necessary, repeat the last word that pops into your head until a new one comes along. Don't think too deeply; just keep focusing on the subject and let the language take you where it will. Here's a fragment of freewriting:

> Hemingway those hills big elephants hot white shade. He buys the drinks that girl she's in pain she wants the man he wants to have fun stay in hotels—spent nights—you know I worry, how I get when I worry but he doesn't worry about her just get her to do what he wants—simple operation—shadow of a cloud—I worry—I worry how I get when I worry—Please, please, please be quiet stop talking I can't bear to think of that line and you'll love me and things will be like they were . . .

LOOPING.   Looping is just **enhanced freewriting.** After you've freely explored your subject for ten or fifteen minutes, go back and underline the most meaningful thing that you've gotten down. Using it as a focus, freewrite again. Keep repeating the process until you find a focus for your writing. Here's the beginning of a looping exercise based on the freewriting above. During freewriting the writer found a fragment of conversation from the story particularly meaningful, and explores the fragment by looping:

> I keep thinking about her worrying about him and how he feels—there's a threat in that you know how I get when I worry I'll pout like teenaged boy withdraw from you You do what I want or else I'll worry she's all concerned he won't think she's bright—no fun a drag on him she just wants to make things as they were by mentioning white elephants see how bright I can be at the end she capitulates I'll be be bright for you so you'll love me I'll order the beer and forget . . .

DOUBLE-ENTRY NOTES.   Some writers begin with double-entry notes. Draw a line down the center of a sheet of paper. On the left side, free-associate **(brainstorm)** and write down as many words about the subject as you can until you have exhausted the possibilities. Then on the right side, **comment on each word.** In your comments, go into more detail—supply examples and evidence, but also record your reflections and conclusive judgments about the specifics that you've listed on the left side of the page. Here's the beginning of a double-entry note exercise:

hills	like white elephants, rare
	a pain in the neck—depends on your perspective—definitely a responsibility
	He says, "I've never seen one,"
	She says, "No, you wouldn't have."
hot, dry	two sides—dry and barren
	also pressure, no relief
	suddenly their relationship is sticky—no more carefree days and nights
grain fields	other side—river, trees, fruitful life—we could have all this—every day *we* make it more impossible—she's always looking into the distance—at hills—at the fields—at the future—he's always looking at her at the table—shortsighted?
he's testy	the minute she speaks, he jumps down her throat—he's "worrying"—he makes her dance around him, she feels she has to be entertaining "sound bright" or he won't love her anymore
station	they must go somewhere from here—things will never be the same again—she "knows" things—that they'll never get their relationship back?—and "they're all so happy" —sarcasm?

SKETCHING Some people are visual. If you find that you usually grab a pencil and start sketching when you want to explain something, you may be a naturally **visual** person, and sketching may be a good tool for generating the ideas that you will then put into written language. Whether you're naturally visual or not, sketching can be a useful way of exploring either a process or the setting in a literary work. Here's a sketch of the setting in "Hills Like White Elephants."

CLUSTERING Like the brainstorming that you do in double-entry notes, clustering is a way of **free-associating** about the subject of your writing. The difference is that because it is visual, it allows you to see relationships among your subtopics. Here's an illustration of clustering based on Hemingway's "Hills Like White Elephants."

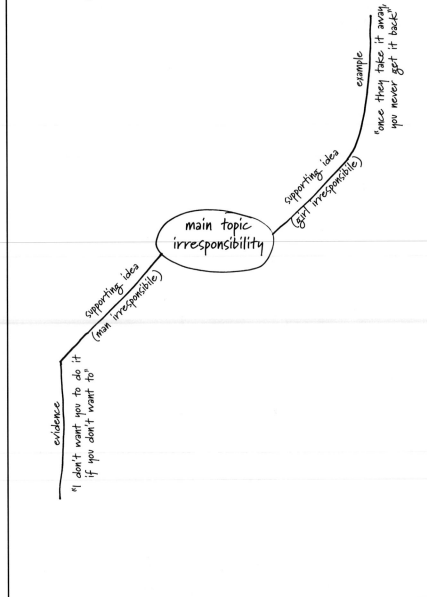

SUMMARIZING.   When you summarize, you **condense** a large amount of material into a smaller form. The primary purpose of writing a summary is to focus on what's significant in a particular text or situation in order to get at its meaning. Summarizing involves making claims about what's important in a subject and what isn't.

OUTLINING.   Outlining is most likely to be useful after you've explored a subject by freewriting or writing double-entry notes. A detailed double-entry note exercise can give you a place to start an outline. Outlining can help you **structure** a paper. In addition, you can use outlining to explore the causal relationships in processes, controversial situations, or works of literature. Here's the beginning of an outline of the couple's argument in the short story "Hills Like White Elephants."

 I. There's already tension between the couple
  A. She's being "bright"
   1. Hills look like white elephants
  B. He's ready to be irritated
   1. "I've never seen one"
   2. "That's the way with everything"
 II. They argue about the abortion
  A. He
   1. "awfully simple"
   2. "natural"
   3. "fine afterward"
  B. She
   1. Looks at ground
   2. Doesn't speak
   3. Doesn't think they'll be fine afterward

 Outlining is especially useful when employed in combination with one of the following "bridge strategies," which are discussed more fully under "Problems with Arrangement."

BRIDGE STRATEGIES

Because the strategies listed below are natural and familiar ways in which we humans think and communicate, they can be used as critical thinking strategies for **prewriting** and **developing** texts, and they can also be used as strategies for **arranging** entire texts or single paragraphs. Writers often use one or more of these strategies after they've warmed up their minds freewriting, clustering, or writing double-entry notes. Like "bridges," these strategies can carry you from free-form, writer-based **prewriting** into structured, audience-based **drafting.**

- Illustrating a Judgment
- Comparing and Contrasting
- Defining
- Considering Causes and Effects
- Dividing and Classifying
- Narrating
- Analogy
- Describing

PROBLEMS WITH ARRANGEMENT

COLLABORATE TO ASSESS THE PROBLEM.   If your readers often comment that your writing "goes off track," is "disorganized," or is "hard to follow," then you most likely have habitual problems with arrangement. A well-arranged text moves logically from one cluster of judgments and evidence to another without including unrelated material. In addition, a well-arranged piece of writing contains transitional words and phrases that connect one cluster of judgments and evidence to another.

Problems with arrangement often arise when a writer fails to distinguish between the prewriting stage of the writing process and the active drafting stage. Usually, you "write" your way into a text during the process of writing—your draft flows out of your prewriting. However, you then have to go back and amend and organize your text (revise it) into a form that is easily accessible to your audience. If you have problems with arrangement, **analyze** why. You may need to **cut** material that leads readers away from your message, you may need to **rearrange** sentences and paragraphs into a more logical order, or you may need to **add transitional words and phrases** to link one sequence of ideas to another.

PROBLEMS WITH LOGICAL ORDER

Like many problems with arrangement, lack of logical order often occurs when the writer fails to distinguish between prewriting and active drafting. When we prewrite, we're often reminding ourselves of what we know, so we don't have to make all the logical connections. However, when we draft, we make the **switch from internal to external audience,** and our external audience has to have all the logical connections laid out for them. Writing that's organized around a *familiar* set of logical relationships is easier to follow than the sometimes random reminders you write for yourself while prewriting.

COLLABORATE TO ASSESS THE PROBLEM.   If your collaborators often comment that your writing is "hard to follow" or "disorganized," you may have a general problem with lack of logical order. Similarly, if your workshop partner's draft seems more like an unformed prewriting exercise than a focused paper, he or she may be writing randomly for an internal audience rather than writing logically for an external audience.

EMPLOY PROCESS-BASED STRATEGIES TO REVISE.   To make your own or your partner's writing more accessible to an external audience, consider the following **familiar logical patterns** as strategies for organizing paragraphs or entire papers. In addition, since the following strategies are natural and familiar ways in which we humans think, they can also be used for focusing and expanding your **prewriting** to help you **develop** your texts fully and logically.

TOPIC SENTENCES, FORECASTING STATEMENTS, AND PARAGRAPHS

It's natural when we talk to people to give them a general idea of what we're going to talk about. If you think about the purposeful conversations you've had recently, you'll realize that many of them began with a statement of some kind. The statement might have been something like "This has been the worst day of my life" or "I want to talk to you about your son." Whatever the statement was, it served as an orientation to the conversation that followed. It's also natural to give our listeners a breakdown of what we're going to talk about, and to reorient them when we switch to a different subject. A breakdown statement following "This has been the worst day of my life" would be something like "You have to hear about how my car got hit, how I got fired, and how my cat needs surgery."

And the same kinds of general statements that help listening audiences follow the movements in spoken conversation also help reading audiences follow the movements in written texts. A **topic sentence** orients readers by telling them the general subject of a paragraph, just as a sentence that states the **message** of a text (a thesis sentence) tells readers what the general subject of the entire text will be. **Forecasting statements** give readers a breakdown of the general categories you'll cover in a text or a paragraph so that readers can anticipate the way the text or paragraph will be developed.

Paragraphing is another way to signal movements in written texts. **Introductory paragraphs** orient readers to the general subjects of texts and supply background information; **concluding paragraphs** discuss implications, offer solutions, or call for action from the reader. **Topic paragraphs** are groups of logically ordered sentences that present and fully develop a single, important aspect of a text's subject. **Transitional paragraphs** are guides that explain logical connections between one topic paragraph and another, or between topic paragraphs and introductory or concluding paragraphs.

BRIDGE STRATEGIES

When writers use any of the following strategies to structure paragraphs, they often cue their readers by identifying the focus of the paragraph in a **topic sentence.**

ILLUSTRATING A JUDGMENT   Illustrating a general judgment or point with specific **examples** or **reasons** is perhaps the most familiar logical pattern used in human communication. In addition to being used to structure paragraphs and whole essays, illustration is a **critical thinking strategy** that you should make a habit of using to test the soundness of your conclusions as you prewrite.

The following paragraph from Joseph Epstein's essay "A Few Kind Words for Envy" begins with a **topic sentence** that **identifies the general topic** of the paragraph and states a point, then ends with a sentence that presents a judgment.

> The second thing I remember envying was Catholics. For a time, from roughly age four to seven, I thought the United States was a Catholic country. This was owing partly to there being a pre-ponderance of Catholic families on our block and partly to the movies of those years, a large number of which seemed to feature Bing Crosby, Barry Fitzgerald, Spencer Tracy, and Pat O'Brien playing priests. I envied the rigmarole of the Catholic church, at least as it came across in the movies and in the bits and pieces of it I was able to pick up from families like the Cowlings. Nothing theological or even religious about this, for I was in fact rather like Valery, who felt that the protestants had made a big mistake and should have gotten rid of God and not the pope. I liked the lighting of candles, the confessional box, the prohibition against meat on Fridays, the clothes of priests and the extraordinary get-ups of nuns. "May I offer you a seat, Sister?" I used to say whenever the opportunity presented itself on Chicago streetcars or el trains. "Excuse me, Father, but would you care to have my seat?" I would announce with just a slight hint of an Irish brogue. Any fisher of souls who knew his business could have had me in the net in fewer than thirty seconds.

COMPARING AND CONTRASTING   Another natural way of thinking and communicating, **comparing and contrasting** things points out their respective **similarities or differences.** In addition to being a useful arrangement strategy, comparing and contrasting can be a useful pre-writing strategy. Comparison and contrast can be used in two ways to structure paragraphs or entire papers. You can use the block form, in which you present all the developmental material about one thing before you go on to the second thing; or you can you use the point-by-point form, in which you alternate between the two things, presenting developmental material about a specific element of each one. Student writer Lance Hummel uses the block form to structure a paragraph contrasting the perspectives of the American and the girl in "Hills Like White Elephants." Notice how Hummel starts the paragraph with a **topic sentence** that is also a judgment, and then later uses the transitional phrase *in contrast* when he shifts to discussing the man in the story. The block form is often used to structure paragraphs in essays that employ a point-by-point form overall.

> Throughout the entire conversation the man and the girl are not talking to each other as much as they are talking past one another. Each of them discusses the abortion on different levels. The girl is concerned with the future of their relationship—if their love can survive, and if they can develop a more responsible, viable union by keeping the child. The man, in contrast, cannot respond to the girl on her level and is only able to consider the problem at hand—terminating the pregnancy.

In the following paragraph, student writer Lauren Davidson uses a point-by-point structure to trace evidence of the American man's dominance over the girl in the same story:

> Signs of the man's domination of the girl are evident in their contrasting responses during conversation; in each case the girl capitulates to the man. At the beginning of the story, when the girl tries to initiate small talk by pointing out the hills, the man is ready to be irritated. In response, the girl caters to his irritation and defensiveness by changing the subject or falling silent after his comments. Later, as the man pressures the girl to have the abortion he reminds her of his superiority by warning her, "You know how I get when I worry," implying she should be worried about his worrying. In contrast, however, he never asks her about *her* feelings on the matter. For him the abortion is "perfectly simple." The girl is obviously dependent on this man. She knows that if she decides to have the child her life with him will terminate, and she is too dependent upon him to let that happen. This is made clear to the reader when the girls asks the man, "And if I do it you'll be happy and things will be like they were and you'll love me?" She needs reassurance of his love because she is not secure in it. She knows their relationship is not stable, but she does not have the courage to give up what little she has.

DEFINING.   You'll most often use definition in conceptual writing. Although you may be asked to write a whole paper defining a concept, you'll more likely use definition in combination with other strategies. In the following paragraph from "Being Black and Feeling Blue" Shelby Steele defines the concept of the anti-self as a way of setting up his personal concept of the "internal racist."

> I mention this experience as an example of how one's innate capacity for insecurity is expanded and deepened, of how a disbelieving part of the self is brought to life and forever joined to the believing self. As children we are all wounded in some way and in some degree by the wild world we encounter. From these wounds a disbelieving "anti-self" is born, an internal antagonist and saboteur that embraces the world's negative view of us, that believes our wounds are justified by our unworthiness, and that entrenches itself as a lifelong voice of doubt. This anti-self is a hidden but aggressive force that scours the world for fresh evidence of our unworthiness. When the believing self announces its aspirations, the antiself always argues against them, but never on their merits (this is a healthy function of the believing self). It argues instead against our worthiness to pursue these aspirations and, by its lights, we are never worthy of even our smallest dreams. The mission of the anti-self is to deflate the believing self and, thus, draw it down into inertia, passivity, and faithlessness.

CONSIDERING CAUSES AND EFFECTS.   Since we live in a world of causal relationships, it's likely that some form of causal analysis will be a useful part of each prewriting activity you engage in. Most of the formal Responsive Writing Assignments in this book ask you to engage in causal analysis by exploring the **motives** and **actions** of the active participants in a text or situation, and the **consequences** of those actions. However, in addition to being a highly useful prewriting strategy, causal analysis can be used to structure entire texts or single paragraphs, like the one that follows from Steele's "Being Black and Feeling Blue."

> This vulnerability begins for blacks with the recognition that we belong quite simply to the most despised race in the human community of races. To be a member of such a group in a society where all others gain an impunity by merely standing in relation to us is to live with a relentless openness to diminishment and shame. By the devious logic of the anti-self, one cannot be open to such diminishment without in fact being inferior and therefore deserving of such diminishment. For the anti-self, the charge verifies the crime, so that racial vulnerability itself is evidence

of inferiority. In this sense, the anti-self is an internalized racist, our own subconscious bigot, that conspires with society to diminish us.

DIVIDING AND CLASSIFYING.   Dividing and classifying are both ways of analyzing things. When you divide, you **separate** the elements that constitute a thing to discover their meaning or significance in relation to the whole. When you classify, you **group** elements into categories according to their similarities. Like the other strategies in this section, classifying and dividing are useful for **prewriting** and **development** as well as **arrangement.** In the following paragraph, writer Paul Keegan divides a phenomenon into constituent parts both to inform and communicate a judgment to his readers.

> Sexual assault, if that is what happened here, goes on at every college in America. About one woman student in eight is raped, according to a government survey. Ninety percent of these are victims of "acquaintance rape," defined as "forced, manipulated, or coerced sexual intercourse by a 'friend' or an acquaintance." Its most repugnant extreme is gang rape. Bernice Sandler of the Association of American Colleges says she has documented evidence of more than seventy incidents of this nationwide in the past four or five years. They usually involve fraternities and drugs or alcohol, she says, and the men nearly always contend that it wasn't rape, that they were merely engaged in group sex with a willing partner.

NARRATING.   The elements of narrative writing are **character, action,** and **setting.** Narratives are stories and are arranged chronologically according to time. Narratives can proceed along a straight time line, or they can employ flashbacks or flashforwards. You can use narration to structure and develop an entire text, or you can tell a story as a way of illustrating a judgment. In the following narrative paragraph from "Being Black and Feeling Blue," Shelby Steele uses a story to communicate a judgment about the consequences of racism:

> The sin I was made to carry was the sin of stupidity. I misread a sentence on the first day of school, and my fate was sealed. He made my stupidity a part of the classroom lore, and very quickly I in fact became stupid. I all but lost my ability to read and found the simplest math beyond me. His punishment for all my errors rose in meanness until one day he ordered me to pick up all the broken glass on the playground with my bare hands. Of course,

this would have to be the age of the pop bottle, and there were sections of the playground that glared like a mirror in sunlight. After half and hour's labor I sat down on strike, more out of despair than rebellion.

ANALOGY.   An analogy is an **imaginative comparison.** Comparing the similarities in things that are dissimilar is often an effective and subtle way to communicate a judgment. In the following paragraph from the essay "Marriage and Love," Emma Goldman uses an analogy to convey a powerful negative judgment about marriage:

> Marriage is primarily an economic arrangement, an insurance pact. It differs from the ordinary life insurance agreement only in that it is more binding, more exacting. Its returns are insignficantly small compared with the investments. In taking out an insurance policy one pays for it in dollars and cents, always at liberty to discontinue payments. If, however, woman's premium is a husband, she pays for it with her name, her privacy, her self-respect, her very life "until death do part." Moreover, the marriage insurance condemns her to life-long dependency, to parasitism, to complete uselessness, individual as well as social. Man, too, pays his toll, but as his sphere is wider, marriage does not limit him as much as woman. He feels his chains more in an economic sense.

DESCRIBING.   When you write descriptively, you ask the reader to imaginatively recreate a bit of the **physical** world. You want the audience to use their minds to recreate what you have received through some or all of your five senses. The following descriptive passage is from Beverly Lowry's "Getting to Know Mister Lincoln."

> The sun sets behind the Lincoln Memorial, at an angle from its southernmost corner. That night it had already gone down, but that time of year sunset blessedly lasts for what seems like hours, and the sky was wildly ablaze, framing the memorial in a pulsating glow of deep reds, wild pinks and hot golds as lush and beautiful and vulgar as a cheap chiffon scarf.

TRANSITIONAL DEVICES

Transitional words and phrases are connecting devices that make the meaning of text easier to follow. Transitions tell the reader how sentences or paragraphs in a text are **logically, temporally,** or **spatially** related to one another.

COLLABORATE TO ASSESS THE PROBLEM.   If your collaborative partners often comment that your writing "jumps" from one idea to the next, you may tend to underuse transitions. Similarly, if your workshop partner's text seems to "lurch" from one sentence or paragraph to another, he or she may need to clarify connections by **adding transitional devices.**

In the following persuasive paragraph, Emma Goldman's frequent use of transitions to signal **logical connections** pushes the reader along and is partially responsible for the passionate tone of her created voice.

> From infancy, almost, the average girl is told that marriage is her ultimate goal; *therefore* her training and education must be directed toward that end. *Like* the mute beast fattened for slaughter, she is prepared for that. *Yet,* strange to say, she is allowed to know less about her function as wife *and* mother than the ordinary artisan of his trade. It is indecent *and* filthy for a responsible girl to know anything of the marriage relation. Oh, for the inconsistency of respectability, that needs the marriage vow to turn something which is filthy into the purest *and* most sacred arrangement that none dare question or criticize. *Yet* that is exactly the attitude of the average upholder of marriage. The prospective wife *and* mother is kept in complete ignorance of her only asset in the competitive field—sex. *Thus* she enters into life-long relations with a man only to find herself shocked, repelled, outraged beyond measure by the most natural and healthy instinct, sex. It is safe to say that a large percentage of the unhappiness, misery, distress, *and* physical suffering of matrimony is due to the criminal ignorance in sex matters that is being extolled as a great virtue. *Nor* is it at all an exaggeration when I say that more than one home has been broken up because of this deplorable fact.

Following is a list of frequently used logical transitional words and phrases.

To introduce an illustration or example
    for example
    for instance
    particularly
    to illustrate

To indicate a contrast
    in contrast
    however

on the other hand
but
yet
nor
conversely
on the contrary

To introduce a cause or result
therefore
thus
consequently
so
because
since
for

To introduce a new item in a series
first
second
in addition
next
finally
and

To introduce a conclusion
in conclusion
finally
in summary
to sum up

Writers also use transitions to signal **temporal** and **spatial connections**—most often in creative and process writing, in responses to literature, and in personal essays. However, since temporal transitions are markers of the order of events in time, any narrative passage in a text might be improved with the addition of transitions. The following paragraph from Paul Keegan's "Dangerous Parties" contains both **temporal** and **spatial** transitional devices:

The boys arrived at the Wildcat that *Thursday night sometime between nine-thirty and ten o'clock* and drank about six beers apiece. *At about twelve-fifteen* they went out into the freezing night and headed back to their dorm *where* they encountered an eighteen-year-old freshman named Sara who had been drinking heavily at a fraternity party. *One by one*, each of the three boys had sex with her. *As the incident proceeded*, witnesses said, Jon bragged in the hallway that he had a "train" going in his room and *then* gave his friends high fives, as a football player might do after scoring a touchdown.

Following are temporal and spatial transitional words and phrases.

TEMPORAL

To signal particular time
    then
    now
    last Thursday
    on Monday
    next summer
    before

To signal the beginning
    in the beginning
    at first
    at the start of

To signal the middle
    meanwhile
    then
    as this was happening
    simultaneously

To signal an end
    finally
    eventually
    at last
    afterwards

SPATIAL

To signal direction
    up
    down
    beside
    around
    to the left or right
    across
    west or east

To signal closeness or distance
> here
> there
> near
> far
> close to
> in the distance
> against
> on the other side

INCLUSION OF UNRELATED MATERIAL

We've all known people who confuse us by suddenly veering off into another subject during the course of spoken conversation. "Veerers" are exhausting to talk to, and we usually think of them as being scatter-brained. And the same thing that is true in spoken conversation is also true in a written text: material that does not in some way **relate to the message** of your text drags your readers off in irrelevant directions, undermining the **unity** of your text and undercutting your **credibility.**

COLLABORATE TO ASSESS THE PROBLEM.   If your editors or workshop partners often question the "relevance" of passages in your text or say your writing "goes off track," you may be a habitual includer of unrelated material. Similarly, if your partner's draft contains passages that lead you away down unconnected paths, he or she has probably included evidence or judgments that aren't related to the text's message.

PROCESS-BASED STRATEGY   The strategy you use to get rid of unrelated material will depend on the scope of your problem. Minor problems can be remedied simply by **cutting the unrelated passages** that your collaborator has helped you identify. However, if you've included large quantities of unrelated material, it's probably best to **return to your prewriting** to cut or add developmental material, or even to reconsider your working message.

PROBLEMS WITH MECHANICS

COLLABORATE TO ASSESS YOUR PROBLEMS. As with all writing weaknesses, problems with spelling, punctuation, and mechanics are specific and habitual. One writer may repeatedly misuse semicolons; another writer may repeatedly create comma splices. The habitual errors you make in spelling, punctuation, and mechanics aren't mysterious and insurmountable; instead, they merely indicate gaps in your knowledge of the conventions of writing. Filling in those gaps is simply a matter of identifying your specific problems and learning the proper conventions.

MAP YOUR ERRORS IN MECHANICS. If you have problems with usage, identify and analyze your specific areas of weakness by **mapping** them with the help of a collaborator (your instructor, a writing lab tutor, or a *knowledgeable* fellow student). To map:

- Identify
- Determine scope
- Prioritize
- Define
- Discuss
- Practice

1. Ask your collaborator to **identify** the mistakes in mechanics in your text by marking them.
2. Determine the **scope** of your problems by connecting similar mistakes with a continuous line. For example, with the help of your collaborator, locate the first comma splice in your text and draw a line from it to the second comma splice, then to the third, and so on. Follow the same process with other specific errors.
3. **Prioritize** your problems. Concentrating on your problems one at a time will make overcoming them easier. For example, if you have problems with sentence fragments and comma splices, use the list of Common Problems with mechanics that follows to determine which problem to concentrate on first, and write out your **priority list.**

COMMON PROBLEMS WITH MECHANICS

Run-on Sentences
Lack of Comma in Compound Sentence
Lack of Commas to Separate Items in a Series
Lack of Commas Around Nonrestrictive Elements
Lack of Comma After Introductory Element
Incorrect Semicolon Use
Omission of Apostrophe to Signal Possession
Incorrect Colon Use
Incorrect Dash Use
Problematic Words:
   its/it's
   supposed to/used to
   there/their/they're
   whose/who's
   have/of
   past/passed
   to/too

4. Work through your priority list (give yourself a couple of days to concentrate on each problem). Pre-read and then read thoroughly the section that defines the problem and provides strategies for solving it.
5. Discuss the definition with your knowledgeable collaborator. Talking through the definition and your problem will clear up any misunderstanding you may have and help **set the proper use of the convention in your mind.**
6. Practice the correct use of the convention by revising the sentences you identified as incorrect in step one. Have your priority list on hand whenever you write (even in your journal), and continue to **practice** the proper conventions.

RUN-ON SENTENCES

BLATANT RUN-ONS   A blatant run-on sentence, also called a fused sentence, is created when a writer combines two or more sentences with no punctuation between them. Blatant run-ons are a significant problem for two reasons: first, they confuse the reader; second, they undercut the writer's credibility because they indicate a very basic gap in the writer's knowledge of the conventions. To overcome the writing of blatant run-ons, keep in mind that a whole sentence contains a subject and a complete verb.

Run-on   The American man is selfish he wants to continue his carefree lifestyle.

Revised   The American man is selfish. He wants to continue his carefree lifestyle.

Run-on   Goldman is against the institution of marriage she believes it enslaves both women and men.

Revised   Goldman is against the institution of marriage. She believes it enslaves both women and men.

COMMA SPLICE RUN-ONS.   Comma splices are the most frequently created kind of run-on sentence. A comma splice is created when a writer "splices" two independent sentences by connecting them with a comma.

Comma splice   The American is selfish, he wants to continue his carefree lifestyle.

Revised   The American is selfish. He wants to continue his carefree lifestyle.

Comma splice   Goldman is against the institution of marriage, she believes it enslaves both women and men.

Revised   Goldman is against the institution of marriage. She believes it enslaves both women and men.

EXERCISE FOR PRACTICE

Practice the proper convention by revising the following passage. Then check your work by conferring with a knowledgeable collaborator.

The field of medicine faces many human conditions whose mysteries have yet to be solved Alzheimer's, AIDS, multiple sclerosis and Lou Gehrig's disease are constant reminders of how much we don't know, these diseases inflict a great deal of physical and emotional pain on those afflicted.

For ways of revising run-on sentences by using semicolons, see the section on semicolon use.

LACK OF COMMA IN COMPOUND SENTENCE

A compound sentence is composed of two or more independent sentences joined together with a comma plus a coordinating conjunction *(and, or, but, for, nor, yet, so)*. A good way of remembering this convention is to think of a comma plus a coordinating conjunction as having the same power as a period:

, + and, or, but, for, nor, yet, so = .

Examples   We each bring our own abilities and gifts to the relationship, *and* the combination of these abilities makes the home into a more loving, caring environment than either of us could provide individually.
The man wants the pregnancy to be terminated, *but* he does not want to force the girl to have the abortion against her will.

EXERCISE FOR PRACTICE

Practice the proper convention by constructing three correctly punctuated compound sentences. Check the sentences you construct by conferring with a knowledgeable collaborator.

LACK OF COMMAS TO SEPARATE ITEMS IN A SERIES

To avoid confusing your readers, separate items in a series with commas.

Confusing   My favorite authors are Amanda Quick Catherine Hart Madeline Baker and Johanna Lindsey.
Revised   My favorite authors are Amanda Quick, Catherine Hart, Madeline Baker, and Johanna Lindsey.
Confusing   I've read western romances Civil War romances pirate romances Regency romances travel romances and futuristic romances.

EXERCISE FOR PRACTICE

Practice the proper convention by constructing three sentences in which you use commas to set off items in a series. Check the sentences you construct by conferring with a knowledgeable collaborator.

Revised   I've read western romances, Civil War romances, pirate romances, Regency romances, travel romances, and futuristic romances.

LACK OF COMMAS AROUND NONRESTRICTIVE ELEMENTS

A nonrestrictive element is a word or group of words that can be taken out of a sentence without changing the essential meaning of that sentence. Nonrestrictive elements provide the reader with additional information about a preceding part of the sentence without restricting or changing the meaning of that part. To avoid confusing your readers about what is essential in a sentence, you should set the nonessential elements off with commas or with a comma.

Confusing   The couple was waiting for the express from Barcelona which was due to come in forty minutes.
Revised   The couple was waiting for the express from Barcelona, which was due to come in forty minutes.
Confusing   The man of course wants the pregnancy to be terminated.
Revised   The man, of course, wants the pregnancy to be terminated.
Confusing   My father who is a well-known violinist often travels to Europe.
Revised   My father, who is a well-known violinist, often travels to Europe.

EXERCISE FOR PRACTICE

Practice the proper convention by constructing three sentences in which you use commas to set off nonrestrictive elements. Check the sentences you construct by conferring with a knowledgeable collaborator.

LACK OF COMMA AFTER INTRODUCTORY ELEMENT

To avoid confusing your readers, set off an introductory element with a comma.

Confusing	In contrast Jig, as the man sometimes refers to her, is aware of what the man wants.
Revised	In contrast, Jig, as the man sometimes refers to her, is aware of what the man wants.
Confusing	Because of his lack of foresight and selfishness the American man can't empathize with the girl.
Revised	Because of his lack of foresight and selfishness, the American man can't empathize with the girl.
Confusing	In fact the girl sees other problems in their relationship.
Revised	In fact, the girl sees other problems in their relationship.

EXERCISE FOR PRACTICE

Practice the proper convention by constructing three sentences in which you correctly use a comma after an introductory element. Check the sentences you construct by conferring with a knowledgeable collaborator.

INCORRECT SEMICOLON USE

A semicolon is most commonly used like a "tight" period to draw two independent sentences together in terms of their meaning.

Separate   I love Mike. He is an adventurous cook.
Together   I love Mike; he is an adventurous cook.

In the first example, the two independent sentences are separated by a period, suggesting that they are two separate assertions about the subject, "Mike." However, in the second example the two sentences are drawn together with a semicolon, which signals a connection between the writer's love of Mike and the assertion that he is "an adventurous cook."

Semicolons can also be used to correct comma splice run-on sentences when the two independent sentences are related in terms of their meaning.

Comma splice   Goldman is against the institution of marriage, she believes it enslaves both men and women.
Revised   Goldman is against the institution of marriage; she believes it enslaves both men and women.

In addition, to avoid confusing your readers, use semicolons to separate items in a series when the items contain commas.

Confusing   Mike's favorite recipies are Autumn Pasta, a pasta dish made with anchovies and black olives, Potage Bon Femme, a rich pea soup, and Coyote Fajitas, fajitas with salmon and goat cheese.
Revised   Mike's favorite recipes are Autumn Pasta, a pasta dish made with anchovies and black olives; Potage Bon Femme, a rich pea soup; and Coyote Fajitas, fajitas with salmon and goat cheese.

EXERCISE FOR PRACTICE

Practice the proper convention by constructing three sentences in which you use semicolons correctly. Check the sentences you construct by conferring with a knowledgeable collaborator.

OMISSION OF APOSTROPHE TO SIGNAL POSSESSION

Apostrophes tell the reader that one thing is possessed or owned by another thing. To form the possessive of most singular nouns and indefinite pronouns—pronouns that don't refer to specific nouns (*somebody, anybody, anyone, nobody*)—add an apostrophe and -*s*. Omitting apostrophes can confuse your readers about whether nouns are plural or singular.

Confusing   The girls hat was on the table.
Revised   The girl's hat was on the table.
Confusing   Hemingways short story is set in Spain.
Revised   Hemingway's short story is set in Spain.
Confusing   After the train left, the woman found somebodys luggage
                    next to the station.
Revised   After the train left, the woman found somebody's luggage
                    next to the station.
Confusing   Nobodys luggage was lost in transit.
Revised   Nobody's luggage was lost in transit.

Form the possessive of plural nouns that end in *-s* by adding the apostrophe *after* the *-s*.

Confusing   The students final papers were all brilliantly written.
Revised   The students' final papers were all brilliantly written.
Confusing   The dogs tails wagged in unison.
Revised   The dogs' tails wagged in unison.

Form the possessive of plural nouns not ending in *-s* by adding an apostrophe and an *-s* as with singular nouns.

Confusing   The childrens jackets were piled on a table.
Revised   The children's jackets were piled on a table.
Confusing   The womens trucks were parked in the alley.
Revised   The women's trucks were parked in the alley.

EXERCISE FOR PRACTICE

Practice the proper convention by constructing three sentences in which you use apostrophes correctly. Check the sentences you construct by conferring with a knowledgeable collaborator.

INCORRECT COLON USE

Colons should be used after a *complete statement* when a list follows.

Incorrect   I like: Brittany spaniels, Labrador retrievers, and Scottish
                    terriers.
Correct   I like the following breeds: Brittany spaniels, Labrador retriev-
                    ers, and Scottish terriers.

EXERCISE FOR PRACTICE

Practice the proper convention by constructing three sentences in which you use colons correctly. Check the sentences you construct by conferring with a knowledgeable collaborator.

INCORRECT DASH USE

Overusing dashes will clutter your writing and make it seem gushing. Therefore, use dashes *sparingly* to signal an abrupt change in thought or to emphasize what follows.

Overused dash	Best of all—stand on the south corner of Ryman Street at nightfall. On winter evenings—the sky—cools slowly into a deep frosty blue.
Revised	Best of all, stand on the south corner of Ryman Street at nightfall. On winter evenings the sky cools slowly into a deep frosty blue.
Sparing dash use	I slept like a baby—every two hours I woke up screaming.

EXERCISE FOR PRACTICE

Practice using dashes by constructing three sentences in which you use dashes sparingly. Check the sentences you construct by conferring with a knowledgeable collaborator.

PROBLEMATIC WORDS

Following is a list of words that student writers often confuse or use incorrectly.

ITS/IT'S   *Its* is a possessive pronoun, meaning "belonging to it" or "of it." Like *his* or *hers, its* doesn't contain an apostrophe.

Examples   The dog wagged its tail.
The tree lost its leaves.

On the other hand, *it's* is a contraction, meaning "it is" or "it has." When you take the second *i* of it *it is* or the *ha* out of *it has* to make it one word, you put in the apostrophe to mark what you've taken out.

Examples   It's a long way from Maine to California.
It's funny that you say that.
It's been over for hours.

EXERCISE FOR PRACTICE

Practice the proper convention by constructing three sentences in which you use *it's* correctly and three sentences in which you use *its* correctly. Check the sentences you construct by conferring with a knowledgeable collaborator.

SUPPOSED TO/USED TO   The correct form of both of these expressions takes the *ed* ending ("I am suppos*ed* to go to New York in the morning"; "I us*ed* to go to New York every January"). However, many student writers write *suppose to* and *use to* because the *d* at the end of *supposed* and *used* isn't pronounced in spoken conversation.

EXERCISE FOR PRACTICE

Practice the proper convention by constructing three sentences in which you use *supposed to* correctly and three sentences in which you use *used to* correctly. Check the sentences you construct by conferring with a knowledgeable collaborator.

THERE/THEIR/THEY'RE.   *There* refers to place.

Example   I left my sweater over there.

Their is a possessive pronoun, meaning "belonging to them."

Example   Their books were scattered all over the room.

They're is a contraction of *they are.*

Example   They're going to New York in the morning.

EXERCISE FOR PRACTICE

Practice the proper convention by constructing three sentences in which you use *there* correctly, three sentences in which you use *their* correctly, and three sentences in which you use *they're* correctly. Check the sentences you construct by conferring with a knowledgeable collaborator.

WHOSE/WHO'S.   *Whose* is the possessive form of *who.*

Example   Whose book is this?

Who's is a contraction of *who is.*

Example   Who's going with me in the morning?

EXERCISE FOR PRACTICE

Practice the proper convention by constructing three sentences in which you use *whose* correctly and three sentences in which you use *who's* correctly. Check the sentences you construct by conferring with a knowledgeable collaborator.

HAVE/OF.   Like *suppose to* for *supposed to, of* is often used where *have* should be because the two words sound the same when spoken. ("I should of gone" sounds like "I should have gone"). However, *have* is part of a verb and *of* isn't.

Examples   I would have caught the train if the bus had been on time.
She could have gone to the movies.

EXERCISE FOR PRACTICE

Practice the proper convention by constructing three sentences in which you use *have* correctly. Check the sentences you construct by conferring with a knowledgeable collaborator.

PAST/PASSED.   *Passed* is the past-tense form of the verb *pass*.

Example   The train passed here at three o'clock.

Past is an adjective or a noun that refers to events that have already occurred.

Example   If he'd been thoughtful, he might have learned from the mistakes of the past.

EXERCISE FOR PRACTICE

Practice the proper convention by constructing three sentences in which you use *past* correctly and three sentences in which you use *passed* correctly. Check the sentences you construct by conferring with a knowledgeable collaborator.

TO/TOO.   *Too* either means "also" or "an excessive amount."

Examples   I'm an excellent skier too.
            The soup is too hot.

To usually refers to direction or movement.

Example   Greg is going to Ben's house after dinner.

EXERCISE FOR PRACTICE

Practice the proper convention by constructing three sentences in which you correctly use *to* and three sentences in which you correctly use *too*. Check the sentences you construct by conferring with a knowledgeable collaborator.

INDEX

Academic community research,
115–116
Academic freedom, 115
Acknowledging sources, 135
Active drafting
for controversial issues, 294
described, 187
of process writing, 237–238
using, 94–95
See also Drafting
Active essay writing, 362
Active listening, 495
Active observation, 104–105
Active revising, 451–452
Active rewriting
on controversial issues, 295–296
described, 187–188
of essay, 362–363
of process writing, 238
See also Rewriting
Active secondary research, 115
Ad hominem fallacies, 528
Almanacs, 121
American Psychological Association
(APA), 470
Analogy, 541
Apostrophe, 552–553
Arrangement
considered during drafting,
93–94
of controversial issues, 279, 294
described, 49–50
of essay writing, 356–357,
361–362
of fiction/film writing, 407–408,
451
of personal experience text, 174,
186–187
problems with, 535–545
in process writing, 219–220, 237
used in collaborative assignment,
80
using computer for, 94
Article citations, 474–475
Atlases, 121–122
Attitudes, 71, 92
See also Writers
Audience
considered during drafting, 91
of controversial issues, 273, 288,
291
determining the, 72

of essay writing, 258, 353, 355
of exams, 497–498
of fiction/film writing, 403, 445,
448
focus on, 90
internal vs. external, 535
of personal experience text, 170,
181, 184
persuasion processes used for,
77–80
for process writing, 214, 231, 234
writer's choices on, 47–52, 86–87
writing arrangement and, 49–50
writing purpose and, 5–6, 22–23
writing situations and, 22
Author card, 462

"Bachloresque Dad" (Richter), 36–37
Bandwagon fallacy, 528
"Beautiful Fire" (Silberman),
478–489
"Beauty Helpline" column
(*Cosmopolitan*), 7
"The Beekeeper" (Hubbell), 202–205,
237
Begs the question, 527
"Being Black and Feeling Blue"
(Steele), 62–68, 539–540
"Being a Man" (Theroux), 501
Bevis, William, 9, 12
Bibliographic Index, 120
Bibliographies, 120, 123
Biographical dictionaries, 121
Blatant run-on sentence, 547–548
Book citation, 473–474
Brackets, 469
Brainstorming, 232, 530
Bridge strategies
to structure paragraphs, 537–
541
used in development, 533–534
"Bringing Home the Red Lantern"
(Wayman), 220–225
Bruck, David, 308
Burke, Kenneth, 3, 4

Carver, Raymond, 416
Casual voice, 511–512
"Cathedral" (Carver), 416–431
Causality, 216
Causes and effects, 539–540
CBE Style Manual, 470

Central catalogue (library), 119–120
Citation conventions, 470–472
Classifying, 540
Cliff, Michelle, 152
"Clint Eastwood and the Machinery
of Violence" (Tibbetts),
386–399
Closed questions
during interview, 99
in questionnaire, 107–109
Collaboration
on development problems,
525–526
on inclusion of unrelated
material, 545
informal, 20, 507
prewriting exercise, 35
on primary research, 98–99
to assess arrangement problems,
535
to assess transitional problems,
542
to assess voice problems, 509–513
to assess writing problems, 508
two students on process of,
228–229
writer's choices used in, 79–80
writing and, 20–21
Collaboration writing assignment
on controversial issues, 278–279
for essay exam question, 502
for essay writing, 315–316
for expressive writing, 69–72
for fiction/film writing, 373–379,
401–404, 405–408, 446
process of, 30, 32, 35–36
on process writing, 213–220
to explore meaning of
experiences, 169–170
to improve personal experience
writing, 173–174
Collaborative research assignments,
124–125, 171
College library sources, 118–122
Colon, 553
Comma splice run-on sentences,
548–549
Commas
after introductory element, 551
compound sentences and, 549
nonrestrictive elements and,
550–551

Commas (*cont.*)
    to separate items in series,
        549–550
Common knowledge, 468
Communication
    evidence-supported writing for,
        92
    meaning to create purpose in, 5
    using divisions to, 540
    See also Conversation
Compare and contrast, 537–538
Compound sentences, 549
Computers
    accessing library sources by, 119,
        461–463
    for editing development
        materials, 93
    used in arrangement, 94
    used in research paper writing,
        458
    used to access Internet, 118
    used to create voice, 92
    writing with, 16
Concluding paragraphs, 536
Conclusions
    about subject, 59–61
    critical pressure on, 93
Connotation, 523–524
Consequences, 539
Continents in Motion, 241
Controversial issues
    encountering subject of, 270–271
    meaning of, 272–274
    prereading of, 242–270
    research on, 271, 272, 274, 289
    rewriting, 295–296
    techniques for responding to,
        242
    writers and, 240–242
Controversial issues writing
    assessing past performance and,
        287–288, 296
    drafting to revise, 292–294
    exploring situation of, 288–289
    guide to process of, 287
    perspective on, 279–287
    persuasion focus on, 274–278
    prewriting for, 289–292
Conversation
    critical thinking through, 495
    writing as, 3–4
    See also Communication
Course journal, 15
Credibility
    faulty denotation/connotation
        and, 524
    persuading through, 78–79
    in process writing, 218
    of research sources, 101
    of specialized sources, 123

unrelated material impact on,
    545
Crenshaw, Theresa L. 260, 275
Critical reading
    described, 4
    as essay question study strategy,
        496
    learning through, 75–77
    for meaning in text, 59–68
    model for, 61
    of personal experience text,
        171–173
    preread as part of, 61–68
    primary research and, 99
    as research activity, 19
    of specialized sources, 124
    student on, 73–75
Critical secondary research, 115
Critical thinking
    about fiction/film writing
        performance, 452
    described, 4
    drafting for revising, 38–39
    during secondary research, 115
    as essay question study strategy,
        495–496
    in expressive writing, 7–9
    student writer on, 9–12
    summarizing as, 109–110
    to assess voice, 513, 524
Critical writing
    assessing essay performance by,
        503
    assessing performance by, 53, 96,
        239
    described, 4
    as essay question study strategy,
        497
    student writer on, 9–12
    See also Writing

"Dangerous Parties" (Keegan),
    316–333, 543–544
Dangling modifiers, 517
Daniels, Harvey A. 125
Dashs, 554
Davidson, Lauren, 410, 538
"Death and Justice: How Capital
    Punishment Affirms Life"
    (Koch), 303–308
"The Death Penalty" (Bruck),
    308–313
Denotation, 523–524
Describing, 541
Development
    common problems with, 525–534
    considered during drafting to
        revise, 92–93
    of controversial issues, 278–279,
        293–294

described, 49
of essay writing, 356, 360–361
of fiction/film writing, 406–407,
    450
of personal experience text,
    173–174, 186
in process writing, 219, 236–237
used in collaborative assignment,
    80
Dewey Decimal System, 463
Dictionaries, 121
"Different Environment Different
    Me" (Richter), 37–38
Dividing writing elements, 540
Documentation
    conventions of, 467
    of sources, 468–469
    specific to disciplines, 135
    styles of, 470
    See also Research
Double-entry notes, 530
Drafting
    controversial issue writing,
        292–294
    of essay writing, 359–362
    of fiction/film writing, 449–451
    personal experience text, 185–187
    process writing, 235–238
    of research paper, 466–468
    revising your thinking by, 38–39
    to revise, 91–95
    using active/recursive, 94–95,
        187, 237–238, 294

Earling, Debra, 9
Eastwood, Clint, 372
Electronic sources citations, 475–476
Elliot, Gary D., 381
Ellipsis, 469
Emotional fallacies, 527–538
Emotions
    persuading with, 78
    of speaker, 70–71
    See also Pathos
Encyclopedias, 121
Epstein, Joseph, 537
Essay exams
    assessing performance on, 503
    practicing strategies for, 500
    strategies for studying for,
        497–499
    strategies for taking, 499–500
Essay questions
    long-term study strategies for,
        494–497
    sample answer to, 501
Essay writing
    assessing past performance for,
        352
    brief anthology of, 316–345

drafting to revise, 359–362
encountering subject of, 313–314
guide to process of, 352
meaning of, 315–316, 354–355
perspective of, 345–351
persuasion in, 355–357
prereading for, 302–313
prewriting, 357–359
research for, 314, 354
rewriting, 362–363
techniques for, 302
writer's scenario for, 301–302
writing situation for, 352–353
Ethical fallacies, 528–529
Ethos
    for controversial issues, 276–278
    described, 78–79
    in fiction/film writing, 405
    for personal experience text, 172
    in process writing, 218
Evidence
    critical pressure on, 93
    developing specific, 49
    as essay question study strategy,
        496
    supporting judgments, 18–20
Explicitly expressive writing, 68–69
Expression, 6–9
Expressive writing
    critical thinking in, 6–9
    implicitly/explicitly, 68–69

Fallacious thinking, 526–527
False analogy, 528
Faulty denotation, 523–524
Faulty pronoun reference, 520–521
Faulty pronoun-antecedent
    agreement, 518–519
Faulty subject-verb agreement,
    517–518
"A Few Kind Worlds for Envy"
    (Epstein), 537
Fiction anthology, 414–444
Fiction/film writing
    analyzing for meaning, 373–379
    assessing past performance of,
        444–445
    drafting to revise, 449–451
    encountering subject of, 385, 399,
        445
    guide to response, 414
    meaning of responses to, 400–404
    prereading fiction, 367–372
    previewing film, 372
    prewriting for, 447–449
    primary fiction text and, 414–444
    research for, 373, 385, 400, 401,
        404
    rewriting of, 451–452
    secondary responses to, 379–385

student responses to, 408–413
techniques for responding to, 367
using persuasion in, 405–408
writer's response to, 365–367
writing situation of, 445–446
Films (suggested viewing list), 444
Final form
    of controversial issues writing,
        296
    editing to, 96
    of essay writing, 363
    of fiction/film writing, 452
    of personal experience text, 188
    of process writing, 239
"Fire on the Plains" (Richter), 39–47
Fletcher, Mary Dell, 383
Forecasting statements, 536
"Forestry: Only God Can Make A
    Tree, But . . ." (Frome),
    243–252
Formal collaboration, 21
Fragmented sentences, 515–516
Freewriting, 529
Frome, Michael, 243
Fused sentence, 547–548

Gadbow, Grady, 280
"Gays In Arms" (Weisberg), 252–260
"Getting Into Bob Weir Hot
    Springs" (Ricker and Pollner),
    225–228
Getting Started (journal entry), 14
"Getting To Know Mister Lincoln"
    (Lowry), 147–152, 541
"Girl" (Kincaid), 414–415
Goldman, Emma, 333, 541, 542
Green, Tripp, 408
Guilt by association, 528–529

Han, Lutfi, 83
Harjo, Joy, 141
Hasty generalization, 527
Have/of, 556
Hemingway, Ernest, 368
"Hemingway's 'Hills Like White
    Elephants' " (Elliot), 381–382
"Hemingway's 'Hills Like White
    Elephants' " (Fletcher),
    383–385
"Hemingway's 'Hills Like White
    Elephants' " (Kobler), 380–381
"Hills Like White Elephants: Critical
    Analysis" (Green), 408–410
"Hills Like White Elephants"
    (Davidson), 410–412, 538
"Hills Like White Elephants"
    (Hemingway), 368–372,
    379–385
"Hills Like White Elephants"
    (Hummel), 538

"HIV Testing: Voluntary,
    Mandatory, or Routine?"
    (Crenshaw), 260–270
"Howling" (McNamer), 110–113
Hubbell, Sue, 202
Hummel, Lance, 348–351, 538
Hypothesis (research paper),
    458–459

"I Can Wash My Rugs on Sunday"
    (Straw-Gusé), 176–178
"If I Could Write This in Fire, I
    Would Write This in Fire"
    (Cliff), 152–168
Implicitly expressive writing, 69
"In Defense of American Education"
    (Skinner), 283–287
Inappropriate connotation, 523–
    524
Inconsistent voice, 510–511
Indexes, 120, 123
Informal collaboration, 20, 507
Interlibrary loan, 122
Internet, 118
Interview citations, 476
Interviewing
    experts, 117–118
    as primary research, 99–103
    on process, 233
    research mentor, 460
    student on research paper
        performance, 490–493
    to encounter subject, 168
Introductory element, 551
Introductory paragraphs, 536
Its/it's, 554–555

"Journal Entries of a College
    Freshman" (Plath), 25–32
Journals
    entry by Jesse Richter, 36–38
    evidence-supported judgments
        in, 25
    keeping a personal, 15
    learning to write, 14–15
    as part of essay study strategy,
        497
    research, 458
    responsive writing in, 17, 24, 33,
        72–73
Judgments
    comparing collaboration group,
        76–77
    development to support, 49
    illustrating, 537
    making evidence-supported,
        18–20
    through critical thinking, 495
    using division to communicate,
        540

Judgments (*cont.*)
within expressive writing, 7–9
within journal writing, 25

Keegan, Paul, 316, 540, 543
Kincaid, Jamaica, 414
Kobler, J. F., 380
Koch, Edward I., 303
Kramer, Mark, 205, 237

Leading questions, 107
Learning
through collaboration, 21
through critical reading, 75–77
"Learning to Read" (Malcolm X),
191–201
Libraries (college), 118–122
Library of Congress Classification
System, 463–464
Library search
cataloguing system used in,
462–464
computers used in, 119, 461–463
on controversial issues, 271
on process, 233
Logical fallacies, 526–527
Logical order, 535–536
Logos
for controversial issues, 275–276
described, 77–78
in personal experience text,
171–172
in process writing, 218
Looping, 529–530
Lowry, Beverly, 147, 541

McNamer, Deirdre, 110
Malcolm X, 191
Mapping mechanic errors, 50–52,
546–547
Mapping voice problems, 513
"Marriage and Love" (Goldman),
333–341, 541
"Marriage and Love" (Hummel),
348–351
"Marriage and Love" (student
author), 345–348
Meaning
analyzing fiction/film for,
373–379
clarity of, 92
communication to create, 5
of controversial issues, 272–274
critical reading for, 59–68,
169–170
essay question study strategy
and, 496
of essay writing, 315–316,
354–355
expressive writing and, 8

of process, 213
reading critically to discern, 4
of responses to fiction/film,
400–404
writing mistakes which affect,
507
Mechanics
apostrophes, 552–553
colon use, 553
commas, 548–551
described, 50
mapping, 50–52, 546–547
problematic words and, 554–557
problems with, 546–557
of quoted material, 468–469
semicolon, 551–552
using collaboration for, 507
using dashs, 554
See also Punctuation
Meek, Jonathan, 412
Message
considered during drafting, 91
of controversial issues, 273
determining the, 71
development to support, 49
in essay writing, 316, 355, 359
of fiction/film writing, 403,
448–449
focus on working, 91
of personal experience text,
169–170, 185
of process writing, 214, 235
veering away from, 545
Microforms, 122
Misplaced modifiers, 517
*MLA Handbook for Writers of Research
Papers*, 470
Modern Language Association
(MLA), 470
Motives, 539

Narrating, 540–541
Non sequitur fallacies, 526–527
Non-parallel sentence structure, 516
Nonrestrictive elements, 550–551
Notes
double-entry, 530
during observing, 105
for essay question study, 495–
496
interviewing, 102

Observational site, 104
Observing
primary research and, 103–106
processes, 232–233
Open questions
during interview, 99
in questionnaires, 107–109
"Ordinary Spirit" (Harjo), 141–147

O'Reilly, Jane, 341
Outlining, 533

Paragraphs, 536
Parallelism
Paraphrasing material, 469–470
Past performance
assessed for controversial issue
writing, 287–288, 296
assessed for essay writing, 352
assessed for fiction/film writing,
444–445
assessed for personal experience
writing, 179
assessed for process writing, 230
assessing your, 52–53, 86
on exams, 497
See also Performance
Past/passed, 556–557
Pathos
for controversial issues, 276
described, 78
in fiction/film writing, 405
for personal experience text, 172
in process writing, 218
See also Emotions
Pattern of organization, 49
Performance
assessing essay writing, 363–364
assessing personal experience
text, 188
assessing process writing, 239
assessing voice, 513
critical thinking about fiction/
film writing, 452
critical writing for assessing, 53,
96
student interview on, 489–493
See also Past performance
Performance citations, 476
Periodicals, 120
Periodicals citations, 474–475
Person shifts, 521
Personal experience text
drafting to revise, 185–187
encountering subject of, 168
meaning in, 169–171
perspective of, 171–178
prereading, 149–168
prewriting, 182–184
research and, 182
responding to, 179–182
rewriting, 187–188
Personal experiences
scenario of writer's, 139–140
subject encountered through,
168, 180
techniques for responding to, 140
Perspective
on controversial issues, 279–287

developed for process writing, 220–228
developed through writing, 81, 85, 174–178
of essay writing, 345–351
of fiction/film, 377
of fiction/film writing, 413
researching variety of, 122
responding to changing, 168, 170
Persuasion
  on controversial issues, 274–278
  in essay writing, 355–357
  in fiction/film writing, 405–408
  using evidence to back up, 94
  writing for, 5
  writing techniques for, 77–79
Plagiarism, 135, 467–468
Planning
  for observations, 104
  primary research, 101–102
Plath, Sylvia, 25
"The Politics of Prohibition and the Death of the American Dream" (Gadbow), 280–283
Pollner, T. Anthony, 21, 225
Post hoc fallacy, 527
Prereading
  of controversial issues, 242–270
  for essay writing, 302–313
  example used for, 62–68
  fiction, 367–372
  guidelines for, 61–62, 88
  personal experience text, 140–168
  on processes, 191–213
Pretentious voice, 509–510
Previewing film, 372
Prewriting exercises
  for controversial issue writing, 289–292
  described, 33–35
  for essay writing, 357–359
  of fiction/film writing, 447–449
  for personal experience writing, 182–184
  for process writing, 232–234
  for process-based revision, 526
  for research paper, 457–458, 458–460
  See also Responsive prewriting exercises
Prewriting strategies, 529–533
Primary research
  analyzing results of, 110
  collaborative, 98–99
  critical reading and, 99
  described, 97–98
  example of text from, 110–113
  interviewing as, 99–103
  observing and, 103–106

questionnaires as, 106–109
for reference papers, 461, 465–466
summarizing results of, 109–110
See also Research
Process writing
  assessing performance of, 230
  causality in, 216
  collaborative writing assignment for, 213–220
  drafting to revise, 235–238
  guidelines for, 230
  prereading on, 191–213
  responsive prewriting exercise on, 233–235
  rewriting of, 238–239
  techniques for responding to, 190
  writer's purpose and, 190–191
  writer's response to, 189–190
  writing situation of, 230–232
Pronoun reference, 520–521
Pronoun-antecedent agreement, 518–519
Proofreading
  of controversial issues writing, 296
  of essay writing, 363
  of fiction/film writing, 452
  as final step, 96
  of personal experience writing, 188
  of process writing, 239
Publication Manual of the American Psychological Association, 470
Punctuation. *See* Mechanics
Purpose
  analyzing, 33
  considered during drafting, 91
  of controversial issue writing, 288, 292
  determining the, 72
  in essay writing, 316, 353, 355, 358
  of fiction/film writing, 403–404, 445, 449
  focus on, 91
  of personal experience text, 170, 181, 184
  of process writing, 215, 231, 234–235
  of questionnaire, 107
  of text, 5, 23
  writer-based/audience-based, 5–6
  writer's choices on, 87
  See also Writing purpose

Questionnaires, 106–109
Quotation marks, 469
Quoted material, 468–469

Reader's Guide to Periodical Literature, 120
Reason, 77–78
Recursive drafting, 187, 294
Recursive writing, 24, 94–95, 362
Reference books, 121–122
Reference librarians, 118–119
Reference sources, 116–122
Research
  collaborative assignments using, 124–125, 171
  for controversial issues, 271, 272, 274, 289
  as essay question study strategy, 496
  for essay writing, 314, 315, 354
  evidence-supported judgments through, 18–20
  example of text using, 125–135
  for fiction/film writing, 373, 385, 400, 401, 404
  for personal experience text, 169, 182
  primary, 97–113
  primary vs. secondary, 114
  for processes, 212–213, 215–216
  for research paper, 460–466
  secondary, 114–135
  for unknowns, 70
  using Internet for, 118
  See also Sources
Research journal, 458
Research mentor, 100, 460
Research papers
  avoiding plagiarism in, 467–468
  citations in, 470–472
  drafting of, 466–468
  lists of sources in, 472–476
  paraphrasing material in, 469–470
  prewriting/hypothesis for, 458–459
  quoted material in, 468–469
  researching for, 460–466
  rewriting of, 477–489
  special considerations for, 457–458
  student interview on performance in, 490–493
"Response To Unforgiven" (Meek), 412–413
Responsive journal writing
  on changing perspective, 168, 170
  on controversial issues, 271, 273–274
  on critical reading, 72–73
  on essay writing, 314, 316
  on fiction/film writing, 386, 400–401, 404
  on process research, 213, 215

Responsive journal writing (*cont.*)
  on process writing, 33
  on "writing place" 17
  on writing weaknesses, 24
Responsive prewriting exercises
  for controversial issues, 290–292
  for essay writing, 357–358
  guidelines for, 88–90
  on processes, 233–235
  on Sylvia Plath, 34, 36
  See also Prewriting exercises
Responsive writing
  examples of student, 81–85
  prewriting exercise on, 34, 88–90
Responsive writing assignment
  on controversial issues, 287
  on critical reading, 85
  on essay exam, 502
  on essay writing, 352
  on personal experience, 178
  on process writing, 230
  on Sylvia Plath, 32
Review
  of interview, 102–103
  of observation, 105
  of research sources, 123–124
Revision strategies, 526–534
  See also Drafting
Rewriting
  controversial issue writing,
    295–296
  essay writing, 362–363
  of fiction/film writing, 451–452
  interviewing notes, 103
  of observation notes, 106
  personal experience text, 187–188
  process of, 95–96
  of process writing, 238–239
  research papers, 477–489
  revising by, 39–52
Richter, Jesse
  "Fire on the Plains" 39–47
  journal entries by, 36–38
  Sylvia Plath assignment by,
    34–35
Ricker, Brian T., 21, 225
"Roman Fever" (Wharton), 431–444
"The Roots of Language
    Protectionism" (Daniels),
    125–135
"The Ruination of the Tomato"
    (Kramer), 205–212, 237
Run-on sentences, 547–549

Sakai, Shiro, 174–176
Schuyler, Jason, 507
Secondary research
  in academic community, 115–
    116
  described, 114–115

reference/specialized sources for,
    116–124
  for research papers, 461–466
  See also Research
Self-critical internal audience, 8
Semicolon, 551–552
Shifts in person, 521
Shifts in tense, 521–522
Silberman, Micha, 477, 478, 485
Sketching, 531–532
Skinner, Hadley, 283
"Smelling Foreigner" (Han), 83–85
Sources
  acknowledging, 135
  in college library, 118–122
  conventions for lists of, 472–476
  documentation of, 468–469
  reference, 116–122
  for reference papers, 461–466
  secondary research, 116–117
  specialized, 117, 122–124
  thanking your, 103
  using credible, 101
  See also Research
Spatial connections, 543–545
Speakers
  analyzing the, 70–71, 213–214
  controversial issue, 272–273
  emotions/attitudes of, 70–71
  essay writing, 315
  evidence-supported judgement
    of, 169
  of fiction/film writing, 402
Specialized sources, 117, 122–124
Steele, Shelby, 62, 76, 78, 539
Steenberg, Anne, 81
Straw-Gusé, Susan, 176
Subject
  conclusions about, 59–61
  of controversial issue, 270–271,
    288
  encountered through
    experiences, 168, 180
  of essay writing, 313–314, 353
  of fiction/film writing, 385, 399,
    445
  processes as, 212, 231
  writer's choices on, 86
  writing, 14–15
  writing situation and, 22
  writing to encounter, 25–32
Subject card, 462
Subject-verb agreement, 517–518
Summarizing, 109–110, 533
Supposed to/used to, 555
"Sylvia Plath-Agreement Statement"
    (Richter), 34–35

Temporal connections, 543–545
Tense shifts, 521–522

Text
  collaboration to assess, 20
  computer tip for writing, 16
  conversation through, 3–4
  critical reading for meaning in,
    59–68
  critical reading of, 19
  example of research used for,
    125–135
  purpose of, 5
  unique nature of, 22
  See also Writing
Theme (fiction/film), 378–379
There/their/they're, 555–556
Theroux, Paul, 7–8, 501
Think tank, 99
Thinking critically, 4
Thinking time, 18
"Three Faces of Greed" (O'Reilly),
    341–345
Time
  for controversial issue writing,
    289
  for essay writing, 353
  for exam taking, 499–500
  for fiction/film writing, 446
  for personal experience text, 181
  for primary research, 100
  for process writing, 232
  for writing research paper, 457
Title card, 462
Tone (fiction/film), 378
Topic paragraphs, 536
Topic sentences, 536
To/too, 557
Transitional devices, 541–545
Transitional paragraphs, 536

UNCOVER, 120
Unforgiven (film), 372, 386–399

Veiled threats, 527–528
Voice
  casual, 511–512
  collaboration to assess, 509–513
  considered during drafting, 92
  of controversial issues, 278, 293
  creating your, 92
  described, 48–49
  of essay writing, 355–356,
    359–360
  of fiction/film writing, 406, 450
  inconsistent, 510–511
  of personal experience text, 173,
    185–186
  pretentious, 509–510
  in process writing, 219, 236
  technical problems with, 513–524
  used in collaborative assignment,
    79–80

Wayman, Marci, 220
Weisberg, Jacob, 252
Welch, Lois, 9
Wharton, Edith, 431
Whose/who's, 556
Wing, Stephanie, 9–12, 14, 19, 20
"Without Success There Can Be No
   Motivation" (Steenberg),
   81–82
Word processors, 16
   See also Computers
Works cited conventions, 472–476
Writer-based purpose, 5–6
Writers
   controversial issue writing and,
      2, 240–242, 288–289
   conversation with student, 50–52
   essay writing by, 301–302, 353
   personal experiences used by,
      139–188
   of process writing, 231–232
   responding to fiction/film,
      365–367, 446
   responding to processes, 189–190

speaker element of, 70–71
unique creation by, 22
writer's choices and, 87
Writer's choices
   listed, 47–52
   used in collaborative
      assignments, 79–80
Writer's tools, 15–16
Writing
   assessing past performance in,
      86
   assessing problem areas in, 508
   controversial issue, 240–296
   as conversation, 3–4
   essay, 301–364
   as expression, 6–9
   finding time for, 18
   as persuasion, 4–6
   recursive nature of, 24
   the research paper, 457–493
   responding to fiction/film,
      365–493
   responding to personal
      experiences, 139–188

role of collaboration in, 20–21
student writer on, 50–52
subjects of, 14–15
tools of, 15–16
using bridge strategies in,
   533–534
writer-based/audience-based
   purpose to, 5–6
   See also Critical writing; Text
Writing place, 16–17
Writing process, 23–25, 86
Writing situations
   choices/constraints in, 86–87
   for controversial issues, 288–289
   defining, 22–23
   for essay writing, 352–357
   of fiction/film writing, 445–446
   for personal experience, 179–
      182
   process of, 23–25
   for process writing, 230–232
   writing to analyze the, 32–33

Yearbooks, 121

CREDITS

David Bruck, "The Death Penalty" from *The New Republic*, May 20, 1985. Reprinted by permission of The New Republic, © 1985, The New Republic, Inc.

Raymond Carver, "Cathedral" from *Cathedral*. Copyright © 1981 by Raymond Carver. Reprinted by permission of Alfred A. Knopf, Inc.

Michelle Cliff, "If I Could Write This In Fire, I Would Write This In Fire" from *The Land of Look Behind* by Michelle Cliff. Copyright © 1985 by Michelle Cliff. Reprinted by permission of Firebrand Books, Ithaca, New York.

Theresa L. Crenshaw, "HIV Testing: Voluntary, Mandatory, or Routine?" from *The Humanist*, Vol. 48, No. 1 (Jan/Feb 1988), pp. 29–34. Reprinted with permission of the publisher, American Humanist Association, copyright 1988.

Harvey A. Daniels, "The Roots of Language Protectionism" from *Not Only English: Affirming America's Multilingual Heritage*, edited by Harvey A. Daniels, NCTE 1990. Reprinted by permission of NCTE, Urbana, IL.

Lauren Davidson, excerpt analyzing Hemingway's *Hills Like White Elephants*. Reprinted by permission of the author.

Gary D. Elliot, "Hemingway's *Hills Like White Elephants*" from *The Explicator*, Vol. 35, No. 4, Summer 1977. Reprinted with permission of the Helen Dwight Reid Educational Foundation. Published by Heldref Publications, 1319 Eighteenth St., NW, Washington, DC 20036-1802. Copyright © 1977.

Mary D. Fletcher, "Hemingway's *Hills Like White Elephants*" from *The Explicator*, Vol. 38, No. 4, Summer 1980. Reprinted with permission of the Helen Dwight Reid Educational Foundation. Published by Heldref Publications, 1319 Eighteenth St., NW, Washington, DC 20036-1802. Copyright © 1980.

Michael Frome, "Forestry: Only God Can Make a Tree, But . . ." from *Conscience of a Conservationist*, © 1989 by The University of Tennessee Press. Reprinted by permission of The University of Tennessee Press.

Grady Gadbow, "The Politics of Prohibition and the Death of the American Dream." Reprinted by permission of the author.

Emma Goldman, "Marriage and Love."

Tripp Green, response to *Hills Like White Elephants*. Reprinted by permission of the author.